LOCKHEED AIRCRAFT
SINCE 1913

A Lockheed P-38F-1-LO over the Sierra Nevada during the testing of 165-gal drop tanks in the spring of 1942. (*Edric Guy Francillon*)

Frontispiece illustration selected with much paternal pride and in grateful remembrance for the 'double queues' of my childhood.

LOCKHEED
AIRCRAFT

SINCE 1913

RENÉ J. FRANCILLON

PUTNAM
AN IMPRINT OF THE BODLEY HEAD

BY RENÉ J. FRANCILLON

Japanese Aircraft of the Pacific War
McDonnell Douglas Aircraft since 1920

British Library Cataloguing
in Publication Data
Francillon, René J.
Lockheed aircraft since 1913.
1. Lockheed airplanes – History
I. Title
629.133'34   TL686.L/

ISBN 0–370–30329–6

© René J. Francillon 1982
Printed in Great Britain for
Putnam & Company Ltd
9 Bow Street, London, WC2E 7AL
by Thomson Litho Ltd, East Kilbride
Set in Times
First published 1982

CONTENTS

vi

Preface and Acknowledgments

Like many other young people raised in occupied Europe during the Second World War, I first associated the name Lockheed with the P-38s criss-crossing the sky in their hunt for Luftwaffe aircraft and Wehrmacht vehicles. In particular, I remember vividly a day in 1944 when a 'double queue' from one of the Fifteenth Air Force's Fighter Groups left an unexploded 20 mm shell embedded in the law library of the top-storey tenant in our apartment building. A quarter of a century later I was part of a Douglas team engaged in a fierce competitive struggle while marketing DC-10s against Lockheed's L-1011s.

Whether as a child, when my enthusiasm for aviation was sparked in part by wartime Lightnings, or as an adult, whose professional future depended on helping to outdo the TriStar team, I came to admire greatly the aircraft bearing the Lockheed name. I was thus delighted when, after I had completed the manuscript of *McDonnell Douglas Aircraft since 1920*, I was asked by Putnam to undertake a companion volume on Lockheed Aircraft since 1913.

In undertaking this task I have greatly benefited from the earnest co-operation of the Lockheed Corporation and of its staff at corporate headquarters, the Lockheed-California Company, the Lockheed-Georgia Company and the Lockheed Aircraft Service Company. Once again, in the process, my admiration for the company and its people was renewed. Not only have they helped to design, produce and support many of the world's most successful civil and military aircraft but in doing so they had the foresight to maintain very adequate historical records. Access to this wealth of information certainly made my task easier and more pleasurable. To all past and present Lockheed employees, who patiently bore with my questions and requests, I wish to express my sincere gratitude. I especially single out Herb Boen, Harvey Christen, Bert Dubell, Robert Ferguson, Don Phillips, Wayne Prior, James Ragsdale and Bill Slayton for their generous assistance and delightful hospitality.

From outside Lockheed, help, guidance and photographs came from many directions. First and foremost, this assistance was rendered by friends and fellow aviation historians: Peter M. Bowers, John F. Brindley, Ian Geddes (of Canadair Limited), Jean-Michel Guhl, H. L. James, Peter M. Keefe, William T. Larkins, Howard Levy, Peter J. Mancus (of Cloud 9 Photography), David W. Menard, Jay Miller, Robert C. Mikesh, B. C. Reed, and Gordon S. Williams. Then there was the staff of the Air Force Museum, the National Air and Space Museum, the Museu Aéroespacial, and the South African Air Force Museum. Repeatedly I could also rely on the courteous and efficient co-operation of the public relation officers of airlines throughout the world which have operated, or are currently operating, Lockheed airliners. On the military side, outside the United States, much help came from long established contacts among the Commonwealth air forces, while I was able to enroll the support of the air attachés—and through them of their respective air forces/naval air arms—of many nations on all continents. Finally, as always in the past, I was most fortunate to receive the sterling co-operation of public affair officers of the National Aeronautics and Space Administration, the Department of Defense, the Department of the Air

vii

Force, and the Department of the Navy, at headquarters as well as at operational bases and on board aircraft carriers.

I also wish to acknowledge the pioneering research efforts of fellow aviation writers Richard S. Allen (early Lockheed single-engined aircraft), Warren Bodie (P-38/XP-49/XP-58), and Peter M. Bowers and William T. Larkins (Models 10, 12, 14 and 18, Ventura and Harpoon), which provided a solid base for my own research. In particular, I recommend wholeheartedly to readers with a special interest in the early Lockheed aircraft the book by R. S. Allen (*Revolution in the Sky*, The Stephen Greene Press, Brattleboro, Vermont, 1964).

With the encouragement of my wife, and the willing co-operation of my employer—International Engineering Company Inc, I took four months leave of absence from my consulting work to write the manuscript of this book. Carol's advice certainly was as wise as her support was steadfast and the writing task became substantially easier than when I wrote the McDonnell Douglas book while concurrently trying to find time for a full-time job, our family life and four moves across the United States within eight years. This time I was able to lock myself peacefully in the midst of my papers and photographs and 'endure' the joyful teasing of family and friends to whom I became known as the 'house husband' (. . . grudgingly they admit that this time I was more pleasant to live with!). Thanks for tolerating, or rather encouraging the enthusiasm I display toward my 'fichue aviation'.

Finally, I do not intend to forget my gratitude to the late L. E. Bradford, Michael Badrocke and Clem Watson, who produced the general arrangement drawings in this book, and to John Stroud, the General Editor of the Putnam Aeronautical Books. The care with which John and his wife, Patricia, have edited this typescript—as well as those of my two previous Putnam titles—has led some to insist that I am not a naturalized American citizen but rather that I am a native of Brooklyn . . . not quite so will anyone assert who has ever heard me speak with my 'unmistakable' French accent!

René J. Francillon

Albany
California
1981

Author's Notes

This book follows the format used in my earlier *McDonnell Douglas Aircraft since 1920* and generally complies with that of most other titles in the Putnam series. Its content has been deliberately limited to cover only the history of the aircraft and of the companies which built them, as this is an aircraft history series as clearly set in the title of these books. Therefore, greater depth in recording corporate affairs, the biographies of the founders and other key figures, and non-aircraft undertakings, was considered to be outside the proper scope of this book. Obviously, economic considerations necessitated restricting length as book-production costs have more than sextupled over the twenty-one years separating the publication by Putnam of their first aircraft manufacturer history—*Hawker Aircraft since 1920* by F. K. Mason—and that of the present volume. Nevertheless, having been educated as a business economist, I have attempted within this limit to provide, as in the McDonnell Douglas book, some details on the financial results of the corporation. Needless to say, and as clearly demonstrated in 1971 when Lockheed survived only after obtaining Government guarantees for its borrowings, technical success cannot be sustained if cash flow problems interfere.

In most chapters in the main text devoted to the major aircraft types, a paragraph listing the Related Temporary Design Designations (*see* Appendix A for an explanation of this term) has been included before the technical data. It is hoped that these paragraphs will provide readers with an understanding of the vast number of projected developments undertaken by Lockheed. Most of the concepts remained on the drawing boards and, due to space limitations, only a few are described in the 'Selected Projects' section of this volume.

In the U-2 and SR-71 chapters it has not been feasible to maintain the customary thoroughness associated with titles in the Putnam series as these programmes remain heavily shrouded under a security mantle. Therefore, I regret that the design and production history of these fascinating aircraft cannot be fully told at this time. However, it may prove opportune to upgrade these chapters in a later edition. Meanwhile, they contain some educated guesses and many omissions.

Similarly, and even though for the past few years it has been repeatedly rumoured that Lockheed was working on a 'Stealth' aircraft—with the first flight of such an aircraft believed to have taken place in 1977—nothing further can be included in this first edition. Sublata causa, tollitur effectus.

Advanced Development Projects

This brief note on Lockheed Advanced Development Projects was held back as long as possible in the hope that further information would become available. For this reason it appears out of sequence.

Now officially known as Advanced Development Projects (ADP), the renowned 'Skunk Works' is headed by Ben R. Rich. Its administrative and engineering offices are located in Burbank and its manufacturing facilities in Palmdale.

It is generally reported that current activities encompass the design and construction of the TR-1 and ER-2 developments of the U-2, as well as overhaul, engineering support and modernization of the Air Force fleet of SR-71s. However, virtually nothing about more recent projects has been made public. Obviously, this talented group, with an extraordinarily successful record and unrivalled ability to design, build and test systems in complete secrecy, has not rested on its laurels since its SR-71 was first flown on 22 December, 1964.

Neither Lockheed nor its contracting US government agencies are prepared to comment on projects undertaken in the past seventeen years. Consequently, the following sketches, gleaned from public records, represent merely the author's attempt to summarize what little is known.

Stealth projects: To minimize aircraft detectability by radar or other devices, ADP has worked for many years on the so-called Stealth technology. It is believed that Lockheed, working under an ARPA-funded contract from the USAF's Flight Dynamics Laboratory, built two prototypes of a single-seat development aircraft. Powered by two 12,000-lb (5,443-kg) thrust turbojets, the first of these aircraft is reported to have been flown in 1977. It is further rumoured that both prototypes have since crashed. Production of an initial batch of twenty aircraft has been funded for delivery during the period 1981–83. However, no illustrations or details had been cleared for publication when this book went to press.

Hypersonic project: Even less is known about this project but the author believes that ADP has flown at least one prototype of a hypersonic research aircraft. Apparently, this manned vehicle has demonstrated its ability to cruise at Mach 6.

Origin and Corporate History

Vega, Sirius, Orion, Electra, Lodestar, Constellation, Shooting Star, Neptune, Hercules, Galaxy . . . these names, symbolic of the vastness of our universe, have also been borne by trend-setting aircraft designed by Lockheed, one of the most innovative aerospace manufacturers and certainly one with a keen sense of publicity. Like their namesakes, these aircraft have enlarged human horizons and, in the process, have turned Lockheed into one of the best-known aviation firms in the world. Yet, while its products captured the attention of the public and realized some of the greatest feats in the history of aviation, the company has led an unusually challenging life with successes followed by periods of cliff-hanging suspense. Even though blessed throughout its history with many of the most outstanding engineering talents in the industry — Allan Loughead, Jack Northrop, Jerry Vultee, Hall Hibbard, Kelly Johnson, . . . — and guided by brilliant managers — Carl Squier, Bob Gross, Dan Haughton, Bob Haack, Roy Anderson, . . . — Lockheed has had a difficult time in translating technical successes into a steady business climate. Thus, Lockheed's nearly 70-year history, that of the more than fifty types of aircraft it designed and built, and its diversification endeavours, provide some of the most interesting elements in the development of the US aerospace industry.

Having survived, among other major upheavals, the bankruptcy of its parent company in 1932, a major cash-flow crisis in 1971, and a serious loss of confidence in its business practices in 1975, Lockheed remains a giant in the aerospace

Allan Loughead (1889–1969) when he was working at Lockheed shortly before his death, and (right) Hall L. Hibbard at the time of his retirement. The long-time chief engineer had joined the Lockheed Aircraft Corporation in 1932 as an assistant to Richard A. Von Hake. (*Lockheed*)

1

industry with annual sales exceeding the $3-billion mark since 1974. Its activities range from civil and military aircraft design to missiles and space vehicles, aircraft maintenance, air traffic control systems, construction management for aviation facilities, military electronics, shipbuilding, engineering research and development in the fields of pure science and energy, and to undersea mining and farming.

This remarkable company adopted its present corporate title in September 1977 when the Lockheed Aircraft Corporation, which had been organized in June 1932, became the Lockheed Corporation. It carries forward the proud name of Lockheed, inherited from the proper phonetic rendering of the family name of its founders—the Loughead brothers, who had built their first aircraft in 1913. The progressive change in spelling from Loughead (often mispronounced 'log head') to the more familiar spelling, with its less offensive pronunciation, was initiated by the oldest brother when in 1909 he published two books under the name of Victor Lougheed. Eight years later the spelling Lockheed was adopted when Malcolm Loughead formed with other associates the Lockheed Hydraulic Brake Company and was also used in parenthesis on advertising brochures of the Loughead Aircraft Manufacturing Company. Finally, the current spelling was first legally used in the brothers' aviation business when in December 1926 the Lockheed Aircraft Company was incorporated with Allan Loughead as its vice-president and general manager.

Before providing a synopsis of the corporate history of the Lockheed Corporation and its forebears, with emphasis on their financial and managerial affairs, a brief biography of their founding fathers is in order.

The Loughead brothers

All three sons of John Loughead and Flora Haines Loughead—Malcolm (1887–1958), Allan (1889–1969), and their half-brother, Victor, from a previous marriage of their mother and adopted by John Loughead—showed an early interest in aviation. Educated as an engineer, Victor was better prepared than his younger brothers and his training led him to write *Vehicles of the Air* and *Aeroplane Designing for Amateurs* which were published in 1909–10 by the Reilly and Britton Co in Chicago. During these early years, Victor also acted as a negotiating agent for James E. Plew, the Chicago distributor of White automobiles and trucks, securing the manufacturing rights for a glider, designed by Professor James Montgomery of the University of Santa Clara, which Plew wanted to convert into a powered aeroplane.

Malcolm and Allan were equally mechanically-minded and in 1904 the former began working as an automobile mechanic for the White steam car agency, with Allan following suit two years later. As all three brothers resided in San Francisco and as Victor had become a respected theorist of aerodynamics, it was only natural that they spent much time together discussing aviation. By 1910, Allan could resist the lure of aviation no longer and, with Victor's help, was hired by James Plew to work in Chicago as a mechanic on the Montgomery glider and a Curtiss Pusher. Shortly after his arrival in Chicago during the summer of 1910, Allan became associated with members of the Aero Club of Illinois and was invited by one of them, George Gates, to fly in Gates' homebuilt pusher biplane. In the process the youngest of the Loughead brothers gained some limited flying experience which came in handy in December 1910 when Plew's Curtiss Pusher refused to get airborne. After two of Plew's pilots, Jack Hogan and Otto Brodie,

The Loughead brothers in the cockpit of their F-1 flying-boat; Malcolm is in the starboard seat and Allan in the port. (*Lockheed*)

had been unable to fly the Curtiss, Allan Loughead readjusted its 35 hp engine and obtained approval to attempt flying the recalcitrant machine. Following a first unsuccessful attempt, due to Allan Loughead's unfamiliarity with the system of shoulder harness operating the ailerons, the novice pilot managed to get airborne, flew uneven circles around the field and landed without accident. The exhilarated Allan had become a self-taught pilot and was now eager to carry on with his aeronautical plans.

Later, after Jack Hogan had crashed Plew's first Curtiss Pusher, Loughead rushed to complete a second machine of the same type. The new aircraft, taken on its first flight in January 1911 by Allan Loughead, unfortunately was unstable and crashed. Temporarily forced to return to work as an automobile mechanic, the frustrated young aviator was called back by James Plew to repair the two damaged Curtiss Pushers in time for the 1911 summer exhibition programme. In June 1911, while working on these aircraft, young Allan took time to marry Miss Dorothy Watts. The newlywed, not prepared to give up flying in spite of his additional responsibilities, flew the first rebuilt Curtiss.

The other Curtiss, however, crashed on 13 July, 1911, killing its pilot, Don Kraemer, and Plew withdrew from the flying business. True to his Scottish ancestry, Allan Loughead, a more determined man than Plew, subsequently obtained a job as an instructor and exhibition pilot for the International Aeroplane Manufacturing Company. This new job almost proved to be the end of his flying career, as on 18 September, 1911, when attempting to fly a rain-soaked and underpowered Curtiss, Allan failed to reach sufficient height to clear some telegraph wires. The aircraft was totally wrecked but the lucky pilot walked away with only minor cuts. Nevertheless, it was time for a re-evaluation and Allan Loughead and his bride agreed that he should give up barnstorming but not aviation.

3

By that time the young Loughead had conceived an aeroplane of his own design and soon he had some milled wooden parts made in Chicago. Returning in early 1912 to San Francisco with his bride and the few parts of his aeroplane, he resumed work as a mechanic and proceeded to convince his brother Malcolm to join him in building the Model G aircraft. For the previous eight years Malcolm Loughead had worked as an automobile mechanic during which time he had first conceived the hydraulic brake for which he later became well-known. He had, nevertheless, retained his interest in aviation and thus enthusiastically agreed to work with his brother. Although the two Lougheads first worked together as individual entrepreneurs, they soon were forced to seek additional outside financing to organize the Alco Hydro-Aeroplane Company, as detailed later.

Following the demise of this company in 1913, Allan and Malcolm sought their fortune by prospecting in the California gold country until 1914. Allan then, once again, went back to work as a mechanic while Malcolm acquired a Curtiss biplane which he shipped to Hong Kong to set up a sales and service agency. When his aircraft was seized as contraband by the Royal Navy, Malcolm Loughead went to Mexico where he briefly served as 'chief engineer' for the lone aircraft used by the forces of President Venustiano Carranza fighting Pancho Villa and his rebels. Working together again, the two brothers, with the financial assistance of a certain Mr Meyer, then restored their Model G and entered a bid for a passenger-flying concession at the 1915 Panama-Pacific Exposition in San Francisco. When the aircraft of the bid winner crashed on its first flight, the Loughead–Meyer partnership stepped in and, in fifty flying days, carried 600 passengers on $10 ten-minute rides.

Moving down the California coast to Santa Barbara in 1916, Malcolm and Allan Loughead, joined by other investors, used part of their profits to organize the Loughead Aircraft Manufacturing Company which was liquidated in 1921 after building the F-1 flying-boat, manufacturing two Curtiss HS-2Ls, and unsuccessfully attempting to market the S-1 lightplane. Malcolm had left the company two years before the liquidation to form the Lockheed Hydraulic Brake Company with other associates. Succeeding in this venture, Malcolm sold his company to Bendix in 1932.

In December 1926 Allan Loughead was back in aviation when, with outside capital, he put together the Lockheed Aircraft Company. In thirty-one months the new organization built a solid reputation with its remarkable Vega, Air Express and Explorer. Capitalizing on this success, and luckily completing the sales agreement four months before the October 1929 stock market crash which triggered the Great Depression, the Board of Directors outvoted Allan Loughead and elected to sell 87 per cent of its capital to Detroit Aircraft Corporation. The disappointed Allan attempted once more with brother Malcolm to go into aircraft manufacture and, in 1930, organized with others the Loughead Brothers Aircraft Corporation at Glendale, California. This company was wound up in 1934 but the persevering Allan Loughead formed the Alcor Aircraft Corporation in Oakland, California, in February 1937. The sole product of each of these two companies is described with the accompanying illustrations. The loss of Alcor's C.6.1. Junior Transport forced the Corporation out of business.

After this failure Allan and Malcolm no longer pursued actively their aeronautical interest and, like Victor had already done since the 1910s, they became involved in a variety of other undertakings. Of the three brothers, only Allan returned to the fold when, shortly before his death in 1969, he became a part-time consultant for the Lockheed Aircraft Corporation.

4

During its less than five years of existence (1930–34) the Loughead Brothers Aircraft Corporation produced only one aircraft: the Olympic-Duo, or Duo-6 (X962Y). Retaining the basic configuration of the Vega, the new aircraft was built as a demonstrator for a novel powerplant installation. Two 130 hp Menasco B-6 Buccaneer six-cylinder inline engines were faired on each side of the nose with minimum separation for safe clearance of the propeller arcs. In this way, it was hoped to minimize directional control problems in the event of an engine failure. Limited tests were encouraging but the aircraft was destroyed during a low-level pass at Rosamond Dry Lake. This accident, coupled with the insufficient capitalization of the company, spelled the end of the venture. (*Lockheed*)

The Alcor C.6.1 (for Commercial, six-passenger, first model) Junior Transport was first flown at Oakland, California, on 6 March, 1938. Of modern, low-wing design with a retractable main undercarriage, the C.6.1 (NX15544) retained the powerplant configuration of the Duo-6 but used two 260 hp Menasco C6S-4 six-cylinder inline air-cooled engines. It was destroyed during a high-speed dive test over San Francisco Bay on 27 June, 1938, shortly before the anticipated completion of its certification trials. With the demise of the Junior Transport came that of the Alcor Aircraft Corporation. Span 49 ft (14·94 m); length 31 ft 8⅛ in (9·66 m). Empty weight 4,141 lb (1,878 kg); loaded weight 6,200 lb (2,812 kg). Maximum speed 211 mph at 5,500 ft (339 km/h at 1,675 m); cruising speed 190 mph (306 km/h); single-engined cruising speed 129 mph (208 km/h); initial rate of climb 1,350 ft/min (411 m/min); ceiling 24,000 ft (7,315 m); single-engined ceiling 12,600 ft (3,840 m); range 835 miles (1,345 km). (*Lockheed*)

The Alco Hydro-Aeroplane Company, 1912–13

To help finance the construction of their Model G, which they had undertaken in a garage at Pacific and Polk Streets in San Francisco and on which they laboured whenever they had some spare time, Allan and Malcolm Loughead continued to work as automobile mechanics. The income they earned in this manner, however, was not sufficient to cover all costs and especially to finance the acquisition of an engine. It thus became necessary for the Lougheads to seek outside financing. Fortunately, with both of them having worked for many years for several of the top automobile specialists in the San Francisco area, they were well-known to wealthy people in this field. Soon they were able to convince Max Mamlock, head of the Alco Cab Company, to add $1,200 to their own $1,800 investment. Other investors provided another $1,000 to obtain the $4,000 required to complete the Model G and see it through its initial flight demonstrations.

The Model G floatplane taxi-ing back to a slip on San Francisco Bay. (*Lockheed*)

When, during the summer of 1913, soon after the first four flights of the Model G on 15 June, the aircraft was damaged at San Mateo, the Alco Hydro-Aeroplane Company became dormant. However, shortly before the opening of the 1915 Panama-Pacific Exposition in San Francisco, Allan and Malcolm Loughead bought out the interests of Max Mamlock and the other investors and acquired control of the Model G.

Loughead Aircraft Manufacturing Company, 1916–21

The Lougheads' second aircraft venture, the first to bear their name, was incorporated in California in early 1916. The main stockholder was Berton R. Rodman, the owner of a machine-shop in Santa Barbara. Accordingly, the new company set up offices in this Southern California coastal town and Rodman became its president. The other officers were the Loughead brothers, with Allan as vice-president and Malcolm as secretary/treasurer. Renting space in the rear of a garage on State Street, one block from the waterfront, the fledgling company embarked upon the design of a large twin-engined flying-boat. Anthony

A 1920 advertisement illustrating the early Loughead aircraft and pointing the way to the later spelling of the company's name. (*Lockheed*)

Stadlman, who had worked for James E. Plew in Chicago with his friend Allan Loughead, was then hired as factory superintendent. Shortly after, in addition to adding workmen, the firm hired a 21-year old architectural draughtsman who quickly made a name for himself in the aviation industry, John K. 'Jack' Northrop.

The ambitious nature of the flying-boat design, Northrop's methodical stress analysis, and the company's meagre finances limiting the size of the work force, combined to slow the completion of the F-1 until March 1918, two years after the organization of the Loughead Aircraft Mfg Co. By then the United States had been at war with the Central European Powers for almost a year and the Lougheads were anxious to offer their flying-boat for evaluation by the US Navy. The F-1 was first airborne on 28 March, 1918, and shortly after was flown to North Island, San Diego, where for three months it underwent Navy flight and structural trials. The flying-boat was not purchased by the Navy but the Service was sufficiently impressed with the Loughead team to sign a contract with the company for the production of two Curtiss HS-2L single-engined flying-boats. The two machines were completed before the end of the war. However, the company lost between $4,000 and $5,000 on this $90,000 contract — the value of which had been calculated on the estimated cost plus a 12½ per cent fee (the Lockheed forebears was already underestimating costs on military contracts!) as it had attempted to improve the Curtiss design, notably by experimenting with bullet-proofing its 141-US gallon (534-litre) fuel tanks. In July 1918 the Loughead Aircraft Mfg Co had also received a Navy contract for the production of fifty scouts, but this contract was cancelled before the completion of a single aeroplane.

When in August 1918 the F-1 was returned by the Navy, the company decided to modify it as a landplane with revised central nacelle, twin-wheel main undercarriage units and single nosewheel, and other aerodynamic improvements. Unfortunately, during an attempted Santa Barbara–Washington transcontinental flight in November 1918, the modified F-1A was damaged on take-off at Gila Bend, Arizona. Rebuilt as a flying-boat the machine was used in 1919–20 for passenger charter flights, for which it could carry the pilot and ten people, to fly King Albert and Queen Elisabeth of Belgium to and from Santa Cruz Island on 11

Dwarfed by a sign more impressive than the company's real contribution to the war effort, this Loughead-built HS-2L is seen here on the beach at Santa Barbara. (*Lockheed*)

Destined to remain in prototype form, the F-1 flying-boat was an excellent but ambitious design for a fledgling company. (*Lockheed*)

October, 1919, and as an aerial camera platform for Hollywood film studios. It was finally sold to a group which planned to use it on regular service between the Los Angeles area and Catalina Island. The plan failed to materialize and, after earning a final income for the Loughead Aircraft Mfg Co, the F-1 was abandoned by its new owner on the beach at Santa Barbara.

In 1919, the company was reorganized, with Allan Loughead taking over the presidency from Berton Rodman, and it went on to develop the small S-1 sport biplane, the first aircraft to use the moulded plywood monocoque fuselage developed by Jack Northrop, Tony Stadlman and the Lougheads. In spite of its delightful handling characteristics and its remarkably low operating costs, the S-1 failed to penetrate a market glutted with cheap surplus Jennies. After sinking $29,800 in this venture the Loughead Aircraft Manufacturing Company had to be liquidated in 1921.

Lockheed Aircraft Company, 1926–29

Another short-lived company was incorporated in Nevada on 13 December, 1926, and, for the first time, to benefit from the reputation of Malcolm Loughead's Lockheed Hydraulic Brake Company, included in its corporate title the Lockheed spelling. It came into being to produce the new single-engined cabin monoplane conceived by Jack Northrop, then working for the Douglas Company in Santa Monica, and Allan Loughead, then associated with the California distributor of his brother's hydraulic brakes and moonlighting by selling real estate in the Los Angeles area. In order to hire Northrop away from Douglas and to proceed with the design and construction of the new aircraft, Allan Loughead first needed to raise the necessary capital to organize a proper company. Assisted by W. Kenneth Jay, an accountant and former Air Service flying instructor, Allan Loughead and Northrop prepared a stock prospectus. At Jay's suggestion the prospectus was shown to Fred E. Keeler, a wealthy brick and tile manufacturer. Liking what he saw and confident in the ability of the Northrop/Loughead team, Keeler agreed on the spot to acquire 51 per cent of the common stock of the proposed company for $2,550 and all of its preferred stock for $20,000. Allan Loughead invested $2,450 to secure the balance of the remaining stock, thus providing the Nevada corporation with a total paid-up capital of $25,000. In return for his controlling interest, Keeler assumed the presidency of the Lockheed Aircraft Company and appointed his attorney, Ben Hunter, as executive vice-president. Completing the management team were Allan Loughead, as vice-president and general manager, and W. Kenneth Jay, as secretary/treasurer. Key personnel were Jack Northrop as chief engineer and Tony Stadlman as factory superintendent who, together with a dozen carpenters and helpers, were the only full-time employees of the new company.

The trend-setting Vega in the summer of 1927. This aircraft, X3625, the second Vega 1, was powered by a 225 hp Wright Whirlwind J5. (*Van Rossen/Lockheed*)

Construction of the company's first aircraft, the beautifully streamlined Vega cantilever monoplane, was undertaken in a rented building at Romaine and Sycamore Streets in Hollywood. While the Vega was under construction, the Lockheed Aircraft Company succeeded in selling it to George Hearst Jr, the wealthy publisher of the *San Francisco Examiner*, who wished to enter it in the August 1927 Oakland-to-Honolulu Dole Derby. Even though taking a $5,000 loss on this sale — the agreed purchase price for the aircraft was $12,500 whereas its cost was $17,500 — the company rushed the first Vega to completion and got it into the air at Inglewood on Independence Day 1927. Following flight trials and modifications to its vertical surfaces, the aircraft, flown by John Frost and Gordon Scott, took off from Oakland on 16 August, 1927, bound for Oahu. Although the first Vega disappeared on its way to Hawaii, its advanced design had already attracted other customers and the Lockheed Aircraft Company, before being forced to move to larger quarters in the partly occupied building of the Mission Glass Works on Empire Avenue in Burbank, completed four more Vegas and began the construction of the Air Express and Explorer. Off Empire Avenue behind the factory, a narrow piece of land some 1,500-ft (455-m) long was graded to serve as the company's own airstrip.

Three months after the March 1928 move to Burbank, Jack Northrop and Ken Jay left the company and were replaced by Gerald F. 'Jerry' Vultee, as chief engineer, and Whitley C. Collins, as secretary/treasurer. Going on from success to success while being flown by many of the most famous pilots of the time, the hand-built Vegas were produced at a remarkably high rate (two in 1927, 29 in 1928, and 40 during the first six months of 1929 with many more under construction). In addition, the company completed two Air Expresses in 1928 and five of this type during the first six months of 1929. The first Explorer, which had been started in 1927, was also completed during the first half of 1929.

With business booming and a healthy cash flow fuelled by a steady stream of orders, Fred Keeler saw an opportunity of realizing a large profit by selling the Lockheed Aircraft Company while the going was good. Over the protest of Allan Loughead, Keeler began in April 1929 to negotiate the sale of the company with Edward S. Evans, the president of Detroit Aircraft Corporation. The sale agreement, which became final in July 1929, says much for Keeler's business acumen as three months later the 1929 stock market crash plunged the United States into the Great Depression and the bottom fell out of the aircraft market.

Lockheed Aircraft Corporation, a Division of Detroit Aircraft Corporation, 1929–31

Upon acquiring 87 per cent of the assets of Lockheed in July 1929, the Detroit Aircraft Corporation—a Michigan holding corporation with controlling interest in various aviation ventures including aircraft manufacturers (Ryan and Eastman), an airport (Grosse Isle in Detroit), the Park Air College in East St Louis, and other entities—reorganized the company as a division. To head the new Lockheed Aircraft Corporation the Detroit group sent Carl B. Squier (the founder of one of its other subsidiaries, Eastman Aircraft) as general manager and retained Jerry

The cantilever wing and narrow fuselage of the Vega are seen to advantage in this view of an aircraft under construction. (*Van Rossen/Lockheed*)

11

Charles Lindbergh's Sirius during an early test flight near Burbank. (*Lockheed*)

Vultee as chief engineer. On the surface it appeared that the change of owners was not going to affect the business and the operationally independent Burbank team went on producing Vegas, Air Expresses and Explorers.

Besides producing these well-established types, the sale of which provided much needed cash to the Detroit Aircraft Corporation after the stock market crash, Lockheed introduced the Sirius (the first of which was completed for Charles Lindbergh in 1929 and was followed by twelve aircraft in 1930 and two in 1931), the Altair (the first Lockheed aircraft with a retractable undercarriage) and the superb Orion (first appearing in April 1931). Most of these aircraft were built with the company's traditional plywood monocoque fuselages but, beginning in February 1932 when the first DL-1 Vega was completed in Michigan, Detroit Aircraft Corporation built nine Vegas, and one Sirius with metal fuselage of Detroit construction and Lockheed-built wooden wings. Detroit, using the same

Y1C-23 Altair of the US Army Air Corps, modified from the Sirius DL-2 with Detroit-built metal fuselage and Burbank-produced wooden wing. (*Peter M. Bowers*)

combination, also built in 1931 the XP-900 two-seat fighter prototype. Initial design work for an Army observation biplane and an exceptionally clean flying-boat was also undertaken but lack of funds prevented the realization of these projects.

In spite of this flurry of activity in the midst of the Great Depression, the future looked bleak for Lockheed as rising losses from other operations of its parent company drained it of its own profit. Finally, having lost $733,000 in 1929 and seeing its stock (with a par value of $15) plummet to 12½ cents, the Detroit Aircraft Corporation could no longer survive. On 27 October, 1931, it went into receivership with its Lockheed Aircraft Corporation subsidiary being placed under the aegis of the Title Insurance and Trust Company of Los Angeles. With Carl Squier remaining as general manager, a skeleton work force built two more Orions and one Altair but, on 16 June, 1932, the doors were finally locked. Before this event, parts for two more Vegas were acquired by two groups of former employees; one aircraft was completed in May 1932 under the direction of Firman Gray, and the other was completed in March 1933 by Richard A. Von Hake, who in 1930 had succeeded Jerry Vultee as the last chief engineer of the Detroit Aircraft Corporation's Lockheed subsidiary.

The rebirth of the Lockheed Aircraft Corporation

Only five days after the Title Insurance and Trust Company had shut the doors of the company for which it acted as receivers, a new Lockheed Aircraft Corporation was born. Led by Robert Ellsworth Gross, a 35-year old San Francisco investment broker, a group of investors submitted to the US District Court in Los Angeles a $40,000 bid for the assets of the defunct company. There being no other bids District Judge Harry Holzer accepted Gross' offer on the day of its presentation, 21 June, 1932. Lockheed was now owned by four investors: Walter T. Varney, the owner of Varney Speed Lanes who provided $20,000, Mr and Mrs Cyril Chappellet, who jointly contributed $10,000, and R. C. Walker and Thomas Fortune Ryan III, who each provided $5,000. For this sum the investors acquired physical assets worth $129,961 as valued by the receivers and including work in progress, raw material, machine tools, office and engineering equipment, and furniture. At 30 cents in the dollar it was not a bad investment if one had confidence in the aviation business at a time when the country was at the bottom of the Great Depression.

For their management team the investors elected Lloyd C. Stearman, already a well-known aircraft designer and who later achieved even higher repute for his wartime PT-13/PT-17 Kaydet trainers, as president and general manager. Stearman was initially assisted by Carl Squier, as vice-president and sales manager; Robert Gross, as treasurer; Cyril Chappellet, as secretary; Richard Von Hake, as chief engineer; and Hall L. Hibbard, as assistant chief engineer. Their initial tasks were to complete four Vegas, one Altair and seventeen Orions, with all twenty-two aircraft to be delivered by 1934, and to initiate the development of a new product line.

At first the new company planned to build a ten-seat, single-engined, metal transport which Stearman and Hibbard had conceived earlier while working for Stearman-Varney Inc. However, convinced that the future of passenger transport would depend on the development of clean and fast twin-engined aircraft — such as the ten-passenger Boeing Model 247 then under construction — Robert Gross convinced his associates that they should abandon their single-engined design and undertake that of a twin-engined aircraft. The Stearman-Von Hake-Hibbard team immediately set to work. During wind-tunnel testing of a model of the new twin-engined transport at the University of Michigan under the supervision of Professor Edward Stalker, the Lockheed team first noted a talented aeronautical engineering student when he alerted them to potential instability and control problems. This gifted young man was Clarence L. 'Kelly' Johnson who joined Lockheed shortly after and who, more than any other single individual, did so much to establish the company's reputation for advanced engineering concepts culminating with the YF-12/SR-71 series of Mach 3 aircraft.

The 135th Electra, a Model 10-A, before delivery to Aeroput in Yugoslavia. (*Lockheed*)

In the light of the unpromising financial results of the company's first six months of operations—with losses of $9,500* on revenues of $23,000 by the end of 1932—the bold decision to proceed with the development of the Model 10 Electra twin-engined transport created an urgent need for more capital. Thus, with the guidance of the Los Angeles investment firm of G. Brashears and Company, Lockheed restructured its capital. At the time of its inception, Lockheed Aircraft Corporation had an authorized capital of 50,000 shares of non-par stock; 4,800 of these shares, with a stated unit price of $10, were distributed as follows among the original investors and Robert Gross: 2,000 shares to Varney, 1,000 to the Chapellets, and 500 each to Ryan and Walker in return for their $40,000 investment, with 800 shares going to Gross for goodwill and the rights to the planned single-engined transport. Soon after, Thomas Fortune Ryan III purchased an additional 500 shares for $5,000 and William L. Graves acquired 700 shares at $10 per share. The 6,000 shares then outstanding were transferred to a holding company organized as Lockheed Aircraft Corporation of Delaware (the State of Delaware having particularly favourable corporate laws) but known later as the Southern California Aviation Corporation.

When in early 1933 the need for additional capital was recognized, the company's directors authorized an issue of 500,000 shares at a par value of $1. Ninety thousand of these shares were given to the Southern California Aviation Corporation in exchange for the 6,000 shares of the original Lockheed stock (thus providing the original investors with a fifty per cent return in less than one year

*Annual sales and profit/loss figures, which are quoted for some years in the text, are given for every year between 1932 and 1980 in a table on page 48.

. . . quite an achievement in the midst of the Great Depression!). Southern California Aviation also received 34,000 of the new shares to cancel loans for operating funds made by its stockholders to Lockheed. Additional shares were sold on the open market and by April 1934 289,471 shares (almost 58 per cent of the authorized capital) were outstanding. The successful underwriting of the new stock and the $25,962 profit realized during 1933 insured the soundness of the company. Moreover, before its maiden flight in February 1934, the Model 10 Electra was ordered by Northwest Airways. Lockheed's future looked bright.

Development of the Electra reached a critical stage on 11 August, 1934, when the aircraft was granted its Approved Type Certificate by the Aeronautics Branch of the Department of Commerce and was placed in service by Northwest Airlines (the name was changed from Northwest Airways in April 1934). This work, however, continued to drain the company's finances. None-the-less, as Lockheed had a respectable order book for the Electra, it was able to obtain in September 1934 a $200,000 revolving credit line from the government's Reconstruction Finance Corporation and thus could finance quantity production. While this was taking place changes were being made at the top of the company. Walter T. Varney disposed of his Lockheed stock in May 1933 to concentrate on his airline ventures and Lloyd Stearman was also planning to depart. Thus Hall Hibbard took over as chief engineer in 1933 and Robert Gross succeeded Stearman as president on 15 December, 1934.

During 1934 Lockheed delivered its last Vega and its last four Orions as well as its first ten Electras; nevertheless, the year ended with a $190,891 loss on sales of $562,759. Renegotiations of the Electra sales price, which increased by ten per cent to $55,000, and the delivery of 36 of these aircraft restored profitability in 1935 when a 10·4 per cent ($217,986) profit was realized on sales of $2,096,775. It was thus possible for Lockheed to undertake the design and construction of the Model 12 Electra Junior, a scaled-down version of the Model 10 specially intended as a fast executive transport to be entered in a Department of Commerce

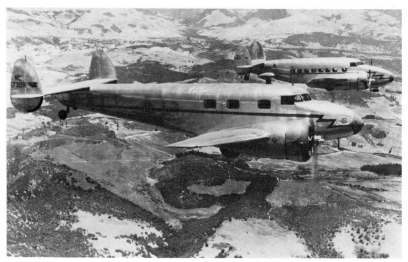

Two of the Lockheed transports operated by California-based Santa Maria Airlines: Model 12-A Electra Junior NC17309 and Model 14-H2 Super Electra NC18993. (*Lockheed*)

15

design competition. This design competition failed to have concrete results. Yet, the company was able to find a ready market for its Model 12 and eventually produced 130 of these aircraft for civil and military customers between 1936 and 1942. The year 1936, which ended for Lockheed with a $100,126 profit, also saw the company deliver its first military aircraft (the Navy XR2O-1 and Coast Guard XR3O-1 versions of the Electra) and obtain its first Air Corps contracts (AC8805 for the XC-35 high-altitude research aircraft and three Y1C-36 staff transports). Lockheed also undertook during that year to design the Model 14 Super Electra and purchased the 108,000 sq ft (10,000 sq m) plant facilities it had previously leased. To finance this expansion programme two stock issues were made and brought in an additional $1·6 mn in capital.

Five weeks before the first flight of the Model 14 on 24 July, 1937, Lockheed was awarded by the War Department Contract AC9974 for a prototype of its Model 22 twin-engined interceptor. Designed by Kelly Johnson and Hall Hibbard, after the Lockheed Model 11 (Air Corps designation XPB-3, later XFM-2) had lost an earlier competition to the Bell XFM-1, the Model 22 was submitted to meet the requirements of the Air Corps' specification X-608 of February 1937. First in the Lightning series, the XP-38 brought the Lockheed Aircraft Corporation into the major league of aircraft manufacturers. The advanced nature of the Model 22 design, however, resulted in a fairly protracted gestation, with construction of the XP-38 beginning in July 1938 and its first flight not taking place until 27 January, 1939. Meanwhile, Lockheed continued to produce Model 10, 12 and 14 transports in the light of intense competition from the Douglas Aircraft Company which dominated the prewar airliner market with its DC-2s and DC-3s (prior to the war, Douglas sold 623 DC-2s and DC-3s, not including initial orders for C-47 and C-53 military models, versus 391 Lockheed 10s, 12s and 14s). Thus, by the spring of 1938 Lockheed's order book was down to only a few aircraft when the aggressive promotion of the Model B-14 by Kenneth Smith won for the company its first largescale contract, an order for 200 to 250 Hudson general-reconnaissance aircraft, signed by the British Air Ministry on 23 June, 1938. To fulfil this initial order and follow-on contracts for Hudsons and P-38s, the Lockheed work force exploded and from its nadir of 332 people in 1934 went to 7,000 employees on 31 March, 1940, and to 16,898 one year later.

The birth of a new fighter: a YP-38 taking off at the Lockheed Air Terminal.
(*USAF*)

16

Even though it had by then obtained a foothold on the military market, Lockheed, spurred by rising profits ($137,920 in 1937 and $442,111 in 1938), wanted to increase its commercial business and, to that end, undertook a two-pronged effort. On the one hand it incorporated on 17 August, 1937, a wholly-owned subsidiary, the AiRover Company, while on the other its engineering staff studied several new transport designs which eventually culminated in the Model 49, the famous Constellation. Before dealing with some of these design studies and the wartime achievements of the Lockheed Aircraft Corporation a brief synopsis of the short-lived AiRover Company and its successor follows.

The first product of the Vega Airplane Company, the Unitwin-powered Starliner, after the fitting of twin vertical tail surfaces. (*Lockheed*)

From the AiRover Company to the Vega Aircraft Corporation, 1937–43

When it was founded in August 1937, under the presidency of Mac V. F. Short, the AiRover Company moved into an old red-brick building at 923 East San Fernando Road, Burbank, next door to Lockheed. Its initial tasks were to build from available spares a modified Altair for use as a flying testbed for a powerplant consisting of two C6S-4 Menasco engines coupled to drive a single propeller, and to design a five-seat feeder transport, the Starliner, powered by this coupled engine. Completed in December 1937, the modified Altair, named *Flying Test Stand*, proved the Menasco powerplant to be reliable and, after the AiRover Company had been renamed the Vega Airplane Company during 1938, was followed into the air on 22 April, 1939, by the Starliner. However, the Starliner was found to be too small and its development was abandoned when the war in Europe dictated a better use for the limited plant capacity of Lockheed and its subsidiary. The Vega Airplane Company went on to build five Model 40 target drones of its own design and four NA-35 primary trainers designed by North

American, with the trainers being the first aircraft manufactured in the new 750,000 sq ft (70,000 sq m) plant built on a 30-acre (12-hectare) lot adjacent to the Union Air Terminal, and a mile from the parent Lockheed plant. At about the same time Courtlandt Gross, Robert Gross' younger brother, took over the presidency of the Vega Airplane Company and Mac V. F. Short became its vice-president of engineering. Earlier, Lockheed, which with its officers controlled the stock of Vega, distributed 51,666 ⅔ shares of Vega stock (par value of $1.50) as a dividend to Lockheed stockholders.

In its new plant the Lockheed subsidiary built Ventura bombers under British and Lend-Lease contracts and, as a member of the BVD (Boeing/Vega/Douglas) team, played a major role in building B-17F and G Flying Fortresses for the USAAF. Vega's design work included the PV-2 Harpoon and XP2V-1 Neptune for the US Navy and the XB-38 and XB-40 derivatives of the Flying Fortress. Its corporate identity was changed on 31 December, 1941, when it was merged with Lockheed (its stockholders receiving one share of Lockheed for three of Vega) and its assets were transferred to the Vega Aircraft Corporation. Finally, on 30 November, 1943, the Vega Aircraft Corporation was absorbed into the Lockheed Aircraft Corporation and its facilities became Lockheed's plant A-1.

Lockheed Aircraft Corporation
Wartime Expansion, 1939–45

As indicated earlier, Lockheed in the late thirties pursued its efforts to increase its share of the commercial aircraft market and studied a number of new designs including the Model 18 — a stretched version of the Super Electra, a three-engined eighteen-seater, a very fast twin-engined aircraft for fourteen passengers, an eighteen-seater with four engines, a thirty-passenger transport with two Allison liquid-cooled engines buried within the wings, and the short-range Model 16

Not a typical view of a Southern California residential area but the Lockheed factory under wartime camouflage. (*Lockheed*)

Plant A-1 at the Union Air Terminal, Burbank, during the final phase of construction. (*Lockheed*)

which combined the Model 14 fuselage with the wings and engines of the Model 10. Of these designs only the Model 18 progressed beyond the preliminary stage. First flown on 21 September, 1939, the Model 18 was produced to the tune of 625 aircraft including civil and military models. Of unusual interest was another twin-engined project, the Model 27, which featured canard control surfaces but was not built. Another project was the Model 44 Excalibur which started out in 1939 to be a four-engined aircraft capable of carrying 18 passengers at a top speed of 241 mph (388 km/h) but which, at the behest of Pan American Airways, grew into 30- and then 34-passenger projects while top speed increased to 270 mph (435 km/h) and then 300 mph (483 km/h). In its last form the project proceeded to the full-scale mock-up stage but, in turn, was abandoned in favour of a still larger aircraft with full cabin pressurization which became the Model 49 Constellation and was put into production in 1940 when TWA ordered nine aircraft.

In an unrelated move Lockheed increased its commercial activities during 1940 when it purchased for $1·5 mn the Union Air Terminal in Burbank previously owned by United Air Lines. Organized as a subsidiary under the presidency of Cyril Chappellet, the Lockheed Air Terminal continued to be used by airlines and for general aviation operations, and enabled Lockheed to expedite test and delivery flights for the aircraft coming off its assembly lines at this airport. Thirty-eight years after acquiring this airport, Lockheed sold it to the Hollywood-Burbank Airport Authority for $51 mn, of which $35·5 mn came from federal grants by the Department of Transportation to the cities of Burbank, Glendale and Pasadena, and was thus able to include in its income for the year 1978 a $36·3 mn gain from this sale.

Between 1 July, 1940, and 31 August, 1945, Lockheed produced 19,077 aircraft, representing 6·6 per cent of the US total during the period or, expressed in terms of airframe weight, 9 per cent of the national total, and thus ranked as the fifth largest United States aircraft manufacturer. Almost 70 per cent of these aircraft—consisting mainly of Lightnings (P-38, F-4 and F-5), Hudsons, Lode-

19

At last the big time! Parallel production lines for Hudson Vs and Lodestars in 1940.
(*Lockheed*)

stars, Shooting Stars and Constellations—came from the assembly lines at plant
B-1, with the remainder–mainly Venturas, Harpoons and Flying Fortresses—
being produced at plant A-1. To produce this large number of aircraft the company was forced to augment its facilities, with floor area increasing from
550,000 sq ft (51,000 sq m) in the summer of 1939, to 1,600,000 sq ft (149,000
sq m) at the end of 1940, and to a wartime peak of 7,700,000 sq ft (715,000 sq m)
in mid-1943. Most of this expansion took place at plants A-1 and B-1 but Lockheed also operated a system of ten feeder plants in California—two each in
Bakersfield, Fresno, East Los Angeles and Santa Barbara, and one in both
Taft and Pomona—and, beginning in March 1942, a modification and service centre in Dallas, Texas. Another service centre was opened in early
1944 at the Van Nuys Airport, California, to handle modifications of Navy
aircraft.

Overseas, Lockheed had set up during 1938 a parts depot in Amsterdam and
the British Reassembly Division, LAC Ltd, at Speke, the Liverpool airport. The
Liverpool facility, together with similar units at Renfrew and Abbotsinch near
Glasgow, handled the task of receiving and assembling the British-ordered
Hudsons. Reassembly facilities were also set up in Australia to handle the
Hudsons of the RAAF. This experience proved useful when on 3 December, 1941,
the company was asked by the Air Service Command to establish a maintenance
and overhaul base in the British Isles, with repair shops and accessories for 33
types of aircraft. Its proposal was accepted and Lockheed was awarded a contract
in February 1942. Three months later Lockheed Overseas Corporation set up
operations at Langford Lodge, twenty miles west of Belfast in Northern Ireland.

Before it closed in July 1944 the facility reassembled and modified 3,250 aircraft, serviced 11,000 more, and overhauled 450,000 components; late in 1943 its employment peaked at about 6,000.

In spite of many difficulties in obtaining and retaining qualified workers—almost 24,000 company employees joined the Services and 394 of them died while on duty—Lockheed employment jumped during the first years of the war and from its already high level of 18,724 on 31 March, 1941, reached a peak of 94,329 in mid 1943 (a level since exceeded only in 1968–69). To obtain the necessary employees the Lockheed Aircraft Corporation, in common with other members of the aircraft industry, was forced to innovate. Largescale training programmes were organized to train unskilled personnel, including high school students—who worked four hours a day in addition to continuing their daily academic studies for four more hours—and women. It was the era of 'Rosie the Riveter' with women constituting some 40 per cent of Lockheed's peak wartime employment and handling a wide variety of tasks on the assembly lines and in engineering offices.

As work experience increased and the benefits of the learning curve were felt—with, for example, man-hours required to build a P-38 decreasing from 360,000, for the first production aircraft, to 17,000 for the 500th machine, and to only 3,800 for the last examples—Lockheed was able to reduce its work force. Thus by the end of 1944 employment had declined to 62,657 and it dropped another 25 per cent by VE-Day. In the process, serious problems with shortages of employees' housing and transport facilities were finally alleviated.

Changing of the guard! The P-80 and P-38 lines sharing the same assembly hall at Plant B-1 in the spring of 1945. (*Lockheed*)

21

In terms of new aircraft the war years were marked at Lockheed by the first flight of the Ventura (31 July, 1941), the XB-40 (10 November, 1942), the XP-49 (14 November, 1942), the XB-38 (19 May, 1943), the Constellation (9 January, 1943), the Harpoon (3 December, 1943), the XP-80 (8 January, 1944), the XP-58 (6 June, 1944), the Little Dipper (August 1944), and the Neptune (17 May, 1945). Of particular interest to the company's postwar future were the debuts of the piston-powered Constellation and Neptune, and of the jet-powered XP-80.

Work on jet propulsion projects had begun at Lockheed during 1939–40 when the Hibbard-Johnson team, including Phil Colman, Willis Hawkins and Gene Frost, undertook preliminary studies for a series of novel twinjet aircraft of highly unconventional design, including the L-133 all-steel aircraft with canard surfaces, which Lockheed had planned to use for its proposed Model 27 transport mentioned earlier. In addition, Nathan Price designed for Lockheed the L-1000 turbojet (military designation XJ-37) which incorporated several then extremely advanced features such as axial-flow, two-spool turbine stages, high compression ratio and afterburner. Neither the L-133 aircraft nor the L-1000 turbojet projects went into production but later Menasco built a few XJ-37s and Lockheed sold some of its turbojet patents to Curtiss-Wright. Fortunately for the company, the XP-80 contracted for by the USAAF on 24 June, 1943, led to the production of 8,507 related aircraft (F-80, T-33, F-94 and T2V-1) between 1943 and 1958. Together with the Constellation family (856 Constellations/Super Constellations/Starliners) and 1,051 Neptunes, they assured the well-being of the Lockheed Aircraft Corporation well into the late fifties.

The Lockheed L-1000 axial-flow turbojet with its designer, Nathan Price (*right*), and the company's chief engineer, Hall Hibbard (*left*). (*Lockheed*)

Neptune MR.1 (P2V-5) WX505 of No.217 Squadron, R.A.F. (*M.O.D.*)

Lockheed Aircraft Corporation
Postwar transports, the jet age, and the Skunk Works, 1945–65

The elation with which the Japanese surrender was received was followed by the hard realization that with it would come the mass cancellation of military contracts and a drastic curtailment of operations. The Lockheed management first ordered a five-day shutdown for its employees to celebrate the victory while key officers analysed the impact on the company and charted a new course. On the one hand, military contracts for Lightnings and Constellations were terminated and that for Harpoons was reduced; on the other, the prospects for civil Constellations appeared bright, as did the prospect for the jet-powered P-80 and, to a lesser extent initially at least, for the Neptune. Furthermore, increased volume during the war years had enabled the company to accumulate a substantial cash surplus (during the five years ending at December 1944 Lockheed realized a $30·4 mn profit on sales of $1,980·7 mn; although a profit of over $30 mn appears large, and indeed was almost ten times the total profit realized by the company during its first eight years of operations, it represented a return on sales of only 1·5 per cent!).

23

The Little Dipper as originally completed with open cockpit. (*Lockheed*)

In charting a new course for the company its directors and officers decided to bank heavily on the anticipated boom in commercial and general aviation. For the latter, Lockheed had the Little Dipper, first flown during the last year of the war, and the Big Dipper, which was being readied for a first flight toward the end of 1945. For the airlines it had prototypes of the Saturn feeder-liner under construction and was anticipating a potential market for its 92-ton (83·5-tonne) Constitution, of which two prototypes had been ordered in 1942 by the US Navy at the behest of the airline operating its trans-Pacific logistic network, Pan American Airways. Lockheed's trump, however, was the Constellation.

Ordered by TWA before America's entry into the war, the Constellation was commandeered by the USAAF and was first flown on 9 January, 1943, in Air Force camouflage but with the experimental registration NX25600. This aircraft, together with thirteen more C-69s and one C-69C, were delivered to the USAAF; however, five partly completed aircraft were cancelled. Cruising 50 mph (80 km/h) faster than the DC-4, carrying a larger payload (18,400 lb/8,346 kg versus 14,200 lb/6,441 kg) over a longer still-air range (2,635 miles/4,240 km versus 2,140 miles/3,445 km), and having full cabin pressurization, the Constellation held a decisive advantage over the older, unpressurized, Douglas four-engined transport and was available eighteen months earlier than the pressurized DC-6. The Constellation had an even more commanding lead over newer four-engined transports under development by Boeing (the Stratocruiser which entered service only in September 1948) and by Republic (the Rainbow was built in prototype form as the high-speed, long-range XF-12 reconnaissance aircraft for the USAAF but never developed into the hoped-for commercial transport).

During the five-day plant shutdown in mid-August 1945 Lockheed considered developing an advanced version of the Constellation but rejected this idea as it would have cut the Constellation's lead over its rivals and would not have provided immediate jobs for the assembly-line personnel. Instead, the company elected to proceed with immediate production of Model 049 Constellations using C-69 surplus tooling, materials, components and five uncompleted airframes purchased back from the US Government. In this way Lockheed was able to begin commercial deliveries of Constellations in November 1945 and the type went into scheduled service on 3 February, 1946. Unfortunately, a Constellation crashed five months later due to an inflight fire and fifty-eight L-049s were grounded for six weeks while the cause of the fire was investigated and corrective modifications made (a similar misfortune befell the Constellation's main competitor, the DC-6, which was grounded for 19 weeks beginning in November 1947). Reflecting settlements on cancelled contracts, 1945 ended with a $5·5 mn profit, exceeded only by profits in 1943 and 1944, even though the number of aircraft delivered dropped from 5,864 in 1944 to 2,828 in 1945. Included in these aircraft were the first nine commercial Constellations. The year 1945 also saw in October the organization of the Airquipment Company, a subsidiary providing engineering, production and sales of ground handling equipment for airlines, airports and general aviation owners.

The beautiful Constellation—in this instance *Flagship Copenhagen*, a Model 049 of American Overseas Airlines—helped Lockheed to stay in business after the mass cancellation of wartime military contracts. (*Lockheed*)

The first full year of peace, even though it ended with a net income of $3·1 mn in spite of a $21·9 mn operating loss, was a difficult one for Lockheed; the July-August grounding of its Constellation had been preceded in January by the crash of the Big Dipper, and the Shooting Star was experiencing a high rate of accidents. Furthermore, although initial attempts at operating commercial servicing bases at Linden in New Jersey and Shannon in Eire ran into trouble, the company stuck to the concept and at the end of 1946 organized Lockheed Aircraft Service (LAS) as a wholly-owned subsidiary to handle servicing and modifications of Lockheed's own aircraft as well as those of other manufacturers. A third of a century later, LAS is still a profitable part of the Lockheed Corporation. Other favourable developments during 1946 included the first flight of both the Saturn (17 June) and the Constitution (9 November), the introduction of the first postwar version of the Constellation (the L-649), and the 11,235·6 mile (18,081·98 km) nonstop flight by the P2V-1 *The Turtle*, which set a world's record for piston-engined aircraft still standing in 1981.

At the end of 1946 the financial picture appeared bleak, for Lockheed's operating loss for the year had been $21·9 mn (almost three-quarters of its wartime profit of $30·4 mn realized from 1940 through 1944!) before income tax. A federal income-tax credit reduced this loss to $10·7 mn and a transfer of $13·8 mn from a reserve fund set up during the war to finance transition to peacetime operations enabled the company to post a $3·1 mn net income.

25

One of Lockheed's less successful business ventures, the Saturn programme, found itself without a market due to a glut of surplus military aircraft. (*Lockheed*)

Moreover, Lockheed was forced to borrow up to £40 mn to finance continued operations.

The following year, 1947, ended with a $2·5 mn loss, which this time could no longer be offset by transfer of funds from reserves. It came about as a result of the intense competition between Lockheed and Douglas, with the DC-6 starting to overtake the Constellation's lead, the reduced delivery rate for the Shooting Stars, and the realization that sales of the Saturn feeder-liner would not materialize in the face of the availability of large numbers of cheaper surplus aircraft (mainly Beech C-45s and Douglas C-47s) while the Constitution proved too large to attract airline orders. Fortunately, in spite of the competition from the DC-6, the Constellation was still doing well and accounted for 47 per cent of the $134·4 mn sales realized by the company during 1947. During that year Lockheed, as a private venture, also undertook design of a two-seat advanced trainer version of the Shooting Star. While the decision to proceed with this aircraft proved wise, few people, within or outwith the company, could foresee that it would result in Lockheed's second largest programme in terms of aircraft produced. A total of 5,771 T-33//RT-33/TV-2s were built in Burbank while the T-bird* became the first Lockheed type to be built abroad under licence, with Canadian and Japanese production adding 866 aircraft.

The increase in world tension following the start of the Berlin blockade — which saw C-121s, military versions of the Model 749 Constellation, making trans-atlantic cargo/passenger flights in support of the Berlin Airlift, and LAS obtaining a three-year Air Force contract to operate facilities at Keflavik Airport in Iceland — and the realization that the strength of the US Armed Forces had been allowed to dwindle alarmingly since the end of the war had a positive impact on Lockheed. New or additional orders were placed for F-80Cs, T-33As and P2Vs, while development of the all-weather F-94 interceptor was authorized by Letter

*T-bird was the affectionate nickname given to the T-33 by United States pilots.

The two-seat version of the Shooting Star, in this case an early TV-2 of the US Navy, had its origin in a private venture and succeeded beyond the most sanguine hopes of the company.
(*Lockheed*)

Contract in November 1948, thus enabling the company to increase its year-end backlog from $154 mn in 1947 to $195·9 mn in 1948. At the same time, increased deliveries of civil and military 649/749 Constellations boosted annual sales to $125·6 mn, of which 93 per cent was derived from military contracts. A net profit of $6·2 mn was realized and, more importantly, bank loans were reduced by 85 per cent to $6 mn. Furthermore, after dropping to a postwar low of 13,286 in April 1948, employment started to pick up. This favourable trend continued during 1949 with the year-end backlog increasing to $230 mn and a net profit of $5·5 mn being obtained on sales of $117·7 mn (79 per cent of which were military). The forties ended for Lockheed with the first flight of the XF-90 penetration fighter prototype (6 June, 1949) and YF-94 (1 July, 1949), and the start of the development for the Super Constellation series.

Initially ordered by Eastern Air Lines in April 1950, with military orders first being placed in Fiscal Year 1951 for both the USN and USAF, the Super Constellation outsold its forebear 2·4 to 1, with 259 civil models being supplemented by 320 military transport, airborne early-warning and reconnaissance models. Most of the military Super Constellations procured were part of the

Lockheed 1049G Super Constellation PP-VVD of Varig, now the Brazilian flag carrier.
(*Varig*)

27

The Marietta plant in Georgia which includes the world's largest aircraft assembly hall under a single roof. (*Lockheed*)

massive orders received by Lockheed during the Korean War period. These contracts were for already existing types (T-33As, F-94s, P2Vs, and C-121/R7Vs) and for new designs leading to the development of the XFV-1 VTOL research aircraft, which was initiated in August 1950, the YC-130, in mid-1951, and the XF-104, in November 1952. Whereas the XFV-1 and pre-Korean War XF-90 projects did not lead to production contracts, the XF-104 and YC-130 fathered the Starfighter and Hercules programmes which had long-term impacts on the company's workload and profit.

Late in 1950 the Air Force asked Lockheed to reopen a government plant at Marietta, Georgia. Built by the Defense Plant Corporation, a subsidiary of the Reconstruction Finance Corporation, this 4·5 mn sq ft (418,000 sq m) facility had been operated during the war by the Bell Aircraft Corporation to produce 356 Boeing B-29-BAs but had been shut down at the end of the war. Reopened in January 1951, it was initially used by Lockheed to de-cocoon and prepare for operations 120 B-29s which had been stored for several years at Pyote, Texas, and went on to be used for the assembly of eight Boeing-designed B-47B-LM Stratojets and the production of 386 B-47E-LMs. Later, the Marietta plant was assigned responsibility for the production of the Hercules and JetStar (two prototypes of each type being built in Burbank before the transfer of production to Marietta). Since then the Lockheed-Georgia Company, which was organized in 1961 to succeed Lockheed's Georgia Division, has been the prime manufacturer of military transport aircraft.

In addition to the opening of the Marietta facility and modernization of the main installations in Burbank, Lockheed opened in early 1951 a new facility at Palmdale Airport, California, to supplement the Van Nuys Airport's production flight test centre for jet aircraft. In 1953, following the crash of a T-33A at Van Nuys, in which a housewife was killed, Lockheed transferred all jet production flight activities to Palmdale. Moreover, Lockheed Aircraft Service—which earlier had moved its East Coast facilities from Linden, New Jersey, to MacArthur Field on Long Island, New York, and finally to Idlewild (now New York's John F Kennedy International Airport)—relocated its main base from the crowded Lockheed Air-Terminal in Burbank to Ontario, California, in October 1952.

By the end of 1950 the company's backlog had skyrocketed to $447 mn and during the Korean War Lockheed posted steadily gaining sales figures: $173·3 mn in 1950, $237·2 mn in 1951, $438·1 mn in 1952 and $820·5 mn in 1953, with net income during these four years totalling $37·5 mn, or 2¼ per cent of sales. Clearly, in spite of continued Super Constellation production for the airlines, the bulk of sales was generated by defence contracts; military sales accounted respectively for 85, 88, 92 and 89 per cent of total sales in 1950 to 1954.

B-47E-40-LM, one of 394 Boeing B-47 Stratojets built by Lockheed in the Marietta plant.
(*David W. Menard*)

Continued dependence to such an extent on military sales was a worrisome situation in post-Korean War days. In the commercial field, the heated competition between Lockheed and Douglas was not turning in favour of the Burbank company as between 1945 and 1958, the year in which the last of the piston-powered transports were produced, it delivered 510 commercial Constellations/ Super Constellations/Starliners versus 878 Douglas DC-4s/DC-6s/DC-7s. Even when including deliveries of military versions of these aircraft, Lockheed was outsold 856 to 1,045 (or to 2,210 if wartime C-54s are included in the Douglas total). It was not that Lockheed was lax in its efforts to improve the Constellation series as in fact it outpaced Douglas in introducing, or attempting to introduce, significant improvements. Thus, it pioneered in 1953 the commercial use of Turbo-Compound engines, when on 17 February the L-1049C was first flown, and in 1954 the use of propeller-turbines on a US transport aircraft, when on 1 September the R7V-2 began flight trials. However, the Douglas DC-6 and DC-7 series benefited from the use of a circular fuselage of constant cross section, which made stretching easier and less expensive, and of Pratt & Whitney R-2800 engines, which were more reliable than the Wright R-3350s used in the Constellation series and thus proved more economic and longer-lived.

Prior to gaining experience of propeller-turbines as powerplants for transport aircraft with the Pratt & Whitney T34-powered Model 1249A Super Constellation (R7V-2 for the USN and YC-121F for the USAF) Lockheed had begun ground

29

testing the Allison XT40-powered XFV-1 in late 1953. This aircraft became inadvertently airborne on 23 December, 1953, but officially flew for the first time on 16 June, 1954. By then, however, the construction of YC-130 prototypes was well underway and the turbine-powered Hercules was first flown on 23 August, 1954. Lockheed, which for a while had been considering offering turbine-powered Super Constellations to the airlines, had also made preliminary studies for a shorter-range turbine transport primarily intended for the US domestic trunk carriers. One of these designs, the CL-303 airliner with a high wing and two propeller-turbines, came close to being built, but insufficient interest on the part of the airlines forced its abandonment in 1954. Thus, before returning to this segment of the market, Lockheed temporarily concentrated its commercial efforts on its last piston-engined aircraft, the L-1649 Starliner. The company also studied some 300 jet transport configurations including the double-decked L-193 with swept wing and tail surfaces and four turbojets attached to the fuselage, aft of the wing. This 1954 design lost out to the Boeing 707 and Douglas DC-8, and the first Lockheed jetliner, the TriStar, did not fly until 16 November, 1970.

In the military jet aircraft field Lockheed continued during the mid-fifties with the largescale production of T-33As and with the manufacture of T2V-1s, a naval development of the T-33A. Its P2V Neptune also continued strongly, with Kawasaki acquiring in 1958 the licence rights for the production of P2V-7s in Japan. Above all, however, this period was marked by the debut of the XF-104, which was first flown on 4 March, 1954, and of two highly classified programmes: research into nuclear-powered aircraft and the U-2. The first of these programmes had been started in great secrecy in 1949 and its existence was not revealed until October 1953, and even then only in a guarded statement. Three

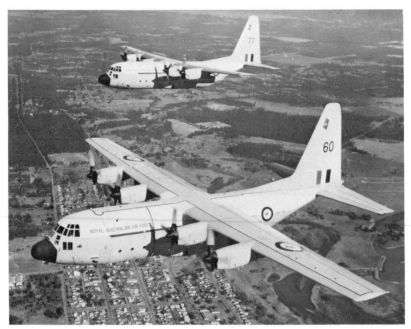

A pair of C-130Es from No.37 Squadron, RAAF. (*Australian Department of Defence*)

F-104A-15-LO in service with the US Air Defense Command. (*via Cloud 9 Photography*)

years later Lockheed undertook the construction of a $13 mn specialized laboratory near Dawsonville, Georgia, for this programme; however, little else has been released for publication and no nuclear-powered aircraft were actually built by Lockheed.

Just about as heavily classified was the work of a special engineering team led by Kelly Johnson in an off-limit area of Burbank which housed the Advanced Development Projects section, better known as the 'Skunk Works'.* Johnson, whose technical genius was greatly respected in industry and Department of Defense circles, had long been critical of pure research aircraft (even though his own F-104 owed much to the work of Frank Fleming's X-3 Stiletto team at Douglas) which, he claimed, were a wasteful way of spending limited funds. Instead, Johnson advocated designing high-performance aircraft which not only would serve to advance the state-of-the-art but would also have specific operational use. He got a chance to practice what he preached when he was secretly apprised of the need of the Air Force and the Central Intelligence Agency for a long-range reconnaissance aircraft with such performance that interception by potential adversaries would be virtually impossible. How well Johnson succeeded with his U-2, which was first flown on 6 August, 1955, can be judged by the fact that for several years it repeatedly made 3,800-mile (6,115-km) flights across the USSR without being intercepted, until 1 May, 1960, when Lieut Francis Gary Powers was brought down near Sverdlovsk, and by the fact that it has been ordered back into production as the TR-1.

In an amazing demonstration of the benefits of free enterprise Kelly Johnson and his team, freed from most governmental red tape and company bureaucracy

*The nickname 'Skunk Works' was coined at the onset of the XP-80 programme when Kelly Johnson and his staff were housed in temporary quarters next to a plastics factory. One of the team engineers began referring to the buildings by the same name as the foul-smelling factory in Al Capp's 'Li'l Abner' comic strip. In spite of Kelly Johnson's initial dislike for the nickname, it stuck. Indeed, the classified nature of the operations undertaken by the Advanced Development Projects makes its buildings nearly as unapproachable as if they were inhabited by mammals of the genus Mephitis.

due to the highly secret nature of the U-2 programme, got the first aircraft ready to fly within eight months of the project go-ahead. Later, the first twenty U-2s and spares for the USAF were not only completed within the $21 million budget but, when the inventory of spares was determined to exceed requirements, Lockheed used these spares to build six additional aircraft for only the cost of labour. Thus, the USAF obtained twenty-six U-2s ahead of schedule and at the remarkably low unit cost of less than $900,000. Furthermore, working with a project and manufacturing staff running a mere 7 to 25 per cent of that of similar, non-classified, programmes at Lockheed, the Advanced Development Projects group has reportedly obtained since that time profit margins reaching 12 per cent, or more than double the average on most other military contracts. Quite an achievement indeed for a contractor often accused by the press and some members of Congress of being careless with its cost and schedule controls on military contracts!

Clarence L. 'Kelly' Johnson, Lockheed's technical and project management genius, in a 'proud father' pose in front of a U-2. (*Lockheed*)

Even though some of its preliminary design experts had begun working in 1949 on what became the X-7 ramjet research vehicle, Lockheed was a late comer in the missile field and its Missile Systems Division (now the Lockheed Missiles & Space Company Inc) was not formed until late in 1953. MSD began operating in January 1954 at Burbank, with a move three months later to Van Nuys, and a further move to new facilities in Sunnyvale, Northern California, in September 1956. Since then MSD and the Lockheed Missiles & Space Company have been involved in several highly successful programmes including the X-17 hypersonic research vehicle, the Agena space vehicle and, above all, the Polaris/Poseidon/Trident submarine-launched strategic missiles. Although of considerable importance to the overall viability of the Lockheed Aircraft Corporation/Lockheed Corporation as, for example, they contributed 37·3 per cent of the company's revenues and 45·9 per cent of its programme profits in the five-year period ending in December 1978, further discussion of Lockheed's missile, space and electronics activities is not included in this volume as they fall outside its scope.

When in 1955 Lockheed again activated its preliminary design study efforts for a turbine-powered airliner to meet American Airlines' requirements, it faced stiff competition from Boeing, Convair, Douglas and North American. In particular, it could then be feared that Douglas would have an edge as American Airlines,

Beset by technical troubles during its early service life, the propeller-turbine Electra went on to achieve an excellent reputation after Lockheed spent $25 mn to overcome its problems. (*Lockheed*)

since acquiring its first DC-2s in 1934, had been a staunch Douglas client and had become the launch customer for the DC-3, DC-6 and DC-7. However, apparently displeased by a dispute over DC-7 pricing, American Airlines was ready to consider alternative suppliers. Thus, after working with Lockheed and Eastern Air Lines in refining the requirements for the four-engined propeller-turbine transport, American Airlines became, on 8 June, 1955, the Electra's launch customer with an order for 35 aircraft. By the end of the year Lockheed had received orders for 61 more aircraft and had a $211 mn Electra backlog. The future appeared bright for the new type which made its first flight on 6 December, 1957. Unfortunately, following two accidents, the Federal Aviation Agency imposed on 25 March, 1960, a speed restriction on the aircraft. Following completion of a modification programme funded by Lockheed, this restriction was lifted on 5 January, 1961. The cost of this modification programme, together with loss of revenues when production had to be ended with the delivery of the 170th Electra, drained Lockheed of an estimated $25 mn. By then, however, the Electra had spawned the P-3 Orion long-range patrol aircraft which has remained in

P-3B-85-LO Orion of Patrol Squadron Four (VP-4) based at NAS Barbers Point, Hawaii. (*Cloud 9 Photography*)

N9201R, the first production JetStar 6 built in the Marietta plant. (*Lockheed*)

continuous production since the 25 November, 1959, first flight of its YP3V-1 prototype (the 500th P-3 was delivered to the US Navy in December 1979). When viewed jointly, the Electra and Orion programmes have been solid money-makers for their manufacturer.

Even though its design had been started only in early 1957, almost two years after Lockheed had received an initial order for its Electra, the prototype of the JetStar business jet and light military transport was first flown on 4 September, 1957, three months before that of the Electra. Anticipated largescale military orders for these twin-engined (prototypes) and four-engined (production models) jet transports did not materialize. Even though the sixteen C-140A/Bs and VC-140Bs for the USAF were supplemented by 146 commercial JetStars and 40 JetStars IIs, with the two prototypes being built in Burbank and all production aircraft being built in Marietta, the programme did not prove financially satisfactory for Lockheed. Also relatively unsuccessful was the Lockheed-Azcarate 60 single-engine light utility aircraft intended for mass production in Mexico, Argentina and Italy under Lockheed licences. The first of the two Marietta-built prototypes was flown on 15 September, 1959, and was followed by eighteen Mexican-built machines. The Argentine programme was never undertaken but, in Italy, Macchi was more fortunate with its development of the basic design.

While the JetStar and Electra were undergoing flight trials, Lockheed was also engaged in a ruthless competitive battle with other US aircraft manufacturers as well as with British and French companies to supply the West German Luftwaffe with its first supersonic fighters and to provide similar weapons systems to other allied air forces. Helped in part by the world's records (absolute speed, absolute ceiling and seven time-to-height records) it set, and in part by the company's aggressive marketing, the F-104 was a strong contender. Its first and decisive victory in this competition was won on 6 November, 1958, when the German Federal Republic's defence committee announced its selection of the F-104G, a specially developed all-weather multi-mission version of the Starfighter, as that nation's standard interceptor, fighter-bomber and reconnaissance aircraft, with limited production to be undertaken by Lockheed and larger-scale manufacturing to be initiated in Germany. During the following year the Starfighter was also selected by Canada (CF-104A/D) and Japan (F-104J/DJ), whilst in 1960 the multi-national programme was expanded to include Belgium, Italy and the Netherlands. This largescale undertaking eventually added 1,789 Starfighters to Lockheed's own production of the F-104 and contributed $1·39 billion to the US balance of payment. For Lockheed, it was a major coup which greatly contributed to the company's financial success in the late fifties and early sixties, and funded in great part its diversification programme.

Having acquired the Lockheed Air Terminal in 1940, organized the Lockheed Aircraft Service in 1946, and activated its Missile Systems Division in 1953, the Lockheed Aircraft Corporation was better prepared than most other aircraft manufacturers when a 1957 announcement of drastic cutbacks in military aircraft expenditures made it advisable for these companies to diversify their business. For the Burbank firm which had missed entering the commercial jetliner field, unlike Boeing, Convair and Douglas, the search for new endeavours led in 1959 to going intensively into electronics with the formation in March of the Lockheed Electronics and Avionics Division and the acquisition in May of Stavid Engineering; these two entities were later combined into the Lockheed Electronics Company, a wholly-owned subsidiary which now remains active in military electronics. During 1959 Lockheed also bought the Puget Sound Bridge and Dry Dock Company, a major construction, shipbuilding, and ship repair firm. After being operated for five years under its original name this subsidiary was reorganized in 1964 as the Lockheed Shipbuilding and Construction Company; fifteen years later, in 1979, LSCC accounted for 3·2 per cent of the total corporate sales.

To complement its missile and space activities, Lockheed acquired in February 1960 a fifty per cent interest in Grand Central Rocket Company of Redlands in California. After its remaining stocks had been acquired this rocket engine design and manufacturing company was renamed the Lockheed Propulsion Company. However, disappointing results, notably with the SRAM (Short Range Attack Missile) solid-fuel rocket, and failure to win follow-on contracts, forced the closure of this subsidiary in 1975.

The year 1957 saw Lockheed begin in the Van Nuys facility its fifteen-year effort to break into the helicopter business. Although its development of rigid-rotor systems, first demonstrated in flight when the CL-475 began trials in November 1959, gave it a strong competitive edge, Lockheed fought an uphill battle. This led to the development of the high-speed XH-51 and L-286 series and,

Representing a bold jump in the state-of-the-art, the AH-56A Cheyenne became the source of many technical and contractual problems. (*Lockheed*)

more significantly, to the award in March 1966 of a US Army contract for engineering development of an Advanced Aerial Fire Support System helicopter. Designated AH-56A and named Cheyenne, this weapons system was first flown on 21 September, 1967. Unfortunately, plagued initially with teething troubles and caught in a controversy with the Department of Defense, the Cheyenne programme was terminated in August 1972. The final cancellation of the AH-56 development ended the company's work in the helicopter field, one of Lockheed's least satisfactory diversification ventures. In the VTOL field the Lockheed-Georgia Company first flew, on 7 July, 1962, its VZ-10 augmented jet-ejector vertical-lift research aircraft under US Army contract. One of the two experimental aircraft was later modified as the XV-4B jet-lift research vehicle for the USAF, but neither the XV-4A nor the XV-4B led to production programmes.

In its more traditional aircraft business Lockheed proceeded during the first half of the sixties with its existing Starfighter, Hercules, JetStar, Orion and U-2 programmes, and concluded production of the Neptune and Electra. New aircraft types committed to production during this period included the C-141 StarLifter, first flown on 17 December, 1963 — on the sixtieth anniversary of the first powered, sustained, and controlled flight by the Wright brothers — and the YF-12/SR-71, the superb product of the Skunk Works which began flight trials on 26 April, 1962. Furthermore, after participating in a preliminary design competition for a very large military logistics transport, in December 1964 Lockheed became one of the three contractors invited to participate in the C-5 competition. Thus, at the end of 1964, Lockheed, which then had a backlog of just over $2 US billion, a working capital of $161 mn, a capital of $75 mn and retained earnings of $164 mn, appeared to be in a comfortable position. Serious troubles, however, were soon to beset its

The C-141A StarLifter production line at Marietta. (*Lockheed*)

Two of the most famous products of the Skunk Works (F-80C-10-LO, 49-696, and YF-12A, 60-6935) at the US Air Force Museum in November 1979. The F-80, obtained from the Fuerza Aérea Uruguaya, has been repainted in the markings it once bore while serving in Korea. (*David W. Menard*)

new management (Robert Gross, who died on 1 September, 1961, had been succeeded as Chairman of the Board by his brother Courtlandt, and Daniel J. Haughton had become President in 1961 when Courtlandt Gross had taken his new position).

Lockheed Aircraft Corporation
TriStar, Tribulations and Trinkets—The Crisis Years, 1965–77

The first year in the most difficult period in the history of the company saw Lockheed win in October 1965 the hotly contested C-5 competition when its Marietta division was awarded the contract for the first type of aircraft powered by the new generation of high-bypass-ratio turbofans in the 40,000 lb (18,144 kg) thrust class. This award, however, was one of the first under the total package procurement system. The unworkable application of this novel type of contracting to a high technology programme, combined with a sharp increase in inflationary pressures in the United States and with increased difficulties in obtaining and retaining skilled workers at a time when sharply rising production of military aircraft and jetliners (due respectively to the intensifying of the Vietnam hostilities and a boom in the air transport industry) forced the manufacturers into a sharp competition for staff, and resulted in substantial cost overruns on the company's programmes, notably that of the C-5A Galaxy. Bad as it was, the overrun in the Galaxy programme was further aggravated by the reduction in production programme from 115 to 81 aircraft which was announced in November 1969 and gave rise to a legal dispute over the applicability of a repricing formula contained in the C-5A contract.

The cutback in C-5 production had come six months after Lockheed had been informed that the US Army, alleging default, was terminating the AH-56A Cheyenne Phase III production programme. Indeed, the development of this very advanced compound helicopter had run into difficulties as the AH-56A could not initially meet some of its performance requirements, while its cost rose sharply over the ceiling of 115 per cent of the bid price, forcing the company to absorb substantial losses. During the next three years most of the technical deficiencies were corrected but cost remained excessive. As the Army was

Still the heaviest and largest aircraft in the USAF inventory, the C-5A Galaxy is being given a new lease on life through a major wing rebuild programme. (*Lockheed*)

inexperienced in the management of complex aircraft programmes, and as it was fighting with the USAF to justify the development of a weapons system competing with fixed-wing aircraft to provide support for ground forces, the Cheyenne was finally terminated in August 1972. Lockheed was then unsuccessful in its attempt to be selected as one of the two contractors to design and test prototypes of a less complex attack helicopter (eventually resulting in the ordering in December 1976 of the Hughes AH-64A) and was forced out of the helicopter business after incurring substantial losses.

Lockheed Propulsion Company also ran into troubles with the development of the solid-fuel engine which it developed under subcontract from Boeing for the Short Range Attack Missile. Claiming increased costs attributable to unexpected and exceptionally difficult technical challenges encountered in developing the test propulsion motors for the SRAM,* Lockheed was forced in December 1969 to submit a $50 mn claim to the Boeing Company and asked the Department of Defense for a $25 mn provisional payment under this claim pending its resolution. Lockheed and Boeing negotiated an agreement and Lockheed received $20 mn in full settlement of its claim in October 1970. The SRAM engine was then successfully developed but, at the conclusion of this programme, LPC was inactivated.

In the military aircraft business not all had been bad for Lockheed during 1969,

---

*The author, and more especially his children, remember vividly a spectacular pyrotechnic display when an SRAM engine blew up on the day of their move in 1969 to a new home located one mile from the LPC plant in Redlands. The wisdom of this move remained in doubt for some months . . .

as in August of that year it had won the VSX competition. The resulting S-3A Viking was first flown on 21 January, 1972, but, although it met all of its contractual requirements, the Viking only had a short production life (187 S-3As, including prototypes, were built whereas the aircraft it replaced, the Grumman S-2 Tracker with its Canadian-built version, and TF-1/C-1 Trader and WF-2/E-1 Tracer derivatives, had a combined production run of 1,461 aircraft).

Having opted out of the competition for the first generation of US jetliners, Lockheed did not intend to let its long tradition as a manufacturer of commercial transports lapse permanently. Beginning in 1956 the company had studied many configurations for supersonic transports and was thus in a good position to answer the requests for proposals for an SST Phase 1 design study issued by the Federal Aviation Agency in August 1963. Its CL-823 proposal for a 218-passenger transport with a take-off weight of 450,000 lb (204,117 kg) was selected in June 1964 for further development in parallel with a Boeing proposal. During the ensuing Phases 2A through 2C of the US SST programme the Lockheed design evolved into the L-2000-7 which retained the double-delta configuration and Mach 3 cruising speed of the CL-823 but grew steadily until it reached a take-off weight of 590,000 lb (267,620 kg). Two versions were proposed, the L-2000-7A intercontinental model, with an overall length of 273 ft 2 in (83·26 m) and accommodation for up to 266 passengers, and the L-2000-7B domestic model, which was larger (293 ft/89·31 m) and could carry up to 308 passengers but had a reduced fuel load. These two variants were entered against the Boeing 2707 but the latter was announced the winner on 31 December, 1966.*

*The selection of the Boeing design, thought by most airlines to be inferior to the L-2000, can probably be explained by geopolitical considerations. Three equally large contracts were to be awarded in 1965–66 by the US Government. For the MOL (Manned Orbiting Laboratory) Lockheed and Douglas in California competed with Boeing in Washington; for the C-5A the same three companies, but with Lockheed being represented in that instance by its Georgia division, were at odds, while the SST pitted Boeing in Washington against Lockheed in California. The award of the MOL contract to Douglas took care of that company and of the State of California; thus, after the C-5A had gone to Lockheed and the State of Georgia, only Boeing and the State of Washington remained to be taken care of.

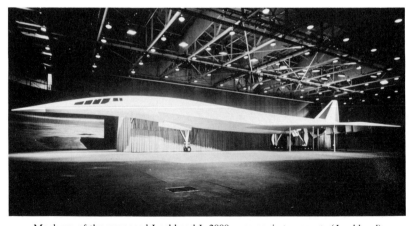

Mock-up of the proposed Lockheed L-2000 supersonic transport. (*Lockheed*)

After losing the SST competition, Lockheed half-heartedly proposed its L-500 commercial version of the C-5A but banked its re-entry in the commercial transport market on a 250-passenger, wide-bodied jetliner to meet an American Airlines requirement for a lower capacity, shorter-range, companion to the Boeing 747. Evolving from an original twin-engined study to a three-engined design, the L-1011 lost the initial competition to the McDonnell Douglas DC-10 as American Airlines ordered the Long Beach-designed trijet on 19 February, 1968. Gloom in Burbank was short-lived as forty days later Lockheed was able to announce the largest-ever launching orders for an airliner: 172 orders and options, worth $2·5 US billion, from TWA, Eastern, Delta, Northeast, and Air Holdings Ltd. The Air Holdings order was not as binding as it initially appeared but its inclusion helped defuse criticism for the selection of a British-made engine, the Rolls-Royce RB.211, in preference to US-made units from either Pratt & Whitney or General Electric. The success of the TriStar (the name selected in January 1969 from suggestions made by employees) programme, however, soon ran into turbulence as the proposed intercontinental L-1011-8—a fairly major redesign of the domestic L-1011-1 version—lost out in June 1969 to the DC-10-30 which was a more straightforward development of the McDonnell Douglas trijet.

The Palmdale plant which was specially built to house final assembly of the L-1011 TriStar.
(*Lockheed*)

As a result of the disputes between Lockheed and its main customer (89 per cent of the company's sales in 1969 were to the US Government) over the C-5A, AH-56A, SRAM engine, and shipbuilding programmes, and of the increased cash requirements to finance the development, testing, and production of the L-1011, it became apparent in early 1970 that the company would require additional borrowings from its bankers. The firm had ended 1969 with a loss of $32·6 mn and was anticipating further deficit in 1970 in spite of its record backlog of $5·1 US billion. At that time it had $230·7 mn in retained earnings and a capital of $90·4 mn but it owed $336·3 mn in long-term debt (a Credit Agreement between Lockheed

Early TriStar production at Palmdale with two aircraft for Eastern Air lines and TWA, one for Air Canada and one for Court Line. (*Lockheed*)

After bringing their respective manufacturers to the brink of disaster, the Rolls-Royce RB.211 and the Lockheed TriStar have now earned high marks from operators, airline passengers and residents of communities near airports. (*Peter M. Keefe*)

and its lenders, dated 1 May, 1969, provided a ceiling of $400 mn). A tentative agreement to raise this limit to $500 mn was reached in January 1971 but, before it could be executed, Lockheed was dealt another near fatal blow: Rolls-Royce, the manufacturer of the engine for the aircraft on which the company relied to end its over-dependency on military and space prógrammes, announced it would not fulfil its contract to develop and produce the RB.211 and placed itself in the hands of a receiver. The L-1011 programme, which had entered its flight-trial phase on 16 November, 1970, ground to a halt. The new Credit Agreement was held back, and the Lockheed Aircraft Corporation was on the verge of bankruptcy.

The only workable solution to this new threat to Lockheed's viability was to revive Rolls-Royce. Weeks of deliberation between Lockheed, Rolls-Royce, the British Government, and L-1011 customer airlines, brought forth a plan: engine prices were revised upward and large airlines increased their advance payments for L-1011s by $100 mn. Nevertheless, Her Majesty's Government desired assurances from the United States Government that it would likewise stand behind Lockheed, for it was obvious that the aircraft manufacturer's weakened financial condition would suffer further from the months of interrupted TriStar production.

By all normal banking standards Lockheed's balance sheet in the spring of 1971 no longer warranted an extension of credit past the previously agreed ceiling of $400 mn. To go beyond this limit the lenders insisted on some unusual form of guarantee and suggested that the company seek assistance from the government. Consequently, in order to avert Lockheed's bankruptcy and the resultant national economic and defence impacts, legislation was introduced in Congress in May 1971 to provide for a Government guarantee of up to $250 mn of commercial loans. These loans would be in addition to the existing $400 mn line of credit and to the $100 mn in additional advance payments by customer airlines. Following exhaustive hearings and debate by Congress, the Emergency Loan Guarantee Act, Public Law 92–70—which provided for the establishment of a Guarantee Board comprising the Secretary of the Treasury as Chairman, and the Chairmen of the Board of Governors of the Federal Reserve System and of the SEC (Securities and Exchange Commission), and authorized it to guarantee up to £250 mn of private bank loans—was passed on 2 August, 1971, and was signed by President Nixon one week later.

The Emergency Loan Guarantee Act gave authority to guarantee or make commitments to guarantee lenders against loss of principal or interest on loans that met the following requirements: (1) the loan be needed to enable the borrower to continue to furnish goods and services; (2) credit not otherwise be available to the borrower under reasonable terms and conditions; and (3) the lender certify that it would not make the loan without such guarantee. The Guarantee Board found that Lockheed met the requirements of the Act and committed on 9 August, 1971, its entire guarantee capacity to Lockheed.

The company immediately drew $100 mn in guaranteed loans, and its borrowing under the Act peaked at $245 mn in September 1974. The last $60 mn in guaranteed loans were converted to conventional bank loan on 14 October, 1977, and, since then, the company has had access to the credit market under conventional terms and conditions without further utilization of the Government guarantee. Lockheed had been saved. It is worth noting, however, that the banks were the ones actually lending funds to the company—the Government only provided its guarantee and no taxpayers' money was lent to Lockheed. In return for this guarantee the Government earned over $31 mn, net of administrative expenses of slightly less than $1 mn, between August 1971 and October 1977. These earnings, which were transferred to the Treasury to be used as general funds, included approximately $25 mn in cumulative guarantee fees (at an annual rate of 2 per cent) on the borrowings, $2 mn in commitment fees (at an annual rate of $\frac{1}{4}$ per cent) on the unused portion of the credit, and $5 mn in cumulative interest on the fees. Furthermore, throughout the period of its guarantee commitment, the Government's position was fully secured by a first lien on Lockheed assets which consistently were valued in excess of the maximum authorized loan guarantees by both the GAO (General Accounting Office) and the Guarantee Board.

With the implementation of the Emergency Loan Guarantee Act and the assurance that the initial batch of 555 engines would be delivered by Rolls-Royce (1971) Ltd under a renegotiated contract, Lockheed could again get back to work in earnest on the TriStar programme, and 9,000 employees, who had been laid off at the time of the Rolls-Royce receivership, were rehired. The L-1011 received its FAA Type Approval on 14 April, 1972, and entered scheduled service with Eastern Air Lines twelve days later. Other aircraft programmes which could then be continued were those for the Orion and Viking at CALAC (Lockheed-California Company), and for the Hercules, JetStar and Galaxy at GELAC (Lockheed-Georgia Company). The new financing was indeed much needed by Lockheed as, after taking into account a change in accounting practice to charge development costs against current earnings, it reported net losses of $187·8 mn in 1970, $39·4 mn in 1971 and $7·2 mn in 1972. Profitability was restored in 1973, with net profits of $18·2 mn being reported for that year and of $23·2 mn for 1974. Likewise, the following five years brought a total profit of $260·8 mn. As the company's management, staff and backers were finally able to breathe sighs of relief, a new calamity struck.

In the post Southeast Asia War period the American public and press became increasingly suspicious of big business in general and more especially of the companies from the military-industrial complex. In particular, the so-called questionable practices involving a double standard—one standard of propriety for sales in the United States and a quite different standard for sales in foreign countries—came under close scrutiny. Thus, in June 1975 allegations of improper payments abroad by Lockheed began appearing in the press as a result of a Senate Subcommittee's investigation of similar practices by the Northrop Corporation. Lockheed's independent auditor, Arthur Young and Company, then requested that certain company officers sign a letter stating that: (1) All payments were made in accordance with agreements and were duly recorded on the books of Lockheed; (2) No employee or official of any foreign government, or any director, officer or employee of a customer was a party to any of the agreements; and (3) No director, officer, or managerial employee of Lockheed or an affected subsidiary had knowledge of the disposition of payments made to consultants.

Dan Haughton, the company's Chairman of the Board, did not allow the officers in question to sign the requested letter. This refusal led to a joint investigation of commissions and questionable payments by a special review committee of the Board of Directors and Arthur Young and Company. As a result, tight controls on the hiring of foreign consultants and the payment of overseas marketing commissions were adopted by the Board in September 1975. Finally, on 13 February, 1976, Haughton resigned as chairman of the Board and A. Carl Kotchian, vice-chairman and president, was forced to do so. On the same date a new top echelon, with Robert W. Haack as chairman, Roy A. Anderson as

The old guard and the new guard in the sixties: from left to right Courtlandt S. Gross, Daniel J. Haughton, A. Carl Kotchian and Robert E. Gross. (*Lockheed*)

Roy A. Anderson, chairman of Lockheed Corporation since January 1978 (*left*) and Lawrence O. Kitchen, president and chief operating officer. (*Lockheed*)

vice-chairman, and Lawrence O. Kitchen as president and chief operating officer, took over to implement the new policy and restore confidence in Lockheed. Outside the company the bribery scandal and related allegations resulted in the fall of foreign government officials and in the dismissal of officers from airlines and trading companies.

For Lockheed the final phase in this regrettable affair, which also plagued other US corporations and remains a sad fact of life involving non-US companies, came on 13 April, 1976, when the Securities and Exchange Commission filed a complaint against Lockheed Aircraft Corporation and its two former top executives, Haughton and Kotchian. The main thrust of the complaint was that Lockheed had violated the Securities Exchange Act of 1934 by failing to disclose that it (1) had made payments to foreign government officials, (2) had used secret funds for that purpose, and (3) had hidden these activities by falsifying its financial records and reports. On the same day, without conceding the truth of the facts alleged, or admitting the illegality of any of its conduct, Lockheed consented to the entry of a permanent injunction and filed an undertaking which together: (1) enjoined it from any activities of the kind described in the complaint; (2) provided for the establishment of a special review committee to conduct an investigation into the matters alleged in the complaint; (3) provided the procedure under which the committee should make its report to the Board of Directors and the procedures under which the directors should transmit it to the SEC and to the Court; and (4) provided that Lockheed could seek an order from the Court sealing material, disclosure of which could injure the interest of Lockheed and its stockholders. The report and recommendations of the Special Review Committee were transmitted on 16 May, 1977.

Lockheed Corporation since 1977

To reflect the changes in its top management and its practices overseas, to project a new image, and to acknowledge the fact that by then aircraft and related services accounted for only 58 per cent of its sales, the company changed its name to Lockheed Corporation on 1 September, 1977. It continued to be led by Robert Haack until 29 September, 1977, when, having successfully polished the tarnished image of the firm, he retired. At that time Roy Anderson became Chairman of the Board and chief executive officer while Lawrence Kitchen continued as president and chief operating officer.

Since its name change, Lockheed has not been able to launch, officially at least, a completely new major aircraft programme. Conversely, it concluded production of the S-3A in 1978. Thus, by the end of that year only four aircraft types remained in production — the P-3 and L-1011 in Burbank, and the C-130 and the JetStar II in Marietta — and, for the first time since the late thirties, total deliveries fell below the 80-aircraft mark. The year 1980 saw the delivery of the last JetStar II but also marked the resumption of manufacturing of one of the company's most famous types as the U-2 production line was reopened to produce the TR-1A (single-seat) and TR-1B (two-seat) tactical reconnaissance versions of the U-2 and their ER-2 derivative for NASA. The Advanced Development Projects group, the Skunk Works, under the leadership of Ben R. Rich since Kelly Johnson's retirement, has also been rumoured since 1977 to be working on the highly-classified 'Stealth' programme.

During the last three years of the seventies two of the well-established aircraft programmes passed significant milestones with the delivery of the 1,500th

Overhead view of Plant A-1, corporate headquarters and the Hollywood-Burbank Airport in December 1978. (*Lockheed*)

Hercules in March 1978 and of the 500th Orion in December 1979. As for the L-1011, progress has been slow, with deliveries totalling only 197 aircraft by the end of 1980 whereas the company had, optimistically, announced 172 orders and options back in the spring of 1968. However, the problems of its DC-10 rival following the May 1979 crash in Chicago of an American Airlines aircraft, coming almost three years after the August 1976 launch order for the L-1011-500 by British Airways, and Pan American's selection of the same type in April 1978, have injected new life in the programme. Combining the wide-bodied customer appeal with a seating capacity tailored to the less dense long-range route, and with advanced features such as its active aileron system and improved avionics/electronics (notably its Flight Management System), the fuel-efficient TriStar 500 bids fair to erase the memory of the failure of the L-1011-8 in the initial competition against the DC-10-30 for the intercontinental trijet market.

At the beginning of the eighties the Lockheed Corporation comprised the following operating companies and principal subsidiaries:

Lockheed-California Company (CALAC), with headquarters in Burbank next

One of the safest aircraft currently in service with the US Navy, the S-3A Viking has had its effectiveness limited by budgetary restrictions which resulted in insufficient spares provisioning. (*US Navy*)

46

to those of CORLAC—the Lockheed Corporation itself, has plant facilities in Burbank, Palmdale, Rye Canyon and Watts-Willowbrook. Operating semi-independently is the Advanced Development Projects group. CALAC principal activities include the L-1011 and P-3/CP-140 programmes, aerospace research and the classified work of the Skunk Works.

Lockheed-Georgia Company (GELAC) based in Marietta, with additional facilities at Charleston in South Carolina, Clarksburg in West Virginia, and Meridian in Mississippi. It is now responsible for the C-130, C-141B and C-5A wing modification programmes,

Lockheed Missiles & Space Company Inc (LMSC) in Sunnyvale, California, and other facilities in Alabama, California, Florida, South Carolina, and Washington, is primarily responsible for the company's submarine-launched ballistic missiles, and its military and NASA space activities. LMSC is also engaged in ocean mining, deep submergence rescue and research submarines, and alternate energy development.

Lockheed Aircraft Service Company (LAS), headquartered in Ontario, California, has facilities in Europe, the Middle East and Africa. Its activities include aircraft maintenance and modification, air traffic and air defence systems management and operations. At Luke AFB, Arizona, LAS has been since 1964 maintenance manager for the Luftwaffe F-104 training programme. In Singapore it handled the modification and modernization of the Douglas A-4S/TA-4S Skyhawks for the Singapore Air Defence Command.

Lockheed Electronics Company Inc (LEC) in Plainfield and Denville, New Jersey, provides a variety of electronic products, systems, and services to military (radar and gunfire control systems), industrial, and commercial (air traffic control) customers.

Lockheed Shipbuilding and Construction Company (LSCC) has three shipways in two yards fronting on the deepwater port in Seattle, Washington. Among the ships built by LSCC have been ferries, light cruisers, drill vessels, barges, destroyer escorts, hydrofoils, bulk carriers, assault transports, icebreakers, and submarine tenders.

Lockheed Engineering and Management Services Company Inc (LEMSCO), with headquarters in Houston, Texas, and offices in Missouri, Nevada and New Mexico, provides key technical support to NASA and other federal agencies.

Lockheed Air Terminal Inc (LAT) provides operational services at the Burbank-Glendale-Pasadena Airport (owned by Lockheed until 1978), and fuelling and other services at 25 airports in the United States, Panama and Guam. LAT also offers airport consulting services.

Lockheed Finance Corporation (LFC) in Burbank finances or arranges financing for buyers of Lockheed products, services and related projects, as well as general equipment for airlines and the aerospace industry.

Murdock Machine and Engineering Company of Texas in Irving, Texas, machines and assembles components for the L-1011, the McDonnell Douglas F-15 and the LTV A-7. It also manufactures the Lockheed joint which had been developed earlier by the Lockheed Propulsion Company for use in ships, submarines and oil pipelines.

Since 1 June, 1981, Dialog Information Services Inc has operated as a wholly-owned subsidiary with headquarters in Palo Alto, California, providing information retrieval service to customers in more than 60 countries.

During 1980 the Lockheed Corporation realized a profit of $27·6 million on sales of $5,395·7 million.

Annual Employment, Net Sales and Net Income
Lockheed Corporation and forebears, 1932 to 1980

Fiscal Year	Number of employees (year's end)	Net Sales US$	Net Income US$
1932	64	NA	NA
1933	253	355,990	25,692
1934	332	562,759	(190,891)
1935	500	2,096,775	217,986
1936	1,200	2,006,501	100,126
1937	1,989	5,209,986	137,920
1938	2,977	10,274,503	442,111
1939	7,000	35,308,150	3,132,918
1940	16,898	44,936,595	3,165,676
1941	54,043	144,728,154	6,608,622
1942	74,354	491,160,471	8,163,721
1943	90,853	697,408,167	7,988,420
1944	62,657	602,482,245	4,522,848
1945	30,631	415,076,381	5,469,888
1946	17,156	112,682,732	3,058,785
1947	14,555	134,364,006	(2,471,695)
1948	15,905	125,620,700	6,239,380
1949	16,676	117,666,803	5,490,670
1950	20,241	173,330,839	7,209,934
1951	39,523	237,229,666	5,793,463
1952	47,750	438,122,395	9,058,026
1953	51,548	820,466,739	15,462,079
1954	45,974	732,872,237	22,445,966
1955	58,007	673,588,647	17,332,172
1956	61,912	742,591,206	15,073,011
1957	49,465	868,314,701	16,309,388
1958	54,591	962,679,211	18,556,883
1959	57,504	1,301,565,000	8,733,000
1960	61,050	1,332,289,000	(42,934,000)
1961	70,250	1,444,510,000	26,096,000
1962	80,155	1,753,074,000	37,199,000
1963	78,296	1,930,488,000	43,254,000
1964	74,602	1,601,012,000	45,108,000
1965	81,302	1,814,085,000	51,517,000
1966	90,355	2,084,759,000	58,883,000
1967	92,267	2,335,456,000	54,359,000
1968	95,404	2,217,366,000	44,476,000
1969	97,600	2,074,639,000	(32,642,000)
1970	84,600	2,535,603,000	(187,800,000)
1971	74,700	2,852,365,000	(39,400,000)
1972	69,600	2,472,732,000	(7,200,000)
1973	66,900	2,756,791,000	18,200,000
1974	62,100	3,279,100,000	23,200,000
1975	57,600	3,387,200,000	45,300,000
1976	55,100	3,202,700,000	38,700,000
1977	55,100	3,372,800,000	55,400,000
1978	61,500	3,485,000,000	64,900,000
1979	66,500	4,057,600,000	56,500,000
1980	74,600	5,395,700,000	27,600,000

LOCKHEED CORPORATION AND FOREBEARS

ANNUAL AIRCRAFT DELIVERIES

(1913-1929)

	1913		1918		1920		1927	1928	1929	Totals By Type
Model G	1		–		–		–	–	–	1 (1913)
F-1	–		1		–		–	–	–	1 (1918)
HS-2L	–		2		–		–	–	–	2 (1918)
S-1	–		–		1		–	–	–	1 (1920)
Vega	–		–		–		2	29	60	Continued to 1934
Air Express	–		–		–		–	2	5	7 (1928-29)
Explorer	–		–		–		–	–	2	Continued to 1930
Sirius	–		–		–		–	–	1	Continued to 1931
Annual Totals	1		3		1		2	31	68	106

49

ANNUAL AIRCRAFT DELIVERIES

(1930-1939)

	1930	1931	1932	1933	1934	1935	1936	1937	1938	1939	Totals by Type
Vega	28	4	1	3	1	-	-	-	-	-	128 (1927-34)
Explorer	2	-	-	-	-	-	-	-	-	-	4 (1929-30)
Sirius	12	2	-	-	-	-	-	-	-	-	15 (1929-31)
Altair	-	3	1	-	1	-	-	1	-	-	6 (1931-37)
Orion	-	14	3	13	3	2	-	-	-	-	35 (1931-35)
XP-900	-	1	-	-	-	-	-	-	-	-	1 (1931)
Electra	-	-	-	-	10	36	28	45	14	7	Continued to 1941
Electra Jr	-	-	-	-	-	-	8	37	8	34	Continued to 1942
Super Electra	-	-	-	-	-	-	-	8	79	22	Continued to 1940
Hudson	-	-	-	-	-	-	-	-	-	287	Continued to 1943
Lightning	-	-	-	-	-	-	-	-	-	1	Continued to 1945
Starliner	-	-	-	-	-	-	-	-	-	1	1 (1939)
Annual Totals	42	24	5	16	15	38	36	91	101	352	720

ANNUAL AIRCRAFT DELIVERIES
(1940-1949)

	1940	1941	1942	1943	1944	1945	1946	1947	1948	1949	Totals by Type
Electra	1	8	–	–	–	–	–	–	–	–	149 (1934-41)
Electra Jr	15	14	14	–	–	–	–	–	–	–	130 (1936-42)
Super Electra	3	–	–	–	–	–	–	–	–	–	112 (1937-40)
Hudson	319	1127	858	350	–	–	–	–	–	–	2941 (1939-43)
Lightning	1	265	1421	2497	4186	1553	–	–	–	–	9924 (1939-45)
Lodestar	54	95	181	295	–	–	–	–	–	–	625 (1940-43)
Model 35	–	4	–	–	–	–	–	–	–	–	4 (1941)
Ventura and Harpoon	–	25	913	1203	421	466	–	–	–	–	3028 (1941-45)
XP-49	–	–	1	–	–	–	–	–	–	–	1 (1942)
Flying Fortress	–	–	68	887	1244	551	–	–	–	–	2750 (1942-45)
Constellation	–	–	–	1	3	21	57	55	22	17	Continued to 1951
Shooting Star	–	–	–	–	8	237	400	259	257	360	Continued to 1951
XP-58	–	–	–	–	1	–	–	–	–	–	1 (1944)
Little Dipper	–	–	–	–	1	–	–	–	–	–	1 (1944)
Neptune	–	–	–	–	–	–	5	47	74	34	Continued to 1962
Big Dipper	–	–	–	–	–	–	1	–	–	–	1 (1946)
Saturn	–	–	–	–	–	–	2	–	–	–	2 (1946)
Constitution	–	–	–	–	–	–	–	–	–	2	2 (1949)
T-33	–	–	–	–	–	–	–	–	20	86	Continued to 1959
F-94	–	–	–	–	–	–	–	–	–	1	Continued to 1954
Annual Totals	393	1538	3456	5233	5864	2828	465	361	373	500	21011

ANNUAL AIRCRAFT DELIVERIES
(1950-1959)

	1950	1951	1952	1953	1954	1955	1956	1957	1958	1959	Totals by Type
Constellation	37	20	-	-	-	-	-	-	-	-	233 (1943-51)
Shooting Star	207	4	-	-	-	-	-	-	-	-	1732 (1944-51)
Neptune	66	51	81	241	163	72	36	29	34	33	Continued to 1962
T-33	137	258	984	1265	1044	870	317	289	256	165	5691 (1948-59)
F-94	120	344	48	254	87	-	-	-	-	-	854 (1949-54)
XF-90	-	-	2	-	-	-	-	-	-	-	2 (1952)
Super Constellation	-	4	25	73	92	117	135	89	40	4	579 (1951-59)
B-47	-	-	-	38	143	120	84	9	-	-	394 (1953-57)
T2V-1	-	-	-	-	-	-	17	103	30	-	150 (1956-58)
F-104	-	-	-	-	-	1	17	48	164	67	Continued to 1967
XFV-1	-	-	-	-	-	2	-	-	-	-	2 (1955)
Hercules	-	-	-	-	1	1	10	140	62	56	Still in production
U-2				←——	Classified	Information	——→				Classified
Starliner (L1649A)	-	-	-	-	-	-	-	35	9	-	44 (1957-58)
JetStar	-	-	-	-	-	-	-	1	1	-	Continued to 1980
Electra (L-188)	-	-	-	-	-	-	-	-	12	110	Continued to 1962
Orion (P-3)	-	-	-	-	-	-	-	-	-	1	Still in production
CL-475	-	-	-	-	-	-	-	-	-	1	1 (1959)
Annual Totals	567	681	1140	1871	1530	1183	616	743	608	437	9376 (+ U-2s)

52

ANNUAL AIRCRAFT DELIVERIES
(1960-1969)

	1960	1961	1962	1963	1964	1965	1966	1967	1968	1969	Totals by Type
Neptune	25	38	22	-	-	-	-	-	-	-	1051 (1946-62)
F-104	29	48	110	142	54	28	23	10	-	-	741 (1955-67)
Hercules	53	55	112	131	139	90	67	65	63	46	Still in Production
U-2				Classified Information							Classified
JetStar	-	17	21	7	7	18	22	18	17	12	Continued to 1980
Electra (L-188)	22	21	5	-	-	-	-	-	-	-	170 (1958-62)
LASA-60	2	-	-	-	-	-	-	-	-	-	2 (1960)
Orion (P-3)	-	6	25	29	51	48	50	45	42	29	Still in Production
SR-71				Classified Information							Classified
Hummingbird	-	-	-	2	-	-	-	-	-	-	2 (1963)
L-186 & L-286	-	-	-	2	1	2	-	-	-	-	5 (1963-65)
C-141	-	-	-	4	9	58	103	107	4	-	285 (1962-68)
Q-Star & YO-3A	-	-	-	-	-	-	-	2	12	3	17 (1967-69)
Cheyenne	-	-	-	-	-	-	-	5	5	-	10 (1967-68)
C-5A	-	-	-	-	-	-	-	-	1	5	Continued to 1974
Annual Totals	131	185	295	317	261	244	265	252	144	95	2189 (+U-2/SR-71s)

ANNUAL AIRCRAFT DELIVERIES

(1970-1980)

	1970	1971	1972	1973	1974	1975	1976	1977	1978	1979	1980	Totals by Type
Hercules	42	39	35	47	46	71	72	54	35	37	35	Still in Production 204 (1957-80)
JetStar	1	7	8	7	-	-	3	17	9	7	4	204 (1957-80)
Orion (P-3)	24	23	13	24	17	14	12	11	19	16	23	Still in Production 81 (1968-74)
C-5A	20	24	19	10	1	1	-	-	-	-	-	81 (1968-74)
TriStar	-	-	17	39	41	25	16	11	8	14	24	Still in Production 187 (1971-78)
S-3A	-	1	6	7	38	50	44	33	8	-	-	187 (1971-78)
Annual Totals	87	94	98	134	143	161	147	126	79	74	86	1,229(+TR-1/Stealth)

54

The Model G at San Francisco. Note the shape of the main float and wingtip floats, location of ailerons between the wings, and cruciform tail. (*Lockheed*)

Loughead Model G

Having survived two crashes in Curtiss Pushers within nine months, Allan Loughead was not very keen on having a relatively heavy engine mounted aft of the pilot. Thus, while working as an instructor and exhibition pilot for the International Aircraft Manufacturing Company, he conceived a tractor biplane as the first aircraft to bear the Loughead name. Of fairly advanced concept for its day, the machine was completed as a floatplane in 1913 and, until 1918, when its builders dismantled it and sold its engine, it was a money-making venture for Allan and Malcolm Loughead. Of not many single contemporary aeroplanes could such a claim be justly made.

Even though Allan Loughead had begun to have some wooden parts milled while he was working in Chicago, most of the work remained to be done when in early 1912 he joined forces with his brother Malcolm in San Francisco. Renting space in a small frame garage at Pacific and Polk Streets on the waterfront, the brothers worked on the aircraft during evenings and week-ends. Finally, with the formation of the Alco Hydro-Aeroplane Company, they obtained sufficient funds to complete the work and acquire a six-cylinder Kirkham engine.

Of three-bay biplane design, with upper and lower wing spans of 46 and 36 ft (14·02 and 10·97 m) respectively, the aircraft had its ailerons mounted between the two wings, and cruciform tail surfaces hinged as a unit on a universal joint.* Beneath the forward fuselage was installed a sled-type pontoon, and cylindrical floats were attached beneath the lower wing. Accommodation was provided for a pilot and one, later two, passengers in tandem open cockpits located below and aft of the top wing.

*A three-in-one control arrangement was used, with the wheel operating the rudder, and the stick, to which the wheel was attached, operating the elevators and ailerons.

Designated Model G, to imply that it was their seventh design, the seaplane at the time of its completion was powered by a Kirkham six-cylinder engine with a distinctive horseshoe-shaped radiator. However, this powerplant was unreliable and after fifteen minutes of ground running time its crankcase split. The Lougheads returned the engine to Kirkham, in the unwarranted hope of obtaining a refund, and switched to an 80 hp Curtiss O V-8 engine. Initially they retained the horseshoe-shaped radiator for the Curtiss engine.

Launched onto San Francisco Bay from the slipway at the foot of Laguna Street, the Model G was flown by Allan Loughead on 15 June, 1913. After a brief flight he alighted to pick up Malcolm and together they flew for twenty minutes, cruising over the shores of the Golden Gate, over Alcatraz Island and back to the beach. A similar flight was made with R. L. Coleman as a passenger, but a fourth flight had to be cut short when stronger winds and choppy waters required prudence. Later during the summer of 1913 the Model G suffered minor damage, including a broken propeller and torn pontoon, when Allan Loughead hit a levee on alighting at San Mateo while taking Ferdinand Theriot on a charter flight. The seaplane was transported back to San Francisco where it was repaired and a conventional frontal radiator replaced the old Kirkham horseshoe unit. However, the Model G then remained in storage for some eighteen months while Malcolm Loughead went on wild adventures to China and Mexico.

Seeing in the Panama-Pacific Exposition an opportunity to recoup their investment, the Lougheads, with the help of capital provided by a Mr Meyer, bought the Model G from the other investors of the Alco Hydro-Aeroplane Company. Underbid by Bob Fowler for the passenger-flying concession at the Panama-Pacific Exposition, which opened in San Francisco in February 1915, the Loughead-Meyer partnership took over from Fowler when the latter's aeroplane was destroyed. In fifty days of flying they obtained a $4,000 profit from the $6,000 income realized by carrying 600 passengers on ten-minute joy rides.

The horseshoe-shaped Kirkham radiator as originally fitted to the Model G. (*Lockheed*)

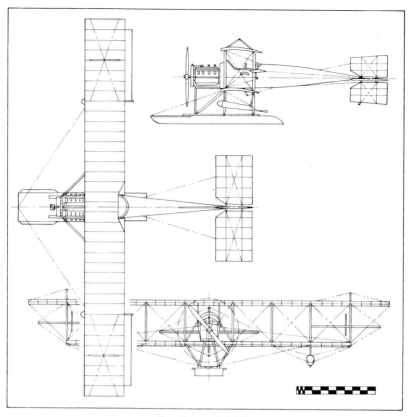

Loughead Model G

Upon investing their profit in the Loughead Aircraft Manufacturing Company, which they organized at Santa Barbara with other investors, Allan and Malcolm Loughead had the Model G taken by flat-car to that community down the coast of California. There the Model G continued to earn income for its owners by flying joy rides and charters. It was even used to make the first air crossing of the Santa Barbara Channel, carrying two passengers sixty miles in one hour. Finally, in 1918 the Model G's wooden airframe and fabric covering were showing signs of age and the Lougheads realized a last income from their aircraft by selling its Curtiss engine.

Span 46 ft (14·02 m) upper, 36 ft (10·97 m) lower; length 30 ft (9·14 m); height 10 ft (3·05 m).
Empty weight 1,616 lb (733 kg); loaded weight 2,200 lb (998 kg); fuel capacity 8 US gal (30 litres).
Maximum speed 63 mph (101 km/h); cruising speed 51 mph (82 km/h).

The Model F-1 which was completed at Santa Barbara in March 1918. (*Lockheed*)

Loughead F-1

Undertaking the design and construction of a ten-seat, twin-engined flying-boat was a daring venture, whether for so small a firm as the newly organized Loughead Aircraft Manufacturing Company or for such an inexperienced designer as Allan Loughead then was. Nevertheless, after a two-year gestation the F-1 (Flying-boat One) was first flown on 28 March, 1918, and soon made the then longest overwater flight when it was delivered to North Island, San Diego, for evaluation by the US Navy. It then had a brief career after being modified to landplane configuration and then re-converted to a flying-boat.

Preliminary design work was undertaken in early 1916 by Allan Loughead, with some assistance from his brother Malcolm. In mid-summer of that year the Loughead brothers got additional design help when they hired a 21-year-old mechanic and architectural draughtsman, John K. Northrop. A self-taught engineer, Northrop began working on the wooden hull of the new flying-boat and soon demonstrated his creative talent. Accordingly, he took over responsibility for the design and stress analysis of the fabric-covered unequal span wings. The lower wing was attached to the fuselage nacelle, which had open accommodation for two pilots side by side and eight to ten passengers, and was linked to the high-mounted upper wing by steel interplane struts. Between the wings were attached the two 160 hp Hall-Scott liquid-cooled engines driving two-blade tractor propellers. The tail surfaces were carried by twin uncovered booms, with directional control being provided by two fins and three rudders, the central unit being all movable. There were side curtains between the fore and aft kingposts above the upper wing. The stabilizing wingtip floats were attached directly to the wing.

Construction of the F-1 — under the direction of Anthony 'Tony' Stadlman, a friend of Allan Loughead since their barnstorming days in Illinois — proceeded very slowly at first as the company was undercapitalized and understaffed. However, the United States' entry into the war in 1917 lent a new impetus to the project as the Loughead brothers were keen on selling their aircraft to the US Navy. Nevertheless, eleven more months elapsed until the F-1 was first launched on Santa Barbara Bay and Allan Loughead took it for its first flight on 28 March,

The Loughead F-1 in its original form.

1918. Flight characteristics were found generally satisfactory, the only modification required being a reduction in the area of the ailerons which extended beyond the upper wingtips. Nevertheless, the rudders were heightened and provided with horn balances. Shortly after the F-1, carrying Allan and Malcolm Loughead, Carl Christofferson, and a newspaper man, was flown nonstop to San Diego covering the 211 miles (340 km) between Santa Barbara and North Island in 3 hr 1 min. The US Navy evaluation of the aircraft was generally favourable but by then that Service had already ordered large quantities of Curtiss HS-2Ls which, each powered by a single 330 hp Liberty engine, were lighter and slightly faster than the Loughead F-1. Consequently, the Navy did not buy the F-1 but, as a consolation prize, awarded Loughead Aircraft Manufacturing Company a contract for the construction of two HS-2Ls and another, cancelled at the end of the war, for the production of fifty single-seat naval scouts.

After the F-1 had been returned by the Navy in August 1918 the Loughead brothers decided to modify it to attract attention to their fledgling company. The original fuselage and hull were replaced by a streamlined nacelle, and a tricycle undercarriage was installed to convert the aircraft into the long-range F-1A

The F-1 flying-boat with increased rudder area. (*Lockheed*)

In its landplane version the Loughead twin-engined aircraft had a short life. (*Lockheed*)

landplane. To reduce drag further, Jack Northrop devised streamlined wooden fairings for the steel interplane struts. In this form the aircraft was readied in late November 1918 to attempt a US transcontinental flight. As at that time of the year the weather was not favourable over the most direct route, the crew—pilots O. S. T. 'Swede' Meyerhoffer and A. R. 'Bob' Ferneau, and mechanic L. G. Flint —chose a more southern route skirting the Mexican border. On the first leg of the transcontinental trip they nevertheless ran into bad weather and strong headwinds and, after covering 415 miles (688 km) in 6 hr 10 min, the aircraft was forced down at Tacna, Arizona, with a broken valve spring. After a fast repair

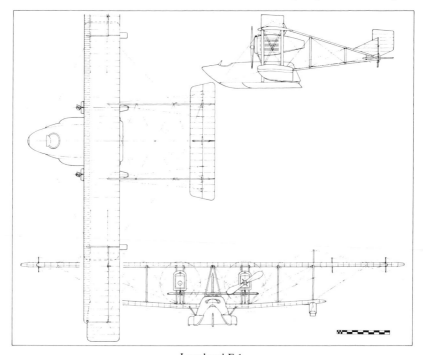

Loughead F-1

60

the F-1A continued to Gila Bend, Arizona, where it was refuelled. On take-off from Gila Bend, a propeller hit a mesquite bush and, after reaching an altitude of 50 ft (15 m), the F-1A came down on its nose. There was no alternative but to abandon the transcontinental attempt and ship the aircraft back to Santa Barbara for repairs.

In Santa Barbara the aircraft was rebuilt as a flying-boat to be used during the 1919 summer tourist season to offer joy rides at $5 per passenger. The F-1 proved so reliable in this job that in October 1919 the US State Department chartered it for King Albert and Queen Elisabeth of Belgium. The royal couple and their entourage were flown by the Loughead brothers from Santa Barbara to Santa Cruz Island, off the coast of southern California, and their services earned for Allan and Malcolm the award of the Belgian Order of the Golden Crown. After this, the F-1 was again operated on commercial charters, specially for use in films for which the Loughead brothers charged $150 per flying hour and $50 an hour for standby time. The F-1 was also hired by a couple who wished to become the first to have their marriage ceremony performed aloft.

After earning a sizeable sum for the Loughead Aircraft Manufacturing Company, the F-1 was finally sold in 1920 to provide cash to cover the cost of the S-1 sports biplane. Its new owners planned to use it for an air service to their resort and amusement centre on Catalina Island. This plan, however, never materialized and the F-1 finally succumbed to vandalism on the beach at Santa Barbara.

Specifications for the F-1 flying-boat version. Span 74 ft (22·56 m) upper, 47 ft (14·33 m) lower; length 35 ft (10·67 m); height 12 ft (3·66 m).
Empty weight 4,200 lb (1,905 kg); loaded weight 7,300 lb (3,311 kg); power loading 22·8 lb/hp (10·3 kg/hp).
Maximum speed 84 mph (135 km/h); cruising speed 70 mph (113 km/h); range 510 miles (820 km).

Loughead S-1

Although the tiny S-1 single-seat sports biplane failed to achieve the commercial success its designers had hoped for, it gave Allan Loughead and Jack Northrop an outstanding research vehicle for their new method of construction for wooden monocoque fuselages. Indeed, the S-1 was a remarkably advanced design providing the technical basis for another trend-setting machine, the Lockheed Vega, which first flew eight years later and soon obtained considerable fame.

Seeking to capture a share of the market for private aircraft which was anticipated to result from the return of wartime pilots to civil life, Allan Loughead and Jack Northrop, assisted by Tony Stadlman, conceived in 1919 a light single-bay biplane. Its design incorporated several novel features including manually-folded wings to ease ground transport and facilitate storage in a garage. For lateral control the aircraft used neither ailerons nor wing-warping but its entire lower wing surfaces could change angle differentially on a fuselage pivot point. Furthermore, to reduce landing speed both halves of the lower wing could be rotated simultaneously on this pivot point to act as air brakes. Even more remarkable was its fuselage construction, with two plywood half-shells glued on concentric wooden circles. These shells were obtained by placing in a specially-built, full-length concrete tub three thicknesses of spruce plywood, with the grain

Even though it was inexpensive to operate and easy to fly, the S-1 sports biplane did not go into production. (*Lockheed*)

The Loughead S-1 in front of San Francisco City Hall. (*Lockheed*)

laid alternatively, and coated with casein glue. To achieve adequate bonding and proper shaping, a rubber bag was inserted in the tub and, after a cover had been clamped over, was inflated to a pressure of 20 lb/sq in (1·4 kg/sq cm). After twenty-four hours, the ⅛-in (3 mm) thick shells were ready for installation, with longitudinal seams above and beneath the fuselage. The result was a very clean body combining light weight with ample strength.

The concrete tub in which Lockheed formed the plywood fuselages of its early single-engined aircraft from the Vegas to the Orions. (*Lockheed*)

As no adequate powerplants were readily available—plans to use the British-built Green engine foundered when its manufacturer went out of business—Allan Loughead drew up the desired specification and Tony Stadlman designed the XL-1 two-cylinder, horizontally-opposed, liquid-cooled engine developing 25 hp at 1,800 rpm. With this engine driving a two-blade Paragon propeller the S-1 was first flown at Redwood City, California, in late 1919 or early 1920, by Gilbert C. Budwig. It immediately demonstrated good handling characteristics and, after the installation of a propeller also designed by Tony Stadlman, good performance with a top speed of 70 mph (113 km/h) and landing speed of only 25 mph (40 km/h), even without the use of the lower wing as an air-brake.

Unfortunately for Allan Loughead and his team, the single-seat S-1, after being demonstrated over much of California and gaining the attention of such noted aviators as Lieut H. H. Arnold—who was to become Chief of the Army Air Forces—failed to attract customers as its purchase price far exceeded that of brand-new two-seat Curtiss Jennies sold as surplus at a unit price as low as $350. A quarter of a century later the Lockheed Aircraft Corporation had to learn the

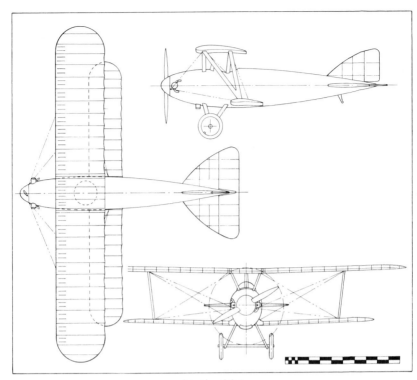

Loughead S-1

This view of the S-1 shows to advantage the very clean fuselage. (*Lockheed*)

same lesson when the higher acquisition price of its Saturn and Little Dipper could not be offset by their operating costs, even though substantially lower than those of surplus aircraft.

After investing $29,800 in its S-1 sports biplane the Loughead Aircraft Manufacturing Company was forced to go out of business in 1921. Six years later, however, the S-1 construction method resurfaced in the Vega, the first aircraft to bear the Lockheed name.

Span 28 ft (8·53 m) upper, 24 ft (7·32 m) lower; length 20 ft (6·10 m); height 7 ft 3 in (2·21 m).

Empty weight 375 lb (170 kg); loaded weight 825 lb (374 kg); power loading 33 lb/hp (15 kg/hp).

Maximum speed 70 mph (113 km/h); initial rate of climb 700 ft/min (213 m/min); service ceiling 12,000 ft (3,658 m); maximum endurance 8 hr on 8 US gal (30 litres) of petrol.

Lockheed 1, 2 and 5 Vega

In the years following the demise of the Loughead Aircraft Manufacturing Company, Allan Loughead sold real estate and also acted as agent for the hydraulic brakes developed by his brother Malcolm. Jack Northrop was more fortunate in finding engineering employment with the Douglas Company. In spite of their temporarily separate professional paths the two occasionally got together to discuss aircraft design and both were convinced that the manufacturing process which they had developed for the S-1 offered substantial potential. From these discussions eventually emerged the concept for a high-speed cabin monoplane with accommodation for a pilot and four passengers. Allan Loughead was so confident in the potential of the new design from Northrop's creative genius that in 1926 he set out to obtain capital for a new company. Finally, in December of that year his efforts were rewarded with the incorporation of the Lockheed Aircraft Company. Jack Northrop, resigning from Douglas, immediately went to work on the aircraft and suggested it be named Vega. Thus he not only provided a suitable name for the fast single-engined aircraft but also started the Lockheed tradition of naming its aircraft after stars and planets.

Combining a wooden monocoque fuselage — built by the same method as used for the S-1 — with a wooden, internally-braced, cantilever wing as pioneered by Anthony Fokker, the first Vega was started as a private venture. It featured an adjustable tailplane and a clean undercarriage attached to the fuselage sides by single main struts and braced to the fuselage underside by V-struts. To power this aircraft its designer selected a 200 hp Wright Whirlwind J5 nine-cylinder radial driving a two-blade Standard steel propeller. While under construction, the aircraft was brought to the attention of John W. Frost, an ex-Air Service Lieutenant, and, with the help of his brother Ezra, Jack Frost succeeded in convincing George Hearst Jr to purchase it. A San Franciscan controlling an influential chain of newspapers, George Hearst intended to enter the aircraft in the Oakland to Hawaii race sponsored by James D. Dole and his Hawaiian Pineapple Company and scheduled to start on 12 August, 1927.

Sold to Hearst for $12,500, which was less than its cost as Lockheed realized the prestige to be gained from having its aircraft acquired by Hearst and entered in the Dole Race, the first Vega was built in a rented building in Hollywood. Upon completion the fuselage and wings were towed separately to a large hayfield at Inglewood, now part of the Los Angeles International Airport. There the aircraft, bearing the original registration 2788, was reassembled and on Independence Day (4 July) 1927 was flown by Edward 'Eddie' A. Bellande. For its entry in the Dole Race the first Vega had been considerably modified internally and its originally planned accommodation for four passengers was replaced by two 100-US gal (379-litre) tanks, which supplemented the normal 160-gal (606-litre) tank in the wing, and by a navigator's station in the aft part of the cabin; a hatch with folding windshield on the upper fuselage was provided for the navigator. To improve flotation in case of a forced alighting at sea, the undercarriage could be dropped, special seals were provided for all openings, the base of the fuselage was padded with cork, and flotation bags — to be filled in less than one minute by carbon dioxide — were installed beneath the pilot's seat and in the aft fuselage. In addition, the aircraft carried the most modern navigation equipment, a liferaft, water and food, a radio receiver, and distress signal equipment, and was fitted with an earth inductor compass generator.

The *Golden Eagle* being readied in Oakland just before the Dole Race. (*Peter M. Bowers*)

Before entering the Dole Race the first Vega was tested as intensively as the limited time permitted. In the process it established a number of point-to-point records with various payloads and demonstrated its high speed by flying from Los Angeles to Oakland in 3 hr 5 min. Finally, the aircraft was readied in Oakland for the scheduled date of the race. However, its pilot, Jack Frost, and its navigator, Gordon Scott, initiated a move to postpone the departure to enable some of their competitors to complete their preparation. Thus, the eight-aircraft Dole Race started on 16 August, 1927, six weeks and one day after the first flight of the Vega. By then re-registered NX913 and named *Golden Eagle*, the Vega, painted orange with red trim, was the second aircraft to leave Oakland. In spite of its heavy load, with fuel alone accounting for some 2,410 lb (1,093 kg), the aircraft was easily pulled aloft by its 200 hp Wright Whirlwind engine and set off for the Hawaiian Islands, some 2,439 miles (3,925 km) out in the Pacific. Four of the competitors failed to start or were forced to return, leaving the race to Jack Frost and Gordon Scott in their Lockheed Vega *Golden Eagle*, Martin Jensen and Paul Schlater in their Breese monoplane *Aloha*, Art Goebel and Bill Davis in their Travel Air monoplane *Woolaroc*, and Augy Pedlar and Mildred Doran in their Buhl biplane *Miss Doran*. According to all accounts, the beautifully clean Vega was the favourite. Tragically Jack Frost and Gordon Scott vanished with the

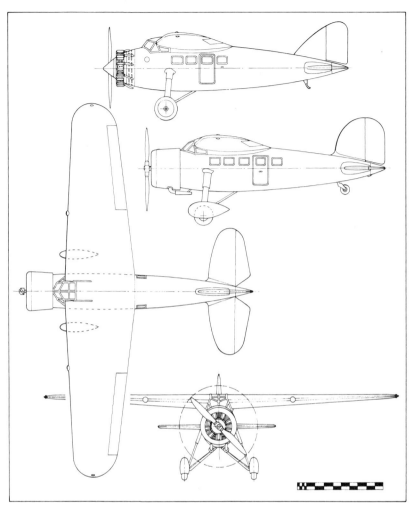

Lockheed Vega 5C, with side view of Vega 1

Golden Eagle, as did Augy Pedlar and Mildred Doran in their *Miss Doran*. The $25,000 first prize was won by the crew of the *Woolaroc* and the $10,000 second prize by that of the *Aloha*.

The mysterious disappearance of the *Golden Eagle* did not spell the end of the Vega, and the Lockheed Aircraft Company, Detroit-Lockheed and individuals went on to produce a total of 128 of these aircraft. In addition, parts of fourteen additional Vegas were built and either remained uncompleted or were used in rebuilding damaged aircraft included in the production total. Several of these aircraft were used by airlines in the United States and Latin America, others were operated as private transports by corporations and wealthy individual owners but, more importantly, several took part in many spectacular flights between 1928 and

1935. While details of several of the most notable flights are given further on in this chapter, the following partial listing provides a clear idea of the achievements of the Lockheed Vega:

15/20 April, 1928, Vega 1 (c/n 4, X3903): Capt G. H. Wilkins and Carl Ben Eielson: first trans-Arctic flight from Alaska to Spitzbergen.

19/20 August, 1928, Vega 5 (c/n 7, X4769) *Yankee Doodle*: Arthur Goebel and Harry Tucker: first eastbound nonstop US transcontinental flight, from Los Angeles to New York in 18 hr 58 min.

24/25 October, 1928, Vega 5 (c/n 7, X4769): C. B. D. Collyer and Harry Tucker: east–west nonstop US transcontinental flight in 24 hr 51 min. Tucker thus became the first passenger to have flown nonstop across the United States in both directions.

16 November, 1928, Vega 1 (c/n 4, X3903): Sir Hubert Wilkins and Carl Ben Eielson: first exploratory flight over Antarctica.

February 1929, Vega of Bobby Trout: 17 hr 5 min 37 sec solo endurance record for women.

28/29 May, 1929, Vega 1 (c/n 35, NC34E): Herb Fahy: 36 hr 56 min 36 sec solo endurance record.

November 1929, Vega 5A Executive (c/n 107, NC538M): Amelia Earhart: women's speed record over one mile: 184·17 mph (296·38 km/h) average.

18/19 February, 1930, Vega 5A Special *Miss Silvertown* (c/n 79, NC308H): Leland Schoenhair: 100-km speed record at 185·5 mph (298·5 km/h) with 500 kg (1,102 lb) load and 176 mph (283·2 km/h) with 1,000 kg (2,204 lb) load.

June 1930, Vega DL-1 (c/n 135, NC497H): Amelia Earhart: 100-km women's world speed record without load at 174·9 mph (281·4 km/h), and with 500 kg (1,102 lb) load at 171·4 mph (275·8 km/h).

6 March, 1931, Vega 5A Special *The New Cincinnati* (c/n 619, NR496M): Ruth Nichols: American altitude record for women 28,743 ft (8,761 m).

13 April, 1931, Vega 5A Special *The New Cincinnati* (c/n 619, NR496M): Ruth Nichols: women's speed record over 3-km course: 210·685 mph (339·059 km/h).

23 June/1 July, 1931, Vega 5B *The Winnie Mae* (c/n 122, NC105W): Wiley Post and Harold Gatty: 15,474-miles (24,902-km) around-the-world flight in 8 days 15 hr 51 min.

14 February, 1932, Vega 7 *Miss Teanek* (c/n 14, NR7426): Ruth Nichols with 225 hp Packard DR-980 diesel engine: 19,928 ft (6,074 m) world altitude record for diesel-powered aircraft.

20/21 May, 1932, Vega 5B (c/n 22, NC7952): Amelia Earhart: first trans-atlantic solo flight by a woman, Newfoundland to Ireland in 15 hr 18 min.

August 1932, Vega 5B (c/n 22, NC7952): Amelia Earhart: first woman's nonstop transcontinental flight, Los Angeles to Newark, 2,447·8 miles (3,939·3 km) in 19 hr 5 min, constituting also new international distance record for women.

15/22 July, 1933, Vega 5B *The Winnie Mae* (c/n 122, NC105W): Wiley Post: first solo around-the-world flight, 15,596 miles (25,099 km) in 7 days 18 hr 43 min.

Although the Vegas used for these outstanding flights and those performing more mundane undertakings were handbuilt machines and therefore few of them were identical to other aircraft in the series, they can generally be grouped in the following categories.

The Vega 1 X3903 of Capt George H. Wilkins seen in Alaska before the flight from Point Barrow to Spitzbergen in April 1928. (*Lockheed*)

NC308H *Miss Silvertown*, a Vega 5A (c/n 79), operated by the B. F. Goodrich Rubber Company as an executive and experimental aircraft. Later fitted as a testbed for de-icing boots, it was destroyed at Vineland, Ontario, Canada, on 16 May, 1931. (*Lockheed*)

Vega 1: Powered by a 225 hp Wright Whirlwind J5, J5A, J5AB, J5B, or J5C nine-cylinder radial, aircraft of this model were basically five-seaters with the pilot sitting ahead of the wing and the four passengers in an enclosed cabin below the high-mounted wing. However, not all passenger seats were installed when the aircraft were operated for special purposes such as the Dole Race or the Wilkins expeditions to the Arctic and Antarctica. After c/ns 1 and 3 had been built, the shape of the vertical surfaces was revised. Twenty-eight Whirlwind-powered Vega 1s were built (c/ns 1, 3, 4, 6, 8 to 12, 12B, 14 to 17 and 28 to 41). To suit individual customers, special features, such as a fuselage hatch aft of the wings and observation windows beneath the fuselage as fitted to c/n 4 for Captain George H. Wilkins' Arctic expedition in 1928, were often incorporated. Furthermore, the conventional undercarriage could be replaced by skis (first used on c/n 4) or twin floats (initially installed on c/n 17, Wilkins' second Vega 1). C/n 33 of California Aerial Transport became the first Lockheed to be used as an air ambulance.

Built in 1929 as a Whirlwind J5 powered Vega 1, c/n 40 was fitted with a Wasp Jr in 1931. It remains the oldest airworthy Lockheed aircraft. (*Peter M. Bowers*)

Post-delivery modifications resulted in the addition of a Townend cowling ring on four aircraft (c/ns 12, 16, 36 and 41), and in changes of engine types to seven aircraft. The re-engined aircraft included c/n 9, which became a Vega 5C with 420 hp Pratt & Whitney Wasp C; c/n 11, with a 450 hp Pratt & Whitney R-985 AN-1; and c/n 30 with a 300 hp Wright Whirlwind J6 engine in a 9-in (23-cm) shorter fuselage. One aircraft, c/n 38, was first modified as a Vega 5 with a 420 hp Wasp C1 and subsequently became a Vega 2D with a 300 hp Wasp Jr; c/n 40 was also brought up to the same standard with a Wasp Jr engine. Two aircraft, as described later, were fitted with diesel engines (c/ns 14 and 28).

Vega 2: Differing primarily from the preceding model in being delivered with a 300 hp Wright Whirlwind J6, the five Vega 2s bore the c/ns 56 to 58, 60 and 64. Subsequently c/n 58 was converted to Vega 5 configuration with Wasp engine and then as a Vega 2D with Wasp Jr. Likewise, c/n 60 was successively re-engined with a Wasp C as a Vega 5B, and with a Wasp C1 as a Vega 5C.

Powered by a Wright Whirlwind J6, this Vega 2 (c/n 30) of Canadian Airways later went to the warmer climate of Central America. (*Lockheed*)

Vega 2A: One aircraft (c/n 83) built as Vega 2 but gross weight increased from 3,853 lb (1,748 kg) to 4,220 lb (1,914 kg).

Vega 2D: Not a production model. Designation given to the re-engined c/ns 38 and 40 (ex-Vega 1s) and c/n 58 (ex-Vega 2).

Vega 5: Main production version with 35 aircraft (c/ns 7, 18, 20 to 27, 48 to 55, 59, 63, 67, 69, 70, 71, 73, 78, 81, 82, 84, 85, 87, 94 and 97 to 99) built with a 410 hp Pratt & Whitney Wasp A, 450 hp Wasp B or 420 hp Wasp C1 nine-cylinder radial. The first Vega 5 was completed in March 1928 and five months later was used to make the first nonstop Los Angeles–New York flight. Accommodation, in addition to the pilot, was increased from four to five or six passengers. One aircraft (c/n 69) was delivered with dual control but all other Vega 5s had provision for a passenger seat next to the pilot. Most Vega 5s were fitted with a NACA* cowling, either after delivery or during production. Twin floats, which increased normal weight from 4,033 lb (1,829 kg) to 4,698 lb (2,131 kg) and reduced top speed by 8 mph (13 km/h), were frequently fitted. Landplane versions could be fitted with streamlined wheel fairings.

*National Advisory Committee on Aeronautics, forerunner of the present NASA.

Vega 5 (X7441, c/n 21) before delivery to the Schlee-Brock Aircraft Corp, the Lockheed distributor in Detroit. (*Van Rossen/Lockheed*)

Built in 1929, this Vega 5 (N47M, c/n 99) was operated for sixteen years by Alaska Coastal Airlines until it crashed near Tenakee, Alaska, on 15 January, 1958. (*Lockheed*)

In-service modification resulted in c/n 18 being converted into a Whirlwind J5-powered Vega 1, while c/ns 22 and 54 became Vega 5Bs with increased empty and loaded weights. Still heavier—with a loaded weight of 4,500 lb (2,041 kg) versus 4,265 lb (1,935 kg) for the Vega 5Bs—were the seven aircraft (c/ns 23, 26, 49, 50, 63, 73 and 99) modified as Vega 5Cs with larger fin and rudder.

Vega 5A Executive: Nine aircraft (c/ns 72, 79, 80, 88, 89, 96, 107, 108 and 132) with Wasp engines were delivered with de luxe interiors, raising loaded weight by 637 lb (289 kg) as compared to that of stock Vega 5s; standard interior fittings included chemical toilet, table and typewriter. Many were later converted back as airliners, while c/ns 72, 96 and 108 were brought up to Vega 5C standard with enlarged vertical surfaces.

N926Y (c/n 134), acquired from the Shell Oil Company in 1935, and named *Lituanica II*, this Vega 5B failed in an attempt to fly nonstop from New York to Lithuania in September 1935. (*Lockheed*)

72

This Vega 5B (NC105N, c/n 117) was acquired by the Standard Oil Company in 1929 and was destroyed seven years later in the State of Minas Gerais, Brazil. (*Lockheed*)

Vega 5B: Characterized by heavier operating weight to enable normal operation as seven-seaters, the twenty-eight Vega 5Bs (c/ns 61, 62, 66, 68, 74, 90, 100, 101, 103, 105, 106, 109, 112, 117 to 129, 133 and 134) had the same powerplant options as the Vega 5 and could also be fitted with NACA cowling and/or twin floats. Other Vega 5Bs were obtained by post-delivery conversions. Six of the original Vega 5Bs (c/ns 100, 101, 109, 121, 124 and 127) were modified as Vega 5Cs while c/n 122, the famous *Winnie Mae*, was extensively modified as described later.

Vega 5C: Five aircraft (c/ns 138, 160, 170, 203 and 210) were delivered with larger vertical tail surfaces and higher operating weights, with other aircraft being later brought up to the same standards. Two other aircraft in this series were the Vega High-Speed Special 5C (c/n 171) and the Vega 5C Special (c/n 194). A

NC14236 the last Lockheed-built Vega (c/n 210), a Model 5C, was impressed as the UC-101 during the Second World War but crashed at El Paso, Texas, in June 1945 after being returned to the civil register. (*Lockheed*)

unique Vega 5C was c/n 76 which was built as an Air Express and, after operating in this guise for more than three years, had its wing lowered to bring it to Vega 5C standard; more details of this hybrid are given in the Air Express section.

Vega: Not assigned a model number, c/n 19 was the only Vega to be powered by a 525 hp Pratt & Whitney Hornet A. Ordered by Lieut-Col William K. Thaw, a former commander of the Lafayette Escadrille, this aircraft was specially built as an entry in the nonstop New York–Los Angeles event of the 1928 National Air Races. Completed nine days before this race, the aircraft (X7430) was ferried to Roosevelt Field, New York, where Thaw could not resist realizing a quick $5,000 profit by selling his aircraft for $35,000 to Bernard Macfadden, a wealthy publisher. On the day of the race, 13 September, 1928, the Macfadden-owned Vega with Jack Morris as pilot and Thaw as navigator was the last of the nine competitors to take off. Unfortunately, following a drop in oil pressure, it was destroyed in an emergency night landing near Decatur, Indiana; although badly hurt, the two aviators survived their ordeal. None of the other entries made it nonstop to Los Angeles.

Vega Special: Also not assigned a model number, c/n 102 (NC32M) was a Wasp C-powered machine built in 1929 for a Detroit newspaper, the *Evening News*. With this owner the aircraft was operated for five years with wheels, floats and skis. Resold in 1934, it was converted to Vega 5C during the following year. In 1935–36 it was flown to Africa by Philip Whitmarsh. Finally, it was acquired in 1942 by Lineas Aéreas Mineras S.A. and was registered XA-DAI in Mexico; with this identity the aircraft burned up at Parral, Chihuahua, on 23 June, 1943.

DL-1: Following the acquisition of the Lockheed Aircraft Company by the Detroit Aircraft Corporation in July 1929, a modernized version of the Vega 5C was developed by the new parent company. Powered by a 450 hp Pratt & Whitney C1, three DL-1s (Detroit-Lockheed One) were assembled in Detroit with a duralumin fuselage built in that city and wooden wing made in Burbank. The first of these DL-1s (c/n 135) was completed in February 1930 and was initially used by Amelia Earhart to set three NAA women's speed/load records. The next two aircraft were completed later in 1930 and one of them survived in Mexico until 1946.

DL-1B: Also powered by the Pratt & Whitney Wasp, the three DL-1Bs (c/ns 136, 137 and 154) were generally similar to the DL-1s. However, they were especially intended for use by airlines as six-passenger transports.

DL-1 Special: Specially built for the export market, the five-seat, Wasp-powered c/n 155 (NC372E) was completed in October 1930 for Lieut-Cdr Glen Kidston and re-registered in the United Kingdom as G-ABGK. While on the British register, this aircraft set a number of speed records (London–Paris and London–Capetown in 1931) and was entered in the 1934 London–Melbourne Mac.Robertson race. After being damaged in Syria during the race, it was shipped to Australia where it was rebuilt and registered VH-UVK. In November 1941, it was impressed into RAAF service as A42-1, but subsequently flew only 46 hours in service with Nos.24 and 23 Squadrons and No.3 Communications Unit before being scrapped in October 1945. With the exception of c/n 30—a Vega 1 sold to Canada in early 1929 as CF-AAL and resold to Nicaragua fifteen years later—c/n 155 was the only Vega to be used in the British Commonwealth.

Y1C-12: Basically a 450 hp Wasp (R-1340-7) powered DL-1, the Y1C-12 (c/n 158) was acquired for evaluation by the US Army Air Corps as a fast command transport. Assigned the military serial 31-405, this aircraft flew 999 hours in military service before being scrapped in May 1935. The Y1C-12 was the first aircraft of Lockheed design to be acquired by the US Armed Forces; some twelve years earlier the US Navy had evaluated, but not purchased, the Loughead F-1 twin-engined flying-boat and had ordered two Loughead-built, but Curtiss-designed, HS-2L single-engined flying-boats.

Y1C-17: Specially fitted with a wire-braced, spatted main undercarriage and a faired doughnut-tailwheel, this DL-1B Special (c/n 159) was powered by a 500 hp Pratt & Whitney R-1340–17. When completed in December 1930, serial 31-408 was the fastest aircraft of the Army Air Corps with a top speed of 221 mph (356 km/h). Accordingly, the Service decided to entrust it to Capt Ira C. Eaker for an attempt at breaking the eastbound nonstop transcontinental record. When it took off from Long Beach, California, on 10 March, 1931, the Y1C-17 had been specially fitted with auxiliary cabin tanks in place of its four passenger seats. Clogging of the fuel line forced Eaker to attempt an engine-off landing in a Kentucky meadow and the Y1C-17 was damaged beyond repair. Before its crash the aircraft had covered 1,740 miles (2,800 km) in 7 hr 20 min at an average speed of 237 mph (381 km/h) with the help of favourable winds.

Operated by the US Army Air Corps for less than four months, the Y1C-17 (c/n 159) had only been flown for 33 hours when it was damaged beyond repair at Tolu, Kentucky, on 10 March, 1931. (*USAF*)

UC-101: In 1942 the US War Department acquired for use by the Corps of Engineers the last Lockheed-built Vega (Vega 5C, c/n 210, ex NC14236) and this aircraft was given the military serial 42-94148 and assigned a designation in the UC (Utility Transport) category. In 1944 the aircraft was returned to the civil register as NC48610; it was destroyed in a crash at El Paso, Texas, on 9 June, 1945.

Vegas built by others: The first of these aircraft was completed in March 1930 by William S. Brock and Edward F. Schlee before liquidating their Schlee-Brock Aircraft Corp, which had acted as a Lockheed distributor in Detroit. This Vega 5 Special with Wasp C engine used a fuselage specially built by Lockheed with the c/n 619, and wings and other parts available to Schlee-Brock. It was followed by another aircraft (c/n 139) assembled in Patterson and New Orleans, Louisiana, by Wedell-Williams Air Service Inc, and using Lockheed-built parts; c/n 139 was completed in March 1931 as a Vega 5B and later converted as a Vega 5C (NC997N).

Following the demise of Detroit-Lockheed, Richard Von Hake and other laid-off employees completed in March 1933 a DL-1B Special (c/n 161) with Wasp SC1 engine, a Detroit-built metal fuselage and Lockheed-built wooden wings. Ten months earlier, other laid-off employees had assembled a Wasp-powered Vega 5C (c/n 191).

Special Vega modifications: Even though all Vegas were not, in the modern sense, assembly-line products, they could generally be categorized in the series previously described. Some of these aircraft, however, were further modified drastically after initial delivery and deserve to be described separately by constructor numbers.

C/n 14: Completed in September 1928 as a Vega 1, this Wright Whirlwind powered aircraft served as a transport aircraft before being acquired, engineless, by Chamberlin Flying Services of Jersey City, NJ. Its new owner obtained from the Packard Motor Company the loan of one of its experimental 225 hp DR-980 diesel engines. Besides being used as a flying testbed for its diesel powerplant, the aircraft, named *Miss Teanek* but affectionately known as the 'flying furnace', was loaned on several occasions in early 1932 to Miss Ruth Nichols. On 14 February, 1932, the noted aviatrix used this aircraft to set a still-standing world's altitude record for diesel-powered aircraft of 19,928 ft (6,074 m). Retaining its Packard DR-980 diesel engine, this experimental aircraft (NR7426) was destroyed at Roosevelt Field, NY, in May 1937.

C/n 28: Also starting life as a Whirlwind-powered Vega 1, this aircraft was flown in 1932–33 with a 240 hp Guiberson diesel engine. With this powerplant it was flown nonstop from New York to Los Angeles by A. Harold Bromley. In the spring of 1933 it was converted back to Vega 1 standard, before being lost in July of that year.

C/n 69: Pilot fatigue being the main problem on long endurance flights, James J. Mattern decided to modify the Vega 5 he had acquired from Cromwell Air Lines. A second cockpit was fitted with a partial set of controls so that he and Bennett Griffin could share the flying during their attempt at beating the round-the-world record set by Wiley Post and Harold Gatty in June–July 1931. The second cockpit of Mattern's and Griffin's *Century of Progress* was provided in the fuselage aft of the wings and was usable only in flight, with all take-offs and landings being made from the forward cockpit. In this form the aircraft left Floyd Bennett Field in New York on 5 July, 1932, and, with a refuelling stop in Harbor Grace, Newfoundland, went on to Berlin. It then continued eastward but, following the inflight loss of a hatch, it was damaged during an emergency landing at Borisov, in the Soviet Union. The damaged aircraft was shipped back to the United States where it was rebuilt and where its dual controls were removed in preparation for Jimmie Mattern's unsuccessful solo flight around the world.

C/n 79: After being damaged in June 1929, the Vega 5A Executive owned by the B. F. Goodrich Company was rebuilt with the fuselage of an uncompleted Vega (c/n 95). In early 1931 this aircraft (X308H, *Miss Silvertown*) was modified by Goodrich to test the pulsating rubber leading-edge devices which the company had developed to prevent accumulation of ice on the wing and tail surfaces. The aircraft was lost at Vineland, Ontario, on 16 May, 1931, but the Goodrich de-icers were soon widely adopted as standard for many years to come.

C/n 619: The oddly-numbered Vega built by Schlee-Brock was acquired by Crosley Radio Corp of Cincinnati, Ohio, in the summer of 1930. Fitted with the second Hamilton-Standard controllable-pitch propeller ever made and flown by Miss Ruth Nichols, it was used to set women's transcontinental speed and altitude

Ruth Nichols in the cockpit of c/n 619, a Vega 5 Special built by Brock and Schlee in 1930 from parts supplied by Lockheed. (*Lockheed*)

records. In the spring of 1931, the aircraft was modified by Clarence Chamberlin in preparation for Miss Nichols' unsuccessful transatlantic flight. Damaged on landing at St John, New Brunswick, during that attempt, the aircraft was rebuilt by Chamberlin, and Miss Nichols flew it in October 1931 from Oakland, California, to Louisville, Kentucky. Unfortunately, it was damaged by fire at Louisville, preventing Miss Nichols' continuing to New York and, once again, Clarence Chamberlin was given the task of rebuilding this indestructible Vega. In the process NR496M had its wing lowered 14 in (35·6 cm), was provided with a bubble hatch over its cockpit and was fitted with a droppable undercarriage and a heavy wooden skid beneath the fuselage. This last set of modifications did not bring luck back to the aircraft as on 4 November, 1932, it was damaged beyond repair when Miss Nichols was taking off from Floyd Bennett Field for a planned nonstop flight to Los Angeles.

Four months after the tragic disappearance of the *Golden Eagle* on its way to Hawaii, Lockheed completed the second Vega 1 (c/n 3) as a company demonstrator. After being sold to Bernard Macfadden, this aircraft showed its capability by flying from New York to Mexico City in August 1928; however, seven months later it crashed during an attempt to fly nonstop from Los Angeles to New York. Thus, it was the next aircraft in the series which first brought fame to Lockheed and its revolutionary Vega. Specially ordered by Captain George Hubert Wilkins, an already well-known Australian explorer, c/n 4 was completed in January 1928 and was intended for the Wilkins' Arctic Expedition sponsored by the *Detroit News*.

Sir Hubert Wilkins' famous Vega 1 (X3903, c/n 4) after being fitted with floats for the first of two expeditions to Antarctica. (*Peter M. Bowers*)

Having left California with its original conventional undercarriage, in Alaska Wilkins' Vega was fitted first with metal and then with wooden skis. A first take-off attempt from the frozen and snow-covered Barrow Lagoon failed and forced a switch to the nearby and larger Elson Lagoon. Finally, on 15 April, 1928, Wilkins and his pilot, Carl Ben Eielson, took-off for their pioneering flight over the Great North. After flying twenty hours over the Arctic Ocean and the northern tip of Greenland, the Vega was low on fuel and had to be landed on Doedmansoeira (Dead Man's Island) in a storm. After waiting for the weather to clear, the two indomitable flyers took off again to terminate their 2,200-mile (3,540-km) flight at Green Harbour, in Spitzbergen. For their remarkable feat in a wooden aeroplane powered by a 225 hp engine, Wilkins was knighted (as Sir Hubert) by HM King George V and Ben Eielson received the 1928 Harmon Award and the USA's Distinguished Flying Cross.

The second Vega 1 of Sir Hubert Wilkins (X7439, c/n 17) being brought back on land in the autumn of 1928. (*Lockheed*)

Upon the successful completion of his Arctic Expedition, Sir Hubert ordered a second Vega 1 (c/n 17). This aircraft, the first Vega to be flown as a floatplane, took part with c/n 4 in Sir Hubert's expeditions in Antarctica in 1928–29 and 1929–30. Flown during the first of these by Ben Eielson and Joe Crosson, the two Vegas charted unknown territory and Sir Hubert named several geographical points in honour of the designers of his aircraft and of their engine (*e.g.* Lockheed Mountains, Cape Northrop, Whirlwind Glaciers). In the second expedition, which like the first one was sponsored by George Hearst Jr, the San Francisco newspaper magnate, the Vegas were flown by Parker Cramer and Al Cheesman. Even though the two aircraft had been left to survive the Antarctic winter of 1929 with limited protection, they were used to chart an additional 1,200 miles (1,930 km) of coast in 1929–30. They were then given to the Argentine Government but, unfortunately, neither got the permanent display place they deserved.

The first of the Wasp-powered Vega 5s (c/n 7) was acquired in 1928 by Harry J. Tucker and was named *Yankee Doodle*. With Leland Schoenhair as pilot and its owner as passenger, the aircraft failed in a first attempt to fly nonstop eastbound across the United States when fog forced a precautionary landing in Ohio. With Arthur Goebel replacing Schoenhair as pilot, and Harry Tucker refilling the wing tanks in flight by means of a hand-pump and five-gallon cans carried in the fuselage (*Yankee Doodle* was a standard aircraft and did not have additional fuselage tanks), the aircraft made the first eastbound, nonstop transcontinental flight on 19–20 August, 1928, from Mines Field, Los Angeles, to Curtiss Field, New York, in 18 hr 58 min. Two months later, with Charles Collyer as pilot, Tucker and his Vega returned nonstop to California to become the first passenger and first aircraft to fly both ways across the United States. Sadly, Tucker was driven to beat his own record, and ten days later he died with Charlie Collyer when *Yankee Doodle* crashed near Palace Station, Arizona.

Following its unsuccessful participation in the Dole Race, the brilliantly executed Arctic and Antarctic expeditions of Hubert Wilkins and the transcontinental records of *Yankee Doodle*, the Vega remained in the limelight for many years. Space limitations prevent us from recording the achievements of many noted Vega pilots but the exploits of Wiley Post and *The Winnie Mae* deserve to be recorded here. As the pilot of F. C. Hall, a wealthy Oklahoma oilman, Post had flown Hall's first *Winnie Mae* (Vega 5, c/n 24). However, it was in the second *Winnie Mae* (Vega 5B, c/n 122) that the one-eyed pilot gained fame. In this aircraft Post beat four other Vegas and one Air Express to win the 1930 National Air Races by flying nonstop from Los Angeles to Chicago in 9 hr 9 min. The following year, with Harold Gatty as his navigator, Wiley Post set out to obtain a new round-the-world record. Taking off from Roosevelt Field, New York, on 23 June, 1931, Post and Gatty proceeded eastward and refuelled at Harbor Grace, Newfoundland, before the Atlantic crossing. Flying via England, Germany, the Soviet Union, Alaska and Canada, *The Winnie Mae* and its crew landed back at Roosevelt Field on 1 July, having gone around the world in 8 days 15 hr and 51 min (seven years earlier the first round-the-world flight by two Douglas DWCs had taken 175 days!).

Not content with this success, Wiley Post sought a solo record around the world. Leaving Floyd Bennett Field on 15 July, 1933, Post flew to Berlin in 25 hr 45 min, thus making the first nonstop New York to Berlin flight, and soon continued on his race against the clock. In spite of damage to the propeller and undercarriage when he was forced to land at Flat, Alaska, to check his position, Wiley Post managed to reach New York in 7 days 18 hr and 43 min. Flying alone, he had succeeded in cutting 21 hours from his previous record! Yet, this outstanding achievement was not the end for Wiley Post and *The Winnie Mae*. Working with the B. F. Goodrich Company, Post used a specially-built pressure suit to develop high-altitude flying techniques and, if possible, beat the world's altitude record of 47,352 ft (14,433 m) then held by Italy. Three times his attempts were marred by technical difficulties (an unofficial record of 55,000 ft (16,764 m) could not be registered on the third flight due to failure of the recording barograph) and a fourth was curtailed by sabotage. For this last attempt *The Winnie Mae* had been fitted with a jettisonable undercarriage and had to be landed on a metal belly skid. In this form the aircraft was used three times in attempts to break the transcontinental speed record by flying in the less dense atmosphere. Unfortunately, these 1935 flights were unsuccessful. Wiley Post died with Will Rogers on 15 August, 1935, in the crash of the Orion-Explorer at Walakpi, Alaska.

With the American women pilots of the thirties, the Lockheed Vega was a favourite and several of the best known aviatrices achieved spectacular results whilst flying this type. With the possible exception of Wiley Post, Amelia Earhart was probably the best proponent of the Vega and, between 1929 and 1935, she used no fewer than six. Her first Vega was an already well used Vega 1 (c/n 10) which she briefly owned in 1929 and traded in for c/n 36, another Vega 1. With the latter she entered the 1929 'powder-puff derby' and was placed third in that Santa Monica to Cleveland race. During the same year she was loaned c/n 107, a Wasp-powered Vega 5A Executive, and with it established a new women's speed record, at the Los Angeles Metropolitan Airport, of 184·17 mph (293·38 km/h) over a 3-km course. In June 1930 she was also loaned the first metal-fuselage DL-1 (c/n 135) and with it set three women's speed/load records at the Grosse Isle Airport, Michigan. During 1930 she exchanged her second Vega 1 for a Vega 5 (c/n 22) but this aircraft was damaged and had to be rebuilt as a Vega 5B by using

NR105W *The Winnie Mae* (c/n 122) of Wiley Post after being modified for high-altitude experiments. Note the under-fuselage skid and jettisonable undercarriage. (*Lockheed*)

The Vega 5C Special NC965Y (c/n 171), the last of six Vegas of Amelia Earhart, in which the famous aviatrix became the first woman to fly from Hawaii to California, in January 1935. The lettering on the tail reads—N.Y. Los Angeles 14 hrs, Honolulu Oakland 18 hrs, Los Angeles Mexico City 12 hrs, Mexico City New York 14 hrs. It is in capitals and without punctuation. (*Lockheed*)

the fuselage of c/n 68. With this rebuilt aircraft Amelia Earhart gained considerable fame by becoming the first woman to fly solo across the Atlantic, from Harbor Grace in Newfoundland to Culmore in Ireland, in 15 hr 18 min on 20/21 May, 1932, and nonstop across the United States from Los Angeles to Newark on 24 August, 1932, in 19 hr 5 min. Finally, in 1933 she acquired c/n 171, originally built as a Vega High-Speed Special 5C but by then modified as a standard Vega 5C, with which she became the first woman to fly over the Pacific, from Wheeler Field on Oahu to Oakland, 2,408 miles (3,875 km) in 18 hr 16 min on 11/12 January, 1935. In the same aircraft, she flew from Los Angeles to Mexico City on 19/20 April, 1935, and, finally, on 9 May, 1935, made the first ever nonstop flight from Mexico City to Newark, New Jersey.

Miss Ruth Nichols, the other famous contemporary aviatrix, made most of her record flights in the Vega 5 Special (c/n 619) assembled by Schlee-Brock and loaned to her by Powell Crosley of the Crosley Radio Corp. She first used it in November–December 1930 to set a women's round-trip transcontinental record of 30 hr 21 min flying time from Roosevelt Field, New York, to Burbank, California, and back. The westbound flight was started on 24 November and made with four intermediate stops, whereas the return trip was made with a single stop at Wichita, with the final landing at Roosevelt Field on 10 December. In the same aircraft Miss Nichols set a women's world altitude record of 28,743 ft (8,761 m) over the Jersey City Airport on 6 March, 1931, and a 3-km women's world speed record of 210·685 mph (339·059 km/h) at the Grosse Isle Airport on 13 April of that year. Two months later, while trying to become the first woman to fly solo across the Atlantic, Miss Nichols damaged her aircraft while landing at St John, New Brunswick. After her aircraft had been repaired, and whilst still wearing a back brace due to her accident, on 24–25 October, 1931 she broke the women's distance record by flying from Oakland to Louisville, a distance of 1,977 miles (3,182 km). Her aircraft, however, was damaged by fire on the ground as she was preparing to leave for New York. This time, while her faithful c/n 619 was being rebuilt with its wing lowered as described earlier, she borrowed the Packard diesel-powered c/n 14 and on 14 February, 1932, set an all-time altitude record for that class of aircraft, reaching 19,928 ft (6,074 m), after which Miss Nichols' association with the Vega ended.

Although Vegas are best remembered for their many record flights, leading its manufacturer to boast 'it takes a Lockheed to beat a Lockheed', the aircraft was operated for more mundane uses, such as corporate flying, ambulance work, passenger and cargo transport. The last two roles saw Vegas being used by at least forty-one airlines in the United States, with the largest fleet being that of Braniff Airways—which between 1930 and 1939 owned ten Vegas and leased briefly an eleventh—and by six airlines abroad. Outside the United States, Mexico was the main operator of Vegas, with no fewer than 26 appearing on its register, the largest user being Lineas Aéreas Mineras S.A. of Mazatlan. Other Vegas were registered in Nicaragua (two aircraft), and Argentina, Australia, Canada, Costa Rica, Norway, Panama, and the United Kingdom (one aircraft each).

This metal fuselage DL-1 (NC8495, c/n 156), was one of ten Vegas used by Braniff Airways.
(*Braniff International*)

At least one Vega 5B (c/n 103, ex NC534M, XA-BHI and XB-AAD) found its way to the Republican forces during the Spanish Civil War. It is reported to have served primarily as a personnel and supply transport as well as, on occasions, a light bomber. Its ultimate fate has not been traced.

The historic Lockheed Vega can still be found more than half of a century after the maiden flight of the ill-fated *Golden Eagle*. Wiley Post's *The Winnie Mae* (c/n 122) is in the collection of the National Air and Space Museum, Washington, DC, while Amelia Earhart's c/n 22 is exhibited by the Franklin Institute in Philadelphia. Four other Vegas (c/ns 40, 72, 161 and 203) were still believed to be in existence in 1980, with at least the first of these in flying condition.

83

Dimensions (landplane versions): span 41 ft (12·49 m); length 27 ft 6 in (8·38 m); height 8 ft 4½ in (2·55 m) for Vega 1 and 8 ft 6 in (2·59 m) for later models; wing area 275 sq ft (25·548 sq m).

Empty weight ranging from 1,650 lb (748 kg) for Vega 1 to 2,565 lb (1,163 kg) for Vega 5C in landplane configuration and 3,153 lb (1,430 kg) for Vega 5C in seaplane configuration; corresponding loaded weight 2,900 lb (1,315 kg) to 4,500 lb (2,041 kg) and 4,880 lb (2,214 kg); corresponding wing loading 10·5 lb/sq ft (51·5 kg/sq m) to 16·4 lb/sq ft (79·9 kg/sq m) and 17·7 lb/sq ft (86·7 kg/sq m); corresponding power loading 13·2 lb/hp (6 kg/hp) to 10 lb/hp (4·5 kg/hp) and 10·8 lb/hp (4·9 kg/hp).

Maximum speed ranging from 135 mph (217 km/h) for Vega 1 to 185 mph (298 km/h) for Vega 5C with NACA cowling and in landplane configuration, and 175 mph (282 km/h) for Vega 5C with NACA cowling and in seaplane configuration; other performance for same models: cruising speed 118 mph (190 km/h) to 165 mph (265 km/h) and 160 mph (257 km/h); initial rate of climb 850 ft/min (259 m/min) to 1,300 ft/min (396 m/min) and 1,100 ft/min (335 m/min); service ceiling 15,000 ft (4,570 m) to 19,000 ft (5,790 m) and 17,000 ft (5,180 m); normal ranges 900 miles (1,450 km) to 725 miles (1,165 km) and 620 miles (1,000 km).

Lockheed 3 Air Express

Although the type was especially conceived as a mail or passenger transport for Western Air Express, as evidenced in part by its name, only one Air Express was acquired by this airline and its only scheduled flight ended in a landing accident. Yet, after repair this aircraft and her six sister ships were used for many notable flights and did much to enhance the reputation of the young Lockheed company.

The performance of the Lockheed Vega, which was markedly superior to that of the Douglas M-2 biplanes with which the fledgling airline had begun operations over Air Mail Route 4 (CAM No.4, Los Angeles–Salt Lake City), had attracted the interest of Western Air Express. However, in the opinion of senior pilots of WAE, an aft cockpit location was preferable to the forward position as used on the Vega (an odd preference in view of the Vega's better approach visibility) and

As originally finished in black and silver, this Air Express (NR3057, c/n 75) became known as The Black Hornet. (*Lockheed*)

the Whirlwind-powered Vega was underpowered for operations with full load over the Sierra Nevada. To overcome these objections, Jack Northrop redesigned the Vega into the Air Express by relocating the cockpit aft of the wing. To improve forward visibility from the relocated pilot's seat, which incidentally was now in the open, the wing was raised 18 in (46 cm) to a strut-braced parasol position. In the process, wing span and area were increased from 41 ft to 42 ft 6 in (12·49 m to 12·95 m) and from 275 sq ft to 288 sq ft (25·548 sq m to 26·756 sq m), thus improving the aircraft's weight-lifting capabilities. This performance was further improved by powering the aircraft with a 410 hp Pratt & Whitney Wasp. Commercial load, consisting of up to 100 cu ft (2·8 cu m) of mail or four passengers, was carried in a cabin ahead of the pilot's open cockpit. Three cabin windows were provided in each side of the fuselage.

Construction of the first Air Express (c/n 5, registration number 4897) for WAE was undertaken in late 1927 in the original building rented by Lockheed at Romaine and Sycamore Streets, Hollywood, but was completed in April 1928 in the new Burbank factory. As originally built, the aircraft had a triangular fin, as used on the first two Vegas, but before delivery to WAE the vertical tail surfaces were changed to the more familiar rounded shape of greater area. The Air Express first flew in April 1928, and after being tested for over two months, including at least once by Charles Lindbergh, it was delivered to WAE and readied for its inaugural flight on the Los Angeles–Las Vegas–Salt Lake City route. Unfortunately, on its very first landing, the aircraft was badly damaged by striking a cement T marking the centre of the Las Vegas landing strip. The aircraft was returned to Lockheed for repair but neither it nor others of the type were again flown by Western Air Express.

As the rebuilt aircraft and subsequent machines are of unusual interest, their history is detailed here in order of constructor's numbers:

EX-2: Upon return to Lockheed the original c/n 5 was totally rebuilt and, fitted with a new Wasp engine, was given the special construction number EX-2 and the new registration 7955 (later NR7955 and NC7955). It was initially tested at Burbank with an uncowled powerplant but, by the time it was ready to be ferried to New York for an exhibition, it had acquired the first NACA cowling to be fitted to a commercial aeroplane. To ferry this Air Express, Lockheed obtained the temporary service of Capt Frank M. Hawks. This noted pilot, with the manufacturer's enthusiastic support, decided to use the ferry flight as an attempt to beat the transcontinental nonstop record then held by *Yankee Doodle*, the Vega 5 of Harry Tucker. As the Air Express did not have sufficient internal tank capacity for the nonstop flight, a Lockheed employee was taken along to hand-pump fuel from 5-gallon cans carried in the cabin. The scheme worked perfectly and on 4/5 February, 1929, Frank Hawks and his Air Express flew from Los Angeles to New York in 18 hr 22 min, cutting 36 minutes from the time achieved with *Yankee Doodle*.

After this record flight, Frank Hawks convinced his regular employer, The Texas Company, to acquire the aircraft which then received the fleet number Texaco 5. During the next eleven months, while the aircraft was progressively modified with the addition of wheel spats and the replacement of the original fuselage with that of c/n 91, Frank Hawks flew Texaco 5 on many news-making flights, while Charles Lindbergh borrowed it to help in the search for the wreckage of a Western Air Express Ford Tri-motor. The most spectacular of these flights were out-and-back westbound and eastbound nonstop transcontinental flights made by Frank Hawks: 19 hr 11 min westbound on 27 June and,

The first Air Express as it appeared after being rebuilt and given the new c/n EX-2. (*Lockheed*)

after resting for only seven hours, 17 hr 38 min eastbound. Seven months later, and only eight days after receiving its new fuselage, Texaco 5 was destroyed at West Palm Beach, Florida, when Frank Hawks ran into some parked aircraft shortly after getting airborne from a muddy field.

C/n 65: Powered by an uncowled 420 hp Pratt & Whitney Wasp C, NC514E was used as a demonstrator after being completed in March 1929. In January of the following year it was acquired by NYRBA (New York, Rio & Buenos Aires Line) for service on that carrier's South American network. Its use, primarily in Argentina, continued after NYRBA was absorbed by Pan American in September 1930, and this aircraft became the only Air Express to be operated on twin floats. In January 1931, its US registration was cancelled and it eventually found its way to Brazil where it was flown as a floatplane with Brazilian registration. Its subsequent fate is unknown.

C/n 75: Most famous of all the Air Expresses, this machine was originally fitted with an uncowled Wasp but, while still in Lockheed's hands, it was re-engined with a 525 hp Pratt & Whitney Hornet A and fitted with square-cut wheel spats. Flown by Herb Fahy, it was used for an unsuccessful nonstop transcontinental flight before being sold in August 1929 to the General Tire & Rubber Company. On its delivery flight to its new owner, NR3057 was flown by Henry Brown and was entered in the 1929 National Air Races from Los Angeles to Cleveland, winning this event in 13 hr 15 min at an average speed of 156 mph (251 km/h).

A little over six months later it was resold to the Gilmore Oil Company which entrusted it to the flamboyant Roscoe Turner. Named the *Gilmore Lion*, after its new owner and Turner's pet lion cub, c/n 75 was fitted with a new Hornet engine and spats of revised shape. Among the many important flights made by Roscoe Turner in the *Gilmore Lion* were a new eastbound transcontinental record of 18 hr 45 min, including a brief stop in Wichita, in May 1930; a 9 hr 14 min flight from Vancouver, British Columbia, to Agua Caliente, Mexico, in July 1930; and fifth place in the 1930 Los Angeles–Chicago National Air Races. In November 1931 the aircraft was again re-engined with a Wasp and, nine months later, was acquired by Roscoe Turner as his personal aeroplane. By then registered NC3057 and renamed *Ring-free Express*, it was damaged in March 1935 but soon repaired. By late 1938 dry rot in its wooden structure kept it grounded and two years later it had to be dismantled.

NR3057 (c/n 75) in its famous livery as *The Gilmore Lion*. Roscoe Turner's pet lion cub can be seen on the ground in line with the cabin window. (*Lockheed*)

NC3057 (c/n 75) when owned in 1932–38 by Roscoe Turner and named *Ring-free Express*. (*Peter M. Bowers*)

C/n 76: Delivered to Texas Air Transport in Dallas as NC306H, with a NACA-cowled Wasp engine, this aircraft served for less than four months before being damaged at Big Springs, Texas, on 12 September, 1929. C/n 76 was then rebuilt by Southern Air Transport with a specially-built fuselage (c/n 93) supplied by Lockheed. With this carrier and with American Airways, which had acquired

Southern in 1931, this Air Express was used from February 1930 until the winter of 1932–33. At that time the aircraft was converted by former employees of the Detroit Aircraft Corporation and, with its wing lowered, re-emerged as a Wasp-powered Vega 5C. In this guise the aircraft was successively operated by Rapid Airlines and Hanford-Rapid Air Lines after their merger in December 1933 before being destroyed in a hangar fire at Rickenbacker Field, South Dakota, on 20 January, 1937.

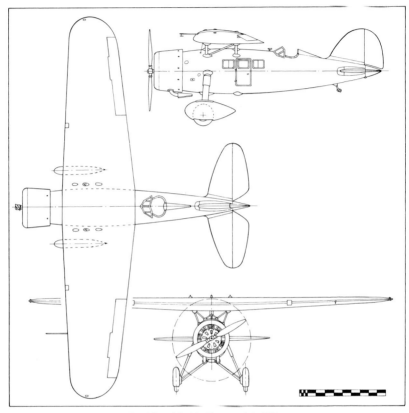

Lockheed 3 Air Express (c/n 75)

C/n 77: Built for NYRBA, with its engine initially uncowled and with four windows on each side instead of three as other Air Expresses, this Wasp-powered aircraft was not taken up by its owner until ten months after its completion in May 1929. Like c/n 65, it was operated by NYRBA/Pan American in South America until late in 1930. In 1932, after its engine had been removed, it was shipped back to the United States. Restored to the US register as NC307H and fitted with a NACA cowling, it was successively owned by Katherine Daufkirch (1932–33), Bernard Macfadden (1933–34), Air Engineers Inc (1934–36), and Mr and Mrs Charles Ewan (1936–38). Finally, in 1938 it was acquired as an instructional airframe by the Lindsay-Hopkins Vocational School in Miami.

C/n 92: Even though NC522K had five owners in less than four years, including two members of the wealthy and air-minded Guggenheim family, it had a fairly undistinguished career. Nevertheless, as proved when it was flown through thirty-two States in two weeks during the 1932 Presidential campaign, it was a reliable machine. It was lost on 27 April, 1934, when bad weather over Georgia forced its pilot and mechanic to bale out.

C/n 130: The last Air Express, NR974Y, was completed in May 1931 with a cowled Wasp, wire-braced high-speed undercarriage, and four cabin windows in each side. After delivery to the Atlantic Exhibition Company of New York, the cabin windows were covered up and extra tanks were fitted to bring total capacity up from 100 to 650 US gal (379 to 2,461 litres). So modified, the aircraft was to be used in 1931 by Laura Ingalls in her attempt to become the first woman to fly solo across the Atlantic, but leaky fuel tanks prevented its realization. In 1933, however, Miss Ingalls acquired the aircraft and it was again fitted with cabin windows and reduced fuel tankage. In this form the aircraft, now named *Auto-da-Fé (Act of Faith)*, was flown by Laura Ingalls on a 16,897-mile (27,192-km), 23-nation tour of Latin America and crossed the Andes between Santiago, Chile, and Mendoza, Argentina. For her 28 February–25 April, 1934, flight Miss Ingalls received that year's Harmon Award. After that flight she traded her aircraft for a Lockheed Orion and, eventually, c/n 130 was acquired by two Japanese-Americans and then by Pacific Airmotive Corp. After the Japanese attack on Pearl Harbor this last airworthy Air Express was flown to Sky Ranch, Nevada, where it was destroyed a month later during a wind storm.

In its basic Wasp-powered configuration the Air Express had the following characteristics and performance:

Span 42 ft 6 in (12·95 m); length 27 ft 6 in (8·38 m); height 8 ft 4½ in (2·55 m); wing area 288 sq ft (26·756 sq m).

Empty weight 2,533 lb (1,149 kg); loaded weight 4,375 lb (1,984 kg); wing loading 15·2 lb/sq ft (74·2 kg/sq m); power loading 10·4 lb/hp (4·7 kg/hp).

Maximum speed 167 mph (269 km/h) at sea level without cowling or 176 mph (283 km/h) at sea level with NACA cowling; cruising speed 135 mph (217 km/h) without cowling or 151 mph (243 km/h) with cowling; initial climb rate 1,460 ft/min (445 m/min); service ceiling 17,250 ft (5,260 m); normal range 750 miles (1,207 km).

Lockheed 4 and 7 Explorer

The least successful of the early Lockheed aeroplanes, both in terms of number of aircraft built and actual achievements, was the Explorer. This type, which combined the basic Vega/Air Express wooden fuselage with cantilever, low-mounted wooden wing, was conceived by Jack Northrop at about the same time as the Vega. In fact, construction of a first example of this type had been started in 1927 in the Sycamore and Romaine Streets building but was temporarily held up. However, when Sir Hubert Wilkins, after his Arctic flight, sent a tentative order for a floatplane to be used on his coming expedition to Antarctica, Northrop proposed to resume construction of the low-wing monoplane and fit it with a central float and retractable outrigger stabilizing floats; but this configuration was judged impractical for operation in Antarctica, and construction of the Explorer, so named in honour of Sir Hubert, was once again halted in favour of a float-equipped Vega (c/n 17).

The unlucky first Explorer 4 NR856H (c/n 2) with experimental tail surfaces. (*Lockheed*)

In the post-Lindbergh New York–Paris flight euphoria, the Japanese *Asahi Shimbun* offered a $25,000 prize for the first nonstop, trans-Pacific flight between Japan and the United States. This would be much more difficult than the Atlantic crossing, not only because the distance was longer—7,000 km (4,350 miles)—but also because the shorter great-circle route would take the aircraft over the Kuriles, the Aleutians and Alaska, where weather conditions were seldom favourable. Obviously, a very special machine would be required, and John Buffelen, a wealthy lumber dealer, and members of the Tacoma Chamber of Commerce, keen on promoting their region, put up funds to purchase such an aircraft. Together with their pilot, Albert Harold Bromley, the Tacoma businessmen contacted several West Coast manufacturers and in early 1929 came to Lockheed. Neither the Vega nor the Air Express could be modified to take the required fuel load, but Jerry Vultee, who had by then succeeded Jack Northrop as chief engineer, proposed resurrecting the unfinished Explorer. Agreement was soon reached and the aircraft (c/n 2, NR856H, *City of Tacoma*) was completed on 18 June, 1929, and first flew that month.

To provide the necessary weight-lifting capability, the then basic Lockheed fuselage was mated to a low-mounted wing of substantially increased span and area, 48 ft 6 in (14·78 m) and 313 sq ft (29·077 sq m) versus 41 ft (12·49 m) and 275 sq ft (25·548 sq m) for the Vega. A conventional non-retractable under-carriage was attached beneath the wing's centre section, and the single cockpit

The first Explorer 4 with another set of tail surfaces, and named *City of Tacoma*. (*Lockheed*)

was located well aft of the wing trailing edge. While the aircraft was undergoing trials in June 1929, three different shapes of vertical tail surfaces were tried before settling on a rounded fin and squared-off rudder. The original tailskid was then replaced with a wheel to enable take-off at the maximum weight of 9,008 lb (4,086 kg), nearly three times the aircraft's empty weight. Power was supplied by a 450 hp Pratt & Whitney Wasp driving a two-blade propeller.

For the trans-Pacific attempt a special inclined take-off ramp was built at the Pierce County Airport, Washington, and the fuselage and fuel tanks were topped up in the cool early morning hours of 28 July, 1929, to hold 902 US gal (3,414 litres) of petrol. Carelessly, no thought had been given to the fact that fuel in the overfilled tanks would expand as temperature rose, and on his take-off run for Tokyo, Harold Bromley was blinded by the petrol spewing off the filler cap forward of the cockpit. Losing control of the Explorer, Bromley veered off the strip and his aircraft ended up on its nose. Luckily it did not catch fire and Bromley escaped; the aircraft, however, was beyond repair and only its engine and a few parts could be salvaged. Undaunted, the pilot and his Tacoma financial backers ordered a replacement aircraft.

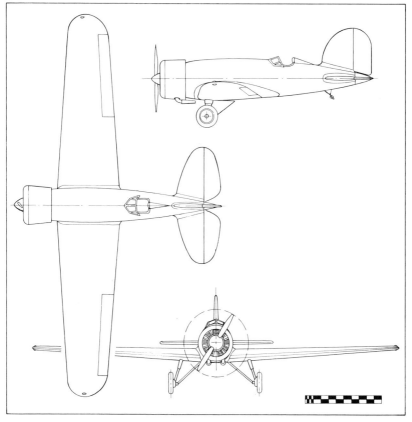

Lockheed 7 Explorer

Bearing the c/n 116 and incorporating some parts and the engine from the first Explorer, the second *City of Tacoma* was completed in September 1929. Like the first Explorer, it had no wing dihedral but modifications incorporated during its construction included a jettisonable undercarriage, to reduce drag and thus increase its range, and at the completion of its hoped-for trans-Pacific flight it was to be landed on a metal belly skid. Still not satisfied with the size and shape of the vertical tail surfaces, Jerry Vultee had a horn-balanced rudder fitted to the second Explorer. This last change brought about c/n 116's quick demise for during its maiden flight on 18 September, 1929, the aircraft developed violent tail flutter. Intending to show the problem to the engineering staff, test pilot Herb Fahy made a low pass over the Burbank airport; the flutter grew more violent and, after the vertical tail surfaces broke off, the aircraft crashed on the edge of the field. Fahy got out with only minor injuries (he was eventually killed on 25 April, 1930, in the crash of the Lockheed Sirius c/n 142) but the second *City of Tacoma* was a total write-off; Lockheed had no recourse but to start building a third Explorer to satisfy the standing order from Bromley and the Tacoma businessmen.

Proving once again that bad luck runs in threes, the next Explorer also crashed before achieving the elusive goal of flying to Japan nonstop. As this aircraft featured several modifications, it's full designation was changed from Explorer 4, as used for the first two aircraft of this type, to Explorer 7. Obviously, the changes included the incorporation of redesigned vertical tail surfaces, but also the use of a slightly more powerful engine, a 450 hp Wasp C, and the adoption of two degrees of dihedral to improve handling characteristics. During the two months following its March 1930 completion, the third *City of Tacoma*, which was registered NR100W whereas its two predecessors both carried the registration NR856H, was intensively tested by Lockheed pilots and by Harold Bromley. Everything appeared satisfactory and it remained for the manufacturer to demonstrate the ability of the aircraft to take off when lifting its full fuel load. This task was given to test pilot Hugh W. Catlin, and the aircraft was moved to Muroc Dry Lake where its tanks were filled to capacity. After being delayed by a fuel-tank leak the pilot was forced to take off in the heat of the day on 24 May, 1930, as the company's insurance policy was expiring the next day. The aircraft barely got airborne before settling back in the thin hot air of the California high desert. It broke up on impact and soon was ablaze. Catlin walked out of the burning wreckage but died hours later from extensive burns. The history of the Explorer as a trans-Pacific contender had ended tragically.

Arthur Goebel, the winner of the 1927 Dole Race in a Travel Air and the pilot who had made the first eastbound, nonstop transcontinental flight in a Vega (c/n 7, *Yankee Doodle*), had also ordered an Explorer to attempt a new speed record between New York and Paris; but perhaps dismayed by the bad luck of the Explorer, he did not take delivery of this aircraft. Essentially similar to c/n 147, this Explorer 7 (c/n 148, NR101W) differed in having its maximum fuel capacity reduced from 900 to 800 US gal (3,407 to 3,028 litres). Completed in April 1930, it was acquired later in the year by Pure Oil Company and, named *Blue Flash*, was entrusted to Roy W. Ammel. Various long-distance flights were planned but, before they could take place, *Blue Flash* was damaged at Gila Bend, Arizona. After repair by Lockheed it was flown on 9/10 November, 1930, by Roy Ammel to make the first nonstop flight from New York to the Canal Zone, Panama. This brief streak of good fortune ended eleven days after this flight when *Blue Flash* was badly damaged at Ancon in the Canal Zone. Parts were shipped back to the United States and its wing was eventually mated to an Orion fuselage to produce

The only partly successful Explorer 7 NR101W *Yankee Doodle* as completed for a projected Paris–New York flight by Col Arthur C. Goebel. (*Lockheed*)

the equally unfortunate Orion-Explorer hybrid in which Wiley Post and Will Rogers were killed at Walakpi in Alaska on 15 August, 1935.

Fortunately for Lockheed, the tragic saga of the Explorer was never to be repeated in the company's history.

Span 48 ft 6 in (14·78 m); length, 27 ft 6 in (8·38 m); height 8 ft 2 in (2·49 m); wing area 313 sq ft (29·077 sq m).

Empty weight 3,075 lb (1,395 kg); loaded weight 9,008 lb (4,086 kg); wing loading 28·8 lb/sq ft (140·5 kg/sq m); power loading 20 lb/hp (9·1 kg/hp).

Maximum speed 165 mph (265 km/h); maximum rate of climb 1,200 ft/min (366 m/min); maximum range 5,500 miles (8,850 km).

Data for first Explorer 4.

Lockheed 8 Sirius

After flying a Lockheed aircraft for the first time, WAE's Air Express, Charles Lindbergh discussed with Jerry Vultee his desire to purchase a high-performance, low-wing monoplane at a price not to exceed that of a standard Vega. On the basis of this discussion at the 1929 National Air Races in Cleveland, Vultee, as Lockheed's chief engineer, undertook to adapt the Explorer design to meet Lindbergh's requirements. Like its forebear, the new aircraft was to combine a wooden fuselage of the basic Vega type with a low-mounted wing. Given two degrees of dihedral to improve handling characteristics, the wing had a shorter span and smaller area, as Lindbergh's aircraft required less fuel capacity (416 US gal/1,575 litres, in two fuselage and two wing tanks) and lower gross weight. Accommodation for the pilot and one passenger were provided in open tandem cockpits, with baggage and other equipment stowed in a compartment between the engine and the front cockpit. The aircraft was powered by a 450 hp Pratt & Whitney Wasp and was fitted with a non-retractable, conventional undercarriage. Lindbergh approved the specifications for his new aircraft in October 1929 and also requested that Lockheed undertake the design and construction of a

The first Sirius (c/n 140) when fitted with a 450 hp Wasp engine and 'outriggers' on the sides of the fin. (*Lockheed*)

modified wing which, incorporating a retractable undercarriage, could be substituted for the original unit.

Bearing the c/n 140, Lindbergh's aircraft was completed and flown in November 1929 and was tested in Burbank initially by Marshall Headle and then by Lindbergh himself. During the next five months the Sirius was progressively modified, with the small 'outrigger elements'* on both sides of the rudder being eliminated, wheel spats added, the original propeller replaced by an hydraulic unit, and the propeller spinner removed. Externally, the most significant change was the fitting of a sliding canopy over the tandem cockpits, an improvement suggested by Anne Morrow Lindbergh. Finally satisfied with their aircraft, the Lindberghs left Glendale, California, in the morning of 20 April, 1930. Stopping briefly in Wichita, to refuel, they continued eastward and landed in New York after setting a new transcontinental record, with a total flying time for the two-stage trip of 14 hr 45 min 32 sec.

Acting as a consultant to Pan American Airways, Lindbergh planned a number of survey flights for future overwater routes. In preparation, his Sirius (NR211, the same number as his famous *Spirit of St. Louis*) was fitted with a 575 hp Wright Cyclone in August 1930 and, early in the following year, with twin Edo metal floats. At that time the arrangement of the forward fuselage compartment and of the fuel tanks was revised to provide additional storage space and fuel capacity. These objectives were achieved by removing a 200-US gal (757 litre) fuselage tank and by installing a 150 gal (568 litre) tank in each float, thus bringing total capacity up from 416 to 516 gal (1,575 to 1,953 litres). So modified, and redesignated Sirius Special, the aircraft was flown by the Lindberghs to Alaska, the North Pacific and China between 27 July and 2 October, 1931. Though it often flew in difficult weather conditions and had to be maintained under less than ideal conditions, the

*Described by Lockheed as 'outrigger elements', these were vertical metal strips just outboard of the rudder hinge. Their true purpose has not been recorded.

Sirius performed reliably. This survey flight, however, ended in Hankow, as a result of an unfortunate accident when the aircraft was damaged while being lowered from the aircraft carrier HMS *Hermes* to the swirling water of the Yangtze River.

The damaged floatplane was shipped back to Burbank, where in 1932 Lockheed rebuilt the aircraft as a landplane before returning it to its famous owners. For their next survey flight the Lindberghs had a 710 hp Cyclone, driving a controllable-pitch propeller, substituted in June 1933 for the earlier and less powerful version of the Wright engine, and had the twin Edo floats re-installed. Between 9 July and 6 December, 1933, they took their Sirius Special on a 30,000-mile (48,280 km) survey flight around the North and South Atlantic. It was in Greenland during this flight that the aircraft acquired its name *Tingmissartoq* (Eskimo for *the one who flies like a big bird*). At the completion of this flight *Tingmissartoq* was donated to the American Museum of Natural History in New York. It was later transferred to the Air Force Museum in Dayton, Ohio, before becoming part of the collection of the National Air and Space Museum in Washington.

The first Sirius with 710 hp Cyclone engine, twin floats and enclosed cockpits. (*Lockheed*)

The individual history of the fourteen other aircraft in the Sirius series — five of which were subsequently modified as Altairs with retractable undercarriages — is related in the sequential order of their serial numbers.

C/n 141: Powered by a 420 hp Pratt & Whitney Wasp C and registered NC349V, this aircraft was completed in February 1930 with tandem open cockpits and spatted undercarriage. Sold to Shell Oil Company, it was flown on cross-country and demonstration flights, including an unofficial 206 mph (331 km/h) speed record at Alameda, California. It was badly damaged at Tracy, California, in October 1930 after developing violent wing flutter. The damaged Sirius was returned to Lockheed but was not repaired.

C/n 142: Ordered by Roberto Fierro, a colonel in the Fuerza Aérea Mexicana, the third Sirius was retained by Lockheed as a demonstrator. It differed from the previously described machine only in having the slightly increased fuel capacity of 440 US gal (1,665 litres). On 25 April, 1930, less than six weeks after its completion, NR12W was destroyed in a take-off attempt from a rough field at Roscommon, Michigan. The demonstrator pilot, Herb Fahy, died two days later but his wife survived the accident.

C/n 143: Fitted with enlarged vertical tail surfaces and completed in March 1930, the fourth aircraft in the series was designated Sirius 8A and also had tandem open cockpits. Powered by a Wasp engine and registered NC13W, it was owned and flown by Joan Fay Shankle and Capt C. E. Shankle for two years until converted to an Altair 8D with retractable undercarriage. Its history in the latter guise is covered in the Altair chapter.

C/n 144: Built as a company demonstrator, this Wasp-powered Sirius 8 (NC14W) with tandem open cockpits was destroyed less than one month after its completion. Its early demise came on 11 April, 1930, when a prospective buyer, Stafford Lambert, and his passenger, Herbert Condie, were forced to bale out following violent aileron and wing flutter leading to the complete disintegration of the aircraft in flight.

C/n 145: This Wasp-powered Sirius 8A (NC15W) served as a demonstrator for slightly over a year before being converted to an Altair with retractable undercarriage.

C/n 146: In spite of Stafford Lambert's unlucky experience with c/n 144, in May 1930 he acquired a Wasp-powered Sirius 8A (NC16W) which was specially fitted with counter-balanced ailerons to prevent flutter recurrence. Twenty-six months later Lambert sold his Sirius to the Texas Oil Company which had the original Wasp C replaced by a Wasp SC1 and used it for one year as their *Texaco 16*. For two and a half years this aircraft was owned by Diversified Shares Inc until it was sold to the Republic of Cuba. Modified as a single-seater, with its rear open cockpit sealed off, it was flown by Cuban Navy pilot Lieut Antonio Menendez y Palaez from Cuba to Spain and back via Trinidad, British Guiana, Brazil, and French West Africa, between 9 January and 14 February, 1936. It was reportedly destroyed in a hangar fire in 1945 after being kept as an historical aircraft.

X-BADA *Anahuac*, the Sirius 8 (c/n 149) of Col Roberto Fierro. (*Lockheed*)

The clean design of the four-seat Sirius 8C is clearly apparent in this view. (*Lockheed*)

C/n 149: Purchased as a quasi-military aircraft with the proceeds from public, state and military donations, this Mexican-registered Sirius 8, X-BADA, was a Wasp-powered machine with tandem open cockpits. First test flown by Col Roberto Fierro of the Fuerza Aérea Mexicana and named *Anahuac*, it was used by Col Fierro and Capt Arnaulfo Cortes on 23 June, 1930, to make the first nonstop flight between New York and Mexico City, 2,152 miles (3,463 km) in 16½ hours. Five years later it was shipped from Mexico to Spain where it was modified as a fighter-bomber by the Republicans. It was apparently shot down by anti-aircraft fire during 1937.

C/n 150: Acquired in July 1930 by H. Walter Blumenthal, this Wasp C powered aircraft was characterized by its accommodation, comprising pilot and co-pilot in tandem, canopy-covered cockpits and two passengers in an enclosed cabin between the engine and the pilot's cockpit, and necessitating a reduction in fuel capacity to 288 US gal (1,090 litres). Designated Sirius 8C and initially registered NR116W, this special machine became NC116W after being certificated in August 1931. Successively sold to Miss Katherine Daufkirch in August 1933 and to Samuel R. Sague a few weeks later, NC116W was finally destroyed in Detroit in September 1935.

C/n 151: The rather undistinguished career of NC117W, a Wasp C powered Sirius 8A with tandem enclosed cockpits, saw this aircraft starting as a company demonstrator and, then, changing hands three times and being involved in one major accident before being acquired by United Air Services in 1936. With its last owner c/n 151 was re-engined with a Wasp SC1 and fitted with open cockpits to be used for air photography. In this role, on 9 May, 1940, the aircraft collided with the prototype Vultee 48 while photographing its maiden flight. The pilot and two passengers in the Sirius were killed but test pilot Vance Breese succeeded in landing the damaged Vultee 48 safely.

97

Sirius 8A NC117W (c/n 151) before delivery to Air Services Inc, New York, in the spring of 1930. (*Lockheed*)

Sirius 8A NC117W equipped as a cinematographic aerial platform; it was lost on 9 May, 1940, after an inflight collision with the Vultee 48 fighter prototype. (*Lockheed*)

The single-seat Sirius 8A NR118W *City of Virginia* (c/n 152) which was to have been used in 1930 for a record attempt over the North Atlantic; it later became the Altair 8D of Sir Charles Kingsford Smith. (*Lockheed*)

C/n 152: After being flown for less than an hour, this Sirius 8A (NR118W) was badly damaged by its pilot-owner, Capt George R. Hutchinson, during a take-off at the Los Angeles Municipal Airport on 2 August, 1930. It was a one-off, Wasp-powered aircraft with reinforced spars and an additional fuselage tank replacing the front cockpit and bringing total capacity to 633 US gal (2,396 litres). Following its accident it was rebuilt by Lockheed, its additional tank being removed and a second cockpit added forward. It was then sold in 1931 to Victor Fleming and Douglas Fairbanks Sr. In August 1932, it was sold back to Lockheed to be modified as an Altair 8D and then achieved fame as Sir Charles Kingsford Smith's *Lady Southern Cross*.

C/n 153: After five months as a company-owned demonstrator, this Wasp C powered Sirius 8A (NR119W) was modified by Lockheed as the first Altair to become the Army Air Corps' Y1C-25 as described in the following chapter.

C/n 165: Assembled and tested in Detroit with DAC-built metal fuselage and LAC-produced wooden wing, the sole Sirius DL-2 (NR8494) was operated as a demonstrator between August 1930 and April 1931; it was powered by a Wasp C

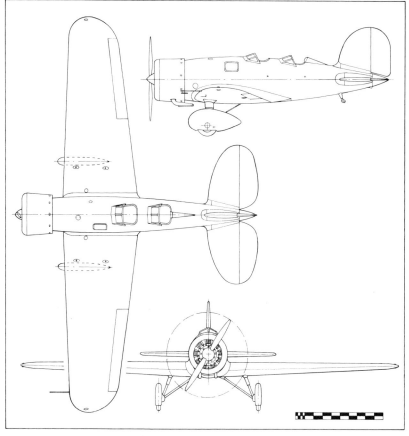

Lockheed 8 Sirius (c/n 149)

and had tandem enclosed cockpits. It was subsequently fitted with a retractable undercarriage as the Altair DL-2A and became the Y1C-23 with the Army Air Corps.

C/n 166: Specially ordered by US residents of Hungarian origin to be used in a transatlantic flight to Hungary to publicize the alleged unfairness of the Treaty of Trianon, this Wasp C powered Sirius 8A (NR115W *Justice for Hungary*) was completed in April 1930. It had tandem enclosed cockpits and increased fuel tankage of 633 US gal (2,396 litres). Following careful preparation and additional fund-raising activities, Sandor Wilczek, a Hungarian residing in Canada, and Capt George Endres of the Hungarian Army left Roosevelt Field, New York, for Harbor Grace, Newfoundland. Thence the pair flew nonstop to Hungary on 15/16 July, 1931, but fuel exhaustion forced them to make an emergency landing at Bicske, just short of their destination, Budapest. Ten months later the *Justice for Hungary* crashed on landing at Rome, and George Endres and J. Pitany were killed.

C/n 167: Receiving the registration NC167W upon being completed in July 1930 as the last aeroplane in the Sirius series, this Wasp-powered Model 8A with tandem enclosed cockpits was delivered to Wedell-Williams Air Service Inc. During the following four and a half years it was sold several times until finally acquired by Bowen Air Lines. For this owner, it was modified in 1935 by Lockheed as a Sirius 8C with revised vertical tail surfaces and open cockpits. Leased by Bowen to Delta Air Lines, NC167W crashed on landing at Charleston, South Carolina, on 24 December, 1935, at the end of a mail flight. The pilot survived but the aircraft was written off.

The following characteristics and performance apply to Charles Lindbergh's Sirius 8 in its Wasp-powered, landplane configuration.

Span 42 ft 9¼ in (13·04 m); length 27 ft 1 in (8·25 m); height 9 ft 3 in (2·82 m); wing area 294·1 sq ft (27·32 sq m).

Empty weight 4,289 lb (1,945 kg); loaded weight 7,099 lb (3,220 kg); wing loading 24·1 lb/sq ft (117·8 kg/sq m); power loading 15·8 lb/hp (7·2 kg/hp).

Maximum speed 185 mph (298 km/h); cruising speed 150 mph (241 km/h); initial rate of climb 1,280 ft/min (390 m/min); service ceiling 26,100 ft (7,955 m); range 975 miles (1,570 km).

The following data apply to the Sirius DL-2:

Span 42 ft 10 in (13·06 m); length 27 ft 10 in (8·48 m); height 9 ft 2 in (2·79 m); wing area 294 sq tt (27·31 sq m).

Empty weight 2,958 lb (1,342 kg); loaded weight 5,170 lb (2,345 kg); wing loading 17·6 lb/sq ft (85·9 kg/sq m); power loading 11·5 lb/hp (5·2 kg/hp).

Max speed 175 mph (282 km/h); cruising speed 145 mph (233 km/h); initial rate of climb 1,100 ft/min (335 m/min); service ceiling 18,000 ft (5,485 m); range 870 miles (1,400 km).

First Lockheed aircraft to be fitted with a retractable undercarriage, the Altair originated in a request by Charles Lindbergh to have this feature incorporated as an alternative for his Sirius. (*Lockheed*)

Lockheed 8 Altair

While negotiating the purchase of his Sirius, Charles Lindbergh requested that Lockheed design an alternate wing set housing a retractable undercarriage. To satisfy this request, a team comprising James Gerschler, Richard Palmer, and Richard Von Hake, devised a novel undercarriage retraction system. Whereas the contemporary Boeing Monomail had its main wheels retracting aft into the wing, with the wheels partly protruding, and the Grumman XFF-1 had its narrow-gauge undercarriage retracting into the fuselage, the Lockheed design had the wheels and struts retracting inwardly and fully flush with the wing. Thus, it was the true prototype of the modern retractable undercarriage. Retraction was achieved by means of a hand crank and with the help of cables and pulleys.

As Lindbergh elected not to have his Sirius modified to the retractable-undercarriage configuration, the specially built wing set was mated to the fuselage of a company-owned Sirius 8A (c/n 153). Ground testing, with the aircraft supported on jacks, began in September 1930 and the modified Sirius was flight tested by Marshall Headle before the end of the month. Bearing the experimental registration X119W, the Wasp C powered aircraft was redesignated Altair 8D and was demonstrated for some six months by Headle and Vance Breese, the latter setting with it an unofficial 92-minute record between Oakland and Burbank. Re-engined with a Wasp B, the first Altair 8D was then loaned to the US Army Air Corps and entrusted to Capt Ira C. Eaker. On 11 April, 1931, Eaker and his Altair were prevented from breaking the transcontinental speed record when on the second leg of their flight supercharger problems necessitated a precautionary landing at Port Columbus, Ohio. None the less, Eaker and the Air Corps were impressed with the aircraft and in November 1931, after it had received a Pratt & Whitney R-1340-17, the aircraft was purchased by the War Department. Designated Y1C-25 and assigned the military serial 32-393, the first Altair was damaged beyond repair seven months later after accumulating a total of 153 flying hours.

NC13W was completed in March 1930 as Sirius 8A c/n 143 and in October 1932 converted to Altair 8D configuration as illustrated. (*via Robert C. Mikesh*)

This first Lockheed aircraft with a retractable undercarriage was followed by four other modified Sirius airframes and by six aircraft built from the onset as Altairs. Their individual history follows:

C/n 143: Converted in August 1932 from its original Wasp-powered Sirius 8A configuration to the Altair 8D standard, NC13W had, as did subsequent Altairs, an hydraulically-operated undercarriage retraction system in place of the hand-operated mechanism used on the prototype. Like most other Altairs, it had accommodation for a crew of two beneath a canopy faired into the aft fuselage decking and had a baggage compartment forward of the cockpits. Registered to Louise Ashby, this aircraft was primarily flown by her husband, Clarence Chamberlin, until sold in 1940 to Charles H. Babb. Its subsequent acquisition by the US Army Corps of Engineers and reported crash near Bakersfield, California, are unconfirmed.

C/n 145: Fourteen months after being completed as a Wasp C powered Sirius 8A demonstrator, NR15W became an Altair 8D and was sold to James Goodwin Hall, an ardent advocate of the repeal of the Eighteenth Amendment to the US Constitution—the prohibition of the manufacture, sale and transportation of intoxicating liquors. Naming his Altair *The Crusader*, James Hall flew it extensively. Notable achievements included a flight from Vancouver in Canada to Agua Caliente in Mexico, in 7 hr 49 min, and one from New York to Havana, in 8 hr 35 min. On 21 September, 1931, Hall was forced to bale out of *The Crusader* but his passenger and a housewife on the ground at Meiers Corner on Staten Island were killed in the crash.

The Altair 8D *Lady Southern Cross* in which Sir Charles Kingsford Smith and P. G. (later Sir Gordon) Taylor flew from Australia to California in October–November 1934. (*Peter M. Bowers*)

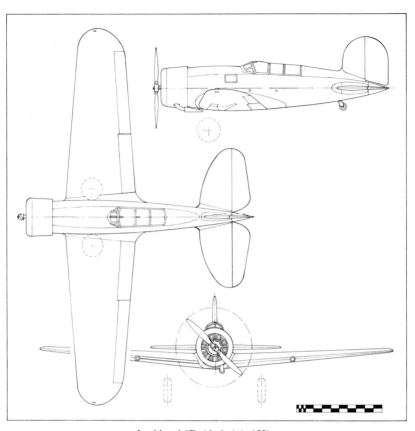

Lockheed 8D Altair (c/n 152)

C/n 152: The most famous Altair, VH-USB, also began as a Sirius 8A and, later, as Sirius 8 Special, was owned by Victor Fleming. Lockheed bought it from Fleming in 1934, and fitted it with a retractable undercarriage as Altair 8D (X118W). Intending to enter it in the October 1934 Mac.Robertson London–Melbourne Race, Sir Charles Kingsford Smith acquired this aircraft shortly after it had been converted to an Altair. Its purchase by the noted Australian pilot had been made possible by Australian public donation, including a contribution by the race sponsor Sir MacPherson Robertson. Originally named *Anzac* but, due to governmental objections to the use of this name, renamed *Lady Southern Cross* and registered in Australia as VH-USB, Sir Charles' aircraft could not take part in the race because there was no time to repair cracks in its cowling. Feeling that he had to sell back his aircraft to compensate his sponsors, Sir Charles decided to fly it back from Australia to the United States. With P. G. Taylor as his navigator he left Brisbane on 20 October, 1934, for the long Pacific crossing. Flying via Fiji and the Hawaiian Islands, Sir Charles and Taylor reached Oakland on 4 November achieving the first eastbound flight from Australia to the United States. Reversing his decision to sell his aircraft, Sir Charles had its engine modified from Wasp C to

Wasp SC1 standard and had *Lady Southern Cross* shipped to England, where it was re-registered G-ADUS. One year after his Pacific flight, Sir Charles decided to attempt to lower the record time between England and Australia. Tragically, Sir Charles and his navigator, Tommy Pethybridge, were lost on 7 November, 1935, when G-ADUS disappeared in the Andaman Sea on the Allahabad–Singapore leg of the flight.

C/n 153: The history of the Y1C-25 was detailed earlier in this chapter.

Y1C-23, the metal fuselage Altair DL-2A operated by the US Army Air Corps from 1931 until 1942. (*Lockheed*)

C/n 165: The last of the Altairs obtained by modifying an existing airframe was originally the Detroit-built DL-2 (NR8494). As an Altair DL-2A it was fitted with a retractable undercarriage and re-engined with a 500 hp Pratt & Whitney SR-1340E in the spring of 1931. Later during that year it was acquired as the Y1C-23 (32-232) by the Army Air Corps. After initial service testing at Wright Field the Y1C-23 was assigned to Bolling Field as a staff transport for use by the Assistant Secretary of War, the Chief of the Air Corps, and other key officers. During its seven-year military flying career this aircraft survived at least five wheels-up landings before being assigned as a ground instructional airframe to Chanute Field, Illinois, after having flown a total of 1,075 hours. It was finally scrapped at the Middletown Air Depot, Pennsylvania, in June 1942.

C/n 176: The first aircraft to be built as an Altair was unique both in being the only civil version of the type to be powered by a 645 hp Wright Cyclone R 1820 F2 nine-cylinder radial and, at the special request of its owner, Bernard Macfadden, in having a substantial external area covered with gold leaf (thus contributing some $8,000 to its $32,000 price). Known as the Altair Special it was completed in July 1931, named *The Gold Eagle* and registered NC998Y. In April 1932 this Altair Special made the first nonstop Montreal–Havana flight (9 hr 3 min) while flown by Macfadden and Lou Reichers. One month later, after extra tanks were added to bring fuel capacity to 465 US gallons (1,760 litres) and its name changed to *Miss Liberty*, the aircraft was used by Lou Reichers in an attempt to halve Lindbergh's New York–Paris time. After flying from New York to a refuelling stop at Harbor Grace, Newfoundland, Reichers left for Dublin. After getting lost, he came close to exhausting his fuel supply and was forced to ditch close to the ss *President Roosevelt* some seventeen miles south of Kinsale Harbour in County Cork. Reichers was rescued but the Altair Special sank.

BuNo 9054 (c/n 179) was an Altair DL-2A with metal fuselage and was designated XRO-1 by the US Navy. It is seen here as it appeared on 8 October, 1931. (*US National Archives*)

C/n 179: This Altair DL-2A with metal fuselage was ordered by the Department of the Navy and was assembled in Detroit with Lockheed-built wooden wing. It was powered by a 645 hp Wright Cyclone R-1820E and, as the XRO-1 (BuNo 9054), was completed in September 1931. After only two years of use from NAS Anacostia, DC, primarily as a command transport by the Assistant Secretary of the Navy and flag officers, it was placed in storage.

C/n 180: Powered by a Wasp E, this Detroit-built Altair DL-2A with metal fuselage (X12222) was leased to Transcontinental & Western Air in September 1931. On 10 October of that year it was damaged in a wheels-up landing at Columbus, Ohio, while being flown by TWA as a mailplane. Returned to Lockheed, it was rebuilt at Burbank as an Orion 9C Special. Its subsequent history is given in the Orion chapter.

C/ns 188 and 213: These two Wasp S1D1 powered aircraft were exported to Japan for use by the *Mainichi Shimbun* as passenger and cargo aircraft. They had the standard tandem enclosed cockpits but their forward fuselage compartments were modified to carry either two passengers or cargo. The first (X12230, J-BAMC) was an Altair 8E and was completed in January 1932 whilst the second

The AiRover Altair 8G NX18149 used as a testbed for the Menasco Unitwin engine. (*Lockheed*)

105

(X14209, J-BAUC) was completed two years later as an Altair 8F. J-BAMC made the first Tokyo–Manila round trip between 10 and 26 November, 1935; on 12 April, 1937, it crashed at Osaka. The second Japanese-registered Altair lasted until autumn 1944 when it was destroyed at Haneda Airport, Tokyo, during a bombing raid by B-29s of the US Twentieth Air Force.

C/n 214: Assembled by the AiRover Company towards the end of 1937 from parts left over from previous production, the Altair 8G (NX18149, *Flying Test Stand*) was the first product of the new Lockheed subsidiary. It was intended to serve as a testbed for the Menasco Unitwin engine, which consisted of two 260 hp Menasco C6S-4 six-cylinder inline engines coupled to drive a single propeller. This aircraft was initially assigned the AiRover c/n 1. After helping with the successful testing of the Menasco Unitwin engine, which had been selected to power the Vega Starliner, this aircraft was re-engined with a Wasp C and was sold as an Altair 8D (c/n 214 in the Lockheed series, and registered NC18149) to Howard Batt in September 1940. In 1942 it was acquired by the California Aircraft Corporation and, later during that year, by the Bechtel-Price-Calahan consortium to carry personnel and equipment for a construction project in Northern Canada.

Span 42 ft 9 in (13·03 m); length 28 ft 4 in (8·64 m); height 9 ft 6 in (2·90 m); wing area 293·2 sq ft (27·238 sq m).

Empty weight 3,235 lb (1,468 kg); loaded weight 4,895 lb (2,220 kg); wing loading 16·7 lb/sq ft (81·5 kg/sq m); power loading 9·8 lb/hp (4·4 kg/hp).

Maximum speed 207 mph at 7,000 ft (333 km/h at 2,135 m); cruising speed 175 mph (282 km/h); climb to 7,000 ft (2,135 m) in 9·4 min; service ceiling 23,800 ft (7,255 m); range 580 miles (935 km).

Data for Y1C-23

Lockheed 9 Orion

The Model 9 Orion reverted to the fuselage configuration of the Vega with its enclosed cockpit just behind the engine and an enclosed passenger cabin aft. The Orion design, however, combined this fuselage arrangement with the NACA cowling first fitted on the Air Express, the low-wing configuration initiated with the Explorer, and the retractable undercarriage introduced with the Altair. Thus, when the first of the new aircraft (c/n 168, X960Y) was completed in February 1931 it incorporated virtually all the aerodynamic features to be found half a century later in the present generation of single-engined, low-wing, general aviation aircraft. But its wooden structure, advanced as it was at the beginning of the thirties, would not compare as favourably with today's types and their metal or composite construction. The Orion first flew in February or March 1931.

Primarily intended as a passenger transport, the Orion had an enclosed cabin for six passengers (three rows of single seats on each side of a central aisle) with the pilot seated centrally forward. The first Orion, powered by a 410 hp Pratt & Whitney Wasp A and fitted with an hydraulically-operated retractable under-carriage, was flight tested by Marshall Headle between March and May 1931 and received its Approved Type Certificate on 6 May, 1931, before being delivered to Bowen Air Lines in Fort Worth as NC960Y. It was followed by thirty-four additional Orions, also with wooden fuselages, and by one metal-fuselage Altair

Mexican-registered Orion 9 (c/n 181) operated by Lineas Aéreas Occidentales S.A. in 1934–35. It bears the title Varney Speed Lines Inc on the fin. (*Lockheed*)

DL-2A (c/n 180) which was modified to Orion 9C Special configuration. The Orion's initial success would probably have resulted in larger-scale production — as already by the spring of 1930 Lockheed had sufficient plant capacity to build as many as twelve single-engined aircraft per month — had it not been for the bankruptcy of the Detroit Aircraft Corporation in October 1931 resulting in the suspension of Orion production after the completion of the first seventeen aircraft. None-the-less, after the organization of the new Lockheed Aircraft Corporation, a further eighteen Orions were built and, as already mentioned, the Altair DL-2A was rebuilt as the Orion 9C Special. These thirty-six aircraft appeared in seven basic models (9 to 9F) with several of these models having sub-variants.

Orion 9: The fourteen aircraft of this model were powered by either a 410 hp Wasp A (c/ns 168/169, 177, 181/182 and 184/185) or 420 hp Wasp C (c/ns 172/175, 178, 183 and 186). With the exception of c/n 174, NC988Y, which went to Asa G. Candler Jr as an executive transport, all Orion 9s were delivered as airliners. Most Orion 9s had a fairly short life, with the first loss occurring on 5 November, 1931, when c/n 178 crashed at Camden, New Jersey, and the last four or five aircraft ended their lives during the Spanish Civil War. Another Wasp A powered aircraft in this series (c/n 192, NC12277) used the uncompleted fuselage of an Air Express, to appear in December 1932 as a cargo aircraft under the designation Orion 9 Special. Less than six months later it was modified as a passenger-carrying Orion 9E before delivery to Transcontinental & Western Air. While in service with that carrier it crashed near Kansas City on 28 July, 1933.

Orion 9A Special: The single aircraft of this model (c/n 187) differed from the Orion 9 in being powered by a 450 hp Wasp SC, in having the dihedral increased from two to three degrees and its forward fuselage lengthened by 6 in (15 cm), and in having a retractable tailwheel. Fitted as an executive transport, it was acquired as NC12229 *Spirit of Fun* by Hal Roach Studios Inc in early 1932. During the summer of that year it was shipped to China to be flown via Southeast Asia and the Middle East to Africa. Its pilot, James B. Dickson, was killed when it crashed at Victoria Falls on 17 November, 1932, but two passengers survived.

107

The red and white Orion 9B (c/n 189) of Swissair at the factory with both Swiss registration, CH-167, and US temporary experimental registration, X12231. (*Lockheed*)

Orion 9B: Powered by a 575 hp Wright Cyclone R-1820-E, the Model 9B was a standard airliner. The two aircraft of this type (c/ns 189 and 190), after being tested as X12231 and X12232, were delivered to Swissair in 1932 and registered CH-167 and CH-168 (later HB-LAH and HB-LAJ). In September 1935 the Swiss airline disposed of its two Orion 9Bs which, apparently, found their way to the Spanish Republicans. Their ultimate fate is unknown.

Orion 9C: After serving with Transcontinental & Western Air on lease from Lockheed, the Altair DL-2A (c/n 180) was returned to the manufacturer and, retaining its original 500 hp Wasp E engine, was converted as the sole metal-fuselage Orion 9 Special. Acquired during the summer of 1932 by the Shell Petroleum Corporation, this aircraft was primarily flown by James H. Doolittle as NC12222, *Shellightning*. Shortly after being re-engined with a 650 hp Wright Cyclone SR-1820-F2, *Shellightning* was extensively damaged at St Louis on 7 May, 1936, and was disposed of by Shell. Rebuilt by the Parks Air College, NC12222 went in 1938 to Paul Mantz, then to five other owners before being re-acquired by Mantz in 1955.

NR12222 (c/n 180) originally completed as a DL-2A Altair, was converted to an Orion 9C Special in June 1932. It is seen here in the later form as used by the Shell Aviation Corp. (*Lockheed*)

108

For some years this Orion was displayed outdoors at Orange County Airport, Santa Ana, where its condition deteriorated. It was purchased in 1976 by the Swiss Transport Museum at Lucerne, flown to Frankfurt in a Boeing 747F, and then taken to Zürich where the 'Fokker Team' of ex-Swissair employees rebuilt it, although it could not be restored to flying condition. Finished in overall red livery with white trim and representing Swissair's first Orion, CH-167, it was handed over to the Museum on 10 August, 1978, as the sole surviving example of the type.

Orion 9D: The thirteen Orion 9Ds appeared in four variants (9D, 9D-1, 9D-2 and 9D Special), all powered initially by the 550 hp Wasp S1D1, with 3-degree dihedral wing, and horizontal tail surfaces span increased from 15 to 16 ft (4·57 to 4·88 m). In addition, the seventh aircraft in the series (c/n 205) became the first Lockheed aircraft to be fitted with landing flaps. Those without flaps (c/ns 197 to 202) were built in 1933 for American Airways as Orion 9Ds and were followed in 1933–34 by three flap-equipped Orion 9Ds (c/ns 205 to 207) for Northwest Airways. A tenth Orion 9D (c/n 209) was acquired in 1934 by Michel Détroyat, a then well-known French racing pilot. Registered F-AKHC, this aircraft was fitted by Morane-Saulnier with a 575 hp Hispano-Suiza 9V nine-cylinder radial, and with additional fuel tanks in its stripped-down cabin in preparation for its planned entry in the 1934 Mac.Robertson Race. Tests with the French engine were completed too late for Détroyat to take part in the race and, instead, his F-AKHC was tested by the Centre d'Essais en Vol du Matériel Aérien (CEMA) at Villacoublay. It later went to Spain for use by the Republican forces.

The Orion 9D-2 NC799W *Early Bird* (c/n 208) of the Detroit News/Evening News Association with camera pod on the wing leading-edge. (*Lockheed*)

The sole Orion 9D-1 (c/n 204) which did not have landing flaps, had an executive interior, with a couch and three chairs in place of the six standard passenger seats; it was delivered in December 1933 to the Mabee Consolidated Corp as NC232Y, *Sheridan of Oklahoma*. Delivered during the early autumn of 1934 to the Evening News Association, the Orion 9D-2 (c/n 208, NC799W, *Early Bird*) was specially fitted with broadcasting equipment and a camera pod on the wing leading edge; in 1942 it was acquired by the Defense Supplies Corp and was impressed into the USAAF under the UC-85 designation (*qv*). The last Model 9D was specially built for Laura Ingalls, the noted aviatrix, as an Orion 9D Special (c/n 211, NR14222, *Auto-da-Fé*) and had its fuel capacity increased from the standard 116 US gal (439 litres) to 650 gal (2,461 litres). With it on 11 July, 1935, Miss Ingalls made the first nonstop transcontinental flight from Burbank to Newark, in 13 hr 34 min 5 sec and was also placed second in the 1936 Bendix Race. Her Aircraft went to Spain during the Civil War.

Orion 9E: In addition to c/n 192, the previously described aircraft which had originally been completed as an Orion 9 Special, Transcontinental & Western Air also acquired two other Orion 9Es (c/n 193 and 195). In spite of bearing the E suffix as part of their designation, these aircraft did not incorporate the improvements introduced on the earlier Model 9D. Powered by the 450 hp Wasp SC1, the first of these two aircraft (NC12278) was fitted with Goodrich de-icers five months after entering service with TWA; after two accidents it was repurchased by Lockheed in early 1937 but was not repaired. The other Orion 9E, NC12283, served with TWA for two years until acquired in 1935 by Wiley Post to be modified as the Orion-Explorer (*qv*).

Orion 9F: Two executive aircraft with special interiors were built. The first (c/n 196, NC12284) had no landing flaps and was powered by a 645 hp Wright Cyclone R-1820-F2 whereas the Orion 9F-1 (c/n 212, NC14246) had flaps and a 650 hp Cyclone SR-1820-F2 engine. Respectively delivered in July 1933 to George A. MacDonald and in August 1934 to Phillips Petroleum Co, both the Orion 9F and 9F-1 went to Spain in 1937.

UC-85: After being acquired in 1942 by the Defense Supplies Corporation, the Orion 9D-2 (c/n 208) was impressed into the USAAF. After less than two years as a military utility transport (42-62601), the UC-85 was restored to the civil register as NC799W in 1944. One of its three postwar owners exchanged its original Wasp S1D1 engine for a 600 hp Pratt & Whitney R-1340-49 from a surplus North American AT-6A. After crashing at Los Angeles during November 1947 the Orion 9D-2 was scrapped.

NR12283, the Orion-Explorer modified from the third Orion 9E (c/n 195). (*Lockheed*)

Orion-Explorer: After less than two years of service with TWA, the third Orion 9E (c/n 195) was purchased by Charles H. Babb, a used-aircraft dealer, who in February 1935 replaced its damaged wing with the wing of the fourth Explorer (c/n 148), increasing the span from 42 ft 9¼ in (13·04 m) to 48 ft 6 in (14·78 m). At that time the half-breed Orion-Explorer was fitted with a non-retractable undercarriage and was re-engined with a Pratt & Whitney Wasp S3H1 driving a three-blade propeller, and rated at 600 hp for take-off and 500 hp at 5,000 ft (1,525 m).

The hybrid aircraft was then purchased by Wiley Post who, together with Will Rogers, planned to use it for a westbound round-the-world flight even though its modification, and the later replacement of the fixed undercarriage with twin Edo floats, were not approved by the manufacturer. Now registered NR12283 and fitted with its floats in Seattle, the Orion-Explorer left for Alaska in August 1935. On the 15th of that month, while on his way to Barrow, Wiley Post was forced to alight at Walakpi, in Alaska, to get his bearings. Tragedy struck minutes later as the Wasp engine stopped when the aircraft was barely airborne. The nose-heavy Orion-Explorer set down abruptly and came to rest on its back in the shallow water of a tidal river, killing Wiley Post and Will Rogers.

C/n 169, an Orion 9 of Pan American's Mexican subsidiary, Aérovias Centrales S.A. (*Pan American*)

The Orion made its debut in the spring of 1931 on the route network of Fort Worth-based Bowen Air Lines but this carrier went out of business in 1934 and its surviving Orion 9 then appeared on the Mexican registry as X-ABEI (later NC 13977 with Pan American and finally XA-BAY back in Mexico). Twelve other United States airlines operated Orions: American Airways, and Varney Air Service* (six aircraft each); Northwest Airways, TWA, and Wyoming Air Service (each with three aircraft); Air Express Corporation, Continental Airways, Inland Air Lines, New York and Western Air Lines, and Pan American (two aircraft apiece); and Alaska Star Airlines, and New York, Philadelphia and Washington Airway (each with a single Orion). However, as aircraft changed hands only 25 Orions were used in airline service in the United States. The last of these aircraft was an ex-American Airways Orion 9D (c/n 201) which was operated by Alaska Airlines (previously known as Alaska Star Airlines) until shortly after the end of the Second World War.

Abroad, Swissair was the only carrier to buy, directly from Lockheed, two new aircraft. Its two Orion 9Bs were flown on passenger and fast mail services in Europe between 1932 and 1935 before being sold and ending their lives in Spain. Of the twelve Orions which appeared on the Mexican register nine were flown by airlines, beginning in 1934 when Varney Air Service suspended its US operations and registered its five surviving Orion 9s to its associate Lineas Aéreas

*Trading as Varney Speed Lanes.

111

NC12225 Orion 9 (c/n 183) of Varney Air Service. This aircraft ended its life in Spain during the civil war. (*Lockheed*)

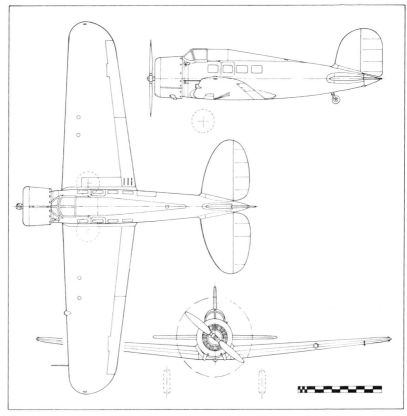

Lockheed 9 Orion (c/n 183)

Occidentales S.A. for service between Los Angeles and Mexico City. Other Mexican airlines operating the type were Aérovias Centrales S.A. (a subsidiary of Pan American which had three Orions; two of these aircraft then went to another Pan American subsidiary, Mexicana de Aviacíon) and Lineas Aéreas Mineras S.A. (one Orion 9). The only other foreign registered Orions were the Hispano-Suiza powered Orion 9D of Michel Détroyat (F-AKHC) and three other aircraft temporarily registered in France on their way to Spain.

Immediately after the civil war had started in Spain on 17 July, 1936, the government forces (Republicans) began seeking additional aircraft to fight the Nationalists led by General Francisco Franco. Benefiting from the sympathy of much of Europe — with the exception of Germany and Italy — and of Mexico, as well as from the business greed of aircraft dealers in the United States, the Republicans were soon able to acquire a large but widely assorted collection of aircraft to supplement the combat types supplied by the USSR beginning in October 1936. Among the many types they received from sundry sources were some fifteen to seventeen single-engined Lockheed aircraft (at least one Vega, one Sirius, and 13 to 15 Orions). The first Orion to appear in Spain was first seen in Madrid during November 1936, and c/ns 181, 183, 185, 186, 189, 190, 196, 202, 204, 205, 209, 211 and 212 were positively known to have been received by the Republicans, while c/n 172 (ex XB-AHQ of Lineas Aéreas Mineras) and c/n 182 (reported by some as having crashed in Rumania in 1935) are thought to have also been flown during the Spanish Civil War. In service with the Republican forces these aircraft bore a code in the TK series. Only one of these Orions survived this conflict but it was scrapped soon after being captured by the Nationalists.

With the end of the last Spanish aircraft in 1939, only four of the thirty-six Orions were still airworthy as, in addition to the thirteen to fifteen aircraft lost in Spain, fourteen had been destroyed earlier in the United States, while three or five Orions had crashed abroad. The survivors continued in use into the 1940s but by November 1947 c/n 180 had reached its present status as the last of the breed.

Orion 9
Span 42 ft 9¼ in (13·04 m); length 27 ft 8 in (8·43 m); height 9 ft 8 in (2·95 m); wing area 294·1 sq ft (27·32 sq m).

Empty weight 3,420 lb (1,551 kg); loaded weight 5,200 lb (2,359 kg); wing loading 17·7 lb/sq ft (86·3 kg/sq m); power loading 12·4 lb/hp (5·6 kg/hp).

Maximum speed 220 mph (354 km/h) at sea level; cruising speed 175 mph (282 km/h); initial rate of climb 1,450 ft/min (442 m/min); service ceiling 22,000 ft (6,705 m); normal range 750 miles (1,205 km).

Orion 9D
Dimensions as Orion 9 except length 28 ft 4 in (8·64 m).

Empty weight 3,640 lb (1,651 kg); loaded weight 5,800 lb (2,631 kg); wing loading 19·7 lb/sq ft (96·3 kg/sq m); power loading 10·5 lb/hp (4·8 kg/hp).

Maximum speed 225 mph at 5,000 ft (362 km/h at 1,525 m); cruising speed 205 mph (330 km/h); initial rate of climb 1,400 ft/min (427 m/min); service ceiling 22,000 ft (6,705 m); normal range 720 miles (1,160 km).

With a top speed of 235 mph (378 km/h), the two-seat YP-24 was faster than contemporary single-seat pursuit aircraft of the US Army Air Corps. (*Lockheed*)

Detroit-Lockheed XP-900 (YP-24)

Designed by Robert J. Woods in Detroit, the XP-900 (later YP-24) was the Detroit-Lockheed organization's only original design and, until the advent of the XP-38 later in the thirties, the only combat aircraft to bear, although hyphenated, the Lockheed name. Its career was brief but its end was due not to design problems but to the manufacturer's financial failure.

Being most impressed with the good performance of its versions of the Vega (Y1C-12 and Y1C-17) and Altair (Y1C-23), notably their top speed, the US Army Air Corps was prepared to make a drastic change in its policy and to consider acquiring a low-wing monoplane fighter with retractable undercarriage. Yet, as its budget had been curtailed as the result of the Depression, the War Department was not in a position to order prototypes. To circumvent this difficulty, Detroit-Lockheed undertook to develop privately the prototype of a two-seat fighter based on the Altair. Accordingly, a mock-up was completed in March 1931 under the supervision of Robert Woods and construction of a prototype started. Bearing the Wright Field project number XP-900, the experimental fighter combined a slim metal fuselage and metal tail surfaces built by Detroit Aircraft, and Altair wooden wings built by Lockheed in Burbank; final assembly and initial testing of the aircraft were undertaken in Detroit by the parent company. The powerplant was a 600 hp Curtiss Conqueror V-1570C (military designation V-1570-23) liquid-cooled twelve-cylinder vee engine driving a three-blade propeller. The crew of two, pilot and gunner, was housed back to back in enclosed cockpits, and the aircraft was armed with two synchronized machine-guns (one 0·30-in and one 0·50-in) in the nose and one flexible 0·30-in gun firing upward and to the rear.

At the conclusion of brief manufacturer's trials conducted in Detroit during the summer, the XP-900 was delivered to Wright Field on 29 September, 1931. At that time the aircraft was purchased by the Army Air Corps and designated YP-24 (serial 32-320). Tested as a potential replacement for the Berliner-Joyce P-16, the

YP-24 proved to be not only 40 mph (64 km/h) faster than that two-seater but also 20 mph (32 km/h) faster than the Curtiss P-6E single-seater, then the Air Corps' most important fighter. Satisfied with the potential of the Detroit-Lockheed prototype, the War Department awarded a $250,000 contract for five Y1P-24 two-seat fighters and four Y1A-9 attack aircraft. The latter were to differ from the fighter version in being powered by a V-1570-27 rated at a lower altitude and carrying heavier forward-firing armament plus bombs.

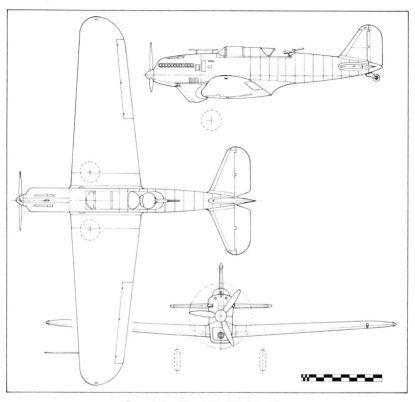

Detroit-Lockheed XP-900 (YP-24)

As the Air Corps' first low-wing monoplane fighter with retractable under-carriage and enclosed cockpits, the Y1P-24 seemed to have a promising future. However, on 19 October, 1931, the YP-24 prototype was lost when its pilot, Lieut Harrison Crocker, was ordered to bale out instead of attempting a wheels-up landing after the undercarriage control lever had broken off. The problem was a relatively minor one and could have been quickly fixed.

Unfortunately, for reasons unrelated to the YP-24 accident, the Detroit-Lockheed Corporation could no longer avoid bankruptcy and could not under-take manufacture of the Y1P-24s and Y1A-9s. The project was tentatively shelved until after Robert Woods had joined the Consolidated Aircraft Corp. The Detroit-Lockheed design was then developed into the all-metal Consolidated Y1P-25 which, in turn, gave place to the Consolidated P-30/P-30A series

(PB-2/PB-2A). Production by the latter company included one Y1P-25, one Y1A-11 and fifty-eight P-30s, P-30As and A-11s.

Span 42 ft 9½ in (13·04 m); length 28 ft 9 in (8·76 m); height 8 ft 6 in (2·59 m); wing area 292 sq ft (27·126 sq m).
Empty weight 3,010 lb (1,365 kg); loaded weight 4,360 lb (1,978 kg); wing loading 14·9 lb/sq ft (72·9 kg/sq m); power loading 7·3 lb/hp (3·3 kg/hp).
Maximum speed 235 mph (378 km/h); cruising speed 215 mph (346 km/h); initial rate of climb 1,820 ft/min (555 m/min); service ceiling 25,000 ft (7,620 m); range 556 miles (895 km).

The prototype Model 10 Electra with the original reverse-slope windshield with which it was first flown. (*Lockheed*)

Lockheed 10 Electra

Upon acquiring in June 1932 the assets of the Lockheed Aircraft Corporation, a subsidiary of the defunct Detroit Aircraft Corporation, Robert Gross and his fellow investors planned to have the reorganized firm build a ten-seat, all-metal transport designed by its president Lloyd Carlton Stearman. However, before the construction of this single-engined aircraft could proceed, the new Lockheed management team agreed with the conclusions of Robert Gross' informal market study and decided to develop a twin-engined airliner. The wisdom of this decision was confirmed within the next two years when the new Lockheed found itself competing against the slightly larger Boeing 247 and Douglas DC-1/DC-2, also twin-engined metal aircraft, and when from October 1934 single-engined transports operating in the United States were forbidden to carry passengers on scheduled services at night or over terrain unsuitable for emergency landings.

Continuing with the aircraft model numbering and naming systems of its immediate forebear, the new Lockheed Aircraft Corporation designated the twin-engined aircraft Model 10 and named it Electra after the lost Pleiad in the cluster of stars in the constellation Taurus. Its design was undertaken by Hall Hibbard assisted by Richard Von Hake and, to a lesser extent by Lloyd Stearman. The configuration evolved from the preliminary design work was for a cantilever low-wing monoplane, with a heavy truss passing through and over the cabin floor to join the wing spars. It had accommodation for a crew of two and ten passengers (five seats on each side of the central aisle, aft of the cockpit). Its two Pratt & Whitney Wasp Jr radials were to be enclosed in NACA cowlings and, to obtain a reasonable landing speed in spite of the relatively high wing loading, split flaps were to be installed on the wing trailing edge. All these features were carried on to the final design and production aircraft; but three other initial design characteristics—single vertical tail surfaces, wing-to-fuselage fillets, and forward raked windshield—were not retained, the first two having been identified as likely to cause problems by Clarence 'Kelly' Johnson, then working as an assistant to Professor Edward Stalker, the University of Michigan aerodynamicist who had been entrusted with testing of a Model 10 model in the university's wind tunnel.

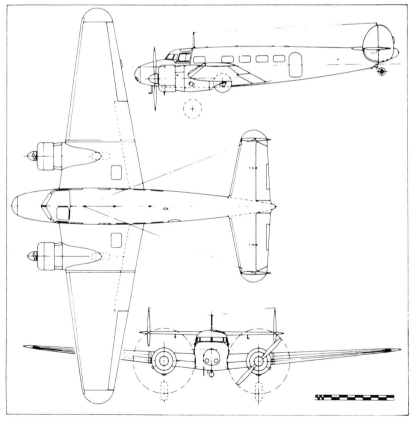

Lockheed Model 10-A Electra

117

Although Johnson's report was not fully endorsed by Stalker, he was invited to join Hall Hibbard's staff and, for his first assignment with Lockheed, was asked to redesign the tail surfaces. After wind-tunnel testing of additional end-plate fins near the end of the tailplane, Johnson adopted a twin fin and rudder design—for long thereafter a Lockheed 'trademark'—and this was incorporated in the prototype during its construction. This aircraft (c/n 1001, X233Y), however, initially retained the wing fillets and forward-raked windshield, and was completed in this form during February 1934. On the 23rd of that month the Electra prototype was taken by Marshall Headle on its maiden flight from the company's airstrip at Burbank. It was powered by a pair of Wasp Jr SB engines rated at 450 hp for take off, 450 hp at 3,500 ft (1,065 m) and 400 hp at 5,000 ft (1,525 m), and driving two-blade variable-pitch propellers.

Initial trials confirmed Kelly Johnson's second recommendation and the wing fillets were soon removed. Another change introduced during that period was the replacement of the original windshield with a shallow unit blending with the nose of the aircraft, but it was not satisfactory and had to be replaced with more conventional V-panes; this final configuration was introduced on the line during the construction of the fifth Electra and was retrofitted on at least two aircraft by Northwest Airlines' maintenance personnel. With these improvements, performance and handling characteristics gave complete satisfaction and the Electra completed its preliminary C A A airworthiness trials at Mines Field, Los Angeles, in the spring of 1934. Unfortunately, when returning to the company's airstrip in Burbank, the aircraft experienced an undercarriage malfunction. After dumping most of its fuel and the lead ballast used in the C A A's full-weight tests, the Electra was taken by Marshall Headle to the Union Air Terminal where a successful one-wheel landing was made. Damage was slight and, after repair and the offending undercarriage shaft replaced, the aircraft was awarded its Approved Type Certificate on 11 August, 1934.

This prototype was followed by 148 production Electras, delivered between 4 August, 1934, and 18 July, 1941, in four commercial and five military versions.

Model 10-A: More than two-thirds of the Electras were Wasp Jr SB powered Model 10-As with standard accommodation for ten passengers. The 101 aircraft of this type were delivered to four US carriers, ten overseas airlines, American and foreign private customers, and to the Venezuelan Government, with the last Model 10-A being delivered to LAN-Chile. They were normally fitted with

Electra 10-A CF-AZY (c/n 1063) of Canadian Airways; from October 1939 until May 1946 this aircraft, then bearing the military serial 1529, served with the RCAF. (*Gordon S. Williams*)

NC14259 (c/n 1006), a Model 10-C fitted with cold-weather cowling for service with the Alaska Division of Pan American Airways. (*Lockheed*)

variable-pitch two-blade propellers, but later some aircraft received constant-speed units. Goodrich de-icer boots were also available as options.

Model 10-B: The eighteen Model 10-Bs were, together with the generally similar XR3O-1 for the US Coast Guard, the only Electras not to be powered by Pratt & Whitney engines as they were certificated with 440 hp Wright R-975-E3 Whirlwinds. Beginning in September 1935, when c/n 1036 was delivered to Eastern Air Lines, the Model 10-Bs went to three US airlines, one foreign carrier and one private customer (Dr J. R. Brinkley's NC16054, c/n 1066). The last Model 10-B delivery was made to Ansett Airways in July 1937.

Model 10-C: Pan American Airways expressed an early interest in the Electra but requested that Lockheed modify it to use the 450 hp Wasp SC1 as the airline had a surplus of these engines. Upon receiving Lockheed's agreement to redesign and obtain certification of the Model 10-C with its specified engines, Pan American became the second customer for the Electra. Eventually all eight Model 10-Cs produced were acquired by this carrier for its Alaska Division, and its subsidiaries, Aérovias Centrales and Cubana. The first (c/n 1004, X14257/NC 14257) was the fourth Electra to be built and was delivered in September 1934; the last Model 10-C delivery was made to Aérovias Centrales eight months later.

Model 10-D: Projected military development; none built.

The Electra 10-C NC14259 (c/n 1006) of Pacific Alaska Airways, seen with non-retractable main and tail skis. (*Pan American Airways*)

119

Model 10-E: Powered by a pair of 600 hp Wasp S3H1s, the fifteen Model 10-Es were the most powerful Electras and were developed for Aérovias Centrales after Pan American had exhausted its supply of Wasp SC1s. This version also found a ready market with private owners seeking high-performance aircraft. By far the most famous of these aircraft was c/n 1055, NR16020, in which Amelia Earhart disappeared near Howland Island on 2 July, 1937.

XR2O-1: Ordered in 1935 and delivered in February 1936, this aircraft (c/n 1052, BuNo 0267) was the first military version of the Electra. Powered by two 450 hp Pratt & Whitney R-985-48s, it was based at NAS Anacostia for use as a staff transport by the Secretary of the Navy.

The XR2O-1 (BuNo 0267, c/n 1052) before delivery to the US Navy. (*Lockheed*)

XR3O-1: Initially intended to be identical to the XR2O-1, this aircraft (c/n 1053, USCG serial 383, later V-151) was delivered in March 1936 with a pair of 440 hp Wright R-975-E3s and with a convertible interior arrangement providing for rapid change from command transport to ambulance. After the Second World War, it was sold to a private owner and was modified to the Wasp S3H1 powered Model 10-E standard. In this configuration it became one of the last Electras to be used as an airliner, but this 31-year old veteran was finally ditched on a beach in Massachusetts Bay on 27 August, 1967, while operated by Provincetown-Boston Airline.

XC-35: The unique aircraft in the Electra series (c/n 3501 — note that Lockheed assigned to this aircraft a special construction number rather than one falling within the 1001 to 1148 range as given to other Electras— military serial 36-353) was ordered in June 1936 by the War Department as a research vehicle for pressurized-cabin and high-altitude operations. Under the leadership of project engineer Ferris Smith, Lockheed designed a new fuselage of circular cross-section with heavy doors and internal bracing but retained the standard wing and tail surfaces of the Electra. Sealing of the pressure cabin was first planned to be achieved by using strips of cloth soaked in marine glue and placed between each riveted fuselage section. This process, however, failed under test and the XC-35 was completed with the new neoprene sealing tape especially developed by E. I. Du Pont de Nemours. To provide cabin pressurization and the necessary altitude performance, the XC-35 was powered by two 550 hp turbosupercharged Pratt & Whitney XR-1340-43 radials. Accommodation was provided for a crew of six but, due to the 10 lb/sq in (0·7 kg/sq cm) differential between inside and outside pressure, the large cabin windows of the standard Electra were dispensed with.

The XC-35 'sub-stratosphere' research aircraft of the US Army Air Corps photographed on 2 August, 1937. (*USAF*)

Ground testing of the XC-35, nicknamed *The Boiler* by project personnel, provided some excitement when faulty gaskets and fittings around the doors leaked noisily when pressure was first applied. After replacement of the offending items, these tests were satisfactorily concluded. Flight testing began at Burbank on 7 May, 1937, and the aircraft was delivered to Wright Field in August of that year. With military pilots at the controls, notably Lieut Ben Kelsey, an engineering graduate from the Massachusetts Institute of Technology, the XC-35 provided the Air Corps and the aircraft industry with useful experience in cabin pressurization and turbosuperchargers. Moreover, it made some spectacular flights such as that between Chicago and Washington when, helped by tailwinds, it averaged 350 mph (563 km/h) at 20,000 ft (6,095 m). For sponsoring the development of the XC-35 and doing most of its testing, the Army Air Corps was awarded the Collier Trophy in 1937 as it was judged that the XC-35 programme had made the most valuable contribution to aircraft development during that year. At the conclusion of its trials, the XC-35 was set aside for preservation and it is now part of the collection of the National Air and Space Museum in Washington.

Y1C-36: In addition to the XC-35, the Army Air Corps ordered three Lockheed 10-As (c/ns 1071, 1073 and 1074, serials 37-65/37-67) powered by 450 hp Pratt & Whitney R-985-13s. The first Y1C-36 was damaged beyond repair in February 1938, fifteen months after its delivery. The other two, by then redesignated C-36-LOs, were transferred to the Fôrça Aérea Brasileira during the war. Both crashed during the early 1950s after going onto the Brazilian civil register.

C-36A (UC-36A-LO): Early after America's entry into the war, fifteen commercial Model 10-As were impressed into the USAAF as C-36As with the military serials 42-32535, 42-38341/42-38344, 42-56638/42-56641, 42-57213/42-57216, 42-57505 and 42-68362. Powered by 450 hp Pratt & Whitney R-985-13s, these aircraft were redesignated UC-36A-LOs in the utility transport category in January 1943. Surviving aircraft were returned to the civil register beginning in 1944.

C-36B (UC-36B-LO): In a similar fashion, five Model 10-Es with 600 hp Pratt & Whitney R-1340-49s were impressed into the USAAF and assigned the serials 42-32533, 42-32534, 42-38289, 42-38296 and 42-38304.

121

C-36C (UC-36C-LO): Completing the series of impressed Electras were seven Model 10-Bs with 440 hp Wright R-975-13s. Upon impressment they were serialled 42-38345 and 42-57217/42-57222.

Y1C-37 (C-37 and UC-37-LO): The only aircraft of this model (c/n 1104, serial 37-376) was ordered by the War Department shortly after the three Y1C-36s. Like these latter aircraft, it was powered by two R-985-13s but instead of going to the Army Air Corps it was delivered to the National Guard Bureau. In the Guard, which used it as a staff transport assigned to its Chief, the Y1C-37 was the first multi-engined aircraft. After the war this aircraft was sold and in January 1947 it crashed in Honduras.

Model 10-B (c/n 1040, NC14962) of Chicago & Southern Airlines. (*Delta Air Lines*)

Jumping the gun, Northwest Airlines was the first to put the Electra into service and one of its aircraft, the second Electra, crashed on 7 August, 1934—four days before the CAA award of an Approved Type Certificate! In spite of this unfortunate beginning the Model 10 played a significant part in assuring the commercial success of Northwest in the immediate post-Air Mail Emergency period. Like the larger Boeing 247 and Douglas DC-2, the Electra offered a degree of comfort not previously experienced in American aircraft, and its high cruising speed—190 mph (306 km/h), the same as that of the DC-2 even though the latter had nearly sixty per cent more power—endeared it to passengers. Its seat-mile cost, however, was slightly higher and, combined with its limited capacity, somewhat reduced the Electra's attractiveness to major carriers at a time when fierce competition and rapid rate of growth required the use of larger and more economic airliners. None-the-less, the type was operated in the United States during the second half of the thirties by Chicago & Southern, Continental, Delta, Eastern, Hanford, National Airways (later Boston-Maine Airways and then Northeast), Northwest and Pan American (Alaska Division).

During the late thirties and early forties several of these airlines replaced or supplemented their Electras with larger-capacity aircraft and by 1942 only sixteen Model 10s—out of a total US domestic trunk fleet of 322 aircraft—were operated by Delta, Mid-Continent (previously Hanford), National, Northeast (ex-Boston-Maine) and Northwest. Typical of these carriers was Northwest Airlines which in 1942 retained only four Electras from its original fleet of thirteen Model 10-As. After the war, Electras were operated by a number of smaller scheduled and non-scheduled carriers, with the last commercial Electra service being flown by Provincetown-Boston Airlines in the early seventies.

Photographed at Rio Vista, California, on 30 November, 1980, this Model 10-A, N38BB (c/n 1026), of Naples Airlines & Provincetown-Boston Airline had been originally delivered to Braniff Airways as NC14937 on 10 June, 1935. It is seen here with additional rear windows and downward-opening airstairs. (*H. L. James*)

In the United States, as well as to a lesser extent abroad, Electras were also acquired as executive transports and special-purpose aircraft by private owners. The most famous (c/ns 1055 and 1065, both Model 10-Es with the more powerful Wasp S3H1 engines) made the headlines during the spring and summer of 1937. Ordered by Purdue Research Foundation for Amelia Earhart and registered NR16020, the first was delivered in July 1936. Specially fitted with fuselage tanks bringing total capacity up from 200 to 1,200 US gal (757 to 4,542 litres) and with additional navigation equipment (notably a D/F loop atop its fuselage), this Model 10-E Special had most of its cabin windows blanked out. In the 1936 Bendix Trophy Race, from Los Angeles to New York, it was flown into fifth and last place by Amelia Earhart and Helen Richey. However, Amelia Earhart had more ambitious plans for her Electra and, with Fred Noonan as her navigator, she left Oakland on 17 March, 1937, for a westbound round-the-world flight. The flight was terminated on the first landing when the aircraft was ground-looped at Honolulu. Following repairs and minor modifications to NR16020, Earhart and Noonan decided to fly eastward for their second attempt. Six weeks after leaving Oakland on 20 May, Amelia Earhart and her navigator had reached the Central Pacific when, on 2 July, 1937, they disappeared at sea in the vicinity of Howland Island. For years it was rumoured that the flyers had been carrying out covert activities over Japanese-controlled territories and had been captured; but there now appears to be little or no foundation to this story.

Miss Earhart's Model 10-E Electra, NR16020 (c/n 1055), at Oakland, California, on 20 March, 1937. (*USAF*)

Delivered in August 1936 to its wealthy original owner, Harold S. Vanderbilt, c/n 1065/NC16059 was acquired a few months later by financier Ben Smith to be used by H. T. 'Dick' Merrill and J. S. Lambie for a special round-trip crossing of the Atlantic. After extra tanks had been installed, the aircraft was re-registered NR16059, to denote its restricted certificate, and named *Daily Express*. In May 1937, Merrill and Lambie flew from New York to London carrying newsreels of the *Hindenburg* crash and returned to New York with the first photographs of the Coronation of HM King George VI. For piloting the *Daily Express* on what was billed as the first commercial round-trip flight over the Atlantic, H. T. Merrill was awarded the 1937 Harmon Trophy. Whether the carriage of newsreels and photographs constituted a commercial undertaking may be debatable but, none-the-less, this feat brought to the Lockheed twin-engined transport its second major trophy. Three months after its transatlantic flight, this Model 10-E was purchased by Amtorg, the Soviet trading company, to be flown by Sir Hubert Wilkins and Herbert Hollick-Kenyon in the Arctic search for the missing Russian flyers, Levanevski and Levchenko. After the unsuccessful conclusion, this Electra, which had received the Soviet registration SSSR-N-214, was shipped to the USSR.

When N-214 reached the Soviet Union the Model 10 had already achieved considerable foreign success as the type had been ordered directly from Lockheed by airlines in Australasia, Europe, Japan, and Latin America, and by the governments of Argentina and Venezuela. Excluding the Cuban and Mexican registered aircraft, which had been ordered and paid for by Pan American Airways for two of its foreign subsidiaries, the first genuine export order was that placed by a Japanese trading firm, Okura & Co, for one Model 10-A (c/n 1017 delivered in March 1935). Other single examples of the Electra, acquired second-hand, found their way to Spain. One, believed to be c/n 1033, was among the prizes of war obtained when the Nationalists captured the ss *Mar Cantábrico* on 5 January, 1937, and served subsequently with Grupo 42; the other one, assumed to be c/n 1035, did reach the Republicans. The first major overseas customer was LOT Polish Airlines which received the first (c/n 1045, SP-AYA) of its ten Electra 10-As in November 1935. Other major European Electra operators in the prewar period were British Airways (six Model 10-As), LARES of Rumania (seven

Delivered to Union Airways of New Zealand Ltd in April 1937 ZK-AFC crashed on take-off at Auckland on 10 May, 1938. (*Lockheed*)

124

Originally delivered with the registration CC-228, this Model 10-A Electra (c/n 1147) of LAN is seen over Santiago, Chile, after being re-registered CC-LIN. (*Lockheed*)

10-As) and Aeroput of Yugoslavia (eight 10-As). These four carriers operated their Electras on scheduled European services — with British Airways also using G-AEPR, c/n 1083, to fly Prime Minister Neville Chamberlain to Germany on his quest for 'peace in our time' when meeting the German Chancellor, Adolf Hitler in September 1938. One year later, when the Prime Minister's efforts had come to naught and war broke out, twenty-six of these thirty-one European registered aircraft were still in flying condition. Two other Electras were then in Europe, an ex-Northwest Airlines' 10-A acquired by British Airways as a replacement for G-AEPP which had been lost on 13 December, 1937, and c/n 1114 (OK-CTA), an executive transport for the Bata Shoe Company (this Czechoslovak firm had also acquired two Model 10-As for its US subsidiary).

Three British Commonwealth nations also placed new Electras on their civil registers. In Australia, the Model 10-A was purchased by Guinea Airways (three aircraft beginning with VH-UXH (c/n 1060) delivered in June 1936) and Mac.Robertson-Miller (two aircraft), while Ansett acquired three Model 10-Bs. In New Zealand, Union Airways obtained five Model 10-As beginning in April 1937. Finally, in northern climes, Canadian Airways received the first of its two Model 10-As in August 1936. Later these two aircraft were acquired by Trans-Canada Air Lines. In service with the new Canadian flag carrier they were joined by three similar machines ordered by Fairchild Aircraft Ltd on behalf of TCA.

Latin American customers for the Electra included the Argentine Army and Navy, which respectively received one Model 10-E in October 1937 and May 1938, the Ministerio de Guerra y Marina in Venezuela (two Model 10-As), and three airlines: LAV in Venezuela (eight Model 10-As), Servicio Aéreo Colombiano (two 10-Es), and LAN-Chile (six 10-As). The aircraft for LAN, together with the two Venezuelan military aircraft, constituted a batch of eight aircraft produced after an eleven-month hiatus (February 1940 through January 1941) in Electra assembly. The last of these aircraft (c/n 1148) was delivered to LAN on 18 July, 1941, and ended the production history of the Electra. Fourteen years later

125

the name was resurrected by Lockheed for another transport, the turbine-powered Model 188.

Whereas the US military Electras were used almost exclusively within CONUS (Continental United States), those of the Royal Air Force saw widespread service. The RAF acquired its first Electra on the day of Britain's declaration of war on Germany, and this aircraft, still carrying its civil registration G-AEPR, was operated by No.24 Squadron for over a month before being returned to British Airways. In April 1940, three other British Airways Electras were impressed as W9104/W9106 for service in the United Kingdom with the same squadron; the last one was struck off charge in July 1942. At least four, and possibly five Electras (three ex-Aeroput Model 10-As, the ex-Czechoslovak registered 10-A of the Bata Shoe Company and one ex-Chicago & Southern Model 10-B) are believed to have gone to the RAF in 1941. However, only four military serials (AX699/AX701 and AX766) have been recorded, while the previous identity of AX700 is in doubt as it has been reported to be either c/n

This RAF Electra, AX700, was assigned in 1945 as the personal transport of the Governor of Bengal. (*Peter M. Bowers*)

1123, YU-SBA, or c/n 1114, OK-CTA. These aircraft served in the Middle East and Africa, with AX700 being finally transferred to India where it was crash-landed near Calcutta on 11 July, 1946. The two British Airways Electras which had not been impressed in 1940 were operated by BOAC for two years on East African and Middle Eastern routes. This airline had also been scheduled to receive five ex-LOT Model 10-As which had been flown out of Poland in 1939; they were assigned the registrations G-AGAF/G-AGAJ, but were impounded in Rumania on their way to Egypt.

Another wartime operator was the Royal Canadian Air Force which, from October 1939 until May 1946, had twelve Model 10-As (Canadian military serials 1526/1529, 7631/7633, 7650/7652, 7656 and 7841) and three 10-Bs (serials 7634, 7648 and 7649) on strength and used them for communications and at Flying Instructor Schools. During the war the Fôrça Aérea Brasileira also obtained four 10-As (FAB serials 1002, 1219, 1439 and 1796) and one 10-B (FAB 1325), while the Fuerza Aérea Hondureña later had one Model 10-A (FAH 104).

As an airliner the Electra had already been on its way out when the United States had joined the fighting powers. Thus, it was not surprising to see the type being restricted after the war to use by a few feeder lines, small and mostly unscheduled overseas carriers, and to private operators. None-the-less, Model 10s then appeared on a number of new Latin American registers including those of Brazil, Costa Rica, Ecuador, Honduras, Nicaragua and Panama. Finally, the Electra slowly faded out and was virtually extinct by the seventies. Luckily, some Model 10s, together with their more historically significant XC-35 derivative, have been preserved, thus keeping alive the first twin-engined type to bear the Lockheed name.

Model 10-A

Span 55 ft (16·76 m); length 38 ft 7 in (11·76 m); height 10 ft 1 in (3·07 m); wing area 458·5 sq ft (42·59 sq m).
Empty weight 6,454 lb (2,927 kg); loaded weight 10,300 lb (4,672 kg); wing loading 22·5 lb/sq ft (109·7 kg/sq m); power loading 11·4 lb/hp (5·2 kg/hp).
Maximum speed 202 mph at 5,000 ft (325 km/h at 1,525 m); cruising speed 190 mph (306 km/h); rate of climb 1,140 ft/min (347 m/min); service ceiling 19,400 ft (5,915 m); normal range 810 miles (1,305 km).

XC-35

Dimensions as for Electra 10-A.
Empty weight 7,940 lb (3,602 kg); loaded weight 10,500 lb (4,763 kg); wing loading 22·9 lb/sq ft (111·8 kg/sq m); power loading 9·5 lb/hp (4·3 kg/hp).
Maximum speed 236 mph at 20,000 ft (380 km/h at 6,095 m); cruising speed 214 mph (344 km/h); rate of climb 1,125 ft/min (343 m/min); service ceiling 31,500 ft (9,600 m).

Lockheed 12 Electra Junior

For use as a private transport or as a feeder-liner, the Model 10 was initially found to be too large. Thus, by the end of 1935 Carl Squier, vice-president sales, identified the potential for an aircraft substituting the Model 10-A's size and capacity for more spritely performance on the power of the same pair of 450 hp Pratt & Whitney Wasp Jr SB engines. The need for such a feeder-liner was also recognized by the Bureau of Air Commerce which invited manufacturers to submit small twin-engined aircraft for its evaluation. Hall Hibbard, Kelly Johnson and their staff set to work diligently, as the Bureau of Air Commerce had specified that it would only consider aircraft flown before the end of Fiscal Year 1936 (30 June). Designated Model 12 and named Electra Junior, the Lockheed design was a scaled-down Electra providing accommodation for a crew of two and up to six passengers in a fuselage 4 ft 3 in (1·3 m) shorter than that of the Model 10. As an executive transport, the aircraft could be fitted with more luxurious accommodation including club chairs or a sofa, table, typewriter, etc; as in the feeder-liner, this version included a lavatory. All-up weight was reduced by over eighteen per cent from 10,300 lb (4,672 kg) for the Model 10-A to 8,400 lb (3,810 kg) for the Model 12.

By working overtime the Lockheed team completed the prototype (c/n 1201, NX16052) before the end of June 1936 and, symbolically, Marshall Headle made the first take-off at precisely 12.12 hr on the 27th of that month. Performance, with a top speed of 225 mph at 5,000 ft (362 km/h at 1,525 m) and a cruising speed of 213 mph (343 km/h), and handling characteristics, met the manufacturer's most sanguine expectations, and the Bureau declared the Electra Jr the winner. It received its Approved Type Certificate on 14 October, 1936, by which time c/ns 1202 and 1203 had already been delivered, to the Tela Railroad Company and the Herschbach Drilling Company respectively.

In spite of having won the competition, the Electra Jr had limited success as a feeder-liner, with only six of the ninety Wasp Jr SB powered Model 12-As (including the prototype) being acquired by US airlines while c/n 1236 went to Associated Airlines Pty in Australia. One of the six US-registered feeder-liners, which as NC18137 (c/n 1229) had been delivered in August 1937 to Varney Air Transport, was later used briefly by TWA as a high-altitude and weather research aircraft until replaced by a Lockheed 18. Two other Model 12-As were acquired by British Airways but, as detailed later, this airline purchase was a front for the activities of Sidney Cotton.

Model 12-A Electra Junior (c/n 1209, NC17309) of Santa Maria Airlines Inc. (*Lockheed*)

Initial operators of the other 81 Model 12-As included private operators in the United States (39 Electra Jrs) and abroad (six aircraft), US government agencies (25 aircraft) and foreign governments (eleven Model 12-As). The most unusual privately-owned Electra Jr was delivered to the Republic Oil Company in June 1937. Specially equipped to be entered by Jimmy Mattern in a planned, but later cancelled, New York–Paris Derby, c/n 1225 was registered NR869E and named *The Texan*. In preparation for a projected trans-Polar flight Mattern used the aircraft to conduct inflight-refuelling trials with a Ford Tri-motor as tanker. Noteworthy among foreign private operators were the Maharajahs of Jodhpur (c/n 1237, VT-AJN), of Jammu and Kashmir (c/n 1238, VT-AJS, ex-G-AFCO) and of Jaipur (c/n 1274, VT-AMB, ex-G-AFXP), with the first of these aircraft being flown on delivery from Amsterdam to India at an average speed of 210 mph (338 km/h) despite four refuelling stops. Two closely-related developments of these first Electra Juniors were the Models 12-B and 12-25. Two of the former, the only Model 12-B Electra Jrs (powered by 440 hp Wright R-975-E3d), were obtained by the Argentine Army in September 1937 (c/n 1228) and May 1938 (c/n 1249), while two Model 12-25s with 450 hp Wasp Jr SB3s were delivered in September 1941 to US private operators.

The 'hot-wing' Electra Junior (c/n 1268, NACA 97); note central fin and heated air exhaust slots in the upper surface of the wing. (*Lockheed*)

Of interest among the aircraft operated by United States non-military government agencies were c/n 1272 which, before being delivered to the Tennessee Valley Authority, was used by Lockheed as an experimental aircraft with a non-retractable undercarriage, and c/n 1268. The latter was ordered in April 1940 by the National Advisory Committee for Aeronautics as a flying testbed for a wing de-icing system using exhaust heat. This system, previously tested in Germany by Junkers, was developed by project engineer Jay Cowling and was the first to be fitted to a US aircraft. As first designed, engine exhaust was deflected into the wing leading-edge and was vented out at the wingtips and at two slots just ahead of each aileron. Another modification to this otherwise standard Model 12-A consisted of the addition of a central fin to increase directional stability while the aircraft was flown in search of heavy icing conditions. Flight tests were begun on 7 May, 1941, and the 'hotwing' aircraft (NACA 97) was delivered thirteen days later. Initial results, however, were unsatisfactory as heat was excessive close to the engines and insufficient near the wingtips. Moreover, the untreated exhaust gases caused corrosion problems and cracking of the wing surfaces. These difficulties were solved after the aircraft was returned to Lockheed for modifica-

An Electra Junior of the Brazilian Aviação Militar at Campo dos Afonsos, Rio de Janeiro. (*Lockheed*)

tions through the use of a heat exchanger, to remove the corrosive elements from the exhaust gases, and of a blower, to push the hot air towards the wingtips. These proved successful and the 'hotwing' Model 12-A provided the basic data for similar wing de-icing devices used on later US multi-engined aircraft. The aircraft was later re-converted to the standard 12-A configuration.

On the same day, 23 September, 1937, as the first Model 12-B was delivered to the Argentine Army, two Model 12-As were handed over in Burbank to representatives of the Brazilian Ministry of Aeronautics. The same agency received two more Model 12-As in February 1940 and a final batch of four in April 1941. In Brazilian service these aircraft, which were designated C-40s and were based at Campo dos Afonsos on the outskirts of Rio de Janeiro, initially bore the serials D.Aé.01 to D.Aé.08. However, in the spring of 1945 they were respectively reserialled 2656 to 2663 in the new system then being implemented by the Fôrça Aérea Brasileira. The only other Latin American military operator of the Electra Jr was Cuba which during the war received an ex-USAAF C-40A, 38-547, which became IM-18 in that country.

The C-40A mentioned was part of a batch of ten (serials 38-539/38-548) Pratt & Whitney R-985-17 powered aircraft which was delivered to the Army Air Corps in February and March 1939 to follow three generally similar C-40s (38-536/38-538). The first C-40, which had been built as a Lockheed-owned Model 12-A demonstrator (c/n 1247, NC18965) was evaluated at Wright Field during the summer of 1938 (two years after the Model 12 prototype had been tested briefly by the Army Air Corps) and was acquired by the War Department on 30 September of the same year. The Army Air Corps also took delivery nine months later of a single C-40B (c/n 1266, 38-582) experimental aircraft with a non-retractable tricycle undercarriage. After completion of its special tests, the C-40B was brought to C-40A standard in November 1940. By the time the United States entered the war, the Army Air Forces still had all of its C-40s and these were supplemented as utility transports by eleven Model 12-As impressed as UC-40Ds (42-22249, 42-38346/42-38352, 42-38380, 42-57504 and 42-66386). In US military service these Electra Jrs had been preceded by seven aircraft ordered by the Navy Department. The first of these, the single JO-1 (c/n 1227, BuNo 1053), had been delivered on 9 August, 1937, for use by the US Naval Attaché in Brazil. It was followed by five Pratt & Whitney R-985-48 powered JO-2s (BuNos 1048/1051 and

Model 12-A NX18964 (c/n 1272) which was experimentally tested with a non-retractable undercarriage before being delivered to the Tennessee Valley Authority with a conventional retractable undercarriage. (*Lockheed*)

2541) used as command and staff transports by the Navy and Marine Corps, and by one XJO-3 (BuNo 1267). The latter, which was the first Electra Jr to have a non-retractable tricyle undercarriage, was briefly tested in August 1939 aboard the uss *Lexington* to evaluate the compatibility of this type of undercarriage with carrier operations. A wartime impressment (c/n 1287, ex-NC33615, BuNo 02947) was designated R3O-2, even though this designation was an anomaly as the XR3O-1 had been a version of the Model 10-B Electra, not of the Model 12-A Electra Jr.

The first production Model 212 before delivery to the Air Division of the Royal Netherlands Indies Army (ML/KNIL). One Dutch and four Australian airmen made a daring escape to Ceylon in this aircraft on 8 March, 1942. (*Lockheed*)

The largest single operator of the type was the Netherlands East Indies Government, with its own orders and that for four aircraft taken over from KNILM before delivery accounting for no fewer than 36 out of the total of 130 Electra Jrs built by Lockheed. The initial order from the Batavia Government had been placed on behalf of the ML/KNIL (Air Division of the Royal Netherlands Indies Army) for a bomber crew training version. Designated Model 212, this aircraft was first proposed by Lockheed in July 1938 and was fitted with a dorsal turret having a 0·303-in machine-gun, a fixed forward-firing weapon of the same calibre, and under-fuselage racks for up to eight 100-lb (45-kg) bombs. To serve as a crew trainer prototype, during the winter of 1938–39 the company modified the ex-Western Air Express Model 12-A (c/n 1243, NC18955). Re-registered NX18955 and temporarily given the new c/n 212-13, the experimental machine was subsequently brought back to Model 12-A standard before being delivered to the RCAF in June 1940. This aircraft was followed by sixteen aircraft for the ML/KNIL (c/ns 212-01/212-12 and 212-14/212-17, Netherlands Indies military serials L201/L216) which were each powered by two 450 hp Pratt & Whitney R-985AN-4s. The Netherlands Indies order for Model 212s, which was fulfilled between February 1939 and June 1940, was soon after supplemented by a military contract for sixteen Model 12-26 transports powered by the same engines and by a KNILM contract for four identical machines; all twenty Model 12-26s (c/ns 1295/1314) eventually were given Netherlands Indies military serials (L2-27/L2-46).

All the Model 212s and four of the military Model 12-26s had reached Java when the East Indies came under Japanese attack. During the next three months the Model 212s were used for maritime patrols, a role in which they were closely

131

Model 12-A CF-CCT, c/n 1219, which was delivered to the Canadian Department of Transport on 25 April, 1937. This aircraft, which is seen here at Vancouver in July 1937, is now part of the National Aeronautical Collection, Ottawa, Canada. (*Gordon S. Williams*)

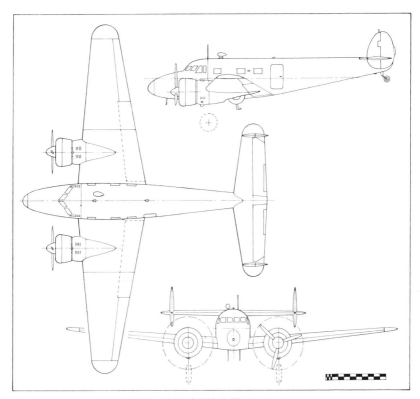

Lockheed Model 12-A Electra Junior

comparable to the Avro Ansons operated in the same theatre by the RAAF, but only the first of these aircraft (L201) survived. Although damaged, this aircraft was used on 8 March, 1942, by a Dutch cadet-pilot and four Australian sergeant pilots for a daring escape to Ceylon. With its internal tankage supplemented by two petrol drums hoisted into its fuselage, L201 was successfully navigated some 2,000 miles (3,200 km) by the five gallant men using a simple map from an ordinary atlas. Three of the Model 12-26s also escaped from Java before the Japanese occupation, while a fourth survived into the seventies with the Indonesian Air Force. Other Netherlands-ordered Model 12-26s, which had not yet reached the East Indies at the time of the Japanese onslaught, were either diverted to Ceylon and Australia or retained for training and communications in the United States. While four of these machines were briefly operated in the West Indies by KLM, the Dutch aircraft were later shipped to Australia for service with No.18 Squadron NEIAF. Finally, five Model 12-26s were operated in the postwar period by the KLu in the Netherlands; the last three were sold in 1952.

Although generally, and with good reason, considered a commercial design, the Electra Jr was remarkable in that nearly half the number of aircraft of this type were originally delivered to military customers in four countries. Fittingly, the adaptability of the Model 12 to military applications was never better demonstrated than with the civil-registered aircraft operated by Sidney Cotton on covert activities for the United Kingdom and France. The first aircraft (c/n 1267, G-AFKR) used by the Australian-born pilot and specialist aerial photographer was procured in January 1939 as an apparent order from British Airways. In fact, Cotton was acting on behalf of the French Deuxième Bureau, and with the agreement of British Intelligence, to fly a high-speed civil aircraft from which to photograph military establishments in Germany and Italy. Equipped with either a single large camera of French design or with three British F-24 cameras in the fuselage, this aircraft was flown over Germany and Italian aerodromes in Tripolitania between February and April 1940 before being handed over to France as F-ARQA. Another British Airways ordered Model 12-A (c/n 1270, G-AFPF) was apparently similarly modified and became F-ARPP, while Cotton resumed his operations with a third Electra Jr (c/n 1203, ex NC16077, registered G-AFTL in the United Kindom). Working by then directly for British Intelligence and the RAF, Sidney Cotton modified his new aircraft by fitting two 70-Imp gal (318-litre) fuselage tanks, bulged cockpit windows to provide downward view, and cameras (initially three fuselage-mounted F-24s, with the subsequent addition of two Leica cameras in the wing leading-edge and two hand-held Leicas). From May until August 1939 G-AFTL was flown repeatedly over Germany and Italian Somaliland, providing up-to-date photographic data on the eve of the war. At that time Sidney Cotton organized the Photographic Development Unit at Heston and G-AFTL was taken on strength. Damaged in a German bombing raid on 19 September, 1940, this Electra Jr was later repaired and in December 1942 was sold to British West Indian Airways as VP-TAI.

Whereas G-AFTL was not given a military serial, at least nineteen other Electra Jrs did receive British serials. In the United Kingdom these aircraft included three ex-British-registered Model 12-As (c/ns 1206, 1212 and 1265 which became R8987, X9316 and HM573), five ex-UC-40Ds (LA619/LA623) and four other unidentified machines (LV700 and LV760/LV762). In Britain, one Dutch Model 12-26 (c/n 1295) for the use of Prince Bernhard was assigned serial NF753. In the Southeast Asia theatre the RAF took over the three ex-Indian-registered Electra Jrs which became V4732, AX803 and HX798, as well as two ex-Dutch

Photographed in 1980, this Electra Junior did not look out of place next to 40-year younger aircraft. Note downturned wingtips on this aircraft (c/n 1214) used by Frontier Aviation for cargo charters. (*Howard Levy*)

Model 12-26s and one Model 212 (British serials unknown). With the RCAF, ten Model 12-As received Canadian military serials (1531, 7640/7641, 7645/7647, 7653/7654 and 7837/7838) while the modified Model 212 prototype became 7642; these aircraft were on strength from June 1940 until May 1945.

With the delivery of the last Netherlands Model 12-26 in May 1942, production of the Electra Jr was ended as by then Lockheed had more pressing business. Thus, the type was overshadowed by the generally similar Beech 18 which, including its numerous military utility transport and training versions, remained in production for twenty years (estimated total deliveries more than 7,066 aircraft). In spite of its limited production, the Model 12 remained popular as a private transport long after it had come off the Burbank assembly line, and nearly a quarter of the 130 aircraft built between 1936 and 1942 were still flying a third of a century later.

Related Temporary Design Designations: L-110 and L-126

The following specifications and performance apply to the standard Model 12-A with the Pratt & Whitney Junior SB, rated at 450 hp for take-off and 400 hp at sea level, with variable pitch two-blade propellers:

Span 49 ft 6 in (15·09 m); length 36 ft 4 in (11·07 m); height 9 ft 9 in (2·97 m); wing area 352 sq ft (32·7 sq m).
Empty weight 5,765 lb (2,615 kg); normal loaded weight 8,400 lb (3,810 kg); maximum weight 8,650 lb (3,924 kg); wing loading 23·9 lb/sq ft (116·5 kg/sq m); power loading 9·3 lb/hp (4·2 kg/hp).
Maximum speed 225 mph at 5,000 ft (362 km/h at 1,525 m); cruising speed 213 mph (343 km/h); initial rate of climb 1,400 ft/min (427 m/min); service ceiling 22,900 ft (6,980 m); range 800 miles (1,290 km).

Lockheed 14 Super Electra

Entering service three and a half years after the Douglas DC-2 of similar capacity, the Lockheed Model 14 Super Electra was of far more advanced design and had more powerful engines, giving it a more than twenty per cent higher cruising speed. When compared with the DC-3, which had a fifty per cent larger capacity and similar engines but which preceded it into service by fourteen months, the Super Electra still benefited from roughly the same speed advantage but was less economic. Thus, except when it was evaluated by carriers placing high value on exceptional cruise performance, the new Lockheed airliner started with a distinct disadvantage when pitted against the Douglas transports. Technically, the Lockheed 14 introduced a number of significant features such as its Fowler flaps, the first to be used on a production type, optional fixed wing slots (later standardized), fully-feathering propellers and integral fuel tanks. Moreover, to attract customers, Lockheed offered a broad choice of powerplants, including two versions of the Pratt & Whitney Hornet, five of the Wright Cyclone and one of the Pratt & Whitney Twin Wasp. None-the-less its belated entry into the market could never be overcome and only 112 Model 14s were built as opposed to 430 prewar DC-3s.

As early as autumn of 1935, when Douglas was proceeding with the final design of its DST/DC-3 series, Hall Hibbard and Kelly Johnson identified the need for an aircraft larger than the Lockheed Electra to compete against the new Douglas transport. Unfortunately, impeded both by lack of capital and by the fact that its limited engineering staff was already burdened with work on the Model 12, the relatively young Burbank firm could not proceed with the development of another design as fast as it would have liked. The slower pace of this programme, however, enabled the Hibbard/Johnson team to consider the use of several novel features to endow the projected aircraft with outstanding performance. Key to these improvements was the decision to adopt a highly-loaded wing of relatively small span and area (65 ft 6 in and 551 sq ft versus 85 ft and 939 sq ft for the DC-2) in order to achieve a higher cruising speed. To offset the resultant excessive approach and take-off speeds, Fowler flaps were adopted. These surfaces not only increased drag to lower approach speed as did conventional flaps but also augmented effective wing area to reduce take-off distance. Another early design choice was a deeper fuselage, thus eliminating the need for passengers to step over the wing truss as in the Models 10 and 12. Moreover, cabin length was increased to accommodate either fourteen passengers in single seats on each side of the central aisle or ten to eleven passengers, with galley and a cabin attendant.

Construction of a prototype powered by two Pratt & Whitney Hornet S1E-Gs, rated at 875 hp for take-off and 750 hp at 7,000 ft (2,135 m), was undertaken in early 1937 under the guidance of project engineer Don Palmer. Following its maiden flight on 29 July, 1937, with Marshall Headle at the controls, this aircraft (c/n 1401, X17382) went through an uneventful trial period culminating on 15 November, 1937, with the award of an Approved Type Certificate covering the Hornet S1E-G powered Model 14-H and the Model 14-H2 with Hornet S1E2-Gs. This company-owned aircraft—which had been painted in the markings of Northwest Airlines, the first Model 14 customer— was actually delivered late

Although it is seen here in the markings of Northwest Airlines, X17382, the prototype Model 14 Super Electra was never operated by this carrier. (*Gordon S. Williams*)

in December 1937 to Transportes Aéreos Centro-Americanos (TACA) as AN-AAH. However, it was soon re-acquired by Lockheed and modified as a demonstrator for the proposed C-14H-1 cargo transport. This modification, together with the civil and military versions of the Model 14, are now described.

Model 14-H and 14-H2: A total of 52 Hornet-powered Super Electras were built between July 1937 and June 1940 and included twenty Model 14-Hs with S1E-G engines (the prototype, eight production aircraft for Northwest Airlines, c/n 1418/VH-ABI for Guinea Airways, and ten Polish-registered machines for LOT) and thirty-two Model 14-H2s with S1E2-G radials (sixteen of which being delivered to Trans-Canada Air Lines, with the other sixteen aircraft going to five other airlines and one private customer—Max Fleischmann). Subsequently, one Model 14-H was modified as the C-14H-1, one 14-H (c/n 1404) and two 14-H2s (c/ns 1483 and 1486) were rebuilt as Lodestars, and twelve of the sixteen Model 14-Hs of TCA were re-engined with 1,200 hp Pratt & Whitney Twin Wasp S1C3-Gs as Model 14-08s. Post-delivery modifications to early production Super Electras of this model included the replacement of the original rudders with balanced surfaces as developed for the Model 14-WF62.

The Model 14-H2 CF-TCK (c/n 1474) of Trans-Canada Air Lines taking off from Boeing Field, Seattle, in July 1939. (*Gordon S. Williams*)

136

Model C-14H-1: After being operated briefly by TACA, c/n 1401 was taken back by Lockheed to be modified as a prototype cargo version. To enable the carriage of bulkier loads, notably aircraft engines, its fuselage was hunchbacked and fitted with a large loading door. The C-14H-1, which was re-registered NX18962, was briefly tested at Wright Field during the spring of 1938 but was found unsuitable by the Army Air Corps. Consequently, it was converted back to Model 14-H standard and was returned to passenger service in Brazil, as PP-AVB, and, later, Nicaragua, as AN-TAB.

Model 14-08: When, during the war, spare parts for the original powerplants of its Model 14-H2s became difficult to get, and also to provide some commonality with its fleet of Lodestars, TCA undertook replacement of the 875 hp Hornet S1E2-Gs in its Super Electras with 1,200 hp Twin Wasp S1C3-Gs. Twelve aircraft (c/ns 1429/1430, 1450/1451, 1471/1474, 1476, 1499/1500 and 1502) were so modified and redesignated Model 14-08s. Contrary to some reports, c/n 1429, which went on the British register in 1947 as G-AKPD, had been converted to Model 14-08 standard during the war in Canada; not in 1947 by Scottish Aviation Ltd.

Wartime scene at Winnipeg: Model 14-H2 CF-TCD (c/n 1429), re-engined with Twin Wasps as a Model 14-08, with horse-drawn ground support equipment riding on bare metal rims! (*Air Canada*)

Model 14-WF62:* Produced exclusively for the export market, this version differed from the Model 14-H in being powered by two Wright Cyclone SGR-1820-F62s, rated at 900 hp for take-off and 760 hp at 5,800 ft (1,770 m), and in having modified rudders incorporating static balances to prevent tail flutter. The twenty-one aircraft of this version were all exported, with eleven going to KLM and KNILM, beginning in February 1938, eight to British Airways, and the last two being delivered in May 1939 to Aer Lingus in Ireland.

Model 14-WG3B: With the exception of four aircraft delivered in August 1938 to Rumania, all Model 14-WG3Bs, or 14-G3Bs as they were also recorded, were exported to Japan. Twenty of these Super Electras, together with the licence production rights, were acquired in 1938 by Tachikawa Hikoki KK (Tachikawa Aeroplane Co Ltd). This manufacturing firm acted as agent for Nihon Koku KK (Japan Air Transport Co Ltd) and, as related later, undertook licence production of a version with Japanese engines. The Japanese carrier also acquired directly another ten Model 14-WG3Bs. Aircraft of this version were each powered by two Wright Cyclone GR-1820-G3Bs, rated at 900 hp for take-off and 840 hp at 8,000 ft (2,440 m).

*Also known as Model 14-F62

137

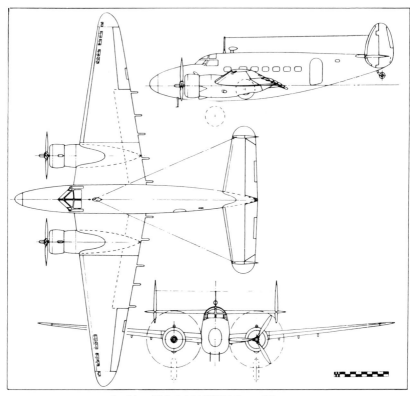

Lockheed Model 14-WF62 Super Electra

Model 14-N:* Whereas all but one of the aircraft in the previous series had been built as airliners, these four Super Electras powered by the more powerful Wright Cyclones of the G-series, with take-off rating of 1,100 hp and maximum rating of 900 hp between 6,000 and 6,700 ft (1,830 and 2,040 m) depending on model, were built for private owners. Two Model 14-Ns, with GR-1820-G105 engines, and one Model 14-N3 with -G105As, were finished with de luxe interiors as executive transports, whereas the GR-1820-G102 powered Model 14-N2 was especially built for Howard Hughes' round-the-world flight. For this undertaking, which Hughes wished to make with as few stops as possible to take full advantage of the 235-mph (378-km/h) cruising speed of his Super Electra, the standard fuel arrangement, consisting of four integral tanks in the wing, was supplemented by fuselage tanks increasing total capacity from 644 to 1,844 US gal (2,438 to 6,980 litres). Additional radio and navigational equipment, as well as supplies and flotation bags, were installed in the fuselage. Accommodation was provided for a crew of five (three forward and two aft of the cabin tanks), with a rest area right aft. As with its full fuel load the Model 14-N2 would have a high take-off weight (equivalent to 226 per cent of its empty weight) exceeding the value in its

*The Model 14-Ns were also known by engine designation as, for example, Model 14-G102 for the N2.

138

Approved Type Certificate, special dispensation had to be given by the CAA. Consequently, the aircraft (c/n 1419) was given the experimental registration NX18973 when it was delivered on 20 May, 1938.

XR4O-1: Powered by two 850 hp Pratt & Whitney R-1690-52s, the XR4O-1 (c/n 1482, BuNo 1441) was a staff transport version of the Model 14-H2 delivered to the US Navy on 15 October, 1938, and struck off strength six years later.

C-111: In March 1942, four Model 14-WF62s of KNILM, to avoid capture, were flown to Australia where they were purchased by the USAAF for service with the ADAT (Allied Directorate of Air Transport). One crashed almost immediately but the other three – c/ns 1414, 1442 and 1443 — were designated C-111s and were respectively assigned the US military serials 44-83233/44-83235 and the Australian call signs VH-CXI/VH-CXK.

Type LO: Exercising its licence rights, in 1939 Tachikawa Hikoki KK developed a military personnel transport version powered by Mitsubishi Ha-26-I (900 hp Army Type 99 radial Model 1) fourteen-cylinder air-cooled engines. Production for the Imperial Japanese Army was undertaken both by Tachikawa and by Kawasaki Kokuki Kogyo KK (Kawasaki Aircraft Engineering Co Ltd), which respectively produced 64 and 55 aircraft between 1940 and 1942. In military service these machines were designated Army Type LO Transports. During the war the Allies assigned the code name Thelma to these Japanese-built aircraft and that of Toby to the civil Model 14-WG3s purchased from Lockheed in 1938. A later Japanese development with a stretched fuselage received the code name Thalia and is described in the chapter on the Model 18 Lodestar.

SS-1: Following the lead of Lockheed with the XC-35 development from the Model 10, during the war Tachikawa designed a research version of the Type LO for experiments with cabin pressurization. Designated SS-1, this aircraft combined a new fuselage of circular cross-section with the wing and tail surfaces of the Type LO, née Lockheed 14-WG3. Powered by two 1,080 hp Mitsubishi Ha-102 fourteen-cylinder radials, the SS-1 was completed in 1943.

Having previously operated Lockheed Orions and then Electras, Northwest Airlines was the logical launch customer for the Super Electra. It ordered nine Hornet-powered Model 14-Hs before the first flight of the type and had received five of them before the award of an Approved Type Certificate. Northwest thus introduced the type into service, between Twin Cities and Chicago, in October 1937, and soon acquired four Model 14-Hs, including one substituted for the undelivered 14-H prototype and one replacement aircraft for c/n 1439 which had crashed before delivery. Initial reaction from the travelling public was favourable, with passengers and flight crews praising the high cruising speed, but the aircraft soon ran into bad luck, with three of the eleven Model 14s accepted by Northwest crashing during the first fifteen months of operations. Tail flutter had been diagnosed as the cause of the first crash (c/n 1407 on 10 January, 1938) and was soon cured by retrofitting balanced surfaces. None-the-less, after the third but unrelated fatal accident, the US public lost confidence in the Super Electra and Northwest was forced to dispose of its fleet during the summer of 1939 and switch to the slower Douglas DC-3. The only other US carriers to operate Lockheed 14s before the war were Santa Maria Airlines, which took delivery of a single 14-H2 in December 1938, and Continental Airlines, which acquired two ex-Northwest aircraft.

Overseas, the type had considerably greater success, with six major carriers taking delivery of twenty-one Hornet-powered and fifty-three Cyclone-powered

An immaculately clean Model 14-WF62 (PJ-AIM, *Meeuw—Seagull*, c/n 1441) of KLM's West Indies Division. The Fowler flaps are well shown. (*Gordon S. Williams*)

aircraft (including twenty acquired for resale by Tachikawa), with a further seven Super Electras going to three smaller airlines. The first of the operators were KLM and its East Indies subsidiary KNILM which received eleven Model 14-WF62s between February and June 1938. Perhaps more than any other carrier, KLM/KNILM could take full advantage of the Super Electra's spritely performance, as on their long Amsterdam–Batavia route its speed proved more attractive than the greater comfort offered by the wider cabin of the DC-3. KLM also operated four of its Super Electras in the West Indies. High cruising speed was also of interest to British Airways, already an established Lockheed customer, which initially ordered four Model 14-WF62s for its projected route from the United Kingdom to West Africa and on to South America. In the event, after using its first Super Electra to fly Prime Minister Chamberlain to Munich, on 15 September, 1938, British Airways introduced the type between London and Stockholm on 18 September. Later they made survey flights over part of the proposed South American route, but were mainly used on European routes including services to Berlin and Warsaw. Its fleet was later supplemented by four new 14-WF62s and by one ex-KLM machine.

Other European airlines ordering Super Electras were LOT (ten Model 14-Hs), LARES (four Model 14-WG3s), Aer Lingus (two Model 14-Hs) and Régie Air Afrique (five Model 14-Hs for service between France and its African colonies). LOT made history in May 1938 when Super Electra SP-LMK was flown from Burbank to Central and South America, across the South Atlantic, over West Africa and on to Europe to accomplish the first transoceanic delivery flight of an airliner. Trans-Canada Air Lines, with its order for sixteen Model 14-Hs, became Lockheed's largest airline customer. However, when adding to its own order for ten Model 14-WG3s, the twenty machines it acquired through Tachikawa, Japan Air Transport, later renamed Dai Nippon Koku KK (Greater Japan Air Lines), was by far the largest operator of the type.

Of the four aircraft sold by Lockheed to private owners only c/n 1419 achieved fame. Flown by Howard Hughes — with a crew consisting of Harry Connor (copilot and navigator), Tom Thurlow (navigator), Richard Stoddart (radio-operator) and Ed Lund (flight engineer) — NX18973 left Floyd Bennett Field, New York, on 10 July, 1938, for an abbreviated round-the-world flight. After intermediate stops at Paris, Moscow, Omsk, Yakutsk, Fairbanks and Minneapolis, Hughes and his crew landed back at Floyd Bennett on 14 July. Total elapsed time for the 14,672 miles (23,612 km) was 91 hr 14 min 10 sec, with a flight time of 71 hr 11 min 10 sec at an average speed of 206·1 mph (331·6 km/h). In 1940, Howard Hughes sold his Model 14-N2 to the Canadian Department of National Defence but its subsequent wartime use is not known.

Better known for their wartime service were the Japanese machines (thirty Lockheed-built Model 14-WG3s and 119 locally-produced Type LOs) which served until August 1945 with both Dai Nippon Koku and the Imperial Japanese Army Air Force. Flown primarily as personnel transports, with the Type LO also seeing limited use as paratroop transports, these aircraft operated mainly in Japan, Korea, the Philippines, China, Manchukuo, Malaya and the Netherlands East Indies. Early in the war their appearance in the same theatre as the RAAF Hudsons and the KNILM Model 14-WF62s, created some recognition problems as those types used the same wing and tail surfaces as their Japanese cousins. With British Commonwealth nations, the wartime use of Super Electras was much more limited. BOAC operated eight Model 14-WF62s (five inherited from British Airways and three LOT aircraft which had escaped from Poland in 1939)

The Wright GR-1820-G102 powered Model 14-N2 NX18973 (c/n 1419) in which Howard Hughes and a crew of four flew around the world during July 1938. (*Gordon S. Williams*)

primarily on services to France, before June 1940, and to Portugal as well as on trans-African routes to Cairo (at first from Dakar and then from Lagos). The R A F acquired two ex-British Airways Model 14-WF62s (c/ns 1485 and 1491), which both received two British military serials (HK982 to VF247, and HK984 to VF251); a Model 14-N (c/n 1417, AX681) and a Model 14-N3 (c/n 1496, AX682) were also obtained in the United States. In Canada, TCA continued to operate its fleet of Super Electras after modifying them to Model 14-08 standards. In Australia, the war years saw four ex-KNILM aircraft, of which three were assigned US military serials as C-111s, and five Guinea Airways aircraft (of which four were second-hand machines) in service with the Allied Directorate of Air Transport.

Seen here after being re-registered from SP-BNK to SP-LMK, this Model 14-H (c/n 1425) was one of ten Super Electras acquired by LOT Polish Airlines. (*Lockheed*)

Second-hand Super Electras began appearing on foreign registers as early as December 1937 when TACA in Nicaragua received the 14-H prototype. Used Model 14s were subsequently flown by operators in at least twelve countries (Belgium, Brazil, Colombia, Costa Rica, El Salvador, Guatemala, Honduras, Mexico, Peru, Portuguese East Africa, Sweden, and Venezuela) in addition to those previously mentioned. Most of these operators acquired their aircraft after

Ex-Northwest Airlines Model 14-H NC17384 (c/n 1403) of TACA de Honduras at Toncontin Airport, Tegucigalpa, in Honduras. (*TACA*)

the Second World War but made limited use of the type. In the same period many other Super Electras were operated as executive transports in the United States but the type disappeared from the scene rather more quickly than its predecessors, the Lockheed Electra and Electra Junior. None-the-less, the Model 14 had a significant impact on aviation history in general, and on that of Lockheed in particular, as it was the stepping stone from which the more successful Hudson, Lodestar and Ventura/Harpoon were developed.

Related Temporary Design Designation: L-119

	14-H	14-WF62	14-WG3	14-N
Span, ft in	65 6	65 6	65 6	65 6
(m)	(19.96)	(19.96)	(19.96)	(19.96)
Length, ft in	44 4	44 4	44 4	44 4
(m)	(13·51)	(13·51)	(13·51)	(13·51)
Height, ft in	11 5	11 5	11 10	11 5
(m)	(3·48)	(3·48)	(3·61)	(3·48)
Wing area, sq ft	551	551	551	551
(sq m)	(51·19)	(51·19)	(51·19)	(51·19)
Empty weight, lb	10,300	10,750	11,025	11,000
(kg)	(4,672)	(4,876)	(5,001)	(4,990)
Normal loaded weight, lb	15,200	15,650	15,650	15,900
(kg)	(6,895)	(7,099)	(7,099)	(7,212)
Maximum weight, lb	17,500	17,500	17,500	17,500
(kg)	(7,938)	(7,938)	(7,938)	(7,938)
Wing loading, lb/sq ft	27·6	28·4	28·4	28·9
(kg/sq m)	(134·7)	(138·7)	(138·7)	(140·9)
Power loading, lb/hp	8·9	8·7	8·7	7·2
(kg/hp)	(4·1)	(3·9)	(3·9)	(3·3)
Maximum speed, mph/ft	247/7,000	250/5,800	248/8,000	260/6,000
(km/h /m)	(397/2,135)	(402/1,770)	(399/2,440)	(418/1,830)
Cruising speed, mph	215	215	240	235
(km/h)	(346)	(346)	(386)	(378)
Rate of climb, ft/min	1,490	1,520	1,580	1,800
(m/min)	(454)	(463)	(482)	(549)
Service ceiling, ft	24,300	24,500	24,700	26,000
(m)	(7,405)	(7,470)	(7,530)	(7,925)
Normal range, miles	1,500	850	—	950
(km)	(2,415)	(1,370)	—	(1,530)
Maximum range, miles	2,060	2,125	1,600	—
(km)	(3,315)	(3,420)	(2,575)	—

A Hudson Mk.III (V9092, c/n 414-3717) during an acceptance test at Burbank before installation of its dorsal turret; the Fowler flaps are down as the aircraft is about to touch down. (*Peter M. Bowers*)

Lockheed Hudson

Hitler's assumption of dictatorial power in 1934, one year after becoming Chancellor of Germany, markedly increased tension in Europe and led the British Government to undertake an R A F expansion scheme. As part of this programme a new class of military aeroplane made its appearance when an initial order for 174 twin-engined, land-based, general reconnaissance aircraft, the Avro Anson I, was awarded to A. V. Roe & Co Ltd. When on 6 March, 1936, the first of these entered service with No.48 Squadron it not only became the first monoplane with retractable undercarriage to serve with the R A F but also initiated the trend of using land-based aircraft for maritime reconnaissance. Today this trend is still going strong, with the British Aerospace Nimrod, Breguet-Dassault Atlantic, Ilyushin Il-38, and Lockheed P-3 Orion, being produced for many of the world's air forces.

Lockheed's role in the development and production of land-based maritime reconnaissance aircraft, unbroken for more than forty years, began 25 months after the Anson's entry into service when—capitalizing on a February 1938 preliminary study for a bomber version of the Model 14 airliner—the company undertook as a private venture to build a mock-up of a general-reconnaissance aircraft. The work on this wooden mock-up, as well as preliminary engineering data, had been started when Lockheed learned of the impending visit of a British Purchasing Commission and was completed in five days and nights of frantic work. The gamble paid off as a few days later Lockheed was invited to send a delegation to London for negotiations with the Air Ministry.

As originally shown in April 1938 to the British Purchasing Commission, the mock-up of the proposed B14 (for bomber version of the Model 14) general-reconnaissance aircraft retained the wing, tail surfaces and engines of the Lockheed 14-WF62. It featured a modified fuselage with nose and dorsal turrets

145

(each having a single flexible gun), bomb storage in the centre fuselage, and a navigator's station (with a ventral flexible aft-firing gun) behind the wing trailing-edge. While this arrangement would have been satisfactory had the type been intended as a conventional bomber, it did not meet the RAF requirements for a general-reconnaissance aircraft in which the navigator played a vital role. Accordingly, the British Purchasing Commission suggested that the navigator be located in a glazed nose, closer to the pilot, and this suggestion was incorporated in a revised mock-up within 24 hours.

Several factors favoured the Lockheed proposal in the eyes of the BPC. First of all, two of the competing designs—proposed versions of the Boeing B-17 and Douglas B-18—were more expensive and would not be available in sufficient quantity within the desired time, whilst a third—a proposed amphibian version of the Consolidated 28 Catalina—was not favourably considered initially. Second, the British were already impressed with the qualities of the civil Lockheed 10, 12 and 14, the first two types having been in service in Great Britain for over a year and the third being on the point of joining the British Airways fleet. Finally, the company's eager development of a satisfactory mock-up and its obvious willingness to speed up deliveries sealed the British interest.

During two months of intensive meetings in London, Lockheed's team, including Courtlandt Gross, Kelly Johnson, Carl Squier, Richard Von Hake and Robert Proctor, negotiated with the Air Ministry. In the course of these discussions agreement was reached to replace the proposed US dorsal turret with a Boulton Paul unit housing two 0·303-in machine-guns and to mount in the nose twin fixed, forward-firing guns of the same calibre. Engines were to be 1,100 hp Wright GR-1820-G102As, instead of the originally proposed 900 hp GR-1820-F62s. With agreement on the technical specifications, negotiations concentrated on financial terms and delivery schedule and culminated on 23 June, 1938, with the signing of a $25 million contract for two hundred Model B14Ls (at a unit cost of £17,000) plus as many more as could be delivered by December 1939, up to a maximum of 250 aircraft.

The first unarmed, but fitted with a mock dorsal turret, Model B14L (Hudson Mk.I, serial N7205) began flight trials at Burbank on 10 December, 1938. Being a fairly straightforward development of the proven Lockheed 14, the type completed its trials rapidly and without notable problems. By then the Australian Government had placed an initial order for fifty Model B14Ss with Pratt & Whitney Twin Wasps. Deliveries of Hudson Mk.Is to the RAF began on 15 February, 1939, and production slowly gained tempo, with 48 aircraft being completed by June 1939. Spurred by the incentive of producing a further 50 aircraft, beyond the guaranteed initial British contract for 200 machines, if they could be delivered before the end of 1939, Lockheed increased its workforce and subcontracted a substantial amount of parts assembly to Rohr Aircraft in San Diego, including the complete powerplant package with hydraulic and electrical equipment. The company's efforts succeeded and the 250th Hudson was rolled out seven and a half weeks ahead of the December 1939 deadline. Lockheed had finally joined the ranks of the world's leading aircraft manufacturers and the future of the Hudson programme was assured.

Between December 1938 and May 1943, a total of 2,941 Hudsons came off the production lines in Burbank and included 1,338 aircraft under direct purchase orders, 1,302 machines under Lend-Lease contracts, 300 AT-18/AT-18As for the USAAF, and one civil B14S for Sperry. In the following narrative the many versions of the Hudson are grouped under each of these three main categories.

146

The 197th Hudson Mk.I (N7401, c/n B14L-1800) at Floyd Bennett Field, New York, at the completion of its transcontinental delivery flight to its port of embarkation. (*Gordon S. Williams*)

Direct Purchases

Hudson Mk.I: Beginning with a contract for 200 aircraft (British military serials N7205/N7404) the British Purchasing Commission ordered a total of 350 Model B14Ls (with additional serials P5116/P5165 and T9266/T9365). Another Mk.I (R4059) was built by Lockheed as a replacement for N7260 which had been written-off before delivery. These aircraft were powered by two Wright GR-1820-G102A nine-cylinder radials (1,100 hp for take-off and 900 hp at 6,700 ft) driving three-blade two-position propellers. Armament consisted of two 0·303-in forward-firing (fixed) guns in the upper nose decking, twin 0·303-in guns in a Boulton Paul turret (installed in the United Kingdom after delivery) and 1,400 lb (635 kg) of bombs or depth-charges in an internal bomb bay beneath the floor of the cabin. The normal crew was five. Following the 10 December, 1938, maiden flight of N7205, deliveries were made by sea to Liverpool—beginning on 15 February, 1939, with the arrival of N7206—with final assembly being made by the British Reassembly Division, Lockheed Ltd, at Liverpool's Speke Airport. All but 31 of these aircraft were assigned to the RAF while one (N7260) was destroyed before delivery and two (P5163 and P5164) went to the South African Government. The remaining twenty-eight Hudson Mk.Is went directly to the RCAF and were given Canadian serials 759/786 (corresponding to British serials N7344/N7350, N7352, N7354/N7356, N7360, N7370/N7371, N7375, N7380/N7381, N7373, N7382, N7384, N7383, N7387, N7385/N7386 and N7388/N7391). In RAF service N7220 was converted to a VIP transport and N7364 became G-AGAR while serving with No.2 Camouflage Unit.

Fifty other aircraft, initially known to the RAAF as Hudson Mk.Is, were powered by Pratt & Whitney Twin Wasp SC3-Gs and were Lockheed Model B14Ss. They were later redesignated Hudson Mk.IVs.

A16-73, an Australian Hudson II from No.1 OTU operating from East Sale, Victoria. (*via Frank F. Smith*)

Hudson Mk.II: Differing from the Mk.I in having constant-speed propellers, the twenty Mk.IIs (T9366/T9385) were Model 414s with strengthened airframe components. All but the last one, which retained its British serial upon delivery to the RCAF, were delivered to the RAF. One of the RAF aircraft (T9367) was used by BOAC but retained its military serial. The aircraft, initially known as MK.IIs to the RAAF, were Model 414s and were later redesignated Mk.IVs.

Hudson Mk.III: Combining the airframe improvements of the Mk.II with more powerful GR-1820-G205A engines (1,200 hp for take-off and 1,050 hp at 7,500 ft) driving constant-speed propellers, the Model 414 Hudson Mk.III had increased defensive armament. Three flexible 0·303-in machine-guns were added, one in a retractable ventral position and one each in beam positions. Before the transfer of existing direct-purchase orders to Lend-Lease contracts, a total of 428 Mk.IIIs were delivered by Lockheed against British orders (T9386/T9465, V8975/V8999, V9020/V9069, V9090/V9129, V9220/V9254, AE485/AE608 and AM930/AM953). During the course of production, extra fuel tanks, increasing maximum capacity from 644 to 1,028 US gallons (2,438 to 3,892 litres) were added to 241 aircraft which became Mk.III(LR); the initial production aircraft then became Mk.III(SR). The 428 British-ordered Mk.IIIs were distributed among the RAF (371 aircraft), the RCAF (three with British serials), and the RNZAF (54 with serials starting with NZ2001). Some of the Hudson Mk.IIIs were later modified to carry Mark I airborne lifeboats on air-sea rescue missions. For use as transports BOAC received V9061 (G-AGDC *Loch Lomond*), AE581 (G-AGDO *Loch Loyal*) and two unidentified aircraft (G-AGDF c/n 3772 *Loch Leven* and G-AGDK c/n 3757 *Loch Lyon*). Two ex-BOAC aircraft (G-AGDC and G-AGDK) were returned to the RAF as Hudson C.Mk.IIIs and received new military serials: VJ416 and VJ421.

Hudson Mk.IIIA: Lend-Lease aircraft described under the A-29A-LO heading.

Hudson Mk.IV (RAAF Mk.I and Mk.II): As the Commonwealth Aircraft Corporation had acquired the licence rights for the Pratt & Whitney Wasp S1H-1G and as many components of this single-row engine were common to those

148

in the fourteen-cylinder Twin Wasp, the RAAF elected to have Pratt & Whitney Twin Wasp SC3-Gs (1,050 hp for take-off and 900 hp at 12,000 ft) fitted to the fifty aircraft it ordered shortly after the British had ordered their first 200 Hudson Mk.Is. Built as Model B14S and assigned the Australian serials A16-1 to A16-50, these aircraft were shipped to Melbourne with initial delivery taking place on 9 February, 1940. They were initially known as Mk.Is but, to avoid confusion with the Cyclone-powered Mk.Is of the RAF, they were later redesignated Hudson Mk.IVs. The first batch of aircraft was delivered without dorsal turrets and had a flexible gun in a dorsal hatch.

One additional B14S (c/n 1930) was built for and delivered on 28 February, 1940, to the Sperry Gyroscope Co. Registered NX21771, this unarmed aircraft was used by Sperry as a flying testbed for aircraft instruments.

A follow-on order for fifty aircraft (A16-51/A16-100) was placed by the RAAF and the aircraft in this batch incorporated a number of minor improvements. Accordingly, these Twin Wasp powered aircraft were at first known as Hudson Mk.IIs in the RAAF; later, again to avoid confusion wtih the RAF designation, they became Hudson Mk.IVs. Thirty aircraft (AE609/AE638) generally similar to the Mk.IIs of the RAAF were ordered for the RAF, with twenty-three of them going into British service and seven being delivered to Australia.

Hudson Mk.IVA: Lend-Lease version (*see* A-28-LO) of which 52 were delivered to the RAAF.

Hudson Mk.V: Powered by Twin Wasp S3C-4Gs (1,200 hp for take-off and 1,100 hp at 2,550 ft) the Mk.Vs had airframes and increased defensive armament similar to those of the Mk.IIIs. The first 202 aircraft (AE639/AE657 and AM520/AM702) had the original fuel tanks and were designated Hudson Mk.V(SR). All but seven were delivered to the RAF—including AM633, AM667, AM668 and AM688 which were later transferred to the USAAF in Britain—while AM576 went to the RCAF and AM589/AM594 were shipped to Auckland to serve with the RNZAF as NZ1019/NZ1024. They were followed by 207 Hudson Mk.V(LR)s with increased tankage and serials AM703 to AM909. One of these aircraft (AM707) was used between June and August 1941 by BOAC as G-AGCE while 42 aircraft were delivered to the RCAF.

Hudson Mk.VI: Lend-Lease version built as A-28A-LO.

Lend-Lease Contracts

After President Roosevelt had signed on 11 March, 1941, the Lend-Lease Bill, outstanding British contracts for Hudsons — as well as other aircraft types— were taken over under Department of the Army contracts and these 1,302 aircraft were produced with USAAF designations.

A-28-LO: Assigned USAAF serials 41-23171/41-23222 for contractual purposes and powered by Pratt & Whitney R-1830-45s (the USAAF version of the Twin Wasp SC3-G), these 52 aircraft were delivered to the RAAF with which they served as A16-101/A16-152 under the designation Hudson Mk.IVA.

A-28A-LO: Basically similar to the Hudson Mk.V, but powered by 1,200 hp R-1830-67s (Chevrolet-built military version of the Twin Wasp S3C4-G), the 450 A-28A-LOs (42-6582/42-6681 and 42-46937/42-47286) were intended for British Commonwealth air forces and were also given the British military serials EW873/EW972 and FK381/FK730. They were delivered as Hudson Mk.VIs to the RAF (410 aircraft, of which at least three were transferred to the USAAF, and one went to Portugal's Aviação Naval), the RCAF (36 aircraft which

Glider tug A-28A-LO (42-47164) at Bowman Field, Kentucky. (*USAF*)

retained their British serials) and the RNZAF (four aircraft within serial range up to NZ2094). A number of RAF machines had their armament removed and were operated as Hudson C.VI transports.

A-29-LO: Whereas the A-28s and A-28As had Pratt & Whitney engines, the A-29s and A-29As had 1,200 hp Wright R-1820-87 nine-cylinder radials. The A-29-LOs were identical to the Hudson Mk.III(LR) and were designated Hudson Mk.IIIAs in Commonwealth service. When originally ordered by the British, 616 aircraft had been assigned serials BW361/BW766, BW768/BW777 and FH167/FH366; however, upon becoming Lend-Lease items they became 41-23223/41-23628, 41-23630/41-23639 and 41-36968/41-37167 as A-29-LOs. The first twenty aircraft were delivered to the US Navy as PBO-1s (BuNos 03842/03861); the remaining aeroplanes went to the RAF and RCAF (32 and 133 aircraft, respectively, with their original British serials), the RAAF (41 aircraft within serial range up to A16-247), the RNZAF (14 aircraft within the serial range up to NZ2094), the Chinese Air Force (23 aircraft) and the USAAF (153 aircraft with a flexible 0·50-in machine-gun in an open dorsal position in place of the Boulton Paul turret); twenty-four became A-29B-LOs.

A-29A-LO: Differing from the A-29s in having a convertible interior for troop transport, but retaining their armament and Hudson Mk.IIIA designation, the 184 aircraft of this type had both British and US serials assigned (BW767, 41-23629, FH367/FH466, 41-37168/41-37267, and FK731/FK813, 42-47287/42-47369). The RAF received 289 of these aircraft, the RAAF took delivery of

With a hand-held 0·50-in machine-gun replacing the dorsal turret of the British Hudsons, this A-29-LO (41-23386) is seen at Drew Field, Florida, early in the war. (*USAF*)

150

65 machines (serials up to A16-247), the RNZAF obtained 23 aircraft (including BW767), the RCAF was the recipient of four aircraft and the Chinese Air Force added three A-29A-LOs to its inventory of twenty-three A-29-LOs.

A-29B-LO: Twenty-four of the A-29-LOs which had been retained by the USAAF were converted under this designation as photographic-survey aircraft.

USAAF Contract

On 8 May, 1942, the USAAF awarded Lockheed its own contract AC22346 for 300 advanced trainers. The first 83 aircraft were navigational trainers with the remainder being built as gunnery trainers.

AT-18-LO: Powered by 1,200 hp Wright R-1820-87s, the 217 AT-18 gunnery trainers (42-55568/42-55784) had twin 0·50-in machine-guns in a Martin dorsal turret as used on most USAAF wartime bombers.

AT-18A-LO: Retaining the R-1820-87 engines, the eighty-three AT-18As (42-55485/42-55567) were unarmed navigational trainers with accommodation for pilot, instructor and three students.

AT-18-LO (42-55593) over Laredo AAF, Texas, on 8 February, 1944. The full c/n is painted on the nose. (*USAF*)

With the RAF, Hudson Mk.Is entered service with No.224 Squadron Coastal Command at Gosport in the summer of 1939 and by the outbreak of the war on 1 September, 1939, were also serving with No.233 Squadron, whilst Hudson Mk.IIIs were in the process of replacing Avro Ansons with No. 220 Squadron. On 8 October, 1939, one of the first unit's Hudsons became the first aircraft of American design to destroy an enemy aircraft, a Dornier Do 18D of 2./Kü.Fl.Gr. 106 off Jutland. Four months later, a Hudson Mk.III of No.220 Squadron directed HMS *Cossack* and her boarding party to the hideout of the Kriegsmarine prison ship, *Altmark*, in Norwegian waters and so helped bring freedom to many captured British seamen. During the first year of the war, the Coastal Command Hudson squadrons, with the first three being progressively joined by Nos.206 and 269 Squadrons, flew regular maritime patrols and anti-shipping sorties, and their effectiveness was increased beginning in early 1940 by the installation of ASV (air-to-surface-vessel) radar. They also played a vital role during the Norwegian campaign (April–June 1940) and in covering the withdrawal of Allied troops from Dunkirk in May 1940. Other Hudsons also served in the reconnaissance role during 1939–40 with No.2 Camouflage Unit (later Photographic Development Unit and, from July 1940, No.1 Photographic Reconnaissance Unit) and flew low-level and bad-weather sorties, not only over Germany and occupied Europe, but also over the USSR, the latter missions being flown by N7364 which flew over Baku and Batumi from RAF Habbaniyeh in Iraq under the 'civil' registration G-AGAR.

In the anti-submarine role, Hudsons were operated by the RAF beginning in August 1940 when detachments from several squadrons flew out from Aldergrove in Northern Ireland to cover the Western Approaches. Seven months later a detachment from No.269 Squadron began ASW patrols from Kaldardanes, Iceland, and on 27 August, 1941, one of its aircraft, under the command of Sqn Ldr J. H. Thompson, damaged the surfaced U-570. The submarine crew surrendered and U-570 was taken in tow to become the first U-boat captured by

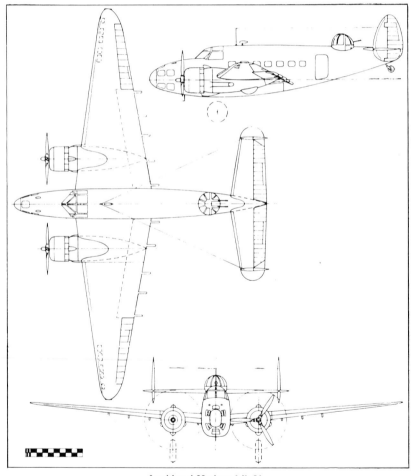

Lockheed Hudson Mk.V

the R A F. As time went on, R A F Hudsons flew anti-submarine patrols not only from the British Isles and Iceland but also from NAS Quonset Point, Rhode Island; Waller Field in the British West Indies; NAS Norfolk in Virginia; Gibraltar; North Africa (from where an aircraft of No.608 Squadron became the first R A F aircraft to sink a U-boat with rockets fired from underwing racks); Lydda in Palestine; and from Sicily, Italy and Corsica.

Besides hunting U-boats, the Coastal Command and Mediterranean Air Command Hudsons continued to fly convoy escort, maritime reconnaissance and occasional bombing sorties (notably during the night of 25/26 June, 1942, when Nos.59, 206 and 224 Squadrons contributed 35 Hudsons to R A F Bomber Command's Operation Millenium II, the second 1,000-bomber raid against Germany). As a bomber the Hudson also saw much use in the Far East, beginning in early 1942 with No.62 Squadron in Malaya, and in this theatre it went on to serve with Nos.139, 194, 217, 353 and 357 Squadrons in the bombing, convoy escort and supply-dropping roles.

Spirit of Lockheed-Vega Employees, the presentation Hudson III T9465 of No.269 Squadron, RAF. (*Lockheed*)

By May 1943, when Hudson production ended, the type was becoming obsolete in its intended role and the R A F increasingly used it for other duties including meteorological flights, air-sea rescue sorties—for which the aircraft was adapted to carry a Mark I airborne lifeboat beneath its fuselage—the dropping of agents in enemy-occupied territory, operational training, and transport work (notably in the Mediterranean). The type was also operated by B O A C in support of the Atlantic Ferry, and, from November 1940, Hudsons were flown across the Atlantic instead of being shipped. Finally, the Hudson was retired from R A F service in April 1945 when No.251 Squadron completed its conversion to Boeing Fortresses.

Between 15 September, 1939, when the first two of twenty-eight Hudson Mk.Is, which were diverted from the original British contract and were given Canadian serials 759/786, were delivered to No.11 Squadron, and November 1942, the RCAF received a total of 248 Hudsons (all but the already mentioned 28 aircraft from the first batch retained their British serials whilst in Canadian service; they included one Mk.II, three Mk.IIIs, 137 Mk.IIIAs, forty-three Mk.Vs and thirty-six Mk.VIs). In the maritime patrol and ASW roles, RCAF Hudsons were operated by Nos.11, 113, 119 and 120 Squadrons until 1943. In addition, No.407 Squadron (RCAF) operated British Hudsons in the United Kingdom as part of Coastal Command. Their most important duty in Canada, however, was training and Hudsons were flown by Nos.31, 34 and 36 Operational Training Units, No.1 Central Flying School and No.4 Air Observer School. Noteworthy was the success of one of No.31 OTU's aircraft which, during a training sortie on 4 July, 1943, damaged and possibly sank a U-boat off Nova Scotia. In Canadian service, Hudsons remained in use after the end of the war. BW430, a Hudson Mk.IIIA, last serving with No.123 Search and Rescue Flight during 1947, was finally struck off strength on 13 December, 1948.

Following the R A F lead, the R A A F had ordered an initial batch of fifty Twin Wasp powered aircraft in late 1938. Known in Australian service as Hudson Mk.Is (A16-1 to A16-50), even though they had Pratt & Whitney engines and, accordingly, were later redesignated Mk.IVs in the British numbering system, these aircraft were delivered by sea beginning on 9 February, 1940. A follow-on order for fifty aircraft (A16-51 to A16-100, Mk.IIs in the R A A F nomenclature and Mk.IV according to the RAF) was supplemented by 96 Lend-Lease Hudson Mk.IIIAs diverted from R A F allotments (95 of which were given Australian serials A16-153 to A16-247) and by 52 Hudson Mk.IVAs (A16-101 to A16-152) which had originally been ordered by the R A A F but were completed under Lend-Lease as A-28-LOs. With the exception of a handful of R A A F Hudson Mk.Is, the first 100 aircraft to arrive in Australia during 1940 came from the diverted R A F allotment. These aircraft entered service with No. 1 Squadron at Laverton, Victoria, and by the beginning of July 1940 this unit was on its way to Singapore. On the eve of the Japanese attack, the R A A F had eight Hudson squadrons: No.1 at Kota Bharu and No.8 at Kuantan, Malaya; Nos.2 and 13 Squadrons at Darwin with detachments at Koepang, Timor, and Laha, Ambon, in the Netherlands East Indies; No.24 Squadron at Rabaul; and Nos.6, 7 and 23 Squadrons in process

Hudson Mk.Is (Mk.IVs in the RAF nomenclature) of No.8 Squadron, RAAF, with an escorting Commonwealth CA-3 Wirraway of No.21 Squadron, over Malaya before the Japanese onslaught. (*Australian War Memorial*)

154

For the first two years of the war Twin Wasp powered Hudsons were the main bombers in service with the RAAF during operations against the Japanese. (*Australian War Memorial*)

of conversion in Australia. Alerted by the sound of gun-fire on the beaches, No.1 Squadron flew out of Kota Bharu in the darkness to locate and bomb Japanese invasion forces. From then on, the two Malaya units fought against overwhelming odds and suffered heavy losses, with attrition being partially offset by the transfer of RAF Hudsons flown from India.

Forced to leave the Malay peninsula on 29 January, 1942, Nos.1 and 8 Squadrons continued the fight in the East Indies where they joined the similarly-equipped Nos.2 and 13 Squadrons. Likewise, No.24 Squadron fought from Rabaul against strong Japanese forces from 15 December, 1941, until it was forced to evacuate in late January 1942. By March 1942, the advancing Japanese forces were ready to take on Allied troops in New Guinea and once again the RAAF Hudsons were forced to provide the main Allied bombing power, with elements of Nos.2 and 13 Squadrons being regrouped into a new No.32 Squadron. Other elements from these two squadrons repeatedly flew from north-western Australia to bomb Japanese installations on Timor. Finally, the Hudsons were replaced in the bombing role during autumn 1943 and in the maritime patrol role during the spring of 1944. All told, Australian Hudsons had served at home and in the SWPA theatre in no fewer than eleven Squadrons (Nos.1, 2, 6, 7, 8, 13, 14, 23, 24, 25 and 32), four Communication Units (Nos.1, 3, 4 and 6), No.1 Operational Training Unit, No.1 Rescue and Communication Unit, No.2 Air Ambulance Unit, and the RAAF Survey Flight. The last Hudson was not phased out of the RAAF until 1949. Hudsons with British serials had also been operated by two RAAF Squadrons (Nos.459 and 464) serving in the United Kingdom with RAF Coastal Command.

In their fight against Japanese forces, the RAF and RAAF Hudsons were joined by RNZAF aircraft, with that Service receiving, by transfer from RAF allotments, fifty-four Mk.IIIs, thirty-seven Mk.IIIAs, six Mk.Vs and four Mk.VIs (94 of which received New Zealand serials NZ2001 to NZ2094 and seven retaining British serials). In RNZAF service these aircraft equipped five Bomber Reconnaissance Squadrons (Nos.1, 2, 3, 4 and 9) and two Transport Squadrons (Nos.40 and 41). In the bomber role they entered service during 1941 with Nos.1, 2 and 4

An A-29-LO in Chinese markings during operations on the Asiatic mainland. (*Lockheed*)

The one and only 'Hudstar', an hybrid aircraft produced by Rausch Aviation by matching the forward fuselage, wing and powerplant of an AT-18A with the rear fuselage and tail surfaces of a Lodestar. (*Howard Levy*)

A surplus Cyclone-powered Model 414 with Brazilian registration. (*Gordon S. Williams*)

Squadrons and were phased-out by No.3 Squadron in 1944; in the transport role they served from 1943 until the end of the war. After flying maritime patrols from New Zealand, Fiji, and New Caledonia, the RNZAF Hudsons went into action in earnest in late November 1942 when No.3 Squadron joined the fight on Guadalcanal. During its tour of duties in the Solomons, No.3 Squadron's Hudsons, prior to giving way to Lockheed-Vega Venturas, gained two firsts for the RNZAF: first aerial victory on 2 April, 1943, and first submarine sunk on the next day.

The assignment of US serial numbers to 1,302 Lend-Lease Hudsons is misleading as regards the type's importance in USAAF service, as only 153 A-29-LOs — with a flexible 0·50-in machine-gun replacing the Boulton Paul dorsal turret of the standard aircraft — were actually retained by the USAAF for its own use. Considered only as an interim type pending the availability of more modern equipment, the A-29-LOs were retained in the States and distributed, along with a variety of other aircraft, among a number of Bombardment and Anti-Submarine Squadrons on both the East and West Coasts. One of these A-29s became the first USAAF aircraft to claim an enemy submarine when it sank the U-701 on 7 July, 1942. After their brief service on ASW duty, the A-29-LOs were used by the USAAF for crew training, supplemented in this role by the specially-built AT-28s and AT-28As. Twenty-four of the A-29s were modified by the USAAF as A-29B photographic-reconnaissance aircraft and this Service also operated in the liaison/transport role a handful of Hudsons obtained from RAF stocks in Britain.

Although the US Navy received only twenty A-29-LOs, which were redesignated PBO-1s and assigned BuNos 03842/03861, it used these aircraft to form in October 1941 an operational patrol squadron, VP-82. Operating from Argentia in Newfoundland and NAS Quonset Point, Rhode Island, VP-82 flew patrols over the Atlantic convoy routes with its PBO-1s which retained the standard Boulton Paul dorsal turret. In the process, the unit sank on 1 and 15 March, 1942, the first two submarines claimed by United States aircraft.

The Fôrça Aérea Brasileira, as part of the mix of equipment it needed to equip some of its Grupos de Bombardeio Medio (Medium Bombardment Groups), received twenty-eight A-28As after Brazil had declared war on Germany and Italy on 22 August, 1942. Assigned to the Grupo de Patrulha and operating from the 12° Corpo de Base Aérea at Galeão, Rio de Janeiro, one of these aircraft caught the submarine U-199 on the surface on the morning of 31 July, 1943. In spite of suffering heavy damage from anti-aircraft fire, the A-28A forced the German submarine to remain on the surface where twenty minutes later it was sunk by a Catalina of the same Brazilian unit. In 1945, these aircraft received the Brazilian serial numbers 6028 to 6055 under the new numbering system then being implemented by the Fôrça Aérea Brasileira. Subsequently aircraft 6042, 6051 and 6053 were modified as transports, with the Brazilian designation C-28, and were numbered 2900 to 2902 respectively.

The Chinese Air Force, though it was the recipient of twenty-three A-29-LOs and three A-29A-LOs, made little operational use of the Hudson. Most were written off in accidents, but a few flew some bombing sorties in central China.

After an eventful combat career, during which it was credited with the sinking of their first submarine by several air forces, the Hudson faded out rapidly after 1945 as it was then retained in service only by the RCAF and RAAF. At least 36 found their way on to civil registers, with some 18 aircraft used in Australia as transports and aerial-survey aircraft and 12 more in Canada for similar duties.

Related Temporary Design Designations: L-100/L-101, L-103, L-107/L-109 and L-114

Hudson I

Span 65 ft 6 in (19·96 m); length 44 ft 4 in (13·51 m); height 11 ft 10 in (3·61 m); wing area 551 sq ft (51·19 sq m).

Empty weight 11,630 lb (5,275 kg); loaded weight 17,500 lb (7,938 kg); wing loading 31·8 lb/sq ft (155·1 kg/sq m); power loading 8 lb/hp (3·6 kg/hp).

Maximum speed 246 mph at 6,500 ft (396 km/h at 1,980 m); cruising speed 220 mph (354 km/h); rate of climb 2,180 ft/min (664 m/min); service ceiling 25,000 ft (7,620 m); range 1,960 miles (3,155 km).

Hudson IV

Dimensions as Hudson I.

Empty weight 13,195 lb (5,985 kg); loaded weight 18,500 lb (8,391 kg); maximum weight 22,360 lb (10,142 kg); wing loading 33·6 lb/sq ft (163·9 kg/sq m); power loading 7·7 lb/hp (3·5 kg/hp).

Maximum speed 284 mph at 15,000 ft (457 km/h at 4,570 m); cruising speed 224 mph (360 km/h); rate of climb 2,160 ft/min (658 m/min); service ceiling 27,000 ft (8,230 m); range 2,160 miles (3,475 m).

The beautifully clean lines of the XP-38 are shown to advantage in this photograph taken at March Field, California. (*Lockheed*)

Lockheed P-38 Lightning

Truly one of the great fighters of the Second World War, the Lightning was the only American pursuit aeroplane to remain in continuous production throughout the war, with its first service model being delivered to the U S A A F in June 1941 and contracts for its final variants being cancelled after VJ-Day. In fact, even though later types of fighters were then in full production, deliveries of P-38s peaked only in 1944 when 4,186 Lightnings were produced by Lockheed and Consolidated-Vultee started on the production of one hundred and thirteen P-38L-5-VNs. Besides its longevity, the P-38's claims to fame included notably the destruction of

YP-38s at the Lockheed plant in Burbank. The first two aircraft are Nos.9 and 10.
(*Lockheed*)

the first German aircraft by a U S A A F fighter, the first round-trip mission to Berlin by United Kingdom-based fighters, the shooting down of Admiral Isoroku Yamamoto's transport, and its exclusive use by the two top-scoring American pilots, Majors Richard I. Bong and Thomas B. McGuire Jr. Furthermore, this twin-engined, single-seat fighter proved highly amenable to fulfilling other roles and was developed into an outstanding photographic-reconnaissance aircraft, a fighter-bomber carrying a load heavier than the standard bomb load of the contemporary B-17 and B-24 four-engined bombers, and, during the last year of the war, the best night fighter of the U S A A F.

After its XPB-3/XFM-2 multi-seat fighter proposal had come in a close second to Bell's in the 1936 competition which resulted in the XFM-1 Airacuda, Lockheed was rewarded for its efforts by being invited, along with Boeing, Consolidated, Curtiss, Douglas and Vultee, to take part in the Air Corps' Design Competition X-608 for a twin-engined high-altitude interceptor. Immediately, Kelly Johnson began studying a number of configurations, ranging from a conventional twin-engined layout, to still fairly orthodox airframes but with engines buried in the fuselage and driving either tractor or pusher propellers by means of extended drive shafts, to a twin-boom design with engines fore and aft of the cockpit in a central nacelle, and to twin-boom models with each boom extending aft of the engine and the pilot sitting either in an enclosed cockpit on the port boom or in a central nacelle. The latter configuration formed the basis for the Model 22-64-01 proposal as submitted in April 1937. The proposed design was characterized by its twin booms—each housing a 1,150 hp Allison V-1710C

159

twelve-cylinder liquid-cooled engine, the aft-retracting main undercarriage units, and exhaust-driven turbosupercharger—and its central nacelle—providing space for the forward-firing armament consisting of one cannon—either 0·90-in/22·9 mm T1, 23 mm Madsen, or 37 mm M4—and four 0·50-in machine-guns, the nosewheel and the single-seat cockpit. Tail surfaces consisted of a fin and rudder at the end of each boom, and horizontal tailplane and elevator between the booms. Fowler flaps were fitted between the ailerons and the booms, and between the booms beneath the trailing edge of the wing centre-section.

In spite of its radical design, as well as some scepticism about its calculated top speed of 400 mph (644 km/h)—more than ten per cent above the Air Corps' requirements—the Model 22 won Design Competition X-608 and on 23 June, 1937, Lockheed was awarded Contract AC-9974 for one XP-38 prototype (37-457, c/n 022-2201). Following contract award, detailed design proceeded under the guidance of project engineer James Gerschler, and the XP-38, construction of which had begun in July 1938, was completed in December of that year. After being taken to March Field, California, the fighter prototype was re-assembled and Lieut Benjamin S. Kelsey, the Air Corps' Project Officer, began its high-speed taxi-ing trials. Major damage to the XP-38 was narrowly avoided during one of these tests when the aircraft skidded off the end of the runway when grease on a brake shoe led to ineffective braking. Soon after, it was found necessary to add a hand-operated pump to boost brake pressure and to change the brake linings, but these modifications had not yet been made when on 27 January, 1939, Kelsey first flew the XP-38 for 34 minutes. This maiden flight, however, was marred by violent vibration of the flaps and by the rupture of three of the four flap support rods. Repairs to the flaps and modifications of the brake system were made before the second flight, on 5 February. In spite of continuous minor problems during the next four test flights, it was decided to attempt a record transcontinental flight before delivering the XP-38 to Wright Field. Thus, on 11 February, 1939, Ben Kelsey left March Field for Mitchel Field, New York, with refuelling stops at Amarillo, Texas, and Wright Field, Ohio. On the last leg of the flight, after just over seven hours' flying time and an elapsed time of about 7 hr 43 min—some fifteen minutes more than the then standing transcontinental record of Howard Hughes in his H-1 racer—the XP-38 lost power as Kelsey was slowing down to land at Mitchel Field behind other traffic. Crashing on a golf course 2,000 ft short of the field, the prototype, which by then had accumulated less than twelve hours in the air, was damaged beyond repair; fortunately, Kelsey was unhurt.

On 27 April, 1939, some two and a half months after the loss of the XP-38, Lockheed was awarded a $2 m contract for thirteen YP-38s (39-689/39-701) and one structural test airframe. These service test aircraft (Model 122-62-02) differed from the prototype in being powered by V-1710-F2 engines, installed so that the handed propellers rotated outboard instead of inboard as on the XP-38,* as well as incorporating several other minor improvements and revised armament. The first YP-38 was flown by Marshall Headle on 17 September, 1940, at Burbank, with subsequent YP-38s being used by the USAAC/USAAF for accelerated service tests. During trials, the YP-38s ran into a tail buffet problem and, when this was improperly diagnosed as elevator flutter, external mass balances were added above and below the elevator; the real problem, tail buffet,

---

*That is, the port propeller turned anti-clockwise when seen from the rear and the starboard propeller turned clockwise.

A YP-38 over the Los Angeles metropolis. (*Lockheed*)

was solved later by adding large wing-root fillets. Even before the first flight of the YP-38, the new Lockheed twin-engined fighter's future had been assured by the issue on 20 September, 1939, of a contract for 66 aircraft (delivered as P-38s, XP-38A and P-38Ds) and on 30 August, 1940, for a follow-on contract for 410 aircraft (delivered as P-38E and P-38F fighters, and F-4, F-4A, F-5 and F-5A photographic-reconnaissance aircraft). These and other versions of the Lightning for the USAAF are described later, after details are given of the export Model 322s—whose order preceded the delivery of production variants of the P-38.

In France, as early as the spring of 1939, the Comité du Matériel and the Etat Major had begun considering the P-38 as a substitute for the Breguet 700, Potez 671, and Sud-Est S.E.100 twin-engined aircraft, then under development to fulfil the C 2 (two-seat fighter) and CN 2 (two-seat night fighter) requirements of the Armée de l'Air. Eventually this early interest led in April 1940 to the placing by the Anglo-French Purchasing Committee of a contract for 667 aircraft, thus lending a hefty boost to the programme as, up to then, and including the prototype and service test aircraft, the US Air Corps had ordered only eighty P-38s. The two versions ordered by the European allies were respectively designated Models 322-61-03 (or 322-F) for France and 322-61-04 (or 322-B) for Britain and were to be powered by Allison V-1710-C15s rated at 1,090 hp at 14,000 ft (4,265 m), with the French version to be fitted with French instruments, radio and armament, and to have the engine throttles operating in the opposite direction. The selection of the unsupercharged version of the Allison engine was carefully arrived at by the Anglo-French Purchasing Committee in order to standardize on the same powerplant as used on the Curtiss H-81A—the P-40 version for the Armée de l'Air and the Royal Air Force—and to optimize performance for medium-altitude combat as was then taking place in Europe. With these engines, guaranteed top speed was 400 mph at 16,900 ft (644 km/h at 5,150 m).

After the fall of France in June 1940, the entire contract for Model 322s was taken over by Britain and shortly after was amended to provide for the delivery of 143 Lightning Is (British military serials AE978/999 and AF100/220) with the originally specified V-1710-C15 engines, and the remaining 524 aircraft (AF221/AF744) to be Lightning IIs (Model 322-60-04) with turbosupercharged V-1710-F5Ls and -F5Rs boosting guaranteed top speed to 415 mph at 20,000 ft (668 km/h at 6,095 m). Following unsatisfactory testing of the Lightning I at Boscombe Down and a contract dispute with Lockheed, the RAF refused delivery of the type after receiving only three Lightnings. The remaining 140 Lightning Is were completed by Lockheed and taken over by the USAF in December 1941 as P-322s (P for pursuit and 322 for the Lockheed Model designation); twenty retained their V-1710-C15 engines (USAAF designation V-1710-33) with unhanded propellers, and were assigned to operational use in the critical days following United States entry into the war; the remaining 120 P-322s, which also kept their British serials, were fitted with handed engines (V-1710-27 and -29) but, lacking turbosuperchargers, were used as operational trainers with reduced armament (two 0·50-in and two 0·30-in machine-guns). Only one Lightning II (AF221) was completed and, with US national markings and the USAAF designation P-38F-13-LO, was used by Lockheed for testing smoke-laying canisters on racks between the booms and the nacelle, and for air dropping of two torpedoes from the same racks. Twenty-eight other British-ordered aircraft were completed as P-38F-13-LOs for the USAAF, 121 as P-38F-15-LOs, 174 as P-38G-13-LOs and 200 as P-38G-15-LOs.

Ordered as a Lightning I, this aircraft (British serial AF126) was used by the USAAF as an operational trainer under the designation P-322. (*USAF*)

Including the 667 French- and British-ordered aircraft, Lockheed and Vultee produced 10,037 Lightnings which received the following USAAF designations in the P- (Pursuit) and F- (Photographic Reconnaissance) series:

XP-38 (Model 22-64-01): First flown on 27 January, 1939, the prototype (37-457) was powered by 1,150 hp Allison V-1710-11/-15 engines with General Electric B-1 turbosuperchargers and driving inward-rotating three-blade propellers. Armament, not actually installed before the 11 February, 1939, crash, was to have included one 20 mm cannon with 60 rounds and four 0·50-in machine-guns (210 rpg).

YP-38 (Model 122-62-02): Service test batch of thirteen aircraft (39-689/39-701) with 1,150 hp Allison V-1710-27/-29 engines, B-2 turbosuperchargers and driving outward-rotating propellers. The revised powerplant installation, with spur reduction gear instead of the former epicyclic type, resulted in the raising of the engines' thrust-line, the use of twin cooling intakes in place of the XP-38 lip intake, and the adoption of enlarged coolant radiators on both sides of the tail booms. Armament was revised to substitute two 0·30-in machine-guns with 500 rpg for two of the four 0·50-in guns (210 rpg) and a 37 mm cannon (15 rounds) for the 20 mm weapon.

P-38-LO (Model 222-62-02): First production model of which 29 were built (40-744/40-761 and 40-763/40-773). Same powerplants as YP-38 but armament changed to one 37 mm cannon and four 0·50-in machine-guns. Operational items added on this model included armour plate, bullet-proof glass and fluorescent instrument lighting for night flying. The first P-38 (40-744) was later modified to study the effects on flight crews of asymmetric cockpit location. The turbosuperchargers were removed from this modified aircraft, with the unit in the left boom being replaced by a cockpit for a flight surgeon. In 1942, the P-38-LOs were redesignated RP-38s with the R prefix denoting their restricted, non-combat status.

163

The first production P-38 as modified to test the effects of asymmetrical cockpit location on flight crew. (*USAF*)

XP-38A-LO (Model 622-62-10): A change order to the initial production contract provided for the completion of one P-38-LO (40-762) as a prototype with a pressurized cockpit. To partly offset the added weight of the cockpit, the 37 mm cannon was to have been replaced by a 20 mm weapon but no armament was actually fitted to this experimental aircraft. Design work on the XP-38A was done under the direction of project engineer M. Carl Haddon and provided useful experience later incorporated in the XP-49 design. Manufacturer's trials were done by Joe Towle between May and December 1942 and the XP-38A was accepted by the USAAF at the end of that year. The engines were the V-1710-27 and -29.

P-38B and P-38C: Designations reserved for two versions proposed by Lockheed in November and October 1939, respectively, but not proceeded with.

P-38D-LO (Model 222-62-08): Thirty-six P-38Ds (40-774/40-809) with V-1710-27/-29 engines differed from the P-38-LOs in having a low-pressure oxygen system, bullet-proof fuel tanks and retractable landing light. Normal fuel capacity remained 210 US gal (795 litres) but maximum internal fuel capacity was reduced from 410 to 300 gal (1,552 to 1,136 litres). Later redesignated RP-38Ds as combat trainers.

P-38E-LO (Model 222-62-09): The first major production version—with 210 P-38Es (see Appendix B for listing of serials) being produced—had the 37 mm cannon with its 15-round magazine replaced by a 20 mm cannon with 150 rounds. The P-38Es also had improved instrumentation and revised hydraulic and electrical systems. Not yet considered combat-ready, most P-38Es were redesignated RP-38Es while others were used for a variety of tests. Among the latter was 41-1983 in which were tested several features of the P-38J and P-38K (notably the revised powerplant installation with beard radiators). Some P-38Es were later modified by Lockheed to carry drop tanks as developed for the P-38F-1-LO and subsequent models.

Of greater interest were the modifications made in the spring of 1942 to 41-1986 in support of a projected twin-float version. This seaplane development, which would have retained its retractable undercarriage, was to be fitted with two large floats attached to the centre section. So equipped, this model could have been ferried more easily to combat units in the Pacific islands but it was intended that

164

the floats would be removed before combat operation from forward air bases. The scheme, however, necessitated finding a way to keep the tailplane free of spray. Accordingly, 41-1986 was first fitted with lengthened tail booms, its fins and rudders were recontoured and the tailplane raised 16 inches (40·6 cm). Later, the booms were returned to their normal length, the vertical surfaces were redesigned, the tailplane was raised 33 inches (83·8 cm) above its normal position, and an engineer/observer's seat installed aft of the pilot in the place of some of the radio equipment. Thus, this aircraft became during the summer of 1942 the first of many two-seat conversions. With either type of revised tail surfaces, 41-1986 was only flown as a landplane. The proposed twin-float revision was never tested, as by the end of 1942 the US Navy could provide adequate shipping for aircraft and materiel sent to the Southwest Pacific Area.

The P-38E (41-1986) used to test modified tail surfaces for the proposed twin-float version of the Lightning. (*Lockheed*)

Also of interest was the modification of 41-2048 which was converted in 1942 as a two-seater with elongated central nacelle extending aft of the wing trailing-edge. Intended as a research vehicle to find ways of reducing drag, this aircraft was the only P-38 to have a full dual set of flight controls. Later in the war, this experimental aircraft was fitted with enlarged laminar-flow wing sections—with slots and boundary layer control by means of exhaust bleed air—just outboard of the booms.

An unidentified P-38E was used in 1942 at Orlando to demonstrate the feasibility of towing a Waco CG-4A glider, and a proposal was made to modify Lightnings for towing 'trains' of up to three of these troop-carrying gliders.

P-38F-LO Series: The first combat-ready version of the Lightning included 377 US-ordered aircraft and 150 originally ordered under French and British contracts. All were powered by 1,325 hp V-1710-49/-53 engines and carried the same forward-firing armament as the P-38Es, but a series of changes led to five different batches. The 149 P-38F-1-LOs (Model 222-60-15) differed from the initial batch of 128 P-38F-LOs (222-60-09) in being modified after delivery to carry under the wing centre-sections either two 155/165-US gallon (568/625-litre) drop tanks or two 1,000 lb (454 kg) bombs, whereas one hundred P-38F-5-LOs (222-60-12) were

165

Seen over the snow-covered Sierra Nevada, this P-38F-1-LO was one of the Lightnings used in developing drop tanks in preparation for Operation Bolero, to ferry combat-ready P-38s across the North Atlantic. (*USAF*)

built from the onset with provision for drop tanks. The latter also featured revised landing-lights, desert equipment, identification lights and other minor improvements. The twenty-nine P-38F-13-LOs and 121 P-38F-15-LOs were ex-British aircraft and were Model 322-60-19s; the P-38F-15-LOs differed from the former in being fitted with manoeuvring flaps incorporating an 8 deg setting to tighten turning radius.

P-38G-LO Series: In a similar manner, the six blocks of P-38Gs with 1,325 hp V-1710-51/-55 engines included 708 US-ordered Model 222-68-12s of which 80 were P-38G-1-LOs generally similar to the P-38F-15-LOs, but with the new engines, improved oxygen equipment and more reliable radio; twelve were P-38G-3-LOs with B-13 turbosuperchargers; 68 were P-38G-5-LOs with revised instrumentation; and 548 P-38G-10-LOs combining the improvements introduced in the two previous blocks with winterization equipment, provision for

A P-38G in overload condition with two 165-US gal drop tanks and four triple-cluster rocket launchers. (*Lockheed*)

166

carrying 1,600 lb (726 kg) bombs beneath the wing centre-section, or a triple cluster of 4·5-in (11·4-cm) rocket launchers on each side of the central nacelle. The 374 Model 322-68-19s (174 P-38G-13-LOs, equivalent to the P-38G-3-LOs, and 200 P-38G-15-LOs, corresponding to the P-38G-5-LOs) came from the British contract for Lightning IIs. One P-38G-5-LO (42-12866) was used as a testbed for the proposed XP-49 armament (two 20 mm cannon and four 0·50-in guns). The USAAF also undertook at Wright Field preliminary design for a proposed derivative of the P-38G which was to have carried a 75 mm cannon in a revised and enlarged central nacelle, but the concept did not reach the hardware stage.

P-38H-LO (Model 222-81-20): The 226 P-38H-1-LOs were powered by 1,425 hp Allison V-1710-89/-91 engines and fitted with automatic oil radiator flaps to solve a chronic engine overheating problem and enable military power above 25,000 ft (7,620 m) to be increased from 1,150 to 1,240 hp. In other respects this model was identical to the P-38G-10-LO, but the 375 P-38H-5-LOs were fitted with B-33 instead of B-13 turbosuperchargers.

P-38J-LO Series: With this version Lockheed switched to producing aircraft with revised powerplant installation—with the intercooler air-intake being sandwiched between the oil radiator intakes in a deeper lower nose—as initially tested on a modified P-38E (41-1983). The P-38J also had redesigned Prestone coolant scoops on the tail booms. All P-38Js retained the V-1710-89/-91s of the P-38Hs but their more efficient installation enabled military rating at 27,000 ft (8,230 m) to be

Droop Snoot P-38J-15-LO in India on 8 April, 1945. There is a bombardier station in place of the forward-firing guns and three additional aerials beneath the port boom. (*Peter M. Bowers*)

increased from 1,240 to 1,425 hp while at that altitude war emergency rating was 1,600 hp. The 1,010 Model 422-81-14s included ten service test P-38J-1-LOs, 210 P-38J-5-LOs with two 55-US gallon (208-litre) additional tanks in the space previously occupied by the intercoolers and thus restoring maximum internal fuel capacity to 410 gal (1,552 litres), and 790 P-38J-10-LOs with flat windshields. They were followed by Model 422-81-22s in two blocks: 1,400 P-38J-15-LOs with revised electrical system, and 350 P-38J-20-LOs with modified turbo regulators. Finally, 210 P-38J-25-LOs (422-81-23) were fitted with power-boosted ailerons and electrically-operated dive-flaps beneath the wing outer panels. With the increased use of the Lightning as a light bomber, the type was modified to carry in place of the forward-firing armament either a bombardier with a Norden sight in a glazed nose enclosure, or a 'Mickey' B.T.O.* bombing radar in the nose with operator station between the radar and the pilot's cockpit. These installations were developed at the Lockheed Modification Center in Dallas. A few surviving aircraft became F-38Js in 1948. Two P-38J-20-LOs (44-23544 and 44-23549) were modified in Australia during autumn 1944 as single-seat night fighters, with AN/APS-4 radar in a pod beneath the starboard wing, and were tested in New Guinea and the Philippines. Similarly, a P-38J-5-LO (42-67104) was tested at Wright Field and Orlando, Florida, as an experimental night fighter with a radar operator on a jump seat, aft of the pilot. In this example the AN/APS-4 radar was initially installed under the fuselage in a pod aft of the nosewheel. It proved to be easily damaged by stones thrown up by the nosewheel and was repositioned in a pod beneath the starboard wing but this resulted in interference from the adjacent engine nacelle. This experience led to adoption of a nose pod for the P-38M version.

TP-38J-LO: Unofficial designation given to a number of P-38Js modified in service as two-seat 'piggy-back' trainers with jump seat aft of the pilot. Some of these aircraft carried an AN/APS-4 radar pod beneath the starboard wing and were used to train P-38M crews.

P-38K-LO (Model 422-85-14): This prototype (42-13558) combined a P-38G-10-LO airframe with 1,425 hp V-1710-75/-77 engines in nacelles similar to those of the P-38Js, and driving broader-chord propellers.

P-38L-LO (Model 422-87-23): The final production version of the Lightning was delivered by Lockheed in two blocks and was powered by 1,475 hp Allison V-1710-111/-113 engines with war emergency rating of 1,600 hp at 28,700 ft (8,750 m) and military rating of 1,475 hp at 30,000 ft (9,145 m). Except for their new engines, the 1,290 P-38L-1-LOs were similar to the P-38J-25-LOs; some were modified by the USAAF as two-seat familiarization trainers and were designated TP-38L-1-LOs. The 2,520 P-38L-5-LOs had submerged fuel pumps and, after the unsatisfactory testing of fourteen 5-in HVAR on zero-length launchers beneath

*Bombing Through Overcast.

P-38L-1-LO 44-23856 of a training group from the US Fourth Air Force, with its starboard propeller feathered, demonstrates one of the Lightning's attributes. (*USAF*)

the wing outer panels, underwing rocket 'trees' for ten 5-in projectiles. The racks beneath the wing centre-sections were strengthened to enable the routine use of either 2,000 lb (908 kg) bombs or 300-US gal (1,136-litre) drop tanks. Like the P-38Js, the last Lightning production model could be fitted with either a glazed bombardier station or bombing radar in the nose. The small number of aircraft remaining in USAF service in 1948 became F-38Ls.

P-38L-5-VN: Improvements progressively incorporated by Lockheed into the Lightning had resulted by 1944 in a most capable combat aircraft for which the USAAF had a pressing need. Accordingly, Lockheed's production capability was to be supplemented by that of the Consolidated-Vultee Aircraft Corporation in Nashville, Tennessee, and in June 1944 this company was awarded a contract to manufacture 2,000 P-38L-5-VNs similar to Lockheed's last production variant. Delay in getting the new assembly line started resulted in only 113 P-38L-5-VNs being completed by August 1945 and, shortly after VJ-Day, the remaining 1,887 aircraft were cancelled. A similar fate befell 1,380 P-38L-5-LOs then on order from Lockheed.

P-38M: Early in 1943 at least two unidentified P-38Fs were modified by the Fifth Air Force as single-seat night fighters by fitting an SCR540 radar with yagi antennae on the nose, on both sides of the central nacelle, and above and below

P-38M Night Lightning modified from a P-38L-5-LO (44-27234, c/n 422-8238). Note radome under the nose and launching racks for HVAR rockets beneath the wing. (*Lockheed*)

the wings. To make room for this, two of the 0·50-in guns and their ammunition boxes had to be moved forward. Three P-38Js were also modified in the field as experimental night fighters. Finally, in 1944 Lockheed undertook to convert a P-38L-5-LO (44-25237) as a prototype night fighter. Retaining its natural metal finish, the P-38M test aircraft was a two-seater, with the radar operator sitting aft of the pilot under a raised section of the canopy. The aircraft was fitted with AN/APS-6 radar in an external radome beneath the nose, relocated radio equipment and anti-flash gun muzzles. The success of this modification—which provided the USAAF with a night fighter having a top speed of 406 mph at 15,000 ft (653 km/h at 4,570 m) versus only 369 mph at 20,000 ft (594 km/h at 6,095 m) for its Northrop P-61A—led to a contract change calling for the Lockheed Modification Center in Dallas to convert 75 additional P-38L-5-LOs into P-38Ms. Painted glossy black overall, the P-38Ms were just entering service when the war ended.

RP-38, RP-38D, RP-38E: The three initial Lightning versions, which were not fit for assignment to combat units, had their designations prefixed in 1942 by the letter R for Restricted.

P-322/RP-322: USAAF designation for the French and British-ordered Lightning Is it took over in December 1941.

F-4-1-LO (Model 222-62-13): Ordered as P-38Es, but completed by Lockheed as unarmed photographic-reconnaissance aircraft, the ninety-nine F-4-1-LOs were powered by 1,150 hp V-1710-21/-29 engines and carried four K-17 cameras in a modified nose. In service these aircraft carried a pair of 150/165-US gal (568/625-litre) drop tanks. Most were retained for training and their restricted use status was reflected by their redesignation as RF-4-1-LOs.

F-4A-1-LO (Model 222-60-13): Twenty P-38F-1-LO airframes with 1,325 hp V-1710-49/-53 engines were completed by Lockheed to a standard similar to that of the F-4-1-LOs with four K-17 cameras.

F-5A-LO Series: With the exception of the single F-5A-2-LO (Model 222-62-16) modified from a P-38E (41-2157) with V-1710-21/-29 engines, all F-5As (Model 222-68-16) had P-38G airframes and 1,325 hp V-1710-51/-55 engines. Twenty F-5A-1-LOs, twenty F-5A-3-LOs and one hundred and forty F-5A-10-LOs had the same modifications as P-38G variants with corresponding block numbers. All were unarmed and carried five cameras instead of four as in the F-4/F-4As.

F-5B-1-LO (Model 422-81-21): Photographic-reconnaissance version built by Lockheed with camera installation as on F-5A-10-LO but with airframe and engines (V-1710-89/-91) identical to those of the P-38J-5-LO. A Sperry automatic pilot was standard on the F-5Bs and subsequent versions. The two hundred built brought Lockheed production of the reconnaissance aircraft to an end. All subsequent F-5 versions were modified after delivery from P-38 airframes.

F-5C-1-LO: P-38J airframes converted at the Dallas Modification Center to a standard basically similar to that of the F-5B-1-LO but with improved camera installations. A total of 123 aircraft is believed to have been so modified.

XF-5D-LO: One F-5A-10 (42-12975) modified as an experimental two-seat reconnaissance aircraft. Camera operator located in a glazed nose compartment with two forward-firing 0·50-in machine-guns. Three K-17 cameras were installed, one beneath the nose and one in each tail boom.

An F-5B-1-LO of the 28th Photographic Reconnaissance Squadron, Seventh Air Force, on Wontan Airstrip, Okinawa, on 10 July, 1945. (*USAF*)

F-5E-2-LO: A total of one hundred P-38J-15-LOs were modified in Dallas to a standard similar to that of the F-5C-1-LO.

F-5E-3-LO: Similar conversion of one hundred and five P-38J-25-LO airframes.

F-5E-4-LO: A total of five hundred P-38L-1-LO airframes converted to comparable standard. One K-17 trimetrogon camera could be substituted for one of the four K-17 or K-18 cameras normally fitted.

F-5F-LO: One F-5B-1-LO (42-68220) modified with revised camera installation.

F-5F-3-LO: Photographic-reconnaissance version combining P-38L-5-LO airframes and engines with F-5F camera installation.

F-5G-6-LO: Last photographic-reconnaissance version of the Lightning modified in Dallas from P-38L-5-LO airframes. Revised nose contours to provide more space for photographic equipment and a wider selection of cameras.

FO-1: Designation given by the US Navy to four F-5Bs obtained by that Service in North Africa. They were assigned the BuNos 01209/01212.

In addition to the Lightning versions described above—and for which the Modified Model Numbers 22, 122, 222, 322, 422 and 622 were assigned by Lockheed—the company proposed the Model 522, which was developed into the XP-49 as described separately, the Model 722—which would have resulted in a standardized version of the Models 222, 322 and 622 with either V-1710-49/-53s or V-1710-51/-55s—and the Model 822. The Model 822 was to have been a carrier-based aircraft, with folding wings and arrester hooks, and combining a suitably strengthened P-38H airframe with V-1710-89/-91 engines. The Navy, however showed little interest in this comparatively large aircraft, requiring excessive deck space and powered by liquid-cooled engines.

Having conducted service testing of the YP-38 in the late spring of 1941, the 1st Pursuit Group at Selfridge Field, Michigan, was selected to become the first unit to receive P-38s and P-38Ds. Within weeks of receiving its early Lightnings, which were not yet fitted with their cannon, the 1st PG participated with some success in the Louisiana manoeuvre of September 1941 and in the process quickly built up experience on the type. Thus, two days after Pearl Harbor had been attacked, the unit moved to NAS San Diego and joined the March Field based 14th Pursuit Group, then converting to P-38D/P-38Es. Although their aircraft were not yet combat ready, these two groups had on strength the only truly modern fighters then available to the USAAF and bolstered the West Coast defence at a time when Japanese attacks were thought likely. Even though the measures to contain this threat initially received priority, the USAAF began in the spring of 1942 planning the deployment of Lightning-equipped groups to Britain.

This contemplated deployment created a serious logistic problem as by then U-boats had made shipping across the Atlantic extremely risky. However, development by Lockheed of reliable drop tanks, increasing the ferry range of P-38F-1-LOs from 1,300 to 2,200 miles (2,090 to 3,540 km)—test pilot Milo Burcham even demonstrated a maximum range of over 3,100 miles (5,000 km)—made it possible to plan the ferrying of Lightnings from Maine to the United Kingdom, via Goose Bay (Labrador), Bluie West One (Greenland), Reykjavik (Iceland) and Prestwick (Scotland). Thus, after the US Navy had defeated the Japanese Navy in the Battle of Midway during the first week of June 1942, the USAAF was ready to proceed with the deployment to the United Kingdom of its 1st and 14th Fighter (redesignated from Pursuit in May 1942) Groups. By early

A P-38-LO from the 94th Pursuit Squadron which was based at Selfridge Field, Michigan, when in 1941 as a component of the 1st Pursuit Group it became the first unit to fly Lightnings. It has metal fairings in place of nose guns. (*USAF*)

August 1942, eighty-one P-38Fs of four of the six squadrons of the 1st and 14th FGs had arrived in Great Britain to complete the first transatlantic crossing by single-seat fighters. Two other Lightning squadrons, the 27th and 50th, were temporarily held in Iceland to assist the Curtiss P-40Cs of the 33rd Fighter Squadron assigned to the Iceland Base Command and flying defensive patrols over the Atlantic. One of these P-38Fs, flown by 2nd Lieut Elza Shaham of the 27th FS, shared with a P-40C the destruction of an Fw 200C-3 to obtain on 14 August, 1942, the USAAF's first victory against the Luftwaffe.

After flying 347 practice and sweep sorties during which there was no contact with the Luftwaffe, the 1st and 14th Fighter Groups along with the similarly-equipped 82nd FG which had arrived in Northern Ireland in November 1942,

A flight of P-38L-5-LOs from a training unit of the Fourth Air Force based in the western United States. (*USAF*)

172

were transferred from the UK-based Eighth Air Force to the Twelfth Air Force in North Africa. Flying their aircraft from Britain to Algeria, with pilots of the 82nd FG being credited with the destruction of two Ju 88s whilst in transit over the Bay of Biscay, the three Lightning groups were soon flying regular combat sorties, with the first being flown on 19 November, 1942, when the 1st FG escorted B-17s on a bombing raid to El Aouina airfield at Tunis. During the North African campaign, which ended on 13 May, 1943, with the surrender of the Axis forces in the area, the three P-38 groups had done much in establishing local air superiority and causing havoc to the enemy airlift. Notably, on 5 April twenty-six P-38Fs of the 82nd FG claimed the destruction of 31 enemy aircraft for the loss of only six Lightnings. Already, prior to the Axis defeat in Tunisia, the Northwest African Air Forces, of which the Twelfth Air Force was a component, had begun softening-up Sicily. This action, along with attacks against the islands of Pantelleria and Lampedusa, was soon stepped up in preparation for Operation Husky—the invasion of Sicily on 10 July, 1943—and the Lightnings continued to be in the midst of the fray until Sicily fell on 17 August. The three P-38 Fighter Groups then concentrated their efforts against the Italian mainland but, on 1 November, 1943, they were transferred to the Fifteenth Air Force. By that time they counted 37 aces including the top scoring Twelfth Air Force pilot, Lieut W. J. Sloan of the 82nd FG with twelve victories, and Lieut H. T. Hanna of the 14th FG who had become an ace-in-a-day by destroying five Ju 87s on 9 October, 1943.

A P-38J-15-LO from the 27th Fighter Squadron, 1st Fighter Group, Fifteenth Air Force. (*USAF*)

Following their transfer, the 1st, 14th and 82nd Fighter Groups concentrated on escorting B-17s and B-24s of the Fifteenth Air Force to targets in Austria, the Balkans, France, Greece and Italy; on occasions, however, they also continued escorting medium bombers of the Twelfth Air Force. Beginning in February 1944, the P-38s began flying with bombers attacking aircraft factories in southern Germany, while in April of that year they escorted the bombers to the oil refinery at Ploesti in Rumania, a target which became the Lightnings' own when on 10 June, 1944, forty-six aircraft of the 82nd FG, each carrying a 1,000 lb (454 kg) bomb, attacked the Romano Americana Oil Refinery under the protective umbrella of forty-eight P-38s of the 1st Fighter Group. Good bombing and strafing results were obtained, but, in the ensuing encounter with the Luftwaffe, twenty-two P-38s were lost while claiming 23 enemy aircraft. Six weeks later the 82nd FG flew the first P-38 shuttle mission to Russia and returned to their Italian base on 25 July after three days at a Soviet base in the Ukraine; together with their

P-51 escort they had shot down thirty German aircraft and destroyed twelve more on the ground. The Lightnings' last shuttle mission was flown on 4/6 August and was marked by the daring rescue of a downed pilot by Lieut R. J. Andrews who landed his Lightning in an open field to pick up Capt R. E. Willsie. The three Lightning groups also took part in August 1944 in the Allied landing in southern France for which the 1st and 14th FGs temporarily operated from Corsica. The P-38s then returned to providing fighter escort for bombers operating against strategic targets until VE-day, and at war's end they counted twenty-eight aces among their pilots. In the North African and MTO campaigns, Lightnings had equipped three of the fifteen Fighter Groups of the Twelfth and Fifteenth Air Forces but in the autumn of 1945 these Groups were inactivated.

The departure of the 1st and 14th Fighter Groups for North Africa in November 1942 left the Eighth Air Force without P-38s until September 1943 when the 55th FG arrived at Nuthampstead in Hertfordshire. Flying P-38Hs, this unit began combat operations on 15 October, 1943, and drew blood for the first time on 3 November. The following month it converted to P-38Js and with these the 55th flew on 3 March, 1944, to Berlin, thus giving the Lightning the distinction of being the first type of fighter to fly the 1,300-mile (2,100-km) round trip to the German capital. Other Lightning units with the Eighth Air Force were the 20th, 364th and 479th FGs which respectively became operational in December 1943, March 1944 and May 1944. Two significant new uses of the Lightning were pioneered in April 1944 when the 20th FG began low-level fighter sweeps and the 55th FG first used the Droop Snoot P-38J with bombardier station to act as leader for other Lightnings bombing the Coulommiers airfield from an altitude of 20,000 ft (6,095 m). Both types of operation proved most successful and were later extensively used by P-38 units of the Ninth Air Force. With the Eighth Air Force however, the P-38s were already on their way out as the 20th, 55th and 364th FGs converted to North American P-51 Mustangs during July 1944; two months later the 479th Fighter Group also exchanged its P-38Js for P-51Ds.

With the Ninth Air Force, which was assigned a tactical role as opposed to the strategic mission of the Eighth Air Force, P-38J/P-38Ls had only a slightly longer service life. Its first Lightning group was the 474th which flew its first war mission on 25 April, 1944. This unit was almost immediately joined by the 367th and 370th FGs but during March 1945 these two groups converted to P-47Ds and P-51Ds respectively. Thus by VE-Day the 474th was the only P-38-equipped Fighter Group operating among sixteen Mustang-equipped and fifteen Thunderbolt-equipped groups. Even though by then the Lightning had been overshadowed in this theatre of operations by other types of fighters, it was still playing a major role as a reconnaissance aircraft at the time of the German surrender.

In the war against Japan the honour of being the first Lightnings to be deployed from the 48 contiguous states went to a small number of P-38Ds and P-38Es which were rushed to Fairbanks and Anchorage for service with the Alaska Defense Command. However, these aircraft were not considered combat ready. As soon as feasible they were replaced by P-38Es of the 54th Fighter Squadron which were modified by Lockheed to a standard approaching that of the P-38F-1-LO and could carry two drop tanks. Following the Japanese invasion of Kiska in June 1942, the 54th FS moved with its modified P-38Es to an airstrip at Ft Glenn on Umnak Island in the Aleutians. On 4 August, Lieuts K. Ambrose and S. A. Long from that unit each shot down two four-engined Japanese flying-boats to claim first blood for the Lockheed fighter. Thereafter, while escorting bomber and reconnaissance aircraft operating against Japanese-held Kiska, the Lightnings encountered some opposition from Nakajima A6M2-N floatplane fighters. Soon, however, they gained full control of the air and by July 1943 the Japanese forces had to leave the Aleutians. In this theatre, the initial batch of P-38Es of the 54th FS were soon supplanted by a specially winterized version of the Lightning, the P-38G-10-LO, and later by P-38Js. However, the Eleventh Air Force was never able to receive enough Lightnings fully to equip its 343rd Fighter Group; three of the four squadrons from this unit flew a mix of P-38s and P-40s alongside the P-38 equipped 54th FS. Going on the offensive in 1944, the 343rd FG flew its Lightnings on fighter sweeps and escort sorties to the Kurile Islands until VJ-Day.

Four P-38Js from the 1st Fighter Group, one of the Fifteenth Air Force's three groups which flew Lightnings until the war's end. (*USAF*)

Lightnings never were available in sufficient numbers to equip a full Fighter Group in either the Tenth or Fourteenth Air Forces operating in the China–Burma–India theatre of operations. In India, P-38Hs were first operated by the 459th Fighter Squadron of the 80th FG in September 1943 and this squadron went on to fly P-38J/P-38Ls until the end of the war whereas the three other squadrons in this group flew P-40s and P-47s. Similarly, the 449th FS of the 51st FG flew Lightnings in China while the group's other squadrons had a mix of aircraft. Finally, the 33rd Fighter Group flew a motley assortment of P-38s and P-47s in Burma.

The first batch of twenty-five P-38Fs to reach Australia during 1942 was assigned to the 39th Fighter Squadron of the 35th Fighter Group and this unit converted from Bell Airacobras to Lightnings at Amberley in Queensland before returning to combat operations from Jackson Airfield at Port Moresby in Papua. After more than two months of relatively uneventful operations, the 39th FS had its first major success on 27 December, 1942, when its pilots claimed eleven enemy aircraft for the loss of only one P-38F. Two of these kills were the first for Lieut R. I. Bong who, by then a major, obtained his 40th victory on 17 December, 1944, to become the all-time American top-scorer. Already Maj-Gen Kenney, CO of the Fifth Air Force, was strenuously endeavouring to have the long-range P-38 adopted as his main fighter type. However, the production rate was still insufficient to meet all the USAAF's requirements and the limited number of P-38F/P-38Gs arriving in the Southwest Pacific Area in late 1942 and early 1943 had to be used to make up attrition in the 39th FS and to equip only a single squadron in each of the 8th and 49th Fighter Groups of the Fifth Air Force in New Guinea, and of the 18th and 347th FGs of the Thirteenth Air Force on Guadalcanal. Of exceptional interest among these early Lightnings were two P-38Fs of the 6th Fighter Squadron/18th Fighter group which, equipped with radar as single-seat night fighters, were operated from Cactus Strip, Henderson Field, to curb the activities of 'Bedcheck Charlie', the Japanese raider flying nuisance sorties over Guadalcanal. Two P-38J-20-LO single-seat night fighters, each fitted at Townsville with AN/APS-4 radar in a pod beneath the starboard wing, were also operated in the winter of 1944-45 by the 547th Night Fighter Squadron. One, operating from Tacloban, Leyte, was in successful combat on 9 January, 1945.

Combining performance markedly superior to that of contemporary Japanese aircraft with the added safety factor inherent in operating twin-engined aircraft over long stretches of water and forbidding jungle, and possessing a range significantly better than that of the P-39s, P-40s and P-47s available in 1943 in the SWPA, the P-38 was ideally suited to operations in this theatre. Its only drawback was its manoeuvrability which, although outstanding in view of its size and twin-engined configuration, was inferior to that of the exceptionally nimble Japanese fighters. However, the use of appropriate tactics—notably the avoidance of dogfighting at low speed and the reliance on fast diving attacks—enabled the few fortunate P-38 squadrons in New Guinea and the Solomons to achieve impressive results, thus confirming General Kenney's enthusiasm for the Lightning. Likewise, successive commanders of the Thirteenth Air Force in 1943–44 (Generals Twinning, Owens and Harmon), who were responsible for operations in the Solomons where the P-38's range was a major asset, kept pressing the AAF Headquarters for more Lightnings. Unfortunately, because lower priority had been given to operations in the Pacific once the Japanese onslaught had been checked and only some 2,300 P-38s had been accepted by the AAF up to June 1943, requests from the Fifth and Thirteenth Air Forces remained mostly unheeded for many months.

In spite of the small number of P-38s available in the southwest Pacific, the Lockheed fighter had a significant impact on operations against Japanese forces, not only in countless routine escort and sweep sorties but also in the course of a well-planned and perfectly-executed mission on 18 April, 1943. After US Navy cryptographers had ascertained that on that date Admiral Isoroku Yamamoto, the C-in-C of the Rengo Kantai (Combined Fleet), the spearhead of the Japanese Navy, would be flown to Ballale airfield on Shortland Island, the Thirteenth Air

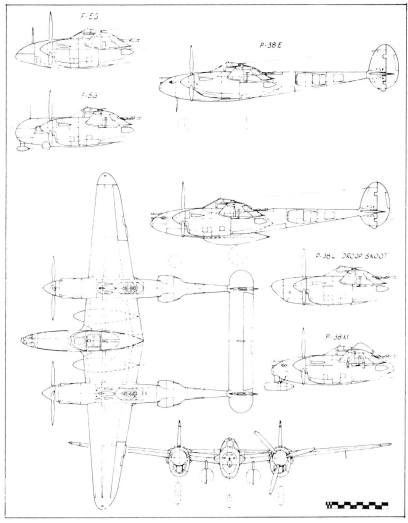

Lockheed P-38J Lightning, with side view of P-38E. Upper left: F-5B and F-5G; right: P-38L 'Droop Snoot' and P-38M

Force was ordered to attempt to intercept Yamamoto's aircraft. Accordingly, sixteen P-38F/P-38Gs from the 18th and 347th FGs — led by Maj John Mitchell and carrying an asymmetrical mix of 165- and 310-gallon drop tanks — flew 500 miles (800 km) from Henderson Field, Guadalcanal, to Shortland Island, and reached their target on schedule. Two bomber-transports and at least five Japanese fighters were shot down by the Lightnings at the cost of one P-38, and Capt Thomas Lanphier Jr was credited with downing the aircraft in which Admiral Yamamoto had been flying.

177

P-38Fs from the 39th Fighter Squadron, 35th Fighter Group, Fifth Air Force, at Jackson Airfield, Port Moresby, in late 1942. (*Australian War Memorial*)

In August 1943, the first all-Lightning Fighter Group of the Fifth Air Force, the 475th, began combat operations. However, later in the year, continuing shortage of P-38s forced both the 35th and 49th FGs to convert their single P-38 squadron to P-47Ds, thus leaving the Fifth Air Force at the end of 1943 with only four P-38 squadrons versus eight squadrons with P-47s and three with P-40s (at that time the Eighth Air Force in England had six squadrons of P-38s, and twenty-seven P-47 squadrons). By the summer of 1944 when, in preparation for the American return to the Philippines, the Fifth and Thirteenth Air Forces had been reorganized into the Far East Air Forces under General Kenney, the supply situation had somewhat improved and Kenney's new command could field five groups fully equipped with P-38s (the 8th, 18th, 49th, 347th and 475th). The last of these groups, in particular, achieved much fame as it counted among its personnel the three top-scoring aces (the previously mentioned Majors Bong and McGuire, and Col C. H. MacDonald with 27 kills) as well as, at war's end, no fewer than 38 other pilots who had reached ace status while flying exclusively P-38s. Charles Lindbergh was then in the Pacific as a technical representative for United Aircraft Corporation, and he flew a number of combat missions with the 475th FG in June/August 1944 as a civilian to instruct pilots on improving their cruise control technique. In the process, Lindbergh not only succeeded in enabling pilots to get increased range and endurance from their P-38Js but, on 28 July, shot down a Japanese Mitsubishi Ki-51 over Elpaputih Bay, off Ceram Island in the Netherlands East Indies.

By the time war ended, when P-38s were flying from bases on Ie Shima and in the Philippines on far-ranging sorties to Formosa, Korea and the Ryukyus, they were credited with the destruction of more Japanese aircraft than any other type of US fighter. Fittingly, a Lightning was the first type of Allied aircraft to land in Japan after that nation had surrendered on 15 August, 1945.

More than one in eight Lightnings were either completed by Lockheed as photographic-reconnaissance aircraft or were so modified after delivery, with cameras replacing the forward-firing armament of the P-38s. Thus, in view of the large number of aircraft involved (over 1,400 F-4s and F-5s were accepted by the USAAF whereas this Service received less than 500 F-6s, the reconnaissance version of the more numerous North American P-51 Mustang), photographic-reconnaissance Lightnings saw widespread service throughout the war. In North Africa, F-4s were first flown in combat beginning, respectively, in November and December 1942, by the 5th and 12th Photographic Reconnaissance Squadrons. Later these two units and the two other squadrons of the 3rd PRG operated various models of the F-5. In the same theatre, in 1943, the 154th Reconnaissance Squadron obtained its own camera-equipped Lightnings when its maintenance personnel modified in the field a number of P-38Fs. Also equipped with F-5s and, initially, assigned to the Twelfth Air Force, the 5th PRG became operational in September 1943 but was transferred to the Fifteenth Air Force thirteen months later. In the European theatre where the 3rd PRG had been briefly based before transfer to North Africa, the first operational sorties were flown by F-4As of the 7th PRG on 28 March, 1943. This group successively operated F-4As, F-5As, F-5Bs, F-5Cs and, finally, during the last year of the war, F-5Es. Operating initially from bases in England but later moving to the Continent, the Ninth Air Force had four PRS (30th, 31st, 33rd and 34th) which flew various versions of the F-5 from the spring of 1944 until the end of the war. Reconnaissance Lightnings were also flown in the war against Japan, with F-4s being initially operated in the summer of 1942 by the 28th Composite Group in Alaska, the 8th PRS in New Guinea, and the 9th PRS in India. In all these theatres, the F-4/F-5s usually flew alone without fighter escort and in spite of heavy losses, especially when facing radar-controlled Luftwaffe fighters, they proved of unequalled value.

With the exception of fifteen P-38J/P-38L fighters delivered to China late in the war and later supplemented by a similar number of F-5Es and F-5Gs, the only Lightnings handed to the Allies during the Second World War were photo-graphic-reconnaissance aircraft. The RAAF received three F-4-1-LOs in August/September 1942 and assigned them to its No.1 Photographic Reconnaissance Unit. Two of these aircraft (A55-1 and A55-3) were written off in landing accidents, while A55-2 was returned to the USAAF three-and-a-half months after it had entered Australian service. The Forces Aériennes Francaises Libres were the only other wartime recipient of Lightnings, with six F-4s being assigned for conversion training to Groupe de Reconnaissance II/33 at Oujda, Morocco, in April 1943. Re-equipped with F-5s and operating as an attached squadron with the 3rd Photographic Reconnaissance Group of the Twelfth Air Force, USAAF, the Free French unit counted among its pilots Commandant Antoine de Saint-

An F-5E from the 8th PRS, 6th PRG, Fifth Air Force. (*USAF*)

Seen taking off on 17 May, 1945, from Lingayen Airstrip, Luzon, this reconnaissance Lightning was assigned to the 26th PRS, 6th PRG. (*USAF*)

Exupéry, the noted author and pioneer pilot. Tragically, Saint-Exupéry was lost off southern France on 31 July, 1944, while on a combat sortie from Bastia, Corsica. Redesignated GR I/33 'Belfort' on 1 January, 1945, this unit continued flying Lightnings (F-5A/F-5B/F-5F/F-5G) after the war from Lahr in Germany, and Cognac in France, until 1952 when it was re-equipped with specially modified Republic F-84G Thunderjets.

During the war two other air forces operated P-38s on a limited basis. After two P-38s of the 1st Fighter Group, USAAF, had been forced to land at Lisbon while

An F-5A-LO of Groupe de Reconnaissance II/33 during wartime operations. (*ECPA*)

180

on their ferry flight from England to Algeria, the Portuguese Government obtained American approval to retain them. Assigned the Portuguese serials 300 and 301, the two P-38Fs served with Esquadrilha OK at Base Aérea 2, Ota. Similarly, but obviously in this case without the accord of the US Government, the Regia Aeronautica obtained a P-38G when it landed at Capoterra, Sardinia, on 12 July, 1943, due to compass problems during a Gibraltar–Malta flight. Repainted in Italian markings, this aircraft was flown to the experimental centre at Guidonia for evaluation. From there it was flown on 11 August, 1943, by Col Angelo Tondi to intercept USAAF bombers, and Tondi probably shot down a Consolidated B-24D. Shortly after, however, the Italian P-38G had to be grounded because of lack of parts and corrosion of its fuel tanks. Six years later, after Italy had become a NATO member, the Aeronautica Militare Italiana

NX5101N, Glenn H. McCarthy's *Flying Shamrock*, a surplus P-38G, with standard drop tanks between the centre nacelle and the engine/tail booms, and with additional tanks carried à la P-80 beneath the wingtips. (*Lockhead*)

received fifty Lightnings (P-38Js, P-38Ls, and F-5Es) which served with the 3a and 4a Aerobrigate until replaced with jet equipment. The only other foreign military operator of the Lightning was the Fuerza Aérea Hondureña which received a dozen P-38Ls in the late 1940s.

With the USAAF the Lightning hardly survived the end of hostilities and large numbers were scrapped. A few were sold as surplus, some being used for aerial survey and others being flown in postwar National Air Races. A limited number of military machines did manage to find their way into the USAF and in June 1948 were redesignated F-38Js and F-38Ls. This was, however, the swan song of a remarkable warplane and, since the retirement of the last Honduras aircraft, the Lightning has survived only as a museum aircraft and a much valued antique.

Related Temporary Design Designations: L-102, L-111 and L-124

Lockheed Lightning

Dimensions for all versions: span 52 ft (15·85 m); length 37 ft 10 in (11·53 m); height 12 ft 10 in (3·91 m); wing area 328 sq ft (30-472 sq m).

	XP-38	P-38D	P-38H	P-38L	F-5G
Empty weight, lb	11,507	11,780	12,380	12,800	12,800
(kg)	(5,219)	(5,343)	(5,615)	(5,806)	(5,806)
Loaded weight, lb	13,964	14,456	19,500	20,700	18,400
(kg)	(6,334)	(6,557)	(8,845)	(9,389)	(8,346)
Maximum weight, lb	15,416	15,500	20,300	21,600	21,600
(kg)	(6,993)	(7,031)	(9,208)	(9,798)	(9,798)
Wing loading, lb/sq ft	42·6	44·1	59·4	63·1	56·1
(kg/sq m)	(207·9)	(215·2)	(290·3)	(308·1)	(273·9)
Power loading, lb/hp	6·1	6·3	6·8	7	6·2
(kg/hp)	(2·8)	(2·9)	(3·1)	(3·2)	(2·8)
Maximum speed, mph/ft	413/20,000	390/25,000	402/25,000	414/25,000	418/25,000
(km/h / m)	(665/6,095)	(628/7,620)	(647/7,620)	(666/7,620)	(673/7,620)
Cruising speed, mph	—	300	250	290	290
(km/h)	—	(483)	(402)	(467)	(467)
Rate of climb, ft/min	20,000/6·5	20,000/8	20,000/6·5	20,000/7	20,000/6·5
(m/min)	(6,095/6·5)	(6,095/8)	(6,095/6·5)	(6,095/7)	(6,095/6·5)
Service ceiling, ft	38,000	39,000	40,000	44,000	44,500
(m)	(11,580)	(11,885)	(12,190)	(13,410)	(13,565)
Normal range, miles	890	500	350	450	500
(km)	(1,430)	(805)	(565)	(725)	(805)
Maximum range, miles	1,390	975	2,400	2,600	2,600
(km)	(2,235)	(1,570)	(3,860)	(4,185)	(4,185)

The Starliner in its original single-tail configuration. (*Lockheed*)

Vega Starliner

In mid-1935 Lockheed's chief engineer, Hall Hibbard, began discussing with Al Menasco, the president of the Menasco Manufacturing Company in Burbank, the merits of coupling two Menasco six-cylinder inline engines, mounted side by side and driving a single propeller. As this arrangement provided twin-engined reliability in a single-engined configuration, Lockheed decided two years later to use the novel powerplant in an aircraft to be designed by its new subsidiary, the AiRover Company. Moreover, before proceeding with the design, Lockheed asked AiRover to assemble from available components an Altair 8G intended to serve as a flying teststand for the twin Menasco engine. This testbed was first flown in December 1937 and soon confirmed the merits of its powerplant, thus leading to the decision to proceed with the design of a similarly-powered five-seat feeder-liner.

During 1938, by which time the AiRover Company had been reorganized as the Vega Airplane Company, its president, Mac V. F. Short, undertook to design the new feeder-liner. With Jack Wassall as project engineer, the aircraft was built in the new plant A-1 and emerged in the spring of 1939 as a low-wing cabin monoplane with conventional tail surfaces. Its tricycle undercarriage retracted aft, with the wheels partially protruding beneath the nose and wing. The powerplant, known as the Unitwin, consisted of two 260 hp Menasco C6S-4 engines driving a single, two-blade, variable-pitch propeller.

Named the Starliner and bearing the experimental registration NX21725, the first totally new aircraft of the Vega Airplane Company made its maiden flight at Burbank on 22 April, 1939, with Vern Dorrell as pilot and J. B. Kendrick as engineering observer. This first flight, however, ended with an emergency when the propeller accidently slipped into fine pitch. Vern Dorrell succeeded in landing on a vacant field, with minimum damage to the aircraft. Soon repaired, and fitted at that time with twin vertical tail surfaces, the Starliner resumed its trials but was

The Vega Starliner after installation of twin tail surfaces. Note the partially protruding wheels which saved the aircraft from suffering severe damage when its nosewheel failed to lower. (*Oliver R. Philips, via Peter M. Bowers*)

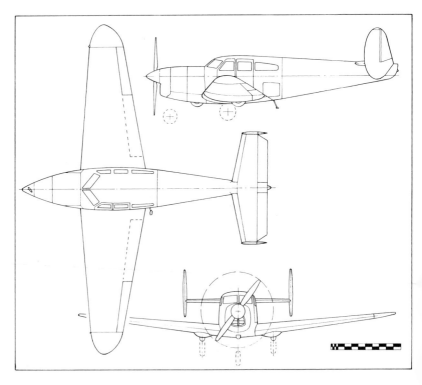

Vega Starliner

damaged again when Bud Martin had to land it on its mainwheels when the nosewheel failed to come down. With the nose protected by the partially protruding front wheel, the aircraft again escaped with only slight damage to its lower cowling. Once more repaired, the Starliner satisfactorily completed a total of 85 flying hours; but its limited capacity, pilot and four or five passengers, was found to be too small to satisfy the needs of the airlines. Moreover, by then Lockheed needed Vega Airplane Corporation's factory for military aircraft production, and development of the Starliner was discontinued. It ended its life as a non-flying machine with a film studio.

Related Temporary Design Designations: V-100/V-103.

Span 41 ft (12·5 m); length 32 ft 5 in (9·88 m); height 8 ft 6 in (2·59 m).
Empty weight 4,190 lb (1,901 kg); loaded weight 6,000 lb (2,722 kg); power loading 11·5 lb/hp (5·2 kg/hp).
Maximum speed 210 mph at 7,500 ft (338 km/h at 2,285 m); cruising speed 178 mph (286 km/h); initial rate of climb 1,350 ft/min (411 m/min) or, on one engine only, 350 ft/min (107 m/min); service ceiling 21,500 ft (6,555 m); range 640 miles (1,030 km).

Lockheed 18 Lodestar

The somewhat disappointing debut of Lockheed's Model 14 in the United States, with Northwest Airlines disposing of its fleet during 1939, together with the high seat-mile cost of this aircraft, forced the company to seek out ways of improving its then largest transport. The redesign work was assigned to a team led by project engineer Jake Cowling and resulted in a length increase of 5 ft 6 in (1·68 m) to increase directional stability and allow two more rows of seats. As calculated performance and, more significantly, operating economics of the modified air-craft were promising, Lockheed decided to suspend production of the Model 14

The first production Model 18 Lodestar (NX25604, c/n 18-2001) with the tailplane in its original position. (*Lockheed*)

185

in favour of the redesigned machine. At that time, even though this was only a minor modification of the Model 14, the aircraft was redesignated Model 18 and named Lodestar to divorce it in the public's mind from the unpopularity of the Super Electra.

As the production switch from Model 14 to Model 18 could not be accomplished immediately, the company decided to modify as a Model 18 prototype the fourth Super Electra (c/n 1404, NC17385) which it had taken back from Northwest. Assigned the c/n 1404A, later 18-1954, and the experimental registration NX17385, the modified aircraft retained the wing, tail surfaces and two 875 hp Pratt & Whitney Hornet S1E-Gs of the Model 14-H. It was first flown on 21 September, 1939, by Marshall Headle and Louis Upshaw, and was soon followed by two other Model 14-H2s (c/ns 1483 and 1486) modified to the same standards as c/ns 18-1956 and 18-1957. The first production Lodestar (c/n 18-2001, NX/NC25604), which like the three modified aircraft had its tailplane in the same position as that of the Super Electra, was first flown on 2 February, 1940. Trials revealed that the Lodestar was prone to 'elevator nibble' which caused its controls to oscillate back and forth while the aircraft was in flight. Initial attempts at curing the problem by splitting the elevators and adding servo tabs failed to have the desired result. Partial improvement was achieved by raising the tailplane by one foot (30·5 cm), with ultimate solution being provided by the addition of a trailing-edge extension to the wing. Together these modifications took the tail surfaces out of the wing turbulence and the Lodestar successfully completed its trial programme to receive its Approved Type Certificate on 30 March, 1940. The type entered service in March 1940 with Mid-Continent Airlines.

In offering the Lodestar to potential customers, Lockheed pursued its policy of providing a wide choice of powerplants. As by then the company had adopted a new system of designation for its aircraft—with basic model number being followed by a hyphenated two-digit suffix indicating the type of engines fitted to a particular aircraft—this resulted in the following variants being offered to civil customers: Model 18-07 with 875 hp Pratt & Whitney Hornet S1E2-Gs; 18-08 and 18-10 with 1,200 hp Pratt & Whitney Twin Wasp S1C3-Gs; 18-14 with 1,200 hp Twin Wasp S4C4-Gs; 18-40 with 1,200 hp Wright Cyclone GR-1820-G104As; 18-50 with 1,200 hp Cyclone GR-1820-G202As; and 18-56, 118-56 and 218-56 with 1,200 hp Cyclone GR-1820-G205As, R-1820-40s or R-1820-87s.

PP-PBK, a Model 18-10 Lodestar of Panair do Brasil. (*Varig*)

186

Model 18-40 (c/n 18-2108) of the Netherlands East Indies Air Force on final approach to the Lockheed Air Terminal, with Fowler flaps extended. (*Peter M. Bowers*)

In airline service these Lodestar variants were normally arranged to carry either fifteen or eighteen passengers, depending on whether or not a cabin attendant and full galleys were provided. Therefore, as the Model 18-07s had the same installed horsepower as the Model 14-Hs, these Lodestars offered substantially lowered seat-mile costs and even came close to matching the operating economics of the Douglas DC-3. Seat-mile costs were further reduced when the Lodestar was fitted with bench-type seats along the cabin walls to carry 26 passengers; at least one of the National Airlines' aircraft was so equipped for the high-density route to Puerto Rico. Nevertheless, as most major American carriers were already committed to DC-3 fleets when the type was certificated in March 1940, it attracted only limited commercial orders in the United States. Deliveries to domestic airlines included two 18-07s to Catalina Air Transport,* two 18-08s and three 18-10s to Continental Airlines, two 18-10s to Dixie, one 18-08 to Inland Air Lines, three 18-07s and one 18-10 to Mid-Continent Airlines, three 18-50s to National Airlines, twelve 18-10s to Pan American Airways and its Panair do Brasil associate, and four 18-10s to United Air Lines. In addition, private and corporate customers in the United States received nine Lodestars during 1940–41 while Pratt & Whitney took delivery in 1943 of a Model 18-10 (c/n 18-2359) which had been ordered by the Chilean airline LAN but was delivered to the engine manufacturer on the instructions of the USAAF.

Fortunately for Lockheed, the Model 18 was far more successful with foreign customers, both airlines and governments. The latter group included the Union of South Africa (one 18-07), the Norwegian government-in-exile (three 18-40s), and the Netherlands East Indies (twenty 18-40s and nine 18-50s). Overseas airlines ordering Lodestars were Air Afrique (five 18-07s), Air France (three 18-07s), BOAC (nine 18-07s), LAV (one 18-10), Navegação Aérea Brasileira (two 18-40s), South African Airways (which, with twenty-nine Model 18-08s, was the

*This was a paper transaction only. They were delivered to the United Kingdom under Lend-Lease.

largest Lodestar customer apart from the US military), TCA (twelve 18-10s) and Yukon Southern Airways (two 18-10s).

As it had already done with the Electra and Electra Junior, the Navy Department placed the first US military orders for the Lodestar when during 1940 it ordered one XR5O-1, two R5O-1s, one R5O-2 and two R5O-3s. During the war the Navy also received 88 Lodestars which were either impressed or diverted from USAAF contracts. By far, however, the Army Air Forces were the main customer as they acquired both impressed aircraft — the C-56 series with Cyclone engines, the C-57 with Twin Wasps, the C-59s with Hornets, and the single Twin Wasp-powered C-66 — as well as the specially-built C-60 series. The following US military designations were given to Lodestars:

XR5O-1: This staff transport ordered for the US Coast Guard was the first Lodestar to be powered by 1,200 hp Wright Cyclones. Assigned the serial V188 on delivery, this Model 18-40 was registered postwar in South Africa and finally in the United States.

R5O-1: Also equivalent to the civil 18-40, the two R5O-1s (BuNos 4249 and 4250) were naval staff transports powered by 1,200 hp Wright R-1820-97s.

R5O-2: The initial order placed by the Navy Department also included one Model 18-07 which was designated R5O-2 (BuNo 7703) and was powered by 850 hp Pratt & Whitney R-1690-25s. In spite of its later Bureau Number, this aircraft preceded the two R5O-1s in service and was delivered to the US Navy during the autumn of 1940.

R5O-3: For use as VIP transports, two R5O-3s (BuNos 01006 and 01007) were delivered with luxurious interiors each with accommodation for four passengers; later a more spartan seating arrangement was installed. Powered by 1,200 hp Pratt & Whitney R-1830-34As, these aircraft corresponded to the civil 18-10 version.

R5O-4: During the war twelve aircraft, which had been laid out as Cyclone-powered Model 18-56s for commercial customers, were impressed before completion and were delivered as seven-seat naval staff transports. Powered by 1,200 hp Wright R-1820-40s, they were assigned the BuNos 05046/05050 and 12447/12453.

R5O-5: Also impressed during construction, the forty-one Lodestars of this model (BuNos 12454/12491 and 30148/30150) were generally similar to the R5O-4s but were fitted as fourteen-seat staff transports.

R5O-6: Produced as eighteen-seat paratroop transports in the midst of a batch of C-60A-5-LOs, 35 aircraft were assigned to the USN/USMC and were completed with the BuNos 39612/39646.

C-56 Series: A total of 36 commercial Lodestars was impressed during 1942–43. Depending upon the types of engines fitted and their accommodation, they were designated as C-56-LO (ex-Model 18-50, 41-19729 with Wright R-1820-89s), C-56A-LO (ex-Model 18-07, 42-38261 with Pratt & Whitney R-1690-54s), C-56B-LO (thirteen ex-Model 18-40s, with R-1820-97s, and serials 42-38262/42-38263 and 42-68347/42-68357), C-56C-LO (twelve ex-Model 18-07s, serials 42-53494/42-53503, 42-57212 and 42-68690), C-56D-LO (seven ex-Model 18-08s with R-1690-25s, and serials 42-53504/42-53507, 42-57223/42-57224 and 42-62602) and C-56E-LO (two Model 18-40s, 43-3278/43-3279, with R-1820-97s).

C-57 Series: Impressed under different contracts, a further twenty Twin Wasp powered Lodestars were designated in this series. They included thirteen C-57-LOs (ex-Model 18-14 with R-1830-53s, and serials 41-19730/41-19732, 41-23164/41-23170 and 43-34921/43-34923) and seven C-57B-LOs (ex-Model 18-08 with

R-1830-53s, and serials 43-3271/43-3277). The designation C-57A-LO was reserved for another variant of impressed Model 18s but was not taken up, while the three C-57C-LOs were ex C-60A-LOs re-engined with 1,200 hp Pratt & Whitney R-1830-43s. One of these aircraft later became the sole C-57D-LO when it was fitted with R-1830-92s.

C-59-LO: Designation given to ten impressed Model 18-07s with Pratt & Whitney R-1690-25s. They were intended for Lend-Lease transfer to the RAF as Lodestar Mk.IAs (British military serials EW973/EW982) but, for contractual purposes, they were given USAAF serials 41-29623/41-29632. The first three C-59-LOs were actually retained by the USAAF

C-60-LO: Thirty-six Model 18-56s were impressed and, powered by 1,200 hp Wright R-1820-87s, were assigned serials 41-29633/41-29647, 42-32166/42-32180 and 42-108787/42-108792. Lend-Lease transfers to the RAF as Lodestar Mk.IIs accounted for the first sixteen machines (EW983/EW997 and FK246) but fourteen additional aircraft, for which serials FK247/FK260 were reserved, were retained by the USAAF as were the last six C-60-LOs. One aircraft (c/n 18-2170, 42-108971) went to TWA as NC33604 to serve as a flight-research laboratory and executive transport.

C-60A Series: Whereas all previous versions of the military Lodestars were inpressed aircraft, the fifty-two C-60A-LOs (42-32181/42-32232), forty-five

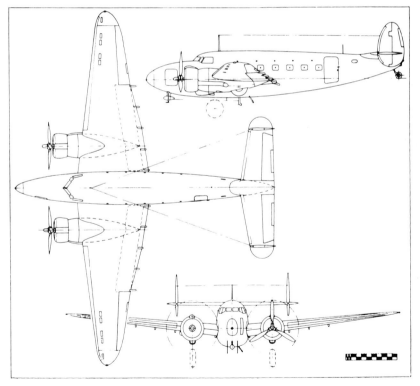

Lockheed C-60A Lodestar

A C-60A-LO of the US Army Air Forces on take-off from Wright Field, Ohio. (*USAF*)

C-60A-1-LOs (42-55845/42-55859 and 42-55861/42-55890) and 227 C-60A-5-LOs (42-55891/42-56084 and 43-16433/43-16465) were directly ordered for the USAAF. Fitted as eighteen-seat paratroop transports, these aircraft were powered by 1,200 hp Wright R-1820-87s. Many were diverted to the Allies while three of the USAAF aircraft were converted as C-57C-LOs, with one of these being further modified as the C-57D-LO. In 1948, the last Lodestars in USAF service were redesignated ZC-60A-LOs.

XC-60B-LO: One of the new aircraft ordered by the USAAF was modified during construction to test a hot-air de-icing system. Bearing the Lockheed designation Model 218-56, this R-1820-87 powered machine was assigned the serial 42-55860 and the c/n 218-2250. After the war it became N66170 on the US civil register.

C-60C-LO (C-104A-LO): Proposed military transport development (Lockheed Model 118-56) with accommodation for 21 troops and installation of long-range tanks. Specifications for the C-104A, later redesignated C-60C, were submitted by Lockheed in February 1943, but construction of a prototype and further developments were not undertaken.

C-66-LO: One Model 18-10 (c/n 18-2148) was taken over during construction by the Defense Supply Corporation and assigned the serial 42-13567. Powered by two 1,200 hp Pratt & Whitney R-1830-53s and fitted with an executive interior (seven airline-type seats, a three-seat settee, removable table, galley and lavatory), the C-66-LO was delivered to Brazil for use by President Getulio Vargas. In 1945 this aircraft was given the Brazilian military serial 2008 and continued in service with the Fôrça Aérea Brasileira.

As twin-engined military transports the C-60s and other versions of the Lodestar were greatly outnumbered in USAAF and USN service by Douglas Skytrains and Curtiss Commandos. Nevertheless, the USAAF Lodestars saw widespread use during the war years on general logistic missions, principally in the continental United States, the Southwest Pacific, the Caribbean and Panama Canal Zone, and South America. Few of these aircraft were retained after the end of the war but some did remain in use into the late forties. Likewise, the type performed usefully but without glamour in USN and USMC service during the war.

Within the British Commonwealth, the Lodestar was in great demand for military and para-military duties. Thus, BOAC operated no fewer than thirty-eight Lodestars for nearly seven years beginning in March 1941. BOAC's first nine Lodestars (G-AGBO/P and G-AGBR/X) were Hornet-powered Model 18-07s ordered directly from Lockheed, whereas the remaining aircraft were second-hand airliners (three Hornet-powered 18-07s, nine Twin Wasp powered Models 18-10 and 18-14, and four Cyclone-powered Models 18-40 and 18-50) or military transports (five C-59, one C-60 and seven C-60A-5-LOs) acquired through the RAF. Initially, due to the pressing need to keep as many aircraft as possible in service over a wide-ranging network, BOAC operated these Lodestars with their original powerplants. However, order was later restored when the airline converted seventeen aircraft to Model 18-56 standard with Wright R-1820-87s as used in its C-60/C-60As to obtain a fairly homogenized fleet of twenty-seven aircraft. Before and after their change of engines, the Lodestars were operated by BOAC on routes between Scotland and Sweden, across Africa, to Malta, within East Africa and the Middle East. During wartime service six of these aircraft were lost, while five were returned to the RAF during 1943 and seven transferred in July 1945 to be operated in Norwegian military service. Another Model 18-07 (c/n 18-2093, ex NC33617 of Catalina Air Transport) was originally reserved for BOAC as G-AGCL but instead was transferred to the Free French Air Force to be used as the personal transport of General de Gaulle. The last six aircraft in the BOAC fleet, part of the batch of nine Lodestars originally ordered by the airline, were sold to East African Airways Corporation in February 1948.

British military serials were assigned to seventy aircraft, a much greater number of Lodestars than was actually operated by the RAF. This was due to the fact that many of these machines went straight into BOAC service, whilst others were retained by the USAAF. Instances of serial duplications were also noted

Lodestar G-AGCM *Lake Mariut* of BOAC over Cairo during the Second World War. This aircraft (c/n 18-2093) had originally been delivered to Catalina Air Transport as the Model 18-07 NC33617 but was modified as a Model 18-56 for service with BOAC.
(*British Airways*)

with, for example, c/n 18-2001—ex NC25604—being given the serial AX722 when destined for the RAF under Lend-Lease but going to BOAC as G-AGCT; in 1943 it was returned to the RAF as HK974. With the RAF, Lockheed 18s were designated Lodestar Mk.Is (ex-civil aircraft), Mk.IAs (ex-C-59s) and Mk.IIs (ex-C-60/C-60As). Only some thirty aircraft did reach the RAF and were operated in the Middle East, notably by Nos. 117 and 167 Squadrons.

Of the twenty-nine Lodestars ordered by South African Airways, two crashed during their delivery flights and all others were taken over by the SAAF upon arriving in South Africa in 1940–41. Together with two second-hand Model 18-07s acquired by the Red Cross, these aircraft were allocated serials 231/249 and 1370/1378. Most were operated as transport/ambulance aircraft by No.5 Wing based at AFS Germiston (Johannesburg) and flew a shuttle service up the length of Africa during the war. Thirteen of these Lodestars were temporarily modified as bombers in 1942 for use in Madagascar to boost the defence of that island against the potential threat of Japanese invasion. Not all of these aircraft were fully modified but at least serial 249 (c/n 18-2055) was fitted with a bomb-aimer's compartment in the nose, provision for external carriage of up to 2,200 lb (998 kg) of bombs on ten wing racks and two racks beneath the centre section, and two forward-firing 0·50-in machine-guns. Beginning in 1944, nineteen of the surviving SAAF Lodestars—including the bombers which had been restored as transports—were progressively returned to SAA ownership and this carrier used the type until 1955; but before use by SAA, one of these (c/n 18-2030, serial 234) was retained by No.28 Squadron as a VIP transport for the Prime Minister.

In the SWPA (Southwest Pacific Area), Lodestars were operated not only by the USAAF and the Netherlands East Indies Air Force—the Dutch having ordered twenty Model 18-40s and nine 18-50s, and also receiving a C-60A-5-LO—but also by the RAAF and RNZAF. The RAAF received ten C-60A-5-LOs, which became A67-1 to A67-10, five ex-NEIAF aircraft on lease (LT9-31 to LT9-35), and, on loan from July 1943 until March 1944, at least three ex-USAAF Lodestars. With this Service, Lodestars were operated by No.37 Squadron, Nos.1 and 4 Communication Units and No.5 ARD; some were also transferred

Model 18-08 Lodestar, c/n 18-2055, ZS-ATI of South African Airways. (*SAA*)

192

NZ3507, ex-USAAF C-60A-5-LO (42-55945, c/n 18-2381) in service with the RNZAF during the war. (*via John Regan*)

to ANA for service with the Allied Directorate of Air Transport. The surviving aircraft with Australian serials were sold in 1947 but the last two of the ex-NEIAF Lodestars were not disposed of until July 1950. With the RNZAF, nine C-60As (NZ3507/NZ3515) were operated by Nos.40 and 41 Transport Squadrons in 1943–45.

Eighteen C-60As (Canadian serials 551 to 568) were operated by the RCAF between January 1943 and February 1948 and were assigned to the Eastern and Western Air Commands, Nos.164 and 165 Squadrons, and No.1 Air Command to provide logistic support within the national territory. Another ally, Brazil, operated Lodestars, as the Fôrça Aérea Brasileira received seven C-60A-5-LOs and the sole C-66-LO during the war; in 1945 these aircraft received the new FAB serials 2001 to 2008.

Although not genuine Model 18s, the 121 aircraft built by Kawasaki and operated during the war by the Japanese Army must be included in this narrative as they were close relatives of the Lodestar. As indicated under the Model 14 section, Japan had acquired the manufacturing rights for the Super Electra. Working without Lockheed's assistance, a design team led by Takeo Doi began in September 1939—in the same month as that of the first flight of the prototype Model 18—to develop a stretched version of the Type LO, the Japanese-built version of the Lockheed 14-WG3. Specially intended as a military cargo transport, the fuselage was lengthened by 1·5 m (4 ft 11 in)—versus a stretch of 5 ft 6 in (1·68 m) for the Model 18—and a large cargo-loading door was provided on the port side of the aft fuselage. The version differed further from the Model 18 in retaining the original location of the tailplane atop the rear fuselage, and in being powered by two 950 hp Army Type 99 (Nakajima Ha-25) fourteen-cylinder radials. Designated Ki-56, the first of two prototypes was flown in November 1940. These two aircraft were followed between August 1941 and September 1943 by 119 production machines, which were designated Army Type 1 Freight Transports in the Japanese nomenclature and were assigned the code name Thalia by the Allies. First operated in combat in early 1942 during the Japanese invasion of Sumatra, they saw widespread service until the end of the war.

At the end of the war the surplus Lodestars were already obsolescent and did not find favour with major carriers, whilst their relatively high operating costs and lack of cargo-carrying capability respectively precluded their use by local carriers and all-cargo airlines. A few did see service with smaller operators, mostly non-scheduled, in the United States and abroad, but the main outlet for these surplus aircraft was the executive and corporate markets for which the Lodestar's high speed and adequate capacity were valuable assets. This potential was further exploited by companies which modified Lodestars to improve their performance and fitted them with special interiors to meet the needs of the most demanding customers. Typical among these executive transport conversions were those undertaken by Howard Aero which fitted elongated nose and tail sections to reduce drag, large rectangular windows in place of the series of smaller panes, and de luxe interiors. The Howard 250 version retained 1,200 hp Wright R-1820-56As as its powerplants whereas the Howard 350 used a pair of 2,500 hp Pratt & Whitney Double Wasp CB17s.

N12L the prototype of the high-performance Learstar developed by Bill Lear from the Lodestar. (*Howard Levy*)

Another interesting conversion of the Model 18 was the Lear Learstar which, on the power of two 1,425 hp Wright R-1820-C-9HDs, achieved a remarkable top speed of 321 mph (517 km/h) and cruised at 280 mph (451 km/h) while carrying twelve passengers in great comfort.

Related Temporary Design Designations: L-123, L-125 and CL-1079

Model 18-07 (powered by Pratt & Whitney Hornet S1E2-Gs)

Span 65 ft 6 in (19·96 m); length 49 ft 10 in (15·19 m); height 11 ft 10 in (3·6 m); wing area 551 sq ft (51·19 sq m).

Empty weight 11,250 lb (5,103 kg); loaded weight 17,500 lb (7,938 kg); maximum weight 19,200 lb (8,709 kg); wing loading 31·8 lb/sq ft (155·1 kg/sq m); power loading 10 lb/hp (4·5 kg/hp).

Maximum speed 218 mph at 8,000 ft (351 km/h at 2,440 m); cruising speed 197 mph (317 km/h); climb to 10,000 ft (3,050 m) in 10·3 min; service ceiling 20,400 ft (6,220 m); normal range 1,800 miles (2,895 km); maximum range 3,200 miles (5,150 km).

C-60A-5-LO

Dimensions as Model 18-07.

Empty weight 12,500 lb (5,670 kg); loaded weight 17,500 lb (7,938 kg); maximum weight 21,000 lb (9,525 kg); wing loading 31·8 lb/sq ft (155·1 kg/sq m); power loading 7·3 lb/hp (3·3 kg/hp).

Maximum speed 266 mph at 17,150 ft (428 km/h at 5,230 m); cruising speed 200 mph (322 km/h); climb to 10,000 ft (3,050 m) in 6·6 min; service ceiling 30,100 ft (9,175 m); normal range 950 miles (1,530 km); maximum range 2,500 miles (4,025 km).

Vega 35

To complement its fast-growing series of basic and advanced trainers powered by radial engines of between 400 and 600 hp, North American Aviation undertook in mid-1937 to design a lower-powered primary trainer. Of low-wing monoplane configuration and all-metal construction, the NA-35 had a conventional non-retractable undercarriage, tandem open cockpits with a protective pylon aft of the front seat, and was powered by a 125 hp Menasco Pirate C4 inline engine. First flown at the end of 1939 with the experimental registration NX14299, the NA-35 lost out to the Ryan STA-1 which was ordered, with the same Menasco engine as its competitor, as the PT-16/PT-20 series for the US Army Air Corps.

As North American already had its existing production capacity tied up with the manufacture of basic and advanced trainers, and as the company was embarking on the full-scale development of its famous B-25 Mitchell bomber, it sought to sell the rights to the NA-35 design to a suitable buyer. It found in Lockheed a willing purchaser as the Burbank company was still needing business for its subsidiary, the Vega Airplane Company. A deal was made in 1940 and Vega went on to produce four of the North American-designed primary trainers, as Vega 35s, with the first of these (NX21760) being tested beginning in January 1941 by Bud Martin at the Lockheed Air Terminal.

Early flight tests indicated the need for various improvements and these were developed by project engineer C. A. 'Zeke' Forter. They included a fifty per cent increase in fin area and, on the third and fourth aircraft, substitution of a 160 hp Menasco Pirate D4-B for the 125 hp Pirate D4 unit fitted to the first two Vega-built trainers which had been found to be underpowered. The Vega-built NA-35

Model 35, the Vega-produced version of the North American NA-35 primary trainer. (*Lockheed*)

195

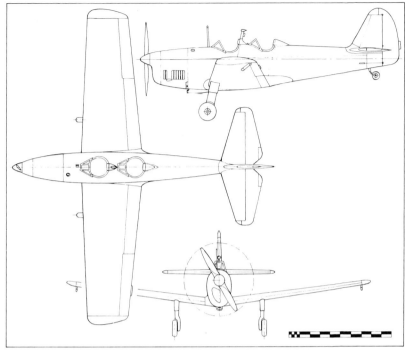

Vega 35

obtained its Approved Type Certificate in February 1941 but, by that time, the project was of limited value to the now very busy Lockheed. Thus, the four aircraft were sold to private individuals and development of the Menasco Pirate powered Vega 35 — as well as that of proposed versions with enclosed cockpits or with Warner Super Scarab, Ranger 6-440C, Kinner R-5 or Lycoming R-680-7 engine — was discontinued. Nevertheless, one of the Vega 35s remained in private use until the mid-fifties.

Related Temporary Design Designations: V-114, V-120 and V-123/V-126

Span 29 ft 9 in (9·07 m); length 25 ft 5$\frac{3}{4}$ in (7·77 m); height 10 ft 0$\frac{5}{16}$ in (3·06 m); wing area 148 sq ft (13·75 sq m).
Empty weight 1,362 lb (618 kg); loaded weight 1,930 lb (875 kg); wing loading 13 lb/sq ft (63·6 kg/sq m); power loading 15·4 lb/hp (7 kg/hp).
Maximum speed 134 mph (216 km/h); cruising speed 129 mph (208 km/h); initial rate of climb 941 ft/min (287 m/min); service ceiling 16,000 ft (4,875 m); range 305 miles (490 km).

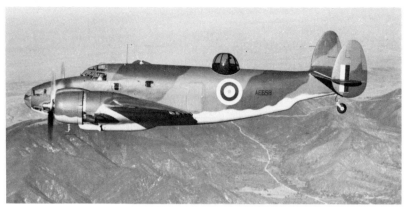

The prototype Ventura, with Royal Air Force serial AE658, during initial trials. (*Lockheed*)

Lockheed-Vega Ventura and Harpoon

Already well-satisfied with the Hudson development from the Model 14, the British Air Ministry received favourably a September 1939 proposal by Lockheed for a similarly produced military version of the Model 18. Bearing the Temporary Design Designation L-108, the Lockheed proposal covered several versions — either retaining powerplants in the 1,000/1,200 hp class as fitted to advanced versions of the Lodestar, or using engines rated at 1,600 to 2,000 hp — to fulfil either the general-reconnaissance role, as a Lockheed Hudson successor, or that of a light/medium bomber, as a Bristol Blenheim replacement. The latter role had a higher priority in the Air Ministry plans and, accordingly, in February 1940 Lockheed was given an initial contract for twenty-five Model 32-94-01 or 132-56-01 bombers. Further discussion with Lockheed, however, soon led to a switch from the Models 32/132 to a more advanced development of the Lodestar: the Model 37-21-01 with 1,850 hp Pratt & Whitney Double Wasp S1A4-G eighteen-cylinder radials. Satisfied with Lockheed's estimates of performance, the RAF order was increased to 300 aircraft (AE658/AE957) in May 1940 and the name Ventura selected for its new bomber; later in that year a contract for 375 additional machines (AJ163/AJ537) was signed.

With this sizeable order in hand, Lockheed decided to have the Model 37 produced in Vega Airplane Company's Plant A-1. Benefiting from the company's experience with the Hudson, the design team led by project engineer Jay Cowling incorporated in its adaptation of the Lodestar as a bomber a number of significant improvements. In particular, gun armament, as compared to that of the Hudson, was both increased and made more effective. The dorsal turret, housing twin 0·303-in machine-guns on initial production aircraft and four on late production machines, was moved forward to allow a wider field of fire. Twin flexible 0·303-in guns were mounted centrally on the tip of the nose and in a ventral position which gave a distinct kink to the aft fuselage. Two fixed forward-firing 0·50-in machine-guns were installed in the upper decking of the nose and 2,500 lb (1,134 kg) of bombs could be carried in an internal bay. Revised fuel-tank arrangement reduced internal capacity from 644 US gal (2,442 litres) for the Lodestar to 565 gal

197

(2,139 litres) for the Ventura but, with the addition of armament and larger engines, normal loaded weight increased from 19,200 lb (8,709 kg) for the Model 18-07 to 22,500 lb (10,206 kg) for the Model 37-21. None-the-less, good airfield performance was preserved by the retention of the Fowler flaps which, extending over 34 per cent of the trailing edge from the ailerons to the fuselage, increased wing area from 551 to 619 sq ft (51·19 to 57·707 sq m) when fully extended.

Painted in full British camouflage and fitted with dorsal turret, but carrying no armament, the first Ventura (AE658) was flown at the Lockheed Air Terminal on 31 July, 1941. Already, as flight trials of the new Lockheed bomber were just getting under way, Defense Agency contracts with Lend-Lease funds were placed for 750 additional aircraft, including 550 to be built in Lockheed's Plant B-1 as Wright R-2600 powered O-56-LOs and 200 as B-34A-VEs from Vega's Plant A-1. Later orders were received from the US Navy for PV-1s and PV-2s, and eventually a grand total of 3,028 aircraft were built between July 1941 and September 1945 in the following versions:

'Ventillation', the fifth Ventura which was used to flight-test the powerplant installation of the Constellation. (*Lockheed*)

Ventura I (Model 37-21-01): Powered by 1,850 hp Pratt & Whitney Double Wasp S1A4-Gs, 188 aircraft (AE658/AE845) were ordered under the original British contract and fitted with the armament already described. Some, including AE659 and AE662, were tested in US markings, with the latter aircraft being retained by Lockheed as a testbed for the powerplant installation of the Constellation. This aircraft, which was powered by two 2,200 hp Wright R-3350s in Constellation nacelles, was nicknamed Ventillation—a contraction of the Ventura and Constellation names. British acceptances began in September 1941 and the RAF Ventura Is were ferried across the North Atlantic, with three aircraft crashing during their delivery flight. Twenty-one of the early production aircraft were retained in Canada for RCAF use (AE658/659, 661, 663/674, 676/678, 696, 703 and 728), at least six (AE690, 694, 727, 752, 754 and 765) went to the SAAF, and one (the Ventillation) was retained by Lockheed. After being phased out of operation as bombers, a number of aircraft were modified as Ventura G.R.Is for service with Coastal Command beginning in autumn 1943.

Ventura II (Model 37-27-01): Generally similar to the Mk.I, the Mk.II differed in being powered by 2,000 hp Pratt & Whitney R-2800-31s built to US military standard (whereas the Double Wasp S1A4-Gs of the Mk.I were built to commercial standard), in having a redesigned bomb bay to carry 3,000 lb (1,361 kg) of bombs or ferry tanks housing 780 US gal (2,953 litres) of fuel. Production totalled 487 aircraft (AE846/AE957 and AJ163/AJ537). Only 196 Ventura IIs went to Commonwealth Air Forces (RAF, RCAF and SAAF), 264 machines were retained by the USAAF as Model 37s (R-Model 37s when in October 1942 the prefix R was added to denote the restricted status of these aircraft); and the last twenty-seven were delivered to the US Navy as PV-3s.

Ventura IIA (Model 137-27-02): Two hundred of these aircraft were ordered under Lend-Lease contract as B-34-VEs and were assigned both British (FD568/FD767) and US (41-38020/41-38219) military serials. The RAF received only twenty-five of these, with the others being retained by the USAAF as RB-34-VEs, B-34A-VEs and B-34B-VEs, or delivered to the RAAF (A59-1/A59-20), the RCAF (45 aircraft with British serials) and the RNZAF (NZ4583/NZ4605). These aircraft differed from the Ventura IIs in being fitted with a Martin dorsal turret (housing twin 0·50-in machine-guns) and other US items of armament and equipment.

Ventura III (Model 137-96-03): The planned delivery of O-56-LOs (B-37-LOs) powered by Wright R-2600-13s, for which the Mk.III designation was retained, did not materialize.

Ventura IV: Designation not used.

Ventura G.R.V: Produced under US Navy contracts for PV-1 patrol bombers, the G.R.V was intended for service with Coastal Command. Technical details of this version are given under the PV-1 designation. British serials (FN956/FN999, FP537/FP684, JS889/JS984 and JT800/JT898) were retained for 387 Ventura G.R.Vs but many of these aircraft were diverted to the RAAF, RCAF, RNZAF and SAAF. Some of the RAF aircraft were later modified for transport duty with No.299 Squadron, Transport Command, as Ventura C.Vs.

Ventura G.R.V (ex-US Navy PV-1, BuNo 48749) bearing the Australian serial A59-64 and the code SF identifying No.37 Squadron, RAAF. (*Eugene Sommerich via Peter M. Bowers*)

B-34-VE (Model 137-27-02): On 13 August, 1941, Lockheed was awarded a Defense Agency contract for 200 aircraft powered by 2,000 hp Pratt & Whitney R-2800-31s. Intended for delivery to Britain under Lend-Lease, they were assigned the USAAF serials 41-38020/41-38219 for contractual purposes. Following US entry into the war, twenty were impressed into USAAF service and in October 1942 their designation was changed to RB-34-VEs to denote their restricted combat capability. Armament consisted of two fixed forward-firing 0·50-in guns in the nose, two 0·50-in guns in a Martin dorsal turret, twin flexible 0·30-in guns in the nose and ventral positions, two flexible 0·30-in beam guns, and 3,000 lb (1,361 kg) of bombs. In service, some of the USAAF's B-34-VEs had the dorsal turret removed and ASV radar antennae installed atop the fuselage and beneath the wings.

B-34A-VE: Taken from the B-34 contract, these aircraft were completed as 66 Ventura IIAs (B-34A-1-VEs) for the RAF, RAAF, RCAF and RNZAF, and as 101 machines for the USAAF (57 B-34A-2-VE bomber trainers, 28 B-34A-3-VE gunnery trainers, and 16 B-34A-4-VE target tugs). In October 1942, the prefix R was added to the designation of the USAAF aircraft. A ground-attack version with heavy forward-firing armament was studied under the Temporary Design Designation V-142.

B-34B-VE: Thirteen other aircraft ordered as B-34-VEs were delivered to the USAAF as B-34B-1-VE navigation trainers and later became RB-34B-1-VEs.

RB-34B-LO: Designation given to the 550 aircraft originally ordered in August 1941 as O-56-LOs. Not built and RB-34B designation reassigned to obsolescent B-34B navigation trainers.

XB-34B-VE: Unofficial designation for a version of the PV-2 proposed to the USAAF (Vega's Temporary Design Designation V-147). Not proceeded with.

B-37-LO (Model 137-96-03): The first US contract for derivative combat versions of the Lodestar was placed on 8 August, 1941, for five hundred and fifty Model 137-96-03s (41-37470/41-38019) to be powered by 1,700 hp Wright R-2600-13s and intended for the armed reconnaissance/observation role. To be built in Lockheed's Plant B-1, whereas all other aircraft in the series were built in Vega's Plant A-1, they were designated O-56-LOs. Before completion of the first O-56-LO, the USAAF dropped its O-Observation series and the aircraft on order were first redesignated RB-34B-LOs and later, to account for the use of R-2600s in place of the B-34's R-2800s, B-37-LOs. As Plant B-1's production capacity was needed for more pressing work, this contract was cancelled after the completion of only eighteen B-37-LOs (41-31470/41-31487). The first R-2600-13 powered

Only eighteen B-37-LOs were completed in Plant B-1 before cancellation of the AAF contract for this version. The side gun port was unique to this version. (*Peter M. Bowers*)

aircraft was flown on 21 September, 1942, and the last was delivered in April 1943. Armament consisted of four 0·30-in machine-guns, five 0·50-in guns, and 2,000 lb (908 kg) of bombs.

O-56-LO: Initial designation for the RB-34B-LO/B-37-LO version.

PV-1 (Model 237-27-01): During the spring of 1942, the USN obtained USAAF concurrence to transfer full responsibility for anti-submarine warfare to the Navy patrol squadrons. While many of the Navy squadrons were to continue operations with flying-boats, others were to be equipped with land-based bombers. Accordingly, on 7 July, 1942, the USAAF agreed to discontinue procurement of Lockheed-Vega B-34s so that the manufacturer could concentrate on the production of a specially outfitted maritime patrol version for the Navy.

Whereas other former USAAF bombers were designated PB-Patrol Bombers, the Vega-produced machines were simply P-Patrol types. To suit them to their primary mission of maritime patrol, the PV-1s had maximum fuel capacity increased from 1,345 US gal/5,091 litres for the B-34s to 1,607 gal/6,083 litres

Fitted with mounts for HVAR rockets beneath the wing, this US Navy PV-1 was photographed at Shanghai in November 1945. (*Peter M. Bowers*)

—including 807 gal/3,055 litres in permanently installed wing and fuselage tanks, two 155-gal/587-litre drop tanks, and 490 gal/1,855 litres in two ferry/long-range patrol bomb-bay tanks. The PV-1 engines remained 2,000 hp R-2800-31s as fitted to the Ventura IIs and B-34s. Defensive armament was reduced to two fixed forward-firing 0·50-in guns, twin 0·50-in guns in the dorsal turret and twin flexible 0·30-in guns in the ventral position, while the bomb bay was modified to carry 3,000 lb (1,361 kg) of bombs, or six 325-lb/147-kg depth charges, or one torpedo. Late production PV-1s carried a three 0·50-in gun pack in place of the bomb-aiming window beneath the nose and could carry eight 5-in HVAR rockets on zero-length launchers beneath the wings. The PV-1s were also fitted with Navy-specified equipment including ASD-1 search radar in a nose radome. Early production PV-1s retained a bombardier's station aft of the radome, with four side windows and a flat bomb-aiming panel beneath the nose, but this was omitted on later production aircraft carrying the gun pack. The PV-1 was first flown on 3 November, 1942, and 1,600 were built on Navy contracts for delivery between December 1942 and May 1944. During the war many were diverted to the RAF, RAAF, RCAF, RNZAF, SAAF and the Fôrça Aérea Brasileira. Moreover, a small number of PV-1s were modified as interim night fighters for use by the USMC; earlier the manufacturer had studied such a version as the V-149. These

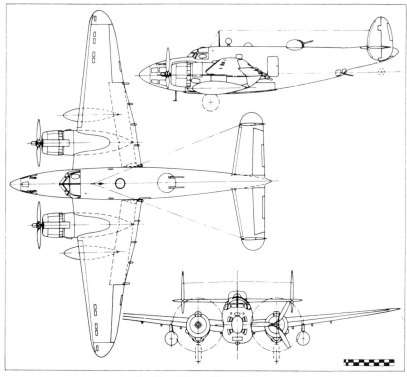

Lockheed-Vega PV-1 Ventura

night fighters had the crew reduced to three (versus a normal crew of five for the patrol aircraft), carried six forward-firing 0·50-in guns, and were fitted with British A.I.Mk.IV radar.

PV-1P: As part of their standard equipment, the PV-1s carried oblique cameras in the fuselage. In addition, a few aircraft were modified as long-range photographic-reconnaissance aircraft and carried additional cameras; they were re-designated PV-1Ps.

PV-2 (Model 15-27-01): When in July 1942 production of the Lockheed twin-engined patrol bomber was transferred to the Navy, this Service and the manufacturer began discussing a major redesign of the aircraft to optimize it for the maritime patrol role. Under the leadership of project engineer C. A. Forter, the redesign work became so major that the Basic Model Number was changed from Lockheed Model 37 to Vega Model 15. In particular, recognizing that when operating with maximum fuel load the PV-1 would have marginal take-off performance, the design team provided the Model 15 with new outboard wing panels, which increased the span by 9 ft 6 in (2·9 m) to 75 ft (22·86 m) and area from 551 to 686 sq ft (51·19 to 63·73 sq m), and with enlarged vertical tail surfaces. Integral fuel tanks were installed in the wing outer panels to bring maximum capacity to 1,863 US gal (7,052 litres)—a 230 per cent increase over the fuel load of the original Ventura I—when bomb-bay tanks and drop tanks were used. Armament was standardized on five 0·50-in nose guns (including three in a pack),

A beautifully clean PV-2 Harpoon in US Navy three-tone camouflage.
(*Clay Janson via Cloud 9 Photography*)

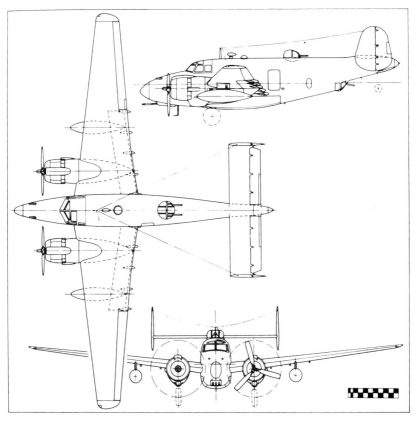

Lockheed-Vega PV-2 Harpoon

two 0·50-in guns in the dorsal turret and in the ventral tunnel position, and eight 5-in HVAR rockets; internal bomb load was increased to 4,000 lb (1,814 kg), and one 1,000 lb (454 kg) bomb could also be carried beneath each wing in place of the rockets. Still powered by 2,000 hp R-2800-31s, the Model 15 was expected to have reduced level and climb speeds but was to have increased range and better field performance. Pleased with these estimates, on 30 June, 1943, the Navy ordered 500 aircraft with the designation PV-2 Harpoon and BuNos 37035/37534. The first thirty were delivered as PV-2Cs, beginning in March 1944, with the remainder being PV-2s. Wartime deliveries to Allies included only five PV-2s for the Fôrça Aérea Brasileira and four for the RNZAF, but postwar transfer from Navy stocks were made to France, Italy, Japan, the Netherlands, Peru and Portugal.

The incident-free first flight of the Harpoon was made at the Lockheed Air Terminal on 3 December, 1943, by a crew captained by Bud Martin. However, initial operations revealed a tendency for the wings to wrinkle dangerously. A quick modification, involving a 6 ft (1·83-m) reduction in span to obtain a uniformly flexible wing, was tested but failed to solve the problem and Lockheed was forced to undertake complete wing redesign. All but thirty of the PV-2s, which had already been completed, were modified by Lockheed in Plant B-9 at Van Nuys, and thus only sixty-nine PV-2s were accepted by the Navy before the end of 1944. The fully-modified aircraft gave complete satisfaction and some were still flown by the Fôrça Aérea Portuguesa against African insurgents during the 1960s.

PV-2C: The first thirty PV-2s (BuNos 37035/37064), which did not have the modified wings, were accepted as PV-2Cs. The integral tanks in the wings, which were built by a subcontractor in Arizona, developed leaks and in service had to be sealed off.

PV-2D: Three follow-on production contracts for 908 Harpoons (BuNos 37535/37634, 84057/84589 and 102001/102275) were awarded but only thirty-five were delivered before the cancellation of contracts after VJ-Day. Forward-firing armament was increased to eight 0·50-in guns and these late-production aircraft were designated PV-2Ds. Final delivery took place in September 1945 to bring to an end the production of Models 37/137/237 Venturas and Model 15 Harpoons.

PV-2T: Designation given to a small number of PV-2s which were modified after the war as unarmed trainers.

PV-3: The last twenty-seven Ventura IIs (AJ511/AJ537) on British contract were taken over by the US Navy and, designated PV-3s, were assigned BuNos 33925/33951.

PV-4: Projected development of the PV-2 with 2,100 hp C-Series R-2800 engines, modified armament and strengthened undercarriage. The proposed V-154 was not proceeded with when war ended.

First delivered to the RAF in September 1941, the Ventura I went into service with No.21 Squadron at Bodney, Norfolk, in May 1942 and flew its first combat sorties on 3 November. Only two other squadrons—Nos.464 (RAAF) and 487 (RNZAF)—serving with No.2 Group, first within Bomber Command and then Fighter Command, flew Ventura I and IIs. Forty-seven Venturas from these three squadrons joined with Bostons and Mosquitos to take part in a daring daylight, low-level, attack on 6 December, 1942, against the Philips radio and valve factory at Eindhoven in the Netherlands. Nine of the Venturas were shot down and 37 damaged but the raid was a success. Switching to medium-altitude operations, the Venturas went on to attack airfields, transport targets and steelworks in occupied

France. On 3 May, 1943, eleven aircraft from No.487 Squadron attacked a power-station in Amsterdam but only one Ventura survived determined attacks by German fighters; the formation leader, Sqn Ldr L. H. Trent, succeeded in shooting down a Messerschmitt Bf 109 with his Ventura's forward-firing guns before being himself shot down. Trent, taken prisoner, survived the war and was awarded the Victoria Cross for his gallantry.

By the summer of 1943, the Venturas were being replaced by faster de Havilland Mosquitos, and the type's last sorties with No.2 Group were flown by No.21 Squadron on 9 September, 1943. A number of aircraft were then modified as Ventura G.R.Is for service along with Ventura G.R.Vs with Nos.519 and 521 Squadrons, Coastal Command, and Nos.13 and 500 Squadrons in the Mediterranean. In this theatre, Venturas were also briefly used by No.624 Squadron for special duties and mine spotting. Mark IIs, modified as transports, were operated by No.299 Squadron.

The RCAF, which received 149 aircraft diverted from British contracts and retaining their RAF serials (21 Mk.Is, 108 Mk.II/IIAs and 20 G.R.Vs), as well as 137 ex-US Navy PV-1s (which were given the Canadian serials 2141/2277), used its Ventura I/IIs to equip No.340 Operational Training Unit at Pennfield Ridge, New Brunswick, and No.1 Central Flying School at Trenton, Ontario. The G.R.Vs and PV-1s were assigned to five maritime squadrons (Nos.8, 113, 115, 145 and 149) in Canada. The first Ventura I was received in June 1942 and the last G.R.V was struck off charge in April 1947. In Canadian service at least one Ventura II (AE680) was fitted with fixed skis.

On 18 May, 1943, the RAAF received the first of twenty Ventura IIAs (B-34A-1-VEs) which became A59-1/A59-20 in Australian service. These aircraft were later supplanted by fifty-five PV-1s (A59-50/A59-104) diverted from the US Navy. The latter batch served primarily in New Guinea with No.13 Squadron until replaced by Australian-built Bristol Beauforts, whereas the Ventura IIAs went to Nos. 4 and 11 Communications Units. The RAAF last used its Venturas during the 1946–47 fiscal year and these aircraft were then either converted to components or stored for disposal. The last two, A59-6 and A59-17, were sold to a private operator in February 1953.

To re-equip its Bomber Reconnaissance Squadrons which, since the start of the Pacific war, had been equipped with Lockheed Hudsons, the RNZAF received 139 Venturas (116 of which were PV-1s with serials NZ4501/NZ4582 and NZ4606/NZ4639, and twenty-three ex B-34A-1-VEs with serials NZ4583/NZ4605). These

Ventura NZ4503 was taken on charge by the RNZAF in June 1943 and was sold for scrap five years later; its original BuNo was 33309. (*RNZAF*)

aircraft were used by Nos. 1, 2, 3, 4, 8 and 9 Squadrons and saw much use in the Solomons where, in addition to flying on bombing operations, they flew reconnaissance and air-rescue sorties. On 24 December, 1943, while flying an air-rescue sortie, for which the Ventura carried extra dinghies, an aircraft of No.1 Squadron was bounced by Japanese Zeke fighters. The crew, captained by Pilot Off D. F. Ayson, succeeded in shooting down three Zekes and damaging two more before returning to Munda. While particularly noteworthy, this feat was not isolated as the Ventura proved well capable of defending itself. The type was phased out of RNZAF service in 1946 when No.2 Squadron was disbanded.

The South African Air Force, which received 135 Ventura Mk.Is and Mk.IIs (SAAF serials 6001 to 6135) and 134 Ventura Mk.Vs (6401 to 6534) diverted from British contracts, used the type to equip five squadrons (Nos.22, 23, 25, 27 and 29) operating at home to protect shipping around the vital Cape route and in the Mediterranean. In particular, No.22 Squadron operated from Gibraltar while No.27 was in the Balkans in late 1944 on anti-shipping and ASW duty. Postwar, the SAAF continued operating Ventura Vs and some of these aircraft operated with No.2 (Maritime) Group until the 1960s.

Bearing the SAAF serial 6499 this modified Ventura Mk.V was photographed in the mid-1950s after it had been fitted with a target-towing winch atop the aft fuselage.
(SAAF via Capt Dave Becker)

A small number of PV-1s were delivered to the Free French beginning in 1944 and these aircraft were operated by Flotille 6F until replaced, early in the postwar period, by Bloch MB 175s. The Aéronautique Navale (Aéronavale) later obtained some PV-2 Harpoons which saw limited service, notably with Escadrille de Servitude 12S, before being transferred to Portugal as more modern equipment became available.

During the war the Fôrça Aérea Brasileira was the only other non-US Service to fly Venturas and Harpoons operationally. This Service received fourteen ex-US Navy PV-1s—which in FAB service were incorrectly designated B-34s and assigned the Brazilian serials 5034/5047—and six new PV-2s—which carried serials 5048/5051, 5074 and 5076, and were designated B-34As. Remaining in Brazilian service into the fifties, some of the earlier aircraft were modified as transports but retained their wing drop tanks.

Although USAAF military serials had been assigned to no fewer than 200 B-34/B-34A/B-34Bs and eighteen B-37s, while 264 British-ordered Ventura IIs were taken over by this Service, the USAAF made limited use of the type. Early

In service with the Fôrça Aérea Brasileira five PV-2s—one of which is seen here at Burbank before delivery—were incorrectly designated B-34As. (*Lockheed*)

in the war some were used for ASW patrols but, by and large, the Lockheed twin-engined bombers were used mostly for training by such Texas-based units as the Bomber Training Group of the Central Instructors School at Randolph Field, the AAF Gunnery School at Laredo, and the AAF Navigation School at San Marcos. The USN and USMC, on the other hand, were major combat operators of PV-1s and PV-2s. With the Marine Corps, PV-1s were modified to equip the Corps' first night-fighter squadron, VMF(N)-531. Commissioned in November 1942 at Cherry Point, North Carolina, this unit became operational at Banika, Russell Islands, in September 1943. Two months later VMF(N)-531 scored its first night kill. Later transferred to Vella Lavella and Bougainville, the unit returned to the States during the summer of 1944.

With the US Navy, the first Venturas were the PV-3s requisitioned from the British and which were assigned in October 1942 to VP-82 operating from Argentia, Newfoundland, on ASW patrols over the Atlantic. The PV-1s followed in service a couple of months later—with VB-127 being commissioned at NAS

B-34-VEs of the Central Instructors School Bomber Training Group, Army Air Forces, operating from Randolph Field, Texas. (*USAF*)

207

A PV-1 over Sanford, Florida, in May 1943. (*USN*)

Deland on 1 February, 1943 — and Ventura crew training was initiated at both this Florida base and Whidbey Island, Washington. The first PV-1 squadron to be deployed to the combat zone was VP-135, which arrived at Adak in the Aleutians in April 1943. In this theatre PV-1s were subsequently operated by VP-131, VP-136 and VP-139. These squadrons of Fleet Air Wing Four flew reconnaissance patrols, and strikes with guns and rockets against Paramushiro, one of the northernmost Japanese islands in the Kurile chain. Being radar-equipped, the PV-1s were also assigned as leaders to USAAF B-24 bomber formations. In the less difficult climate of the Solomon Islands, PV-1s were first operated by VP squadrons from the Russell Islands during autumn 1943, while in November of that year a detachment of VB-145 undertook anti-submarine patrols over the South Atlantic from Fernando de Noronha off the coast of Brazil.

The PV-2 Harpoon was taken into combat in March 1945 when VPB-139 returned to the Aleutians for a second tour of duty after converting from Venturas at Whidbey Island. By and large, however, the Harpoon was too late for large-scale use during the war. New and well liked, the PV-2s saw much postwar use with the US Navy and at one time equipped eleven VP squadrons in the Reserve. Finally, in August 1948 the type was phased out by VP-3. Several of these aircraft were then converted as executive transports. As had been done earlier with Lodestars and Venturas, some of these conversions were rather extensive and resulted in high-performance private transports with de luxe interiors.

Surplus Harpoon N6852C modified for agricultural work, at Falcon Field, Mesa, Arizona, in 1967. (*Robert C. Mikesh*)

Featuring a modified nose with built-in forward-firing guns and a radome, this PV-2 of the Japanese Maritime Self-Defense Force (JMSDF) was photographed at Iwakuni on 8 March, 1955. (*US National Archives*)

Other surplus PV-2 were delivered to friendly nations as follows:

Italy: During the 1950s, the Aeronautica Militare Italiana received enough Harpoons to equip its 86° and 87° Gruppi Antisommergibili. Beginning in 1957 they were replaced in these units by Grumman S2F-1 Trackers.

Japan: Among the first combat aircraft delivered to the Japanese Maritime Self-Defense Force (JMSDF) after that Service came into being in July 1951 were seventeen PV-2s which were initially assigned the serials 4101/4117. One of these aircraft crashed in 1955 and the others were renumbered 4571/4586.

The Netherlands: Pending receipt of its P2V-5s, the Marine Luchtvaartdienst operated between September 1951 and December 1953 eighteen PV-2s (Dutch serials 19-1/19-18) which were assigned to No.320 Squadron at Valkenburg.

Peru: During the 1950s the Fuerza Aérea del Peru received a small number of Harpoons, which were numbered from 421 on and equipped one maritime-reconnaissance squadron until the 1960s.

Portugal: The Fôrça Aérea Portuguesa initially received in 1954 eighteen ex-Dutch Harpoons and subsequently added 24 additional PV-2s (some ex-French). Assigned the Portuguese serials 4601/4642, these aircraft were operated by the Esquadra de Reconhecimento Maritimo at Base Aérea 6, Montijo. Some of the Portuguese Harpoons later served in the counter-insurgency role with Esquadra 93 based at Luanda but operating detachments throughout Angola. By the time Portugal pulled out from its former African colonies, no Harpoons remained in service.

Related Temporary Design Designations: V-116, V-119, V-127, V-132/V-133, V-137/V-138, V-142/V-143, V-145, V-149, V-153, L-116 and L-128 (Ventura); and V-147 and V-154 (Harpoon)

209

	Ventura Mk.I	B-34A-VE	B-37-LO	PV-1	PV-2
Span, ft in	65 6	65 6	65 6	65 6	75 0
(m)	(19·96)	(19·96)	(19·96)	(19·96)	(22·86)
Length, ft in	51 5	51 5	51 5	51 9	52 1
(m)	(15·67)	(15·67)	(15·67)	(15·77)	(15·87)
Height, ft in	11 10½	11 11	11 11	11 11	13 3
(m)	(3·62)	(3·63)	(3·63)	(3·63)	(4·04)
Wing area, sq ft	551	551	551	551	686
(sq m)	(51·19)	(51·19)	(51·19)	(51·19)	(63·73)
Empty weight, lb	17,233	17,275	18,615	20,197	21,028
(kg)	(7,817)	(7,836)	(8,444)	(9,161)	(9,538)
Loaded weight, lb	22,500	25,600	27,000	31,077	33,668
(kg)	(10,206)	(11,612)	(12,247)	(14,096)	(15,272)
Maximum weight, lb	26,000	27,750	29,500	34,000	36,000
(kg)	(11,793)	(12,587)	(13,381)	(15,422)	(16,329)
Wing loading, lb/sq ft	40·8	46·5	49	56·4	49·1
(kg/sq m)	(199·4)	(226·8)	(239·2)	(275·4)	(239·6)
Power loading, lb/hp	6·1	6·4	7·9	7·8	8·4
(kg/hp)	(2·8)	(2·9)	(3·6)	(3·5)	(3·8)
Maximum speed, mph/ft	312/15,500	315/15,500	298/13,500	322/13,800	282/13,700
(km/h / m)	(502/4,725)	(507/4,725)	(479/4,115)	(518/4,205)	(454/4,175)
Cruising speed, mph	272	230	198	170	171
(km/h)	(438)	(370)	(319)	(274)	(275)
Rate of climb, ft/min	2,035/1	15,000/8·2	10,000/5·5	2,230/1	1,630/1
(m/min)	(620/1)	(4,572/8·2)	(3,048/5·5)	(680/1)	(497/1)
Service ceiling, ft	25,000	24,000	22,400	26,300	23,900
(m)	(7,620)	(7,315)	(6,830)	(8,015)	(7,285)
Normal range, miles	925	950	1,300	1,360	1,790
(km)	(1,490)	(1,530)	(2,090)	(2,190)	(2,880)
Maximum range, miles	—	2,600	2,700	1,660	2,930
(km)	—	(4,185)	(4,335)	(2,670)	(4,715)

The first B-17F-1-VE (42-5705, c/n 17-6001) was the forerunner of 2,750 Boeing Flying Fortresses built by Vega. (*Lockheed*)

Lockheed-Vega Flying Fortress

In the spring of 1941 reports reaching the US War Department from Great Britain clearly showed that its Douglas B-18 and B-23 medium bombers and early-model Boeing B-17 heavy bombers were obsolete and lacked both the defensive armament and performance to be successful in day bombing operations against determined opposition. As it then appeared likely that the United States would sooner or later be drawn into the war, the Materiel Command was forced to devise a mass-production programme for both the Boeing B-17 in its later variants and the newer Consolidated B-24. Thus, in April 1941, Maj-Gen Oliver P. Echols called Robert and Courtlandt Gross to invite the Burbank firm to join Boeing and Douglas in mass producing the B-17F. Specifically, General Echols suggested that the Vega Airplane Company should curtail development of a proposed 30- to 40-seat commercial transport. As the market for civil aircraft was clouded by the war in many parts of the world, the Gross brothers saw much merit in the Materiel Command's suggestion and promptly agreed to join the two other manufacturers in forming the B-V-D (Boeing-Vega-Douglas) pool.

After receiving B-17E pattern aircraft and all necessary blueprints from Boeing, Vega began production of the B-17F in its new and large A-1 plant on the edge of the Lockheed Air Terminal. The first B-17F-1-VE (42-5705) flew on 4 May, 1942, six months ahead of the USAAF schedule and 30 days ahead of the company's. Until 28 July, 1945, when production was terminated, Lockheed-Vega built a total of 500 B-17F-1 through –50 and 2,250 B-17G-1 through –110 (*see* Appendix B for list of serial numbers). In the process the company achieved the lowest man-hours per aircraft in the B-V-D pool. In addition, it submitted proposals or prepared design studies for the following advanced models: the

211

V-143 with 2,000 hp Wright R-3350s, the V-144 with two 3,000 hp Pratt & Whitney Wasp Majors, and the V-151 for the Marine Corps with a tail turret having a 180-deg field of fire. None of these studies was proceeded with.

The next model of Flying Fortress to come from the Vega plant was a Boeing-built B-17F-1-BO (41-24341) which was modified as an escort aircraft for standard B-17 bombers. The concept behind this experimental aircraft, which was described as the Vega V-139 in a report dated 21 July, 1942, and became known as the XB-40, was to create a heavily-armed and -armoured version of the Flying Fortress and thus provide the conventional bombers with added protection against enemy fighters. To that end twin 0·50-in machine-guns were added in a chin turret, in a second dorsal turret—which replaced the hand-held 0·50-in gun manned by the radio operator in standard B-17Fs—and in each waist position, in place of the single gun of the bomber version. Together with twin 0·50-in weapons as normally carried by B-17Fs in dorsal, ventral and tail turrets, these additional guns brought total defensive armament to fourteen heavy machine-guns. Normal ammunition load was 11,135 rounds, but this precluded the XB-40 from carrying bombs so as not to exceed the permitted maximum take-off weight; a maximum ammunition load of 17,265 rounds could be carried if fuel load was reduced.

The XB-40 showing the second dorsal turret and the chin turret distinguishing this escort version of the B-17. (*Lockheed*)

First flight of the XB-40 was made on 10 November, 1942, and Vega then developed details for its V-140 proposed production version. However, responsibility for the modification of twenty Vega-built B-17F-VEs (42-5732/42-5744, 42-5871, 42-5920/42-5921, 42-5923/42-5925 and 42-5927) as YB-40 service-test models and of four B-17F-VEs (42-5833/42-5834, 42-5872 and 42-5926) as TB-40 trainers was entrusted to the Tulsa plant of Douglas (whereas that company was building standard B-17F-DLs in its Long Beach plant). Twelve of the YB-40s were assigned for operational tests to the 327th Bombardment Squadron, 92nd Bombardment Group, at Alconbury, in England, and flew their first mission to St Nazaire on 29 May, 1943. However, the YB-40s proved unsatisfactory in combat as they tended to be excessively tail-heavy and, due to the added weight of armour and weapons, were significantly slower than the B-17Fs once the bombers had dropped their loads. Accordingly, the 327th BS retired its YB-40s in July 1943, less than two months after the type had been commissioned. Nevertheless, the Vega-developed XB-40/YB-40s made a favourable impact on the Flying Fortress programme, since the chin turret, covering the weakest spot in the defensive

With its neatly cowled Allison V-1710-89 engines the XB-38 was possibly the most attractive version of the Flying Fortress. (*Lockheed*)

armament, after being fitted to some of the late production B-17Fs, was adopted as standard for the B-17G version.

On 10 July, 1942, Vega had received a contract to implement a USAAF programme to develop a higher-performance version of the Flying Fortress using an alternative powerplant to preclude possible shortages of Wright R-1820s as used on all previous B-17 models. Under the company designation V-134-1, Vega designed the necessary modifications to install 1,425 hp liquid-cooled Allison V-1710-89s in a B-17 airframe. Initially it was planned to build a brand-new aircraft which received the serial 42-73515 but, eventually, it was decided to modify as an XB-38 prototype a Boeing-built B-17E (41-2401) which Vega had received as a pattern aircraft. The new powerplant used the original B-17 engine mounting and

This view of the XB-38 shows the Allison engines to good advantage.

213

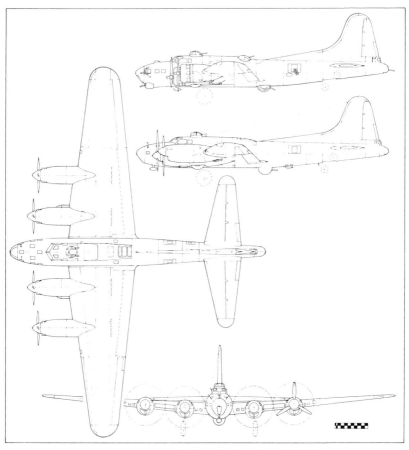

Lockheed-Vega XB-38, with side view of XB-40

had oil coolers beneath and behind the propeller spinner while rectangular glycol radiators were installed in the leading edge of the wing between the nacelles. At the same time the carburettor and intercooler air ducts were enlarged to provide the increased air flow required by the Allisons. Other modifications included the substitution of some standard equipment items to provide space for test instrumentation and, to obtain a valid comparison with contemporary B-17F production models, the substitution of a dummy Sperry ventral turret for the remotely-sighted, retractable Bendix turret as originally fitted to aircraft 41-2401.

After modification work had been temporarily delayed in early 1943 by more urgent tasks, the XB-38 began flight trials on 19 May, 1943. During ground testing and its first five flights, the XB-39 proved remarkably trouble-free. However, by the end of the sixth flight the aircraft had to be grounded for modifications to prevent leakage in its flexible exhaust-manifold joints. The XB-38 resumed its trial programme but, during its ninth flight, on 16 June, 1943, its No.3 engine caught fire in the air and flames started creeping towards the wing fuel tank. Its

214

pilot, Bud Martin, and co-pilot George MacDonald baled out at 25,000 ft but
their parachutes failed to open properly. MacDonald was killed and Martin
seriously injured.

Although the USAAF considered the estimated maximum speed of the XB-38
to be optimistic, plans went ahead to develop the Allison V-1710 powered Vega
V-140 model which was to combine the bombing role of the B-17F with the escort
role of the YB-40 and to have this model go into production at Vega in place of the
B-17F-VEs. However, this plan was turned down in August 1943 by General H.
H. Arnold and his staff as the YB-40 had been found unsatisfactory and as it was
by then unlikely that the Wright R-1820s would be in short supply. In fact, the
B-17G model — which used the YB-40 chin turret and had better performance than
the B-17F due to the use of more powerful R-1820s — was now in production and
negated the value of the V-140 programme. Accordingly, Vega was instructed to
switch from B-17F to B-17G production.

	B-17F	XB-38	XB-40
Span, ft in	103 9	103 11	103 9
(m)	(31·62)	(31·67)	(31·62)
Length, ft in	74 9	74 0	74 9
(m)	(22·78)	(22·56)	(22·78)
Height, ft in	19 1	19 2	19 1
(m)	(5·82)	(5·84)	(5·82)
Wing area, sq ft	1,420	1,420	1,420
(sq m)	(131·923)	(131·923)	(131·923)
Empty weight, lb	34,000	34,750	38,235
(kg)	(15,422)	(15,762)	(17,343)
Loaded weight, lb	40,437	56,000	58,000
(kg)	(18,342)	(25,401)	(26,308)
Maximum weight, lb	56,500	64,000	63,300
(kg)	(25,628)	(29,030)	(28,712)
Wing loading, lb/sq ft	28·5	39·4	40·8
(kg/sq m)	(139)	(192·5)	(199·4)
Power loading, lb/hp	8·4	9·8	12·1
(kg/hp)	(3·8)	(4·5)	(5·5)
Maximum speed, mph/ft	299/25,000	327/25,000	292/25,000
(km/h / m)	(481/7,620)	(526/7,620)	(470/7,620)
Cruising speed, mph	200	226	192
(km/h)	(322)	(364)	(309)
Rate of climb, ft/min	20,000/25·7	—	20,000/48·1
(m/min)	(6,096/25·7)	—	(6,096/48·1)
Service ceiling, ft	37,500	29,600	25,100
(m)	(11,430)	(9,020)	(7,650)
Normal range, miles	2,200	3,300	2,260
(km)	(3,540)	(5,310)	(3,635)
Maximum range, miles	3,800	4,000	2,480
(km)	(6,115)	(6,435)	(3,990)

The XP-49 at Burbank in November 1942. (*Lockheed*)

Lockheed XP-49

On 11 March, 1939, the US Materiel Division distributed its Circular Proposal 39-775 to the industry, calling for a new generation of interceptor fighter. To accelerate the development of these new aircraft, the Air Corps favoured the use of existing airframes matched with more powerful engines and other refinements. Four contractors submitted proposals, with Lockheed offering its L-106, a development of the P-38 Lightning fitted with a pressure cabin and powered by two of the new twenty-four-cylinder Pratt & Whitney X-1800-SA2-Gs (military designation XH-2600) which were expected to develop between 2,000 and 2,200 hp for take-off. Lockheed further proposed that two 2,300 hp forty-two-cylinder Wright R-2160 Tornado radials would be used on production aircraft. Either type of engine was to be fitted with turbosuperchargers to boost altitude performance. With armament comprising two 20 mm cannon and four 0·50-in machine-guns, and Royalin fuel tanks of a new design having a capacity of 300 US gal (1,136 litres)—versus 230 gal (871 litres) for early production P-38s—the aircraft was optimistically anticipated to have a top speed of 473 mph (761 km/h) at 20,000 ft (6,095 m), when powered by Pratt & Whitney XH-2600s, or 500 mph (805 km/h) at the same altitude, when powered by Wright Tornadoes.

Air Corps evaluation of the four proposals was completed on 3 August, 1939, with the Lockheed XP-49 (Model 522) and Grumman XP-50—a proposed development of the XF5F-1 Skyrocket naval fighter—coming respectively in first and second places. The contract for an XP-50 prototype was awarded to Grumman on 25 November, 1939, while Contract W535-AC-13476 for a Lockheed XP-49 prototype was readied five days later and finally executed on 8 January, 1940. Due to more pressing work on the P-38, design activities on the XP-49 proceeded slowly during early 1940. It was then realized by both Lockheed and the Air Corps that with either the Pratt & Whitney XH-2600 or the Wright R-2160, the XP-49 would be overpowered. Accordingly, in March 1940 the decision was made to substitute a pair of the new Continental XIV-1430-9/11 twelve-cylinder liquid-cooled inverted vee engines, rated at 1,540 hp for take-off and driving outward-rotating propellers to counteract torque*. Other agreed changes included the substitution of dummy plates for the originally planned armour to expedite construction of the prototype and alleviate critical procurement problems. Consideration was also given to dispensing with the pressurized cabin, but this decision was not implemented.

Finally, towards the end of 1940, Lockheed was able to release engineering personnel to work on the XP-49 and, on 23 December of that year, detailed design was begun under the leadership of project engineer M. Carl Haddon. Mock-up inspection was completed on 28 August, 1941, and at that time, although favoured by the Air Materiel Command, Lockheed's recommendation to replace the standard 60-round drum for each of the 20 mm cannon by 90-round drums of its own design was not accepted. Construction of the prototype (40-3055) proceeded normally but soon outpaced that of its powerplant, with the first two Continental engines—not yet cleared for flight operations—being received by Lockheed on 22 April, 1942. At last, in November 1942 the XP-49 and its engines were ready for flight and, on the 14th of that month, the experimental aircraft was flown for 35 minutes at Burbank by Joe Towle.

As could be anticipated due to the fact that two-thirds of its airframe components were common with those of the P-38—main differences being found primarily in the engine installation, in the use of a heavier and stronger undercarriage, and of a pressurized cabin similar to that fitted to the XP-38A—the first three flights of the XP-49 revealed no new problems. Nevertheless, the aircraft was grounded within a week to be fitted with XIV-1430-13/-15 engines—rated at 1,350 hp for take-off and 1,600 hp at 25,000 ft (7,620 m)—and to have its Royalin tanks replaced by P-38 self-sealing fuel cells. At the same time a flight-test engineer's jump seat was added aft of the pilot's seat. Flights were resumed in December 1942, but were marred by problems with the hydraulic systems. On 1 January, 1943, while being flown by test pilot Joe Towle and flight-test engineer John Margwarth, the XP-49 suffered an hydraulic line and electrical system failure. In the ensuing single-engined emergency landing at Muroc AAB, the aircraft was damaged when its port undercarriage unit collapsed.

While being repaired, the XP-49 received 7¾-in (19·7 cm) taller vertical tail surfaces and, in this form, was delivered to Wright Field on 26 June, 1943—almost twenty-seven months later than originally scheduled. By then the XP-49 was no

*The port propeller rotating counter-clockwise when viewed from the rear, and the starboard propeller clockwise.

The XP-49 at Wright Field after installation of enlarged tail surfaces. (*Official US Air Force photograph*)

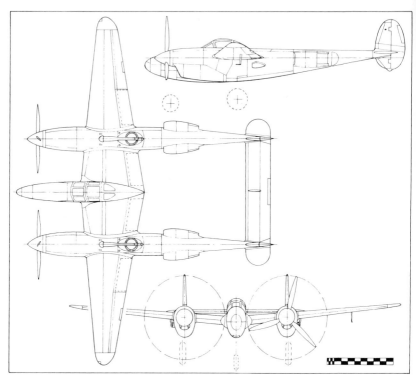

Lockheed XP-49

longer of great interest to the USAAF, as its Continental engines were not to go into quantity production and as its performance was inferior to that of the P-38J already in service. For example, the XP-49 had a top speed of 406 mph at 15,000 ft (653 km/h at 4,570 m) versus the P-38J's top speed of 414 mph at 25,000 ft (666 km/h at 7,620 m). Furthermore, engine maintenance problems and continued fuel-system difficulties — which necessitated a switch to metal tanks — limited the use of the XP-49. Thus, it was flown only briefly before ending its useful life by being dropped from a bridge crane to simulate hard landings. It was finally scrapped at Wright-Patterson AAB in 1946.

Related Temporary Design Designation: L-106

Span 52 ft (15·85 m); length 40 ft 0$\frac{13}{16}$ in (12·22 m); height 9 ft 9$\frac{1}{2}$ in (2·98 m) with original tail surfaces, or 10 ft 5$\frac{1}{4}$ in (3·18 m) with modified surfaces; wing area 327·5 sq ft (30·425 sq m).
    Empty weight 15,464 lb (7,014 kg); loaded weight 19,950 lb (9,049 kg); maximum weight 22,000 lb (9,979 kg); wing loading 60·9 lb/sq ft (297·4 kg/sq m); power loading 7·4 lb/hp (3·35 kg/hp).
    Maximum speed 406 mph at 15,000 ft (653 km/h at 4,570 m) and 347 mph (558 km/h) at sea level; cruising speed 372 mph (599 km/h); initial rate of climb 3,280 ft/min (1,000 m/min); service ceiling 37,500 ft (11,430 m); normal range 680 miles (1,095 km); maximum range 1,800 miles (2,895 km).

Lockheed Constellation

Unquestionably the world's most advanced airliner at the time of its inception and entry into service, the Constellation was one of those outstanding designs combining key virtues: high speed, reliable performance, passenger appeal and sound operating economics. Gifted also with most pleasing lines—with dolphin-like fuselage of circular cross section, clean wing with rounded tips, triple tail surfaces and cleanly-cowled engines—the Constellation was also a crowd-pleaser and attention-getter. Finally, the Model 49 was propitiously-timed; tested by the manufacturer and the USAAF during the war, it became available to the airlines in time for the postwar boom in intercontinental travel. Yet, in spite of all its assets, the type was only moderately successful, as its main competitors—the Douglas family of airliners, started with the more conservative DC-4 which more easily developed into advanced versions—decidedly outsold the Constellation/Super Constellation series both in the civil and military markets.

Even in its drab military camouflage the prototype Constellation was an exceptionally attractive aircraft. (*USAF*)

During 1938 Lockheed had begun studies for a new airliner with passenger seating fitting between that of its fourteen-passenger Model 18 and that of the original Douglas DC-4 (the triple-tailed aircraft, later redesignated DC-4E, which was first flown in May 1938 and accommodated 42 passengers in its original day configuration). Planned to be powered by either four Wright Cyclones or Pratt & Whitney radials (Hornets or Twin Wasps), the Model 44 Excalibur was initially proposed with accommodation for 21 passengers and a top speed of 241 mph (388 km/h). However, discussions with Pan American Airways, which had begun in late 1938, led the manufacturer to increase the seating and speed of the Model 44, first to 30 passengers and 270 mph (434 km/h) and then to 40 passengers and 300 mph (483 km/h), with the aircraft now to be fitted with more powerful double-row radial engines from either Pratt & Whitney or Wright. As airline negotiations progressed, mock-up and wind-tunnel models of the Excalibur were built. Pan American's interest in the Model 44 was close to resulting in a contract when in June 1939, after Transcontinental and Western Air had realized the need for an airliner faster and larger than the 246 mph (396 km/h)/33-seat Boeing 307

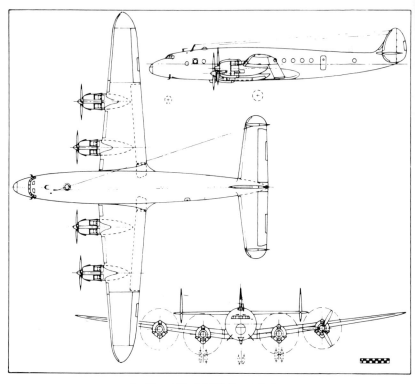

Lockheed Model 049 Constellation

Stratoliners it had on order, Howard Hughes and Jack Frye went to Burbank to discuss TWA's requirements for a pressurized transport with nonstop coast-to-coast capability. A payload of 6,000 lb (2,720 kg), a maximum range of 3,500 miles (5,630 km) without payload, and a speed of more than 250 mph (402 km/h) at 20,000 ft (6,095 m) were required by TWA; furthermore, the airline specified that the aircraft had to fit in its existing maintenance hangars. As it appeared to Lockheed that an aircraft meeting these requirements would be even more attractive to Pan American than the latest Model 44 proposal, the Excalibur project was dropped in favour of a new design, the Model 49 Excalibur A, soon renamed Constellation.

Initially under the direct supervision of its chief engineer and chief aero-dynamicist, Hall Hibbard and Kelly Johnson, but later under a team led by project engineer Don Palmer, in the summer of 1939 Lockheed began initial design work to meet TWA's requirements. Pressurization—with a 4·17 lb/sq in (0·29 kg/sq cm) differential to maintain a cabin altitude of 8,000 ft (2,440 m) when cruising at heights up to 20,000 ft (6,095 m)—necessitated a circular cross section for the fuselage. Its dolphin-like shape was selected to obtain good aerodynamic efficiency and to lower the nose and thus shorten and strengthen the twin-nosewheel unit. Six nose/windshield configurations were also evaluated until a single-curvature conical windshield was retained. Integral tanks were fitted in the twin-spar wing and Fowler flaps were installed between the ailerons and the fuselage. Triple-tail surfaces—consisting of two inset fins and rudders near the ends of the tailplane and a third fin and rudder on the fuselage centre line—were adopted so that the aircraft would clear the doors of existing maintenance hangars. Finally, the design team decided on the use of hydraulically-boosted control surfaces and of a tricycle undercarriage, with the twin-wheel main units retracting forward into the inboard engine nacelles. The latter were first planned to be of the reverse-flow type but were eventually close-fitting units as tested on the fifth Lockheed Ventura.

By the end of November 1939, performance figures for two versions of the aircraft—both planned to accommodate either 44 passengers in double seats on both sides of a centre aisle or 20 passengers in sleeping berths—were ready to be presented to the airlines. The Model 049-16-01 was to be powered by four 2,000 hp Pratt & Whitney Double Wasps whereas the 049-99-01 was to have four similarly-rated Wright Double Cyclones. With either type of powerplant, maximum speed was estimated at 360 mph (579 km/h), cruising altitude at 20,000 ft (6,095 m), ceiling at 35,000 ft (10,670 m), and two-engine ceiling 10,000 ft (3,050 m); moreover, it was anticipated that the Constellation would climb faster on three engines than the Douglas DC-4 could with all four. Performance such as this could only attract the airlines—which then were mainly operating DC-3s with a cruising speed of 200 mph at 8,000 ft (322 km/h at 2,440 m), while the standard USAAF fighter of the time, the Curtiss P-40, had a top speed of 357 mph at 15,000 ft (575 km/h at 4,570 m)—and in early 1940 TWA placed an initial order for nine Double Cyclone powered Constellations. Later this airline increased its order to forty, while Pan American also ordered forty Model 49s and an unidentified customer placed an order for four more to provide Lockheed with an 84-aircraft backlog when the decision to proceed with construction was taken.

While construction of the first of these Model 49s was underway, the United States was drawn into the war and, for the duration of hostilities, manufacture of commercial aircraft was no longer authorized. However, the USAAF needed fast, long-range transports to provide logistic support to forces operating throughout the world and on 20 September, 1942, gave Lockheed authorization to complete the first Constellations ordered by TWA as C-69-LOs (43-10309/43-10317) under Contract AC32089. By Contract AC26610, awarded nine days later, the USAAF ordered 180 additional aircraft (42-94549/42-94728) which were to be finished to full military standards. AAF contracts were subsequently increased to include a total of three hundred and thirteen C-69s of various models but, following cancellations at the war's end, only fifteen military aircraft were delivered. After the programme had been reprieved by the USAAF, it moved forward rapidly, and the first aircraft, powered by four 2,200 hp Wright R-3350-35s was completed in December 1942.

Bearing the civil registration NX25600, but finished in military camouflage and wearing the national insignia (white star on simple blue circle) of the period, the C-69-LO (Model 049-46-10, c/n 049-1961, and assigned the serial 43-10309) was first flown at the Lockheed Air Terminal on 9 January, 1943. Crew on the maiden flight included E. T. 'Eddie' Allen—the noted test pilot on loan from Boeing and who was killed less than two months later in the crash of the second Boeing XB-29—Milo Burcham, Rudy Thoren, Dick Stanton and Kelly Johnson. As everything went well, five more flights were made on that day with the last one ending at Muroc AAB in the Mojave Desert, where critical trials were to take place away from populated areas. Officially accepted by the USAAF in July 1943, the prototype Constellation was then returned to Lockheed for further testing.

Subsequently 43-10309 was scheduled for delivery to Wright Field, Ohio, and, taking advantage of this occasion, it was flown by Howard Hughes and Jack Frye (with three other crew members and twelve important passengers) nonstop from Burbank to Washington National Airport in 6 hr 57 min 51 sec.

Accelerated service tests were conducted at Vandalia Field, a satellite of Wright Field. At their conclusion, the aircraft was returned to Burbank for conversion as the XC-69E (Model 049-39-10), with four 2,100 hp Pratt & Whitney R-2800-83s, and to serve as a flying testbed for the Double Wasp powered version of the Constellation on offer to airlines. Converted back to Double Cyclones, it was sold as surplus to Hughes Aircraft and registered NC25600. In the mid-fifties, it was reacquired by Lockheed and modified once again as a prototype for the Super Constellation series (c/n 1049-1961S, NX67900). Its interesting career in turn saw it fitted to test 600-US gal (2,271-litre) tip tanks for later versions of the Super Constellation, the radar installation of the WV-2 airborne early-warning aircraft, and the engine for the Model 188 Electra (an Allison 501 propeller-turbine was mounted in the No.1 position in place of a Wright R-3350-BD1). Finally, it was sold to California Airmotive which used its nose section to repair a damaged aircraft.

The XC-69E, the sole Pratt & Whitney Double Wasp powered version of the Constellation.

Fourteen other C-69 series aircraft were accepted by the USAAF by the end of the war, when existing contracts were cancelled. However, Lockheed decided to complete the aircraft already on its assembly line as civil Model 049s before proceeding with the all-new Models 649/749. Furthermore, after the war the company built twelve more military Constellations (C-121A, VC-121B and PO-1W) to bring total production of the type to 233 aircraft. In the following paragraphs the military aircraft are described first, and are followed by details of the commercial and projected variants.

C-69-LO (Model 049-46-10): Including the prototype, which was first registered NX25600, nine aircraft ordered initially by TWA were delivered to the USAAF as C-69-1-LOs (43-10309/43-10317). They were followed by five aircraft ordered by the USAAF: one C-69-1-LO (42-94549) and four C-69-5-LOs (42-94551/42-94554). Aircraft 42-94555 through 42-94561 were virtually complete at the war's end but, not accepted by the USAAF, were refurbished before delivery to BOAC and TWA as Model 049s. The C-69s were powered by four 2,200 hp eighteen-cylinder Wright R-3350-35s driving three-blade propellers. Accommodation included 44 seats on the starboard side of the cabin, four folding four-seat benches on the port side, and two lavatories aft. The first aircraft was later converted to become the XC-69E, others were quickly sold as surplus by the War Assets Administration, while a few still in USAF service in 1948 were reclassified as ZC-69-LOs.

222

C-69A-LO (Model 049-43-11): Projected troop transport (100 bench-type seats) with improved R-3350 engines and rifle-firing ports in windows. Not built.

C-69B-LO (Model 349-43-11): Proposed long-range troop transport version with increased fuel capacity. Cancelled.

C-69C-1-LO (Model 049-46-19): VIP transport version of the C-69-1-LO with 42 seats and 2,200 hp R-3350-35A engines. One built (42-94550), which became ZC-69C-1-LO in 1948 before being sold as surplus.

C-69D-LO: Projected development of the C-69C-LO with various improvements, including thermal anti-icing system in place of Goodrich de-icing boots, and 57-seat interior. Three ordered as part of Contract AC1111 but none completed.

XC-69E-LO (Model 049-39-10): First C-69-LO (43-10309) converted as engine testbed with 2,100 hp Pratt & Whitney R-2800-83s and thermal anti-icing system. Later modified back as Double Cyclone powered Model 049.

C-121A-LO (Model 749-79-36): Ten aircraft (48-608/48-617) were ordered in February 1948 for service with the Military Air Transport Service as cargo/personnel transport versions of the postwar Model 749. Nine were actually delivered as C-121A-LOs with reinforced flooring and 112 in by 72 in (2·84 m by 1·83 m) main-deck cargo-loading door on the aft port-side. When fitted as personnel transports they could carry 44 passengers, while for medical evacuation they had provision for 20 litters and medical attendants. Like the Model 749s, they were powered by four 2,500 hp Wright 749C-18BD-1s. In service they were rapidly converted as VC-121A-LO VIP transports, with 48-610 being named *Columbine II* whilst used by President-elect Eisenhower in 1952, 48-613 being used by General MacArthur as *Bataan*, and 48-614 becoming General Eisenhower's first *Columbine*. The last C-121As were phased out by the USAF in April 1968, while 48-613, which had been transferred to NASA in 1966 as NASA 422, was retired in March 1970 and sent to the Army Aviation Museum at Fort Rucker.

Publicity photograph of the sole VC-121B, the VIP transport version of the Model 749, which would have become the Presidential aircraft if Tom Dewey had defeated President Truman in 1948. (*USAF*)

VC-121B-LO (Model 749-79-38): The first aircraft on the C-121A (48-608) contract was completed as a VIP transport for possible Presidential use. It lacked the reinforced flooring and large cargo-loading door of the C-121A/VC-121As and had accommodation for 24 day passengers or 14 night passengers (ten sleepers and four in seats) and a stateroom. It was the first aircraft to serve with the 1254th Air Transport Squadron (Special Missions) at Washington National Airport and, later, at Andrews AFB.

C-121C: This version, as well as later suffixed C-121s, were variants of the Super Constellation and are described in the appropriate chapter.

PO-1W (Model 749A-79-43): To meet a Navy requirement for an AEW (airborne early-warning) aircraft capable of carrying large and heavy radar systems and of functioning as an aerial CIC (combat information centre), project engineer M. Carl Haddon's team undertook in June 1948 the modification of the Model 749A. Main detection equipment consisted of two large radome-housed systems, one beneath the centre fuselage—with adequate clearance being provided by the Constellation's tall undercarriage—and one atop the fuselage. Moreover, its triple-tail configuration was anticipated to result in better directional control than the single-tail configuration of a proposed version of the Douglas DC-6. Additional detection, electronic countermeasure and communications antennae, for a total of 140, were distributed throughout the aircraft. The electronic equipment was installed on the main deck and in underfloor compartments. Primary crew included five flight personnel, as well as a CIC officer and four operators, while accommodation for a ten-man relief crew was provided for long-endurance missions. The first PO-1W (BuNo 124437) was flown at the Lockheed Air Terminal on 9 June, 1949, by Joe Towle, Roy Wimmer and Charles Mercer. After its fins and rudders had been heightened by 18 in (0·46 m) to overcome directional 'stubbornness' caused by the huge height-finder radome atop the fuselage, it was delivered to NAS Patuxent River, Maryland, in August 1949. A second PO-1W (BuNo 124438) was delivered in December 1950 and the two aircraft proved their worth during NATO manoeuvres in 1951–52 (Operations Mainbrace and Mariner). Powered by four 2,500 hp Wright 749C-18BD-1s, the PO-1Ws were redesignated WV-1s in 1952. After serving as prototypes for the PO-2W (WV-2) version of the Super Constellation, the WV-1s had their electronic equipment removed and were sold to the Federal Aviation Agency, with which they were registered N119 and N120, before being transferred in 1966 to the USAF for special tests.

The first PO-1W turning into a north wind for take-off at the Lockheed Air Terminal on 25 January, 1950. (*B. C. Reed*)

F-BAZB, the second Model 049 Constellation acquired by Air France, was operated by the French flag carrier from June 1946 until February 1950 when it was sold to TWA.
(*Air France*)

With the delivery of the second PO-1W in December 1950, the production history of the twenty-seven military Constellations came to an end but a further 206 aircraft were delivered to civil operators between November 1945 and September 1951 as follows:

Model 049: In addition to fifteen military aircraft in the C-69 series, this Modified Basic Model Number included 73 commercial aircraft, construction of which had been started during the war on USAAF contracts. First flight of a commercial Model 049 was made on 25 August, 1945, initial delivery for training purposes was made to TWA on 14 November, and the Approved Type Certificate was granted on 11 December, 1945; final delivery was made in May 1947. The Model 049 was offered with either Wright Double Cyclone (R-3350 series), Pratt & Whitney Double Wasp (R-2800 series) or Bristol Centaurus eighteen-cylinder sleeve-valve engines, but all customers elected to have their aircraft powered by 2,200 hp Wright 745C-18BA-1 Double Cyclones with direct fuel injection. Accommodation at time of delivery varied to meet the specific needs of each customer, but a typical day configuration (Model 049-46-25 for TWA) provided for 51 passengers, flight crew of three, and two cabin attendants. Later, aircraft were modified with high-density, five-abreast seating to carry up to 81 passengers. Certification at higher take-off/landing weights were identified by suffix letters as follows:

049:	86,250/75,000 lb —	39,122/34,019 kg
049A:	90,000/77,800 lb —	40,823/35,289 kg
049B:	93,000/77,800 lb —	42,184/35,289 kg
049C:	93,000/83,000 lb —	42,184/37,648 kg
049D:	96,000/83,000 lb —	43,545/37,648 kg
049E:	98,000/83,000 lb —	44,452/37,648 kg

Model 049s were delivered to TWA (28 aircraft), Pan American (22), American Overseas Airlines (seven), BOAC and Air France (four each), KLM (six) and LAV (two).

After being operated by KLM for four years as PH-TAU *Utrecht* this Model 49 became N86531 *Capitaliner United States* in June 1950 after being acquired by Capital Airlines. (*Lockheed*)

Model 149: No aircraft of this model were built by Lockheed but some Model 049s were retrofitted with additional fuel tanks in the outerwing panels—to bring total capacity up from 4,690 to 5,820 US gal (17,753 to 22,031 litres)—and were redesignated Model 149s. In 1940–41 the Model 149 designation had been assigned to proposed commercial versions (Temporary Design Designation L-122) with reduced gross weight and Wright GR-1820-G3 engines but this project had been dropped.

Model 249: Proposed bomber version with four 2,200 hp Wright R-3350-13s which became the XB-30-LO. Armament consisted of ten 0·50-in machine-guns and one 20 mm cannon in two dorsal turrets, two ventral, one nose and one tail turret; bombload 16,000 lb (7,257 kg). Maximum speed of 382 mph at 25,000 ft

Still bearing the US registration N90827 before its delivery to El Al as 4X-AKA, this Model 149 Constellation had originally been flown as the fifth C-69 (43-10313, c/n 049-1965). (*Lockheed*)

226

(615 km/h at 7,620 m) and range of 5,000 miles (8,045 km) with 6,000 lb (2,722 kg) of bombs were predicted. A contract to prepare preliminary engineering data in competition with Boeing (XB-29), Douglas (XB-31) and Consolidated (XB-32) was awarded on 27 June, 1940, but Lockheed later withdrew.

Model 349: Lockheed's designation for the C-69B-LO long-range troop transport. Contract cancelled on VJ-Day.

Models 449 and 549: Projected passenger versions planned for postwar production but abandoned in favour of Model 649.

Model 649: Design of the first purely civil Constellation was undertaken in May 1945 to take advantage of a more powerful version of the Wright engine and incorporate various improvements, notably in cabin sound-proofing and in the air-conditioning system. Powered by four 2,500 hp Wright 749C-18BD-1s in revised cowlings to facilitate maintenance, the Model 649 had its initial gross weight of 92,000 lb (41,730 kg) later raised to 94,000 lb (42,638 kg). Maiden flight of the first Model 649 (c/n 649-2518, NX101A) took place on 18 October, 1946, but initial trials revealed severe propeller vibration. Five different types of Curtiss and Hamilton Standard propellers were tested until the use of one of the latter solved the problem. Certification was obtained on 14 March, 1947, and fourteen Model 649s were delivered to Eastern Air Lines beginning in May 1947. The Model 649 was the first Constellation version to be fitted with a 400 cu ft (11·3 cu m) ventral pannier ('Speedpak') to carry up to 8,200 lb (3,719 kg) of freight.

Model 649A: Modification of existing Model 649s with additional fuel tanks in outer wing panels (same capacity as on Model 149) and gross weight increased to 98,000 lb (44,452 kg).

YV-C-AMU *José Marti*, a Model 749 Constellation, being readied for delivery to LAV. (*B. C. Reed*)

Model 749: Specially intended for overseas operations, this version was similar to the Model 649 but was fitted during construction with the fuel tanks in the outer wing panels (maximum capacity 5,820 US gal/22,031 litres). The use of a heavier undercarriage enabled gross weight to be increased to 102,000 lb (46,266 kg), and during tests, when 13 short tons (11·8 tonnes) of water were carried in ballast tanks, test pilot Herman Salmon demonstrated that the aircraft could be lifted off at a maximum weight of 133,000 lb (60,328 kg). Lockheed delivered twenty-three Model 749s to US airlines (seven to Eastern, four to Pan American and twelve to TWA), and thirty-seven to foreign flag carriers (five to Aer Linte, one to Aérovias Guest, nine to Air France, three to Air-India, thirteen to KLM, two to LAV and four to Qantas) as well as ten to the USAF (C-121A/VC-121B). Like earlier variants of the Constellation, the Model 749 was also offered with Pratt & Whitney Double Wasp or Bristol Centaurus engines, but all were actually delivered with Wright 749C-18BD-1s.

Model 749A: Retaining the powerplant installation of the Models 649 and 749, as well as the fuel tanks of the latter, the Model 749A had a strengthened structure to enable operation at a maximum take-off weight of 107,000 lb (48,534 kg). Deliveries to US carriers totalled 32 aircraft (six to Chicago & Southern and 26 to TWA) with 27 going abroad to Air France (ten), Air-India (four), Avianca (two), KLM (seven), and South African Airways (four). The last 749A was delivered in September 1951. The two PO-1Ws for the US Navy used Model 749A airframes.

Models 849 and 949: Projected Constellation versions to be powered by four 3,250 hp Wright Turbo-Cyclone compound engines, with exhaust-driven turbines feeding power back to the crankshaft. The Model 849 was offered as a passenger transport and, to the US Navy, as a proposed production version of the PO-1W. The Model 949 was planned in passenger (up to 102 seats when using five-abreast arrangement with reduced pitch), passenger/cargo convertible, or all-cargo (5,000 cu ft/141·6 cu m main-deck capacity) versions. Neither the 849 nor the 949 went into production as Lockheed switched its effort to developing the Model 1049 Super Constellation with stretched fuselage.

The C-69s went into service with Air Transport Command during the final year of the war. After the war's end, and in spite of the USAAF's satisfaction with the type, the Air Force decided to standardize its four-engined transport fleet on the much more numerous Douglas C-54s and twelve of its fifteen C-69s were promptly sold as surplus. Deliveries of the newer C-121As and the VC-121B began in November 1948 when the latter was handed over to the 1254th Air Transport Squadron (Special Missions) at the Washington National Airport for use by the Secretary of the Air Force and the Secretary of Defense, and as a backup for President Truman's Douglas VC-118 *Independence*. Eight of the C-121As were assigned initially to the Atlantic Division of MATS at Westover AFB, Massachusetts, and during 1949 flew transatlantic passenger/cargo runs in support of the Berlin Airlift. They were later converted as VC-121As by Lockheed for service with the 1254th ATS and use by Generals MacArthur (48-613)

Details of the 'Speedpak' installation on a Model 749A (c/n 749-2659, N86523) of Pacific Northern Airlines.

The VC-121B late in its USAF career after the addition of weather radar in the nose.
(*Cloud 9 Photography*)

and Eisenhower (48-614). The C-121A (48-610) not delivered to MATS was first released to Lockheed Air Service International to be used in support of its maintenance facility at Keflavik Airport, in Iceland. In early 1950, it was modified to VC-121A standard and, in this form, was used by President Eisenhower until replaced by the VC-121E Super Constellation (53-7885).

During the 1960s, the aircraft were downgraded to C-121As until the last (48-617) was retired in August 1968 to the Military Aircraft Storage and Disposition Center at Davis-Monthan AFB, Arizona. Six (48-608, 609, 611, 612, 615 and 617) were then modified by civil operators as agricultural sprayers; three of these aircraft found their way to the Canadian register in April 1979, while a fourth, reconverted as a freighter, went to the Dominican Republic in May 1979. Even more unusual was 48-616 which in 1957 was donated by the US Government to Emperor Haile Selassie of Ethiopia; while operated by Ethiopian Airlines as ET-T-35, this aircraft was destroyed in an emergency landing near Khartoum on 10 July, 1957. The VC-121As formerly used by MacArthur and Eisenhower have been preserved.

The first commercial use of the Constellation was made on 3 February, 1946, when Pan American put it into service on its New York–Bermuda route. However, it was TWA which initially took fullest advantage of the type. Having received its first Model 049 in July 1945, TWA had four months to train crews as the Constellation was not certificated until 11 December. The airline then flew a New York–Paris proving flight on 25 November, a special flight for invited guests on 3 December and, finally, inaugurated regular flights between Washington, New York and Paris on 6 February, 1946. This transatlantic route was extended to Cairo on 1 April and New York–Lisbon–Madrid service was begun on 1 May. Nine days after inaugurating its international operations with Constellations, TWA had started US transcontinental service between New York and Los Angeles and, as on the North Atlantic route, the Model 049 soon proved to be the queen of the sky. Its high cruising speed enabled it to cut between two and three hours off the schedule offered by American and United with DC-4s, while its substantially greater passenger appeal enhanced its success. Tragically, on 11 July, 1946, a TWA Constellation (c/n 049-2040, NC86513) on a training flight crashed near Reading, Pennsylvania, after an inflight fire. Pending determination of the cause—later traced to an electrical failure—and modifications, the type was grounded between 12 July and 23 August, 1946. The Model 049s were then returned to service by TWA and, beginning in the late spring of 1947, were joined in US domestic service by the Model 649s of Eastern Air Lines. The only other domestic trunk airlines to fly Constellations were Chicago & Southern (with its 749As going to Delta after C & S was taken over) and, with used aircraft, Braniff, Capital and Western.

Over the North Atlantic, where a USAAF C-69 had made the first crossing for the type in August 1945 (14 hr 12 min nonstop from New York to Paris) and a Model 049 of Pan American had made an initial proving flight to Hurn, on 4 February, 1946—TWA's aircraft were joined in 1946–47 by Constellations operated by American Overseas Airlines, Pan American, BOAC, Air France and KLM. Normal operations on this route required intermediate stops, with Shannon and Gander being the two most frequently used airports. No other major carrier acquired Constellations for use over the North Atlantic but it is interesting to note that in 1949 Swissair had contemplated obtaining five aircraft (one used Model 049 and four 749s). With financial help from the Swiss Government, however, in 1950 this airline was able to purchase the first of its new Douglas DC-6Bs and did not take up its Constellations.

G-ALAL *Banbury* with which BOAC inaugurated its London–Australia Constellation services on 1 December, 1948; this 749 Constellation had previously been operated by Aer Linte as EI-ACS. (*British Airways*)

As more aircraft became available, some of the airlines started operating Constellations on other routes with, for example, BOAC initiating service to Canada on 15 April, 1947, to Australia on 1 December, 1948, and to Chile on 3 October, 1950. Notable users of new Constellations were three British Commonwealth airlines, with service to the United Kingdom beginning in December 1947 (Qantas), June 1948 (Air-India) and August 1950 (South African Airways). From South America, early Constellation operators were Avianca from Colombia, LAV from Venezuela, and Panair do Brasil. The last of these, which obtained its Constellations from Pan American, had inaugurated service on the Rio de Janeiro–Recife–Dakar–Lisbon–Paris–London route as early as May 1947.

Completed as the eighth C-69 (43-10316), this aircraft was acquired by A. Schwimmer to fly armaments to Israel under the flag of convenience of LAPSA in Panama; it is seen at Burbank with US registration and faded LAPSA title. In 1951 it became 4X-AKC with El Al; still operated by this carrier it was shot down over Bulgaria on 27 July, 1955.
(*B. C. Reed*)

With the major carriers the Constellation, which had lost its uncontested supremacy when the Douglas DC-6B had entered service in April 1951 and the Comet inaugurated scheduled jet service in May 1952, was progressively displaced by the Super Constellation and later variants of the Douglas four-engined transports. Initially, used aircraft found a ready market and Constellations appeared over the years on the civil registers of at least twenty-three countries. Among these aircraft three of the seven Israeli registered aircraft (4X-AKA/ 4X-AKC) had an interesting history as, first operated as C-69s by the USAAF, they were acquired in early 1948 by Schwimmer Aviation Service at a unit price of only $15,000 (when new Model 749s were selling for $1,000,000). Using LAPSA (Lineas Aéreas de Panama) as a front, Al Schwimmer had purchased these aircraft to provide the yet-to-be-born State of Israel with a means of ferrying the weapons and ammunition it was acquiring covertly. Later, after refurbishing by Lockheed, the three ex-C-69s appeared in scheduled service with El Al markings. One of them (4X-AKC, c/n 049-1968, ex N90829 and 43-10316), carrying fifty passengers and seven El Al crew on a flight from London to Lydda, was shot down over Bulgaria on 27 July, 1955.

XA-GOQ (c/n 749-2503) of Aérovias Guest S.A. This Constellation, which was used at one time as a flying testbed in France, is now preserved at the Musée de l'Air, Le Bourget, Paris.
(*Lockheed*)

231

In 1960/61 seven Model 749/749A Constellations, which Air France replaced by jetliners, were acquired by the SGACC. With this French government agency, these aircraft retained their civil registrations and were operated for some ten years in the maritime search-and-rescue role. Another Model 749 (c/n 2503 originally operated by Aerovias Guest as XA-GOQ) was acquired from Air France in 1962 by the Armée de l'Air. With the call-sign F-ZVMV, it was used by the Centre D'Essais en Vol (CEV) at Istres as an engine testbed. In 1980 this aircraft became part of the collection of the Musée de l'Air at Le Bourget.

The full advent of the commercial jet age finally displaced the Constellations and their numbers dwindled rapidly. Yet, in 1980 half a dozen were still flying, including three operated by Air International in the United States and one with Aérolineas Argo in the Dominican Republic.

Related Temporary Design Designations: L-117, L-122, L-149, L-151, L-162/ L-163, L-196, L-211, L-214, L-222, L-235, L-244, CL-257 and CL-275

Model 049 (as originally certificated)

Span 123 ft (37·49 m); length 95 ft 2 in (29 m); height 23 ft 8 in (7·21 m); wing area 1,650 sq ft (153·285 sq m).

Empty weight 55,345 lb (25,104 kg); maximum weight 86,250 lb (39,122 kg); wing loading 52·3 lb/sq ft (255·2 kg/sq m); power loading 9·8 lb/hp (4·4 kg/hp).

Maximum speed 329 mph (529 km/h) at sea level; cruising speed 275 mph (442 km/h); initial rate of climb 1,620 ft/min (494 m/min); service ceiling 25,500 ft (7,770 m); range 2,290 miles (3,685 km) with maximum payload of 18,400 lb (8,346 kg), and 3,680 miles (5,920 km) with payload of 7,800 lb (3,538 kg).

Model 749

Dimensions as for Model 049.

Empty weight 58,970 lb (26,748 kg); maximum weight 107,000 lb (48,534 kg); wing loading 64·8 lb/sq ft (316·6 kg/sq m); power loading 10·7 lb/hp (4·9 kg/hp).

Maximum speed 358 mph at 19,200 ft (576 km/h at 5,850 m); cruising speed 327 mph (526 km/h); initial rate of climb 1,280 ft/min (390 m/min); service ceiling 25,000 ft (7,620 m); range 1,760 miles (2,830 km) with payload of 16,300 lb (7,394 kg), and 4,150 miles (6,670 km) with payload of 3,300 lb (1,497 kg).

Lockheed P-80 (F-80) Shooting Star

Development of the XP-80, the prototype of America's first combat-ready jet fighter and its first aircraft to exceed the 500-mph mark, was initiated in the spring of 1943. At that time the USAAF had just introduced into combat the Republic P-47 Thunderbolt, its first single-engined warplane capable of challenging effectively the Luftwaffe's Messerschmitt Bf 109 and Focke-Wulf Fw 190, and was about to go fully on the offensive in Europe. This offensive, however, was soon to be challenged by new and formidable adversaries as the spring of 1943 saw the forming of Erprobungskommando 16, the Luftwaffe's operational testing unit equipped with the Messerschmitt Me 163B-1a—the world's first rocket-powered fighter aircraft—and the flight testing of four Messerschmitt Me 262s.

To meet these new types the Allies were poorly prepared as their development of jet fighters was lagging behind. In the United States the Bell XP-59A, the first

Lulu Belle, the Halford H.1B-powered Shooting Star prototype, at Muroc. (*Lockheed*)

jet fighter for the USAAF, had made its tentative maiden flight on 10 October, 1942, while the McDonnell XFD-1—the progenitor of the new breed for the US Navy—had been ordered in January 1943 but was still two years away from flight trials. In the United Kingdom, the Gloster E.28/39 jet-powered experimental aircraft had flown for the first time on 15 May, 1941, the first Gloster Meteor on 5 March, 1943, and the prototype de Havilland Vampire on 20 September, 1943. Obviously quick action was required if the Allies were to be able to sustain their strategic bombing offensive. A Lockheed team led by Clarence L. 'Kelly' Johnson rose to the challenge and completed the XP-80 prototype 178 days after being formally invited by the USAAF's Engineering Division to submit a fighter proposal around the de Havilland-built Halford H.1B turbojet.

This invitation, which was extended on 17 May, 1943, during a conference chaired by Brig-Gen Franklin O. Carroll, chief of the AAF Engineering Division, formalized preliminary discussions held between representatives of Lockheed and the Air Technical Service Command. Aware of Lockheed's development work on turbojet engines and its proposed L-133 jet fighter, in late 1942 the AAF had transferred to Lockheed the preliminary design studies undertaken by the Bell Aircraft Corporation for the XP-59B single-engined jet fighter and, in March 1943, the specifications and drawings for the Halford H.1B turbojet.

Four weeks after being formally requested to submit a proposal, Lockheed officials were back at Wright Field to present a quotation for $524,920 and reports on 'Preliminary Design Investigation and Manufacturers Brief Model Specifications' for the L-140 project. Two days later, on 17 June, 1943, the AAF gave the go-ahead to the project and action was taken to process a Letter Contract for $515,018.40 (estimated cost of $495,210 plus a four per cent fixed fee versus the six per cent fee originally quoted by Lockheed). Letter Contract No.W535 ac-40680 was approved on 24 June, 1943, for Project MX-409 and was followed on 16 October by a formal contract for the same amount. Subsequent additions, reflecting change orders, the inclusion of wind-tunnel models, and flight testing of the XP-80 and XP-80A brought the final contract cost to $1,044,335.36.

One of the key requirements imposed on Lockheed was the need to complete the first aircraft within 180 days of contract's award. To realize this ambitious goal, Kelly Johnson, assisted by W. P. Ralston and D. Palmer, assembled a team, which at its peak included only 23 engineers and 105 assembly personnel, and adopted a 10-hr day/6-day week schedule. Housed in a temporary building, the start of the 'Skunk Works', near the wind tunnel at Plant B-1, the team set out to finalize the design of the L-140 and to build the prototype XP-80 in record time and complete secrecy.

Adopting from the onset a simple design, Johnson and his team produced a clean aircraft with low aspect ratio, laminar-flow wing, conventional tail surfaces and nosewheel undercarriage. Its Halford H.1B engine was fed by wing-root air-intakes, exhausted through a straight tailpipe, and was attached to a bulkhead on the aft part of the main fuselage section. This section, with the tailpipe and tail surfaces, was detachable for easy access to the turbojet. The pilot sat in an unpressurized cockpit, located well forward of the wing and covered by a rearward-sliding bubble canopy. The nose of the aircraft contained a battery of six 0.50-in machine-guns as well as navigational, radio and electrical equipment.

The mock-up of the XP-80 was ready within four weeks of contract award and was inspected at Burbank on 20–22 July, 1943, by twelve AAF officers, a Navy officer of the Bureau of Aeronautics, and two RAF officers serving with the British Air Commission. Only minor changes were recommended by the inspection team, and construction of the aircraft, which received the AAF serial 44-83020, progressed rapidly. Benefiting from the highest priority, as evidenced by the fact that all its GFE (Government Furnished Equipment) items – such as guns, tyres, instruments, etc — were received by Lockheed within six days of the start of the project, the XP-80 was soon ahead of schedule. Unfortunately for Lockheed and the USAAF, the engine programme was not proceeding apace and delivery of the first, non-flyable turbojet was delayed several times, forcing Lockheed to rely on a wooden engine mock-up for longer than initially anticipated.

Finally the non-flyable engine was received on 2 November, 1943, and fourteen days later, after it had been trucked from Burbank to Muroc AAB, the XP-80 was officially accepted by the Army Air Forces. Although problems beset the aircraft before it could begin its flight-trial programme, Lockheed and Kelly Johnson's team had beaten the schedule by completing the aircraft within 143 days from the date of award of the Letter Contract. Quite a feat, indeed, when one considers the revolutionary nature of the project and the fact that the aircraft was not a mere research aircraft but was the prototype of a genuine fighter aircraft complete with armament!

While the XP-80 was under construction consideration had been given to installing for initial trial purposes a less powerful General Electric I-16 turbojet whereas the contemplated production aircraft were to be powered by the Halford H.1B built under licence by Allis-Chalmers as the J36. However, with the I-16 the XP-80 would have been decidedly underpowered and the proposal was dropped. More successful was Lockheed's proposal for a larger and heavier L-141 version to be powered by a General Electric I-40 (later to be produced by both General Electric and Allison as the J33) which was made in September 1943 and resulted in a 16 February, 1944, contract for two XP-80As. More representative of the production aircraft, the XP-80A was destined to supplant the earlier XP-80 which thus became before its maiden flight an aerodynamic prototype for the new jet fighter.

On 17 November, 1943, while the H.1B installation in the XP-80 was under-going ground testing, both air ducts collapsed without warning when the engine was run up to 8,800 rpm, and ingestion of intake debris cracked the engine's impellers. Failure of the ducts, which were stressed to withstand 4 lb/sq in pressure, was attributed to faulty load distribution. Accordingly, while awaiting delivery of a replacement engine, the ducts were strengthened. Finally, a new engine was received on 28 December and, after installation in the XP-80, successfully passed its ground test. 'Lulu Belle', as the XP-80 had by then been nicknamed, was finally ready to fly.

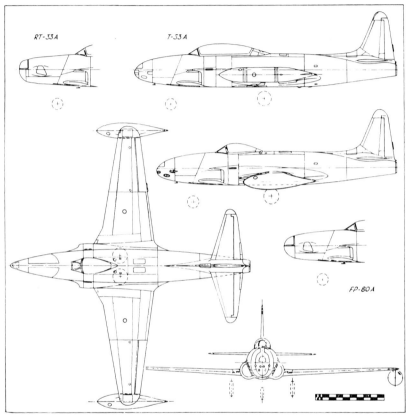

Lockheed F-80C Shooting Star, with nose of FP-80A, and T-33 versions

With Milo Burcham at the controls, the first jet-powered Lockheed aircraft became airborne at 09·10 hr on 8 January, 1944. Unfortunately, undercarriage-retraction failure and pilot's concern over the boosted ailerons' sensitivity led to this flight being aborted after only five minutes. After quick repair of the faulty undercarriage switch, the XP-80 was back in the air and this time Burcham completed a successful flight with a spectacular low-level display of the aircraft's speed and handling capability. Subsequent test flights disclosed a number of problems, including bad stall and spin characteristics, high stick force, unsatisfactory fuel management system, and poor engine reliability and performance. Satisfactory modifications were made progressively and, while under tests, the

235

P-80 reached a top speed of 502 mph at 20,480 ft (808 km/h at 6,240 m). By then the aircraft had been fitted with production-type wing and tail unit tips instead of the original blunt tips and thus could be distinguished from later P-80s only by its shiny green paint scheme, smaller size and the position of its air intake.

In November 1944, following the delivery of the two XP-80As and of the first YP-80A, 'Lulu Belle' was transferred to the 412th Fighter Group for tactical evaluations. It was subsequently returned to Muroc Flight Test Base before being assigned to the AAF Training Command at Chanute Field, Illinois. Finally, on 8 November, 1946, the XP-80 ended its 34-month flying career when it was sent to storage for eventual display at the National Air and Space Museum. In May 1978 restoration of this historic aircraft — the first AAF aircraft to exceed 500 mph in level flight — was completed by the museum staff.

Fitted with cockpit pressurization, a feature which had been considered unnecessary for the XP-80, the two XP-80As were larger and heavier in order to accommodate the General Electric I-40 turbojet. Externally, they were differentiated by the air intakes which were moved aft to a position below the cockpit windshield. The first of these aircraft (44-83021) began flight trials on 10 June, 1944, and was followed on 1 August by the second XP-80A (44-83022), which was fitted with a second seat for an engineering observer. Early in its test programme the XP-80A experienced excessive cockpit temperature — due to a faulty cabin pressurization valve — and unstable duct airflow induced by boundary layer separation along the walls of the duct. This problem, whose cause was properly diagnosed by Kelly Johnson while he occupied the aft seat of 44-83022, was solved by the installation of boundary-layer bleeds and this distinctive feature characterized all production aircraft. Eventually a total of 1,732 aircraft — including prototypes and experimental models — were built between November 1943 and June 1950 in the following versions.

XP-80-LO: Powered by a de Havilland-built Halford H.1B turbojet, with a bench thrust of 3,000 lb (1,361 kg) at 10,500 rpm and an installed thrust of 2,460 lb (1,116 kg) at 9,500 rpm, the Shooting Star prototype (44-83020) was first flown on 8 January, 1944. It carried six 0·50-in machine-guns with 200 rpg, was fitted with an unpressurized cockpit covered by aft-sliding bubble canopy, and had internal fuel capacity of 200 to 285 US gal (757 to 1,079 litres) in two wing and one fuselage self-sealing tanks. The original blunt-tipped wing and tail surfaces were replaced with rounded tips after the fifth flight when sharp leading-edge fillets were added at the wing roots and the tailplane incidence was increased by 1½ deg.

XP-80A-LO: Each of the two production prototypes (44-83021/44-83022) was powered by a 4,000 lb (1,814 kg) thrust General Electric I-40 turbojet fed by intakes located further aft. The span was 2 ft (0·61 m) larger than that of the XP-80 but wing area was marginally reduced by use of a narrower chord. Length was increased from 32 ft 10 in (10 m) to 34 ft 6 in (10·52 m); maximum weight went from 8,916 lb (4,044 kg) to 13,780 lb (6,250 kg) and necessitated a stronger undercarriage. Ammunition for the six machine-guns was increased from 200 to 300 rpg and maximum internal fuel capacity was increased from 285 to 485 US gal (1,079 to 1,835 litres). In addition, the second XP-80A became the first in the series to be fitted to carry a 165-US gal (625-litre) drop tank beneath each wingtip. Boundary-layer bleed was retrofitted to the air-intake system during the course of the trial programme. The first XP-80A crashed on 20 March, 1945, but its test pilot, Tony LeVier, escaped with back injuries suffered in a heavy parachute landing. The second XP-80A (44-83022) was fitted from the onset with a second seat, aft of the pilot, for an engineering-observer. Later the aircraft was used as a testbed for the Westinghouse J34 axial-flow turbojet in support of the XP-90 programme. The intended afterburner for this engine was not initially installed but instrumentation and afterburner fuel lines were housed in a dorsal spine extending from the rear of the canopy to the front of the fin.

YP-80A-LO: Ordered on 10 March, 1944, the thirteen service-test YP-80As (44-83023 to 44-83035) were generally identical to the XP-80As and were also powered by the General Electric I-40 turbojet. After the initial phase of its manufacturer's trials, which had begun on 13 September, 1944, the first YP-80A was specially instrumented and was used by NACA at the Ames Aeronautical Laboratory, Moffett Field, California, for high-speed diving trials. The second was modified during construction as the XF-14 prototype, as described later; the third crashed on its maiden flight, killing Milo Burcham; and the fifth was modified in England by Rolls-Royce to flight test the B-41, prototype of the Nene turbojet. This last aircraft, however, was also lost due to engine failure. The remaining nine YP-80As were used for a variety of purposes including accelerated service trials and operational evaluation in the United States and overseas.

YP-80A-LO over a snow-capped range in Southern California. (*Lockheed*)

P-80A-LO (F-80A-LO): The initial production version of the Shooting Star was ordered on 4 April, 1944, when a Letter Contract covering two batches of 500 aircraft each was issued. Fourteen months later 2,500 additional P-80As were ordered from Lockheed but, following VJ-Day this second contract was cancelled and the first one reduced to 917 aircraft (including P-80A, P-80B, and FP-80A). The first 345 aircraft (44-84992 to 44-85336) were designated P-80A-1-LOs (F-80A-1-LOs after 11 June, 1948). They were powered by 3,850 lb (1,746 kg) thrust General Electric J33-GE-11s (the production version of the I-40 turbojet) or Allison J33-A-9s (a version of the same engine built by the Allison Division of General Motors Corporation). Two of these aircraft were modified respectively as the XP-80B (44-85200) and XFP-80A (44-85201) while, starting with 44-85091, the underwing armament comprising two bombs of up to 1,000 lb (454 kg) could be replaced by eight 5-in HVAR rockets. The next 218 aircraft (44-85337 to 44-85491 and 45-8301 to 45-8363) were put in production as P-80A-5-LOs (F-80A-5-LOs after June 1948) and were powered by 4,000 lb (1,814 kg) thrust Allison J33-A-17s; later, the initial production P-80A-1-LOs had their engines

P-80A-1-LO used in 1947 for testing a novel armament installation which enabled the guns to be rotated and elevated. (*US Air Force Museum*)

brought up to the same standard during regular engine overhauls. Thirty-eight P-80A-5-LOs were actually completed as FP-80A-5-LO reconnaissance aircraft as described later. The first P-80A was accepted by the AAF in February 1945 and the last twelve were delivered in December 1946.

Experimental use of P-80A/F-80A included the transfer of 44-85000, 44-85005, and 44-85235, to the US Navy with which they received BuNos 29667, 29668 and 29689 respectively. Fitted with arrester gear and catapult hook, BuNo 29668 (Lockheed Model 180-41-02) was used for carrier-suitability trials on a dummy deck and aboard the USS *Franklin D. Roosevelt*. Aircraft 44-84995 was used at Wright Field for testing the feasibility of towing the aircraft behind a Boeing B-29A-10-BN (42-93921) in an attempt to increase the fighter's range. The fifty-third P-80A-1-LO (44-85044) successively was tested with a modified rotating nose, housing four machine-guns,which could be elevated up to an angle of 90 deg, and later with a second cockpit installed in the nose in which a pilot lay prone. Armament experiments conducted with yet another P-80A-1-LO (44-85116) included jettisonable racks for 5-in rockets mounted in place of the wingtip tanks and, later, a rocket-launcher gun in a modified nose, while another P-80A was experimentally fitted with four 20 mm cannon. Finally, ramjet trials were conducted with two P-80As: 44-85214 was fitted with a 30-in diameter Marquardt

P-80A-1-LO (44-85214) with tip-mounted Marquardt ramjets. (*Lockheed*)

238

C30-10B unit on each wingtip, while 44-85042 used a pair of 20-in diameter Marquardt C20-85D. The ramjets were first used in flight on 12 March, 1947, and on 17 June, 1948, aircraft 44-85214 was flown briefly on ramjet power alone.

After the end of the Korean War, when F-80s were being phased out of regular Air Force units, 137 F-80As and RF-80As were partially brought up to F-80C standard by Lockheed Aircraft Service and, designated F-80C-11s and RF-80C-11s, were transferred to ANG and USAFR units.

XP-80B: To serve as a prototype for an improved version of the Shooting Star, Lockheed modified the ninth P-80A-1-LO (44-85200) by installing a 4,000 lb (1,814 kg) thrust Allison J-33-A-17 turbojet and fitting a thinner wing. The aircraft was soon modified further as the XP-80R for an attempt at breaking the world's speed record.

F-80B-1-LOs of the 36th Fighter Group seen on 10 February, 1948. (*US Air Force Museum*)

P-80B-LO (F-80B-LO): Initially known as the P-80Z, this postwar version was characterized by a thinner wing with thicker skin. Moreover, to provide space for water-alcohol tanks, the internal fuel capacity was reduced from 470 to 425 US gal—1,779 to 1,609 litres. Other modifications introduced in this version, and later retrofitted to many P-80As, included the installation of a Lockheed-designed ejector seat and provision for JATO bottles. The 0·50-in M-2 machine-guns of the P-80As were replaced with improved M-3 guns of the same calibre while various equipment items were modernized to improve reliability. A total of 240 P-80Bs were delivered between March 1947 and March 1948 and included 209 P-80B-1-LOs (45-8478 to 45-8480, 45-8482 to 45-8565, and 45-8596 to 45-8717) and 31 P-80B-5-LOs (45-8481 and 45-8566 to 45-8595), with the latter being winterized models incorporating canopy defrosting and using special greases and natural rubber for Arctic service in Alaska. After being brought partially up to F-80C standard by Lockheed Aircraft Service, 117 F-80Bs were redesignated F-80C-12-LOs for service with ANG and AFR squadrons.

Special P-80Bs included 45-8557 which became BuNo 29690 in USN service, and at least five aircraft—45-8484, 8485, 8528, 8538 and 8561—which were modified to duplicate the functions and guidance system of the Bell GAM-63 air-to-surface missile during a test programme conducted at Holloman AFB, New Mexico, in 1953–54.

One of the F-80Bs (45-8484) modified to test the guidance system of the Bell GAM-63 missile, with its Boeing DB-50D (48-69) control aircraft during tests at Holloman AFB, New Mexico, between June 1953 and November 1954. Note the modified nose and tip tanks containing the guidance system, the additional vertical control surfaces above and below the wing, and the smoke generator beneath the fuselage. (*USAF*)

P-80C-LO (F-80C-LO): The last production version of Lockheed's first jet fighter were heavier and more powerful developments of the P-80B which, as P-80C-1-LOs (113 aircraft with serials 47-171 to 47-217, 47-1395, 48-382 to 48-396, and 48-863 to 48-912; a further forty-nine P-80C-1-LOs were delivered to the USMC as TO-1s) and P 80C-5-LOs (75 aircraft with serials 47-526 to 47-600; a 76th aircraft, 47-601, was delivered as a TO-1), were initially powered by a 4,600 lb (2,087 kg) thrust J33-A-23 engine. The last 561 aircraft (49-422 to 49-878, 49-1800 to 49-1899, and 49-3957 to 49-3600) had a 5,400 lb (2,450 kg) thrust J-33A-35 engine, were designated F-80C-10-LOs and included four aircraft (49-3957/49-3600) originally ordered by Peru but delivered to the USAF between August and October 1951. Whereas the P-80As and P-80Bs had been built against the original wartime contract, the P-80C/F-80Cs were ordered with Fiscal Year 1947, 1948 and 1949 funds. In service, the armament of these aircraft, which featured improved M-3 guns, was increased by two additional wing pylons and provision for sixteen 5-in rockets was added. Service modifications also included the use of either under-tip 'Misawa' fuel tanks with a capacity of 265-US gal (1,003-litre) or 230-US gal (871-litre) Fletcher centreline tip tanks.

As part of an Air Force structures research programme the first P-80C-1-LO

240

An F-80C-10-LO, the last fighter version of the Shooting Star. (*via Jim Sullivan/Cloud 9 Photography*)

(47-171) was constructed almost entirely from magnesium and was later redesignated NF-80C-LO. Fifty other F-80Cs were delivered to the USN and USMC with which they served under the TO-1 designation (detailed later). Another F-80C airframe was modified during production to the two-seat TF-80C operational-trainer version and served as the prototype for the T-33 series.

F-80D-1-LO: Proposed in July 1948 as a further development of the basic aircraft, the Model 680-33-07 was to have been powered by an Allison J33-A-29 turbojet and to have had improved instrumentation and cockpit arrangement derived from those of the T-33A. It was not proceeded with.

F-80E: Proposed development with swept wing and tail surfaces. It was not proceeded with (*see* Appendix A).

P-80N-NT: North American Aviation was awarded on 19 January, 1945, a contract to produce one thousand P-80As in its Dallas plant under the P-80N designation (North American charge number NA-137). This contract was cancelled shortly after VE-Day and no P-80N was completed.

XP-80R-LO: In compliance with an order from General Arnold, the XP-80B (44-85200) was prepared in the autumn of 1946 for an attempt at breaking the world's speed record of 615·8 mph (991 km/h) set on 7 September, 1946, by Group Capt E. M. Donaldson, RAF, in a modified Gloster Meteor F.4. Redesignated XP-80R, the aircraft was fitted with experimental NACA flush intakes and low-profile canopy. Still powered by a J33-A-17 engine, the XP-80R failed in October

The XP-80R in which Col Albert Boyd set the first FAI-homologated world speed record of more than 1,000 km/h on 19 June, 1947. (*USAF*)

241

1946 to average more than 600 mph in four passes over a 3-km course. Accordingly, it was returned to Burbank where the unsatisfactory flush intakes were replaced by conventional intakes, a 4,600 lb (2,087 kg) thrust Allison Model 400 engine (modified J33 turbojet with water-methanol injection) was installed, and the wings were clipped and fitted with sharper leading edges. Nicknamed 'Racey' and flown by Colonel Albert Boyd, the chief of the flight-test division of the Air Matcriel Command, the highly polished aircraft succeeded in breaking the record on 19 June, 1947. Flying at low altitude over the Muroc Dry Lake, Boyd averaged 623·738 mph (1,003·811 km/h). In recovering the world's speed record for the United States, the XP-80R became the first aircraft to take this record past the 1,000 km/h mark. The XP-80R is now part of the collection of the Air Force Museum at Wright-Patterson AFB, Ohio, where it was joined in 1979 by an ex-Uruguayan F-80C which had earlier seen combat operations in Korea.

P-80Z: This designation initially covered a number of major developments proposed by Lockheed to improve performance and capability significantly. Progressively, these changes resulted in a virtually new design, which was rejected by the AAF but eventually formed the basis for the XP-90 project. The P-80Z designation was resurrected to cover the aircraft delivered as P-80Bs from March 1947 onward.

XF-14-LO (XFP-80-LO): The prototype of the unarmed reconnaissance version of the Shooting Star was the second YP-80A-LO (44-83024) which was modified during construction to house cameras in place of the machine-guns of the fighter version. This aircraft was destroyed in an inflight collision during the night of 6 December, 1944.

XFP-80A-LO: Modified from a P-80A-1-LO airframe (44-85201), the XFP-80A carried more complete photographic-reconnaissance equipment in a modified nose which hinged upward to provide access to the camera.

ERF-80A-1-LO: To test new camera equipment, one F-80A-1-LO (44-85042) was modified by the Air Materiel Command Photographic Center and was fitted with a nose of modified contour.

F-14A-LO (FP-80A-LO/RF-80A-LO): The production version of the Shooting Star reconnaissance aircraft was obtained by converting during construction thirty-eight P-80A-5-LOs (44-85383, 85385, 85399, 85425, 85433, 85439, the odd-numbered aircraft in the batch of 44-85443 to 44-85491 inclusive and the even-

FP-80A (45-8314) of the 363rd Reconnaissance Group based at Langley, Virginia. (*USAF*)

242

An F-14A development aircraft obtained by modifying P-80A-1-LO 44-84998. (*Lockheed*)

numbered aircraft in the batch 45-8302 to 45-8314 inclusive) and by manufacturing a new batch of 114 aircraft (45-8364 to 45-8477). The RF-80A-5-LOs, as the aircraft were designated after June 1948, had a camera nose generally similar to that of the XFP-80A and were initially powered by the 3,850 lb (1,746 kg) thrust General Electric J33-GE-11 turbojet. In 1953, 98 of these aircraft were modernized and re-engined with a 5,400 lb (2,449 kg) thrust Allison J33-A-35 engine. Standard equipment consisted of one K-17 camera with a 6-in (15·24 cm) lens and two K-22 cameras with 24-in (60·9 cm) lens.

RF-80C-LO: To supplement its RF-80A inventory, in 1951 the USAF modified seventy F-80As to reconnaissance aircraft. Partially brought up to F-80C standard, including the installation of J33-A-35 engine, these RF-80Cs had an improved camera installation in a nose of modified contour.

DF-80A-LO: Designation given to F-80As modified as drone directors.

QF-80A-LO: Retaining their standard pilot's controls for ferrying purposes, three aircraft were modified as QF-80A radio-controlled drones. First flight was made on 8 December, 1946, with delivery of the three QF-80As made in June and July 1947.

QF-80C-LO: Similar modification of surplus F-80Cs. Some fitted for radio-active-fallout sampling during atmospheric nuclear device tests.

QF-80F-LO: Modernized QF-80A/QF-80C target drones with improved radio-control equipment and runway arrester hook.

TP-80C (TF-80C/T-33A): Following the TP-80C prototype, as described in the T-33 chapter, 128 TF-80C operational trainers were built under this designation. They later became T-33A-1-LOs.

TO-1 (TV-1): After receiving three P-80A-1-LOs and one P-80B-1-LO, which were used for experimental purposes, the US Navy obtained forty-nine P-80C-1-LOs and one P-80C-5-LO from the USAF to equip operational squadrons. In USN and USMC service these aircraft were designated TO-1s (TV-1s after 1950), with the use of the type letter T indicating that they were considered as jet trainers rather than combat aircraft. Their original USAF serial numbers were replaced by BuNos 33821 to 33870. Lockheed also proposed two fully navalized versions, the Models 380-74-04 and 480-72-04, but neither found favour with the Bureau of Aeronautics.

Still retaining their Air Force tail and buzz numbers, these four TO-1s are shown at the time of their delivery to the US Marine Corps. USMC insignia appears beneath the cockpit. (*Lockheed*)

Five weeks after its maiden flight, the XP-80 was flown for the first time by an Air Force officer when Capt Lien took it up for its sixth and longest flight to that time. From then on, AAF personnel played an ever-increasing role in the testing of the XP-80 and its successors as the Air Force was anxious to have the aircraft readied for combat evaluation. Thus, in spite of the loss of the third YP-80A on 20 October, 1944, four YP-80As were allocated for deployment to Europe to demonstrate their capabilities to combat crews and to help in the development of defensive tactics to be used against the Luftwaffe's jet fighters. Two aircraft were shipped to England in mid-December 1944 but on 28 January, 1945, during its second flight in the United Kingdom, 44-83026 crashed, killing its pilot. The other UK-deployed aircraft, 44-83027, was then lent to Rolls-Royce to be fitted as a testbed for the B-41 turbojet; on 14 November, 1945, it was destroyed in a crash-landing after engine failure. More fortunate were the two aircraft (44-83028 and 44-83029) shipped to the Mediterranean theatre which survived their demonstration period in Italy; back in the United States one crashed on 2 August, 1945, during a ferry flight while the other ended its useful life as a pilotless drone.

Four days after the crash of the seventh YP-80A, Major Richard Bong, the Medal of Honor holder and leading USAAF fighter ace, was killed when his P-80A-1-LO crashed shortly after take off from the Van Nuys airport. Alarmed by the high rate of accidents — by that time eight aircraft had been destroyed, seven had been damaged, and six pilots had been killed — on 7 August, 1945, the AAF ordered the type grounded until satisfactory corrective measures had been taken.

The order was partially rescinded on 1 September to enable flight testing and accelerated service trials to resume, and was fully lifted on 7 November. Unfortunately, this delay was soon compounded by yet another temporary grounding order affecting only the aircraft powered by the J33-A-9 engine. Nevertheless, the aircraft accident rate remained high, with pilot error becoming the main cause, and by September 1946 no fewer than 61 aircraft had been involved in accidents.

With regular Air Force units the Shooting Star began its career in 1945 when the tenth, eleventh and twelfth YP-80As were delivered to the 31st Fighter Squadron, 412th Fighter Group, at the Bakersfield Municipal Airport in California. Soon after, the 412th took delivery of the 14th through 30th P-80A-1-LOs and began its conversion from North American P-51Ds and Bell P-59A/Bs in anticipation of planned deployment, along with a squadron of FP-80As, to the Pacific. The Japanese surrender terminated these plans and the 412th Fighter Group was inactivated in July 1946 after completing for the AAF the operational evaluation of its first two types of jet fighters, the P-59 and the P-80.

Although by the standards of the day, it was a hot aircraft to fly, the P-80 had spectacular performance which the Air Force was keen to publicize. Thus, in addition to the previously related world's record flight of the XP-80R, Shooting Stars took part in many notable flights. The first of these was made on 26 January, 1946, when three P-80A-1-LOs, each fitted with a 95-US gal (360-litre) auxiliary tank in place of guns and ammunition, broke the transcontinental speed record between Long Beach, California, and LaGuardia, New York. Carrying standard 165-US gal (625-litre) tip tanks, Capt Martin Smith's 44-85113 and Capt John Babel's 44-85121 respectively covered the distance in 4 hr 33 min 25 sec and 4 hr 23 min 54 sec, including a refuelling stop in Topeka, Kansas. The fastest time—4 hr 13 min 26 sec for an average speed of 580·93 mph (934·9 km/h) over 2,453·8 miles (3,949 km)—was obtained by Col William Councill, who flew nonstop as his aircraft (44-85123) had been specially fitted with 310-US gal (1,173-litre) drop

Operation Extraversion: two YP-80As, deployed to Italy shortly before the end of the war, fly by Vesuvius. (*USAF*)

245

tanks. Three months later Capt Smith again made the headlines by flying a P-80A from New York to Washington, DC, in 20 min 15 sec. Another P-80A was used in June 1946 by Lieut Henry Johnson to set a 1,000-km speed record at the average speed of 426·97 mph (687 km/h). On the occasion of the first postwar National Air Races, held in Cleveland in August 1946, Shooting Stars won three trophies, including the Bendix Trophy (Van Nuys to Cleveland in 4 hr 8 min by Col Leon Gray in an FP-80A), the Thompson Trophy 180-km closed-circuit race (Col Gustav Lundquist in a P-80A), and the Weatherhead Jet Speed Dash Trophy (Lieut W. Reilly with a speed of 578·4 mph in a P-80A). In 1947 P-80As repeated their Bendix and Thompson wins.

P-80A-1-LO of the Flight Test Division, Air Materiel Command, at Wright Field on 30 April, 1947. On 26 January, 1946, this aircraft had been flown nonstop from Long Beach, California, to LaGuardia, New York, in 4 hr 13 min 26 sec. (*US Air Force Museum*)

Besides these individual feats, Shooting Stars were used for mass cross-country flights. The first was in May 1946 when twenty-five P-80As of the 412th Fighter Group toured the United States. In November 1947, twenty-five P-80Bs were taken to Alaska by the 94th Fighter Squadron, 1st Fighter Group, for six months of cold-weather testing. Sixteen F-80A/F-80Bs of the 56th Fighter Group left Selfridge Field, Michigan, on 7 July, 1948, and made a multi-stop transatlantic flight—the first by jet aircraft in the eastbound direction; they then took part in two weeks of combat training and alert duty at Fürstenfeldbrück, Germany. Later in the summer of 1948, the 36th Fighter Group took eighty F-80Bs from Florida to the Panama Canal Zone before moving permanently to Germany as part of the USAFE.

In Germany, the Shooting Stars of the 36th and 56th Fighter Groups had been preceded by the P-80As of the 38th Fighter Squadron, 55th Fighter Group, which had been briefly based at Giebelstadt before being inactivated in August 1946. In the United States, Shooting Stars served during the late 1940s with SAC, ADC (notably in Alaska with the 57th Fighter Group) and TAC units. With the last-named Command the aircraft served in both the fighter (P/F-80) and reconnais-sance (FP/RF-80) roles. In the Pacific, Shooting Stars had first been issued in 1948 to the 49th Fighter Group at Misawa in Japan, and to the 51st FG at Naha on Okinawa. By the late spring of 1950, F-80Cs equipped twelve Far East Air Forces (FEAF) squadrons—the 7th, 8th, and 9th with the 49th Fighter-Bomber Wing at

Misawa; the 35th, 36th and 80th with the 8th F-BW at Itazuke; the 39th, 40th and 41st with the 35th Fighter Interceptor Wing at Yokota; and the 16th, 25th and 26th with the 51st FIW at Naha—while RF-80As equipped the 8th Tactical Reconnaissance Squadron at Yokota. Being the most modern aircraft in the FEAF inventory, they soon played a major part in the war which broke out in Korea during the early morning hours of 25 June, 1950.

On the morning of 27 June, F-80Cs of the 8th Fighter-Bomber Wing began flying high-altitude escort for the transport aircraft evacuating United States personnel out of Kimpo and Suwon in South Korea. Later in the day four Shooting Stars intercepted eight North Korean Ilyushin Il-10 attack aircraft and Capt R. E. Schillereff and Lieut R. H. Dewald each scored a single kill while Lieut R. E. Wayne shot down two enemy aircraft to obtain the first victories for a USAF jet fighter. On the next day the RF-80As began flying operational sorties while the F-80Cs went on the offensive by flying ground support for the hard-pressed South Korean forces. The pace of operations then increased rapidly for the Shooting Stars, as on 30 June the ban against air operations over North Korea was lifted and the initial commitment of US ground forces was approved.

A detailed account of F/RF-80 operations in Korea falls outside the scope of this volume. However, even the briefest account of this most important phase in the operational life of the Shooting Star must mention the victory scored on 7 November, 1950, by Lieut Russell J. Brown who shot down a MiG-15, to score the world's first victory in air combat between jet fighters. The appearance of the MiG-15, however, marked the beginning of the end for the F-80 as an air superiority fighter and the Shooting Stars were from then on essentially used as fighter-bombers. In this role, as well as in their earlier use, their effectiveness was initially limited by the lack of suitable South Korean airfields. To increase the endurance of the aircraft whilst operating from Japanese bases, personnel from the 49th Fighter-Bomber Wing developed larger tip tanks by inserting sections of Fletcher tanks in the middle of standard F-80 tanks. With a capacity of 265 US gal (1,003 litres), these 'Misawa' tanks were carried beneath the wingtips in the standard Shooting Star fashion and increased the aircraft's radius of action by some 125 miles (200 km) to 350 miles (565 km) when carrying rockets. Later on, new centreline tip tanks, with a capacity of 230 US gal (871 litres), were adopted as standard.

An F-80C-10-LO in Korea in April 1953; it carries napalm tanks beneath the wing and 265-US gal 'Misawa' tanks beneath the wingtips. (*USAF*)

247

The range and endurance deficiencies of its jet fighters and tactical reconnaissance aircraft had already led the USAF to experiment in 1950 with inflight refuelling. While Flight Refuelling Ltd, then the world's leader in this field, modified for the USAF two Republic F-84Es by installing a refuelling probe on their port wing leading edge, the Wright Air Development Center took a simpler approach by fitting a probe on each of the tip tanks of Lockheed F-80Cs, RF-80As and T-33As, and Republic F-84Es, or on the underwing drop tanks of North American F-86As. Success with these trials led to the installation by the Far East Air Materiel Command of similar probes on the tanks of RF-80As of the 67th Tactical Reconnaissance Wing. On 6 July, 1951, three of these aircraft were each refuelled three times by a Boeing KB-29M of the 91st Strategic Reconnaissance Wing, to fly the world's first air-refuelled combat mission. Similar operational trials were made with F-80Cs beginning on 28 September, 1951, when Lieut-Col H. W. Dorris' aircraft was refuelled eight times to fly a 14 hr 15 min combat sortie. The procedure, however, proved cumbersome and was not adopted as standard for the Shooting Star.

Time on station and/or weapon loads were further increased when new air bases were built in South Korea by US engineers. Operating with F-80Cs from these bases were the 8th Fighter-Bomber Wing, which converted to F-86Fs in February/April 1953; the 18th F-BW, which converted to F-86Fs in January/February 1953; the 49th F-BW, which converted to F-84Es in June/August 1951; and the 51st Fighter Interceptor Wing, which acquired F-86Es in October/November 1951. Thus, when the Korean armistice agreement was signed on 27 July, 1953, the only Shooting Stars still flying in combat were the RF-80As of the 67th Tactical Reconnaissance Wing. In thirty-four months of combat operations, the F-80C had distinguished itself as an outstanding, if somewhat ageing, fighter-bomber. It had, however, suffered heavy losses (equal to 35 per cent of the F-80C production) with 14 of their number being shot down by enemy aircraft, 113 being brought down by ground fire and 150 being lost in operational accidents. They had flown 98,515 sorties and had been credited with the destruction of 31 enemy aircraft in the air and 21 on the ground.

F-80C-11-LO (45-8305) modified from a P-80A-5-LO and serving with the Iowa Air National Guard in the mid-fifties. (*Iowa ANG*)

While the Korean War was in progress the F-80A/Bs continued in service in the continental United States where they were primarily used for training jet-fighter pilots; by late 1951 they were finally phased out. With USAFE, F-80Bs were replaced in the 36th Fighter-Bomber Group by Republic Thunderjets during 1950 whilst with the Alaskan Air Command Shooting Stars were replaced by Starfires in 1951. Longer lived were the RF-80A/Cs which remained in USAF service until the end of 1957.

In the Air National Guard the F-80C (with new aircraft being ordered specifically for the Guard whilst others were transferred from USAF inventory) had entered service in June 1948 with the 196th Fighter Squadron (Jet) of the

F-80Cs were operated by the Fôrça Aérea Brasileira from 1958 until 1973. (*Courtesy of Col Werner Brauer, FAB*)

California ANG. At the time of the start of the Korean War, the Guard had six squadrons of Shooting Stars but all converted to other types before being called to active duty for a 21-month period. After the war, the type re-entered Guard service with F-80Cs, including the rebuilt F-80C-11/12-LO versions, equipping twenty-two squadrons and RF-80A/Cs being flown by five squadrons. Phasing-out of the F-80Cs was completed in 1958, while the 105th Tactical Reconnaissance Squadron, Tennessee ANG, became in March 1961 the last US unit to fly Shooting Stars. Air Force Reserve (AFR) squadrons also flew F-80Cs from the summer of 1953 to the autumn of 1957.

To supplement the initially slow delivery of its own jet fighters and to obtain a nucleus of jet pilots, in 1947–48 the Navy Department obtained the transfer of fifty new P-80C-1/5-LOs (47-218/47-224, 47-525, 47-601/47-604, 47-1380/47-1394, 48-382, 47-1396/47-1411 and 48-376/48-381), which respectively were assigned BuNos 33821 to 33870. During the late 1940s and early 1950s these land-based aircraft, designated TO-1s (TV-1s after 1950), served with at least two squadrons: VF-52 in the Navy and VMF-311 with the Marine Corps. When a sufficient number of Grumman F9F Panthers and McDonnell F2H Banshees were received, the TV-1s were transferred to reserve squadrons before being phased out. As previously indicated, the Navy also conducted tests with three P-80As (BuNos 29667, 29668 and 29689) and one P-80B (BuNo 29690).

J-335, an F-80C of Grupo 7, Fuerza Aérea de Chile. (*Chilean Air Attaché, Washington*)

When, in 1958, the F-80s were phased out by the Air National Guard and Air Force Reserve, 113 Shooting Stars—including original F-80Cs and rebuilt F-80C-11/12-LOs—became available for transfer to South American air forces under the US Military Assistance Program (Grant Aid). Thus, the 1° and 4° Grupos de Aviação de Caça of the Fôrça Aérea Brasileira operated thirty-three F-80C-10-LOs (Brazilian serial numbers 4200 to 4232) from Santa Cruz and Fortaleza between 1958 and 1973. During the same fifteen-year period the Fuerza Aérea del Perú—whose original order for four new F-80Cs had been taken over in 1950 by the USAF—obtained sixteen Shooting Stars, with the last being retired in 1973 by Grupo 13 at Chiclayo. Other Latin American operators of the type included the Fuerza Aérea de Chile (eighteen F-80Cs which served at various times with Grupos 6, 7 and 12 and were finally retired in 1974-75 by Grupo 7 at the Cerro Moreno Base, Antofagasta), the Fuerza Aérea Colombiana (sixteen F-80Cs operated by 10° Escuadron de Caza-Bombardeo at the Base Aérea Germon Olana in Palanquero, between 1958 and 1965), and the Fuerza Aérea Ecuatoriana (sixteen aircraft between 1958 and 1965 with the 2112 Escuadrón de Caza-Bombardeo at Taura near Guayaqil). Finally, the Fuerza Aérea Uruguaya, which had obtained fourteen F-80Cs in 1960 to equip its Grupos de Caza 1 and 2 at Carrasco, replaced them with Cessna A-37Bs in 1975.

The phasing-out of the F-80C by the Fuerza Aérea Uruguaya marked the end of the 30-year operational career for Lockheed's first jet aircraft. Designed and built in record time during the hectic days of the war, the Shooting Star had become the first American combat-ready jet fighter and holder of two world records (absolute speed and 1,000-km closed circuit). Although eclipsed by the North American F-86A and MiG-15, the F-80C had distinguished itself as a fighter-bomber during the Korean War and by becoming the first victor in air-to-air combat between jet fighters. Also the Shooting Star led directly to the T-33 series, probably the most important jet trainer yet to have been built in the western world.

Related Temporary Design Designations: L-141, L-157, L-159, L-170, L-172, L-177, L-181 and L-188

250

	XP-80	XP-80A	P-80A	P-80B	F-80C
Span, ft in*	37 0	39 0	38 10½	38 9	38 9
(m)	(11·28)	(11·89)	(11·85)	(11·81)	(11·81)
Length, ft in	32 10	34 6	34 6	34 5	34 5
(m)	(10)	(10·52)	(10·52)	(10·49)	(10·49)
Height, ft in	10 3	11 4	11 4	11 3	11 3
(m)	(3·12)	(3·45)	(3·45)	(3·43)	(3·43)
Wing area, sq ft	240	237·6	237·6	237·6	237·6
(sq m)	(22·29)	(22·07)	(22·07)	(22·07)	(22·07)
Empty weight, lb	6,287	7,225	7,920	8,176	8,420
(kg)	(2,852)	(3,277)	(3,592)	(3,709)	(3,819)
Loaded weight, lb	8,620	9,600	11,700	12,200	12,200
(kg)	(3,910)	(4,354)	(5,307)	(5,534)	(5,534)
Maximum weight, lb	8,916	13,780	14,000	16,000	16,856
(kg)	(4,044)	(6,250)	(6,350)	(7,257)	(7,646)
Wing loading, lb/sq ft	35·9	40·4	49·2	51·3	51·3
(kg/sq m)	(175·4)	(197·2)	(240·4)	(250·7)	(250·7)
Power loading, lb/lb st	3·5	2·4	2·9	2·7	2·3
Maximum speed, mph/ft	502/20,480	553/5,700	558/s1	577/6,000	594/s1
(km/h / m)	(808/6,240)	(890/1,735)	(898/s1)	(929/1,830)	(956/sl)
Cruising speed, mph	—	410	410	497	439
(km/h)		(660)	(660)	(800)	(707)
Rate of climb, ft/min	3,000/1	20,000/4·6	4,580/1	6,475/1	6,870/1
(m/min)	(914/1)	(6,096/4·6)	(1,396/1)	(1,974/1)	(2,094/1)
Service ceiling, ft	41,000	48,500	45,000	45,500	46,800
(m)	(12,495)	(14,785)	(13,715)	(13,870)	(14,265)
Normal range, miles	—	560	780	790	825
(km)		(900)	(1,255)	(1,270)	(1,330)
Maximum range, miles	—	1,200	1,440	1,210	1,380
(km)		(1,930)	(2,320)	(1,950)	(2,220)

*Span without tip tanks

251

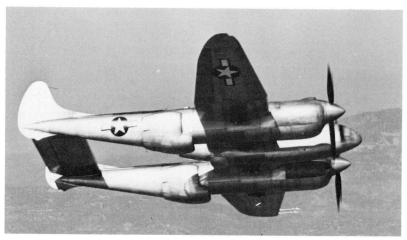

One of the least successful Lockheed designs, the XP-58 had a protracted gestation period. (*Lockheed*)

Lockheed XP-58 Chain Lightning

When in early 1940, some seven months before the maiden flight of the first Model 122 (YP-38), Lockheed was granted War Department authorization to sell to France and Britain its Model 322—a proposed development of the Model 122 to be powered by a pair of Allison V-1710-C15s without turbosuperchargers—the company agreed in exchange to develop and produce at no cost to the US government a prototype of an advanced version of the P-38, formal agreement being signed on 12 April, 1940.

With James Gerschler as project engineer, Lockheed drew up preliminary details for its L-121 fighter. Then intended to be powered by two turbosupercharged Continental IV-1430 liquid-cooled engines, the aircraft was offered in two versions. The single-seat version was to retain the standard P-38 armament —one 20 mm cannon and four 0·50-in machine-guns—while in addition the two-seater was to have one 0·50-in remote-controlled gun at the end of each tail boom. During a meeting at Wright Field in May 1940, the decision was taken to proceed with the two-seat version, which received the XP-58 military designation. Two months later, the Air Corps and Lockheed agreed that with a pair of 1,500 to 1,600 hp Continental engines the two-seater would probably be underpowered and decided to switch to two 1,800 hp Pratt & Whitney XH-2600-9/-11 liquid-cooled engines. Revised specifications for the re-engined XP-58 (Model 20-24) were issued by Lockheed on 10 September, 1940. Forward-firing armament was increased by a second 20 mm cannon, and the impractical tail-boom guns were to be replaced by a remote-controlled Air Arm dorsal turret housing twin 0·5-in guns. With these changes, estimated gross weight increased by some 45 per cent to 24,000 lb (10,886 kg) and guaranteed top speed at 25,000 ft (7,620 m) dropped from 450 mph (724 km/h) to 402 mph (647 km/h). Range on internal fuel was still anticipated to be 1,600 miles (2,575 km).

Barely one month after issuing the specifications for the XH-2600 powered aircraft, Lockheed's new project engineer, Neil Harrison, was informed that Pratt & Whitney was suspending its development. Harrison and his team were forced to find new powerplants for what was becoming known at Lockheed as the 'X-engine airplane'. Design studies around either a pair of Lycoming XH-2470s, Continental XH-2860s, or Pratt & Whitney R-2800s, were prepared, with Lockheed favouring Pratt & Whitney. It was calculated that with two of these 1,850 hp engines, the XP-58 would have a loaded weight of 26,000 lb (11,793 kg) and a top speed of 418 mph (673 km/h) at 25,000 ft (7,620 m). The Air Corps, however, considered performance to be inadequate and suggested that Lockheed adopt the Wright XR-2160 Tornado engine for the XP-58 (Model 20-59).

This 2,350 hp powerplant, a forty-two cylinder, six-row engine of extremely low frontal area, was highly complex; but, though the R-2160 was problem-fraught from the onset, in March 1941 the Air Corps confirmed its support for the Tornado-powered version. Two months later it issued a Government-funded change order to install cabin pressurization for the pilot and for the aft-facing gunner, and to add a remote-controlled ventral turret. This resulted in the estimated gross weight increasing to 34,242 lb (15,532 kg) — more than twice the weight of the original Continental IV-1430 powered version. Yet, the Air Corps insisted on a guaranteed top speed of 450 mph (724 km/h). Estimated range, however, dropped by 300 miles (485 km) to 1,300 miles (2,090 km). By then the XP-58 was scheduled to be delivered in August 1942 and, to meet this deadline, the project team grew to a peak of 187 by October 1941. Following the United States entry into the war in December of that year, a reassignment of engineering staff to more pressing projects became necessary and the XP-58 design team dropped to a low of twelve people by early 1942.

The reduced-size of the design group, however, had little direct impact on the schedule as the XP-58's intended powerplant was lagging much further behind. Nevertheless, at Lockheed's suggestion, the USAAF ordered in May 1942 a

Neither fish nor fowl, the XP-58 was planned for a variety of conflicting missions and its development was impaired by the USAAF's lack of a clear goal. (*Lockheed*)

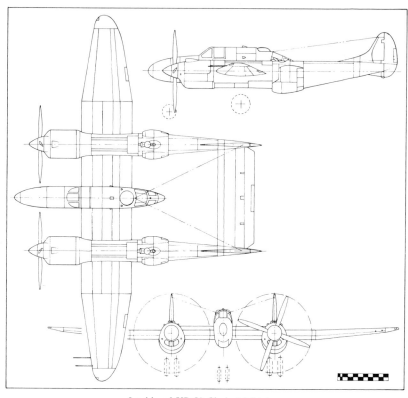

Lockheed XP-58 Chain Lightning

second prototype which was to have increased fuel capacity, and other improvements, to more than double the range to 3,000 miles (4,825 km). Shortly thereafter, thinking within the USAAF began to vacillate and the XP-58 programme was thrown into chaos when it was suggested that forward-firing armament be changed to include a 75 mm cannon, with a 20-round automatic feeder, and two 0·50-in machine-guns. As this armament was not suitable for an escort fighter, consideration was seriously given to switching the aircraft's intended role to low-level attack. In turn, this led to studies of other alternative configurations, including a two-seat attack aircraft with six forward-firing 20 mm cannon, and a three-seat attack/bombing version with a bombardier in the nose, enlarged central nacelle with an internal bomb bay, and with or without the 75 mm cannon.

As better aircraft, including the Douglas A-26 already in production and the promising Beech XA-38, were available to satisfy the USAAF's low-level/light bombing needs, signals were again switched. In November 1942 it instructed Lockheed to complete the two Tornado-powered XP-58s as bomber destroyers, a mission which by then the USAAF was not likely to have to fulfil! The first aircraft was to have four 37 mm forward-firing cannon, while the second was to carry a 75 mm cannon and two 0·50-in guns. Both were again to be fitted with dorsal and ventral turrets, and turbosuperchargers — items which had been deleted from the

254

proposed low-level attack version of the XP-58. By then calculated gross weight had soared to 38,275 lb (17,361 kg), top speed had dropped to 414 mph at 25,000 ft (666 km/h at 7,620 m), and range had been reduced to only 1,150 miles (1,850 km).

In January 1943 Lockheed brought some order to this chaos by recommending that only one prototype be built, with interchangeable nose sections to test both types of forward-firing armament. One month later the Wright Tornado engine programme collapsed and a final powerplant change was submitted by Lockheed. With USAAF concurrence, the sole XP-58 prototype (Model 20-86, serial 41-2670) was to be completed with two turbosupercharged Allison V-3420-11/-13 twenty-four-cylinder liquid-cooled engines, rated at 2,600 hp for take-off and 3,000 hp at 28,000 ft (8,535 m).

With these engines, dummy turrets, and no forward-firing armament, the XP-58 was finally flown by Joe Towle on 6 June, 1944, more than four years after its design had begun, from the Lockheed Air Terminal to Muroc AAB. Some twenty-five flights were made by Lockheed personnel prior to the delivery of the XP-58 to Wright Field on 22 October, 1944. These manufacturer's trials were marred by turbosupercharger torching. At Wright Field, the aircraft, for which the USAAF had no longer any need, remained grounded until early 1945 when it was transferred to be used as a non-flying instructional airframe.

Due to the many powerplant changes during its protracted gestation period, for which Lockheed could hardly be blamed, and to Air Force mismanagement, the XP-58 programme failed to bear fruit. Started at no cost to the Government, it ended costing the taxpayers $2,345,107—$451,556 going for the Air Force's requested changes to the first prototype, and the balance covering the Government-ordered, but then cancelled, second prototype.

As completed, the XP-58 had an 800-US gal (3,028-litre) internal fuel capacity, which, with auxiliary and drop tanks, could be increased to 1,700 gal (6,435 litres). Forward-firing armament, not actually installed on the prototype, would have consisted of either four 37 mm cannon, or one 75 mm cannon and two 0·50-in machine-guns. The dorsal and ventral turrets were to house twin 0·50-in guns. External loads of 4,000 lb (1,814 kg) could also have been carried.

Related Temporary Design Designation: L-134

Span 70 ft (21·34 m); length 49 ft 5½ in (15·07 m); height 16 ft (4·88 m); wing area 600 sq ft (55·74 sq m).

Empty weight 31,624 lb (14,344 kg); loaded weight 39,192 lb (17,777 kg); maximum weight 43,000 lb (19,504 kg); wing loading 65·3 lb/sq ft (318·9 kg/sq m); power loading 7·5 lb/hp (3·4 kg/hp).

Maximum speed 436 mph at 25,000 ft (702 km/h at 7,620 m); cruising speed 283 mph (455 km/h); initial rate of climb 2,582 ft/min (787 m/min); service ceiling 38,200 ft (11,645 m); normal range 1,250 miles (2,010 km); maximum range 2,650 miles (4,265 km).

The Little Dipper after the fitting of its fully enclosed clear canopy. (*Lockheed*)

Lockheed 33 Little Dipper

Conceived as a light monoplane, cheap to build and operate, but safe enough to be flown by relatively inexperienced pilots, this aircraft began as the personal venture of John Thorp, a Lockheed engineer. Developing this project in his own time, Thorp initially planned it as a two-seater with a 40 to 60 hp engine. Once his plans were sufficiently advanced, he showed them to his boss, Mac V. F. Short, the head of Lockheed's special projects group. Short liked what he saw and, after suggesting that the aircraft would be underpowered as a two-seater but would have good performance as a single-seater, obtained in April 1944 the agreement of Robert Gross, the company's president, to have the project taken over as the Lockheed Model 33.

As wartime restrictions and allocations of resources to projects of national interest prevented Lockheed from carrying on the design of an aeroplane for the private market, the company succeeded in attracting to it the attention of the US Army. As proposed to the Army under the name of Air Trooper, the single-seater was suggested as an 'aerial flying motorcycle'. Authorization was granted to Lockheed to proceed with the construction of two prototypes at the company's expense. Fitted with a fixed nosewheel undercarriage and an open cockpit, the aircraft was powered by a 50 hp engine specially developed by Air-Cooled Motors, and using two cylinders from a larger Franklin powerplant to drive a two-blade propeller. The first aircraft (NX18935) began flight trials at the Lockheed Air Terminal in late August 1944, with initial flights being made by Bud Martin.

During these trials the aircraft was fitted with a one-piece canopy hinged on the port side and fully enclosing the cockpit. The little monoplane showed pleasant handling characteristics, with safe flying speed as low as 40 mph (64 km/h) and STOL performance (take off in 100 ft/31 m with clearance of a 50 ft/15 m obstacle being achieved in 400 ft/122 m). None-the-less, with the end of the war fast approaching, the Army lost interest in the project. Lockheed and John Thorp, however, having achieved their goal of developing a prototype for an inexpensive light aeroplane, planned to market it after the war as the Little Dipper private aircraft.

Unfortunately, the market for this type of aircraft failed to materialize in the immediate postwar period and with financial restraints then facing the company, Lockheed was forced to take advantage of an income tax credit by writing off the Little Dipper. Accordingly, the prototype and the partially completed second aircraft were broken up and sold as scrap in January 1947.

Related Temporary Design Designations: V-305 and V-308

Span 25 ft (7·62 m); length 17 ft 6 in (5·33 m); height 7 ft (2·13 m); wing area 104 sq ft (9·662 sq m).
Empty weight 425 lb (193 kg); loaded weight 725 lb (329 kg); wing loading 7 lb/sq ft (34·1 kg/sq m); power loading 14·5 lb/hp (6·6 kg/hp).
Maximum speed 100 mph (161 km/h); cruising speed 90 mph (145 km/h); initial rate of climb 900 ft/min (274 m/min); service ceiling 16,000 ft (4,875 m); range 210 miles (340 km); endurance 2¼ hr.

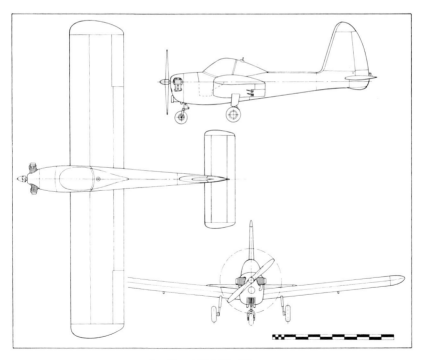

Lockheed 33 Little Dipper

257

The XP2V-1 Neptune (BuNo 48237) with original Neptune nose configuration and its dorsal fin extending forward of the dorsal turret. (*Lockheed*)

Lockheed P2V (P-2) Neptune

On the eve of the United States entry into the war it had become apparent that the US Navy would need a land-based patrol bomber with more range, greater armament load, higher level and climbing speeds and slower approach and landing speeds than provided by the Lockheed Hudson and Ventura. To meet this anticipated requirement, Mac V. F. Short, then vice-president-engineering of the Vega Airplane Company, authorized on 6 December, 1941, the first internal work order for design studies of a new patrol bomber. This private venture, which preceded official interest by fifteen months, eventually led to one of Lockheed's most successful aircraft programmes, with a production life extending over eighteen years or, when including Japanese manufacture of a derivative version, over a third of a century. Moreover, this superb aircraft remains in service in four countries forty years after its inception. Equally remarkable is the fact that one of these aircraft is still the holder of the world's distance record in a straight line for piston-engined aircraft, a record it set back in 1946.

Preliminary project activity was begun in September 1941 by chief engineer John B. Wassall and his Vega team. Then bearing the Temporary Design Designation V-135, the concept called for a twin-engined, high-wing aircraft with a gross weight of 25,000 to 35,000 lb (11,340 to 15,875 kg), power-operated turrets, two torpedoes, bombs or depth charges carried internally, and a nosewheel undercarriage. Engines were to be in the 2,000 hp class, with a pair of eighteen-cylinder Wright R-3350s being the favoured powerplants. Even though by 6 December, 1941, this initial effort had been covered by company work orders, progress initially was slow as Vega and the US Navy had more pressing requirements during the critical months following the Japanese attack on Pearl Harbor. At last, by early 1943 the military situation had stabilized sufficiently for the Navy to switch some of its procurement attention from the acquisition of immediately

258

available aircraft—with the Lockheed-Vega PV and Consolidated PB4Y being the principal land-based patrol bombers—to supporting development of new and more capable types. Accordingly, a Letter of Intent was issued on 19 February, 1943, to the Vega Airplane Corporation for two XP2V-1 prototypes based on the V-146 design study, itself a development of the V-135 with revised tail surfaces, slightly lowered wing, and relocated turrets. This Letter of Intent was followed on 4 April, 1944, by the award of Contract NOa(s)-375 for the two prototypes, and ten days later by that of Contract NOa(s)-3297 for fifteen pilot-line aircraft.

Although at first the development of the PV-2 Harpoon had higher priority than the XP2V-1 in engineering staff and floor space allocation at Plant A-1 (the Vega Airplane Company had become the Vega Airplane Corporation on 31 December, 1941, and had been fully absorbed by its parent company on 30 November, 1943), project engineer R. A. Bailey was able to get the project in high gear during the summer of 1944. Finally, the first XP2V-1 (c/n 26-1001, BuNo 48237) was completed in the spring of 1945 and on 17 May was flown at the Lockheed Air Terminal by a crew captained by Joe Towle. Even though its empty weight fell close to the upper range of the gross weight first envisaged for the V-135, the Neptune prototype was a good performer (top speed was equal to that of the PV-2 but range was from 40 to 75 per cent better, depending on the load carried, while maximum bomb load was one-third greater and defensive armament better distributed). Handling characteristics were smooth—with directional stability, manoeuvrability and single-engine control being particularly good—and the only significant change dictated by the trial programme was the elimination on production aircraft of the prototypes' dorsal fin.

At the time of the XP2V-1's maiden flight Lockheed had received contracts for two prototypes and 116 production aircraft. However, following the end of the war, orders were reduced first by 48 machines and then by a further 52, with actual delivery against wartime contracts including two XP2V-1s, fourteen P2V-1s and fifty-one P2V-2s. Fortunately for Lockheed in the lean postwar years, the Neptune was a substantially more effective patrol aircraft than any other Navy type and a new contract for thirty P2V-2s was added on 13 September, 1946. World instability, the Korean War, and the need to supply aircraft to Western allies combined to keep Lockheed's assembly lines busy with P2Vs until the spring of 1962. Moreover, the type went on to be assembled and developed in Japan to bring total production to 1,181 aircraft in the following versions:

XP2V-1 (Model 026-49-01): Two prototypes (BuNos 48237 and 48238) each powered by a pair of 2,300 hp eighteen-cylinder Wright R-3350-8s driving four-blade propellers. Armament comprised twin 0·50-in machine-guns in nose, dorsal and tail turrets, and 8,000 lb (3,629 kg) of bombs, depth charges, mines or torpedoes, in internal bomb bay. A dorsal fin extended from the base of the vertical tail surfaces to a point just forward of the dorsal turret. The crew of eight consisted of pilot, co-pilot, flight engineer, radio-operator, navigator, and three gunners. First flown on 17 May, 1945, and delivered to the US Navy in May 1946 and June 1947.

P2V-1 (Model 026-49-01): Basically identical to the prototypes—but with the dorsal fin removed and full operational equipment installed—fourteen P2V-1s (BuNos 89082/89085 and 89087/89096) were delivered between September 1946 and March 1947. The engines were 2,300 hp R-3350-8As. Sixteen 5-in HVAR rockets or four 11·75-in Tiny Tim rockets could be carried beneath the wings. The first aircraft (BuNo 89082) was modified during construction in an attempt to set a new world's distance record. All armament was removed, a new and more

259

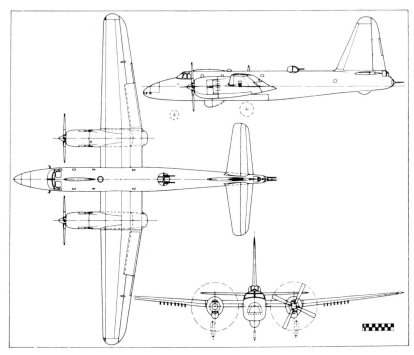

Lockheed P2V-2 Neptune

streamlined metal nose was fitted, and fuel capacity was increased from 3,350 to 8,732 US gal (12,681 to 33,054 litres) by installing extra tanks in the bomb bay and aft fuselage, and by carrying 400-gal (1,514-litre) tanks beneath the wingtips. As related elsewhere, this aircraft — named *The Turtle* — set a still-standing record on 29 September–1 October, 1946. Another unarmed P2V-1, named *Seabiscuit*, was also fitted with long-range tanks for polar exploration.

XP2V-2 (Model 026-52-01): The fifth P2V-1 airframe (BuNo 89086) was modified during construction to serve as prototype for the P2V-2 version. Powered by 2,800 hp Wright R-3350-24Ws with water injection, it was first flown on 7 January, 1947.

P2V-2 (Models 026-52-02 and 126-52-02): Like the XP2V-2 this production variant was powered by R-3350-24Ws driving three-blade propellers. The nose gunner position was replaced by six forward-firing 20 mm cannon in a metal-covered nose, of similar shape to that of *The Turtle*, and provision for carrying sonobuoys was added. The first eight P2V-2s (Model 026-52-02, BuNos 39318/39319 and 39321/39326) retained the Bell tail turret, with twin 0·50-in guns of the P2V-1s, whereas the next seventy-two (Model 126-52-02, BuNos 39327/39368 and 122438/122467) had an Emerson tail turret with two 20-mm cannon. Delivered between June 1947 and August 1948. Two of these aircraft (BuNos 39343 and 39365) were later used by the Marine Corps for airborne electronics aircrew training while BuNo 122467 was modified in 1950 by Lockheed to test a reduced four-crew accommodation optimized for bombing operations (MCR P2V-73, Model 126-52-08). One modified as P2V-3C.

A P2V-2 over NAS Jacksonville, Florida, on 3 July, 1953. (*US National Archives*)

P2V-2N (Model 126-52-07, MCR P2V-79): Two P2V-2s (BuNos 122465/122466) were modified during 1949 for polar exploration (Project Ski Jump). All armament was removed, retractable skis were fitted, and special research equipment—including a retractable tail boom for magnetic-field study—was installed. Cameras were also carried in the fuselage.

P2V-2S (Model 226-52-03): The third P2V-2 airframe (BuNo 39320) was modified during construction as prototype for an anti-submarine version. The installation of an APS-20 search radar in a ventral radome necessitated a reduction in the size of the bomb bay. Additional fuel was carried in fuselage tanks. First flown on 2 April, 1948.

P2V-3 (Model 326-59-02): This version differed from the P2V-2 in being powered by 3,200 hp R-3350-26Ws with jet stack exhaust. Fifty-three were built (BuNos 122923/122951 and 122964/122987) for delivery between August 1948 and January 1950. Eleven were later modified as P2V-3Cs for carrier operations and one as P2V-3B.

P2V-3B: Designation given to one P2V-3 (BuNo 122927), three P2V-3Cs (BuNos 122966, 122969 and 122971) and one P2V-3W (BuNo 124355) modified for close-support trials.

The ski-equipped P2V-2N (BuNo 122465) on 19 September, 1956, during Operation Deepfreeze II. It has RATO bottles aft of the wing on the fuselage sides. (*US National Archives*)

P2V-3C (Model 326-59-05): One P2V-2 (BuNo 122449) and eleven P2V-3 (BuNos 122924, 122927, 122930, 122933, 122936, 122942, 122947, 122951, 122966, 122969 and 122971) were modified as carrier-launched nuclear bombers. The nose cannon, dorsal turret, and other equipment, were removed to reduce weight and enable the P2V-3Cs to carry a 9,700 lb (4,400 kg), 14-kiloton, Mk.I atomic bomb and extra fuel. Delivered between September 1948 and August 1949. Three were later modified as P2V-3Bs. BuNo 122969 was experimentally fitted with an arrester hook beneath the aft fuselage and was used for airfield dummy deck landings at NAS Patuxent River. However, no actual carrier landings were made with this or other Neptunes.

P2V-3W (Models 326-59-04 and 526-59-04): Airborne early warning version with APS-20 radar in ventral radome operated by two specialists. Initially assigned the Modified Basic Model Number 526 but this was changed back to 326 before acceptance by the Navy. Thirty (BuNos 124268/124291 and 124354/124359) were delivered between November 1949 and February 1951. One was later modified as P2V-3B.

P2V-3Z (Model 326-59-09): Two P2V-3s (BuNos 122986 and 122987) were modified as combat transport aircraft with provision to carry six VIP passengers in an armoured cabin in the aft fuselage. Crew complement was reduced to five but the tail turret was retained when the P2V-3Zs were delivered in June and September 1950.

A combat transport P2V-3Z (BuNo 122986) with aft cabin windows (*Lockheed*)

P2V-4/P-2D (Models 426-59-03 and 426-42-03): Equipment of the P2V-4s was similar to that of the P2V-2S but they were the first production Neptunes to be fitted with tip tanks, increasing fuel capacity from the maximum 3,350 US gal (12,681 litres) of earlier variants to 4,210 gal (15,937 litres). The first twenty-five P2V-4s (Model 426-59-03, BuNos 124211/124235) were powered by 3,200 hp R-3350-26WA conventional piston engines but the remaining twenty-seven air-craft (Model 426-42-03, BuNos 124236/124262) introduced compound engines: 3,250 hp Wright R-3350-30Ws. The first of the former was flown on 14 November, 1949, while the variant with Turbo-Compound powerplants began flight trials on 20 March, 1950; deliveries were completed in March 1951. In September 1962 the P2V-4s remaining in service with Reserve squadrons became P-2Ds, as the first Neptunes to be redesignated under the new Tri-Service system.

P2V-5 (Models 426-42-06, 426-42-11, 426-42-13, 426-42-15, 426-42-16 and 426-45-15): Built in larger numbers than any other versions of the Neptune, the P2V-5 appeared in many sub-models. Initially, twenty-three Model 426-42-06s (BuNos 124865/124887) were built. Powered by two 3,250 hp R-3350-30WA Turbo-Compound engines, they differed from the P2V-4s in having an Emerson nose turret with two 20 mm cannon. Enlarged tip tanks, now mounted centrally instead of being underslung, were fitted, with the starboard tank housing a remote-controlled searchlight. They were followed by 147 Model 426-42-11s (see Appendix B for BuNos and foreign serial numbers) for the US Navy, the RAF and the RAAF, in which accommodation was provided for an ECM operator, to increase crew size from eight to nine. The Model 426-42-13s, of which 98 were built for the US Navy (BuNos 127781/127782 and 128327/128422), were fitted during production with a 17-ft (5·18-m) tail 'stinger' extension housing a MAD (magnetic anomaly detection) system. Eighty Model 426-42-15s (BuNos 131400/131479) for the US Navy had the MAD 'stinger' extension, a glazed nose, and defensive armament reduced to two 0·50-in guns in the dorsal turret. The Marineluchtvaartdienst (MLD, Royal Netherlands Naval Air Service) received twelve Model 426-42-16s which were similar to the 426-42-13s (with MAD 'stinger', nose and dorsal turrets) but had revised crew accommodation with a separate aircraft-captain station. Finally, the US Navy was the recipient of sixty-four Model 426-45-15s (BuNos 131480/131543) which differed from the 426-42-15s in being powered by 3,500 hp R-3350-32W Turbo-Compounds. First flight of the P2V-5 was made on 29 December, 1950, with deliveries taking place between April 1951 and September 1954. In service the P2V-5s were progressively modernized, with MAD 'stinger' and glazed nose being generally retrofitted to earlier variants. However, the most significant improvement was the addition of jet pods to produce the P2V-5F model.

P2V-5F/P-2E: Although maximum power had been increased more than forty per cent between the P2V-1s and the early production P2V-5s, maximum gross weight had also increased by over thirty-five per cent and performance was becoming marginal. Accordingly, in 1953 Lockheed devised a power-boosting package consisting of two 3,250 lb (1,474 kg) thrust Westinghouse J34-WE-34

P2V-5F (BuNo 124892) of VW-3; markings for five hurricane-hunting missions are painted beneath the cockpit. (*Lockheed*)

turbojets in underslung wing pods, to increase power on take-off or to boost combat dash speed. First fitted to BuNo 128363, the jet pods proved most successful and were later installed on most US and foreign P2V-5s. At the same time the reciprocating engines were upgraded to 3,500 hp R-3350-32W standard. With the turbojets installed the aircraft were first redesignated P2V-5Fs but, in September 1962, became P-2Es.

P2V-5FD/DP-2E: Designation given to at least nine P2V-5Fs modified to carry, launch, and control drones. Redesignated DP-2Es in 1962.

P2V-5FE/EP-2E: Converted P2V-5Fs with additional electronic equipment.

P2V-5FS/SP-2E: To improve submarine detection capability, some P2V-5Fs were fitted with AQA-3 Jezebel long-range acoustic search equipment and its associated Julie explosive echo-sounding gear.

P2V-6/P-2F (Model 626-42-12): Multi-purpose version of the Neptune of which 67 were built for the US Navy and Aéronavale (respectively 35 and 32 aircraft). Powered by two 3,250 hp R-3350-WAs and fitted with a slightly longer bomb bay with provision for mine-laying and photographic-reconnaissance equipment. Revised tip tanks increased maximum fuel capacity from 3,900 US gal (14,763 litres) for the P2V-5 to 4,200 gal (15,899 litres). First flown on 16 October, 1952, and delivered over the following thirteen months. Some converted to P2V-6F/P-2G and P2V-6T/TP-2F configurations.

P2V-6B/P2V-6M/MP-2F: Anti-shipping version for the US Navy with under-wing racks for two Fairchild AUM-N-2 Petrel missiles. Sixteen (BuNos 131551/131566) delivered to the US Navy in 1953 and successively designated P2V-6Bs, P2V-6Ms and, from September 1962, MP-2Fs.

P2V-6F/P-2G: Designation given to P2V-6s retrofitted with 3,400 lb (1,542 kg) thrust Westinghouse J34-WE-36 turbojets in underwing pods.

P2V-6T/TP-2F: Crew-trainer conversion of a few P2V-6s.

P2V-7/P-2H (Models 726-45-14, 726-45-17 and 826-45-14): The final production version of the Neptune was built by Lockheed in three sub-models with 3,500 hp R-3350-32W Turbo-Compound radial engines and two 3,400 lb (1,542 kg) thrust J34-WE-36 turbojets. All three versions were fitted with twin 0·50-in guns in a dorsal turret and with MAD 'stinger' tail. They were characterized by smaller ventral radome and tip tanks, and revised cockpit with clear, bulged, canopy. The YP2V-7 prototype (BuNo 135544) first flew on 26 April, 1954, and final delivery of a US-made P2V-7 was effected eight years later. A total of 287 Neptunes, including forty-eight assembled in Japan by Kawasaki at Gifu, were built under the P2V-7 designation as Model 726-45-14s (148 aircraft for the US Navy, Aéronavale, and assembly in Japan — c/ns 726-7001 to 726-7157 less five P2V-7Us and four P2V-7LPs — see Appendix B), Model 726-45-17s (114 aircraft, with revised accommodation, for the same customers and the RAAF), and Model 826-45-14 (25 aircraft for the RCAF, delivered without underwing jet pods but with their later addition). Some were later converted in the United States as P2V-7S/SP-2Hs, P2V-7U/RB-69s, AP-2Hs, DP-2Hs, EP-2H and NP-2Hs, while one Japanese machine became the P2V-7KAI.

P2V-7B (Model 726-45-18): Fifteen aircraft built for the MLD with metal-covered nose housing four 20 mm cannon. Later the noses were glazed and aircraft brought up to SP-2H standard.

P2V-7LP/LP-2J: Four P2V-7S (BuNos 140434, 140436, 140437 and 140439) were fitted during construction with retractable skis for use in Antarctica by Antarctic Development Squadron Six (VXE-6). All armament and operational items were removed to make room for survey and photographic equipment.

SP-2H Neptune 145923 from VP-19 over the Oakland Bay Bridge, San Francisco. (*US Navy*)

P2V-7S/SP-2H: Modified P2V-7s with Julie/Jezebel submarine-detection gear. The prototype for this variant was BuNo 140435. Weight of electronics and navigational equipment was nearly 3·8 times heavier than on the original P2V-1 production version. The dorsal turret was frequently removed.

P2V-7U/RB-69A-LO: Electronic-surveillance version for the USAF of which five were built by Lockheed (54-4037/54-4041) and two (54-4042/54-4043) were modified from Navy P2V-7 airframes. Later transferred to the Navy and modified as SP-2Hs.

P2V-7KAI: One Japanese-assembled P2V-7 (ex-BuNo 149109, original JMSDF serial 4637, later 4701) was modified as the P2V-7KAI prototype of the mixed propeller-turbine/turbojet powered P-2J version. It first flew on 21 July, 1966. The KAI suffix was an abbreviation of the Japanese word Kaizo, meaning modified. Another Japanese P2V-7 (ex-BuNo 149127, JMSDF serial 4655) was modified by Kawasaki as a variable-stability research aircraft. The modifications, effected under contract awarded in February 1977 by the Technical Research and Development Institute of the Japan Defense Agency, included the removal of military equipment, the installation of side-force panels above and below each wing, fly-by-wire control system, and special instrumentation. Flight trials began on 23 December, 1977, and the aircraft was later evaluated by the 51st Hiko-tai at Shimofusa, Chiba Prefecture.

An SP-2H of Patrol Squadron Twenty-four (VP-24) near Norfolk, Virginia, on 25 September, 1964. (*US Navy*)

Post-September 1962 designations: When the Tri-Service designation system was adopted in the United States, the versions of the Neptune then in service were redesignated P-2D (ex-P2V-4), P-2E (P2V-5F), DP-2E (P2V-5FD), EP-2E (P2V-5FE), SP-2E (P2V-5FS), P-2F (P2V-6), MP-2F (P2V-6M), TP-2F (P2V-6T), P-2G (P2V-6F), YP-2H (YP2V-7), SP-2H (P2V-7S), and LP-2J (P2V-7LP). The suffix letters A, B and C were not used as the P2V-1, P2V-2 and P2V-3 versions were no longer in service. In addition, the following designations were assigned to post-1962 modifications:

NP-2E: One P-2E (BuNo 131403) was so redesignated after being assigned to a permanent test project.

AP-2H 135620, a P2V-7 modified by E-Systems for the Trails and Roads Interdiction Mission. (*Lockheed*)

OP-2E/AP-2E: A number of modified P-2Es fitted by General Dynamics with specialized sensors for area surveillance in Vietnam were first designated OP-2Es. At least seven were transferred to the US Army and were used as AP-2Es by the 1st Radio Research Group at Cam Ranh Bay.

AP-2H: A number of P-2Hs were modified by E-Systems to carry a special TRIM (Trails & Roads Interdiction, Multisensor) package for special duties in Vietnam with Heavy Attack Squadron Twenty-one (VAH-21).

DP-2H: Designation applying to P-2Hs modified to launch and control drone vehicles.

EP-2H: One P-2H modified by the Navy with UHF telemetry equipment replacing the ASW systems.

NP-2H: BuNo 150283 (ex P2V-7) modified for special tests.

P-2J: Although falling within the US Tri-Service system, this designation applies only to a foreign-built and -operated version of the Neptune. After assembling forty-eight Lockheed-built P2V-7s — the last of which was delivered to the JMSDF on 28 June, 1965, Kawasaki undertook to modify its 21st P2V-7 (JMSDF serial 4637) as the prototype for a more advanced version for which design study had begun in Japan during October 1960. The two R-3350 piston engines were replaced by Japanese-built 2,850 ehp General Electric T64-IHI-10 propeller-turbines driving three-blade propellers, while 3,086 lb (1,400 kg) thrust Ishikawajima J3-IHI-7C turbojets were substituted for the US-made J34. Designated P2V-7KAI, this experimental aircraft was first flown on 21 July, 1966. Following satisfactory results, Kawasaki produced a version with lightened airframe, longer fuselage, APS-80 search radar, twin-wheel main undercarriage, and more powerful Japanese-built engines (3,060 ehp T64-IHI-10E propeller-turbines and 3,417 lb/1,550 kg thrust J3-IHI-7D turbojets). Eighty-two P-2J production aircraft (JMSDF serials 4702 to 4783) were delivered between October 1969 and 15 March, 1979, when 4783 became the last Neptune to be built.

UP-2J: Four P-2Js were modified beginning in 1978 to carry electronic counter-measures and target-towing equipment. More UP-2J conversions are to follow.

With the boost of four RATO bottles *The Turtle* took off in 4,720 ft (1,439 m) at a weight of 85,240 lb (38,664 kg) to set its still-standing world distance record for piston-powered aircraft. (*Lockheed*)

Even before entering squadron service, the Neptune had captured the attention of the public as the Navy used the specially-modified first P2V-1 (BuNo 89082) to shatter the 7,916-mile (12,739-km) world's distance in a straight line record which had been set in November 1945 by a modified, Bell-built, Boeing B-29B of the USAAF with a flight from Guam to Washington, DC. Positioning its special Neptune—which carried the name *The Turtle* but is better remembered by its Navy nickname *Truculent Turtle*—at Perth, Western Australia, the Navy planned to fly it nonstop to Washington, DC, a distance of 11,400 miles (18,346 km). With a crew of four (Cdrs Thomas Davies, Eugene Rankin and Walter Reid, and Lieut-Cdr Roy Tabeling), and 8,592 US gal (32,534 litres) of fuel, and carrying a pet kangaroo as mascot, *The Turtle* weighed 85,240 lb (38,664 kg) when, on 29 September, 1946, it lifted off after a 4,720-ft (1,439-m) run boosted by four 1,000-lb (454-kg) RATO (Rocket Assisted Take-Off) bottles. Flying eastward—to take advantage of prevailing tailwinds in the southern hemisphere when the aircraft was still heavy with fuel—but encountering rain, sleet and ice during some of the flight, *The Turtle* and its crew were forced to land at Port Columbus, Ohio, short of its intended destination. None-the-less, a new absolute world record of 11,235·6 miles (18,081·98 km) in 55 hr 17 min had been established. More than a third of a century later this record still stands as a Class C, Group I (Aeroplanes with piston engines) record and it is doubtful that it will ever be broken. As an absolute record, however, it was just barely surpassed by the 11,377-miles (18,309·54-km) flight of a jet-powered Boeing B-52H in June 1962. *The Turtle* has been preserved for eventual display by the National Air and Space Museum in Washington.

The Neptune's service use began in March 1947 when VP-ML-2 (Patrol Squadron, Medium Land-based Two) received the first of its P2V-1s. With the availability of the P2V-2 and -3 versions, Neptunes replaced Harpoons in more squadrons and, by 1949, the type was solidly established in service. During the preceding year the Navy had begun carrier trials with a modified P2V-2 (BuNo 122449), with the first launch being made on 28 April, 1948, from the deck of the USS *Coral Sea*. The success of this test led to the decision to fully modify this P2V-2 and eleven P2V-3s as carrier-launched P2V-3C strategic nuclear bombers for assignment to Composite Squadrons Five and Six (VC-5 and VC-6). The first of these units was commissioned in September 1948 and the P2V-3Cs retained their specialized role until fully replaced by North American AJ-1s in early 1952.

During the intervening years some of these aircraft were deployed to Port Lyautey, Morocco, for possible assignment to *Midway*-class carriers of the Sixth Fleet in the Mediterranean. Notable proving and training flights included the launching on 7 March, 1949, of three aircraft from VC-5, off the Virginia coast, with one of them dropping its simulated 10,000-lb (4,536-kg) bomb at Muroc, California, and then returning to NAS Patuxent River, Maryland, to end a 23-hr flight. A still longer flight was made, on 8–9 February, 1950, when a P2V-3C, launched from the USS *Franklin D. Roosevelt* off Florida, flew to Panama and then on to San Francisco, for a distance of 5,060 miles (8,143 km) in 25 hr 59 min. The heaviest weight on take-off from a carrier, which as usual was made without the use of a deck catapult but with RATO-boost, was made from the USS *Coral Sea* on 21 April, 1950, at a record 74,668 lb (33,869 kg).

When the United States began to spearhead the United Nations endeavour to contain the North Korean invasion of South Korea, the Navy had to provide anti-submarine patrols, shipping and fishery blockades, weather and coastal recon-naissance, spotting for naval gunfire, rail and road interdiction, and mine spotting. To perform these vital tasks, Patrol Squadrons were assigned to Fleet Air Wings Six and Fourteen for operations in the Japan–Korea area, and to Fleet Air Wings One and Two in the Formosa Straits. In addition to eight flying-boat squadrons and four land-based squadrons operating Consolidated PB4Y-2 Privateers, units controlled by these FAWs included seven Neptune-equipped Patrol Squadrons (VP-1, 2, 6, 7, 22, 29 and 57). The first to be in action was VP-6 which, successively based at Johnson AB, Tachikawa and Atsugi all in Japan, destroyed its first train on 29 July, 1950, with HVAR rockets and 20 mm cannon fire. Altogether the Neptune squadrons flew thirteen tours of duties (four of which being credited to VP-1, the unit remaining the longest in combat) with P2V-3s, P2V-4s and P2V-5s based in Japan and on Okinawa.

RATO-assisted take-off from the USS *Franklin D. Roosevelt* by a P2V-3C of Composite Squadron Five (VC-5) on 26 September, 1949. (*US National Archives*)

The return to peacetime operations, with Patrol Squadrons being normally based in the United States but frequently deployed overseas, did not bring an end to dangerous missions. Thus, while keeping watch on surface and submarine traffic off Siberia, two Neptunes were shot down by Soviet fighters. The first loss took place on 4 September, 1954, when a VP-19 aircraft was forced to ditch, while on 22 June, 1955, a P2V-5 from VP-9 had to crash-land on St Lawrence Island. Other significant uses of the P2V during the 1950s included the establishment in December 1955 of an air link between New Zealand and McMurdo Sound in the

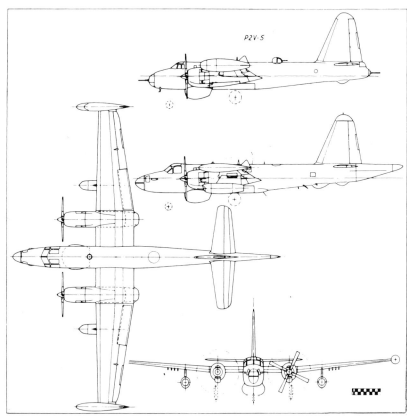

Lockheed P-2H Neptune, with side view of P2V-5

Antarctic by aircraft of VXE-6, and the activation in April 1956 of VP-24 with P2V-6Ms equipped with Fairchild Petrel air-to-surface guided missiles. Nineteen months later this new weapon was also deployed by a Reserve unit, VP-834.

The progressive replacement of Neptunes with propeller-turbine powered Orions began in August 1962, when VP-8 obtained its first P3V-1s, but extended over a fifteen-year period during which P-2s returned to a combat zone. Besides flying anti-submarine and maritime reconnaissance sorties during the early years of the Southeast Asia War, Navy Neptunes were also operated between November 1967 and June 1968 by VO-67. Equipped with twelve AP-2Hs specially fitted with ALARS (Air Launched Acoustical Reconnaissance System) sensors,

54-4037 one of the five RB-69As built by Lockheed for ELINT (Electronic Intelligence) operations with the USAF. (*Lockheed*)

this unit flew as part of Project TRIM (Trails & Roads Interdiction, Multisensor). However, by the start of the seventies, P-2s had been phased out from all Fleet Patrol Squadrons and remained in service only with twelve Reserve Patrol Squadrons. The last of these units, VP-94, relinquished its SP-2Hs in April 1978 to end the Neptune's thirty-one years of operations with the US Navy.

The use of Neptunes by other US Services had been pioneered during the Korean War by the Marine Corps which used two P2V-2s for airborne electronics aircrew training. More exotic was the use, beginning in 1954, of seven USAF RB-69As fitted with SLAR (Side-Looking Airborne Radar) on the starboard side of the aft fuselage, and other classified sensors for ELINT (Electronic Intelligence) gathering from the Soviet and Chinese periphery. Finally, during the Southeast Asia War the 1st Radio Research Group of the US Army used AP-2Es for special missions in Vietnam.

Foreign nations which operated or, in four cases, still operate Neptunes are listed in alphabetical order with brief details of deliveries and service uses:

Argentina: When the Royal Air Force replaced its Neptunes with Avro Shackletons in 1958, a number of ex-British P2V-5s were acquired by the Comando de Aviacíon Naval. Three of these aircraft were still in service in 1981 with the 1 Esc de Exploracíon and were then the oldest Neptunes extant.

AP-2E BuNo131526 (ex-P2V-5F) of the 1st Radio Research Group, US Army, at Pleiku, South Vietnam, in December 1967. (*Robert C. Mikesh*)

271

Australia: The first two Neptunes for the Royal Australian Air Force, the 21st and 22nd P2V-5s built by Lockheed, became the first to go to a non-US operator when they were delivered in 1951. They were followed by ten more aircraft of this model. Initial serials assigned were A89-301 through A89-312 but, at one point, they were replaced by scrambled serials ranging from A89-225 (ex-A89-311) to A89-983 (ex A89-305). These P2V-5s were operated by No.11 Squadron at RAAF Richmond, NSW, and later at RAAF Edinburgh, South Australia, until replaced by P-3Bs beginning in 1969. Twelve P2V-7s (A89-270/A89-281) were acquired in 1961 to equip No.10 Squadron at Townsville, in Queensland, but were replaced by P-3Cs in 1978–79. None of the twenty-four Neptunes remained in RAAF

Neptune MR.4 (A89-281) from No.10 Squadron of the Royal Australian Air Force. (*RAAF*)

service by 1980. In Australia the P2V-5s were first known as Neptune MR.1s but became MR.2s, when the tail turret was replaced by MAD gear and the dorsal turret removed, and MR.3s, after they had been brought up to the jet-augmented P2V-5F configuration by Lockheed Aircraft Service Company. The P2V-7s were the RAAF's Neptune MR.4s. Incidentally, the RAAF considers that its first two aircraft (A89-301 and 302) were P2V-4s; yet, in the Lockheed nomenclature they appear as Model 426-42-11s (c/ns 426-5021/5022) like the other Australian P2V-5s! Minor electrical-system differences did, however, exist between the first two Neptune MR.1s and the ten other aircraft in this batch.

Brazil: Fourteen ex-RAF P2V-5s were acquired in 1958–59 for use by the 1° Escuadrão of the 7° Grupo de Aviação, Força Aérea Brasileira, at Salvador. In Brazilian service these aircraft were designated P-15s and were assigned the serials P-15 7000 to P-15 7013. After flying a total of 22,761hr in Brazil they were progressively phased out, with the last aircraft ending its useful life in June 1976. One aircraft (P-15 7010, ex 51-15952 and WX548) is preserved in the collection of the Museu Aéroespacial at Campo dos Afonsos, Rio de Janeiro.

Canada: Twenty-five P2V-7s, built to a special configuration and initially dispensing with the underwing jet pods, were ordered for the Royal Canadian Air Force in April 1953. Bearing the Canadian military serials 24101/24125, they were delivered between March and September 1955 for service with Nos.404, 405 and 407 Squadrons. By the early 1970s they had been replaced by Canadair CP-107 Argus and many went on the Canadian and US civil registers for fire-fighting.

P2V-5 (FAB serial P-15 7012, ex-RAF WX555) which flew more than 1,400 hours between 12 May, 1959, and 30 March, 1972, while serving with the 1° Escuadrão, 7° Grupo de Aviacão, Força Aérea Brasileira. (*Francisco Pereira via Jackson Flores*)

Chile: Little is known about the Neptunes in service with the Armada de Chile. These four aircraft, believed to be ex-USN SP-2Es, were replaced by Embraer EMB-111ANs in 1978–79.

France: Largest foreign recipient of Lockheed-built Neptunes, the Aéronavale first received thirty-one P2V-6s in 1953 to equip three Flotilles: 21F and 25F in Algeria, and 23F in then French Morocco. Thirty-four P2V-7s then supplemented the earlier aircraft and were operated by Flotilles 23F, 24F and 25F, and by Escadrilles de Servitude 9S and 12S. Replacements of Neptunes with Breguet Atlantics began during 1961 but, twenty years later, P2V-7s were still operated by Flotille 25F at BAN Lann Bihoué in Britanny and by Escadrille 12S at Tahiti-Faaa in French Polynesia. The latter unit had some unusual duties and aircraft since it was formed at Lann Bihoué on 15 April, 1969, to operate P2V-7s in support of the French atomic test and missile programmes. Its first six aircraft were modified as AMOR (Avion de Mesure et d'Observation au Réceptacle) aircraft with missile-

Model 826 as CF-MQX, surplus to RCAF requirements and modified to fight forest fires, seen at Medford, Oregon, on 22 April, 1972. (*via David W. Menard*)

273

tracking equipment in the nose. Four of these modified P2V-7s were operated at any one time over the Landes range off the Atlantic Coast but, eventually, all were converted back to standard configuration. Other Neptunes of Escadrille 12S were used for electronic countermeasures experiments and training. Finally, in 1972 this unit moved to Hao in the Pacific and then to Tahiti-Faaa to provide maritime patrol and surveillance in connection with the Pacific Nuclear Test Centre, as well as search and rescue in the South Pacific. In 1980 only thirteen P2V-7s remained in French service, together with a single P2V-6 instructional airframe.

Great Britain: The fifty-two P2V-5s delivered to the Royal Air Force beginning in January 1952 were ordered under US Navy contracts—the first two under NOa(s)-10487 and the remainder under NOa(s) 51-026—but were built with MDAP (Mutual Defense Assistance Program) funds with USAF serials 51-15914 to 51-15965. In RAF service they were assigned the British serials WX493/WX529 and WX542/WX556 and were designated Neptune M.R.1s. Delivered with nose, dorsal and tail turrets, they were later modified with glazed nose and MAD 'stinger' tail. They entered service with No.217 Squadron at St Eval, in Cornwall, but this unit soon moved to Kinloss in Scotland. Other RAF maritime reconnaissance squadrons equipped with the type were Nos.36, 203 and 210 Squadrons at Topcliffe. Beginning in 1956 the Neptunes were replaced by Avro Shackletons in all four Coastal Command squadrons and the last to relinquish its P2V-5s was No.217 Squadron in March 1957. Earlier, from November 1952 until June 1953, No.1453 Flight, Fighter Command, had also operated four Neptunes (WX499, WX500, WX502 and WX542) in the airborne early warning role from Kinloss and Topcliffe. When the Coastal Command Neptunes were phased out, these MDAP-supplied aircraft had to be returned to the United States; however, authorization was granted to sell some of them to Argentina and Brazil.

Japan: To equip its maritime reconnaissance and anti-submarine patrol units, the Japanese Maritime Self Defense Force (JMSDF) initially received sixteen Lockheed-assembled P2V-7s (Japanese serials 4601/4616) beginning during 1955. Four years later the JMSDF began accepting the first of forty-eight Kawasaki-assembled aircraft of this type (serials 4617/4664), with the last of these P2V-7s

Fitted with a special nose for use in testing sea-skimming missiles, this P2V-7 of Flotille 25F was photographed at Landivisiau in May 1980. (*Jean-Michel Guhl*)

The last Kawasaki-built P-2J (serial 4783), a type nicknamed Owashi (Great Eagle) in service with the Kaijoh Jieitai (JMSDF), in the markings of the Hachinohe-based 4th Kokutai. (*Kawasaki*)

being delivered in June 1965, more than three years after Lockheed had terminated Neptune production. Between October 1969 and March 1979 the JMSDF then accepted eighty-three Kawasaki P-2Js—including serial 4701, the modified P2V-7 which was renumbered from 4637, and 4702/4783 which were production models. The last five P2V-7/SP-2Hs of the JMSDF, which in 1981 were being flown as photographic/chase aircraft, are due to be retired in 1982 but P-2Js will continue to equip five patrol squadrons at Kanoya, Hachinohe (2), Atsugi, and Naha, two training squadrons at Kanoya and Shimofusa, and one flight and one special unit at Shimofusa. Although P-3Cs have already been ordered, the JMSDF aircraft bid fair to become the last operational Neptunes.

The Netherlands: A first batch of twelve P2V-5s (Dutch serials 19-21/19-32) was delivered between October 1953 and January 1954 to re-equip No.320 Squadron, Marineluchtvaartdienst, at Valkenburg. Beginning in 1960 these aircraft were progressively withdrawn from use and by 1962 all had been transferred to Portugal. Fifteen P2V-7Bs (serials 200/214), with four 20-mm cannon in a metal nose, were delivered between September 1961 and February 1962 for operations against Indonesia by No.321 Squadron at Biak, New Guinea. Following the Dutch capitulation in August 1962, these aircraft—less one which had been written off—were moved to the Netherlands. They were soon modified to SP-2H standard with glazed nose and were assigned at Valkenburg for operational duties with No.320 Squadron and training with No.5 Squadron; with these units they were supplemented by four ex-French P2V-7s (serials 215/218). In 1980 No.320 Squadron was still operating seven Neptunes from Valkenburg—with detachment at the Dr Albert Plesman Airport, Curaçáo—but these aircraft were scheduled to be replaced by P-3Cs during 1981.

Portugal: The Força Aérea Portuguesa received twelve ex-Dutch P2V-5s in 1962. Assigned the Portuguese serials 4701/4712, they served at Base Aérea 6, Montijo, until the last four were withdrawn from use at the end of 1977.

Related Temporary Design Designations: V-135, V-146, V-148, V-200, L-165, L-174/L-175, L-178, L-184, L-194, L-198, L-218, L-220, CL-258, CL-260, CL-301, CL-305, CL-353, CL-423, CL-431, CL-438, CL-476, CL-495, CL-557, CL-798, CL-806, CL-886, CL-1018/CL-1020, CL-1034, CL-1041, CL-1043, CL-1046, CL-1062, CL-1065/CL-1066, CL-1068, CL-1151 and CL-1190 (see page 461).

	XP2V-1	P2V-2	P2V-5 (P-2E)	P2V-7 (P-2H)	P-2J
Span, ft in	100 0	100 0	104 0	103 10	101 3½
(m)	(30·48)	(30·48)	(31·7)	(31·65)	(30·87)
Length, ft in	75 4	77 10	78 3	91 8	95 10¾
(m)	(22·96)	(23·72)	(23·85)	(27·94)	(29·23)
Height, ft in	28 6	28 1	28 11	29 4	29 3½
(m)	(8·69)	(8·56)	(8·81)	(8·94)	(8·93)
Wing area, sq ft	1,000	1,000	1,000	1,000	1,000
(sq m)	(92·9)	(92·9)	(92·9)	(92·9)	(92·9)
Empty weight, lb	32,651	33,962	39,900	49,935	42,500
(kg)	(14,810)	(15,405)	(18,098)	(22,650)	(19,278)
Loaded weight, lb	54,527	54,000	72,000	73,139	—
(kg)	(24,733)	(24,494)	(32,659)	(33,175)	—
Maximum weight, lb	58,000	63,078	77,850	79,895	75,000
(kg)	(26,308)	(28,612)	(35,312)	(36,240)	(34,019)
Wing loading, lb/sq ft	54·5	54	72	73·1	—
(kg/sq m)	(266·2)	(263·7)	(351·5)	(357·1)	—
Power loading, lb/hp	11·9	9·6	11·1	—	—
(kg/hp)	(5·4)	(4·4)	(5)	—	—
Maximum speed, mph/ft	289/15,600	320/13,500	353/9,500	403/14,000	403/20,000
(km/h / m)	(465/4,755)	(515/4,115)	(568/2,895)	(648/4,625)	(648/6,095)
Cruising speed, mph	163	178	207	188	230
(km/h)	(262)	(286)	(333)	(302)	(370)
Initial rate of climb, ft/min	1,120	810	2,620	1,760	1,800
(m/min)	(341)	(247)	(799)	(536)	(549)
Service ceiling, ft	23,200	26,000	26,000	22,000	30,000
(m)	(7,070)	(7,925)	(7,925)	(6,705)	(9,145)
Normal range, miles	2,880	—	3,195	2,200	2,765
(km)	(4,635)	—	(5,140)	(3,450)	(4,450)
Maximum range, miles	4,210	3,985	3,885	3,685	—
(km)	(6,775)	(6,410)	(6,250)	(5,930)	—

276

Lockheed 34 Big Dipper

In another attempt to break into the light aircraft market, in October 1944 Robert Gross and Mac Short authorized John Thorp, the designer of the Little Dipper, to start preliminary work on a two-seat aircraft of advanced design. Primarily intended as a research vehicle, it was also seen as a potential 'flying Jeep' for the military or as a 'flying automobile' for the private-owner market. Thorp, under the direction of chief project engineer Robert Reedy, designed a low-wing monoplane with fixed nosewheel undercarriage incorporating several unusual features, including a side-by-side enclosed cabin in the nose and 'all-flying' horizontal tail surfaces. Even more unusual, although it was also featured in the Cloudster II then being designed by the Douglas Aircraft Company, was the engine location in the centre fuselage section. The 100 hp Continental C-100-12 four-cylinder engine was buried aft of the cabin and was fan-cooled, with air exhausting above the fuselage. A non-flexible drive-shaft terminating aft of the rudder drove a two-blade pusher propeller.

The Big Dipper at the Lockheed Air Terminal; note angled-up drive shaft for the pusher propeller. (*Lockheed*)

Construction of the prototype Big Dipper was begun in July 1945 in a small rented building at the Lockheed Air Terminal in Burbank. Upon completion, the aircraft was trucked to Palmdale where flight testing could be undertaken in greater secrecy. There it was first flown on 10 December, 1945, by Prentice Cleaves. With the exception of a vicious root stall during climbs at high angles of attack, the Big Dipper was found to have exceptionally good handling characteristics and its performance also exceeded expectations. After being tested for some 40 hours at Palmdale, the aircraft was flown back to Burbank where it was to have been fitted with a wing-root fillet to eliminate the stall tendencies. However, it was decided to postpone this modification temporarily and the aircraft was ordered back to Palmdale in the afternoon of 6 February, 1946.

To avoid a taxi-ing delay at Burbank, and thus jeopardize the secrecy still surrounding the aircraft, Prentice Cleaves decided to use a shorter, upward-sloping runway. In the process, Cleaves was forced to attempt a steep climb when

This posed photograph clearly shows the layout of the Big Dipper. (*Lockheed*)

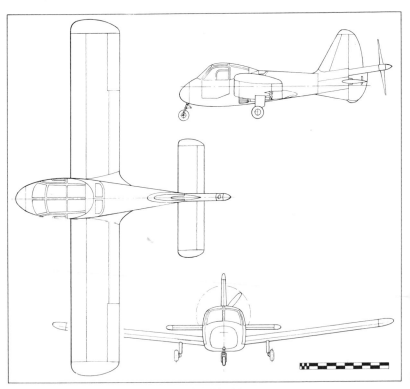

Lockheed 34 Big Dipper

trying to coax the aircraft out of this short strip. Predictably, the Big Dipper stalled and crashed. Cleaves and Frank Johnson, who had replaced John Thorp as project engineer, were hurt and the aircraft destroyed. As by then it had been concluded that the private-aircraft market was glutted, Lockheed dropped further development of the Big Dipper and of its proposed Super Dipper, a four-seat, high-wing monoplane with a 145 hp engine driving a pusher propeller.

Related Temporary Design Designations: V-306, V-309/V-311 and V-314

Span 31 ft (9·45 m); length 22 ft 2 in (6·76 m); height 8 ft 10 in (2·69 m).
Empty weight 935 lb (424 kg); loaded weight 1,450 lb (658 kg); power loading 14·5 lb/hp (6·6 kg/hp).
Maximum speed 136 mph (219 km/h); cruising speed 119 mph (191 km/h); initial climb 840 ft/min (256 m/min); service ceiling 16,000 ft (4,875 m).

Lockheed 75 Saturn

Rather than resting on their laurels after successively introducing into service the Models 10, 12, 14 and 18 airliners, Lockheed engineers and their colleagues at Vega diligently studied a variety of transport aircraft projects ranging in capacity from six to fifty-eight seats and from single-engine feeder-liners to four-engined long-range aircraft. Among these were the Vega Starliners and the Lockheed Models 16, 19, 27, 44 and 49. However, the threat of war and uncertain market conditions prevented the realization of most of these projects and only the Starliner, albeit only in prototype form, and the Lockheed 49 Constellation reached the hardware stage. Later, after the war began to turn in favour of the United States and its allies, Lockheed realized that it would need other commercial types to supplement the anticipated success of its Constellation series. Therefore, early in 1944, teams of market researchers and sales analysts began questioning the airlines about their postwar requirements. As only limited engineering time was available while the war effort was still going on, the decision was soon made to concentrate the company's new commercial efforts on what appeared to be the most promising venture: a twin-engined feeder-liner.

The Saturn feeder-liner programme proved, again, that technical excellence cannot ensure commercial success if it is not matched by competitive price. (*Lockheed*)

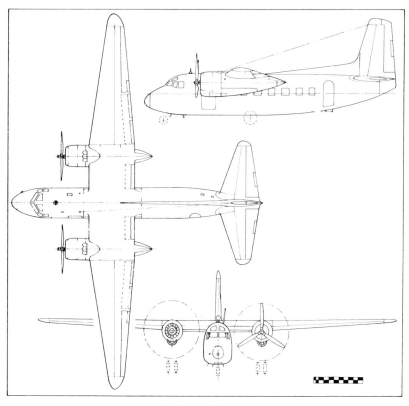

Lockheed 75 Saturn

When in the autumn of 1944, aviation officials gathered in Chicago for an International Air Conference to chart the postwar course of the air transport industry, Lockheed was ready to show them preliminary data for its new feederliner. The same information was presented to airlines and prospective airlines being organized in the United States by investors and airmen, and the feedback was sufficiently encouraging (conditional orders for some 500 aircraft at a unit price of $85,000 were received and provided the illusion of a $4¼ mn order book) for Lockheed to organize a special project group in late 1944. Work on the project, initially under the direction of Don Palmer and later under that of F. A. Smith, proceeded slowly during the last few months of the war but after VJ-Day management gave priority to the development of the Model 75. An idea of the importance given to this project can be gathered from the fact that 189,600 engineering hours went into it, against only 118,900 hours in the XP-80 jet fighter, with part of the effort resulting from the need to upgrade performance to meet the new regulations governing single-engined performance and take-off distance to clear a 50-ft (15-m) obstacle. Close attention was also given to reducing maintenance and operating costs and maximize efficiency. If anything, the Model 75 was over-engineered with the result that its selling price rose to $100,000.

Powered by two 600 hp Continental GR9-A nine-cylinder radials, a Continental development of the Wright R-975 Whirlwind, the Model 075-77-01 Saturn (NX90801) was first flown at the Lockheed Air Terminal on 17 June, 1946, by Rudy Thoren and Tony LeVier. Initial trials revealed a bad stall, soon fully corrected by fitting a strake on the wing leading edge, and serious cooling difficulties with the Continental engines. No satisfactory solution for the power-plant problem could be found, and 700 hp seven-cylinder Wright 744C-7BA-1s were installed in the first Saturn and adopted as standard for the second prototype and the proposed production models. First flight of the Wright-powered Saturn was made on 8 August, 1947. With the new powerplants the Saturn was fully satisfactory, and it was offered to the airlines with accommodation for a flight crew of two and either fourteen seats in two rows (Model 075-57-01), or with a movable bulkhead aft of the cockpit to enable rapid change from fourteen seats and no cargo to all-cargo in an area of 43 cu ft (1·2 cu m), or to any intermediate passenger/cargo combination (Model 075-57-02).

Unfortunately for Lockheed, in 1946–47 the market was glutted with surplus transports, with eight-seat Beech C-45s available at $3,500 and 28-seat Douglas C-47s going for $25,000/30,000. Like other contemporary US and European designs in the same class, the $100,000 Saturn could not compete in spite of its markedly lower operating costs and greater ease of maintenance. The management decided to terminate the Saturn programme and, to take advantage of tax write-off provisions, was forced to have the two prototypes scrapped in early 1948 and take a $6 mn loss on the project.

Related Temporary Design Designations: L-146, L-156 and L-176

    Span 74 ft (22·56 m); length 51 ft 6 in (15·69 m); height 19 ft 10 in (6·05 m); wing area 502 sq ft (46·63 sq m).
    Empty weight 11,361 lb (5,153 kg); loaded weight 16,000 lb (7,257 kg); wing loading 31·9 lb/sq ft (155·6 kg/sq m); power loading 11·4 lb/hp (5·2 kg/hp).
    Maximum speed 228 mph (367 km/h) at sea level; cruising speed 187 mph (301 km/h); initial rate of climb 1,325 ft/min (404 m/min); service ceiling 26,500 ft (8,075 m); range 600 miles (965 km).
    Data for Wright 744C-7BA-1 powered Model 075-57-01.

Lockheed XR6O-1 (XR6V-1) Constitution

Even though in the thirties Pan American Airways, with its fleet of Sikorsky S-42s, Martin M-130s and Boeing 314s, mainly operated large flying-boats on its long over-water routes, it recognized early the advantages of landplanes for its fast-developing network. In 1936 the airline became one of the five sponsors for the original Douglas DC-4, before switching, later in that year, to backing the development of the Boeing 307 Stratoliner with its more attractive pressurized cabin. With Lockheed, Pan American Airways played an active role in the evolution of the Model 44 Excalibur into the Model 49 Constellation. Moreover, Pan American was interested in still larger and longer-range landplanes, thus leading Boeing and Douglas to initiate in early 1942 studies for what respectively became the C-97 and C-74, while shortly after Lockheed began working on its Model 89. These three types were four-engined aircraft whereas Consolidated-

Vultee went on later in the same year to work on the six-engined XC-99. Obviously, with the nation at war, none of these designs could be undertaken as commercial ventures. However, with Pan American Airways operating an extensive network under contracts from the War and Navy Departments, the airline was able to have the Boeing, Convair and Douglas projects sponsored by the USAAF; while the US Navy backed the Lockheed Model 89, with two prototypes being ordered under the XR6O-1 naval designation.

The first XR6O-1 (BuNo 85163) on take-off at Muroc AFB. If it was not for the additional red bar on the national markings of the aircraft on the ground (B-17, B-25, C-45, C-47, P-47 and T-6), the scene could well have been taken at a wartime base. (*Lockheed*)

With Pan American engineers serving as US Navy consultants, the Model 89 was designed by a team led by Willis Hawkins and project engineer W. A. 'Dick' Pulver. Beginning in June 1942, some 28 different layouts were studied before the selection of a four-engined, conventional, mid-wing configuration. Of large dimensions—with its span of more than 189 ft and its length of more than 156 ft being exceeded among Lockheed aircraft only by the much later C-5A Galaxy—the aircraft was anticipated to weigh more than 85 tons. To support this weight Lockheed had to design a new type of main undercarriage with, on each side, two main struts in tandem and two wheels per strut. Furthermore, to reduce stress on landing, the eight main wheels were spun by electric motors before touchdown. The single-strut nose unit also had twin wheels.

The Model 89 originally had four of the new 3,000 hp Pratt & Whitney Wasp Major twenty-eight-cylinder, four-row radials which drove four-blade propellers. The pressurized double-deck fuselage, with each lobe having a diameter of 6 ft 5 in (1·96 m), could carry up to 204 military passengers in maximum density configuration, or 168 military passengers in normal configuration; in its planned postwar civil configuration 51 seated passengers and 58 passengers in sleeper berths as well as 11 crew members could be carried. With passenger accommodation on both decks, circular staircases were provided fore and aft; alternatively, passengers could be carried on the upper deck, with cargo—including Jeep-sized vehicles—being loaded on the lower deck.

Not being given top priority by the Navy, and requiring the construction of a new six-storey hangar to house their bulk, the two XR6O-1 Constitutions (BuNos 85163 and 85164) were not completed until fifteen months after the war's end. Powered by four 3,000 hp R-4360-18s, the first aircraft made its 2 hr 17 min maiden flight from the Lockheed Air Terminal to Muroc AAB on 9 November, 1946. The crew on this first flight consisted of Joe Towle, pilot, Tony LeVier, co-pilot, Rudy Thoren, flight engineer, and Jack Frick and Dick Stanton, assistant flight engineers. Soon after, the R-4360-18s were replaced by 3,500 hp R-4360-22Ws with water injection. This water injection was the cause of the only emergency encountered during flight trials when, in December 1946, it failed to lock at the take-off point on engines 3 and 4. The aircraft yawed violently to the right and began losing altitude but, after the throttles had been retarded in preparation for a crash landing, all four engines settled on equal ratings and the flight was resumed normally. Also powered by the later R-4360-22W engines, the second XR6O-1 was first flown in June 1948.

The first Constitution was delivered to Transport Squadron VR-44 at NAS Alameda on 2 February, 1949, and was followed six months later by the second aircraft. In Navy service, the XR6O-1 proved to be underpowered and to have insufficient range. Thus, for example, on the California–Hawaii run it often had to be flown with substantially reduced payload to have adequate fuel reserves. This range deficiency resulted in part from engine-cooling problems which necessitated keeping the cooling gills partially open and thus increased drag. In 1950, the two Constitutions were redesignated XR6V-1s and, in 1951–52, were returned to Lockheed for major overhaul. Finally, in 1953 when the Navy ran out of spares, they were stored at Litchfield Park, Arizona. Two years later they were sold as surplus for only $98,000. Their new civil owners flew the first XR6V-1 to

This superb picture shows well the clean lines of the Constitution. (*Lockheed*)

The two Constitutions, then serving with VR-44 at NAS Alameda, over the North Beach and Russian Hill areas of San Francisco. (*Lockheed*)

Las Vegas, Nevada, and the second to Opa-Locka, Florida. However, neither obtained an Approved Type Certificate as the necessary work and testing would have been uneconomic. Both were scrapped. Even less successful was a projected ASW version which was too expensive to be seriously considered by the US Navy.

Although the Navy's original specification had called for the XR6O-1s to be easily modified to civil configuration for eventual use by Pan American, this was never done. After the end of the war the airline had decided that the Lockheed Model 189 — the proposed commercial version of the Constitution, which was offered with four 3,500 hp Pratt & Whitney Wasp Major TSB3-Gs, accommodation for either 129 day passengers or 109 night passengers, and a crew of fifteen — the Douglas Globemaster, and the much larger Convair XC-99, were too large for its needs. Instead, Pan American settled on the Boeing 377 Stratocruiser, with accommodation for 55 to 100 passengers, and this type entered airline service two months after the first XR6O-1 had been delivered to the Navy. Lockheed, nevertheless, tried to attract airline interest in two other Wasp Major powered versions — the Models 389 and 489, with the latter offering accommodation for up to 168 passengers and a take-off weight increased from 184,000 to 195,000 lb (83,461 to 88,450 kg) — and in the propeller-turbine powered Model 289. With four 5,500 shp Wright Typhoons, a take-off weight of 240,000 lb (108,862 kg), and high-density accommodation for 154 passengers plus crew, the Model 289 should

284

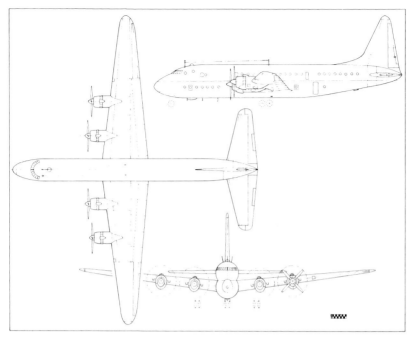

Lockheed XR6O-1 Constitution

have been an excellent performer. Unfortunately, the Wright Typhoon did not go into production and, with the demise of this engine the Constitution was no longer a viable aircraft.

Related Temporary Design Designations: L-150, L-154, L-168 and CL-280

Span 189 ft 1¼ in (57·64 m); length 156 ft 1 in (47·57 m); height 50 ft 4½ in (15·35 m); wing area 3,610 sq ft (335·381 sq m).

Empty weight 114,575 lb (51,970 kg); loaded weight 184,000 lb (83,461 kg); wing loading 51 lb/sq ft (249 kg/sq m); power loading 13·1 lb/hp (5·9 kg/hp).

Maximum speed 303 mph at 20,000 ft (488 km/h at 6,095 m); cruising speed 269 mph (433 km/h); initial rate of climb 1,010 ft/min (308 m/min); service ceiling 27,600 ft (8,415m); maximum range without payload 6,300 miles (10,135 km).

T-33A-5-LO of the 26th Air Division landing at Luke AFB, Arizona. (*Peter J. Mancus/Cloud 9 Photography*)

Lockheed T-33

Early in the development cycle of the P-80, Mac V. F. Short, vice-president in charge of military relations, identified the need for a two-seat training version and suggested that development of such a version be undertaken. However, his suggestion was not taken up until 1947 when the P-80's high accident rate pointed to the urgent need for a jet-transition trainer.

Gambling $1 mn of its own funds, in May 1947 Lockheed assigned the designing of the Model 580 two-seat trainer to a team led by Don Palmer, and three months later obtained Air Force authorization to modify a P-80C airframe to serve as the TP-80C prototype. To provide room for the instructor aft of the student, Palmer revised the fuselage design by inserting a 38·6-in (98-cm) plug forward of the wing and a 12-in (30·5-cm) plug aft, and by reducing the fuselage fuel-tank capacity from 207 to 95 US gal (784 to 360 litres). To offset this fuel reduction, nylon cells were installed in the wings instead of the P-80's self-sealing tank, to bring internal fuel capacity to 353 gal (1,336 litres), as opposed to 425 gal (1,609 litres) for the P-80C. As originally designed, the internal fuel capacity could be increased by the use of two standard 165-US gal (625-litre) drop tanks beneath the wingtips. This arrangement was retained for the early production aircraft but 230-gal (871-litre) centreline tip tanks were later adopted. The tandem ejector seats were housed beneath a clear canopy which was raised electrically or, in an emergency, manually. To conserve weight, the trainer's built-in armament was reduced to two 0·50-in machine-guns.

The successful maiden flight of the first TP-80C (48-356) was made by Tony LeVier on 22 March, 1948, from Van Nuys Airport. Handling characteristics were found equal to those of the P-80C, itself an aircraft well liked by pilots, and operating speeds at comparable engine settings were slightly higher. During the spring of 1948, by which time an initial batch of twenty aircraft (48-356/48-375) had been ordered by the USAF, the TP-80C was sent on a tour of Air Force Bases and Naval Air Stations in the United States. The results of this tour were soon evident as production orders were quickly received for additional TF-80Cs (designation changed from TP-80Cs on 11 June, 1948, and finally to T-33A on 5 May, 1949).

The first production TF-80C was accepted by the Air Force in August 1948. Like other initial production aircraft, it was powered by a 4,600 lb (2,087 kg) thrust Allison J33-A-23; later production trainers were delivered with the 5,200 lb (2,359 kg) thrust J33-A-25 and most aircraft were later re-engined with the 5,400 lb (2,450 kg) thrust J33-A-35. The production of all T-33 versions, including the TV-2 for the US Navy, were under Air Force contracts and covered a total of 5,691 Lockheed-built T-33A-1/-5-LOs in 28 batches ordered with funds from eleven successive Fiscal Years (28 aircraft in FY 48; 144 in FY 49; 140 in FY 50; 1,970 in FY 51; 847 in FY 52; 1,361 in FY 53; 145 in FY 54; 286 in FY 55; 256 in FY 56; 240 in FY 57; and 274 in FY 58). In addition to the basic T-33A for the USAF (*see* Appendix B for listing of serial numbers) there were the following versions:

AT-33A-LO: For delivery to smaller air forces in Latin America and Southeast Asia a small number of T-33As were fitted with underwing pylons and stubs to carry up to 2,000 lb (907 kg) of bombs or eight 5-in HVAR rockets. In addition to their usual training role, the AT-33As could be used for weapons-delivery training and counter-insurgency operations. At least one aircraft was fitted with a gun package, housing twin 0·50-in machine-guns, beneath each wing. Standard T-33As were frequently modified to a similar standard by their recipients.

An AT-33A of the Força Aérea Brasileira (FAB serial TF-33A 4328, ex-USAF 52-9387). Note 0·50-in machine-gun installed in the nose and bomb rack beneath the wing. (*Mario Roberto Vaz Carneiro via Jackson Flores*)

DT-33A-LO: USAF T-33As modified for use as drone directors.

NT-33A-LO: When modified permanently for special tests, a number of T-33As were redesignated NT-33As. Among these one-off aircraft was 51-4120 which was successively used for tests by Lockheed, the Allison Division of General Motors, the USAF Wright Air Development Center, and the Flight Research Department of the Cornell Aeronautical Laboratory (later reorganized as the Calspan Corporation). With Calspan the aircraft was fitted with a larger-volume nose section from an F-94A to accommodate test equipment and computer electronics. Used for variable-stability research and for simulating the flying qualities of a variety of aircraft then under development, this NT-33A was at various times fitted with alternative controls (wheel, stick, two-axis and three-axis side controller), 'fly-by-wire' system, modified tip tanks with electrohydraulically-operated drag petals, and inflight-refuelling probe. In 1980 the Calspan Corporation was still using 51-4120 in a project sponsored jointly by the USAF and USN and known as Display Evaluation Flight Test (DEFT).

287

NT-33A (51-4120) with F-94 nose housing special test instrumentation. (*Roger Besecker via David W. Menard*)

Two other NT-33As were 48-357 and 51-4263; 48-357, the second TF-80C, was used for ejector-seat trials and fitted with aft-focusing camera recording equipment on top of the nose and with an open rear cockpit; 51-4263 was modified by Lockheed to have twin fins and rudders at the ends of the tailplane instead of the standard single tail surfaces. The modified tail was at the time considered for the proposed TV-2 deck-landing trainer. Testing was not fully satisfactory and the new aircraft, the L-245 (T2V-1 in the Navy), had conventional tail surfaces.

QT-33A: During the late seventies ex-USAF T-33As were modified as drones for use by the Navy at the Pacific Missile Test Center at Point Mugu, California, and the Naval Weapons Center at China Lake, California.

RT-33A-LO: Complementing the AT-33A armed-trainer version in the inventory of several smaller air forces, the RT-33A was a photographic-reconnaissance version with vertical and oblique camera installation in a nose of modified contour. Electronic and recording equipment was fitted in the rear cockpit, in the space normally occupied by the instructor. A total of eighty-five T-33As were modified to the RT-33A configuration and came from the 53-4886/53-6152 (75 aircraft) and 54-1522/54-1618 (10 aircraft) batches. Individual serial numbers for the RT-33As are given in Appendix B.

RT-33A-1-LO (54-1548, c/n 580-9179) of the Section de Liaison et Vol Sans Visibilité, 33ème Escadre, at Nancy-Ochey in May 1979. The insignia of the 33ème Escadre—a Cross of Lorraine with the battle-axe of ER 1/33 *Belfort*, the Seagull of ER 2/33 *Savoie* and the paper chicken of ER 3/33 *Moselle*, the three escadrons of this Armée de l'Air unit based at Strasbourg—can be seen on the nose, aft of the camera port. (*Jean-Michel Guhl*)

288

T-33B-LO (TO-2/TV-2): The Navy version of the T-33A-1-LO came directly from the Lockheed assembly line and, for contract purposes, were given USAF serial numbers. In service, these 699 aircraft were given BuNos 124570/124585, 124930/124939, 126583/126626, 128661/128722, 131725/131888, 136793/136886, 137934/138097, 138977/139016, 141490/141558 and 143014/143049. The first 28 were delivered as TO-2s but were later designated TV-2s after the Navy changed the Lockheed identification letter from O (the letter previously identifying aircraft from the main Lockheed plant) to V (the letter which had identified aircraft from the Lockheed-Vega plant). Under the Tri-Service designation system adopted by the Department of Defense on 18 September, 1962, all TV-2s remaining in USN and USMC service were redesignated T-33Bs.

DT-33B (TV-2D): This post-September 1962 designation (and its earlier form) applied to a number of Navy aircraft modified as drone directors.

DT-33C (TV-2KD): Radio-controlled target conversion of T-33Bs (TV-2s) which, for ferrying purposes, could be flown as single-seaters.

Lockheed T-33A-1-LO (FT-34, ex 55-3043) of the 11ème Escadrille (11 Smaldeel), the Instrument Squadron of the Force Aérienne Belge, based at Brusten. (*FAéB*)

Entering service in 1948, the T-33A remained the only USAF jet trainer until the advent of the Cessna T-37A in 1957 and that of the Northrop T-38A in 1961. For thirteen years it thus played a vital role in the training of USAF pilots and aircrew from countless Allied nations. T-33As were also assigned as jet-instrument trainers to operational squadrons of the USAF, the USAFR and the ANG. In this role the type gained in importance after the T-38As supplanted them as the principal type of advanced trainer. Also noteworthy was its use by the 147th Fighter Interceptor Group, Texas ANG, which, beginning in 1957, operated the Jet Instrument School of the Air National Guard. Other T-33As were operated by various USAF Commands and base flights on a variety of duties, including the all important task of keeping up the flying skill of officers assigned to desk jobs.

The Navy Department began procuring TO-2s in 1949 under existing USAF contracts, and these aircraft, along with the follow-up purchases under the TV-2 designations, were built in the midst of T-33A-1-LO batches. With the Navy and Marine Corps the TV-2s (T-33Bs after 1962) served as advanced and instrument trainers, both with specialized units and with operational and reserve squadrons. Like the USAF, the Navy used its aircraft for specialized tests, such as ejector-seat trials by the Naval Parachute Unit at NAAS El Centro, California, as drone directors (designated TV-2Ds from 1951 and DT-33Bs after 1962) and as radio-controlled target or drone-director aircraft (TV-2KD from 1956 and DT-33C after 1962). In naval service the aircraft was replaced by other specialized trainers, beginning in the late fifties, and many were returned to the USAF for eventual disposal, including transfer to friendly nations under the Mutual Defense Assistance Program.

In support of the NATO build-up in the early 1950s, Canada undertook to provide training not only for its own RCAF and RCN aircrews but also for several thousand Allied personnel. To provide the necessary jet-training phase of the programme the RCAF received between May 1951 and March 1952 twenty T-33A-1-LOs, which were designated Silver Star Mk.1s and given the Canadian military serials 14675/14694, and in August 1952 obtained a further ten aircraft (51-6713/51-6717 and 51-6743/51-6747) on loan from the USAF. All these aircraft, except for two which had been written off while in RCAF service, were by 1955 either returned to the USAF or transferred to Greece and Turkey as the RCAF standardized on the Canadair-built version of the T-33.

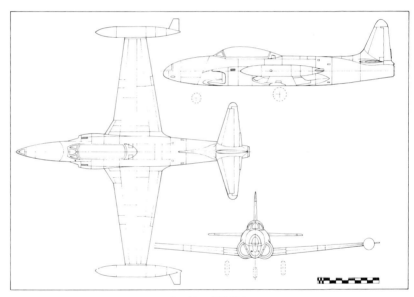

Lockheed T-33A

To serve as pattern aircraft for this version, which differed mainly from the Lockheed-built aircraft in being powered by 5,100 lb (2,313 kg) thrust Rolls-Royce Nene 10s, a T-33A-1-LO (51-4198, c/n 5492, and Canadian serial 14695) was fitted with a Nene on 27 November, 1951. Between 1952—when on 22 December the first Canadian-built aircraft was flown by Bill Longhurst—and 1959, Canadair built 656 Nene-powered T-33AN Silver Star Mk.3s under the company designation CL-30 (c/ns T33-1/T33-656, original RCAF serials 21001/21656 later replaced by 133001/133656 when the Canadian Armed Forces adopted the designation CT-133 for the type). Still equipping No. 414 Squadron in 1981, the Silver Star Mk.3s have served mainly with the training units of the

The 500th Canadair Silver Star 3 (21500), bearing the gold and red livery of the Royal Canadian Air Force's Golden Hawks aerobatic team. (*Robert C. Mikesh*)

RCAF and RCN/Canadian Armed Forces, or as station aircraft and hacks with operational squadrons. In addition, a number of aircraft were transferred to Allied nations, including France, Greece, Portugal, Turkey, and, more recently, Bolivia.

Similarly, in Japan, soon after the formation of the Air Self Defense Force (Koku Jieitai) on 1 July, 1954, Kawasaki undertook production of T-33As powered by the standard J33-A-35 engine. In support of the Japanese production programme, Lockheed supplied two fully-assembled T-33A-1-LOs (54-1584 and 54-1585) and eighteen additional aircraft in knocked-down form. Twenty-seven T-33As were also transferred to the Koku Jieitai from USAF inventory and the US-built aircraft had serials 51-5601 to 51-5647 in Japanese service. Kawasaki then produced 210 aircraft (serials 5201 to 5410 prefixed by 61, 71, 81 and 91 depending on the year of production) between 1956 and 1959. Twenty years later, more than 85 per cent of these aircraft were still serving with the Hiko Kyoiku Shudan (Air Training Command) of the Koku Jieitai.

The use of the T-33 by foreign air forces was certainly not limited to its Canadian and Japanese versions, as at least 1,058 Lockheed-built aircraft were delivered to friendly and neutral nations as part of the Mutual Defense Aid

Lockheed-built T-33A of the Esq.103, Força Aérea Portuguesa, at Base Aérea 5, Monte Real, in August 1978. (*Jean-Michel Guhl*)

T-33A-1-LO of the Centre d'Entrainement en Vol Sans Visibilité 338 (CEVSV 338) at Nancy-Ochey in April 1979. Most Lockheed-built T-33As and Canadair-built T-33ANs in service with the Armée de l'Air were modified to a common standard with Nene turbojets. Those of CEVSV 338, however, retained their Allison engines and have ILS antennae on the nose. (*Jean-Michel Guhl*)

Program and as others were transferred directly from the USAF inventory overseas. NATO members were the main overseas recipients of T-33As (the three largest European operators were the Armée de l'Air with 163 T-33/RT-33As and 61 T-33ANs, the Luftwaffe with 192 T-33As, and the Koninklijke Luchtmacht with 60 T-33As and three RT-33As). With smaller air forces T-33 operators ranged from one European communist country, Yugoslavia, to many Latin American nations—including the Fuerza Aérea Mexicana, with which AT-33As were still the only jet combat aircraft in 1981—and to Southeast Asian, Middle Eastern and African countries. Many of these air forces used their T-33As during armed rebellions, with the latest example of this use being provided by the Fuerza Aérea de Nicaragua which in 1979 strafed and bombed Sandinista strongholds during the waning days of President Somoza's attempt to remain in power.

A surplus T-33A of Murray-McCormick Aerial Surveys Inc at the Sacramento Executive Airport, California, in 1975. (*Peter M. Keefe*)

Outside the United States, one of the most interesting experiments undertaken with a T-33 was Aérospatiale's development of a programme of supercritical wing research. After conducting mathematical and wind-tunnel research in this field, in 1976 the company obtained from the Armée de l'Air the loan of a Canadair T-33AN (ex-RCAF 21064, c/n T33-64). A supercritical wing section was superimposed on the existing Silver Star wing by building up the basic form with balsa and then adding a skin of resin-coated fabric. Flight trials began on 13 April, 1977, and, with interruptions necessitated to improve the wing profile, continued in 1979–80.

At the beginning of the 1980s the T-33A had already been phased out by several air forces and many surplus T-33As had found their way onto the US civil register. Nevertheless, the T-33A will probably still be operated by some air forces until after 1988, forty years after the type's maiden flight. Indeed an amazing achievement in longevity.

Related Temporary Design Designations: L-239, CL-256 and CL-815

Span 38 ft 10½ in (11·85 m); length 37 ft 9 in (11·51 m); height 11 ft 8 in (3·55 m); wing area 234·8 sq ft (21·814 sq m).

Empty weight 8,365 lb (3,794 kg); loaded weight 12,071 lb (5,475 kg); maximum weight 15,061 lb (6,832 kg); wing loading 51·4 lb/sq ft (251 kg/sq m); power loading 2·2 lb/lb st.

Maximum speed 600 mph (965 km/h) at sea level; cruising speed 455 mph (732 km/h); initial rate of climb 4,870 ft/min (1,484 m/min); service ceiling 48,000 ft (14,630 m); normal range 1,025 miles (1,650 km); maximum range 1,275 miles (2,050 km).

Lockheed F-94 Starfire

The appearance over Tushino of three Tupolev Tu-4s, the Russian copy of the Boeing B-29 Superfortress, during the 1947 Soviet Aviation Day, coupled with Intelligence assessment that the USSR would soon have nuclear weapons, had a sobering effect on US military planners as after the war the USAAF had been left without truly modern all-weather fighters. Initially relying on wartime Northrop P-61 Black Widows, the USAF also received 150 North American F-82F/G/H Twin Mustangs in 1948–49. Furthermore, prototypes of jet-powered all-weather fighters had been ordered in December 1945 (Curtiss XP-87) and June 1946 (Northrop XP-89), but development of the first was abandoned in October 1948 while the latter ran into teething troubles and did not enter service until the spring of 1952. Consequently, when in 1948 the USAF realized that the failure of the F-87 programme and the delay in that of the F-89 would leave it for too long without all-weather jet fighters, it began seeking alternatives, including the inconclusive evaluation of the Navy's Douglas XF3D-1, and searched for new designs. From this search were evolved the North American F-86D, which entered service in April 1953, the Convair F-102A, which followed it in squadron use three years later, and the Lockheed F-94.

To solve its immediate need, the USAF had approached Lockheed in March 1948 with the idea of exploring the feasibility of producing an interim all-weather two-seat fighter by fitting a Hughes E-1 fire-control system in a TF-80C airframe, with delivery of the first production aircraft before the end of 1949. Development of the new fighter was entrusted by Kelly Johnson to a team led by project engineer Russ Daniell. It then appeared that the task would be relatively easy, as

A beautifully clean F-94B-1-LO with RATO bottle beneath the fuselage. (*via Jim Sullivan/Cloud 9 Photography*)

the TF-80C airframe had sufficient volume to house the fire-control system in a modified nose and the radar operator's equipment in the aft cockpit. The concept was endorsed by the Secretary of Defense in November 1948, with a Letter of Contract being awarded to Lockheed two months later. Actual design work, however, revealed the need for more substantial changes as on the power of the standard J33 engine of the TF-80C the proposed Lockheed Model 780 all-weather fighter would have insufficient performance because of the additional weight of the electronic equipment and armament. Accordingly, Daniell's team decided to power the aircraft with an afterburning version of the Allison J33-A-33 with dry rated thrust of 4,400 lb (1,996 kg) and developing 6,000 lb (2,722 kg) with reheat. The weight of the afterburner and its increased length aft of the cg were offset by the installation of the E-1 fire-control system in a longer forward-fuselage section, with the APG-32 radar being housed in an upswept nose. Aft of the radar were housed related electronic equipment and the ammunition boxes for the four 0·50-in M-3 machine-guns (weight and space restrictions forced the omission of two of the six guns initially planned). Compared with the TF-80C, the all-weather fighter had enlarged tail surfaces and a reduction of 30 US gal (114 litres) in the fuselage tank. Internal fuel capacity was thus limited to 318 gal (1,204 litres) but the aircraft retained provision for carrying the two standard 165-gal (625-litre) under-wing tip tanks.

To serve as all-weather fighter prototypes, Lockheed modified the first two TF-80Cs (48-356/48-357) which were then redesignated YF-94-LOs. Flight trials, which began on 16 April, 1949, when Tony LeVier and Glenn Fulkerson flew the aircraft out of the Van Nuys airport, were satisfactory from the point of view of handling characteristics but revealed the initial temperamental nature of the afterburner. Frequent flame-outs, with often difficult relights, already experienced during the YF-94 first flight, were eventually solved when Allison and Lockheed engineers developed a flame-holder system for the afterburner. Successful resolution of the problem cleared the F-94 for full production and service and the first F-94 was accepted on 29 December, 1949, to meet the original delivery schedule promised to the USAF. It was followed by 853 other Starfires —including the much-redesigned F-94C version—and became the first jet-powered all-weather fighter to serve with the USAF. The numerous versions were:

294

YF-94-LO: The two modified TF-80Cs (48-356 and 48-357) initially lacked most of the operational equipment fitted to production aircraft. They were, however, put to good use in flight testing the J33-A-33's then-novel afterburner. Armament consisted of four machine-guns mounted in the lower nose section with their muzzles aft of the radome.

F-94A-LO: First ordered in January 1949 by Contract AF-1849, the one hundred and nine F-94As were generally similar to the YF-94s but were fitted with all-operational equipment. The seventeen F-94A-1-LOs (49-2479/49-2495) were practically hand-built models using T-33 airframes taken from the production line, while the ninety-two F-94A-5-LOs (49-2496 and 49-2498/49-2588) started down the line as F-94As. They were accepted by the Air Force between December 1949 and December 1950. Their built-in gun armament could be supplemented by two 1,000-lb (454-kg) bombs for night attacks. Their original under-wing tip tanks were later replaced by Fletcher centreline tanks with a capacity of 230 US gal (871 litres) each, as fitted during production to the F-94Bs. In ANG service a number of F-94As were fitted with two-gun pods on the leading edge to bring forward-firing armament to a total of eight 0·50-in machine-guns.

YF-94B-LO: The nineteenth F-94A airframe (49-2497) was modified during production to test improved equipment and systems as planned for the F-94B model. These items included a Sperry Zero Reader for bad-weather landings, an upgraded hydraulic system, a high-pressure oxygen system, and Fletcher centre-line tip tanks. This aircraft was first flown on 28 September, 1950.

F-94B-LO: Contract AF-9844, which eventually covered one hundred and forty-nine F-94Bs, two YF-94Cs and one hundred and eight F-94Cs, was supplemented by Contract AF-14804 for two hundred and six B models. Incorporating the improvements tested on the YF-94B, the F-94B-1-LOs (50-805/50-876 and 50-878/50-954) were delivered beginning in January 1951. They were followed by the two hundred and six F-94B-5-LOs, which were equipped for Arctic service. The last four F-94B-5-LOs were accepted by the Air Force in January 1952. The F-94Bs were powered by either a J33-A-33 or -33A engine with the same thrust ratings as the turbojet fitted to the YF-94 and F-94A.

Two F-94B-1-LOs, flanking an F-94B-5-LO, in the markings of the 139th Fighter Interceptor Squadron. (*NY ANG*)

The first of two YF-97As, still retaining the nose of the F-94A/B and fitted with non-standard tip tanks, seen over the Mojave Desert. (*Lockheed*)

Proposed derivatives of the F-94B included a two-seat radar combat trainer (Temporary Design Designation L-199) but this project remained on the drawing board.

YF-94C-LO (YF-97A-LO): To improve performance—particularly in terms of speed, rate of climb and endurance—as well as handling characteristics at high altitude, Lockheed had begun in February 1949 (two months before the YF-94-LO's maiden flight) the private venture design of its Model 880. Unofficially referred to as the 'F-94B', the aircraft was to have a thinner wing with increased dihedral, sweptback tailplane, Westinghouse automatic pilot, drag chute, increased fuel capacity, and all-rocket armament and a new engine in a larger fuselage. The Model 880 proposal was initially rejected by the Air Force. However, continued delays with the F-86D and F-89 programmes and Lockheed's efforts finally combined to gain USAF endorsement. In view of the major redesign, the USAF ordered prototypes under the YF-97A-LO designation and retained the F-94B designation for the less drastic improvement of the F-94A already described. The YF-97As (50-877 and 50-955), the 73rd and 151st airframes ordered under the first F-94B contract, were to serve as aerodynamic prototypes and 50-955 was the first to be completed. Retaining the nose configuration, armament, cockpit arrangement, and vertical tail surfaces of the F-94A, this aircraft had the new wing and tailplane as well as tip tanks of modified design.

To provide the YF-97A with the necessary thrust it had been intended to use a licence-built version of the Rolls-Royce Tay turbojet, the Pratt & Whitney J48, but this proposal almost failed to materialize as in the process of being adapted to US requirements the engine had been increased in diameter by $\frac{5}{8}$ of an inch (1·59 cm) and barely fitted in the aircraft. For the initial phase of its trial programme, which began on 19 January, 1950, aircraft 50-955 had an unreheated J48 engine with 6,250 lb (2,835 kg) dry thrust. The second prototype, 50-877, was powered by an afterburning J48-P-5 and introduced a number of aerodynamic refinements including revised air intakes and enlarged tail surfaces with a dorsal spine running from aft of the cockpit to the base of the fin. This aircraft was also used to test the improved fire-control system (Hughes E-5 with APG-40 radar) and revised fuel system with 566 US gal (1,385 litres) in wing and fuselage tanks, 500 gal (1,893 litres) in tip tanks and 460 gal (1,741 litres) in slipper tanks for a total capacity of 1,526 gal (5,019 litres) as opposed to 783 gal (2,964 litres) for the F-94B and F-94A with Fletcher tip tanks. This aircraft was also used to test the all-rocket armament consisting of twenty-four 2·75-in FFAR rockets (in four groups surrounding the APG-40 radome and covered by snap-action doors). Flight trials of the YF-97As (later redesignated YF-94Cs) progressed slowly due to drag-chute difficulties and automatic pilot unreliability, aileron flutter and afterburner problems. These troubles were not resolved until October 1951 after delivery of the first production F-94C.

F-94C-LO (F-97A-LO): Ordered under the F-97 designation but delivered as F-94C-1-LOs, the 387 aircraft of this model (50-956/50-1063, 51-5513/51-5698 and 51-13511/51-13603) were accepted between July 1951 and May 1954. Upon entering service with the 437th Fighter Interceptor Squadron in June 1953, the F-94C became the second type of fighter serving with Air Defense Command to rely on rockets for its primary armament. In the course of its production and service life, the F-94C was progressively improved by installation of new ejector seats, aileron spoilers, variable-position dive-brakes, better drag chute, and doubling of armament. The last of these modifications, which had first been considered in 1951, consisted of the addition of a 12-rocket pod on each wing leading edge and was incorporated on the 100th F-94C leaving the assembly line and retrofitted to early production machines. All production aircraft were powered by J48-P-5 engines with a dry rating of 6,350 lb (2,880 kg) and afterburning rating of 8,750 lb (3,969 kg). The F-94C had a top speed of 640 mph (1,030 km/h) at sea level—a five per cent increase over that of the F-94B—and could just become supersonic in a dive.

DF-94C: At least one F-94C experimentally converted to carry a Hughes GAR-1 Falcon for development of the new guided missile intended to arm later models of ADC interceptors.

YF-94D and F-94D: In January 1951 Lockheed obtained a contract for 113 Model 980-75-14 single-seat ground-attack fighters (51-13604/51-13716) which

F-94C-1-LO (51-13566) of the 179th FIS/148th FIG, Minnesota Air National Guard.
(*Brig-Gen Wayne C. Gatlin*)

were to use the airframe and powerplant of the F-94C. Aircraft 51-13603 was almost completed to serve as the YF-94D test model when the entire F-94D contract was cancelled on 15 October, 1977, to enable the company to concentrate its efforts on F-94C production. Armament was to have included eight 0·50-in guns with a ranging radar and provision for up to 4,000 lb (1,814 kg) of stores on additional wing racks.

First accepted in December 1949, F-94As began replacing North American F-82s with the 317th Fighter Interception Squadron at McChord AFB, Washington, and the 319th FIS at Moses Lake AFB, Washington, in May 1950. By becoming the first jet-powered all-weather fighters in the Air Defense Command and remaining alone in this category for three years, the Starfire played a vital role during the Cold War period. Deliveries of the improved F-94Bs, which entered service in April 1951 with the 61st FIS at Selfridge AFB, Michigan, enabled the ADC to release F-94As for transfer to the Far East Air Forces. Shipped to Japan, these aircraft were assigned to the 68th FIS at Itazuke in March 1951; nine months later the unit began posting two F-94As on strip alert at Suwon AB (K-13), Korea. During the Korean War similar duty was also undertaken by the 339th FIS, which began converting from F-82Gs to F-94Bs in 1951 at Chitose.

By direct orders from USAF Headquarters, the Starfires of these two squadrons on detachment to Korea were forbidden to fly over enemy territory to prevent compromising their secret electronic equipment. The same restrictions initially applied to the F-94B-equipped 319th FIS which began operating from Suwon on 22 March, 1952. However, mounting B-29 losses following the development of night-interception tactics by the Chinese and North Koreans finally led to the lifting of this restriction and in January 1953 the 319th FIS began flying protective patrols 30 miles (50 km) in advance of the medium bombers. The barrier-patrol tactic paid off during the night of 30 January when an F-94B, with Capt B. L. Fithian as pilot and Lieut S. R. Lyons as radar operator, shot down an unseen Lavochkin La-9 piston-engined fighter. During the next six months Korean-based Starfires destroyed three more enemy aircraft but one F-94B and its crew were lost during the night of 12 June when it collided with a Polikarpov Po-2 biplane.

Although the F-94A/Bs proved to be reliable and easily maintained, even under combat conditions, the type's effectiveness against modern bombers was

F-94B-5-LO (51-5502), modified to test the radar and guidance system of the Bomarc missile, during evaluation by the Air Research and Development Command. (*USAF*)

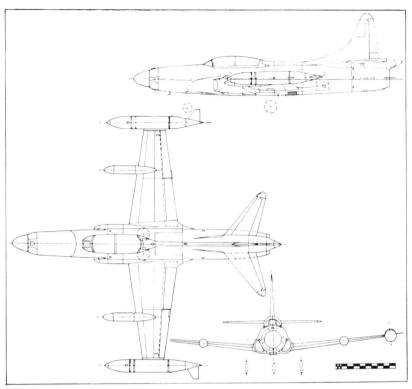

Lockheed F-94C Starfire

strictly limited, as it lacked range, climbing speed and heavy punch. These deficiencies were in part corrected with the F-94C which was first assigned to the 437th FIS at Otis AFB, Massachusetts. Entering service on 7 March, 1953, two years after the original schedule, this model still suffered from teething troubles in spite of its protracted development programme. The unreliability of its E-5 fire-control system and leaking cockpit seal, which caused short-circuits in the electrical system, was eventually corrected and the F-94C became well liked by its flight and maintenance crews. Particularly appreciated, after curing engine flame-out problems when the rockets were fired, was the great accuracy of its armament. In this respect the superiority of the F-94C's armament over that of the F-86D was due to the use of closed-breech launchers which increased the velocity of the 2·75-in FFAR rockets.

The A and B versions of the F-94 were phased out of USAF squadrons by mid-1954 and the F-94C in February 1959. With the Air National Guard, the early versions had first been used by three FIS, the 121st (DC ANG), 142nd (Maine ANG) and 148th (Pennsylvania ANG), while they served on active duty during the Korean War call-up, but the ANG aircraft were retained by the USAF when the three units were returned to State control on 31 October, 1952. F-94A/Bs re-entered ANG service less than eight months later when Starfires replaced North American F-51Hs in the 137th FIS (NY ANG). Before being transferred to the Air

Guard, the F-94A/Bs had their cockpits widened to improve the chance of successful ejections, as the original narrow cockpit had resulted in unfortunate accidents. Their canopies were also reinforced with a metal strap between the two cockpits.

With the F-94A/Bs later supplemented by F-94Cs, Starfires equipped twenty-one FIS of the Air National Guard. The last F-94Cs were phased out from Guard service by the 179th Fighter Interceptor Squadron at the Duluth Municipal Airport, Minnesota, during the summer of 1959.

Related Temporary Design Designations: L-188, L-199 and L-204

F-94B

Span 37 ft 6 in (11·43 m) or, with tip tanks, 38 ft 11 in (11·86 m); length 40 ft 1 in (12·22 m); height 12 ft 8 in (3·86 m); wing area 234·8 sq ft (21·813 sq m).

Empty weight 10,064 lb (4,565 kg); loaded weight 13,474 lb (6,112 kg); maximum weight 16,844 lb (7,640 kg); wing loading 57·4 lb/sq ft (280·2 kg/sq m); power loading 2·2 lb/lb.

Maximum speed 606 mph (975 km/h) at sea level; cruising speed 452 mph (727 km/h); initial rate of climb 6,850 ft/min (2,088 m/min); service ceiling 48,000 ft (14,630 m); normal range 665 miles (1,070 km); maximum range 905 miles (1,455 km).

F-94C

Span 37 ft 4 in (11·38 m); length 44 ft 6 in (13·56 m); height 14 ft 11 in (4·55 m); wing area 232·8 sq ft (21·628 sq m).

Empty weight 12,708 lb (5,764 kg); loaded weight 18,300 lb (8,301 kg); maximum weight 24,184 lb (10,970 kg); wing loading 78·6 lb/sq ft (383·8 kg/sq m); power loading 2·1 lb/lb.

Maximum speed 640 mph (1,030 km/h) at sea level; cruising speed 493 mph (793 km/h); initial rate of climb 7,980 ft/min (2,432 m/min); service ceiling 51,400 ft (15,665 m); normal range 805 miles (1,295 km); maximum range 1,275 miles (2,050 km).

Lockheed XF-90

With the P-80A solidly established in production, Kelly Johnson's advanced design team was able, beginning in July 1945, to turn its attention to conceptual studies for more advanced jet fighters embodying captured information on German research into swept wings as a means of improving transonic characteristics. Within a short period no fewer than 65 different designs were analysed including versions with butterfly tail surfaces, wings of W planform (inboard sections swept back and outer panels swept forward), three engines (one on each wingtip and one in the fuselage), or with swept wings and single engine (this 1946 design bore a strong resemblance to the Hawker Hunter which first flew in the United Kingdom in July 1951). Benefiting from this company-funded work, and enjoying a good reputation with the Air Force thanks to the P-80 programme, Lockheed was well placed in 1946 to answer a USAAF request for a penetration fighter capable of escorting bombers and, if necessary, flying ground-attack sorties.

Ill-defined Air Force specifications for the penetration fighter — combat-range requirements went from 900 to 1,500 miles (1,450 to 2,415 km) and then back to 600 miles (965 km) whilst time to height requirements were increased from 35,000 ft (10,670 m) in ten minutes to 50,000 ft (15,240 m) in less than five minutes — created many problems for the team directed by project engineers Don Palmer

XF-90 (46-687) over North Base, Muroc AFB, in 1949. Thirty-two years later the dry lake seen beneath the rear of this aircraft was the site of the spectacular return of *Columbia*, the first Space Shuttle. (*Lockheed*)

and Bill Ralston. Having received on 20 June, 1946, a contract for two XP-90 prototypes (XF-90 after June 1948; Lockheed Model 090-32-01; 46-687 and 46-688), Lockheed first designed a delta-wing fighter. However, wind-tunnel tests conducted at the California Institute of Technology in Pasadena led to a major redesign, and construction of the delta-winged prototype was halted and its already completed parts were scrapped. The revised design, Lockheed's Model 90, featured swept wings, a sharply-pointed nose, two Westinghouse J34 engines, and proposed armament of six 20 mm cannon. The axial-flow turbojets, selected to provide the added safety of a twin-engined configuration, were of sufficiently narrow diameter to fit within the fuselage and were fed by lateral intakes. The internal fuel tankage could be supplemented by underwing tip tanks bringing total capacity to 1,665 US gal (6,303 litres).

The second XF-90A, with two 1,000-lb (454-kg) bombs. (*Lockheed*)

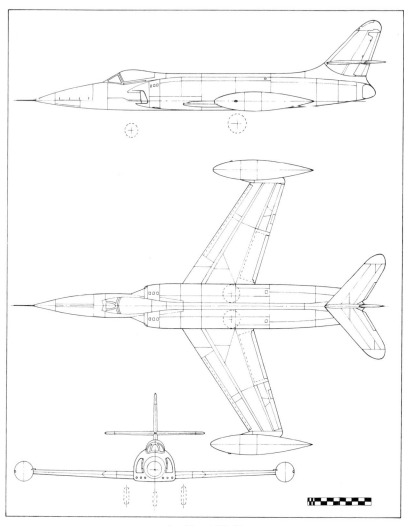

Lockheed XF-90

To enable the aircraft to absorb the high stresses encountered during ground-attack sorties, Lockheed pioneered the use of 75ST aluminium, which was nearly 25 per cent stronger than the then-standard 24ST aluminium alloy, and built the machine with heavy forgings and machined parts. The net result was an aircraft with an empty weight more than fifty per cent heavier than that of its rival, the McDonnell XF-88. As both types used the same pair of turbojets, the Lockheed design had a far less satisfactory power-to-weight ratio. Thus, by the time of its first flight, the XF-90 was doomed to fail.

Powered by two 3,000 lb (1,361 kg) thrust Westinghouse XJ34-WE-11 engines, the first XF-90 (46-687) was completed some seven months after the McDonnell

302

XF-88 and was trucked to Edwards AFB to be readied for its first flight, which, with Tony LeVier at the controls, took place on 3 June, 1949. In spite of disappointing performance due to the insufficient power of its unreheated engines, the XF-90 underwent its trial programme almost without problems until April 1950. To boost performance, Lockheed, capitalizing on its experience with the modified second XP-80A, had planned to use afterburning XJ34-WE-15s with a dry rating of 3,600 lb (1,633 kg) and an afterburning rating of 4,200 lb (1,905 kg), and these were installed in the second aircraft and retrofitted to the first. Designated XF-90As when powered by -15 afterburning engines, the prototypes began exploring the high-transonic portion of their performance envelope and were dived at supersonic speeds (a maximum of Mach 1·12 was reached in a dive on 17 May, 1950). It was during the first of these supersonic flights that one of the XF-90As was almost lost as Tony LeVier experienced great difficulties in pulling out of a dive.

Achieving a top speed in level flight of 668 mph (1,075 km/h), the XF-90A was slightly slower than the North American F-86A which was already in USAF squadron service and was soon to make its combat debut in Korea. Lockheed proposed at least three other developments of the XF-90 which were respectively to be powered by a single Allison J33-A-29 (Lockheed Model 190-33-02), two Westinghouse J46-WE-2s (Model 290-34-03), or one General Electric J47-GE-21 (Model 390-35-02). However, each of these proposed versions would have entailed a major redesign of the intakes and fuselage to accommodate the larger air-flow requirement and diameter of their powerplant. Thus, as no engine combining sufficient thrust with the maximum diameter for installation in the XF-90A was available, the Lockheed design lost out in June 1950 to the XF-88 and development was terminated three months later. The second XF-90A was finally destroyed on the ground during the 1952 atomic bomb tests at Frenchman's Flat, Nevada. The following year the no-longer flyable first prototype was shipped to the NACA laboratory in Cleveland to be used in structural testing, a fitting tribute as the XF-90's small claim to fame was its immensely strong structure.

Related Temporary Design Designations: L-167 and L-169

Span 40 ft (12·19 m); length 56 ft 2 in (17·12 m); height 15 ft 9 in (4·8 m); wing area 345 sq ft (32·05 sq m).

Empty weight 18,050 lb (8,187 kg); loaded weight 27,200 lb (12,338 kg); maximum weight 31,060 lb (14,089 kg); wing loading 78·8 lb/sq ft (384·9 kg/sq m); power loading 3·2 lb/lb.

Performance with XJ34-WE-15 engines: maximum speed 668 mph at 1,000 ft (1,075 km/h at 305 m); cruising speed 473 mph (761 km/h); climb to 25,000 ft (7,620 m) in 4½ minutes; service ceiling 39,000 ft (11,890 m); normal range 1,050 miles (1,690 km); maximum range 2,300 miles (3,700 km).

The long-lived Constellation prototype as it appeared after being modified as the first Model 1049 Super Constellation. (*Lockheed*)

Lockheed Super Constellation

The lively competition between the two Southern California aircraft manufacturers rendered the 1945–1955 period one of the most interesting in the history of commercial aviation. With the Constellation Lockheed had acquired a commanding lead over the unpressurized Douglas DC-4 and retained this lead even after the introduction of the DC-6. However, with the DC-6B's entry into service in April 1951 Douglas had finally overtaken its arch rival from Burbank, thus forcing Lockheed into developing improved versions of its triple-tailed transport. During the following years the lead seesawed between the two firms, with Lockheed winning the most points for technical innovations—notably by introducing compound engines with its Model 1049C and by developing the first very long-range airliner, the Model 1049G—but with Douglas eventually winning, as its DC-4/DC-6/DC-7 series outsold the Constellation/Super Constellation series by a comfortable margin (2,210 to 856 aircraft, when including both civil and military versions, or 878 to 510 aircraft, when counting only commercial versions).

To forestall the anticipated threat of improved DC-6 versions, Lockheed adopted a two-pronged development approach. On one hand, the company studied Constellation versions (Models 849 and 949) to be powered by Wright Turbo-Cyclone compound engines as first used on its P2V-4 in March 1950, while on the other it proposed a stretched model of its airliner to be powered by either standard Wright Double Cyclones or their compound versions. As the increased power of the Turbo-Cyclones could not be effectively utilized on standard Constellations, it was decided in January 1950 to proceed with developing the stretched version. However, as development of the new Wright engines was not going to be completed in time for the new aircraft, the first Super Constellations were to be powered by Double Cyclones even though it was recognized that they would be underpowered.

To serve as a prototype for the Super Constellation, Lockheed took back the original C-69 (c/n 049-1961, NX25600), and spliced new fuselage sections, fore and aft of the wing, to bring its overall length from 95 ft 2 in to 113 ft 7 in (29 to

34·62 m) and increase its tourist-class seating by one-third. Given new serial and registration numbers (1049-1961S, NX67900), the prototype Model 1049 was first flown at the Lockheed Air Terminal on 13 October, 1950, by a crew captained by J. White, to be joined on 14 July, 1951, by the first production aircraft. As anticipated, the Double Cyclone powered Model 1049s were found to be slow, but soon they were followed by aircraft with Turbo-Cyclones, as an R7V-1 for the US Navy began flight trials on 5 April, 1952, and as the similarly-powered Model 1049C was first flown on 17 February, 1953. The commercial versions of the Super Constellation are described first in this narrative, and then come their military derivatives.

Model 1049: The prototype, modified from the first C-69 Constellation, was first flown on 13 October, 1950. Its fuselage was stretched 18 ft 5 in (5·613 m) to increase accommodation in tourist class—in the same arrangement with five-abreast seating and 38-in (96·5-cm) pitch—from 69 to 92 passengers. The aircraft was initially powered by four 2,500 hp Wright 749C-18BD-1s, as fitted to the Models 649 and 749, but was later fitted with the 2,700 hp version of the Wright Double Cyclone as intended for the production version. Subsequently, it was tested as an aerodynamic prototype for the WV-2 (Model 1049A) version with radomes atop and beneath the fuselage, and with wingtip tanks. Finally, with radomes and tanks removed, the veteran aircraft served in the Model 188 Electra development programme by having an Allison 501 propeller-turbine installed in the outer starboard engine nacelle.

The production version of the Model 1049, of which fourteen were built for Eastern Air Lines and ten for TWA, had strengthened fuselage, internally stiffened outer wing panels, and rectangular windows in lieu of the Constellation's circular portholes. The first production Super Constellation was flown on 14 July, 1951, and the type entered service on 7 December, 1951, with Eastern Air Lines; the last Model 1049 was delivered in September 1952. Accommodation at the time of delivery was provided for 88 passengers in Eastern's 1049-53-67s and for 65 (overwater) or 75 (domestic) passengers in TWA's 1049-53-80s. Like later Super Constellations, they could be adapted to carry up to 102 passengers in high-density configuration. Both versions had a flight crew of three and two cabin attendants and were powered by 2,700 hp Wright 956C-18CA-1 eighteen-cylinder radials. Take-off gross weight was 120,000 lb (54,431 kg).

CF-TGC, the third Model 1049C Super Constellation of Trans-Canada Air Lines.
(*Air Canada*)

Model 1049A: Modified Basic Model Number assigned by Lockheed to the military WV-2, WV-3, and RC-121D airborne early-warning versions described separately.

Model 1049B: Lockheed's designation for the USN transport version (R7V-1), the USAF RC-121C and the Presidential VC-121E.

Model 1049C: First commercial transport certificated with Turbo-Compound engines, the Model 1049C was developed to correct the basic shortcomings of the original Model 1049—insufficient power resulting in performance lower than that of the Douglas DC-6B — by taking advantage of the new powerplant developed by the Wright Aeronautical Division of Curtiss-Wright. Adding to the basic Double Cyclone engine three 'blow-down' turbines, which converted the heat energy of exhaust gases into additional power, the Turbo-Cyclone offered a twenty per cent reduction in fuel consumption. In its 872TC-18DA-1 version as fitted to the Model 1049C, this engine was rated at 3,250 hp for take-off and markedly improved performance. Take-off gross weight and maximum landing weight were respectively increased to 133,000 lb (60,328 kg) and 110,000 lb (49,895 kg). The first Turbo-Cyclone powered Super Constellation began flight trials on 17 February, 1953, three months before the similarly-powered Douglas DC-7. Lockheed produced a total of 48 Model 1049Cs, for delivery between June 1953 and June 1954 to Air France (ten aircraft), Air-India (two), Eastern (sixteen), KLM (nine), PIA (three), Qantas (three), and TCA (five).

Model 1049D: Powered by the same engines as the Model 1049Cs, four convertible passenger/cargo aircraft (1049-55-116) were built for Seaboard & Western Airlines in 1954. They were fitted with reinforced flooring and had main-deck cargo loading doors on the port side of the fuselage, fore and aft of the wings. They could carry either 18 tons (16,329 kg) of freight or up to 104 passengers, and had a maximum take-off weight of 135,400 lbs (61,416 kg) and a maximum landing weight of 113,000 lb (51,256 kg).

Model 1049E: Twenty-eight of these aircraft, which were identical to the Model 1049Cs but had the increased operating weights of the Model 1049Ds, were delivered between May 1954 and April 1955 to Air-India (three), Avianca (three), Cubana (one), Iberia (three), KLM (four), LAV (two), Qantas (nine) and TCA (three).

Model 1049F: Lockheed's designation for thirty-three C-121C cargo/personnel transports built for the USAF and fitted with a stronger undercarriage.

Publicity photograph of a Model 1049D Super Constellation of Seaboard & Western Airlines at the Lockheed Air Terminal. The two cargo-loading doors of this first commercial freighter version of the Model 1049 are clearly in evidence. (*Lockheed*)

306

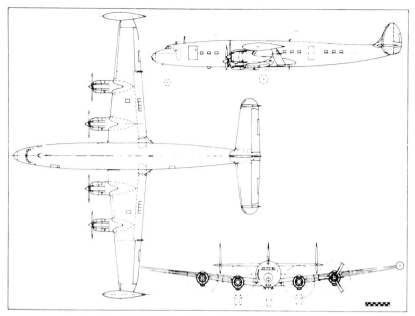

Lockheed Model 1049G Super Constellation

Model 1049G: The most successful version of the Super Constellation, first flown on 7 December, 1954, and introduced by Northwest Airlines on 1 July, 1955, was an improved Model 1049E version with 3,400 hp Wright 972TC-18DA-3 Turbo-Cyclone compound engines. For long-range operations they could be fitted with 600-US gal (2,271-litre) wingtip tanks bringing maximum capacity to 7,750 gal (29,336 litres) — an increase of nearly two-thirds over the tankage of the original Model 49 Constellation. Maximum take-off weight rose to 137,500 lb (62,369 kg) and, in service, some were modified to operate at weights of up to 140,000 lb (63,503 kg). Often known as Super Gs, 42 of these aircraft were delivered to domestic carriers (28 to TWA, ten to Eastern and four to Northwest), 59 went to foreign airlines (14 to Air France, eight to Lufthansa, six each to KLM and Varig, five to Air-India, four to TCA, three each to Cubana, TAP and Thai Airways, two each to Iberia, LAV and Qantas, and one to Avianca), and one went to the Hughes Tool Company.

Model 1049H: The final civil version of the Super Constellation, first flown on 20 September, 1956, and put into service that October, combined the convertible passenger/cargo features of the Model 1049D with the improvements of the Model 1049G. Fifty-three were built: for Aérovias Real (four), Air Finance Corp (three), California Eastern (five), Dollar Airlines (one), Flying Tigers (thirteen), KLM (three), National (four), PIA (two), Qantas (two), Resort Airlines (two), Seaboard & Western (five), Slick Airways (three), TCA (two), TWA (four).

Model 1149: Proposed conversion of 1049Gs and 1049Hs to turbine power with four Allison 501-D2s. Not proceeded with.

Model 1249: Lockheed's designation for the propeller-turbine powered R7V-2 and YC-121F (Model 1249A) for the US military. A commercial version was also proposed as the 1249B.

Super Constellation PP-YSA (c/n 1049H-4833) of the Brazilian carrier Aérovias Real. (*Lockheed*)

Model 1349: Unidentified project.

Model 1449: Proposed development with new wing, fuselage lengthened 55 inches (1·40 m) over that of the Model 1049G, and propeller-turbines.

Model 1549: Further development of the Model 1449 with fuselage 95 inches (2·41 m) longer than that of the Model 1049G. Not proceeded with.

Model 1649: Fitted with a new wing, this derivative of the Super Constellation was, to a large extent, a new design and is described in a separate section.

Eastern Air Lines, the first airline to have ordered the Super Constellation—its contract for fourteen Model 1049s was signed on 20 April, 1950—introduced the type on its New York–Miami route on 15 December, 1951, and thus was able to take advantage of the 1049's additional capacity to absorb the holiday season's rush. Later, this carrier supplemented its initial Super Constellation order by acquiring sixteen 1049Cs and ten 1049Gs. On 30 April, 1961, Eastern used Super Constellations to inaugurate its Air Shuttle no-reservation service on the Washington (National)–New York (LaGuardia)–Boston route. Progressively replaced by Lockheed Electras, Boeing 727-100s and Douglas DC-9-30s, the Super Constellation was retained as back-up aircraft until finally withdrawn on 14 February, 1968, thus ending the 1049's career with major carriers. TWA, having co-sponsored with Eastern the design of the Super Constellation, first used 1049s on its domestic network in September 1952 and, with the availability of higher-performance 1049Cs, went on to start scheduled nonstop transcontinental service on 19 October, 1953, a first for the industry. On its North Atlantic routes TWA made limited use of its early Super Constellation models but on 1 November, 1955, could offer improved service as its Model 1049Gs enabled it to operate nonstop most of the time; however, when headwinds were strong, particularly on westbound flights, or when carrying a heavy payload, the Super G still needed to make one or more intermediate fuelling stops even when wingtip tanks were fitted.

Over the Atlantic and other long-distance routes, the Super Constellation was also operated by several former Constellation operators, notably Air France, Air-India, KLM, LAV and Qantas. New customers—such as Avianca, Cubana,

Iberia, Lufthansa, Northwest (the first to use 1049Gs when it started Seattle–Tokyo service on 1 July, 1955), PIA, TCA, Thai Airways and Varig—joined the list of Lockheed's clients; but others— including BOAC, Pan American and South African Airways—switched from Constellations to Douglas DC-7s. Some carriers, including Eastern and KLM, even went on to operate a mixed fleet of Super Constellations and DC-7s.

When it became evident that the era of piston-engined passenger transports was fast coming to a close, airlines became increasingly hesitant to order aircraft of this type unless they had a pressing need for more capacity. Even in such instances, ways had to be devised to render their purchases more attractive and Lockheed lured them by offering in July 1954 a convertible passenger/cargo version of the Super G. First flown on 20 September, 1956—eleven months after Pan American had placed its order for 45 jetliners (twenty-five Douglas DC-8s and twenty Boeing 707s)—the Model 1049H was sold to fourteen customers. While Flying Tigers, Seaboard & Western, and Slick Airways, operated them mainly as freighters, other carriers used them as passenger transports in the hope that, after their replacement by jetliners, they would easily be sold for use on cargo service. Indeed this second-hand market initially materialized and the 1049Hs were in greater demand during the early 1960s than other Super Constellations; nevertheless, the entry into cargo service of the propeller-turbine powered Canadair CL-44s (with Flying Tigers in June 1961) and of Boeing 707-320Cs and Douglas DC-8-50Fs (respectively with Pan American and Air Canada in mid-1963) soon started to dry up the market. Finally, all versions of the 1049 series became increasingly costly to operate and maintain—with their Turbo-Cyclones proving to be a maintenance nightmare, with frequent failures, leading to the Super Constellations, and the similarly-powered DC-7s, becoming known as the 'world's best trimotors'—and during the 1970s their number decreased rapidly. Thus, at the end of 1980, only four Super Constellations remained in airline service.

View looking aft through the main cabin of a one-class Super Constellation. (*Lockheed*)

The US Navy became on 14 July, 1950, the first military customer for the Super Constellation when it awarded Contract NOa(s) 51-025 for six PO-2W airborne early-warning aircraft. Subsequently, the Navy issued additional contracts and took delivery from Lockheed of 202 Super Constellations in the following versions:

R7O-1/R7V-1 (Model 1049B-55-75): Although first ordered one month after the PO-2Ws, this straightforward cargo/personnel military transport version was delivered to the US Navy eleven months before the AEW version, beginning in November 1952. Powered by four 3,250 hp Wright R-3350-91 Turbo-Compounds, this version had a reinforced floor and a large cargo-loading door on the port side. Navy contracts for sixty-five R7V-1s (briefly designated R7O-1s during 1950) were placed but ten were transferred to the USAF to be completed as RC-121Cs, one was delivered to the USAF as the VC-121E Presidential aircraft, and four were converted during construction as propeller-turbine powered R7V-2s. Thus, the USN took delivery of only fifty R7V-1s (BuNos 128434/128444, 131621/131629, 131632/131649, 131651/131659 and 140311/140313). Thirty-two R7V-1s were later transferred to the USAF as C-121Gs and a few still in Navy service were redesignated C-121Js in September 1962.

R7V-1P: One R7V-1 (BuNo 131624) temporarily equipped with cameras for service with Antarctic Development Squadron Six (VXE-6) for polar ice-pack reconnaissance (Project Birdseye).

R7V-2 (Model 1249A-95-75): Four aircraft (BuNos 131630/131631 and 131660/131661) ordered as R7V-1s were modified during construction as experimental turbine-powered R7V-2s with four 5,550 eshp Pratt & Whitney YT34-P-12A propeller-turbines driving three-blade propellers. Design of the R7V-2 began in August 1951 and BuNo 131630 was first flown on 1 September, 1954. The last aircraft was leased by Lockheed and was modified by Rohr to serve as a testbed for the Allison 501 propeller-turbines for the Electra. Nicknamed the 'Elation', this aircraft was later re-engined with T34-P-6s and delivered to the USAF as a YC-121F-LO.

The fourth R7V-2 (BuNo 131661) while it was fitted with Allison 501 propeller-turbines. Later re-engined with T34-P-6s, it was delivered to the USAF as a YC-121F-LO with serial 53-8158. (*Lockheed*)

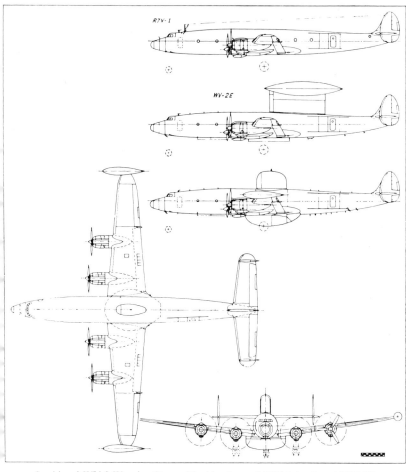

Lockheed WV-2 Warning Star, with side views of R7V-1 (*top*) and WV-2E

WV-2 (Models 1049A-55-70/-86/-91 and -127): First ordered as PO-2Ws but delivered as WV-2s, these machines were airborne early-warning aircraft. In recognition of their duty, these aircraft were known as Warning Stars as were their USAF counterparts, the RC/EC-121s. Fitted with electronic equipment and radomes tested on the PO-1W version of the Constellation, the WV-2s were powered by 3,400 hp Wright R-3350-34 or 42 Turbo-Compound engines and had a maximum take-off weight of 143,600 lb (65,136 kg). They were also fitted with 600-US gal (2,271-litre) tip tanks. Navy contracts were placed for a total of 244 WV-2s but twenty-two were cancelled, one was later modified as a WV-2E, eight were delivered as WV-3 weather reconnaissance aircraft, and 72 were transferred before completion as RC-121Ds for the USAF. The 142 aircraft delivered as WV-2s bore the BuNos 126512/126513, 128323/128326, 131387/131392, 135746/135761, 137887/137890, 141289/141333, 143184/143230 and 145924/145941. Equipment and crew accommodation were progressively upgraded,

Spectacular view of the WV-2E (BuNo 126512), the first AEW aircraft to be fitted with a rotodome. (*Lockheed*)

with corresponding changes in the last two or three digits of the Lockheed Model designation. The last two batches, respectively of 47 and 18 aircraft, were Model 1049A-55-127s with more automated electronic equipment enabling a reduction in crew size from 32 to 28. In September 1962 the WV-2s were redesignated EC-121Ks under the new Tri-Service designation system. Modifications of WV-2/EC-121Ks resulted in the JC-121K, NC-121K, WV-2E (EC-121L), WV-2Q (EC-121M), EC-121P and EC-121R versions described separately.

WV-2E: The first WV-2 (BuNo 126512) was modified as an airborne electronic testbed for the equipment planned for the W2V-1, an airborne early-warning version of the Model 1649 Starliner to be powered by Allison T56-A propeller-turbines and Westinghouse J34 turbojets. Design of the WV-2E was undertaken in January 1954 and, fitted atop of the fuselage with a large dish radome housing the antenna for the APS-82 radar, it was first flown on 8 August, 1956. However, the W2V-1 contract was cancelled and the WV-2E, redesignated EC-121L in 1962, remained experimental. The WV-2E was accepted on 1 March, 1958, and was assigned to the Naval Air Development Unit at NAS South Weymouth, Massachusetts, for preliminary evaluation.

WV-2Q: A small number of WV-2s were modified for electronic counter-measure duties and were first redesignated WV-2Qs and then, from September 1962, EC-121Ls.

WV-3 (Model 1049A-55-95): Eight aircraft (BuNos 137891/137898) retaining the external appearance of the WV-2 but not fitted with tip tanks, were specially equipped during manufacture as weather-reconnaissance aircraft for service with the hurricane hunters of Airborne Early Warning Four (VW-4). For this role special stations were provided for an aerographer and an aerologist, with a total crew of 26. A ninth aircraft was later obtained by modifying a WV-2 (BuNo 141323). In September 1962 the WV-3s were redesignated WC-121Ns and during the late sixties two (BuNos 137895 and 137898) were transferred to the USAF to become the first two EC-121Rs.

The designation C-121, first used by the USAF in 1948 for the C-121A and VC-121B versions of the Constellation, was resurrected when this Service acquired through the Navy the RC-121C/D, VC-121E, and YC-121F versions of the Super Constellations. It later became the designation retained in September 1962 under the Tri-Service system for all military Super Constellations. Redesignations and conversions of existing Navy and Air Force aircraft resulted in the assignment of suffix letters up to T for the EC-121T as follows:

C-121C-LO (Model 1049F-55-96): The USAF transport version of the Super Constellation differed from the Navy's R7V-1 in being powered by 3,400 hp R-3350-34s, in having slightly increased take-off weight (up 3,000 lb/1,361 kg to 133,000 lb/60,328 kg), and rectangular instead of circular windows. Thirty-three C-121Cs (54-151/54-183) were delivered to MATS in 1955 but four were modified as VC-121Cs, two became JC-121Cs, and four ended up as EC-121Ss. On the other hand, one TC-121C (51-3840) had its electronic equipment removed and became a C-121C.

C-121C-LO (54-175) of the 150th Air Transport Squadron, New Jersey ANG. (*Cloud 9 Photography*)

EC-121C-LO: Final designation of eight aircraft ordered as RC-121Cs, and first redesignated TC-121Cs.

JC-121C-LO: Designations given to two C-121Cs (54-160 and 54-178) and one TC-121C (51-3841) modified for systems testing and electronic research.

RC-121C-LO (Model 1049B-55-84): Ten airborne early-warning aircraft (51-3836/51-3845) ordered by the Navy along with WV-2s but delivered to the USAF. Lacking some of the equipment as installed in the ultimate AEW version for the USAF (the RC-121D), nine were redesignated TC-121C and used for AEW training. Powered by 3,400 hp R-3350-34s.

TC-121C-LO: After one of the RC-121Cs (51-3838) had been lost, nine aircraft were redesignated TC-121Cs as AEW trainers. One TC-121C (51-3840) was modified as a C-121C transport and eight became EC-121Cs.

VC-121C-LO: Four C-121Cs (54-167/54-168 and 54-181/54-182) were modified as VIP transports for service with the 1254th Air Transport Squadron (Special Missions), with one aircraft assigned as a backup for the Presidential VC-121E. Later transferred to the ANG.

EC-121D-LO: Redesignated RC-121Ds as the E (Special Electronics Installation) prefix better reflected the aircraft's mission than the R (Reconnaissance) prefix. Some later became EC-121Hs, EC-121Js, EC-121Qs and EC-121Ts.

RC-121D-LO (Model 1049A-55-86): Main AEW version for the USAF of which seventy-two (52-3411/52-3425, 52-533/53-556, 53-3398/53-3403, 54-2304/54-2308, and 55-118/55-139) were procured through diversion from Navy contracts for WV-2s. One more (54-183) was obtained by in-service modification of a C-121C. They differed from the RC-121Cs in being fitted with tip tanks, and in having their equipment and crew stations revised. In 1962 they were redesignated EC-121Ds.

313

VC-121E-LO (Model 1049B-35-97): Ordered by the Navy as an R7V-1 (BuNo 131650), this aircraft was converted during construction as the new Presidential aircraft and, with the serial 53-7885, was assigned to the USAF's 1254th Air Transport Squadron. Named *Columbine III*, the VC-121E was used throughout the Eisenhower administration and, after being replaced in October 1962 by a Boeing VC-137C as the prime Presidential aircraft, it remained in service for a while with the 89th Military Airlift Group (ex-1254th Air Transport Squadron).

YC-121F-LO (Model 1249A-94-75): Ordered as R7V-1s (BuNos 131660/131661) but modified during construction as propeller-turbine powered R7V-2s, these two aircraft were delivered to the USAF as 53-8157 and 53-8158. Powered by four 6,000 eshp Pratt & Whitney T34-P-6 propeller-turbines and fitted with tip tanks, they were operated by the Service Test Squadron (Turboprop) of MATS at Kelly AFB, Texas.

Bearing its original BuNo (131660) instead of its Air Force serial (53-8157), this YC-121F-LO was subsequently operated by the Service Test Squadron (Turboprop) of MATS from Kelly AFB, Texas. (*Lockheed*)

C-121G-LO: After serving with the US Navy, thirty-two R7V-1s were transferred to the USAF during the late fifties and were assigned the serials 54-4048 to 54-4079. Four (54-4050/54-4052 and 54-4058) were modified as TC-121Gs and one of these trainers (54-4051) later became a VC-121G staff transport.

EC-121H-LO: Forty-two EC-121Ds were upgraded and, redesignated EC-121Hs, were fitted with specialized electronic equipment to feed data directly into the SAGE* systems of the joint US-Canadian Air Defense Command (NORAD). Some later became EC-121Ts.

C-121J-LO: Tri-Service designation given in September 1962 to R7V-1s still in Navy service.

EC-121J-LO: Two EC-121Ds (52-3416 and 55-137) were so redesignated after being fitted with additional electronic equipment.

EC-121K-LO: Designation given in September 1962 to the WV-2s of the US Navy. At least one was used for special tests with the YEC-121K designation while others became NC-121Ks.

*SAGE (Semi-Automatic Ground Environment) was a computer-controlled radar and communications defence system.

EC-121K (BuNo 143186) of VQ-1 landing at Atsugi, Japan. (*Hideki Nagabuko via Cloud 9 Photography*)

JC-121K-LO: One EC-121K (BuNo 143196) used for electronic experiments by the US Army.

NC-121K-LO: Modified EC-121Ks operated by the US Navy for a variety of tests at NAS Patuxent River, Maryland, and by Airborne Oceanographic Development Squadron Eight (VXN-8) for Project Magnet — the mapping of the Earth's magnetic field.

EC-121L-LO, EC-121M-LO, and WC-121N-LO: Post-September 1962 designations respectively given to the WV-2E, the WV-2Qs and the WV-3s.

EC-121P-LO: Designation applied to a number of EC-121Ks fitted with updated submarine detection equipment. Three were transferred to the USAF as JEC-121Ps for avionic systems testing but they retained their original BuNos (143189, 143199, and 143200).

EC-121Q-LO: Final designation of some EC-121Ds fitted with more advanced electronic equipment.

EC-121R-LO: Thirty ex-Navy EC-121Ks and EC-121Ps were transferred to the USAF during the Southeast Asia War, and had their radomes and AEW equipment removed. Special electronic equipment was fitted to process data relayed by Beech QU-22Bs from ground monitoring equipment (ADSID — Air Delivered Seismic Intruder Devices) planted along the Ho Chi Minh trail and to direct attacks against such targets. The EC-121Rs were operated from Korat RTAB, Thailand, by the 553rd Reconnaissance Wing between October 1967 and December 1970.

EC-121S-LO: Electronic reconnaissance/counter-measures version operated by the 193rd Tactical Electronic Warfare Group, Pennsylvania ANG. At least five C-121Cs (54-155, 159, 164, 170 and 173) were so modified in the late 1960s and had numerous antennae/radomes protruding from their fuselages.

EC-121T-LO: At least fifteen EC-121Ds, seven EC-121Hs and one EC-121J were upgraded to the EC-121T configuration with improved electronic systems. Most of the EC-121Ts were operated by an AFRES (Air Force Reserve) squadron until October 1978 when the last were consigned to the Military Aircraft Storage and Disposition Center at Davis-Monthan AFB, Arizona.

315

EC-121T (53-550) of the 79th AEW & C Squadron, AFRES. (*Cloud 9 Photography*)

Fifty-five per cent of the Super Constellations built by Lockheed were delivered to the US Navy and USAF and were operated by them for twenty-six years (November 1952 to October 1978). As in June 1948 the Naval Air Transport Service and the Air Transport Command of the USAF had been merged to form the Military Air Transport Service (MATS), the R7V-1s and C-121Cs served side by side in the Atlantic and Pacific Divisions of MATS beginning in early 1953. Initially the Navy-owned R7V-1s carried both MATS and USN markings and retained their BuNos; however, during the 1950s thirty-two were transferred to USAF ownership as C-121Gs but, for a brief period, continued to be flown by

C-121G (54-4052) of Air Transport Squadron Seven (VR-7) over the old dirigible hangar at NAS Moffett Field, California. on 14 August, 1959. (*Robert A. Carlisle/US Navy*)

316

Navy squadrons. Other Navy-owned aircraft fulfilling specific naval logistic tasks (including one Super Constellation assigned as a support aircraft to the Blue Angels demonstration team), and VIP needs, were redesignated C-121Js in 1962. With MATS the C-121Cs and C-121Gs were phased out in 1961 and these aircraft were transferred to the Air National Guard to equip Aeronautical Evacuation Squadrons, beginning with the 183rd ATS, Mississippi ANG. Eventually, the ANG had seven Super Constellation squadrons operating in the aeromedical evacuation (with 47 stretchers and two attendants) and transport roles until the summer of 1973 when the 150th ATS, New Jersey ANG, converted to the C-7A Caribou. The 193rd TEWS flew EC-121S in the electronic counter-measures role from 1967 to 1979 until this unit phased out the last Super Constellation in US military service.

EC-121H of the 551st AEW & C Wing operating from Otis AFB, Massachusetts. (*USAF*)

The first WV-2 Warning Star was accepted by the Navy in October 1955 but three years elapsed before the USN was able to field four Airborne Early Warning Squadrons (VW-2, 3, 11 and 13). These units then kept continuous watch over the North Atlantic until 26 August, 1965, when, after advanced land-based radar had eliminated the need for this mission, an EC-121K of VW-11 flew the last AEW sortie from Keflavik. Phased-out EC-121Ks were then either used for development work, transferred to the USAF for conversion to EC-121Rs, or—as NC-121K, EC-121P and EC-121Q—used in the electronic-reconnaissance role by Tactical Electronic Warfare Squadron Thirty-Three (VAQ-33) and Fleet Air Reconnaissance/Countermeasure Squadron One (VQ-1). On 14 April, 1969, one of the aircraft (BuNo 135749) of VQ-1 made headlines when it was shot down over international waters in the Sea of Japan by fighters of the Korean People's Army Air Force. In a more peaceful yet still demanding setting Airborne Early Warning Squadron Four (VW-4) received WV-2s in 1954 to fly weather reconnaissance/hurricane monitoring sorties over the Caribbean. In 1955 its WV-2s were replaced by specially fitted WV-3s which were retained by VW-4 until the early 1970s. Finally, the last Navy Super Constellation was retired by VQ-1 in 1976.

EC-121R (67-21490, ex WV-2 BuNo 143210) during operations in Southeast Asia in 1969. Note area atop the fuselage from which the radome of the WV-2 has been removed. (*USAF*)

With the USAF the AEW version of the Super Constellation was first assigned to the 552nd Airborne Early Warning & Control Wing at McClellan AFB, California, and then to the 551st AEW & CW at Otis AFB, Massachusetts, to extend the radar coverage of NORAD (North American Air Defense Command). When their contribution to this Command was no longer needed, detachments of EC-121D/Hs were taken to Southeast Asia by the 552nd AEW & CW, with operations taking place first from Tan Son Nhut AB, Saigon, and later from Ubon, Udorn and Korat Royal Thai Air Bases. In this theatre, the EC-121s directed air operations over North Vietnam and Laos, provided air defence control, and acted as airborne communication relay stations. Assigned the call sign Disco, aircraft of this unit flew a total of 98,777 hours in 13,931 combat sorties between April 1965 and August 1973. Another Super Constellation version, the EC-121R as described earlier, was operated in Thailand by the 553rd Reconnaissance Wing. After returning to the United States, the 552nd operated AEW detachments in Iceland and over the Caribbean until the end of 1976. Its duties and aircraft were then transferred to the 79R AEW & C Squadron of the AFRES and this unit retained Super Constellations until October 1978.

The only other military users of the Super Constellation were the Indian Air Force, the Indian Navy and the Indonesian Air Force. The IAF acquired nine Model 1049Gs from Air-India in 1961/62 and, after being modified to serve in the maritime reconnaissance role, these aircraft (Indian Air Force serials BG575/BG583) were operated by No.6 Squadron. Subsequently, five were transferred to the Indian Navy as IN315/IN319 to serve with No.312 Squadron in the same role. At the end of the seventies the Indian Navy's modified 1049Gs were the last Super Constellations in military service. Three unidentified Super Constellations had also been acquired earlier by the AURI (Indonesian Air Force) and had been given the serials T1041/T1043.

Related Temporary Design Designations: CL-255, CL-277, CL-294, CL-323, CL-335, CL-372/CL-375, CL-381, CL-385, CL-395, CL-419, CL-436, CL-545, CL-896, CL-1021, CL-1067, CL-1135, CL-1142, CL-1144, CL-1154 and CL-1225.

	1049	1049G	RC-121D	YC-121F
Span, ft in	123 0	123 5	123 5	119 1
(m)	(37·49)	(37·62)	(37·62)	(36·3)
Length, ft in	113 7	113 7	116 2	116 2
(m)	(34·62)	(34·62)	(35·41)	(35·41)
Height, ft in	24 9	24 9	27 0	24 9
(m)	(7·54)	(7·54)	(8·23)	(7·54)
Wing area, sq ft	1,650	1,654	1,654	1,615
(sq m)	(152·291)	(153·662)	(153·662)	(150·039)
Empty weight, lb	69,210	73,016	80,611	76,162
(kg)	(31,393)	(33,120)	(36,565)	(34,547)
Loaded weight, lb	120,000	137,500	143,600	150,000
(kg)	(54,431)	(62,369)	(65,136)	(68,039)
Wing loading, lb/sq ft	72·7	83·1	86·8	92·9
(kg/sq m)	(355·1)	(405·9)	(423·9)	(453·5)
Power loading, lb/hp	10·7	10·7	11	7·2
(kg/hp)	(4·9)	(4·6)	(5)	(3·3)
Maximum speed, mph/ft	299/11,000	370/20,000	321/20,000	506/20,000
(km/h / m)	(481/3,355)	(595/6,095)	(516/6,095)	(814/6,095)
Cruising speed, mph	255	305	240	421
(km/h)	(410)	(491)	(386)	(677)
Rate of climb, ft/min	960	1,100	845	2,045
(m/min)	(293)	(335)	(258)	(623)
Service ceiling, ft	25,000	22,300	20,600	28,700
(m)	(7,620)	(6,795)	(6,280)	(8,750)
Payload/range, lb/miles	18,800/2,880	18,300/4,140	—	—
(kg/km)	(8,528/4,635)	(8,301/6,660)	—	—
Payload/range, lb/miles	6,100/4,250	8,500/5,250	—	—
(kg/km)	(2,767/6,840)	(3,856/8,445)	—	—
Normal military range, miles	—	—	4,600	2,075
(km)	—	—	(7,400)	(3,340)
Maximum military range, miles	—	—	—	3,140
(km)	—	—	—	(5,050)

Lockheed 'T-33B' Trainer, the private venture L-245, from which the T2V-1 was developed for the US Navy. The shape of the tail surfaces and the exhaust differed significantly from those of the production aircraft. (*Lockheed*)

Lockheed T2V-1 (T-1A) SeaStar

Although Lockheed had developed the TF-80C as a quick, minimum-change of its first jet fighter to provide the Armed Forces with an urgently needed advanced jet trainer, the T-33As and TV-2s achieved success beyond the company's most sanguine hopes. Nevertheless, the manufacturer believed that a much more capable trainer could be developed by incorporating a series of relatively simple changes in the T-33 design, and, accordingly, began in October 1952 privately-funded studies to develop an improved jet trainer.

Under the overall guidance of Kelly Johnson, the design team sought to achieve significant gains in the instructor pilot's work efficiency and in the aircraft's low-speed handling characteristics. The former was to be achieved by raising the instructor's seat six inches (15·2 cm) and by installing a revised canopy, thus greatly increasing the instructor's forward view. The latter by incorporating leading-edge slats, enlarged tail surfaces, and a system of boundary-layer control with compressed air being bled from the engine compressor chambers and discharged through slots over the top of the slats. The combination of these changes was expected to result in a reduction in landing and take-off speeds of 4 kt (7·4 km/h) and 7 kt (13 km/h) respectively over those of the T-33A.

Confident that its projected aircraft, which bore the Temporary Design Designation number L-245, would attract customers, Lockheed decided to proceed with the construction of a demonstrator. To that effect it bought back from the Air Force an uncompleted T-33A airframe (c/n 580-7321, 52-9255) and proceeded to modify it as a prototype of the L-245. Simply named the Lockheed Trainer, and unofficially known as the T-33B, this aircraft was completed at the end of November 1953 and was assigned the civil registration N125D. This company-owned prototype was first flown at the Lockheed Air Terminal on 16

December, 1953, but its initial trials revealed the need for some modifications. In particular, the raised cockpit—which gave the aircraft a distinctive hunchback appearance—resulted in unsatisfactory airflow over the vertical tail surfaces and necessitated the addition of a large dorsal fin. Some redesign of the tailpipe for its 5,400 lb (2,449 kg) thrust Allison J33-A-16A turbojet was also found necessary.

Demonstration of the aircraft to the US Air Force failed to generate interest as it was satisfied with the standard T-33A. The US Navy, however, was impressed by the lower take-off and landing speeds and saw in this aircraft the potential for a much needed jet deck-landing trainer. This interest led in May 1954 to the award of an initial contract for eight T2V-1s (BuNos 142261/142268, Lockheed Model 1080-91-08) to be powered by 6,100 lb (2,767 kg) thrust Allison J33-A-24 or -24A turbojets. These deck-landing trainers were to be fitted with non-jettisonable tip tanks, an arrester hook, and strengthened airframe and undercarriage. The undercarriage, to be capable of withstanding more than twice the sink rate allowed for the TV-2, was characterized by an hydraulically-adjustable nose unit to raise the nose for improved climb and catapult take-off capability.

In advance of the first T2V-1 SeaStar, Lockheed modified its demonstrator into an aerodynamic prototype for the naval trainer by fitting it with the revised nose undercarriage, arrester hook, and revised tail cone. The modified aircraft, painted in USN training colours but retaining its civil registration, was completed in November 1954 and underwent an extensive flight-test programme, followed by structural and functional testing. Simulated catapult take-offs and arrested landings were made at China Lake Naval Testing Station, California, to confirm carrier suitability of structures and equipment, and the experience gained during these tests was incorporated in the final design of the T2V-1 production model.

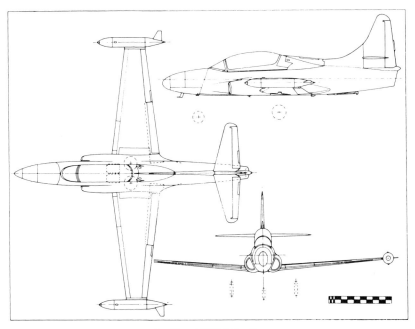

Lockheed T2V-1 SeaStar

321

The first production T2V-1 (BuNo 142261) at the factory. (*Lockheed*)

The first of these aircraft (BuNo 142261, c/n 1080-1001, from the first batch 142261/142268), which differed from the company-owned prototype in having an airframe strengthened to the full production standard and in being fitted with revised main undercarriage, began its flight trials on 20 January, 1956. Eighteen months later, the T2V-1 underwent carrier qualification trials aboard the uss *Antietam* in the hands of personnel from the Flight Test Division, Naval Air Test Center. Four additional batches of T2V-1s were delivered to the US Navy (BuNos 142397/142399, 142533/142541, 144117/144126 and 144735/144764) to bring total production to 150 SeaStars. However, follow-on contracts for 240 T2V-1s (BuNos 144765/144824 and 146058/146237) were cancelled. Among stillborn versions of the SeaStar the CL-330 and CL-340 (proposed lightened models for basic training), CL-341 (a transonic trainer version) and CL-352 (a proposed light-weight all-weather fighter version for use aboard CVS anti-submarine carriers)* are noteworthy.

The T2V-1 (redesignated T-1A on 18 September, 1962) entered service at NAS Pensacola in late 1957. Although proving a docile deck-landing jet trainer, the SeaStar had a relatively short service life as its boundary-layer control sys-tem — the first to be used on a production aircraft in the United States — proved the source of protracted maintenance problems. In any event, the US Navy soon decided to provide initial jet carrier-landing experience with the lower-perform-ance North American T2J-1 (T-2A), with the T2V-1 being used only for advanced training. The availability of the Grumman F9F-8T (TF-9J), which could also be used as a weapons delivery trainer, led to the early retirement of the unarmed SeaStar.

Related Temporary Design Designations: L-245, CL-311/CL-312, CL-330, CL-340/CL-341, CL-352, CL-378, CL-384 and CL-528

Span 42 ft 10 in (13·06 m); length 38 ft 6½ in (11·75 m); height 13 ft 4 in (4·06 m); wing area 240 sq ft (22·297 sq m).

Empty weight 11,965 lb (5,427 kg); loaded weight 15,500 lb (7,031 kg); maximum weight 16,800 lb (7,620 kg); wing loading 64·6 lb/sq ft (315·4 kg/sq m); power loading 2·5 lb/lb.

Maximum speed 580 mph (933 km/h) at 35,000 ft (10,670 m); rate of climb 6,330 ft/min (1,929 m/min); service ceiling 40,000 ft (12,190 m); range 970 miles (1,560 km).

*See Appendix A.

Lockheed F-104 Starfighter

In the afternoon of 1 November, 1950, six sweptwing jet fighters crossed the Yalu River and bounced USAF aircraft operating over North Korea, near the Manchurian border: the MiG-15 had made its combat debut. Soon the new Soviet fighter proved to be a formidable foe which could only be dealt with effectively by the North American F-86 Sabre; even the much-vaunted Sabre achieved air supremacy only through the superior skill and training of its pilots, and its more advanced fire-control system. Moreover, as the current Western trend was toward heavier and more complex fighter aircraft, the MiG-15's performance and manoeuvrability awoke several leading designers to the need to develop lighter and simpler combat aircraft. Thus, in the United Kingdom, W. E. W. Petter began working on light fighter designs, culminating in the Folland Midge and Gnat, while in France several new Intercepteur Léger (light interceptor) projects were launched, including the SFECMAS 1402 Gerfaut, the SE.212 Durandal, the SO.9000 Trident, and the MD.550—the forebear of the superb Mirage series. In the United States, Edward H. Heinemann of Douglas tried to interest the Navy in a light fighter, but instead obtained a contract for a light attack aircraft—the equally famous Skyhawk, while Lockheed's Skunk Works team was also busy with light fighter designs. Finally, Lockheed succeeded in convincing the USAF in December 1952 to proceed with a lightweight and relatively unsophisticated air-superiority day fighter. In the event—and even though Kelly Johnson could justly claim that with the XF-104 Lockheed had brought 'an end to the trend toward constantly bigger, constantly more complicated, constantly more expensive airplanes'—this design achieved its greatest success in later years as the multi-role, heavily-loaded, all-weather F-104G Starfighter.

After June 1950, when its XF-90 had lost the penetration fighter competition to the McDonnell XF-88, Lockheed had gone on to work on a fighter interceptor. Studied under the Temporary Design Designation L-205* and coming close to being built in prototype form as the Model 99, this aircraft had its development contract cancelled by the USAF in January 1951. In May 1952 Lockheed was then offered a new contract for the construction of prototypes of a Wright J67-powered, sixteen-ton interceptor fighter but, as the USAF insisted on a clause forfeiting all patent features and permitting the government to assign the

*See Appendix A.

The prototype Starfighter (XF-104-LO) taking off at Edwards AFB. Note the small size of the air intake and the absence of the shock cone on this J65-powered aircraft. (*Air Force Flight Test Center*)

323

production of the new aircraft to others, Lockheed declined to bid. This refusal to bid was also motivated by the fact that Lockheed's Advanced Design Group, using design and test data on the Douglas X-3 which had been furnished by the USAF, was already working on the CL-246, a relatively simple air-superiority fighter with straight, thin wing. Estimated performance was sufficiently promising for the company, at the behest of Kelly Johnson, to submit an unsolicited proposal in November 1952.

Although the Air Force did not have a standing requirement for this type of fighter, the appeal of Lockheed's proposal was such that within a month the Service prepared a General Operational Requirement calling for a lightweight air-superiority fighter to replace the North American F-100s in Tactical Air Command beginning in 1956, and invited competitive bids from Lockheed, North American and Republic. During January 1953 Lockheed's design was selected and on 12 March, 1953, Letter Contract AF 33(600)-23362 for two XF-104s was issued (Weapon System WS-303A). Under the guidance of Kelly Johnson and project engineer Bill Ralston, the programme then moved swiftly, with mock-up inspection taking place on 30 April and resulting in the substitution of a 20 mm General Electric Gatling-type cannon in place of the two 30-mm cannon suggested by Lockheed. At that time the aircraft's long and pointed fuselage, and its small wing area, already imparted its characteristic 'missile with a man in it' appearance.

To achieve their calculated Mach 2 top speed, the production aircraft were to be powered by a single Wright J65 (a licence-built version of the British-designed Armstrong Siddeley Sapphire) axial-flow turbojet with afterburner. However, the first prototype, construction of which had begun during the summer of 1954, initially received a non-afterburning, Buick-built, XJ65-W-6 with 10,200 lb (4,627 kg) take-off thrust. Trucked to Edwards AFB, the first XF-104 (c/n 083-1001, serial 53-7786) was readied for its maiden flight with Tony LeVier at the controls. After a short and straight hop on 28 February, 1954, the XF-104 experienced undercarriage retraction problems during its first full flight on 4 March, 1954. Subsequently, one of the XF-104s, powered by an afterburning J65, reached a top speed of 1,324 mph/2,130 km/h (Mach 1·79) on 25 March, 1955. The second prototype was lost twenty-four days later, when H. 'Fish' Salmon was forced to eject during gun-firing trials, but the first XF-104 was accepted by the USAF in November 1955.

Already during the first phase of the XF-104 trials it had become evident that, even with the afterburning version of the J65 turbojet, the production aircraft would not be able to reach design maximum speed. Furthermore, directional stability problems and the need to carry more fuel internally required the lengthening of the fuselage. Accordingly, the YF-104A service trial aircraft, and subsequent production versions, had the fuselage lengthened from 49 ft 2 in (14·99 m) to 54 ft 8 in (16·66 m), the T-tail surfaces moved aft, and engines changed to various models of the General Electric J79. In addition, these aircraft were fitted with variable shock-control ramp in the fuselage-side air intakes, forward- (in place of rearward-) retracting undercarriage, and increased fuel capacity.

The first YF-104A was flown on 17 February, 1956, and the programme appeared to move smoothly towards providing the Air Force with its first bisonic fighter. Unfortunately, persistent difficulties in developing the afterburner for the J79 and the USAF decision in April 1956 to add heat-seeking Sidewinder missiles to the aircraft's armament, combined in forcing the schedule to slip, with the first operational Starfighter squadron being formed only during January 1958.

The eleventh YF-104-LO (55-2965) undergoing an afterburner test at night at Edwards AFB. (*Air Force Flight Test Center*)

Moreover, changing TAC requirements and the anticipated early availability of more flexible supersonic fighters, led to a review of the F-104 programme. Finally, by December 1958 the USAF drastically reduced its contracts (at one point orders for 722 aircraft had been placed) and Lockheed went on to produce only 296 Starfighters for the USAF (two XF-104s, seventeen YF-104As, one hundred and fifty-three F-104As, twenty-six F-104Bs, seventy-seven F-104Cs and twenty-one F-104Ds). Fortunately, major foreign MAS- and MAP-funded programmes boosted Lockheed's Starfighter production to 741, and added 48 co-produced aircraft and 1,789 licence-built aircraft, for a grand total of 2,578.

Messerschmitt-built F-104G (c/n 7097) of Marinefliegergeschwader 1 (MFG1), Bundesmarine, at Kleine Brogel in July 1978. (*Jean-Michel Guhl*)

The substantial multi-national F-104 programme had its origin in a Luftwaffe requirement for a supersonic fighter to supplement, and eventually supplant the Canadair Sabres and Republic F-84Fs with which the Jagdgeschwadern and Jagdbombergeschwadern of the Luftwaffe had first been equipped following the rebirth of that Service in 1956. At least nine types of aircraft were considered for German re-equipment (the English Electric Lightning and Saunders-Roe SR.177, the French Dassault Mirage III, the Swedish SAAB Draken, and five US designs: the Convair F-102 and F-106, Grumman F11F-1F Super Tiger, Lockheed F-104 and Republic F-105). By 1958, following British cancellation of the SR.177—which up to then had been one of the front contenders—the competition had narrowed to proposed Mirage and F-104 developments. The F-104 proposal retained the external dimensions and engine—in its improved J79-GE-11A version—of the F-104C but was now proposed as a multi-role, all-weather aircraft with Autonetics F15A NASARR (North American Search and Ranging Radar), provision for 4,000 lb (1,814 kg) of external stores on five hard points, and revised tankage to increase fuel from 1,624 to 1,784 US gal (6,159 to 6,617 litres).

The hotly contested competition—the first of the so-called deals of the century—was won by Lockheed in October 1958 when the F-104G (G for Germany) was declared the winner. A first contract for sixty-six F-104Gs was awarded to Lockheed on 6 February, 1959, and licence-production rights were acquired on 18 March of that year. The European production programme was enlarged during 1960 by the addition of the Netherlands in January, Belgium in March and Italy in November. Meanwhile, on 24 July, 1959, Canada had become the second foreign customer for the Starfighter, and Japan had joined during the same year with the inception of its own Starfighter programme. The complex F-104 production scheme is summarized in the accompanying table, and the Starfighter versions are detailed later:

Starfighter Production Summary

	Lockheed	Co-production	Canadair	Fiat	Fokker	MBB	Messerschmitt	Mitsubishi	SABCA	Total
XF-104	2	—	—	—	—	—	—	—	—	2
YF-104	17	—	—	—	—	—	—	—	—	17
F-104A	153	—	—	—	—	—	—	—	—	153
F-104B	26	—	—	—	—	—	—	—	—	26
F-104C	77	—	—	—	—	—	—	—	—	77
F-104D	21	—	—	—	—	—	—	—	—	21
F-104DJ	20	—	—	—	—	—	—	—	—	20
CF-104	—	—	200	—	—	—	—	—	—	200
CF-104D	38	—	—	—	—	—	—	—	—	38
F-104F	30	—	—	—	—	—	—	—	—	30
F-104G	139	—	140	164	231	50	210	—	188	1,122
RF-104G	40	—	—	35	119	—	—	—	—	194
TF-104G (583C)	29	—	—	—	—	—	—	—	—	29
TF-104G (583D)	88	—	—	—	—	—	—	—	—	88
TF-104G (583E)	13	4	—	—	—	—	—	—	—	17
TF-104G (583F)	42	23	—	—	—	—	—	—	—	65
TF-104G (583G)	—	9	—	—	—	—	—	—	—	9
TF-104G (583H)	—	12	—	—	—	—	—	—	—	12
F-104J	3	—	—	—	—	—	—	207	—	210
F-104N	3	—	—	—	—	—	—	—	—	3
F-104S	(2)	—	—	245	—	—	—	—	—	245
	741	48	340	444	350	50	210	207	188	2,578

XF-104-LO (Model 083-92-01): Two single-seat prototypes (53-7786/53-7787) each powered by a 7,800 lb (3,538 kg) thrust dry and 10,200 lb (4,627 kg) with afterburner Wright XJ65-W-6 turbojet. First XF-104 initially flown on 4 March, 1954, with non-afterburning engine. Downward-ejection seat and provision for single, six-barrel 20-mm Vulcan cannon.

YF-104A-LO (Model 183-93-02): To accommodate the J79 engine and generally improve handling characteristics, the seventeen YF-104A service trials aircraft (55-2955/55-2971) had a 5 ft 6 in (1·67 m) longer fuselage. They incorporated the following other changes: forward-retracting nosewheel, two additional fuel cells in the fuselage, and modified intakes with half-cone centre-bodies. Aircraft initially fitted with the General Electric XJ79-GE-3 turbojet (with maximum thrust rating of 9,300 lb/4,218 kg dry and 14,800 lb/6,713 kg with afterburner); later the J79-GE-3A with improved afterburner was standardized. The first YF-104A was flown on 17 February, 1956, and reached Mach 2 on 27 April. Together with the first thirty-five F-104A production models, the seventeen YF-104As were involved in a protracted flight trials programme during which airframe strengthening and local redesign were progressively introduced, various forms of flap-blowing were tested and a ventral fin was added to improve directional stability at supersonic speed. Some were also used to test wingtip racks for either 170-US gal (644-litre) drop tanks or Sidewinder infra-red guided air-to-air missiles. The seventh YF-104A (c/n 183-1007, 55-2961) was transferred to NASA in August 1956 and, as 818—later N818NA—was operated by this administration until November 1975. It is now on display at the National Air and Space Museum in Washington.

F-104A-25-LO 56-857 of the 157th FIS, one of three Air National Guard squadrons equipped with the first production version of the Starfighter. (*via Cloud 9 Photography*)

F-104A-LO (Model 183-92-02): A total of 153 F-104As (*see* Appendix B for serials) were built by Lockheed in seven blocks—F-104A-1-LO to F-104-30-LO —with final acceptance by the USAF in December 1958. Initially powered by the J79-GE-3A turbojet but retrofitted beginning in April 1958 with the more reliable J79-GE-3B (9,600 lb/4,354 kg dry thrust and 14,800 lb/6,713 kg with afterburner). Design armament consisted of a 20-mm M-61 Vulcan cannon and two wingtip-mounted AIM-9B Sidewinder missiles with AN/ASG-14T-1 fire-control system. However, the early cannon's unreliability forced its removal in November 1957 before delivery of F-104As to operational squadrons; improved cannon were re-installed in 1964. Modifications introduced during Service life included substitution of an upward-firing ejector seat for the initial downward-firing unit, standard installation of the ventral fin and flap-blowing system, and retrofitting of either the J79-GE-19 (17,900 lb/8,119 kg afterburning thrust) on some USAF aircraft or J79-GE-11A (15,800 lb/7,167 kg maximum thrust) on F-104As of the

328

Pakistan Air Force. NASA operated two F-104As between October 1957, when it received 56-734, and December 1962, when 56-749 crashed; a third (56-790) was obtained in December 1966. One F-104A-15-LO (56-770) went to the RCAF as 12700 to serve as a pattern aircraft for the Canadian Starfighter, ten were transferred to Pakistan, at least 25 went to Taiwan, and 32 ended up in Jordan. In addition, three were modified as NF-104As and twenty-four as QF-104As.

NF-104A-LO: Three F-104As, 56-756, 760 and 762, were modified in 1963 to be used in the USAF astronaut training programme conducted by the Aerospace Research Pilot School at Edwards AFB. They were fitted with a 6,000 lb (2,722 kg) thrust Rocketdyne AR-2 auxiliary rocket engine above the jetpipe, 2 ft (61-cm) wingtip extensions, the enlarged vertical surfaces of the F-104G, and hydrogen-peroxide control thrusters at the nose, tail and wingtips.

Details of the Rocketdyne AR-2 rocket fitted above and aft of the J79 exhaust of one of the three NF-104As. (*Air Force Flight Test Center*)

QF-104A-LO: Twenty-four YF-104As and early production F-104As were modified in 1960 as remote-controlled target drones.

RF-104A-LO (Model 383-93-04): Design work on an unarmed photographic-reconnaissance version of the Starfighter had begun in November 1954 but a contract for eighteen aircraft (56-939/56-956) was cancelled in January 1957 before completion of the first RF-104A.

TF-104A-LO: Proposed unarmed, two-seat training version. Not proceeded with as the USAF preferred the combat-capable F-104B.

F-104B-LO (Model 283-93-03): Two-seat, dual-control, combat trainer version of the F-104A of which twenty-six were built in four blocks with J79-GE-3A or -3B. To provide space for the second seat, mounted aft beneath an extended canopy, the 20-mm cannon of the single seater was removed, some of the electronics were relocated, the nosewheel again was made to retract rearward, and internal fuel capacity was reduced from 897 to 752 US gal (3,396 to 2,847 litres); however, provision for two underwing and two wingtip drop tanks — boosting fuel capacity by 730 gal/2,764 litres — was retained. Armament was limited to two AIM-9B Sidewinders with AN/ASG-14T-1 fire-control system. The fin area was increased by 25 per cent and a fully-powered rudder was adopted. The first F-104B-1-LO (c/n 283-5000, serial 56-3719) was flown on 16 January, 1957, and was subsequently used to test the downward-ejection seat initially fitted to all USAF Starfighters. The last F-104B-15-LO was delivered in November 1958. Some F-104Bs were later transferred to Taiwan and Jordan, while 53-1303 was handed over to NASA in December 1959.

F-104C-LO (Model 483-04-05): Tactical strike version combining features of late production F-104As with special modifications to suit the aircraft to its new role. General Electric J79-GE-7 with maximum dry rating of 10,000 lb (4,536 kg) and afterburner rating of 15,800 lb (7,167 kg). In addition to the internally-mounted 20-mm cannon, the F-104C could carry either two wingtip-mounted Sidewinders (later, the aircraft were modified to carry another pair of Sidewinders beneath the fuselage), or bombs/rocket pods on underwing and fuselage points; for nuclear strike an MK-28 special store could be carried beneath the fuselage. A removable inflight-refuelling probe could be fitted on the port side of the fuselage. Fifty-six F-104C-5-LOs (56-883/56-938) and twenty-one F-104C-10-LOs (57-910/57-930) were delivered to Tactical Air Command between September 1958 and June 1959.

F-104C-5-LO (56-914) of the 479th TFW being readied at George AFB, California, for deployment to Southeast Asia. Note external refuelling probe. (*USAF*)

F-104D-LO (Model 383-04-06): Combat trainer version combining the two-seat, dual-control arrangement of the F-104B with the armament, engine and flight-refuelling capability of the F-104C. Twenty-one built in three blocks for delivery to TAC between November 1958 and September 1959.

F-104DJ (Model 583B-10-17): Two-seat trainers with electronics and other items compatible with those of the F-104J version. Twenty built by Lockheed and reassembled in Japan by Mitsubishi for delivery to the Koku Jieitai between July 1962 and January 1964. Bearing the JASDF serials 26-5001 to 26-5009 and 36-5010 to 36-5020, these aircraft were powered by licence-built J79-IHI-11A (15,800 lb/7,167 kg thrust with afterburner) turbojets.

F-104E: Designation not assigned.

F-104F-LO (Model 483-04-08): Minimum-change version of the F-104D two-seat trainer of which thirty were built by Lockheed for the Luftwaffe. They were first assigned USAF serials 59-4994/59-5023 but were later assigned German codes BB360/BB389 and finally, after 1 January, 1968, bore the numbers 2901/2930. They were the first Starfighters to be delivered to the Luftwaffe, beginning in October 1959, but were withdrawn from use in December 1971.

F-104G-LO (Model 683-10-19): By far the most important Starfighter version, the F-104G was the type selected for production in Europe. It was also built in Canada (under US-funded MAP contracts) and in the United States by Lockheed.

Lockheed-built F-104G (c/n 683-2083) of Jagdbombergeschwader 33 at Buchel. (*Bundesluftwaffe*)

Intended as a single-seat, multi-role, all-weather fighter, the F-104G was powered by a 10,000 lb (4,536 kg) dry thrust and 15,600 lb (7,076 kg) with afterburner J79-GE-11A, with the European-built aircraft being fitted with engines co-produced under licence by MAN-Turbo in Germany, the Fabrique Nationale in Belgium, and Fiat in Italy. Most Luftwaffe and Bundesmarine Starfighters were later retrofitted with updated, German-built J79-MTU-J1Ks. Principal differences between the F-104G and the F-104C were the former's strengthened structure, enlarged tail surfaces with fully-powered rudder as used on the two-seat versions, combat manoeuvring flaps, heavier weapons load, and vastly improved electronics, centred around the Autonetics F15A NASARR. The ejector seat fitted at the time of delivery was the Lockheed Model C-2 upward-operating unit but beginning in 1967 replaced by Martin-Baker Mk GQ7(F) 'zero-zero' seats. The first F-104G, a Lockheed-built aircraft (c/n 683-2001), was flown on 7 June, 1960, and the last was delivered by MBB in 1973. Altogether a total of 1,127 F-104Gs, representing nearly 44 per cent of the Starfighter production, were built as

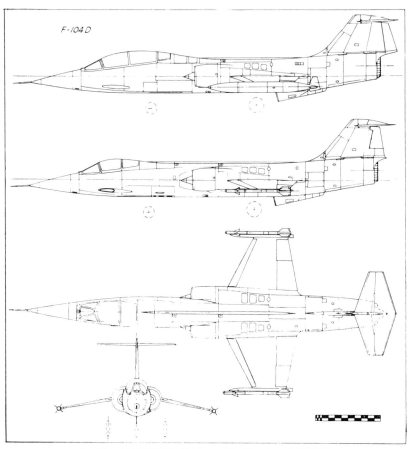

Lockheed F-104C Starfighter, with side view of F-104D

follows: 139 by Lockheed for delivery to the Luftwaffe, Greece, Norway, Turkey, and a pattern aircraft for both Fiat and SABCA; 140 by Canadair (first flight on 30 July, 1963) for Denmark, Greece, Norway, Spain, Taiwan and Turkey; and the balance being built in Europe by four groups for deliveries to Belgium, Germany, Italy and the Netherlands, and later by MBB for Germany. The South Group—led by Messerschmitt and also including Dornier, Heinkel and Siebel—flew its first Starfighter on 5 October, 1960, and delivered 210 aircraft to the Luftwaffe; the West Group—SABCA as leader, and Avions Fairey—flew its first F-104G on 3 August, 1961, and produced 188 aircraft for the Force Aérienne Belge and the Luftwaffe; the North Group—with Aviolanda, Focke-Wulf, Hamburger Flug-zeugbau, Weser Flugzeugbau and its leader Fokker—supplied 231 F-104Gs to the Koninklijke Luchtmacht (KLu, Royal Netherlands Air Force) and the Luftwaffe, with its first F-104G flying on 11 November, 1961; and the Italian Group—led by Fiat and including Aerfer-Macchi, Piaggio, SACA and SIAI-Marchetti—flew its first Starfighter on 9 June, 1962, and delivered its 169 aircraft plus the re-assembled pattern aircraft to Dutch, German and Italian units. Finally, MBB

332

built a batch of fifty replacement aircraft for the Luftwaffe in 1971–73. After being operated by the German training unit at Luke AFB, a Fokker-built aircraft (ex KG313) which had been built as an RF-104G for the Luftwaffe was acquired by NASA in July 1975 and, with all military equipment removed, was operated as an F-104G with the registration N826NA. Two Italian-built F-104Gs (MM6658 and MM6660) were later modified by Lockheed as F-104S prototypes. As part of a control-configured research programme, MBB modified one Fokker-built aircraft (c/n 8100, original German serial KG200 and current serial 2391) with a canard surface atop the fuselage; the modified aircraft first flew on 20 November, 1980.

Under contract from the Luftwaffe, Lockheed undertook tests with the F-104G launched from a special platform with a powerful rocket as part of the ZELL (Zero-Length Launch) programme. The tests were successful but the scheme was not adopted for operational use.

RF-104G-LO (Model 683-04-10): Tactical reconnaissance version of which Lockheed delivered 40, the North Group (Fokker) 119, and the Italian Group (Fiat) 30. The aircraft for the KLu had an external ventral camera pack while most others carried three KS-67A cameras in the forward fuselage; in both cases the cannon and its 725-round magazine aft of the cockpit were removed. In service many of the Starfighters which had been delivered as RF-104Gs were modified to F-104G standard while the reverse, although less frequently, also happened.

TF-104G (Model 583-10-20): Whereas the F-104Fs for the Luftwaffe were pure trainers to be used to convert pilots to the Starfighter, the TF-104Gs were combat-ready aircraft fitted with NASARR, full operational equipment, and underwing racks. Including forty-eight aircraft with components manufactured by the European partners, Lockheed built a total of 220 TF-104Gs in six versions identified by a suffix letter after their Model 583 designation. The Models 583C to 583H were respectively for MAP delivery to the Luftwaffe and the AMI (Italy), and for direct delivery to the KLu, the Luftwaffe, the Force Aérienne Belge and the AMI. One of the Model 583Ds (c/n 583D-5702) was initially retained by Lockheed as a demonstrator, with the registration N104L; it was used by Jacqueline Cochran to set world's records but in May 1965 it was delivered to the KLu with the Dutch serial D-5702. Two ex-Luftwaffe TF-104Gs (c/ns 583D-5755 and -5939) were acquired by NASA in July 1975 and were respectively registered N824NA and N825NA.

TF-104G (2827) of Waffenschule 10 (WS-10) at Jever. (*via Cloud 9 Photography*)

Parachute-assisted landing by a Mitsubishi-built F-104J (36-8526, c/n 683B-3026) of the 205th Hikotai, Koku Jieitai. (*Hideki Nagabuko, via Cloud 9 Photography*)

RTF-104G1: Projected all-weather day and night reconnaissance development of the TF-104G for the Luftwaffe. Cameras, infra-red and sideways-looking radar were to be installed. Not proceeded with as the Luftwaffe selected the McDonnell RF-4E for this mission.

F-104H and TF-104H: Projected single- and two-seat export version with simplified equipment, NASARR not installed and optical gunsight. Not built.

F-104J (Model 683-07-14): Structurally similar to the F-104G but equipped as an all-weather interceptor and powered by a Japanese-built J79-IHI-11A turbojet. Three built by Lockheed, 29 assembled by Mitsubishi from Lockheed components, and 178 built in two batches by Mitsubishi. The first Lockheed-built F-104J was flown on 30 June, 1961, and deliveries by Mitsubishi extended from March 1962 through March 1965, with the final batch being delivered in 1967.

F-104K, F-104L and F-104M: Designations not used.

F-104N: With the N in their designation standing for NASA, the three F-104Ns (c/ns 683C-4045, -4053 and -4058) were built by Lockheed in the midst of a batch of F-104Gs, and were delivered between August and October 1963 as NASA supersonic chase aircraft. They were initially numbered 811 to 813, with the two surviving aircraft later becoming N811NA and N812NA.

F-104P, F-104Q and F-104R: Designations not used.

F-104S: After flight testing some improvements on a modified RF-104G (c/n 683C-4024, serial 61-2624), Lockheed received an Italian contract to modify two Fiat-built F-104Gs (MM6658 and MM6660) as prototypes for an advanced all-purpose aircraft with improved capability both as an interceptor — with an R21G radar and two underwing AIM-7 Sparrow II and/or two AIM-9 Sidewinder missiles — and as a fighter-bomber with a 20-mm Vulcan cannon and up to 7,500 lb (3,402 kg) of bombs, napalm tanks or rocket pods on nine external attachment points. To cope with the F-104S's increased weight and to boost performance, an 11,870 lb (5,384 kg) dry thrust and 17,900 lb (8,119 kg) with afterburner J79-GE-19 was installed. The first Lockheed-modified F-104S was flown in December 1966 and Fiat went on to produce 245 F-104S for the Italian and Turkish Air Forces, with deliveries extending from December 1968 until 1980. In service with the Aeronautica Militare Italiana some aircraft were fitted with a camera package to supplement the RF-104G in the tactical reconnaissance role.

CF-104: Before building one hundred and forty F-104Gs as part of the Mutual Assistance Program, Canadair had manufactured 200 aircraft under a contract awarded by the Canadian Government on 24 July, 1959. Initially designated CF-111s by the Royal Canadian Air Force but later redesignated CF-104s, and bearing the Canadair designation CL-90, these aircraft were basically similar to the F-104Gs. However, they were fitted with equipment specified by the RCAF, were powered by a Canadian-built J79-OEL-7 turbojet (maximum dry rating of 10,000 lb/4,536 kg and 15,800 lb/7,167 kg with afterburner), and retained provision for the removable refuelling probe as fitted to the F-104Cs and F-104Ds of the USAF. They could also carry a ventral reconnaissance pod with four Vinten cameras and electronic sensors produced by Computing Devices of Canada. The first Canadair CF-104 was airlifted to Palmdale, California, where it was first flight tested by Lockheed on 26 May, 1961. The CF-104s were initially assigned the Canadian serials 12701 to 12900 but, effective on 18 May, 1970, they were renumbered 104701 to 104900; at the same time the Lockheed-built F-104A pattern aircraft was renumbered from 12700 to 104700. In recent years a number of CF-104s and CF-104Ds have been transferred to Denmark and Norway, and have been modified to standards respectively approaching those of the F-104Gs and TF-104Gs.

CF-104 104862 of No.463 Squadron, No.1 Air Division, Canadian Armed Forces, at Cambrai, France. Special markings were applied for the 1979 Tiger Meet. (*Jean-Michel Guhl*)

CF-104D (Model 583-04-15): Thirty-eight two-seat trainers built by Lockheed for the RCAF and assigned the Canadian serials 12631/12668; on 18 May, 1970, the serials were changed to 104701/104738. In Canada these trainers, powered by locally-built J79-OEL-7s, were first designated CF-113s. The last sixteen aircraft had slightly different equipment and were designated CF-104D Mk II.

X-27: Beginning in the late 1960s Lockheed endeavoured to breathe some life into the Starfighter programme and marketed unsuccessfully the CL-1200 Lancer. The aircraft retained the basic F-104 fuselage but was to be fitted with shoulder-mounted wing and its tailplane was to be removed from the tip of the vertical fin to the base of the aft fuselage. The engine was to be a Pratt & Whitney turbofan, either the TF30-P-100 or F-100-PW-100. Gross weight was estimated at 35,000 lb (15,875 kg) and top speed at 1,700 mph at 35,000 ft (2,735 km/h at 10,670 m). In support of the programme the USAF considered acquiring one or more Lancers as X-27 research aircraft. However, in November 1970 the primary market for which the Lancer had been conceived was lost to the Northrop F-5E Tiger II and the project shelved.

Other proposed derivatives of the F-104 remained on the drawing boards, including the interesting CL-704 VTOL strike and reconnaissance aircraft which was proposed in 1962. To achieve VTOL operations, the CL-704 was to be fitted with seven vertically-mounted Rolls-Royce RB.181s in each of the enlarged wingtip pods, with a fuselage-mounted Rolls-Royce RB.168R being used as the normal propulsion engine. A larger-wing F-104 development was also proposed as an alternative to the MRCA (Multi Role Combat Aircraft) then being designed as a multi-national European project.

Originally developed as an air-superiority fighter for United States Tactical Air Command units, the F-104A was assigned to the Air Defense Command at the conclusion of its trials, as by then TAC had no use for it while ADC needed some boosting due to delays with the development of the Convair F-106A. Thus, though its lack of all-weather capability and relatively short endurance did not satisfy the requirements for a genuine ADC interceptor, the F-104A was first delivered in January 1958 to the 83rd Fighter Interceptor Squadron at Hamilton AFB, California. Nine months later twelve F-104As from the 83rd FIS were airlifted to Taiwan on temporary deployment to augment Nationalist China's air defence during the Quemoy Crisis. During 1958 two other ADC units—the 56th FIS at Wright-Patterson AFB, Ohio, and the 337th FIS at Westover AFB, Massachusetts—were equipped with F-104As. With the availability of all-weather F-101Bs and F-106As, the F-104As and F-104Bs were phased out from the ADC during 1960 and were transferred to three Air National Guard squadrons: the 151st FIS, Tennessee ANG; the 157th FIS, North Carolina ANG; and the 197th FIS, Arizona ANG.

During the Berlin Crisis these three Guard units were activated between 1 November, 1961, and 15 August, 1962, and were deployed to Europe, with the 151st and 197th being based at Ramstein in Germany, and the 157th at Morón in Spain. When these squadrons were returned to the control of their respective States, their F-104As and F-104Bs were retained by the USAF and re-assigned to ADC units: the 319th FIS at Homestead, Florida, and the 331st FIS at Webb AFB, Texas. Both these ADC units, along with the F-104C/D-equipped 479th Tactical Fighter Wing, were on alert duty during the October 1962 Cuban Missile Crisis. Finally, the F-104A/Bs were phased out when the 319th FIS was deactivated in December 1969.

The F-104C/Ds, which were better suited to Tactical Air Command's needs, were assigned to four squadrons of the 479th TFW at George AFB, California, beginning in September 1958. During the Cuban Missile Crisis they were deployed to Key West, Florida. During the Southeast Asia War, the 479th TFW then deployed a single squadron of F-104Cs to Da Nang AB, Vietnam, in 1965, and to Udorn RTAB, Thailand, in 1966–67, for operations over both South and North Vietnam. However, high losses and insufficient weapons load forced the type's replacement with McDonnell F-4Ds during 1967. A sufficient number of F-104C/Ds were then transferred to the 198th TFS, Puerto Rico ANG, and this unit operated Starfighters until its conversion to LTV A-7Ds in July 1975.

Other notable USAF versions of the Starfighter included the QF-104A target drones, the F-104G/TF-104Gs used in the training of Luftwaffe pilots by the 4510th Combat Crew Training Wing and the 58th Tactical Fighter Training Wing (redesignated 58th Tactical Training Wing in 1977 and still active at Luke AFB, Arizona, in 1981), and the NF-104As. Three of the last were acquired by the Aerospace Research Pilot School at Edwards AFB towards the end of 1963. On 12 December of that year one of these aircraft (56-762) nearly claimed the life of the ARPS Commander — Col Charles Yeager, the first pilot to fly faster than sound in a Bell X-1 — when, after being forced to eject at the end of a flat spin from 104,000 ft (31,700 m) to 11,000 ft (3,350 m), he was burned by the rocket of his ejector seat. On 6 December, 1963, however, Maj R. W. Smith set in another NF-104A an unofficial height record of 118,860 ft (36,229 m) for aircraft taking off on their own power (the official record of 113,829 ft/34,695 m was then held by the Mikoyan Ye-66A, while the air-launched North American X-15A-2 had already reached its still-standing record of 314,750 ft/95,936 m).

Over the years NASA operated eleven Starfighters: one YF-104A, three F104As, one F-104B, one F-104G, two TF-104Gs and three F-104Ns. The first F-104A was acquired by NASA on 23 August, 1956, and at the end of 1980 four Starfighters (one F-104G, one TF-104G and two F-104Ns) were still being used by NASA as chase planes and for research. The third F-104N (c/n 683C-4058, NASA 813) was lost on 8 June, 1966, in an inflight collision with the second North American XB-70; Dr Joseph A. Walker, in the F-104N, and Maj Carl Cross, in the XB-70, were both killed.

In the United States, both military and civil pilots set records in Starfighters. The more important ones are listed here in chronological order:

7 May, 1958: Maj Howard C. Johnson reached 91,249 ft (27,813 m) in a YF-104A at Edwards AFB, California.

16 May, 1958: Capt Walter W. Irwin, flying a YF-104A, averaged 1,404·19 mph (2,259·83 km/h) over a 15/25 km course at Edwards AFB.

December 1958: Flying from NAS Point Mugu, California, an F-104A set three time-to-climb records: 3,000 m (9,842 ft) in 41·35 sec; 15,000 m (49,212 ft) in 131·1 sec; and 25,000 m (82,020 ft) in 266·03 sec.

14 December, 1959: An F-104C boosted the world's altitude record to 103,389 ft (31,513 m), thus becoming the first aircraft taking-off on its own power to exceed the 30,000 m and 100,000 ft marks.

11 May, 1 June, and 3 June, 1964: Flying a TF-104G, Jacqueline Cochran set three women's speed records: 1,429·3 mph (2,299·71 km/h) over a 15/25 km course; 1,303·18 mph (2,097·23 km/h) over a 100-km closed circuit; and 1,127·4 mph (1,814·34 km/h) over a 500-km closed circuit.

24 October, 1977: In a special F-104RB which he had built with help from American Jet Industries Inc of Van Nuys, California, Darryl Greenamyer set the current world's speed record over a 3-km course at restricted altitude: 988·26 mph (1,590·43 km/h) at Mud Lake, Tonopah, Nevada. With this aircraft fitted with 2½-ft wingtip extensions, Greenamyer failed to set a new world's altitude record.

Since October 1959, when the Luftwaffe received its first F-104F trainer, Starfighters have been operated by fourteen countries.

Belgium: The Force Aérienne Belge received a total of one hundred SABCA-built F-104Gs, beginning in February 1963, and twelve Lockheed-built TF-104Gs. They were assigned to four escadrilles: the 23ème and 31ème at Kleine Brogel, and the 349ème and 350ème at Beauvechain (Bevekom). During 1980 the

C/n 583D-5702, the TF-104G in which Jacqueline Cochran set three world records. This aircraft was later delivered to the KLu with the Dutch serial D-5702. (*Lockheed*)

SABCA-built F-104G (FX-65, c/n 9108) of the 10 Wing, Force Aérienne Belge, based at Kleine Brogel. (*FAéB*)

The 117th Canadair-built CF-104. (*Canadair*)

Beauvechain escadrilles converted to General Dynamics F-16A/Bs, while the Kleine Brogel units are to retire their last Starfighters during 1983.

Canada: The Royal Canadian Air Force, which received 200 Canadair CF-104s and 38 Lockheed CF-104Ds, used its Starfighters to equip twelve Europe-based squadrons of its No.1 Air Division, beginning in December 1962 with No.427 Squadron, No.3 Wing, at Zweibrücken, Germany. Other CF-104/CF-104Ds were assigned to No.6 OTU at Cold Lake, Alberta. Attrition, budgetary cuts, and aircraft transfers to Allies have progressively reduced this strength and by the end of 1980 the No.1 Canadian Group only had three Starfighter squadrons (Nos.421, 439 and 441) at Baden-Soellingen, Germany, with No.417 Squadron at Cold Lake functioning as a CF-104 Operational Conversion Unit. Beginning in 1983, the Starfighters are to be replaced in Canadian Armed Forces service with McDonnell Douglas CF-18 Hornets.

Canadair CF-104D of Esk.726, Kongelike Danske Flyvevåben, at Nancy-Ochey in July 1977. (*Jean-Michel Guhl*)

Denmark: Beginning in November 1964, Kongelige Danske Flyvevåben (Royal Danish Air Force) received twenty-five Canadair-built F-104Gs and four Lockheed TF-104Gs to equip two units (Esk 723 and Esk 726) at Aalborg. Attrition has been more than made up by the transfer in 1972–74 of twenty-two ex-Canadian Starfighters—fifteen CF-104s and seven CF-104Ds, with the latter being specially modified for use by Esk 726 in the electronic countermeasures role.

Germany: By far the largest recipient of Starfighters, this nation received a total of 915 aircraft (30 F-104Fs, 96 F-104Gs and 136 TF-104Gs from Lockheed, 255 F/RF-104Gs from the North Group, 210 F-104Gs from the South Group, 88 F-104Gs from the West Group, 50 F/RF-104Gs from the Italian Group, and 50 F-104Gs from MBB)—over thirty-five per cent of all the F-104s! Over the years they have equipped training units at George AFB and Luke AFB in the United States—for which Lockheed Aircraft Service Company has provided maintenance since 1964—a training unit at Norvenich, Germany (Waffenschule 10, WS10), five Jagdbombergeschwadern (JBG31 at Norvenich, JBG32 at Lechfeld, JBG33 at Büchel, JBG34 at Memmingen, and JBG36 at Rheine-Hopsten), two Jagdgeschwadern (JG71 at Wittmundhafen, and JG74 at Neuburg), two Aufklärungsgeschwadern (AKG51 at Ingoldstat/Manching and AKG52 at Leck), and two Marinefliegergeschwadern (MFG1 at Schleswig, and MFG2 at Eggebeck).

The first German Starfighters were F-104Fs, which were initially used in the United States to train a cadre of instructors but were handed over to WS10 at Norvenich. The first operational unit, JBG31, received its first F-104Gs in late

1961 and became fully operational in 1963. In Luftwaffe and Bundesmarine service, however, the type soon got a poor reputation due to a large number of accidents. Comparative analysis of attrition rates for the F-104s in worldwide service and for other contemporary high-performance aircraft does not justify this reputation and actually shows that the Germans did better with their Starfighters than their American, Canadian and Italian allies.

Starfighter phase-out began in 1971 when AKG51 and AKG52 received McDonnell RF-4Es, while the two Jagdgeschwadern re-equipped with F-4Fs in 1973–74 and JBG36 obtained Phantom IIs in 1976. The F-104Gs and TF-104Gs still serving with JBG31, JBG32, JBG33, JBG34, WS10, MFG1 and MFG2 are to be replaced by Panavia Tornados by the end of 1982; at that time the 58th Tactical Training Wing at Luke AFB, which at the end of 1980 still had some fifty German F-104G/TF-104Gs, will be deactivated.

Fokker-built F-104G (63-13690, c/n 8183) of the Bundesluftwaffe in service with the 58th Tactical Training Wing at Luke AFB. (*Peter J. Mancus/Cloud 9 Photography*)

The German Starfighters operated by training units in the United States bore full USAF markings and serial numbers, whereas those in Europe were in Luftwaffe camouflage and carried German serials. Originally these serials (Kennzeichen) consisted of two letters and three digits, but on 1 January, 1968, they were replaced on aircraft then in Luftwaffe service by new four-digit serials as follows:

Lockheed F-104G	2001/2084	were	KF101/KF196
Fiat F-104G	2085/2132	were	KC101/KC150
Messerschmitt F-104G	2133/2326	were	KE301/KE510
Fokker F-104G	2327/2555	were	KG101/KG450
SABCA F-104G	2556/2637	were	KH101/KH188
Lockheed TF-104G	2701/2835	were	KF201/KF272 and KE201/KE233
Lockheed F-104F	2901/2921	were	BB360/BB389

340

Fokker-built F-104G (German serial 2348, c/n 8027) of Jagdbombergeschwader 31 *Boelke* (JBG 31), Bundesluftwaffe, at Norvenich. (*Ben Ullings, via Cloud 9 Photography*)

Greece: Deliveries of thirty-five F-104Gs and four TF-104Gs to the Elliniki Vassiliki Aeroporia (Royal Hellenic Air Force) began in 1965 with these aircraft being distributed in two fighter-bomber squadrons. Subsequently, attrition was made up by the transfer of nineteen F-104Gs and six TF-104Gs from the United States and Spain. In 1981 some thirty Starfighters equipped the 335 and 336 Mire (squadrons) at Araxoi.

Italy: The Aeronautica Militare Italiana (AMI) first received 125 Fiat-built F/RF-104Gs and 24 Lockheed-built TF-104Gs for four interceptor/fighter-bomber gruppi, two reconnaissance gruppi, and one training gruppo. Beginning

TF-104G (62-12274) of the Elliniki Aeroporia. (*Greek Air Attaché, Washington, DC*)

341

Fiat-built F-104S (MM6705) of the 53° Stormo/21° Gruppo, Aeronautica Militare Italiana, at Kleine Brogel, Belgium, in July 1978. (*Jean-Michel Guhl*)

in 1968, these Starfighters were supplemented by the much improved F-104S. In 1981 the earlier versions of the Starfighter were still operated in the training role, by the 20° Gruppo at Grosseto, and in the reconnaissance role, by the 28° and 132° Gruppi at Verona-Villafranca. The F-104S version served alongside RF-104Gs with the last-mentioned gruppi, in the interceptor role with six gruppi (9°, 10°, 12°, 21°, 22° and 23°) and in the fighter-bomber role with four gruppi (102°, 154°, 155° and 156°). Panavia Tornados will eventually replace the Starfighters in AMI service but its last F-104Ss will still be operated at the end of the eighties.

Japan: First entering service in October 1966 with an operational training squadron—the 202nd Hiko-tai at Nyutabaru AB on Kyushu—the two hundred and ten F-104Js, and the twenty F-104DJ operational trainers, have been used exclusively in the interceptor role by seven Hiko-tais (201st-207th) of the Koku Jieitai. In 1981, some one hundred and sixty-five F-104J/F-104DJs were still operated by the 202nd and 204th Hiko-tais at Nyutabaru, the 203rd at Chitose, the 205th at Komatsu, and the 207th at Naha. They are to be progressively replaced by Mitsubishi-built F-15J/F-15DJs beginning in 1982.

Jordan: In 1981, Al Quwwat Aljawwiya Almalakiya Alurduniya (Royal Jordanian Air Force) still had the distinction of operating the oldest Starfighters (F-104A/Bs). Two F-104As and three F-104Bs—ex-USAF and Nationalist Chinese Air Force—were delivered to that Service in the spring of 1967 but were withdrawn to Turkey two days before the June 1967 Six-day War. The US resumed the supply of Starfighters (thirty-two refurbished F-104As and four F-104Bs) in mid-1969 and they were assigned to No.9 Squadron at Prince Hassan Air Base. In November 1972 one of them was used during an abortive coup d'etat when an attempt was made to shoot down the helicopter carrying King Hussein but he escaped with only minor injury.

The Netherlands: By 1984 the last of 138 Starfighters (ninety-five F/RF-104Gs from Fokker, twenty-five F-104Gs from Fiat and eighteen TF-104Gs from Lockheed) acquired by the Royal Netherlands Air Force will have been replaced by European-built General Dynamics F-16A/Bs. Starfighters entered service in December 1962, with No.306 Squadron at Twenthe. In 1963 this unit converted

342

from F/TF-104Gs to RF-104Gs when its responsibility for Starfighter crew training was transferred to the Dutch Masters operational conversion unit. The F-104Gs were operated in the interceptor role by Nos.322 and 323 Squadrons at Leeuwarden, and in the fighter-bomber role by Nos.311 and 312 Squadrons at Volkel. Conversion from F-104Gs was begun by the two interceptor squadrons in 1979 and No.306 Squadron is scheduled to be the last KLu unit to fly Starfighters.

Norway: Kongelige Norske Luftforsvaret (Royal Norwegian Air Force) received the first of nineteen Canadair-built F-104Gs and two Lockheed TF-104Gs in 1963 and the F-104Gs were modified to RF-104G standard for service with No.331 Squadron at Bodø; however, following receipt of Northrop RF-5As for No.717 Squadron, these aircraft reverted to the fighter configuration and still served in the interception role in 1981. Two ex-Luftwaffe TF-104Gs were recently transferred from the United States. A second Starfighter unit, No.334 Squadron also at Bodø, was formed with eighteen ex-Canadian Forces CF-104s and four CF-104Ds; these aircraft were modified to carry Martin Bullpup missiles and operate in the anti-shipping role. Both Nos.331 and 334 Squadrons are to convert to General Dynamics F-16A/Bs.

Pakistan: In 1960 the Pakistan Air Force received twelve ex-USAF Starfighters (ten F-104As and two F-104Bs) to equip one squadron and these aircraft took part in both the August 1965 and December 1971 wars between Pakistan and India. At the end of the second conflict, only seven Starfighters were still operational. However, the Pakistan Air Force then received ten F-104As on temporary loan from Jordan. The Jordanian aircraft were returned in 1972 when Pakistan phased out its last four aircraft.

Spain: Eighteen Canadair-built F-104Gs and three Lockheed TF-104Gs served with the Ejercito del Aire from March 1965 until May 1972. In Spanish service they were respectively designated C.8s (serials C.8-1 to C.8-18) and CE.8s (CE.8-1 to CE.8-3) and were operated successively by Escuadrón 61, Escuadrón 161 and Escuadrón 104 at Torrejón. In 1972 the Spanish Starfighters were returned to the USAF for transfer to Greece and Turkey.

Taiwan: Starfighters first operated from Formosa when the 83rd Fighter Interceptor Squadron was temporarily deployed to bolster the forces of General

A TF-104G, designated CE.8 in Spanish service, at the time of its delivery to Escuadrón 61 at Torrejon. (*Ejercito del Aire*)

343

Chiang Kai-shek, and it is believed that the F-104A/Bs of this USAF unit were the first Starfighters to be supplied in 1960 to the Chinese Nationalist Air Force. These aircraft were supplemented by further F-104A/Bs for a total of twenty-five and two, respectively coded 4201/4225 and 4101/4102. Taiwan also received eight RF-104Gs (4301/4308), forty-two F-104Gs (4309/4350) and a few TF-104Gs, with most of the single-seaters being Canadair-built; in 1981 the survivors still equipped three interceptor/strike squadrons and one reconnaissance squadron.

Turkey: The Türk Hava Kuvvetleri (THK) was initially assigned 36 new Starfighters (32 single-seaters built by Lockheed and Canadair, and four TF-104Gs) to equip two squadrons in 1965–66. These aircraft took part in the 1976 invasion of Cyprus. Subsequently the THK obtained from Italy twenty F-104Gs and forty F-104S, and, in 1980–81, F-104G/TF-104Gs being phased out in Belgium, Germany and the Netherlands began to arrive in Turkey. In 1981, F-104Gs equipped two squadrons of the THK (the 141 Filo at Murted and the 191 Filo at Balikesir) with the F-104S equipping the 142 and 182 Filos at Murted.

N826NA, a Fokker-built F-104G (c/n 8213), which was still operated by the Dryden Flight Research Center at Edwards AFB in 1981. (*NASA*)

Whereas the Starfighter had only a relatively short career with the USAF, the type constituted the backbone of several NATO and Allied air forces during the 1960s and the 1970s. In its F-104S version, and to a rapidly decreasing degree in its F-104G version, the Lockheed supersonic fighter will continue to provide useful service until at least the mid-1980s.

Related Temporary Design Designations: CL-264/CL-265, CL-317, CL-351, CL-354, CL-357, CL-359, CL-369, CL-371, CL-386/CL-389, CL-396/CL-397, CL-403/CL-404, CL-411, CL-446, CL-448, CL-456/CL-458, CL-479, CL-488, CL-509, CL-511, CL-513, CL-521, CL-529, CL-537/CL-539, CL-558, CL-583, CL-586, CL-588, CL-704/CL-705, CL-728, CL-731, CL-739, CL-746/CL-747, CL-772, CL-781, CL-784, CL-799, CL-807, CL-814, CL-829/CL-830, CL-835/CL-837, CL-845, CL-847, CL-849, CL-859, CL-887, CL-901, CL-918, CL-934, CL-937, CL-958, CL-978, CL-981/CL-985, CL-1005/CL-1008, CL-1010, CL-1158/CL-1159, CL-1195, CL-1199/CL-1200 and CL-1600

	F-104A	F-104B	F-104C	F-104G	F-104S
Span, ft in	21 9	21 9	21 9	21 9	21 11
(m)	(6·63)	(6·63)	(6·63)	(6·63)	(6·68)
Length, ft in	54 8	54 8	54 8	54 8	54 9
(m)	(16·66)	(16·66)	(16·66)	(16·66)	(16·69)
Height, ft in	13 5	13 5	13 5	13 5	13 6
(m)	(4·09)	(4·09)	(4·09)	(4·09)	(4·11)
Wing area, sq ft	196·1	196·1	196·1	196·1	196·1
(sq m)	(18·218)	(18·218)	(18·218)	(18·218)	(18·218)
Empty weight, lb	13,384	13,727	12,760	13,996	14,900
(kg)	(6,071)	(6,226)	(5,788)	(6,348)	(6,758)
Combat weight, lb	17,988	17,812	19,470	20,640	21,690
(kg)	(8,159)	(8,079)	(8,831)	(9,362)	(9,838)
Maximum weight, lb	25,840	24,912	27,853	29,038	31,000
(kg)	(11,271)	(11,300)	(12,634)	(13,171)	(14,061)
Wing loading, lb/sq ft	91·7	90·8	99·3	105·3	110·6
(kg/sq m)	(447·9)	(443·5)	(484·7)	(513·9)	(540)
Power loading, lb/lb st	1·2	1·2	1·2	1·3	1·2
Maximum speed, mph at ft	1,037/50,000	1,145/65,000	1,150/50,000	1,146/50,000	1,450/36,000
(km/h at m)	(1,669/15,240)	(1,842/19,810)	(1,850/15,240)	(1,844/15,240)	(2,333/10,975)
Cruising speed, mph	519	516	510	510	610
(km/h)	(835)	(830)	(821)	(821)	(981)
Maximum rate of climb, ft/min	60,395	64,500	54,000	48,000	55,000
(m/min)	(18,408)	(19,660)	(16,459)	(14,630)	(16,764)
Service ceiling, ft	64,795	64,795	58,000	50,000	58,000
(m)	(19,750)	(19,750)	(17,680)	(15,240)	(17,680)
Normal range, miles	730	460	850	1,080	1,550
(km)	(1,175)	(740)	(1,370)	(1,740)	(2,495)
Maximum range, miles	1,400	1,225	1,500	1,630	1,815
(km)	(2,255)	(1,970)	(2,415)	(2,625)	(2,920)

Unusual view of the XFV-1 fitted with its spindly undercarriage for conventional take-off and landing. (*Air Force Flight Test Center*)

Lockheed XFV-1

The high take-off and landing speeds of jet fighters, which resulted in substantially increased runway requirements when operating from land bases or in the need for stronger decking and improved catapult and arresting gear systems in the case of carrier operations, in 1947 led the US Air Force and Navy to study the feasibility of vertical take-off and landing aircraft. Both Services then provided funds for the aircraft manufacturers to make a number of feasibility studies. By 1950 sufficient progress had been made, and with an increased budget following the start of the Korean War, the Navy was ready to proceed with contracts for the design and construction of vertical take-off and landing research vehicles capable of development into operational combat aircraft. A review of industry proposals led in early 1951 to the selection of Convair and Lockheed to develop propeller-turbine powered VTOL machines, the XFY-1s and XFO-1s (soon after the award on 19 April, 1951, of a contract for two aircraft, the designation of the latter was changed to XFV-1).

With Art Flock as project engineer, in August 1950 Lockheed began the design of its Model 081-40-01. Featuring equal-span cruciform tail surfaces each incorporating at their tip a fully-castering strut and wheel, the aircraft was intended to rest vertically on its tail. Vertical take-off and landing was to be achieved through the use of an Allison XT40-A engine (twin T38 turbine driving three-blade contra-rotating propellers) giving a 1·2:1 power-to-weight ratio to the fully-loaded aircraft. Fuel, totalling 508 US gal (1,923 litres), was to be carried in fuselage and wing tanks, as well as in part of the tip tanks. These tip tanks,

346

mounted centrally at the end of tapered broad-chord short-span wings, were also intended to carry test recording equipment initially and, in the proposed production version, armament consisting of either four 20-mm cannon or forty-eight 2·75-in FFAR rockets. The pilot was to sit on an ejector seat under a bubble canopy located forward of the mid-position wings. The proposed production version FV-2 (Model 181-43-02) was to be powered by a more powerful T54-A-16 propeller-turbine, and was to be fitted with bullet-proof windshield, armour, and radar in the forward section of the massive propeller spinner.

For the initial phase of the trial programme it was decided to fly the aircraft in the conventional mode, as the 5,850 hp XT40-A-6 then available was not capable of sustained operation in the vertical mode. Accordingly a temporary non-retractable main undercarriage, with long braced V legs attached to the fuselage, was fitted, and fixed tailwheels were attached to the two lower fins. In this form the first aircraft (BuNo 138657) was trucked to Edwards AFB in November 1953 to undergo its engine ground testing and its taxi-ing trials. During one of these

The XFV-1 in the tail-sitting attitude from which it was to have been operated in the VTOL mode. (*Lockheed*)

tests, when the aft section of the large spinner was not yet fitted, the XFV-1 was taxied by Herman 'Fish' Salmon past liftoff speed and therefore the aircraft was briefly airborne for the first time on 23 December, 1953. However, its engine was not then ready for full flight trials and when, in March 1954, photographs of the XFV-1 were first released, it had not yet been officially flown. Finally, on 16 June, 1954, Salmon made the first conventional flight.

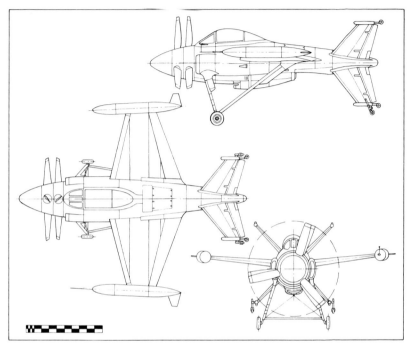

Lockheed XFV-1

Delays with the development of the engine — with elapsed time between project inception and first flight being 47 months for the XFV-1 versus only 16 months for the XF-104 — had already turned the XFV-1 into a research vehicle, as its anticipated top speed of 580 mph (933 km/h) was by then insufficient for a fighter. Furthermore, as its intended 7,100 shp YT40-A-14 engine fully rated for vertical operations never became available, the 'Pogo Stick', as it was known, had made only 32 flights (about 23 hours) when in June 1955 the programme was cancelled. During that period it had been transitioned in flight from the conventional to the vertical flight mode and back, and had been briefly held in hover at altitude. However, without the YT40-A-14 engine it could never have been used for vertical take-off and landing and all flights were made at Edwards AFB with the lightweight spindly undercarriage.

Following programme cancellation, the first XFV-1 was delivered to Hiller Helicopters, in Palo Alto, for ground testing in support of later VTOL projects, while the uncompleted second aircraft (BuNo138658) went to NAS Los Alamitos, California, as a gate guardian. Finally, in December 1979 the first XFV-1 was donated to the San Diego Aerospace Museum.

Span 30 ft $10\frac{7}{64}$ in (9·4 m) with tip tanks; length 36 ft $10\frac{1}{4}$ in (11·23 m); wing area 246 sq ft (22·854 sq m).

Empty weight 11,599 lb (5,261 kg); loaded weight 16,221 lb (7,358 kg); wing loading 65·9 lb/sq ft (322 kg/sq m); power loading 2·8 lb/shp (1·27 kg/shp).

Estimated performance with YT40-A-14 engine: maximum speed 580 mph at 15,000 ft (933 km/h at 4,570 m); cruising speed 410 mph (660 km/h); initial rate of climb 10,820 ft/min (3,298 m/min); service ceiling 43,300 ft (13,200 m); endurance 1 hr 10 min.

Lockheed C-130 Hercules

Operations by Far East Air Forces Combat Cargo Command (FEAF ComCar-Com) at the beginning of the Korean War immediately brought forth the need for a new tactical troop and cargo transport, as the Fairchild C-119, which had entered service a few months before the war started, proved to be underpowered and performed little better than the earlier Curtiss C-46s and Douglas C-47s. Thus, on 2 February, 1951, the USAF issued Request for Proposals to Boeing, Douglas, Fairchild, and Lockheed, for a medium transport complying with a specially-prepared General Operational Requirement. The aircraft was (1) to carry 90 paratroopers over 2,000 miles (3,220 km) or a 30,000-lb (13,608-kg) load over a shorter distance; (2) operate if need be from short and unprepared airstrips; and (3) be capable of slowing down to 125 kt (232 km/h) for paradrops and even more slowly for 'assault' landings. Prompt action was required and proposals were submitted by the four manufacturers during April 1951, with Lockheed being declared the winner on 2 July and awarded a contract for two YC-130 prototypes of the Hercules.

A long and successful line of military and civil transports emanated from these prototypes—with the 1,600th Hercules being delivered, to the Indonesian Air Force, 28 years after that initial contract, and with the type being assured of continued production well into the 1980s. For Lockheed the Hercules has well deserved its name—which both reflects the prodigious strength of the hero of mythology and carries on the company tradition of naming its aircraft after stars and constellations—as it has borne more than its fair share of revenues and profit and ensured the success of the Georgia Division.

A C-130A-45-LM in service with the 304th TAS, AFRES. (*via Cloud 9 Photography*)

To meet and, as far as possible, exceed the demanding specifications of the February 1951 RFP of the USAF, the team of project engineer Art Flock designed under the supervision of Willis Hawkins—then heading the Advanced Design Department—an aircraft which more than made up in functional efficiency what it lacked aesthetically. Key features of the project (Temporary Design Designation L-206) included a 41 ft 5 in/12·62 m long cargo compartment of nearly square cross-section (10 ft/3·05 m wide and 9 ft/2·74 m high) for a total volume of 4,500 cu ft/127·4 cu m, and incorporating a rear loading ramp, a roomy flight deck (normal crew of two pilots, navigator, systems manager and loadmaster) in the extreme nose, high-mounted wing to achieve ease of loading and unloading with a truckbed-height cargo floor, and sturdy undercarriage with mainwheels retracting into fairings on the sides of the fuselage. More unusual, in view of the fact that the L-206 was intended as a medium-sized tactical transport, was the decision to use four instead of two engines, with Allison T56 propeller-turbines being selected. The success of this formula, which resulted in the first turbine-powered transport to reach production in the United States, has been proven by the fact that 96 per cent of the 1,600 Hercules built from 1954 until 1980 have retained the basic dimensions and appearance of the YC-130, while gross weight and horsepower have increased respectively by 45 and 20 per cent.

After the construction of two YC-130s ordered in July 1951 had been undertaken in Burbank, Lockheed proposed to the Air Force that production aircraft be built in the recently opened plant in Marietta. Thus, by the time the first seven C-130As were ordered by the USAF on 10 February, 1953—Contract AF33(600)-22286—most of the design team, by now headed by project engineer Al Brown, had been moved to Georgia. Soon this team and its counterpart in production engineering were making rapid progress while construction of the prototypes proceeded in California. Maiden flight of the type, made with the second YC-130-LO prototype* (c/n 082-1002, serial 53-3397), took place at the Lockheed Air Terminal on 23 August, 1954, with Stanley Betz and Roy Wimmer at the controls. Most of the trial programme was conducted at Edwards AFB, where the Hercules prototypes demonstrated performance far in excess of the original Air Force request (cruising speed twenty per cent faster, and rate of climb and service ceiling thirty-five per cent higher).

The first production C-130A-LM (c/n 182-3001, 53-3129) flew at Marietta on 7 April, 1955, but it was nearly destroyed one week later following an inflight fire in its No.2 engine. Cause of the fire was traced to a loose fuel-hose coupling and the problem was easily solved. More vexing were difficulties with the three-blade propellers. A change from Curtiss-Wright to Aero Product design, first tested on the sixth C-130A, partially cured the problem, with a switch to four-blade Hamilton Standard propellers, initiated with the C-130B model, being the ultimate solution.

Production and service history of the military Hercules are dealt with first in the following narrative, with details of the L-100 civil aircraft given at the end of this section.

YC-130-LO (Model 082-44-01): The two prototypes/service test aircraft (53-3396/53-3397) were the only Hercules built in Burbank. Powered by four 3,250 eshp Allison T56-A-1 propeller-turbines driving three-blade propellers. First flown at the Lockheed Air Terminal on 23 August, 1954.

*The first prototype was initially used for static tests, and flown later.

DC-130A (56-514) of the 6514th Test Squadron at Edwards AFB. A Ryan Firebee can be seen beneath the wing. (*via Cloud 9 Photography*)

C-130A-LM (Model 182-44-03): First production version of which 204 were built in Marietta. Differed from YC-130s in having provision for two 450-US gal (1,703-litre) external tanks outboard of outer engines and in being powered by 3,750 eshp T56-A-1As or T56-A-9s; original three-blade propellers replaced in 1978 by four-blade units. First 27 aircraft delivered without nose radome but later modified to carry AN/APS-42 or AN/APN-59 search radar. First flown at Marietta on 7 April, 1955, with one hundred and ninety-two C-130As delivered to the USAF, beginning in October 1956, and twelve (with T56-A-11 engines) going to the Royal Australian Air Force. In 1972 thirty-five C-130As were transferred by the USAF to the VNAF. A number of C-130As were modified to AC-130A, C-130A-II, DC-130A, GC-130A, JC-130A, NC-130A, RC-130A, TC-130A, C-130D, C-130D-6 and RC-130S configurations. Two C-130As (55-046 and 55-048) were temporarily fitted with underwing refuelling pods for evaluation by the Marine Corps. Generally similar aircraft were built as RC-130As and C-130Ds.

AC-130A-LM: Sixteen C-130A/JC-130As (53-3129, 54-1623, 54-1625/54-1628, 54-1630, 55-011, 55-014, 55-029, 55-040, 55-044, 55-046, 56-469, 56-490 and 56-509) modified as gunships with either four 7·62 mm GAU-2 miniguns and four 20 mm M-61 cannon (first eight AC-130As), or two 7·62 mm guns, two 20 mm cannon and two 40 mm clip-fed cannon (last eight gunships) mounted on the port side of the fuselage to fire obliquely downward. Various items were progressively added, including infra-red sensors, a searchlight, laser illuminator, and an AYK-9 digital computer. First evaluated at Wright-Patterson AFB, Ohio, during the summer of 1967.

C-130A-II-LM: Electronic reconnaissance version obtained by modifying ten C-130As (54-1637, 56-484, 56-525/56-526, 56-530, 56-534/56-535, 56-537 and 56-540/56-541) for service with the 7407th Combat Support Wing.

DC-130A-LM: Originally designated GC-130As, these seven drone directors (55-021, 56-491, 56-514, 56-527, 57-461 and 57-496/57-497) were modified to carry four drones beneath their wings, with specialized guidance-equipment operators in the fuselage. The first two DC-130As were transferred to the Navy as BuNos 158228/158229. Many had an additional radome beneath the nose.

GC-130A-LM: Initial designation given to the DC-130As. Later, one permanently grounded C-130A (54-1621) used as an instructional airframe was so designated.

351

Built as a C-130B (55-21), then modified as the C-130D prototype, this Hercules is seen in its final form as a DC-130A (BuNo 158228) while serving with VC-3 and carrying BQM-34 Firebee target drones. (*US Navy*)

JC-130A-LM: The prefix J identified sixteen C-130As (53-3129/53-3135, 54-1624, 54-1627/54-1630, 54-1639, 56-490, 56-493 and 56-497) modified to track missiles during tests over the Atlantic range. Six later became AC-130As.

NC-130A-LM: Five C-130As (54-1622, 54-1635, 55-022/55-023 and 56-491) temporarily used for special tests; refurbished as C-130As.

RC-130A-LM: This designation covered one TC-130A (54-1632) modified as a photographic-reconnaissance aircraft and fifteen aircraft (57-510/57-524) delivered to this configuration. Most modified back as C-130As.

TC-130A-LM: One C-130A (54-1632) modified to serve as prototype for the proposed crew trainer version; became the first RC-130A.

The JC-130A modified from the fifth C-130A airframe, 53-3133, c/n 182-3005. (*via Cloud 9 Photography*)

C-130B-LM (Model 282): The second production series of which 123 were delivered to the USAF and 33 went to foreign air forces (Canada, Indonesia, Iran, Jordan, Pakistan and South Africa) beginning in December 1958. First C-130B (57-525) flown at Marietta on 20 November, 1958. The C-130Bs differed from the C-130As in having internal fuel capacity increased by 1,820 US gal (6,889 litres) and heavier operating weights, and in being powered by 4,050 eshp Allison T56-A-7s driving four-blade propellers. Thirty-seven USAF aircraft were modified as C-130B-IIs (RC-130Bs), JC-130Bs, NC-130Bs, VC-130B and WC-130Bs, while two Indonesian aircraft became KC-130Bs. Aircraft basically similar to the C-130Bs were built as C-130BLs (LC-130Fs), WC-130Bs, GV-1s (KC-130Fs), GV-1Us (C-130Fs) and R8V-1Gs (SC-130B/HC-130Bs).

Ex-Canadian Armed Forces C-130B being readied at Marietta for re-delivery to the Fuerza Aérea Colombiana. (*Lockheed*)

C-130B-II: C-130Bs modified as electronic reconnaissance aircraft; see RC-130B designation.

C-130BL-LM: See LC-130F designation.

HC-130B-LM: Final designation of the search-and-rescue aircraft initially ordered as R8V-1Gs; twelve delivered to the Coast Guard (USCG serials 1339/1342 and 1344/1351).

JC-130B-LM: Fourteen C-130Bs (57-525/57-529, 58-713/58-717, 58-750, 58-756 and 61-962/61-963) modified with retractable tongs on nose sides for aerial recovery of satellite capsules, and operated by the 6593rd Test Squadron, Air Force Systems Command. Most converted back to C-130B configuration.

KC-130B-LM: Two Indonesian aircraft (T-1309/T-1310) modified as tankers with refuelling pods in place of underwing tanks.

NC-130B-LM: One C-130B (58-712) converted as a prototype for a STOL version and fitted with a boundary-layer control system provided by air bleeds from two Allison YJ56-A-6s operating as gas producers and slung beneath the wings in place of the external tanks. This system was later removed and the aircraft delivered to NASA as N929NA for use in the Earth Survey programme. One JC-130B (58-717) was also designated NC-130B for use on special tests.

RC-130B-LM: Electronic reconnaissance version, initially designated C-130B-IIs, obtained by modifying thirteen C-130Bs (58-711, 58-723, 59-1524/59-1528, 59-1530/59-1533, 59-1535 and 59-1537). Converted back to C-130B.

SC-130B-LM: First redesignation of the R8V-1Gs; later became HC-130Gs and finally HC-130Bs.

The NC-130B modified for STOL operations with boundary-layer control system and YJ56-A-6 turbojets in underwing pods. (*via Jim Sullivan/Cloud 9 Photography*)

VC-130B-LM: One JC-130B (58-714) temporarily modified as a staff transport before returning to the C-130B configuration.

WC-130B-LM: Five weather-reconnaissance aircraft (62-3492/64-3496) built as such by Lockheed and nine C-130Bs (58-725/58-726, 58-731, 58-733/58-734, 58-740/58-741, 58-752 and 58-758) modified to the same standard. Most returned to C-130B configuration but 58-731 went to the National Oceanic and Atmospheric Administration (NOAA), US Department of Commerce, first as N8037 and then as N6541C.

C-130C-LM: Proposed STOL version for which the NC-130B-LM (58-712) had served as a prototype. Not built.

C-130D-LM: Ski-equipped version for service in Alaska and Greenland. The prototype was modified from a C-130A (55-021) but this aircraft later became a DC-130A and went to the Navy. Twelve production C-130Ds (57-484/57-495) were built with C-130A airframes and powerplants.

C-130E-LM (Model 382): Whereas the C-130As and C-130Bs were tactical transports, the third major production version was designed for longer-ranged logistic missions. Internal fuel capacity was increased from 5,050 US gal (19,116

C-130E (A97-181) of No.37 Squadron, RAAF, based at Richmond, NSW. (*RAAF*)

354

litres) for the C-130As to 6,960 gal (26,347 litres) for the C-130Es, while the two 450-gal (1,703-litre) underwing tanks of the earlier version were replaced by 1,360-gal (5,148-litre) units, with the larger external tanks being moved to a position between the engine nacelles. Maximum take-off weight increased from 124,200 lb (56,336 kg) for the C-130A to 175,000 lb (79,379 kg) for the C-130E but the increased weight was partially offset by using 4,050 hp Allison T56-A-7s. During the course of production, beginning with the ninth C-130E, the (6·7 ft by 6 ft/2·04 m by 1·83 m) forward cargo-loading door on the port side was dispensed with. First flight of a C-130E (61-2358, c/n 382-3609) was made at Marietta on 15 August, 1961, with deliveries commencing in April 1962. The USAF received 377 C-130Es and 111 additional aircraft went to nine foreign countries (Argentina, Australia, Brazil, Canada, Iran, Israel, Saudi Arabia, Sweden and Turkey); one generally similar EC-130E and four C-130Gs were built for the Coast Guard and the Navy respectively. USAF C-130Es were modified to fulfil seven roles (prefix letters A, D, E, J, M, N and W) as now described.

AC-130E-LM: Gunship version with two 40-mm and two 20-mm cannon plus two 7·62-mm Miniguns. Flare dispensers between the engine nacelles and ALQ-87 on outer wing racks. Eleven C-130Es (69-6567/69-6577) modified to that standard; all but 69-6571, which had been shot down over South Vietnam, were upgraded as AC-130Hs. Some had a 105-mm howitzer replacing one of the 40-mm cannon.

DC-130E-LM: Launching and guidance aircraft for drones or RPVs (Remotely Piloted Vehicles) carried on underwing pylons. Seven C-130Es (61-2361/61-2364, 61-2368/61-2369 and 61-2371) so modified.

EC-130E-LM: Designation first given to one aircraft fitted during construction with equipment for Loran A & C calibration and delivered to the Coast Guard as USCG 1414. At least eight C-130Es modified for the USAF as ABCCCs (Airborne Battlefield Command Control Centers) were first designated C-130E-IIs but later became EC-130Es before being upgraded as EC-130Hs with more powerful T56-A-15 engines.

HC-130E-LM: Nineteen C-130Es (62-1843, 63-7785, 64-508, 64-523, 64-547, 64-551, 64-555, 64-558/64-559, 64-561/64-568 and 64-571/64-572) modified as C-130E-I-LMs, with crew recovery yoke on the nose for use by the Aerospace Rescue and Recovery Service of the USAF, were redesignated HC-130Es. They were later modified for clandestine operations as MC-130Es.

JC-130E-LM: One C-130E (61-2358) temporarily modified for USAF tests.

MC-130E-LM: Modified HC-130Es as already described (Project Talon); several fitted in 1978 with T56-A-15 engines as C-130H(CT)s.

NC-130E-LM: One C-130E (64-571) used for test; later became an HC-130E/MC-130E/C-130H(CT).

WC-130E-LM: Weather reconnaissance version obtained by modifying six C-130Es (61-2360, 61-2365/61-2366 and 64-552/64-554).

C-130F-LM: Navy utility transport version corresponding to the C-130B of the USAF. Seven delivered as GV-1Us (BuNos 149787, 149790, 149793/149794, 149797, 149801 and 149805) but redesignated C-130Fs in September 1962.

KC-130F-LM: Tanker version for the US Marine Corps ordered as GV-1s and redesignated KC-130Fs in 1962. These 46 aircraft (BuNos 147572/147573, 148246/148249, 148890/148899, 149788/149789, 149791/149792, 149795/149796, 149798/149800, 149802/149804, 149806/149816 and 150684/150690) differed from the C-130Bs and GV-1U/C-130Fs in being powered by 4,910 eshp T56-A-16 engines and in carrying refuelling pods beneath the outer wing panels.

LC-130F (BuNo 148321) of VXE-6 over Christchurch, New Zealand, on 15 October, 1960. (*US Navy*)

LC-130F-LM: Four ski-equipped aircraft (BuNos 148318/148321), with T56-A-16 engines, acquired by the Navy as UV-1Ls, for use by VXE-6 in Antarctica.

C-130G-LM: Four Navy transport aircraft (BuNos 151888/151891) corresponding to the C-130Es but powered by 4,910 eshp T56-A-16s.

EC-130G-LM: Designation given to the four C-130Gs after they had been modified as VLF (Very Low Frequency) communications relay stations with trailing antenna extending from the ventral loading ramp. Operated by Fleet Command and Control Communication Squadrons Three and Four (VQ-3 and VQ-4) under acronym TACAMO (Take Charge And Move Out).

C-130H-LM: First delivered to the RNZAF in March 1965, the C-130Hs are basically similar to the C-130E but are powered by four T56-A-15s normally derated from 4,910 to 4,508 eshp. They are fitted with an improved braking system and redesigned centre-wing-box assembly, as often retrofitted to earlier versions, to improve the service life of the airframe. Remaining in production, the C-130H has been built for the USAF, the Air National Guard—with which the C-130H was the first Hercules variant to be received directly from Lockheed—and 36 foreign customers (*see* table 'Hercules in Foreign Military Use'), with delivery

Hercules CN-AOJ (c/n 382-4783) of the Moroccan Forces Aériennes Royales during a visit to France in 1978. (*Jean-Michel Guhl*)

by the end of 1980 totalling 560 aircraft. Variants obtained by modifying existing C-130H airframes include the DC-130H, NC-130H, VC-130H and WC-130H. Related models are the HC-130H, KC-130H, C-130K, HC-130N, HC-130P, EC-130Q, KC-130R and LC-130R. At least one Saudi Arabian C-130H had been modified by Lockheed as a flying hospital.

C-130H(CT): Designation given to fifteen MC-130Es fitted with T56-A-15s and improved electronic equipment.

C-130H-MP(PC-130H): Maritime patrol/search-and-rescue version of the C-130H initially produced for Malaysia.

C-130H(S): New military production version combining features of the C-130H with the larger fuselage of the L-100-30. First delivered to the Indonesian Air Force during 1980; redesignated C-130H-30s.

AC-130H-LM: Upgraded AC-130Es fitted in 1973 with T56-A-15s and in 1978 for inflight refuelling—with a boom receptacle atop the fuselage, aft of the flight deck.

DC-130H-LM: One HC-130H (65-979) modified as a drone director.

EC-130H-LM: Designation applied to EC-130Es re-engined with T56-A-15s.

HC-130H-LM: Forty-three rescue and recovery aircraft (64-14852/64-14866, 65-962/65-987 and 65-989/65-990) with re-entry tracking radar on top of the fuselage, and folding, nose-mounted, Fulton recovery system to pick up aircrews from the ground. Some were fitted with two 1,800-US gal (6,814-litre) fuselage fuel tanks while others had a refuelling boom receptacle. One modified as a DC-130H, two as JHC-130Hs, and fifteen as WC-130Hs. Twelve essentially similar HC-130Hs were built for the Coast Guard as USCG 1452/1454, 1500/1504 and 1600/1603.

A KC-130H of I Escuadrón de Transporte, Fuerza Aérea Argentina. Note refuelling pods outboard of the outer engines. (*Lockheed*)

KC-130H-LM: Air tankers, with refuelling pods beneath wing, built for the Argentine, Brazilian, Israeli, Saudi Arabian and Spanish air forces.

JHC-130H-LM: Two HC-130Hs (64-14854 and 64-14857) modified for aerial recovery of re-entering space capsules; redesignated NC-130H.

VC-130H-LM: Two Saudi Arabian C-130Hs modified as VIP transports with appropriate accommodation and square fuselage windows.

WC-130H-LM: Fifteen HC-130Hs modified as weather-reconnaissance aircraft with recovery system removed and special equipment fitted.

C-130J-LM: Projected version with increased aileron and rudder chords, wider undercarriage track, and armour protection. Not built.

C-130K-LM: Built by Lockheed, with some components made by Scottish Aviation, the sixty-six C-130Ks (XV176/XV223 and XV290/XV307) were fitted

357

by Marshall of Cambridge (Engineering) Ltd with British electronics, instrumentation and other equipment before delivery to RAF Air Support Command. Although consideration had been given to having these aircraft powered by Rolls-Royce Tynes, all were fitted with Allison T56-A-15s and were similar in most respects to the C-130Hs. The C-130K first flew on 19 October, 1966, and, as the Hercules C.Mk.1, the type entered service with No.242 OCU at Thorney Island in April 1967. One aircraft (XV208) was modified by Marshall for service with the RAF's Meteorological Research Flight at RAE Farnborough. Designated Hercules W.Mk.2 this aircraft, which first flew on 21 March, 1973, has a long instrumentation boom on the nose — forcing the relocation of the radar scanner on a pod above the flight deck; scientific instruments in the fuselage; and instrumentation pods beneath the wing. Thirty C-130Ks are being brought up to standard approaching that of the L-100-30 with the fuselage stretched by nearly 15 ft (4·57 m). The first Hercules brought by Lockheed to C.Mk.3 standard (XV223) was flown at Marietta on 3 December, 1979; the remaining 29 Hercules C.Mk.3s will come from Marshall with the modification programme to be completed in 1982.

C-130L-LM and C-130M-LM: Designations not used.

HC-130N-LM: Fifteen search-and-rescue aircraft (69-5819/69-5833) for recovery of aircrew and retrieval of space capsules.

HC-130P-LM: Twenty combat aircrew recovery aircraft (65-988, 65-991/65-994 and 66-211/66-225) similar to HC-130H but fitted with underwing drogue pods and associated plumbing for inflight refuelling of rescue helicopters.

EC-130Q-LM: Improved version of the Navy's TACAMO airborne communications relay aircraft built with C-130H airframe and powerplants; eleven delivered (BuNos 156170/156177, 159348, 159469 and 160608); more to be delivered.

KC-130R-LM: Fourteen tanker aircraft (BuNos 160013/160021, 160240 and 160625/160628) for the Marine Corps; basically similar to the KC-130H for export customers.

LC-130R-LM: Six ski-equipped version of the C-130H delivered to the US Navy (BuNos 155917, 159129/159131 and 160740/160741).

RC-130S-LM: Two JC-130As (56-493 and 56-497) modified by E-Systems with BIAS (Battlefield Illumination Airborne System) comprising 28 high-powered lights of 6·14 million candlepower. Intended for search-and-rescue night missions, they were assigned to the Ellington AFB, Texas, based 446th Tactical Airlift Wing and were deployed to Southeast Asia.

GV-1, GV-1U, R8V-1G and UV-1L: Navy-type designations initially given respectively to the KC-130F, C-130F, HC-130B and LC-130F versions. The four UV-1Ls were first redesignated C-130BLs before becoming LC-130Fs.

Projected military developments of the Hercules have been numerous and have included the HOW–Hercules-on-Water flying-boat with hydro-ski*— , and the C-130SS (Stretch/STOL) with stretched fuselage, enlarged tail surfaces, double-slotted flaps, roll-control spoilers and aerial refuelling receptacle, which Lockheed proposed as an alternative to the Boeing YC-14 and McDonnell Douglas YC-15. More recently, Lockheed has been offering an improved TACAMO version (ECX-130), an improved tanker (KCX-130), a missile-launching aircraft (C-130H-MSL), a missile control aircraft (C-130-MX ALCC), and a sea control variant (C-130H-SC). The latest of the proposed Hercules developments is

*See Appendix A.

Hercules W.Mk.2 XV208 operated by the Meteorological Flight from RAE Farnborough. (*Paul Bennett*)

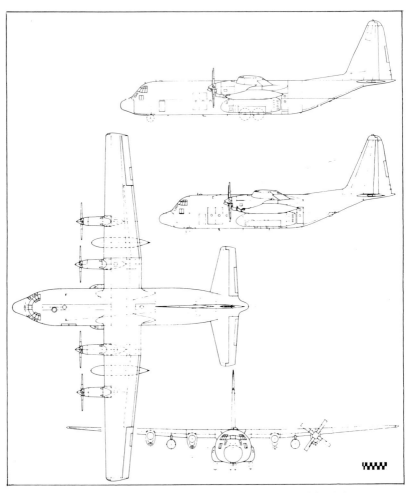

Lockheed C-130K Hercules C.Mk.1, with side view of C.Mk.3

the C-130 ARE (Airborne Radar Extension), an early warning version of the C-130H with the aerial for a General Electric APS-125 radar mounted in a 24 ft (7·3 m) rotodome atop a shortened vertical fin. By June 1981 none of these versions had got further than the drawing board.

The first operational unit to be equipped with Hercules was the 815th Troop Carrier Squadron, 463rd Troop Carrier Wing, at Ardmore AFB, Oklahoma, which received its first five C-130As on 9 December, 1956. This initial C-130 version was also delivered to the 314th TCW at Sewart AFB, Tennessee, the 322nd Air Division at Evreux-Fauville AB, France, and the 483rd TCW at Ashiya AB, Japan. In service with these TAC, PACAF and USAFE units, the C-130As were supplemented by C-130Bs beginning in early 1959 while the ski-equipped C-130Ds first went to the 61st Tactical Airlift Squadron, 314th Tactical Airlift

Wing, at Sewart AFB. The Hercules soon had a taste of emergency deployment during the July 1958 US involvement in Lebanon, the August 1958 crisis over the Quemoy Strait between Formosa and mainland China, and the July 1960 United Nations airlift to the Congo.

With the availability of the longer-ranged C-130E version, delivery of which began in April 1962, the Hercules joined the 1501st, 1608th and 1611th Air Transport Wings of the Military Air Transport Service, while this model was also delivered to units of other Commands. However, beginning in 1964, the MATS Hercules were transferred to Tactical Air Command. Specialized C-130 versions also entered service during the early sixties with the Air Force Systems Command, MATS, and TAC, as drone launchers and weather-reconnaissance aircraft, and for specialized tests.

The all-grey AC-130A (55-011) of the 711th Special Operations Squadron, USAF Reserve, in 1978. (*Peter J. Mancus/Cloud 9 Photography*)

Already well established in service, the C-130s really came into their own during the Southeast Asia War. The main task of the C-130A/B/E, frequently coming under heavy Viet Cong fire, was the resupply of isolated outposts and intra-theatre logistic work. In the process the Hercules crews earned the grateful respect of American and Vietnamese ground forces. During the conflict the AC-130A/E/H gunships were first operated in 1967 by the 14th Special Operations Wing at Nha Trang AB, Vietnam, and were later operated by the 8th and 38th Tactical Fighter Wings at Ubon RTAFB and Korat RTAFB in Thailand. The 14th SOW also operated C-130E-Is for low-level covert transport, while a squadron flew C-130E-IIs for battlefield command and control duties from Vietnamese and Thai bases. Rescue operations were flown by the 38th and 56th Aerospace Rescue & Recovery Squadrons with the HC-130Hs and HC-130Ps. In addition to their all but routine rescue operations, the HC-130Ps were used to refuel Sikorsky HH-53 helicopters during the abortive commando attempt to rescue American prisoners of war from the Son Tay prison in North Vietnam on 20–21 November, 1970.

Following the US withdrawal from Vietnam in early 1973, the USAF underwent re-organization and, beginning in December 1974, all C-130 transport units were transferred to the Military Airlift Command. At the same time Hercules-equipped squadrons of the Air National Guard, which had received its first C-130As in April 1970, and of the Air Force Reserve, began reporting to MAC. At the end of 1980 MAC had fifteen squadrons of C-130E/Hs, four squadrons with HC-130H/N/Ps and two squadrons with WC-130E/Hs, while the ANG and AFRES respectively had eighteen and twelve transport squadrons with Hercules,

The KC-130F (BuNo 149806) used as a support aircraft by the Blue Angels demonstration team landing at MCAS Cherry Point, North Carolina. (*Jim Sullivan/Cloud 9 Photography*)

as well as two and three squadrons with HC-130s. The 193rd Tactical Electronic Warfare Squadron, Pennsylvania ANG, also flies EC-130Es; single squadrons of AC-130s and WC-130s are serving with AFRES. Finally, the Air Force Systems Command has a number of NC-130A/B/Hs and C-130Es.

The first Hercules ordered under Navy Department contract, a GV-1 tanker, was flown on 22 January, 1960. Since then the Marine Corps has received forty-six KC-130Fs (redesignated from GV-1s in 1962) and fourteen KC-130Rs. At the end of 1980 these aircraft were operated by three Marine Aerial Refuelling/Transport Squadrons (VMGR-152, -252 and -352, respectively with the 1st, 2nd and 3rd Marine Air Wings) and Marine Transport Squadron 234 (VMR-234) with the Reserves. One KC-130F (BuNo 149806) has been used as a support aircraft for the Blue Angels demonstration team.* The US Navy obtained two DC-130As, seven GV-1Us (C-130Fs after 1962), four LC-130Fs, four C-130Gs (EC-130Gs),

*Another KC-130F (BuNo 149798), flown by crews from the Naval Air Test Center, was used for carrier trials aboard the USS *Forrestal* in October 1963.

TACAMO EC-130G flying near NAS Patuxent River, Maryland, on 16 April, 1967. (*US Navy*)

362

eleven EC-130Qs (with four more on order), and six LC-130Rs. Ski-equipped LC-130F/Rs are operated by Antarctic Development Squadron Six (VXE-6) while TACAMO-configured EC-130G/Qs were still assigned in 1980 to Fleet Command and Control Communication Squadrons Three and Four (VQ-3 and VQ-4) for service respectively with the Pacific and Atlantic Fleet. The other Hercules operating primarily over water were those of the US Coast Guard, with the survivors of twelve HC-130Bs (ex R8V-1Gs and SC-130Bs), one EC-130E and twelve HC-130Hs being distributed between five Coast Guard stations at Barbers Point, Hawaii; Elisabeth City, North Carolina; Kodiak, Alaska; Sacramento, California; and St Petersburg, Florida.

While in US military service Hercules set a number of unofficial records including the heaviest take-off for a ski-equipped aircraft (124,000 lb/56,245 kg) by a C-130D in February 1958; parachute drop from the highest altitude (44,100 ft/ 13,442 m) by nine Marines jumping from a KC-130F; heaviest weight carried externally (four drones weighing 44,510 lb/20,189 kg) by a DC-130H; and a 27 hr 45 min flight by a modified C-130H refuelled by a Boeing KC-135. More significantly, an HC-130H flown by a crew captained by Lieut-Col E. L. Allison set on 20 February, 1972, the current Class C, Group II (Aeroplanes with propeller-turbines), distance in a straight line record: 8,732·098 miles/14,052·977 km from Taiwan to Scott AFB, Illinois.

Besides being operated by the USAF, USCG, USMC and USN, Hercules have been delivered so far to forty-six foreign air forces, beginning with the Royal Australian Air Force which received its first C-130As in 1957. Foreign military operations of C-130s are summarized in the tables on pages 364–370, with only key uses being detailed in narrative form.

The Heyl Ha' Avir (Israeli Air Force) which acquired twelve C-/KC-130Hs new and obtained twelve C-130Es from the USAF during the Yom Kippur War of 1973, used four Hercules on 4 July, 1976, to mount the daring rescue of hostages held at Entebbe Airport, in Uganda, by the Gaza Commando of the Palestine Liberation Forces. Flying over the Red Sea, Ethiopia and Kenya, the Israeli Hercules landed 245 commandos, who killed the hijackers and freed the hostages in the remarkably successful Operation Thunderbolt.

Not quite as spectacular, but nonetheless vital after the withdrawal of US forces from Vietnam, were the operations of the Hercules of the VNAF. As part of Operation Enhance Plus, thirty-five C-130As were quickly withdrawn from ANG squadrons in the United States and delivered to South Vietnam in November 1972. By April 1975, when the Republic of South Vietnam collapsed, three C-130As had been lost; nineteen other Hercules succeeded then in fleeing to Thailand but thirteen were captured by North Vietnam and subsequently put into service with the Vietnamese People's Air Force, some being used as makeshift bombers during the invasion of Kampuchea in 1978 and when fighting invading Chinese forces.

In 1959 Lockheed announced that Pan American had ordered twelve GL-207 Super Hercules for delivery in early 1962 and that Slick Airways was to receive six later in that year. To be powered by 6,000 eshp Allison T61 propeller-turbines, the Super Hercules were to be 23 ft 4 in (7·11 m) longer than the C-130B, with wing span increased by 12 ft 5in (3·78 m), and were to have a maximum take-off gross weight of 204,170 lb (92,610 kg). A GL-207 version with 6,445 eshp Rolls-Royce Tynes and gross weight of 230,000 lb (104,326 kg) was also proposed during 1960 as was a jet-powered version (four 22,000 lb/9,979 kg thrust Pratt & Whitney JT3D-11 turbofans) with a 250,000 lb (113,398 kg) gross weight and a

Hercules in Foreign Military Use

Country/Operator	No. of aircraft × Model	First and last delivery dates	Serial/Registration when delivered	Use and Status at December 1980
Abu Dhabi				
United Emirates Air Force	2 × C-130H	Mar 75 – Apr 75	1211/1218	Based at Abu Dhabi
Argentina				
Fuerza Aérea Argentina	3 × C-130E 5 × C-130H 2 × KC-130H	Nov 68 – Dec 68 Feb 71 – Apr 75 Apr 79 – May 79	TC-61/-63 TC-64/-68 TC-69/-70	Current with I Esc. de Transporte at El Palomar
Australia				
Royal Australian Air Force	12 × C-130A 12 × C-130E	57 – Mar 59 65 – Feb 67	A97-205/216 A97-159/160, A97-167/168, A97-171/172, A97-177/178, A97-180/181, and A97-189/190	Withdrawn from use in 1978 and returned to GELAC (C-130A) Current with No.37 Squadron at Richmond NSW (C-130E)
	12 × C-130H	July 78 – Oct 78	A97-001/012	Current with No.36 Squadron at Richmond, NSW (C-130H)
Belgium				
Force Aérienne Belge	12 × C-130H	July 72 – May 73	CH-01/12	Current with 20ème Escadrille at Melsbroeck
Bolivia				
Fuerza Aérea Boliviana Transportes Aéreos Militares	2 × C-130H 1 × L-100-30	July 77 – Oct 77 1980	TAM-90/91 CP-1564	Current with Transportes Aéreos Militares at La Paz
Brazil				
Força Aérea Brasileira	11 × C-130E 3 × C-130H 2 × KC-130H	64 – Nov 68 Jan 74 – Nov 75 Oct 75 – Nov 75	2450/2460 2463/2465 2461	Current with 1º Escuadrão, 1º Grupo at Galeão, and for search and rescue with 6º Grupo at Recife

Cameroon Armée de l'Air du Cameroun	2 × C-130H	Aug 77 – Sep 77	TJ-XAC/TJ-XAD	Current
Canada Canadian Armed Forces	4 × C-130B	May 60 – Nov 60	10301/10304	Withdrawn from use in March 1967 and sold back to GELAC (C-130B)
	24 × C-130E 5 × C-130H	Dec 64 – 68 Oct 74 – Feb 75	10305/10327 130329/130333	Current with No.435 Squadron at Edmonton and No.436 Squadron at Trenton (C-130E/H)
Chile Fuerza Aérea de Chile	2 × C-130H	1972 – 1973	995/996	Current with Grupo 10 at Los Cerrillos
Colombia Fuerza Aérea Colombiana	3 × C-130B	Jan 69	1001/1003	Ex-Canadian aircraft; one currently based at Techo; plus two replacement C-130Bs
Denmark Kongelige Danske Flyvevåben	3 × C-130H	Apr 75 – July 75	73-1678/73-1680	Current with Esk 721 at Vaerløse
Ecuador Fuerza Aérea Ecuatoriana	3 × C-130H	July 77 – Apr 79	FAE 743, 748 and 812	Currently based at Guayaquil
Egypt Arab Rep of Egypt AF	20 × C-130H	Dec 76 – Mar 79	SU-BAA/SU-BAF SU-BAH/SU-BAN SU-BAP/SU-BAV	Current
Gabon Forces Aériennes Gabonaises	1 × L-100-30 2 × L-100-20	Apr 75 Dec 76 – Dec 77	TR-KKA TR-KKB/TR-KKC	Current

Greece				
Elliniki Aeroporia	12 × C-130H	Sep 75 – May 77	741/752	Current with No.355 Mira at Eleusi
Indonesia				
Tentara Nasional Indonesia-Angkatan Udara	13 × C-130B 2 × C-130H 5 × C-130H(S) 1 × C-130H(MP)	1959 – 1961 1980 1980 – 1981 on order	T-130/1313 A-1315/1316 A-1317/1321	Current with Nos.31 and 32 Squadrons at Halim; two modified as KC-130B. More Hercules on order.
Gov of Indonesia	3 × L-100-20	July 79 – Sep 79	PK-PLU/PK-PLW	Leased to Pelita Air Services.
Iran				
Iran Revolutionary Air Force	4 × C-130B 28 × C-130E 32 × C-130H	1965 – 1970 Jan 71 – May 75	5-101/5-104 5-105/5-132 5-133/5-162 and 5-8551/5-8552	Sold to Pakistan (C-130B). Eight sold to Pakistan. Current along with some C-130Es.
Israel				
Heyl Ha'Avir	12 × C-130E	1973	4X-FBE, unknown, 4X-FBG/4X-FBJ, 4X-FBL/4X-FBP and one unknown	Transferred from USAF inventory in autumn of 1973; current.
	10 × C-130H	Oct 70 – Sep 76	4X-FBA/4X-FBE, 4X-FBQ, 4X-FBS/ 4X-FBU, and 4X-FBW/4X-FBX	Current
	2 × KC-130H	Apr 76 – May 76	4X-FBY/4X-FBZ	Current
Italy				
Aeronautica Militare Italiana	14 × C-130H	Mar 73 –	MM61988-62001	Current with 50 Gruppo at Grazzanise.
Japan				
Koku Jieitai	2 × C-130H	—		First two on order; more to follow.

Country / Air Force	Aircraft	Dates	Serials	Status
Jordan Royal Jordanian Air Force	4 × C-130B	1976	140/143	Ex-USAF; two sold to Singapore in 1977 and two current.
	2 × C-130H	78 – Apr 79	144 and 345	Current with No.3 Squadron at King Abdullah Air Base.
Kuwait Kuwait Air Force	2 × L-100-20	—	317/318	Current
Libya Libyan Arab Jamahiriya AF	8 × C-130H	1969 – 1971	111/118	Current
	8 × C-130H	—	119/126	Embargoed and held in storage at GELAC since 1973.
Malaysia Royal Malaysian Air Force	6 × C-130H	Mar 76 – Oct 76	FM-2401/2406	Current with No.14 Squadron at Kuala Lumpur; last three used for maritime reconnaissance.
	3 × C-130H(MP)	1980	FM-2451/2453	
Morocco Forces Aériennes Royales	12 × C-130H	May 74 – July 77	CN-AOA/CN-AOL	Current
New Zealand Royal New Zealand Air Force	5 × C-130H	66 – Dec 68	NZ7001/7005	Current with No.40 Squadron at Whenuapai
Niger Force Aérienne du Niger	2 × C-130H	1980	5U-MBD and 5U-MBH	Current
Nigeria Federal Nigerian Air Force	6 × C-130H	Sep 75 – Feb 76	910/915	Current
Norway Kongelige Norske Luftforsvaret	6 × C-130H	May 69 – June 69	BW-A/BW-F	Current with No.335 Squadron at Gardermoen

Pakistan
Pakistan Air Force

2 × C-130B		12646 and 12648	Ex-USAF
4 × C-130B		23488/23491	Ex-Iranian Air Force
4 × C-130B		24140/24143	Delivered new
4 × C-130E	Nov 71	10689, 14726, 64310, 64312	Ex-Iranian Air Force
2 × L-100		64144/64145	Leased from PIA. All current with No.6 Squadron at Chaklala.

Peru
Fuerza Aérea del Peru

6 × L-100-20	Apr 73 – Jan 77	394/396 and 382/384	Current with Grupo 41 at Jorge Chávez; first two were acquired used.

Philippines
Philippine Air Force

4 × L-100-20	Apr 73 – Nov 73	PI-97/PI-100	Three acquired used; both versions operated by No.222 Squadron at Mactan Air Base
3 × C-130H	Nov 76 – Nov 77	4704, 4726 and 4761	

Portugal
Fôrça Aérea Portuguesa

5 × C-130H	Aug 77 – 78	6801/6805	Current with Esc.501 at Lisbon

Saudi Arabia
Royal Saudi Air Force

5 × C-130E	Sep 65 – Nov 68	451/455 and 1606/1608	Current with Nos.4 and 16 Squadrons at Jeddah
26 × C-130H	—	460/470, 1601/1605, 1610/1612, 1614/1615, 1618/1619, MS019 and two yet unnumbered	
6 × KC-130H	Nov 73 –	456/459, 1616/1617 and two yet unnumbered	
2 × VC-130H	July 75 – June 77	111/112	Current with No.1 Squadron

Country / Operator	Type	Serials	Dates	Notes
Singapore Republic of Singapore AF	4 × C-130B 2 × C-130H	720/721 and 730/731 724/725	1977 Feb 80	Two ex-USAF and two ex-Jordanian; operated along with two new C-130Hs by No.121 Squadron at Changi.
South Africa South African Air Force	7 × C-130B	401/407	1961 – 1962	Current with No.28 Squadron at Waterkloof; supplemented by fifteen L-100-30s of Safair Freighters Ltd.
Spain Ejercito del Aire	7 × C-130H 5 × KC-130H	T10-1/10-4 and T10-8/10-10 TK10-5/10-7 and TK10-11/10-12	Dec 72 – Jan 76 –	Current with Esc.311 at Zaragoza. Current with Esc.312 at Zaragoza.
Sudan Sudan Air Force	6 × C-130H	1100/1105	Apr 78 – 78	Current
Sweden Svenska Flygvapnet	2 × C-130E 1 × C-130H	84001/84002 84003	—	Current with Flygflottilj F7 at Såtenäs/Tun; five more C-130Hs on order.
Thailand Royal Thai Air Force	3 × C-130H	60101/60103	—	To be delivered as part of Peace Prince project
Tunisia Tunisian Republic AF	1 × C-130H	—	On order	—
Turkey Türk Hava Kuvvetleri	8 × C-130E	ETI-186/189, ETI-468, ETI-947, ETI-949, and ETI-991	– Feb 74	Current with 222 Filo at Erkilet/Kayseri.

United Kingdom Royal Air Force	66 × C-130K	Dec 66 – Feb 68	XV176/223 and XV290/307	One modified as W.Mk.2 and thirty as C.Mk.3s. Currently equipping Nos.24,30,47 and 70 Squadrons, and No.242 OCU.
Venezuela Fuerza Aérea Venezolana	7 × C-130H	Oct 70 – Dec 78	3556, 4951, 7772, 9508, 4224, 5320, 3134	Current with Esc.1 at Carácas.
Vietnam VNAF	35 × C-130A	1972		Ex-USAF aircraft; nineteen returned in April 1975.
Vietnamese People's Air Force	13 × C-130A	April 1975		Captured from VNAF
Yemen Yemen Arab Republic Air Force	2 × C-130H	1980	1150, 1160	Current
Zaire Force Aérienne Zairoise	7 × C-130H	Feb 73 – May 77	9T-TCA/9T-TCG	Current

maximum cruising speed of 564 mph at 20,000 ft (907 km/h at 6,095 m). However, Pan American and Slick cancelled their orders for GL-207s and other versions did not go beyond the initial study phase. Thus, all commercial versions of the Hercules were straightforward developments of the C-130. So far, civil Hercules have been produced in three versions.

L-100 (Models 382 and 382B): The Lockheed demonstrator (c/n 382-3946, N1130E) made a spectacular first flight on 20/21 April, 1964, when it remained airborne for 25 hr 1 min. It was powered by 4,050 eshp Allison 501-D22s (commercial version of the C-130's T56s) and was used to obtain a Type Certificate on 16 February, 1965. Twenty-one production aircraft (Model 382B) were built, with the first delivery, to Continental Air Services, on 30 September, 1965. Other L-100s were delivered to Airlift International, Alaska Airlines, International Aerodyne, National Aircraft Leasing, Pacific Western Airlines, PIA, and Zambian Air Cargoes. The L-100s did not carry underwing fuel tanks and had most military equipment removed; they could be fitted with retractable combination wheel-skis. The demonstrator and eight Model 382Bs were modified as L-100-20s, and two other L-100s became L-100-30s.

L-100-20 (c/n 382-4706) of the Fuerza Aérea del Peru. (*Lockheed*)

L-100-20 (Models 382E and 382F): As commercial freight seldom has the high density of military cargo, in airline service the L-100s were frequently space limited. To solve this problem Lockheed added a 5 ft (1·52 m) fuselage plug forward of the wing and a 3 ft 4 in (1·02 m) plug aft. Maximum take-off weight remained at 155,000 lb (70,307 kg) and power was supplied by either 4,050 eshp 501-D22 or 4,508 eshp 501-D22A engines. The L-100-20 was certificated on 4 October, 1968, and entered service with Interior Airways one week later. In

L-100-30 PK-PLV, used for the Transmigration project in Indonesia. (*Lockheed*)

addition to nine aircraft modified from existing L-100s, twenty-five L-100-20s were built by Lockheed for delivery to twelve civil and military customers; seven later became L-100-30s. This version is still offered for sale.

L-100-30 (Model 382G): Main commercial version of the Hercules, the L-100-30 remains in production after seven converted aircraft and 35 new ones had been delivered by the end of 1980. Take-off weight and powerplants remain unchanged but the fuselage is stretched by an additional 6 ft 8 in (2·03 m) to bring cabin hold volume from 4,500 cu ft (127·4 cu m) for the L-100 and 5,307 cu ft (150·3 cu m) for the L-100-20 to 6,057 cu ft (171·5 cu m). The L-100-30 entered service with Saturn Airways in December 1970.

In an effort to boost the Hercules' commercial market, Lockheed has proposed, and continues to market, a number of derivatives including the L-100-50 (with a fuselage stretched by another 20 ft/6·10 m), the L-100-30PX passenger transport with 100 seats, the L-100-30QC cargo/passenger convertible and the L-100-30C combined cargo/passenger version. Furthermore, Lockheed announced in January 1980 its decision to proceed with the development and production of the L-400 Twin Hercules, a smaller and lighter version powered by two 4,910 eshp Allison 501-D22Ds; however, this decision was later rescinded and development of the L-400 was shelved, at least temporarily.

The first commercial L-100 operator was Alaska Airlines which on 8 March, 1965, put into service the Hercules demonstrator, on lease from Lockheed. It later leased four more L-100s and purchased one but by the end of the sixties disposed of all of them. Alaska International Air (AIA), known as Interior Airways until 1972, has been much more successful since, following the discovery of oil on the North Slope in 1967, it rapidly built up a fleet of Hercules to become

372

the prime airlifter of heavy construction equipment in the Arctic. Since then, AIA has standardized its fleet on the L-100-30 version and has expanded its operations to worldwide charter and contract work. Other operators of US-registered L-100s have included Airlift International, Delta Air Lines, Flying 'W' Airways, Saturn Airways (absorbed into TIA in 1976 and renamed Transamerica Airlines in 1980), Air America (Continental Air Services), and Southern Air Transport. While the first four of these carriers flew purely commercial operations, Air America and Southern Air Transport flew para-military duties during the Southeast Asia War. At the beginning of 1981, Transamerica Airlines, with a fleet of twelve L-100-30s, remained the largest US operator of the type. A decade earlier, its predecessor, Saturn Airways, had secured a profitable contract to airlift from Belfast to Burbank engine pods manufactured for the TriStar by Shorts.

Over the years Canadian-registered L-100s have also been operated on oil exploration and mine-support operations in the Arctic. In third world countries civil Hercules have joined military C-130s—notably those from Transportes Aéreos Militares in Bolivia, SATENA-Servicio de Aeronavigación a Territorios Nacionales in Colombia, TAME-Transportes Aéreos Nacionales Ecuatorianos in Ecuador, and SATCO-Servicio Aéreo de Transportes Commerciales in Peru—to provide much needed air links in remote jungle and mountain areas where only short and primitive airfields exist. Similar social services are provided on an even larger scale by Pelita Air Services, of Indonesia, with three L-100-30s on loan from the government, which is responsible for airlifting 500,000 families from Java to other, less crowded, islands in the archipelago as part of the Indonesian transmigration programme. Finally, mention must be made of Safair which operates a fleet of sixteen L-100-30s both on commercial flights and as an adjunct to the South African Air Force. In addition, the Hercules has proved repeatedly that it is an outstanding aircraft to airlift emergency supplies following natural catastrophes.

Already in service for twenty-four years, the Hercules was still being produced during 1980 at a monthly rate of three C-130/L-100s. It is undoubtedly the world's most successful cargo aircraft and will continue to be built during most of the decade, to become the type with the longest production life in aviation history. For its manufacturer the Hercules has been a solid money-maker and has helped Lockheed to weather otherwise difficult times.

Related Temporary Design Designations: L-237, CL-415, CL-451, CL-753, CL-1064, CL-1168, GL-101/GL-102, GL-105/GL-111, GL-118/GL-122, GL-127/ GL-129, GL-131/GL-134, GL-137/GL-138, GL-141/GL-142, GL-144, GL-191/ GL-193, GL-199, GL-201, GL-207, GL-212, GL-217, GL-219, GL-221/GL-222, GL-226, GL-231, GL-234/GL-235, GL-237, GL-250, GL-253, GL-257, GL-262/ GL-263, GL-265/GL-266, GL-269/GL-271, GL-273/GL-274, GL-276/GL-279, GL-282, GL-285, GL-288, GL-293, GL-295, GL-297/GL-298, GL-302, GL-304, GL-306, GL-309/GL-310, GL-312/GL-313, GL-319/GL-320, GL-323, GL-326/ GL-328, GL-332, GL-337/GL-343, GL-347/GL-348, GL-353/GL-354, GL-359/ GL-360, GL-362, GL-366, GL-370/GL-371, GL-374/GL-379, GL-381/GL-383, GL-402, LG130-101/LG130-214, LG100-104/LG100-137, LG382-101/LG382-104, LG400-101/LG400-104, LGM-012 and LGM-025

	C-130A	C-130H	L-100-20	L-100-30
Span, ft*	132·6	132·6	132·6	132·6
(m)	(40·42)	(40·42)	(40·42)	(40·42)
Length, ft	97·8	97·8	106·1	112·7
(m)	(29·81)	(29·81)	(32·34)	(34·35)
Height, ft	38·5	38·1	38·1	38·1
(m)	(11·73)	(11·61)	(11·61)	(11·61)
Wing area, sq ft	1,745·5	1,745·5	1,745·5	1,745·5
(sq m)	(162·163)	(162·163)	(162·163)	(162·163)
Empty weight, lb	59,328	76,780	73,412	74,262
(kg)	(26,911)	(34,827)	(33,299)	(33,685)
Loaded weight, lb	108,000	155,000	155,000	155,000
(kg)	(48,988)	(70,307)	(70,307)	(70,307)
Maximum weight, lb	124,200	175,000	—	—
(kg)	(56,336)	(79,379)	—	—
Wing loading, lb/sq ft	61·9	88·8	88·8	88·8
(kg/sq m)	(302·1)	(433·6)	(433·6)	(433·6)
Power loading, lb/eshp	7·2	7·8	9·6	8·6
(kg/eshp)	(3·3)	(3·5)	(4·3)	(3·9)
Maximum speed, mph/ at ft	383/20,400	386/25,000	—	—
(km/h at m)	(616/6,220)	(621/7,620)	—	—
Cruising speed, mph	328	355	361	361
(km/h)	(528)	(571)	(581)	(581)
Initial rate of climb, ft/min	2,570	2,570	1,900	1,900
(m/min)	(783)	(762)	(579)	(579)
Service ceiling, ft	41,300	42,900	—	—
(m)	(12,590)	(13,075)	—	—
Payload/range, lb/miles	35,000/2,090	45,000/2,745	46,588/2,555	50,738/1,825
(kg/km)	(15,876/3,365)	(20,412/4,415)	(21,132/4,110)	(23,014/2,935)
Ferry/range, miles	3,215	5,465	4,215	4,620
(km)	(5,175)	(8,795)	(6,780)	(7,435)

*Lockheed-Georgia dimensions quoted as ft and decimal point, not inches.

374

U-2A of the 4028th SRS/4080th SRW. The marking beneath the tail number is the ribbon of the Air Force Outstanding Unit Award earned by this unit for its role during the Cuban Missile Crisis in 1962. (*Lockheed*)

Lockheed U-2

When the full story of the development and operational use of the U-2 is cleared for publication, it will probably confirm what can only be surmised at this time: that its design, production and service deployment are among the most spectacular achievements in aviation history. Already, what has been released is awe-inspiring. Conceived over a quarter of a century ago, and re-entering production in an improved version in 1980 after a nearly twelve-year lapse, the unnamed U-2 is perhaps the brightest star in the Lockheed aircraft family.

The early fifties, after the Soviet blockade of West Berlin, was a period of intense Cold War activity: actual fighting took place in Korea and Malaya; while in Europe, NATO had been organized to provide for the collective defence of the Atlantic Community and to contain Soviet moves on the European Continent. In the air, Strategic Air Command bombers carrying nuclear weapons were on constant alert and ADC and RCAF interceptors extended a protective umbrella over the United States and Canada. The Soviet Union had detonated its first hydrogen bomb on 12 August, 1953, and the appearance in May 1954 of the Myasishchev Mya-4 (ASCC reporting name Bison) heavy jet bomber made it imperative for the United States to monitor the Soviet threat and plan appropriate defensive measures. Yet, in the face of the ruthless efficiency of the KGB, conventional methods of espionage, even when supplemented by electronic monitoring, did not measure up to the task. The need to develop new intelligence-gathering tools had become urgent. Fortunately, the timely development of mylar-based film by Eastman Kodak, of high-resolution cameras by Dr Edwin

Land and of lenses by the Hycon Corporation made it feasible to consider aerial reconnaissance as a possible answer to the problem.

Although the USAF was already flying photographic and electronic reconnaissance sorties along and across the Soviet borders, its aircraft did not have the performance necessary for deep penetration of Russian airspace. What was needed was an aircraft capable of flying above the effective altitude of Soviet interceptors and possessing sufficient range to fly over most of the USSR. Seeking to obtain the necessary aircraft and acting as a front for the CIA, the USAF's Wright Air Development Center completed at the end of March 1953 the preparation of preliminary specifications (range of 1,750 miles/2,815 km, service ceiling of at least 70,000 ft/21,335 m, and camera/sensor payload of 100 to 700 lb/45 to 315 kg) for a single-seat, high-altitude reconnaissance aircraft, and obtained Headquarters' authorization to contact selected contractors. On 1 July, 1953, Bell, Fairchild and Martin were awarded six-month study contracts for Weapon System MX-2147, Project Bald Eagle. Evaluation of these studies in early 1954 led to the ordering of twenty Martin RB-57Ds—a development of the B-57B tactical bomber with greatly enlarged wing span and area, and two Pratt & Whitney J57-P-37 turbojets—and of the similarly-powered Bell X-16—a brand-new design given an X-experimental designation to conceal its true role. The RB-57Ds were built, and saw service with the USAF and the Chinese Nationalist Air Force, but the X-16 was cancelled when it was overtaken by a private venture from Kelly Johnson's Preliminary Design Department.

Although Lockheed had not been invited to submit a design study for the MX-2147, Kelly Johnson had been aware of its existence and felt that the XF-104, with its anticipated combat ceiling of 60,000 ft (18,290 m), could provide the basis for developing an aircraft with performance as specified by the Wright Air Development Center. Funded by the company, the Preliminary Design Department completed on 4 March, 1954, its Report No.9732 on the CL-282 high-altitude aircraft*. Lockheed's unsolicited proposal was reviewed at Wright-Patterson AFB during the summer of 1954 but was rejected by the USAF as the Service was already committed to the Martin RB-57D, which was to satisfy its most urgent need, and to the Bell X-16, which was expected to have better altitude performance than the RB-57D and was to fill the USAF's longer-term requirements. Had it not been for the intelligence panel of a special Presidential committee, the U-2 would have been stillborn and the X-16 would have gone into production.

Organized by President Eisenhower to study the possibility of a surprise attack against the United States and ways to prevent it, the committee determined an urgent need for improving intelligence gathering on the Soviet missile, strategic bomber, and nuclear weapon programmes. It concluded that reconnaissance overflights of the USSR and the Soviet-bloc countries would be necessary. Accordingly, the committee's intelligence panel reviewed the USAF's RB-57D and X-16 projects, as well as the unsolicited Lockheed CL-282 proposal. The RB-57D was judged to have insufficient performance for long overflights while the X-16 fell victim to Kelly Johnson's forceful lobbying and his guarantee to complete a prototype within a mere eight months from project go-ahead. This accelerated schedule impressed the panel and in November 1954 the Central Intelligence Agency obtained President Eisenhower's approval to proceed with the develop-

*See Appendix A.

ment of the new Lockheed aircraft. Programme management was entrusted to a small group led by Richard M. Bissell Jr of the CIA and Brig-Gen Leo P. Geary of the USAF, with funding to be provided by the CIA and through diversion of USAF money (notably by ordering additional engines under the umbrella of less sensitive aircraft projects). On 9 December, 1954, Trevor Gardner, the assistant secretary of the Air Force for research and development, visited Lockheed and formally gave authorization to proceed with the final design and construction of the aircraft.

Code-named Aquatone, the project immediately went into high gear at the Skunk Works. To meet the more stringent operational requirements established by the committee's intelligence panel, which called notably for greater range and higher ceiling, Kelly Johnson and his team redesigned the CL-282 into what became the U-2 (like the X-16 designation of the Bell project, the U-utility designation of the Lockheed design was assigned to conceal the aircraft's role). To provide space for increased fuel capacity and for a 10,500 lb (4,763 kg) thrust Pratt & Whitney J57-P-37 turbojet, the fuselage was lengthened to 49 ft 7 in (15·11 m) while the higher ceiling was obtained by increasing the span and area of the wing to 80 ft (24·38 m) and 565 sq ft (52·49 sq m). Furthermore, the search for maximum altitude performance led to the drastic application of weight-reducing measures. The glider-like wing, with an aspect ratio of 10·2, weighed only 3 lb per square foot (14·6 kg/sq m)—a third of the weight of conventional jet aircraft wings. Other savings were obtained by dispensing with cabin pressurization (a lighter full-pressure suit being worn by the pilot) and by using a bicycle-type undercarriage. The twin mainwheels and twin small tailwheels retracted forward into the fuselage; for taxi-ing and take-off, jettisonable twin-wheeled outrigger units were fitted beneath the wing at approximately mid-span, while the reinforced wingtips were turned down 90 deg for use as skids during landing. Another weight-saving measure initially adopted was the use of a standard pilot's seat but later ejector seats were retrofitted (current operational versions having zero-zero capability).

Through the unique project organization of the Skunk Works, the tight development schedule was adhered to and the first U-2 was trucked to a dry lake bed at Watertown, northwest of Las Vegas, to be tested in secrecy over the Nevada desert. With Tony LeVier at the controls the 'Angel' first leapt 36 ft into the air during a high-speed taxi run. Its first flight was made on 6 August, 1955, and went satisfactorily until LeVier attempted to land. With its large, lightly-loaded wing, the aircraft just floated above the dry lake and its pilot had to try five times before stalling it back to earth. The aircraft was damaged slightly but was soon repaired and flying again. Accelerated tests revealed a number of problems including fogging of the faceplate of the pilot's pressure suit, and high-altitude engine flameouts which were brought under almost complete control by using a lower volatility fuel (JPTS) developed by the Shell Oil Company. Nevertheless, at least three aircraft were lost during test and pilot training flights in 1955-56. By then, however, production of the aircraft for the CIA was already well underway and the USAF, reversing its earlier decision, cancelled the Bell X-16 and ordered the U-2 for its own use.

The production history of the U-2 remains classified and the manufacturer is not allowed to release details; it is therefore impossible to list all variants and estimate the number of aircraft built, but the following partial listing can be made from declassified information.

U-2A: Initial production version for both the CIA and the USAF. Powered by a 10,500 lb (4,763 kg) thrust Pratt & Whitney J57-P-37 or 11,200 lb (5,080 kg) thrust J57-P-37A turbojet. Cameras and other reconnaissance equipment could be carried in the nose and in a fuselage bay located aft of the pilot and between the air intakes. This Q-bay, basically consisting of a large hole formed by two massive beams which suspended the cockpit some 5 ft ahead of the intakes, could carry up to 750 lb (340 kg) of reconnaissance equipment. The internal fuel capacity of 785 US gal (2,972 litres) could be supplemented by two 105-gal (397-litre) non-jettisonable slipper tanks on the wing leading-edge. Serial numbers 56-6675 to 56-6722 have been reported as assigned to U-2As purchased by the USAF, but several of these aircraft were later modified to other versions (notably U-2C, U-2CT and U-2D). In addition, photographs of an earlier numbered aircraft (55-5741) have been released; however, no details are available on the CIA aircraft and on possible early models for the USAF. Service modifications, dictated by changing mission requirements, resulted in a variety of protrusions appearing on various parts of the aircraft (loops on the aft fuselage, semi-hemispheric fairings above and/or below the fuselage, etc) to house special sensors.

U-2A of the 4080th SRW during a Crow Flight sortie over the South Island of New Zealand. The air-brakes are extended. (*Lockheed*)

WU-2A: Designation given to U-2As of the USAF modified for atmospheric research and radioactivity sampling. For the latter mission a large fairing, with a scoop facing forward, protruded on the port side of the fuselage beneath the equipment bay.

U-2B: Improved version powered by either a 15,800 lb (7,167 kg) Pratt & Whitney J75-P-13 or 17,000 lb (7,711 kg) thrust J75-P-13B turbojet. 'Wet' wings were fitted to bring internal fuel capacity to 1,140 US gal (4,316 litres). It is thought that U-2Bs were built exclusively for the CIA. Several aircraft, which appear to fit in the U-2B series, have been photographed with civil registrations

378

N809X, a civil registered aircraft believed to be one of the U-2Bs produced for the Central Intelligence Agency. Air intakes and dorsal 'canoe' are similar to those of USAF U-2Cs. (*Lockheed*)

(N800X, N803X, N809X, etc) and were probably ordered by the CIA as, even during tests, conventionally-funded US military aircraft carry standard serial numbers or BuNos. At least seven U-2Bs are believed to have been transferred to the Chinese Nationalist Air Force, or flown in CNAF markings by American pilots of Chinese origin, for operations over the Chinese mainland.

U-2C: Development of the U-2A/U-2B—believed to have been obtained by modifying existing aircraft to a common standard with a 17,000 lb (7,711 kg) thrust J75-P-13B turbojet fed by bulged air intakes—specially fitted for electronic intelligence (ELINT) gathering. The nose was slightly lengthened to increase the volume available for equipment, with additional space being provided in a long 'canoe' dorsal spine. The fuel tank arrangement was revised to increase internal capacity to 1,320 US gal (4,997 litres) and total capacity, with two slipper tanks, to 1,530 gal (5,792 litres). Two of these aircraft, originally delivered as U-2As (56-6681/56-6682) to the USAF, were used for carrier trials aboard USS *Enterprise*

U-2C (56-6680) modified from a U-2A airframe. Note enlarged intakes and dorsal 'canoe' housing ELINT (Electronic Intelligence) equipment. (*via Cloud 9 Photography*)

The U-2C N709NA (ex 56-6682) at the Ames Research Center, Moffett Field, California, on 31 January, 1980. Covers above and below the main equipment compartment aft of the cockpit have been removed. (*René J. Francillon*)

before being transferred to the NASA's Ames Research Center in April 1971; they were then registered N708NA and N709NA. After being damaged in an accident, another U-2C (56-6692) was rebuilt as a U-2CT trainer for the USAF.

U-2CT: In addition to the U-2C mentioned above, one U-2D (56-6953) was modified as a two-seat trainer. In these two aircraft an instructors cockpit, with raised seat under a separate canopy, was fitted in place of the main equipment bay.

U-2D: High-altitude research version with a second crew capsule within the fuselage bay normally occupied by sensors. Various sensors for radioactivity, infra-red and other research were carried and resulted in sundry protrusions aft of the pilot's cockpit and above that of the instrument operator. The latter was frequently provided with a rotating periscope, as visibility through two small windows was strictly limited. Serials 56-6951/56-6955 are known to have been applied to U-2Ds. An additional U-2D was obtained by modifying the U-2C 56-6721.

U-2E or U-2F: Designations believed to have been applied to at least one earlier U-2 which was fitted with an inflight-refuelling receptacle (boom method) in the port wing.

Modified from U-2D 56-6953, this aircraft is one of two U-2CT trainers. (*Lockheed*)

U-2C modified to U-2D standard and operated by the Air Force Flight Test Center in 1978.
(*Lockheed*)

U-2EPX: Two U-2Rs were temporarily modified to this configuration for evaluation by the US Navy in the ocean surveillance role (EPX—Electronic Patrol, Experimental). For these tests, they were fitted in 1973 with a Texas Instruments AN/APS-116 radar and other specialized items. These were not adopted by the Navy but modified back to U-2R standard. One of these aircraft (serial 68-10329) was subsequently used to fly test equipment for the TR-1A.

U-2G or U-2J: Two U-2Cs (56-6681 and 56-6682) were tested aboard the USS *Enterprise*. A fully carrier-compatible version may then have been developed and is believed to have had one of these designations.

U-2R: Retaining the familiar external appearance of earlier versions, the U-2R was virtually a complete redesign undertaken to correct a poor engine-airframe match, provide increased equipment volume, and enable operations at higher altitude. When powered by the J75-P-13B engine, earlier versions of the U-2 had been found to have too much thrust for their wing loading and, unless their engine was operated at reduced rating, had been prone to overspeed problems in some flight regimes. The U-2R was thus developed as a significantly larger and heavier aircraft than the U-2C. Span was increased from 80 to 103 ft (24·38 to 31·39 m), area from 565 to 1,000 sq ft (52·49 to 92·9 sq m), and length from 50 to 63 ft (15·24 to 19·2 m). In addition to carrying cameras and sensors in enlarged fuselage bays,

Retaining its USAF serial 68-10339, this aircraft was one of two U-2Rs used for the US Navy's U-2EPX (Electronics Patrol Experimental) programme. The AN/APS-116 radar was carried in the starboard wing pod. (*US Navy*)

Photographed on final approach to RAF Upper Heyford, this U-2R (68-10339) was then used as a development aircraft for some of the electronics for the TR-1. Earlier this aircraft had been tested as one of the two U-2EPXs. (*Paul Bennett*)

the U-2R was provided with wing attachment points for large pods protruding fore and aft. Maximum take-off weight jumped from 22,542 lb (10,225 kg) for the U-2C as operated by NASA to over 40,000 lb (18,145 kg) as a result of the larger airframe, heavier sensor and electronic countermeasures payload, and increased fuel capacity. The J75-P-13B turbojet was retained but the bicycle-type under-carriage was redesigned with the mainwheels being moved aft and the tailwheels relocated further forward than on the U-2C. Twenty-five U-2Rs were ordered for the USAF during Fiscal Year 1968 (serials 68-10329/68-10353).

TR-1A: After a nearly twelve-year lapse in production, the U-2 has been ordered once again. In November 1979 the USAF announced the initial award of a $5 mn contract for pre-production tooling and facilities preparation for the TR-1 high-altitude tactical reconnaissance version. A first production contract for two TR-1As and one ER-2 was announced one month later. Basically using the airframe and powerplant of the U-2R, the TR-1A is a single-seat aircraft equipped with a variety of sensors, carried in fuselage bays and large wing pods, and is intended for high-altitude standoff surveillance of Eastern Europe. Operational equipment includes an Advanced Synthetic Aperture Radar System (ASARS), a UPD-X side-looking airborne radar, ECM, and the Lockheed-developed Precision Location Strike System (PLSS) — a system intended to locate and identify enemy radar, and to direct strike aircraft against these targets. During peacetime operations the TR-1As will loiter high over Western Europe and will be able to 'look' up to 300 miles (485 km) beyond the Iron Curtain. A contract for a first batch of twenty-three TR-1As, with deliveries beginning during 1981, was initially awarded. A further batch of ten TR-1 single-seaters, with different sensors to fulfil another military mission, was ordered later.

TR-1B: Two two-seat trainers, using TR-1A airframes with instructor accommodation similar to that fitted to the U-2CTs, are to enter service with the USAF during Fiscal Year 1982.

ER-2: One of the first aircraft (serial 80-1063, NASA 706) ordered under the TR-1 contract was delivered on 10 June, 1981, to NASA under the designation

ER-2 (ER for Earth Resources). In service with the High-Altitude Missions Branch, Ames Research Center, it is supplementing NASA's two U-2Cs. Sensors payload has been increased from a maximum of 1,450 lb (658 kg) for the U-2C to 3,000 lb (1,361 kg) for the ER-2, with mission equipment being carried in interchangeable nose sections, the Q-bay aft of the pilot's seat, and large wing pods. The ER-2 can transmit data in flight on a real-time basis to increase its effectiveness in co-ordinating its research activities with those of ground-based teams of scientists.

The ER-2 (NASA 706, 80-1063) at Moffett Field on 10 June, 1981, when it was delivered to the Ames Research Center. (*René J. Francillon*)

Training of Central Intelligence Agency U-2 pilots began in the spring of 1956 at Watertown, Nevada, and led to the organization of the 1st, 2nd and 3rd Weather Reconnaissance Squadrons (Provisional). Soon these units moved to RAF Lakenheath in England, Adana in Turkey and Naha on Okinawa, with detachments at Wiesbaden, Germany, and Peshawar, Pakistan. From these bases, and with tacit approval from NATO and CENTO allies, the U-2As began flying photographic and electronic reconnaissance flights across communist borders in Europe and Asia, with the first significant overflight of the USSR taking place on 4 July, 1956. For nearly four years CIA-sponsored flights by U-2As and, from 1959, by U-2Bs were made repeatedly over the Soviet Union, bringing back valuable information which enabled the United States to learn that the Soviet strategic bomber threat was not as serious as had been believed previously and that the much-feared 'missile gap' did not really exist. Then, on 1 May, 1960, the U-2B piloted by Lieut Francis Gary Powers, on a 3,788-mile (6,095-km) mission from Peshawar to Bodø in Norway, was brought down near Sverdlovsk by the nearby explosion of a SAM (surface-to-air missile). Much publicity was derived by the Soviet Union from this incident and President Eisenhower was compelled to forbid U-2 overflights of the USSR. However, flights over mainland China continued as that country did not have sophisticated SAMs in the early sixties. For these flights at least seven U-2s were apparently transferred to the Chinese Nationalist Air Force for operations from Taiwan. Several were lost over the mainland, presumably due in most instances to engine flameouts, forcing the suspension of regular intelligence-gathering flights over China. However, before termination of U-2 flights from Taiwan, CNAF pilots gathered proof during 1964 that China was preparing to explode its first nuclear device.

Within the USAF the U-2A was first assigned to the 4028th Strategic Reconnaissance Squadron, 4080th SRW, Strategic Air Command, at Laughlin AFB, Texas. In addition to flying its regular military missions, which entailed regular deployment to overseas bases—notably Upper Heyford in England, Anderson AFB on Guam, and Albrook AFB in the Panama Canal Zone—the 4028th SRS undertook 'Crow Flights' as part of the High Altitude Sampling Program (HASP) to detect and monitor the presence of radioactive debris in the upper atmosphere. Crow Flights took specially-equipped WU-2As to such distant places as Buenos Aires in Argentina, Lima in Peru, RAAF Laverton in Australia, and Alaska.

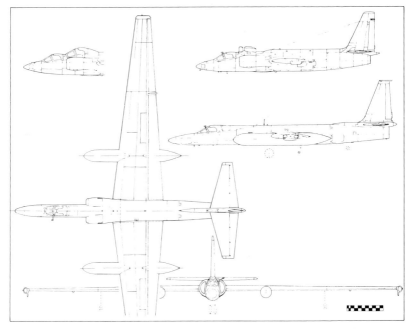

Lockheed TR-1A/ER-2, with side view of U-2D and nose of U-2CT

During the summer of 1962 the Texas-based unit was called to perform a more dangerous task as reports began to be received from refugees that Soviet surface-to-surface IRBM missiles were being deployed to Cuba. On 29 August a U-2 brought back photographic confirmation that offensive weapons had indeed arrived, ninety miles from the US shores. Subsequently, at least seven U-2As and three U-2Ds are known to have been involved in Cuban reconnaissance, and on 27 October one of these aircraft was shot down. Its pilot, Maj Rudolph Anderson Jr, was posthumously awarded the Distinguished Service Medal—the highest decoration bestowed by the United States except in time of war—while other U-2 pilots from the 4028th SRS received Distinguished Flying Crosses for their role in helping to defuse the Cuban Missile Crisis.

In July 1963 the 4028th SRS/4080th SRW was transferred to Davis-Monthan AFB, Arizona, from which it began deploying aircraft and crews to Bien Hoa AB, Vietnam, in July 1964. First redesignated 4025th SRS/4080th SRW on 1 July,

384

The much enlarged U-2R version, as currently operated by the 99th SRS/9th SRW, with large equipment wing pods. (*Lockheed*)

1965, and then 349th SRS/100th SRW on 25 June, 1966, this unit continued to fly U-2Cs and, later, U-2Rs during the Southeast Asia War, with the Bien Hoa detachment being transferred to U-Tapao RTAFB, Thailand, in July 1970. An idea of the intensity of the squadron's operations in this theatre can be gathered by the fact that its U-2s exceeded the 500 flying hours per month mark in January 1973 and the 600-mark in December 1974. Thai-based operations ended during 1975 following the collapse of the Republic of Vietnam.

After return to peacetime operations, the 349th SRS undertook a number of wide-ranging non-military tasks on behalf of government agencies, such as damage-evaluation photographs of Guatemala when in February 1976 an earthquake caused much destruction in this Central American country. This type of activity continues to be performed by the current U-2 unit: the 99th SRS/9th SRW which was organized at Beale AFB following the deactivation of the 349th SRS/100th SRW and the transfer in October 1976 of its personnel and operational

U-2D (56-6954) at Patrick AFB, Florida, on 2 March, 1961. The insignia on the fin is that of the Air Research and Development Center, now the Air Force Flight Test Center. (*USAF*)

385

U-2Rs and U-2C/U-2CT trainers to the California base. During 1980 the trainers were assigned to a new squadron of the 9th SRW, the 5th Strategic Reconnaissance Training Squadron, to train a cadre of pilots for the TR-1As. Two new squadrons will eventually be formed with TR-1A/Bs for operational assignment to the SAC's 7th Air Division at Ramstein AB, Germany. Meanwhile, the U-2Rs, which during most of the seventies kept a watchful eye over the troubled Middle East — operating mostly from RAF Akrotiri on Cyprus where 68-10330 was lost on 7 December, 1977 — played a significant role during the 1980 81 crisis over the taking of US hostages by Iran and in observing the Iran-Iraq war.

In the past, U-2s have also been operated by other USAF units including the AFFTC (Air Force Flight Test Center) and the 6512th Test Group of the ARDC's Special Projects Test Branch, both based at Edwards AFB. The latter unit was responsible for studying the signature of missiles and satellite boosters launched from the Atlantic and Pacific Missile Ranges, and for testing various items of equipment for use in reconnaissance satellites.

Lockheed U-2C (NASA 709) operated by the High Altitude Missions Branch, Ames Research Center, Moffett Field. The last five figures of its old serial, 56-6682, appear on the rear fuselage. (*René J. Francillon*)

The name of the National Advisory Committee for Aeronautics (NACA) was first used as a cover for the U-2, with photographs of Typhoon Kit, allegedly taken by NACA's U-2, being released in early 1957. Three years later a U-2 carrying the serial 55-5741 was hurriedly painted with the letters NASA on a yellow tail band for display to the press following the shooting down of Francis Gary Powers. Although NASA initially took responsibility for this 'accidental overflight' of the USSR, it did not in fact operate the type before April 1971 when it acquired two ex-USAF U-2Cs. Registered N708NA and N709NA and assigned to the Ames Research Center at NAS Moffett, California, these two aircraft have since been operated by NASA for a variety of civil research programmes including water resources survey, land-use evaluation, disaster assessment, collection of extra-terrestrial dust, sensor development, and stratospheric sampling (notably following the eruption of Mount St Helens in 1980). In this role the U-2Cs were supplemented by the ER-2 in June 1981.

Specifications and performance data for the various military models of the U-2 remain classified.

Span 80 ft (24·38 m); length 50 ft (15·24 m); height 15 ft (4·57 m); wing area 565 sq ft (52·49 sq m).

Zero-fuel weight 13,071 lb (5,929 kg); gross take-off weight 22,542 lb (10,225 kg); wing loading 39·9 lb/sq ft (194·8 kg/sq m); power loading 1·3 lb/lb st.

Weight of sensors: 750 lb (340 kg) maximum in bay aft of pilot's seat, 100 lb (45 kg) in dorsal 'canoe' fairing, and 600 lb (272 kg) in two underwing pods; total weight of sensors not to exceed 1,450 lb (658 kg).

Cruising speed 460 mph at 65,000 ft (740 km/h at 19,810 m); operating altitude 65,000/70,000 ft (19,180 to 21,335 m); cruise endurance 6 hr at Mach 0·69; range 2,880 miles (4,635 km).

Data for U-2C operated by NASA.

Span 103 ft (31·39 m); length 63 ft (19·2 m); wing area 1,000 sq ft (92·903 sq m).

Zero-fuel weight 15,101 lb (6,850 kg); take-off weight 34,750 lb (15,762 kg); maximum weight 40,000 lb (18,144 kg); wing loading 34·75 lb/sq ft (169·66 kg/sq m); power loading 2 lb/lb st.

Weight of sensors: 750 lb (340 kg) in bay aft of pilot's seat; 600 lb (272 kg) in nose compartment; and 750 lb (340 kg) in each underwing pod; total weight of sensors not to exceed 3,000 lb (1,361 kg).

Cruising speed 470 mph (756 km/h) at 65,000 ft (19,810 m); operating altitude 65,000/70,000 ft (19,810/21,335 m); endurance 7½ hr; normal range 3,455 miles (5,560 km).

Partial ER-2 data released by NASA.

Lockheed 1649 Starliner

When the competition between the derivatives of the Model 049 Constellation and the Douglas DC-4 reached its peak, Lockheed answered the Douglas challenger—the DC-7C, the first aircraft capable of regularly flying nonstop in both directions across the North Atlantic—with a bolder move entailing the mating of the Super Constellation's fuselage and tail surfaces with an entirely new wing. The resulting Model 1649 Starliner, perhaps the most attractive aircraft in the Constellation series, was unfortunately not able to match its looks with commercial success. Entering service on 1 June, 1957, exactly one year after its DC-7C competitor, it was challenged within six months by the faster, turbine-powered, Bristol Britannia and was rendered obsolete in October 1958 by the commercial debut of the jet-powered Boeing 707-120 and de Havilland Comet 4. Thus, only forty-four Starliners were built and Lockheed was unable to recoup sizeable investment in its last piston-engined transport.

Immediately after learning that, at the request of Pan American, during the summer of 1954 Douglas had begun to develop a version of the DC-7 capable of regular nonstop operations over the North Atlantic, TWA approached Lockheed with a request for a similar development of the Super Constellation. As the fuel needed to meet the range requirement could not be carried in the existing wing design—even when carrying tip tanks, the 1049G often had to make refuelling stops between Europe and the US East Coast—Lockheed had no other recourse but to undertake a major redesign of its aircraft. Providing space for tanks housing 9,600 US gal (36,340 litres) of fuel—versus 6,545 gal (24,766 litres) for the

N1649 the prototype Model 1649, with flaps partially extended and test probe on the tip of the starboard wing. (*Lockheed*)

1049G without tip tanks and 7,750 gal (29,337 litres) when tip tanks were fitted—the new wing increased the span from 123 to 150 ft (37·49 to 45·72 m) and area from 1,650 to 1,850 sq ft (153·291 to 171·865 sq m). The new wing had a higher aspect ratio—12 versus 9·17—and reduced thickness—15 per cent at the root and 11 per cent at the tip versus 18 per cent and 12 per cent respectively for the Super Constellation. Take-off gross weight was increased from 137,500 to 160,000 lb (62,369 to 72,575 kg) and length by 2 ft 7 in (0·79 m), but high-density accommodation (99 seats) remained unchanged from the 1049G to the 1649. Although serious consideration was given to using propeller-turbines, TWA and Lockheed agreed that no such engines were sufficiently proven for commercial use and the Model 1649A-98 went into production with 3,400 hp Wright 988TC-18EA-2 Turbo-Cyclones. However, to reduce cabin noise, these Turbo-Compound engines were mounted 5 ft 2½ in (1·59 m) further outboard than those of the Super Constellation and drove slower-turning, three-blade propellers of increased diameter—16 ft 10 in (5·13 m) versus 15 ft 2 in (4·62 m).

Preliminary design work was undertaken in July 1954 and manufacture began early in 1955 following receipt of a 25-aircraft order from TWA. Flight trials, which began on 10 October, 1956, when the company-owned N1649 (c/n 1649-1001) was first flown at the Lockheed Air Terminal, proceeded rapidly and the Model 1649A was issued a Type Certificate on 19 March, 1957. Six weeks later TWA received its first Starliner and the type went into service (New York to Paris) on 1 June, 1957. The same carrier inaugurated nonstop Starliner service between Los Angeles and London (19 hr 10 min eastbound) on 30 September of that year, with the westbound return to San Francisco being scheduled for 21 hr 5 min.

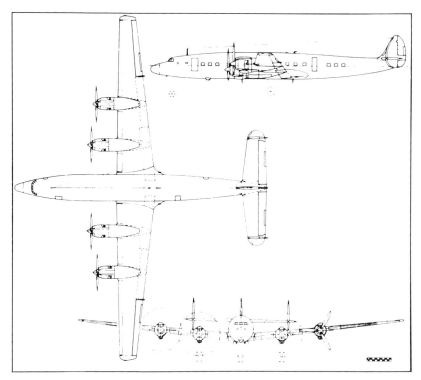

Lockheed Model 1649A Starliner

In addition to the twenty-five aircraft of its initial order, TWA received four Model 1649As ordered by Linee Aeree Italiane but cancelled when LAI was merged with Alitalia. The only other Starliner customers were Air France (ten aircraft including the last 1649A which was delivered on 12 February, 1958) and Lufthansa (four), while Varig converted a letter of intent for two Model 1649As

Known as the Super Star while in Lufthansa service, the Model 1649A Starliner was operated by that carrier from 1957 until 1966. The aircraft illustrated, D-ALOL, was the fourth and last delivered by Lockheed to the German airline. (*Lufthansa*)

An Air Korea Model 1649A (HL4003, c/n 1649-1037) at Da Nang AB in March 1964 during a resupply mission in support of Korean troops operating in Vietnam. (*Robert C. Mikesh*)

into a firm contract for two Model 1049Gs. Lockheed also marketed the Model 1649B, a propeller-turbine powered version of the Starliner, but its development was too late to attract customer interest when jetliners were already on order for delivery beginning during the summer of 1958. The final blow to the programme was struck when the Navy cancelled a contract for the W2V-1, a proposed airborne early-warning development of the Model 1649*.

With its three original customers, the Starliner proved reliable, with the only complaints stemming from its temperamental Turbo-Compound engines. Thus, as it was also well liked by passengers, it is likely that it would have emulated the success of the Super Constellation and perhaps even enabled Lockheed to make inroads among Douglas' customers had it been available three years earlier. Unfortunately, it had preceded the Boeing 707 into service by a mere sixteen months and by the end of the fifties the forty-four Model 1649As were already outnumbered nearly three to one by jetliners (deliveries through December 1959 had included 84 Boeing 707s, 24 Comet 4s and 21 DC-8s). Early retirement from the fleet of the prime carriers was the only solution, and as early as 1960 Air France, Lufthansa and TWA began re-assigning their Starliners to lesser routes. During the same year TWA disposed of some of its 1649As to Transatlantica Argentina, while it returned twelve Starliners to Lockheed Aircraft Service for conversion to all-freight configuration. Two of the Lufthansa aircraft were similarly modified by LAS with reinforced flooring and cargo-loading doors fore and aft of the wing on the port side of the fuselage. From the mid-sixties onwards, Starliners were operated mainly by smaller airlines and charter carriers, as well as by travel clubs, with the last three 1649As being operated in 1976 by Burns Aviation for long-distance cattle charters.

Related Temporary Design Designations: CL-257, CL-344, CL-365, CL-380/CL-381, CL-394, CL-410 and CL-489

Span 150 ft (45·72 m); length 116 ft 2 in (35·41 m); height 24 ft 9 in (7·54 m); wing area 1,850 sq ft (171·865 sq m).
Empty weight 91,645 lb (41,569 kg); loaded weight 160,000 lb (72,575 kg); wing loading 86·5 lb/sq ft (422·28 kg/sq m); power loading 11·8 lb/hp (5·3 kg/hp).
Maximum speed 377 mph at 18,600 ft (607 km/h at 5,670 m); cruising speed 290 mph (467 km/h); initial rate of climb 1,080 ft/min (329 m/min); service ceiling 23,700 ft (7,225 m); range 4,940 miles (7,950 km) with 19,500 lb (8,845 kg) payload or 6,180 miles (9,945 km) with 8,000 lb (3,630 kg).

*See Appendix A.

Lockheed JetStar

Seeking to modernize its fleet of wartime utility transports and twin-engined crew trainers, but lacking funds to sponsor the development of jet-powered aircraft of these types, the USAF informed the industry that, should its budgetary limitations be lifted, it would purchase flight-proven aircraft meeting its UTX (utility trainer experimental) and UCX (utility transport experimental) specifications. As the already sizeable military market could probably be supplemented by an even larger executive aircraft market—the maiden flight of the world's first business jet, the Morane-Saulnier MS.760 Paris, had been made in France on 29 July, 1954—three US manufacturers decided to develop the required prototypes at their own expense. North American wisely concentrated its efforts on the UTX requirement while McDonnell and Lockheed went after the larger and heavier UCX.

N329J, the JetStar prototype, with Bristol Orpheus engines, at Edwards AFB on 6 March, 1958. (*USAF*)

By the end of 1956, Lockheed's management was committed to the development of the light utility jet transport and in January 1957 Kelly Johnson's team went to work on the CL-329. The relatively small size of the aircraft, with its design capacity set at fourteen seats in high-density configuration, or 5,000 lb (2,268 kg) of cargo, dictated the location of the engines on the sides of the aft fuselage, as pod-mounted turbojets beneath the wing would be excessively prone to foreign-object ingestion due to the intakes' close proximity to the ground. This rear-engined configuration, having become fashionable with the SNCASE SE.210 Caravelle first flown in May 1955, was also preferred because of its resulting lower cabin noise. The CL-329 also borrowed from the Caravelle design its tailplane location on the lower portion of the fin. Engine selection, with a twin-engined configuration being favoured, caused some problems as at the time there existed no US-made turbojets in the required thrust class. Fortunately, the Wright Aeronautical Division of the Curtiss-Wright Corporation was planning to build under licence the Bristol Orpheus engine as the TJ37 and, pending availability of domestically-produced powerplants, the prototype CL-329s were to be fitted with British-built 4,850 lb (2,200 kg) thrust Orpheus 1/5 turbojets.

Registered N329J, the first prototype flew at the Lockheed Air Terminal on 4 September, 1957, only 241 days after the start of its design and nineteen months before its McDonnell competitor. Trials of the Orpheus-powered prototypes, the second (N329K) being flown in March 1958, went satisfactorily, and during a sales

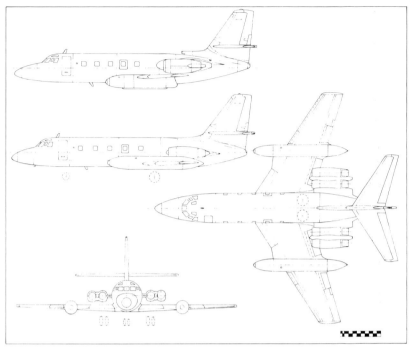

Lockheed JetStar, with (*top*) side view of JetStar II

demonstration campaign in 1958 the type proved its capability by flying a 6,700-mile (10,780-km), multi-stop tour in 18 hours. Unfortunately, in the meantime the bottom had fallen out of the market as the military budget had been slashed during 1957, thus preventing the USAF proceeding with the acquisition of UTX and UCX aircraft. Also during 1958 the US economy was experiencing a recession, thus delaying development of the business jet market. Nevertheless, Lockheed gambled on the future and in November 1958 committed the type to quantity manufacture, with production JetStars to be built at Marietta instead of Burbank. It also marketed the aircraft in two- and four-engined configurations and offered it to the USAF in a crew-trainer version, which succeeded in winning the trainer competition; and in October 1958 the Department of the Air Force announced its intent to acquire it as the T-40A-LM. The USAF, however, changed its selection and adopted the smaller and more economic North American NA-246, with two hundred and eleven T-39 trainers and CT-39 light transports eventually being produced for the USAF and USN.

As the licence-manufacture of the Orpheus by Wright did not materialize and as the USAF was unwilling to acquire aircraft powered by foreign-built turbojets, Lockheed had to study several four-engined versions. Turbojets in the 2,500/3,000 lb (1,135/1,360 kg) thrust class—either Fairchild J83, General Electric J85 or Pratt & Whitney JT12A—were to be mounted in pairs on the rear of the fuselage, as first proposed by Vickers in late 1956 for the project which became the VC10 jetliner. To test this configuration, the second prototype, which earlier had been used to test the installation of 565-US gal (2,139-litre) slipper tanks, was fitted with four 3,000 lb (1,361 kg) thrust Pratt & Whitney JT12A-6s and was first flown in this form in January 1960. Good results achieved with the JT12A-6s led to the decision to fit the Pratt & Whitney turbojets to all production aircraft.

Interest in the JetStar had picked up during 1959 and by February 1960 Lockheed had received conditional orders from corporations and from the Canadian Government for twenty-nine Model 1329 aircraft. During that year the USAF finally placed an initial order for five JetStars to be fitted for calibration of military navigation aids (C-140A-LMs, serials 59-5958/59-5962) while the Navy ordered two UV-1s as staff transports. These military and civil contracts assured the future of the JetStar and the type was subsequently built in the following versions:

JetStar 6: Initial production version for corporate, non-military US Government agencies, and foreign governments. Powered by JT12A-6 or -6As like the modified second prototype and permanently fitted with slipper tanks as tested on the same aircraft, this model differed from the experimental machines in having a slightly longer fuselage (overall length of 60 ft 5 in/18·41 m versus 58 ft 10 in/17·93 m) and in being fitted with rubber-boot de-icers on the leading edge of the wing and tail surfaces. In typical executive layouts the JetStar 6 seated ten passengers in addition to a crew of two. The first production aircraft (N9201R) was flown at Marietta in the summer of 1960 and received its FAA Type Approval in August 1961. Eighty of these aircraft were built but many were later modified as JetStar 8s or JetStar 731s. Among the non-corporate customers of this version were the Federal Aviation Agency (one aircraft), the National Aeronautics and Space Administration (two), the Canadian Ministry of Transport (two), the Luftwaffe (three), and the Indonesian Air Force (three).

One of the NASA aircraft—c/n 5003, N814NA, originally NASA 14—is operated by the Dryden Flight Research Center from Edwards AFB, California, as a General Purpose Airborne Simulator (GPAS). Fitted with an electronic variable-stability and control system, it is able to simulate the handling characteristics of a wide variety of advanced aircraft. Other tests conducted with this aircraft have included evaluation of wing coating and cleaning devices, and, more recently of pylon-mounted propeller-fans.

JetStar 8: Beginning with the 97th production aircraft, Lockheed installed 3,300 lb (1,497 kg) thrust JT12A-8 turbojets, and a number of JetStar 6s were also retrofitted with the more powerful engines. Sixty-six JetStar 8s were built, with

As part of NASA's Aircraft Energy Efficient Program the third production JetStar was modified in 1981 to measure and record acoustical data from a pylon-mounted Hamilton Standard 2-ft diameter SR-3 propeller-fan. (*NASA*)

the last being delivered in 1973 when production of the type was temporarily suspended. Several JetStar 8s were brought up to JetStar 731 standard by AiResearch. Notable foreign operators included the Royal Bank of Canada (one aircraft), the late Shah of Iran (one), the Kuwait Government (one), the Libyan Air Force (one), and the Royal Saudi Air Force (two).

JetStar 731: After the Lockheed-Georgia Company had begun working on a turbofan-powered version of its business jet, the AiResearch Aviation Company undertook the modification of a JetStar to use four TFE 731 1 turbofans developed by its parent company, the Garrett Corporation. First flight of the re-engined aircraft—N731A, the eleventh production JetStar 6 (c/n 5011) which had originally been delivered to the Indonesian Air Force—was made on 10 July, 1974. As the use of turbofans resulted in significant reductions in fuel consumption and noise levels, AiResearch decided to offer TFE 731-1 conversions to JetStar customers. The first production conversion, which also incorporated some aerodynamic and avionics changes, was completed in March 1976. By the summer of 1980, thirty-one JetStar 6s and twenty-four JetStar 8s had been converted to JetStar 731s.

JetStar II (N2MK) of the Morrison-Knudsen Company Inc at its home base: Gowen Field, Boise. (*M-K*)

JetStar II: Built by Lockheed-Georgia as new airframes to be powered by the Garrett turbofans as fitted to the aircraft modified by AiResearch, the JetStar IIs were delivered with 3,700 lb (1,678 kg) thrust TFE 731-3s, They incorporate a number of improvements including new external tanks beneath and forward of the wing but not protruding above and aft as did the slipper tanks originally fitted to the JetStar 6/8s. The revised fuel tank arrangement provides a total of 3,686 US gal (10,168 litres) versus 2,660 gal (10,069 litres) for the earlier models. The first JetStar II (N5527L) was flown at Marietta on 18 August, 1976, and received its FAA certification in December of that year. Forty JetStar IIs have been built—with the last being delivered to the Iraqi Government in 1980—to bring total JetStar production to 204 aircraft, including prototypes.

C-140A-LM: Basically similar to the civil JetStar 6s, these five navaid-calibration aircraft (59-5958/59-5962) were delivered beginning in September 1961 to the 1866th Flight Checking Flight of the Air Force Communications Service at Scott AFB, Illinois. In 1981, the four surviving aircraft were still

C-140A (59-5958) of the Air Force Communications Service at Da Nang in January 1968. (*Robert C. Mikesh*)

operated by this unit, now elevated to squadron status. They are powered by four 3,000 lb (1,361 kg) thrust Pratt & Whitney J60-P-5 (military version of the JT12A-6) turbojets.

C-140B-LM: Utility transport version with passenger/cargo convertible interior. Also powered by J60-P-5s, these five aircraft (62-4197/62-4201) were almost immediately brought up to the VC-140B standard. Although it was the last JetStar version to be ordered by the USAF, the C-140B was first to enter service, doing so in April 1961.

VC-140B-LM: Six JetStar 6s (61-2488/61-2493) powered by J60-P-5s were ordered as VIP transports for use by the 1254th Air Transport Wing, Special Air Missions, at Andrews AFB, Maryland. Along with the five modified C-140Bs, these aircraft were still operated in 1981 by the 1st Military Airlift Squadron, 76th Military Airlift Wing, at Andrews AFB.

C-140C-LM: Designation given in September 1962 to two JetStar 6s ordered for the Navy as UV-1s but not delivered.

UV-1: BuNos 149820/149821 were assigned to two aircraft ordered in 1960 as staff transports by the US Department of the Navy. The contract was cancelled before delivery of these UV-1s.

The first VC-140B in the markings in which it was delivered to the 1254th Air Transport Wing, Special Air Missions. (*USAF*)

Including military-operated aircraft in the United States and abroad, 190 out of the 204 JetStars were still in worldwide service at the end of 1980, with the most numerous version being the AiResearch-modified JetStar 731.

Related Temporary Design Designations: CL-329, CL-976, CL-1049, GL-210, GL-329/GL-330, GL-349, LG140-101/LG140-116, LG1329-101/LG1329-110, LG2329-101/LG2329-106 and LG3329-101/LG3329-102

	Orpheus-powered prototype	C-140B	JetStar II
Span, ft in	53 8	53 8	54 5
(m)	(16·36)	(16·36)	(16·59)
Length, ft in	58 10	60 5	60 5
(m)	(17·93)	(18·41)	(18·41)
Height, ft in	20 6	20 6	20 5
(m)	(6·25)	(6·25)	(6·22)
Wing area, sq ft	523	542·5	542·5
(sq m)	(48·58)	(50·4)	(50·4)
Empty weight, lb	15,139	19,302	24,750
(kg)	(6,867)	(8,755)	(11,226)
Loaded weight, lb	29,333	39,288	41,535
(kg)	(13,305)	(17,821)	(18,840)
Maximum weight, lb	38,841	42,000	44,500
(kg)	(17,618)	(19,051)	(20,185)
Wing loading, lb/sq ft	56·1	72·4	76·6
(kg/sq m)	(273·8)	(353·6)	(373·8)
Power loading, lb/lb st	3	3·3	2·8
Maximum speed, mph at ft	613/36,000	573/36,000	547/30,000
(km/h at m)	(986/10,975)	(922/10,975)	(800/9,145)
Cruising speed, mph	502	507	504
(km/h)	(808)	(816)	(811)
Initial rate of climb, ft/min	6,400	5,600	4,150
(m/min)	(1,951)	(1,707)	(1,265)
Service ceiling, ft	—	38,000	43,000
(m)		(11,580)	(13,105)
Maximum payload range, miles	1,725	2,220	2,995
(km)	(2,775)	(3,570)	(4,820)
Maximum fuel range, miles	—	2,345	3,190
(km)		(3,775)	(5,135)

Lockheed 188 Electra

The first flight of the propeller-turbine Vickers Viscount in July 1948 and of the turbojet de Havilland Comet one year later, and their entry into sustained scheduled service, respectively in April 1953 with BEA and in May 1952 with BOAC, initially had little impact on the US domestic airline industry. Even Pan American's order for three Comet 3s placed in October 1952 went almost unnoticed. However, the ordering of sixty Viscount 744/745s by Capital Airlines between May and November 1954, together with the first flight in July of that year of the Boeing 367-80—the forebear of the 707 series—finally awakened the trunk airlines to the reality of the jet age. Carriers, which earlier had been cool to the idea, scrambled to acquire propeller-turbine and turbojet-powered airliners. Thus, the year 1955 saw the initial ordering of the Lockheed Electra in June, of the Douglas DC-8 in September, and of the Boeing 707 in October.

Electra N5501 (c/n 188-1005), in the markings in which it was delivered to Eastern Air Lines on 31 January, 1959. (*Eastern*)

Before placing its first order for three Viscounts, Capital had approached Lockheed—then the American transport aircraft manufacturer showing the most interest in the propeller-turbine (design of the YC-130 and R7V-2 had both been initiated in 1951)—to see if it would be prepared to develop such an airliner. Indeed the Burbank firm was willing but, following its unsuccessful attempt to interest other US airlines in an aircraft of this type, the manufacturer had to decline Capital's request. The same fate awaited the CL-303—a twin propeller-turbine, high-wing design with 60- to 70-passenger capacity—which was studied in late 1954 to meet an American Airlines' requirement for a short-haul airliner but proved unattractive to other carriers. Undaunted, American Airlines issued revised specifications early the following year and this time was successful.

Coming closer to what other carriers desired, American's updated specification called for a four-engined design with accommodation for 75 passengers and a range of 2,000 miles (3,220 km). The new range requirement, which considerably exceeded the 500 to 800 miles (805 to 1,290 km) sought earlier, nevertheless was not to preclude the aircraft from being profitable when operated on shorter segments. To meet these requirements Lockheed proposed its CL-310 design with low wing, circular cross-section fuselage and either four Rolls-Royce Darts or Napier Elands. American Airlines was pleased, but Eastern Air Lines, the other carrier then ready to select a propeller-turbine powered aircraft, wanted more range (2,500 miles/4,025 km), larger capacity (85 to 90 seats) and a higher cruising speed (350 mph/563 km/h). By switching to Allison 501Ds (a civil version of the T56-A-1 with which the YC-130 had first been flown in August 1954), Lockheed was able to increase the size of the CL-310 and boost its performance while retaining the favourable economics of the earlier version. This time both American and Eastern were satisfied and contract negotiations were successfully completed on 8 June, 1955, when the former ordered 35 aircraft, and on 27 September, 1955, when the latter announced a 40-aircraft order.

With its powerplant installation benefiting from Lockheed's experience with the T56-powered C-130 and more directly with the Super Constellation prototype and one of the R7V-2s—which were respectively fitted with one and four 501D engines for flight trials of the commercial version of the Allison propeller-

397

turbines—the first Model 188 was completed in 26 months. By that time Lockheed had received firm orders for 129 aircraft from six US airlines, three foreign carriers and the manufacturer of the Electra's engines, and conditional orders and options for at least 48 aircraft. It thus appeared that the future of this commercial programme was solidly established—a particularly welcome situation for Lockheed as curtailment of the US defence budget had resulted in the cancellation during 1957 of $119 mn in contracts for F-104s, T2Vs, WV-2s and W2Vs.

On 6 December, 1957, eight weeks ahead of schedule, the first Electra (N1881, c/n 188-1001) was flown from the Lockheed Air Terminal to Palmdale by a flight-test crew captained by 'Fish' Salmon. The remarkably trouble-free trial programme, in which four aircraft took part, led to the award of an FAA Type Certificate on 22 August, 1958. Deliveries to airline customers began on 8 October, 1958, when the seventh Electra was accepted by Eastern Air Lines, and by the end of that year this carrier had received six more Model 188As while four other aircraft had gone to American Airlines. However, pilots' strikes prevented these carriers from beginning Electra service until early in the following year, Eastern introducing the type on 12 January and American on 23 January. Other problems affecting the domestic airline industry, notably the economic recession which hit the United States during 1958, slowed Electra sales. Nevertheless, Lockheed was able to add nineteen firm and conditional orders before the type's entry into service.

The aircraft ordered up to that time were of two versions, the Models 188A and 188C, powered normally by four 3,750 eshp Allison 501D-13s or -13As and also available with 4,050 eshp 501D-15s. Normal accommodation was for 66 to 80 passengers, with six additional seats in a lounge, but the Electra could be adapted to carry up to 98 passengers in high-density configuration. A three-man flight crew and two cabin attendants were standard. The Model 188C was a longer-ranged development of the 188A with increased fuel tankage (6,490 US gal/24,567 litres versus 5,450 gal/20,631 litres) and higher take-off gross weight (116,000 lb/ 52,617 kg versus 113,000 lb/51,256 kg). The first Model 188C, the 57th Electra, was delivered to Northwest Airlines on 19 July, 1959. The Model 188B designation was unofficially used within Lockheed for 188C aircraft (c/ns 188-2001 to 188-2022) which had track-mounted passenger seats, two additional lavatories and a navigator station, and were intended for foreign operators. A total of 116

Model 188C (HC-AZJ, c/n 188-2004) of TAME—Transportes Aéreos Nacionales Ecuatorianos at the Simon Bolivar Airport, Guayaquil, in August 1974. (*René J. Francillon*)

Ansett-ANA's VH-RMC, the last Electra to go through the LEAP modification programme, over Model 188A N9745C in service with Western Airlines. (*Lockheed*)

Model 188As were built and most went to the following original airline customers: American and Eastern (35 aircraft each), National (14), Western (12), Braniff (9), TAA (3), and Ansett-ANA (2); principal customers for the 54 Model 188Cs were: Northwest (18 aircraft), KLM (12), Qantas (4), Garuda, PSA and TEAL (3 each). As detailed later, a series of accidents and passenger preference for jetliners combined to curtail the production of the type, and the last Electra, a Model 188C, was delivered to Garuda on 15 January, 1961.

Entering service with Eastern Air Lines on 12 January, 1959 (New York–Miami), and on 23 January with American Airlines (New York–Chicago), the Electra initially proved very popular with passengers and airlines alike in spite of a fatal accident on 3 February, 1959, which was blamed on pilot error. Service operations, however, revealed the need to correct a propeller resonance problem by changing the incidence of the engine nacelle and this modification programme cost Lockheed $7 mn. More serious was the mid-air disintegration of a Braniff Model 188A which crashed in Texas on 29 September, 1959. No explanation could at first be found for this crash but on 17 March, 1960, a similar accident resulted in the loss of a Northwest Model 188C in Indiana. In fourteen months of service three Electras had been lost. Public confidence in the type vanished, and the press and members of Congress called for its grounding; on the basis of preliminary investigation, the FAA elected instead to impose on 25 March, 1960, a maximum cruising speed reduction from 400 to 316 mph (644 to 508 km/h), and then to 295 mph (475 km/h), while the manufacturer and government agencies sought to determine the cause of the inflight disintegrations.

Weakness of the engine mountings, which led to nacelle vibration and then to wing flexing and final failure at the root, was determined to be the cause. Lockheed accepted responsibility and spent $25 mn on the Lockheed Electra Achievement Program (LEAP) to modify the existing Model 188A/Cs by adding bracing and stiffeners to the engine nacelles and replacing some of the wing skin with heavier-gauge panels. The last twenty-five aircraft were so fitted before delivery. The modification programme was entirely successful and on 5 February, 1961, the FAA lifted its speed restriction. In the process of identifying the cause of the earlier failures, finding a satisfactory cure and modifying the aircraft at its expense, Lockheed's reputation for integrity was enhanced within the airline industry. Unfortunately, this confidence was not shared by the uninformed public — and, in spite of a major advertising campaign, little could be achieved to restore faith in the Electra. Moreover, the trend in short- to medium-haul US operations was already moving in favour of the jetliners (United Air Lines had ordered Sud-Aviation Caravelles in February 1960 and in December of that year had joined with Eastern to launch the Boeing 727 on its record career). No further orders for the Electra were received after the temporary speed restriction had been imposed, with the last firm sales contract (the third Model 188A for Trans-Australia Airlines) being signed on 26 February, 1960.

Seen here in its original PSA markings as N171PS, this Model 188C was first operated by this carrier in 1959. After being used by a number of other operators, it was re-acquired by PSA in August 1975 for service to the Lake Tahoe resort area. (*Lockheed*)

Among the original Electra customers, American became the first to reduce its fleet of Model 188As when during 1962 it disposed of nine aircraft. Other carriers followed almost immediately and this trend was accelerated after the Boeing 727 entered service in 1964. On the other hand, some carriers were highly satisfied with the type. Notably, PSA (Pacific Southwest Airlines) found it to be ideal for its operations within California and supplemented its three new Electras with three used aircraft, but was forced to move to a 727 fleet in 1968–69; nevertheless Electras were again acquired in 1975 when it started serving Lake Tahoe where jet operations were banned. Eastern Air Lines, the type's first operator, used its Electras as back-ups for Douglas DC-9s on the Boston–New York–Washington shuttle until 1977.

The Electra N282F *Resolute*, c/n 188-1084, of Overseas National Airways was delivered to National Airlines as the Model 188A N5006K in December 1955. It was converted to Model 188AF, with two large cargo doors, by Lockheed Aircraft Service Company in the summer of 1968. (*Guido Cortone*)

After displacement from passenger service with the major carriers, the Electras found a ready market in three areas. At least fifty-seven were converted to various freighter configurations—the most important being that undertaken by the Lockheed Aircraft Service Company in 1968 and involving forty aircraft fitted with reinforced flooring and either one or two cargo loading doors on the port side of the fuselage (a 6 ft 8 in by 11 ft 3 in/2·03 m by 3·43 m forward door being standard and a 6 ft 8 in by 8 ft 3 in/2·03 m by 2·51 m aft door optional) — and most of these cargo aircraft were still operated in 1981. Other Electras went to private charter and travel organizations while the type achieved considerable success in Latin America. Particularly noteworthy has been its use on the Ponte Aérea (air bridge or shuttle service) between Rio de Janeiro's Santos Dumont and São Paulo's Congonhas Airports. The use of the Electra on this heavily travelled route (1,650,000 passengers in 1979, with flights every thirty minutes in each direction and an average load factor of 82 per cent) was dictated by the ban on jet operations at the Santos Dumont airport. In 1981, Varig was still contributing

PP-VJO, a Model 188A Electra (ex-American Airlines N6109A, c/n 188-1041), landing at Santos Dumont Airport, Rio de Janeiro, while operated on the Ponte Aérea by Varig. (*Varig*)

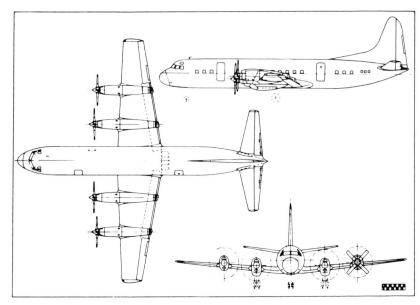

Lockheed Model 188A Electra

twelve Electras and flight crews to the Cruzeiro/Transbrasil/Varig/VASP pool on this route. Also of special interest is the use by Nordair of two specially-equipped Electras which are operated under Canadian Government contract for ice reconnaissance.

Non-airline use of the Electra had begun much earlier, with the sixth aircraft (c/n 188-1006) being delivered in July 1958 to the Allison Division of the General Motors Corporation for use as an engine testbed. Soon after the third Model 188A was modified as an aerodynamic prototype for the P3V-1 Orion patrol aircraft; details of this conversion appear in the Orion chapter. In 1967 this aircraft was acquired by NASA; registered N927NA it was operated by NASA until the late seventies for magnetic, aerodynamic and astronomical research. The US Navy also leased in 1960–61 the 130th Electra which, carrying the registration N181H and fitted with external radomes for tracking equipment, was operated by the Pacific Missile Range at NAS Point Mugu, California, for missile tracking. In 1973 this aircraft was modified by the Lockheed Aircraft Service Company and since then has been operated by the National Center for Atmospheric Research as a heavily-instrumented aircraft.

Victim of a series of highly-publicized accidents early in its operations and quickly rendered obsolete in the eyes of the public by the introduction of pure-jet transports, the Electra had an abbreviated production and first-line service life. Yet, it subsequently proved to be an outstanding airliner, with performance on short routes very close to that of jet-powered aircraft but with much lower fuel consumption. The latter factor led Lockheed to consider re-opening the production line during the late seventies by producing a modernized version based on the Orion but fitted with revised tail surfaces and a longer fuselage. By then, however, it was too late and, much to the sorrow of some airlines' controllers and financial analysts looking with dismay at steadily rising fuel prices and at the high fuel consumption of jetliners, the scheme was stillborn.

Related Temporary Design Designations: CL-292, CL-310, CL-328, CL-355, CL-367/CL-368, CL-390, CL-412, CL-435, CL-470, CL-472, CL-492, CL-501, CL-548/CL-549, CL-559/CL-560, CL-572/CL-573, CL-587, CL-701, CL725, CL-800 and CL-1251.

Span 99 ft (30·18 m); length 104 ft 6 in (31·85 m); height 32 ft 10 in (10 m); wing area 1,300 sq ft (170·77 sq m).

Empty weight 57,400 lb (26,036 kg); maximum take-off weight 113,000 lb (51,256 kg); wing loading 86·9 lb/sq ft (300·1 kg/sq m); power loading 7·5 lb/eshp (3·4 kg/eshp).

Maximum speed 448 mph at 12,000 ft (721 km/h at 3,660 m); cruising speed 373 mph (600 km/h); initial rate of climb 1,970 ft/min (600 m/min); service ceiling 28,400 ft (8,655 m); range 2,200 miles (3,540 km) with maximum payload of 33,800 lb (15,331 kg) or 2,770 miles (4,455 km) with 17,500 lb (7,938 kg) payload.

Data for Model 188A. The Model 188C was dimensionally identical but, operating at a maximum take-off weight of 116,000 lb (52,617 kg) could carry a payload of 11,200 lb (5,080 kg) over a 3,500-mile (5,630-km) sector.

Lockheed LASA-60 Santa Maria

The first aircraft to originate from Lockheed-Georgia was a single-engined light utility transport, with high wing and a fixed nosewheel undercarriage. Designed by the Mooney brothers to meet a specification prepared by General Juan Azcarate of Mexico, this simple machine was generally in the same class as the mass-produced Cessna 180 and 185 and its design was undertaken in January 1959 with a view to attracting a share of this lucrative market. However, as the overheads of a company of the size of Lockheed would excessively burden such a small and relatively low-priced aircraft, it was decided that after the production and testing of two prototypes, quantity manufacture would be undertaken by licensees in countries combining a good potential market with low labour costs.

The second GELAC-built LASA-60 with the Mexican registration in which it was delivered to Lockheed-Azcarate S.A. as a pattern aircraft. (*Lockheed*)

Already, before initiating the design of this six-passenger aircraft, Lockheed had conducted market studies which led it to invest in two foreign companies specially organized to produce this aircraft. In Mexico, the associated company was Lockheed-Azcarate S.A. in San Luis Potosi, while in Argentina it was Aviones Lockheed-Kaiser Argentina; but the Argentine venture, for which a new factory was to have been built in Córdoba, did not come to fruition. The Mexican organization, on the other hand, was more successful, and its acronym, together with the last two digits of the year in which aircraft certification was obtained, supplied the LASA-60 designation to the utility transport from Georgia.

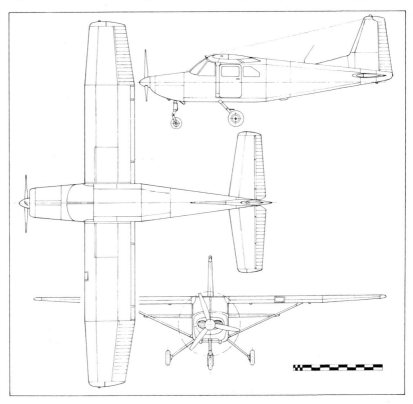

Lockheed LASA-60 Santa Maria

To obtain good field performance at higher elevations, the LASA-60s (design designation L-402) were fitted with high-lift Fowler flaps and were powered by either a 250 hp Continental IO-470R (first prototype) or 260 hp turbo-supercharged TSIO-470B (second aircraft) six-cylinder engine driving a two-blade propeller. The first aircraft, registered N601L in the United States, was flown at Marietta on 15 September, 1959. It was followed shortly after by the second prototype, which was delivered as a pattern aircraft to Lockheed-Azcarate with the registration XB-GUZ. This company produced eighteen LASA-60s—the first of them flying on 21 March, 1961—for service at Cozumel with the 201 Escadrilla Aérea de Buscate y Salvamento of the Fuerza Aérea Mexicana.

Lockheed also sold the licence rights to Aeronautica Macchi, with this Italian firm flying the first of its Aermacchi-Lockheed AL 60B-1s on 19 April, 1961. Macchi had better success with the type and developed the AL 60B-2 with 260 hp TSIO-470B engine and the AL 60B-3 with a 310 hp GIO-470-1 geared engine. A more drastic change was made with the 340 hp Lycoming GSO-480-B1 powered AL 60C-4 which was fitted with a conventional undercarriage and an aft entry door for cargo loading and parachute training. From this latter type was developed the Aeritalia-Aermacchi AM.3C forward air control aircraft, which went on to be built in South Africa by the Armaments Development and Production Corporation (later Atlas Aircraft Corporation) as the Bosbok. The South African company also developed from that aircraft the C4M Kudu which retained the wings and 340 hp Lycoming GSO-480-B1B6 of the AM.3C but had a larger fuselage, with accommodation for eight people. In 1980, Bosboks and Kudus were serving with Nos.41 and 42 Squadrons, SAAF.

Span 39 ft 4 in (11·99 m); length 28 ft 1 in (8·56 m); height 10 ft 8 in (3·25 m); wing area 210 sq ft (19·51 sq m).

Empty weight 2,024 lb (918 kg); loaded weight 3,532 lb (1,602 kg); maximum weight 3,752 lb (1,702 kg); wing loading 16·8 lb/sq ft (82·1 kg/sq m); power loading 13·6 lb/hp (6·2 kg/hp).

Maximum speed 167 mph at 15,000 ft (269 km/h at 4,570 m); cruising speed 130 mph (209 km/h); initial rate of climb 930 ft/min (283 m/min); service ceiling 23,100 ft (7,040 m); range 550 miles (885 km).

Data for the original Lockheed-Georgia built LASA-60.

Lockheed P-3 (P3V) Orion

Nineteen years after entering service with Patrol Squadron Eight (VP-8) at NAS Patuxent River in July 1962, the Orion remains a most important land-based anti-submarine patrol aircraft. Not only does it equip 26 front-line and 12 reserve patrol squadrons of the US Navy, as well as other units of that Service, but it is also flown by the Royal Australian Air Force, the Canadian Armed Forces, the Iranian Revolutionary Air Force, the Royal New Zealand Air Force, Kongelige Norske Luftforsvaret, and the Ejercito del Aire in Spain. Moreover, the type is still to enter service with the Japanese Maritime Self-Defense Force and the Marineluchtvaartdienst. Production of the Orion, which reached an important milestone on 12 December, 1979, when the 500th aircraft was delivered to VP-26 at NAS Brunswick, Maine, was uncertain at the end of 1981. However, if Lockheed's current efforts to continue upgrading the P-3's performance and capability are successful, it may very well proceed until close to the end of the last decade of the Twentieth Century. Should this take place, the Orion would vie with the Hercules to have the longest production life of any aircraft. Quite a tribute, indeed, to the soundness of both of these workhorses!

This maritime patrol aircraft originated in 1957 when Lockheed proposed a straightforward development of the Electra airliner to meet the requirements of the Navy Type Specification No.146. As by then the company was the most experienced American manufacturer of this type of aircraft, and as the Electra had the size and performance necessary for the mission, the Lockheed proposal easily won the competition and an initial research and development contract was awarded in May 1958. Immediately, the pace of the programme was accelerated, with Lockheed flying the modified third Electra (c/n 188-1003, N1883) as a YP3V-1 aerodynamic prototype on 19 August, 1958, the mock-up of the production aircraft being inspected during the following month, and a pre-production contract for long lead-time items being awarded in February 1959.

Whereas the aerodynamic prototype had initially been flown with only limited modifications—including the installation of a dummy magnetic anomaly detection boom and of a fairing which projected beneath the forward fuselage to simulate the weapons bay—it was subsequently converted to a standard more closely matching that of production aircraft. Designated YP3V-1 and assigned the BuNo 148276, it then had a forward fuselage shortened by 7 ft (2·13 m) and was fitted with most of the planned avionics equipment. In this form it was first flown on 25 November, 1959, and its successful evaluation led in October 1960 to the award of a first production contract for seven P3V-1s (BuNos 148883/148889).

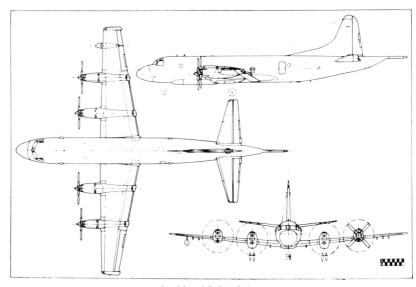

Lockheed P-3A Orion

Retaining the Allison propeller-turbines of the Electra, these P3V-1s had the shorter fuselage and MAD boom of the YP3V-1, and had accommodation for a crew of twelve. The offensive load—including mines, conventional or nuclear depth bombs, rockets or torpedoes—was carried in the forward fuselage bay and on wing racks, while sonobuoys and markers were carried in the aft fuselage. Fuel-tank arrangement was revised to boost internal capacity from 5,450 US gal (20,631 litres) for the Model 188A Electra to 9,200 gal (34,826 litres) for the Model 185 Orion, with the fuel being carried in one fuselage tank and four wing tanks. The first P3V-1 was flown on 15 April, 1961, and since then the type, which was redesignated P-3 in September 1962, has appeared in the following versions:

YP3V-1 (YP-3A): After being used for static tests, the third Electra was modified as an aerodynamic prototype for the Orion, as described earlier, and was first flown in this form on 19 August, 1958. During 1959 its forward fuselage was shortened by 7 ft (2·13 m) and most of the avionic equipment was installed when the aircraft became the YP3V-1. It was redesignated YP-3A in September 1962 and NP-3A later. After completion of sundry tests for the manufacturer and the Navy, it was transferred to the National Aeronautics and Space Administration in 1967. With this organization it was first numbered NASA 927 but in August 1969 was registered N927NA.

P-3A (P3V-1): Powered by four 4,500 eshp Allison T56-A-10Ws, the 157 P-3As (P3V-1s prior to September 1962) were produced, beginning in 1961, as the initial service version for the US Navy. In addition to the shorter forward fuselage, MAD boom, and mission equipment, the P-3As differed from the Electras in having strengthened airframes, salt-water corrosion treatment, and modified engine mountings. Maximum weapons load of 19,252 lb (8,733 kg) could be carried in the fuselage bay and on ten underwing pylons. Principal submarine detection equipment included an APS-80 radar, an ASQ-10 MAD gear, and an ASR-3 detector to sniff the diesel exhaust released by the snorkel of submerged submarines. First tested on the 35th production Orion, the improved 'Deltic' detection equipment was incorporated during production, beginning with the 110th P-3A, and was retrofitted to most earlier aircraft. Moreover, most surviving P-3As were later re-engined with 4,910 eshp T56-A-14s, were equipped with an APU (auxiliary power unit) forward of the weapons bay, and were fitted to carry Martin Bullpup missiles beneath the wing. A number of P-3As were modified as EP-3A, NP-3A, RP-3As, VP-3As, WP-3As, EP-3Bs and EP-3Es, while two batches of P-3As were transferred to the Ejercito del Aire respectively in 1973 and 1978.

EP-3A: One P-3A (BuNo 149673) was modified for electronic reconnaissance experiments, with its MAD boom being deleted and specialized equipment being fitted within radomes beneath the forward fuselage and wing centre-section. The EP-3A was successively operated by the Naval Air Test Center at NAS Patuxent River, the Naval Weapons Laboratory at NAS Dahlgreen, and Air Test and Evaluation Squadron One (VX-1) also at NAS Patuxent River.

NP-3A: Designation applying to both the ex YP-3A before its transfer to NASA and to one specially modified WP-3A (BuNo 149674) which were used for sundry tests.

RP-3A: Two P-3As (BuNos 149667 and 150500) were modified for use by Airborne Oceanographic Development Squadron Eight (VXN-8) at NAS Patuxent River. A third, BuNo 149670, was more extensively modified for electronic experiments at the Naval Research Laboratory.

VP-3A: Three WP-3As (BuNos 149675, 149676 and 150496) phased out from VW-4 in 1975 were converted as staff transports in 1976 for use by the Chief of Naval Operations, and the C-in-C of the Atlantic and Pacific Fleets.

WP-3A: As replacement for the Lockheed WC-121Ns of Weather Reconnaissance Squadron Four (VW-4), four P-3As (BuNos 149674/149676 and 150496) had their MAD boom removed and a large ventral radome added in 1971–72. They were later again modified as an NP-3A and VP-3As.

P-3B: Beginning with the 158th Orion, Lockheed switched to the P-3B version which was delivered with 4,910 eshp T56-A-14s and 'Deltic' detection equipment as fitted to late production P-3As. During the course of production provision for Bullpup missiles was added and this was retrofitted to earlier P-3Bs. The effectiveness of the P-3B has been progressively upgraded, notably through the installation of a TacNav Mod (Tactical Navigation Modification) package. A total of 124 P-3Bs were delivered to the US Navy, ten went to the RAAF (plus one

A Patrol Squadron Four (VP-4) P-3B off Oahu, Hawaii, on 19 July, 1978. (*US Navy*)

replacement aircraft transferred from the US Navy), five were built for the RNZAF and five for Kongelige Norske Luftforsvaret.

EP-3B: Electronic monitoring version obtained by modifying two P-3As (BuNos 149669 and 149678); later upgraded as EP-3Es.

YP-3C: The 240th Orion airframe, built in a batch of P-3Bs, was completed as the prototype for an advanced version. It retained the powerplants and airframe of earlier aircraft but was fitted with the 'A-New' integrated ASW and navigation avionics with ASQ-114 computer system. It was first flown on 18 September, 1968.

P-3C: The current production version of the Orion is basically similar to the YP-3C. Main ASW detection equipment includes an APS-115B search radar, an ASQ-81 magnetic anomaly detector, an AQA-7 Directional Acoustics-Frequency Analysis and Recording (DIFAR) system, and AQH-4 multi-track sonar tape recorder. Since it entered production, the P-3C Orion has been and continues to be fitted with more advanced systems under a series of 'update' programmes. Update I, first tested in the spring of 1974, introduced new avionics and electronics software; it was incorporated on production aircraft delivered after January 1975 to the USN and RAAF, and was retrofitted to earlier aircraft. Update II added the necessary control system for Harpoon missiles, an infra-red detection system, a new sonobuoy reference system, and further electronics improvements; Update II aircraft have been produced since August 1977, and

EP-3B, modified from a P-3A airframe (BuNo 149669) for use in the ELINT (Electronic Intelligence) role. This aircraft was later brought up to EP-3E standard. (*Lockheed*)

many earlier aircraft, including the ten for the RAAF, have been so modified. Finally, Update III—introduced on the assembly line in September 1980 and due to be retrofitted to most earlier P-3Cs of the US Navy—features a new sonobuoy receiver and a more powerful APU to cool the added electronics.

In addition to remaining in production for the US Navy—with proposed budget reductions by the Reagan administration curtailing the planned procurement of Orions—the P-3C is on order for the Marineluchtvaartdienst (thirteen Update II aircraft); and will be built under licence in Japan for the JMSDF. Current plans of the latter Service call for three aircraft to be built by Lockheed, four to be assembled in Japan, and 38 to be produced by Kawasaki; delivery of the first aircraft assembled in Japan will take place in May 1982, with the first domestically-produced Orion to follow in March 1983.

P-3C A9-754 of No.10 Squadron, RAAF, based at Edinburgh, South Australia. (*RAAF*)

RP-3D: The 51st P-3C (BuNo 158227) was modified during construction with all ASW equipment being replaced by specialized gear for atmospheric research and magnetic survey. A 1,200 US gal (4,543 litres) tank was added in the weapons bay to increase total capacity to 10,400 gal (39,369 litres). Besides being operated by VXN-8 in Project Magnet to investigate the earth's magnetic field, the RP-3D was used to set on 4 November, 1972, the current Class C, Group II, world's distance in closed-circuit record. Taking off from NAS Patuxent River, Maryland, this Orion was flown by Cdr R. P. Hite and crew to Hudson Bay and Duluth, Minnesota, and returned to Patuxent River after covering 5,445·6 naut miles (10,085·25 km) in $16\frac{1}{2}$ hours.

WP-3D: Two P-3Cs (BuNos 159773 and 159875) were procured as weather reconnaissance aircraft for the National Oceanographic and Atmospheric Administration (NOAA) of the Department of Commerce. Special sensors, which replaced the ASW equipment, were fitted in a broader tail boom, a ventral radome, and boom projecting forward of the nose on the starboard side. These Miami-based aircraft are registered N42RF and N43RF.

EP-3E: The main electronic surveillance version of the Orion was obtained by modifying ten P-3As (BuNos 148887/148888, 149668, 150494, 150497/150498, 150501/150503 and 150505) and upgrading the two EP-3Bs (BuNos 149669 and

N42RF, the first WP-3D operated from Miami by the National Oceanographic and Atmospheric Administration. (*Lockheed*)

149678). In these aircraft the ASW equipment is replaced by electronic monitoring devices including ALD-8 direction-finding, ALQ-110 radar signal analyser, ALR-60 communications interception and recording system, and a digitally-controlled super heterodyne receiver. Numerous radomes and antennae protrude beneath and above the fuselage of the EP-3Es. In 1981 these twelve aircraft were being operated by Fleet Air Reconnaissance/Countermeasure Squadrons One (VQ-1 at NS Agana on Guam) and Two (VQ-2 at NS Rota in Spain).

P-3F: Six maritime patrol aircraft were ordered by the Imperial Iranian Air Force without the necessary equipment for the ASW mission but with a receptacle for inflight-refuelling by Boeing 707-3J9C tankers of that Service. However, the full ASW gear was fitted before the delivery of these aircraft in 1975.

CP-140 Aurora: At the conclusion of a long and often frustrating effort to acquire a Long Range Patrol Aircraft (LRPA)—during which concern over the

CP-140 Aurora (Canadian serial 140101) with one of the Canadair CP-107 Argus which the Aurora has now replaced in service with the Maritime Group, Canadian Armed Forces. (*Lockheed*)

foreign sales practice of Lockheed, and Canadian budgetary limitations, forced several changes and postponements—the Canadian Armed Forces announced in July 1976 the placing of an order for eighteen advanced maritime patrol aircraft derived from the Orion. Designated CP-140 Aurora, and bearing the Canadian serials 140101/140118, these were to combine the airframe and powerplants of the P-3C with the avionics system and data processing capability of the S-3A Viking (including APS-116 search radar, ASQ-501 magnetic anomaly detector, and AN/AYK-10 computer). Interior arrangement was revised to meet specific Canadian needs, with normal accommodation being provided for a crew of eleven, and the weapons bay was adapted to carry and drop the Canadian-developed SKAD/BR search and rescue kit. Moreover, these aircraft are planned to be fitted later with additional equipment in the weapons bay to undertake alternative civil tasks such as aerial survey, pollution control and resources location. First flight of the CP-140, which initially bore the US civil registration N64996, took place at Burbank on 22 March, 1979. Deliveries to the Canadian Armed Forces began in May 1980 and were completed ten months later.

The first US Navy unit to fly Orions was Patrol Squadron Eight (VP-8) at NAS Patuxent River which began its conversion from P2V-5Fs to P3V-1s in July 1962. During the next five years fourteen other first-line squadrons exchanged Neptunes for P-3As and this version of the Orion also replaced Martin SP-5B Marlin flying-boats in five squadrons. From 1966 onward the P-3As were progressively supplemented in service with the Fleet Patrol Force by P-3Bs and the first version of the Orion joined the Reserve Force in 1970 when it was handed over to eleven squadrons. Six years earlier a P-3A assigned to Air Test and Evaluation Squadron One (VX-1) had completed on 1 May, 1964, a remarkable 18-day, 26,550-naut miles (49,170-km) flight around the world during which it was used for a number of operational and experimental activities. All operational P-3As have since been upgraded with 4,910 eshp T56-A-14s and newer avionics, and in 1981 these aircraft still equipped some US Navy Reserve Patrol Force squadrons. Other reserve units are now equipped with P-3Bs to bring the land-based ASW strength of the US Navy to twenty-four Fleet squadrons with P-3Cs and thirteen reserve units with P-3A/Bs.

The much more potent P-3C entered service with VP-30 in late 1969. This version has now been assigned to all Fleet Patrol Force squadrons and in 1981 these units were assigned to Fleet Air Wing Two (FAW-2) at NAS Barbers Point, Hawaii; FAW-3 at NAS Brunswick, Maine; FAW-5 at NAS Patuxent River, Maryland; FAW-10 at NAS Moffett, California; and FAW-11 at NAS Jacksonville, Florida. In addition to operating from these five bases, P-3Cs are deployed regularly overseas, notably to serve with FAW-1 from Agana, Cubi Point, Kadena, and Misawa. Other recent US Navy operators of the Orion have included VQ-1 and VQ-2 (with EP-3Es) and VXN-8 (with RP-3A/Ds). Current orders and additional scheduled procurement guarantee that the Orion will still be in USN service at the end of the century.

Abroad, the Orion was first received by the Royal New Zealand Air Force in 1966 and five P-3Bs (NZ4201/NZ4205) have since been operated by No.5 Squadron at Whenuapai. In Australia No.11 Squadron has operated ten P-3Bs (A9-291/A9-295, A9-297/A9-300 and A9-605, with the last being a replacement aircraft for A9-296 which had crashed before delivery) from RAAF Edinburgh since 1968, while No.10 Squadron has flown ten P-3Cs (A9-751/A9-760) from the same base since 1978. Other foreign operators of the Orion include the Kongelige

The second P-3B Orion (c/n 185C-5302) for Kongelige Norske Luftforsvaret, in the markings it bore when delivered to No.333 Squadron. (*Lockheed*)

The first of three Lockheed-built P-3C Orions for the Japanese Maritime Self Defense Force, during manufacturer's trials in April 1981. (*Lockheed*)

Norske Luftforsvaret (five P-3Bs, serialled KK-L/KK-P, with No.333 Squadron at Andoya since 1968; this unit was strengthened by the arrival of two ex-US Navy P-3Bs which had been ordered in 1980); the Iranian Revolutionary Air Force (which still had six P-3Fs at Bandar Abbas when war with Iraq broke out late in 1980); and the Ejercito del Aire (with six ex-US Navy P-3As serving in 1981 with Escuadrón 221 at La Parra). Future Orion operators announced prior to 1981, when this was written, were the Japanese Maritime Self Defense Force (45 P-3Cs on order) and the Marineluchtvaartdienst (thirteen P-3Cs to re-equip No.320 Squadron at Valkenburg).

Related Temporary Design Designations: CL-367, CL-427, CL-473, CL-482, CL-490, CL-496/CL-497, CL-505/CL-506, CL-520, CL-544, CL-566, CL-568, CL-580, CL-729, CL-734/CL-735, CL-749, CL-758/CL-759, CL-763, CL-766, CL-768, CL-770/CL-771, CL-773, CL-775, CL-777, CL-779/CL-780, CL-783, CL-785/CL-787, CL-790, CL-792, CL-795/CL-797, CL-801, CL-803, CL-808/CL-809, CL-813, CL-821/CL-822, CL-824, CL-826/CL-828, CL-831/CL-834, CL-842/CL-844, CL-850, CL-856/CL-858, CL-860/CL-861, CL-863, CL-866/CL-867, CL-880/CL-884, CL-886, CL-892, CL-897/CL-898, CL-900, CL-902/CL-910, CL-912/CL-913, CL-921, CL-923/CL-924, CL-926/CL-929, CL-943/CL-944, CL-946/CL-955, CL-960/CL-975, CL-991/CL-994, CL-996, CL-998, CL-1012/CL-1017, CL-1035/CL-1040, CL-1042, CL-1063, CL-1069/CL-1071, CL-1127/CL-1128, CL-1130/CL-1134, CL-1143, CL-1148/CL-1150, CL-1152/CL-1153, CL-1155/CL-1156, CL-1162, CL-1164/CL-1167, CL-1169/CL-1170, CL-1174/CL-1177, CL-1180/CL-1181, CL-1183, CL-1185/CL-1186, CL-1188/CL-1189, CL-1191/CL-1194, CL-1202/CL-1207, CL-1209/CL-1210, CL-1215/CL-1218, CL-1227/CL-1233, CL-1501/CL-1510, CL-1512/CL-1517, CL-1519/CL-1521, CL-1523/CL-1524, CL-1527/CL-1535, CL-1537/CL-1550, CL-1566/CL-1571, CL-1576/CL-1579 and CL-1726*

External dimensions have remained constant from the P-3A to the CP-140 while weights and performance have changed only slightly. The following data apply to the current production models of the P-3C:

Span 99 ft 8 in (30·38 m); length 116 ft 10 in (35·61 m); height 33 ft 8½ in (10·27 m); wing area 1,300 sq ft (120·77 sq m).
Empty weight 61,491 lb (27,892 kg); loaded weight 135,000 lb (61,235 kg); maximum weight 142,000 lb (64,410 kg); wing loading 103·8 lb/sq ft (507 kg/sq m); power loading 6·9 lb/eshp (3·1 kg/eshp).
Maximum speed 473 mph at 15,000 ft (761 km/h at 4,570 m); cruising speed 378 mph (608 km/h); initial rate of climb 1,950 ft/min (594 m/min); service ceiling 28,300 ft (8,625 m); mission radius with 3 hr on station 1,550 miles (2,495 km); ferry range 4,765 miles (7,665 km).

*See also CL-520 in Appendix A.

The CL-475 after installation of its three-blade metal rotor and new gyroscopic ring. (*Lockheed*)

Lockheed CL-475

A very late comer in the helicopter field—Lockheed's CL-475 prototype flying thirty-five years after Etienne Oemichen had set the first helicopter record (360 m in a straight line on 14 April, 1924) confirmed by the Fédération Aéronautique Internationale—Lockheed pioneered the now increasingly accepted rigid-rotor concept. Notwithstanding this technical leap, the company was unable to capitalize on its initial success and, after a thirteen-year struggle, bowed out of the field temporarily when the US Army cancelled the development contract for the AH-56A Cheyenne compound helicopter.

The concept of the rigid rotor coupled to a gyroscope system was developed by an Advanced Concepts Group led by Irven Culver to seek significant improvements in performance, cost, reliability, and handling characteristics of helicopters. Following testing of a small radio-controlled vehicle—with a 5 ft (1·52-m) diameter, two blade, hingeless rotor driven by a McCoy 60 model aeroplane engine—the small design team undertook in July 1959 to design and build an experimental two-seat helicopter for full-scale demonstration of the new concept.

Designated CL-475, this research helicopter had a simple structure with steel and aluminium tubing covered with fabric and a Plexiglass cabin with side-by-side seats. Its 140 hp Lycoming VO-360-AIA four-cylinder air-cooled engine initially drove a two-blade wooden rotor, with gyroscopic control being provided by a double metal 'lollipop' attached to the blades and connected to the swashplate by springs. In this form the CL-475, which was registered N6940C, was completed in autumn 1959 and was trucked to Rosamond Lake in the Mojave Desert where initial trials could be made without attracting undue attention, as Lockheed still wished to keep its helicopter research programme out of the limelight.

Excessive vibration was encountered during the first flight on 2 November, 1959, and forced Irv Culver's team to experiment during the next six months with a variety of three- and four-blade wooden rotor designs. The vibration problem, however, was brought within reasonable limits only after the adoption of a three-blade metal rotor and the installation of a new gyroscopic ring attached directly to the swashplate. The CL-475, which in mid-1960 had been moved to the Lockheed facility at Rye Canyon, was then evaluated by FAA, NASA and military pilots and proved to be easy to fly. In fact, a pilot without previous helicopter experience was once able to ferry it alone. Pleased with the results, Lockheed incorporated the rigid-rotor concept in its entry for the US Army light observation helicopter (LOH) competition in 1961. Although the Army did not select this Lockheed design, it had sufficient confidence in the new concept to order jointly with the Navy two Lockheed XH-51 research helicopters.

At the end of its trial programme, the CL-475 was put in storage until 1975, when it was donated by Lockheed to the National Air and Space Museum, Smithsonian Institution. It has now been loaned to the US Army Aviation Museum at Fort Rucker, Alabama.

Rotor diameter 32 ft (9·75 m); height 9 ft 3 in (2·82 m). Empty weight 1,625 lb (737 kg); loaded weight 2,000 lb (907 kg); power loading 14·3 lb/hp (6·5 kg/hp). Maximum speed 90 mph (145 km/h); ceiling in ground effect 2,000 ft (610 m); range 75 miles (120 km).

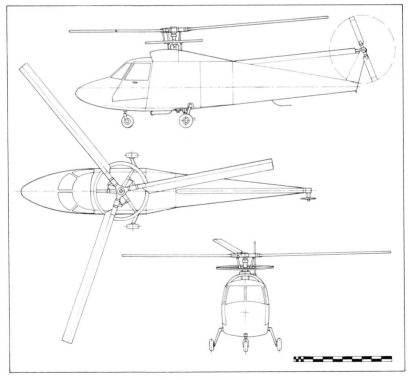

Lockheed CL-475

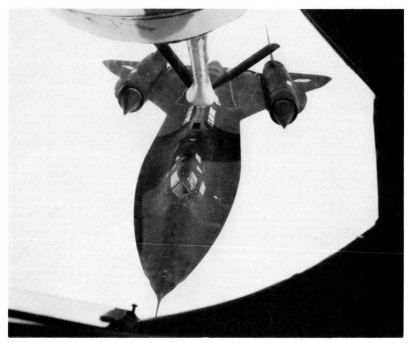

SR-71A-LO (64-17974) about to be refuelled by Boeing KC-135Q-BN 58-0071 over the Mojave Desert, California, on 24 February, 1981. The refuelling receptacle can be seen open atop the fuselage, aft of the cockpit. (*René J. Francillon*)

Lockheed SR-71

Operated in 1981 by the 9th Strategic Reconnaissance Wing at Beale AFB, California, the SR-71A is still the world's fastest and highest-flying operational aircraft. Fifteen years after its entry into service it remains the holder of the official absolute records for speed in a straight line, speed in a closed circuit, and altitude in sustained horizontal flight. Not surprisingly, while some details of its design—such as those pertaining to its unique powerplant system—have been released, most other information is still classified. Notably, particulars about its forebear—the mysterious A-11 announced by President Johnson in February 1964—have been kept heavily shrouded. Therefore, the following narrative represents an attempt to deduce what probably happened and cannot be regarded as an official history.

In March 1954 a British engineer, Randolph Samuel Rae, working for the Summers Gyroscope Company in Santa Monica, California, submitted to the USAF's Air Research and Development Command an unsolicited proposal for a high-altitude aircraft to be powered by a three-stage propeller-turbine using liquid hydrogen and liquid oxygen. Evaluation of this proposal eventually led in October 1955 to the award of a contract to the Garrett Corporation, a Los Angeles firm which a few months earlier had acquired the interests of Rae and the

Summers Gyroscope Co in liquid-hydrogen powerplants. Funds for an aircraft design study were included in the Garrett contract for the Rex I, II and III liquid-hydrogen engines and, in November 1955, the powerplant company awarded a two-month subcontract to Lockheed for this phase of the work. The results of this subcontract came from the Skunk Works in the form of the CL-325 design study. The CL-325-1 had a straight, thin, wing and a slender fuselage, and was designed around two 4,500 lb (2,041 kg) thrust Garrett Rex IIIs. Principal data were: span 79 ft 10½ in (24·35 m), length 153 ft 4 in (46·74 m), take-off weight 45,705 lb (20,731 kg), cruise Mach number 2·5 at 100,000 ft (30,480 m) and range 3,500 miles (5,630 km). The CL-325-2 was of a lighter and smaller configuration, with some of the hydrogen fuel being carried in drop tanks instead of in the fuselage. However, both configurations remained in this early stage as the USAF concluded that Garrett did not have the capability to develop and produce the Rex III engine. Finally, in October 1957, the engine manufacturer was instructed to stop all work after completion of a final study report.

While Garrett was fighting its battle for the Rex programme, Kelly Johnson had become enthusiastic over the potential of liquid hydrogen as fuel for high-altitude aircraft, and in January 1956 Lockheed offered to build two prototypes, with the first to fly within eighteen months from go-ahead. Keenly interested in this offer, the USAF requested proposals for hydrogen-fuelled engines from General Electric and Pratt & Whitney, with the latter being selected. A retroactive contract for the design and construction of the two prototypes was awarded to Lockheed in April 1956 and work on the CL-400 proceeded in earnest. However, within a year Kelly Johnson had serious doubts about the practicality of the exotic fuel and, on his recommendation, development of the CL-400 was cancelled in October 1957.*

Although in the late fifties satellites were expected to provide an increasing share of the reconnaissance over Soviet-bloc countries, the USAF and the CIA still foresaw the need for a specialized aircraft to obtain timely data on a specific target, as it was necessary to wait for the appropriate pass by a satellite, whereas an aircraft could be directed wherever and whenever needed. Accordingly, as the Skunk Works had the necessary experience, Lockheed was directed to proceed, in competition with the Ft Worth Division of General Dynamics, with the development of yet another very-high-performance reconnaissance aircraft. After their two abortive attempts to develop aircraft with hydrogen-fuelled engines, Kelly Johnson and his team decided to use conventional turbojets under development by Pratt & Whitney for the Navy as the JT11D (military designation J58).

Apparently during the early phase of the project, the design team began considering the use of drones to reduce overflight by the manned aircraft and thus undertook development of a specialized remote-controlled vehicle in parallel with that of the aircraft. The latter—which was first mentioned by President Johnson as the A-11, a designation that does not fit either the USAF or Lockheed nomenclatures—was intended to be used either to carry and control the drone, or to operate as the prime reconnaissance system.

The turbojets were installed at about mid-span of the modified delta wing, and inboard-canted, all-moving vertical tail surfaces were situated above the rear of the engine nacelles. In this manner room was also provided atop the fuselage for the D-21 drone designed by the Lockheed Missile & Space Company in close

*See Appendix A.

417

co-operation with Kelly Johnson's team. Bearing a strong resemblance to its A-11 carrier, the single-engined D-21 had a span of 17 ft (5·18 m) and a length of 40 ft (12·19 m), and carried reconnaissance equipment in a forward ventral bay. Details of the high-speed launching of the D-21 from the A-11 are not available, but it is believed that at the end of a mission the trisonic drone was either recovered in flight by specially equipped Lockheed JC-130Bs or parachuted back over designated points. Some forty drones are believed to have been built; they have also been seen with the GTD-21B designation, possibly implying their later modification as target drones.

Lockheed GTD-21B drone in storage at Davis-Monthan AFB, Arizona. (*Ben Knowles via Jay Miller*)

Intended to fly at speeds in excess of Mach 3, the A-11 was built almost entirely of titanium alloys. Yet, in spite of the use of this heat-resistant metal, the airframe was expected to expand during sustained supersonic cruise, thus necessitating the use of chordwise corrugations on the central portion of the wing and the provision of expansion gaps between some panels. The short-span delta wing was supplemented by long chines extending forward on both sides of the fuselage, with these chines contributing to yaw damping at high Mach numbers and providing space for some of the fuel and equipment. The long engine nacelles housing the J58 turbojets, which were designed to burn JP-7 fuel specially blended for low-volatility, were provided with a complex inlet and ejector system, with the inlets contributing as much as 60 per cent of total thrust at Mach 3. Other unusual design features of the A-11 included the use of an undercarriage with three-wheeled main units, and the fitting of fixed fins beneath the nacelle and of a folding fin beneath the rear fuselage.

Flight trials of the A-11 began at Indian Springs Auxiliary AFB, Nevada, on 26 April, 1962. No details have yet been revealed on these tests but it appears that, while the airframe/engine combination was successfully developed, the concept of launching D-21 drones from the A-11 did not fulfil operational expectations. Some twenty-five A-11s were ordered, with known serial numbers including 60-6924 to 60-6948. Some of these machines may have seen limited service with an unidentified unit; eight could still be seen in open storage at Palmdale, California, in 1978. The basic design, however, received a double lease of life as at least four A-11s were modified as YF-12 experimental interceptors while an enlarged version went into limited production as the SR-71.

Following the cancellation of the Mach 3-plus North American XF-108 Rapier in September 1959 due to lack of funds, the USAF found itself without a successor for its Convair F-106 interceptors. Fortunately, the flight-proven A-11 offered a good potential for the development of an interceptor to fulfil the USAF's Specific

YF-12A (60-6934) taking off at the Palmdale Airport. (*Lockheed*)

Science-fiction view of a YF-12A. Note infra-red sensors on the chines and triple-wheeled main undercarriage units. (*Lockheed*)

419

Operational Requirement (SOR) 220. For this role a Hughes AN/ASG-18 pulse doppler fire-control system was installed in the nose of three modified A-11s, which were redesignated YF-12As, while infra-red sensors were fitted at the forward edge of each chine. Armament consisted of four Hughes AIM-47A air-to-air missiles in each of the two chine bays previously used to house the reconnaissance sensors and D-21 control equipment. Known YF-12As include 60-6934/60-6936, while 60-6937 was modified as a YF-12C with equipment changes and chines that extended all the way to the tip of the nose. The existence of a YF-12B version has not been confirmed. The YF-12A/Cs were assigned to the 4786th Test Squadron at Edwards AFB and, besides serving for sundry operational evaluations, were used to set the following world's absolute and Class C, Group III, records at Edwards AFB on 1 May, 1965:

Sustained altitude (Absolute): 80,258 ft/24,463 m
  Col Robert L. Stephens/Lieut-Col Daniel Andre
15/25 km closed-circuit (Absolute): 2,070·102 mph/3,351·5128 km/h
  Col Robert L. Stephens/Lieut-Col Daniel Andre
500 km closed-circuit (Class C): 1,643·042 mph/2,644·225 km/h
  Maj Walter F. Daniel/Maj Noel T. Warner
1,000 km closed-circuit without payload and with 1,000 kg payload (Absolute) and with 2,000 kg (Class C): 1,688·891 mph/2,718·012 km/h
  Maj Walter F. Daniel/Capt James P. Cooney

In spite of its superlative performance, the YF-12 was not adopted as an interceptor mainly because the Southeast Asia War was draining all available funds from the USAF budget. Relegated to the role of research aircraft, the type took part in a comprehensive programme, with NASA pilots joining their USAF colleagues, beginning in December 1969. Eventually, NASA flew all four identified YF-12A/Cs but lost 60-6936 on 24 June, 1971, on the approach to Edwards AFB. The three other aircraft were operated by NASA during most of the seventies until they ran out of airframe hours. Shortly thereafter, on 7 November, 1979, 60-6935 made the last flight for the type when it was delivered to Wright-Patterson AFB for permanent display at the US Air Force Museum. Earlier recognition of the contribution made by the A-11/YF-12 had come in the form of the award of the Collier Trophy to designer Kelly Johnson in 1964. This brilliant aerospace engineer thus became the only person to be so recognized for the second time.

For the strategic reconnaissance mission, Lockheed undertook redesign of the A-11 in February 1963, with the new version appearing as the SR-71A without

SR-71A 64-17967 at Edwards AFB on 27 April, 1967. Some of the sensor covers can be seen beneath the chines. (*USAF*)

Details of the curvature of the chines of the SR-71A-LO. Note canted fins and rudders and large intake cones. (*USAF*)

provision for the D-21 drone but with increased internal fuel tankage. Range could be further extended through inflight refuelling by Boeing KC-135Q, a version of the Stratotanker specially fitted with separate tanks for the JP-7 fuel used by the two 32,500 lb (14,742 kg) thrust Pratt & Whitney JT11D-20B (J58) afterburning turbojets powering the SR-71A. To improve handling characteristics, the chines of the SR-71A were extended forward to the tip of the nose while its tail cone was lengthened to bring overall length to 107 ft 5 in (32·74 m) versus 101 ft (30·78 m) for the YF-12A. Span of 55 ft 7 in (16·94 m) and height of 18 ft 6 in (5·64 m) remained unchanged but gross weight was increased from the YF-12A's 140,000 lb (63,503 kg) to 170,000 lb (77,111 kg). Externally the SR-71A could also be distinguished from the A-11/YF-12A by the absence of the three ventral fins. Cameras and other reconnaissance sensors were housed in the nose section (five different payload configurations) and the chines, enabling the SR-71A to survey over 100,000 sq miles in one hour while flying at Mach 3 above 80,000 ft (24,385 m). Design objectives were a top speed of Mach 4 (about 2,670 mph/4,300 km/h) and a cruising altitude of up to 120,000 ft (36,575 m), but it is not known whether these were actually reached. Reported highest speed and sustained altitude have been respectively 2,193 mph (3,529 km/h) and 85,069 ft (25,929 m) when the SR-71A set the currently standing world's records; yet it is believed that the aircraft was 'held back' during these flights.

By the time of its maiden flight on 22 December, 1964, the type was already committed to production. At least thirty-two aircraft (serials 64-17950/64-17981) were built before production was terminated during 1968. All but three of these aircraft were SR-71As with full reconnaissance capability and crew of two consisting of pilot and reconnaissance systems officer. Two of the exceptions were SR-71Bs (64-17951 and 64-17956) built originally as two-seat trainers—with

The second SR-71B (64-17956) with raised aft cockpit for the instructor. (*USAF*)

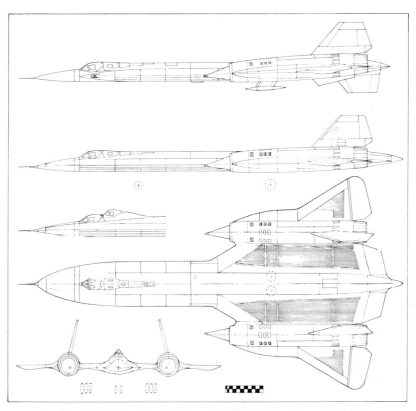

Lockheed SR-71A, with side view of YF-12A (*top*) and nose of SR-71B

instructor's elevated cockpit aft of the pilot's cockpit, and two ventral fins; while the last aircraft (64-17981) was later completed as an SR-71C modified trainer to replace the first SR-71B which had been lost in an accident on 1 November, 1968.

Service use began on 7 January, 1966, with the delivery of 64-17957 to the 4200th Strategic Reconnaissance Wing at Beale AFB, California. Within six months, however, this unit was reorganized as the 9th SRW at the same base. Since then the Wing has been the sole operator of the SR-71A, with its aircraft being regularly deployed to Kadena AB on Guam and to RAF Mildenhall in the United Kingdom. Other deployments, as dictated by current events, have seen the 9th SRW using its 'Blackbirds' — an unofficial name stemming from the special finish intended to absorb heat and distort enemy radar signals — to fly reconnaissance sorties over North Vietnam during the Southeast Asia War, and over the Middle East during the period of tension/war between Israel and its Arab neighbours and during the recent developments in Afghanistan and Iran. In 1981 the 9th SRW continued to be the élite reconnaissance unit of the USAF, with its SR-71A/Bs being kept in top condition through regular overhaul/equipment-modernization programmes performed under contract by the Skunk Works.

In addition to its service duties, the SR-71A has been flown by the USAF to set the following records:

26 April, 1971: 15,000 miles (24,140 km) in 10½ hr with inflight refuelling.
Maj Thomas B. Estes/Maj Dewain C. Vick (the crew was awarded the 1971 Harmon and Mackey trophy for the flight)

27 July, 1976: Height in sustained horizontal flight: 85,069 ft/25,929 m
Capt Robert C. Helt/Maj Larry A. Elliot

27 July, 1976: Speed in a straight line: 2,193·17 mph/3,529·5719 km/h
Capt Eldon W. Joersz/Maj George T. Morgan Jr

27 July, 1976: Speed over a 1,000-km closed circuit: 2,092·294 mph/3,367·2274 km/h
Maj Adolphus H. Bledsoe Jr/Maj John T. Fuller

1 September, 1976: Beale AFB to RAE Farnborough nonstop with air refuelling, including New York to London (3,490 miles/5,617 km) in 1 hr 55 min 42 sec
Maj James V. Sullivan/Maj Noel F. Widdifield

13 September, 1976: London to Los Angeles (5,645 miles/9,085 km) nonstop with air refuelling in 3 hr 47 min 39 sec at an average speed of 1,487 mph (2,393 km/h)
Capt Harold B. Adams/Maj William C. Machorek

Span 55 ft 7 in (16·94 m); length 107 ft 5 in (32·74 m); height 18 ft 6 in (5·64 m).
Take-off weight 170,000 lb (77,111 kg); power loading 2·6 lb/lb st.
Maximum speed 2,250 mph (3,620 km/h); cruising speed Mach 3; ceiling 100,000 ft (30,480 m); unrefuelled range at Mach 3, 3,000 miles (4,830 km).
Estimated characteristics and performance for the SR-71A.

Lockheed VZ-10 (XV-4) Hummingbird

Having proceeded during the late 1950s with the private-venture development of a tethered rig to test the Augmented Jet Ejector Vertical Lift concept, Lockheed-Georgia was able in 1961 to submit to the US Army Transportation Research Command a proposal for a mid-wing VTOL research vehicle. Favourable review of this proposal (Temporary Design Designation GL-224) led to the award in September 1961 of a $2·5 mn contract for the design, construction and testing of two VZ-10 prototypes (Model 330, serials 62-4503 and 62-4504).

Powered by two 3,000 lb (1,361 kg) thrust Pratt & Whitney JT12A-3LH turbojets mounted on the fuselage sides, the VZ-10 Hummingbird was to achieve vertical take-off and landing by directing the jet efflux through a diverter valve in each exhaust. The gases were then ejected at high speed into a mixing chamber by twenty ducts, thus creating a low-pressure area and drawing stream air through doors in the top of the fuselage. Increased mass flow resulted from this mixing and boosted the thrust available for take-off by forty per cent to give the aircraft a VTO thrust-to-weight ratio of 1·17 to 1. The mixing chamber was inclined 12 deg aft to provide a forward-motion component after lift off and, as soon as the speed reached 90 mph (145 km/h), the diverter valve of one engine was to be switched to provide normal thrust. The second engine was then to be similarly switched when speed reached 145 mph (233 km/h). Transition back was to be achieved by reducing speed progressively and then reversing the process.

The first XV-4A in conventional flight mode near Marietta, Georgia. (*Lockheed*)

Intended as a research aircraft, the VZ 10 was relatively small and provided room for only a crew of two side by side, test instrumentation and equipment in two compartments, and 285 US gal (1,079 litres) of fuel in three tanks. The first of these aircraft, which had not yet been fitted with its Augmented Jet Ejector Vertical Lift system, began flight trials in the conventional mode on 7 July, 1962, and was initially used to explore the standard flight envelope. It was then fitted with the diverter valves and ejector ducts for a year of tethered and vertical flights beginning in November 1962. At the onset of this phase, inlet losses, unsatisfactory configuration of the mixing chamber, and deficient roll control prevented the aircraft—which had been redesignated XV-4A in September 1962—achieving vertical take-off. After suitable modifications had been made, this goal was reached on 28 May, 1963, and less than six months later, on 20 November, a full double-transition flight was made for the first time. In February 1964 the two XV-4As were handed over to the US Army but the first was soon lost in an

XV-4B (62-4504). The mainwheels were not fully enclosed. (*Lockheed*)

accident. The second was then transferred to NASA for wind-tunnel testing at the Ames Research Center before being put into storage.

Shortly after the XV-4A trial programme had been terminated, Lockheed undertook to modify the surviving Hummingbird as a direct jet-lift research aircraft to be used in the VTOL Flight Control Technology Program being undertaken at Wright-Patterson AFB, Ohio, by the USAF Flight Dynamics Laboratory. For this purpose its fuselage was slightly enlarged to provide room for four vertically-mounted 3,015 lb (1,368 kg) thrust General Electric J85-GE-19 turbojets, two conventionally-mounted engines of the same type, and increased fuel capacity (740 US gal/2,801 litres). Take-off weight was increased to 12,580 lb (5,706 kg) but, as the exhaust of the two horizontal jets was diverted on take-off and landing through vertical ducts and nozzles to augment the lift of the four vertical J85s, thrust-to-weight ratio for VTO at maximum weight was boosted to 1·44 to 1. The contract for the modified aircraft—Lockheed Model 331, USAF designation XV-4B—was awarded in September 1966 and flight trials began in August 1968. By that time, however, the more pressing budgetary requirements for the Southeast Asia War had resulted in reduced funding for research programmes and the XV-4B's abbreviated career ended on 14 March, 1969, when the aircraft was destroyed in an accident at Marietta.

This view of the XV-4B shows to advantage the engine and undercarriage layout.

425

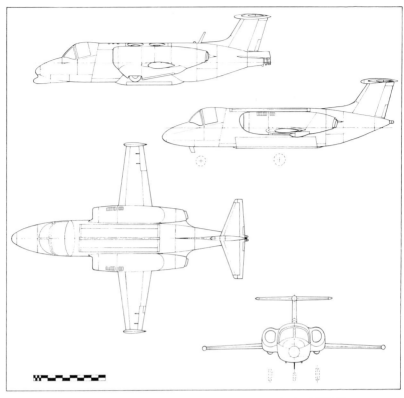

Lockheed XV-4A Hummingbird, with side view (*top*) of XV-4B

Related Temporary Design Designations: GL-204, GL-224, GL-230, GL-233, GL-296, GL-364, GL-380, LG4-101/LG4-102 and LGX-130

XV-4A

Span 25 ft 8 in (7·82 m); length 32 ft 8 in (9·96 m); height 11 ft 9 in (3·58 m); wing area 104 sq ft (9·662 sq m).

Empty weight 4,995 lb (2,266 kg); loaded weight 7,200 lb (3,266 kg); wing loading 69·2 lb/sq ft (338 kg/sq m); power loading 0·85 lb/lb st.

Maximum speed 518 mph at 10,000 ft (833 km/h at 3,050 m); cruising speed 390 mph (628 km/h); initial rate of climb 12,000 ft/min (3,658 m/min); VTO range 335 miles (540 km); maximum range 600 miles (965 km).

XV-4B

Span 27 ft 1 in (8·25 m); length 33 ft 9½ in (10·3 m); height 12 ft 3 in (3·73 m).

Empty weight 7,463 lb (3,385 kg); loaded weight 12,580 lb (5,706 kg); power loading 0·7 lb/lb st.

Maximum speed 463 mph (745 km/h).

The first Model 286 rigid-rotor demonstrator helicopter (*Lockheed*)

Lockheed Models 186 (XH-51) and 286

Satisfactory results obtained with the CL-475 rigid-rotor research vehicle encouraged Lockheed to proceed with the design of a more advanced helicopter combining the novel rotor system with turbine power. Bearing the Temporary Design Designation CL-595, the new helicopter was conceived as a four-seater, with a very aerodynamically-clean, flush-sealed fuselage and retractable aluminium-alloy landing skids to minimize drag, and achieve speeds in excess of 200 mph (322 km/h). Further attention to drag reduction led to the installation of the rotor swashplate within the fuselage and the control rods were brought up through the main rotor shaft. Moreover, the control gyroscope ring of the CL-475 was replaced by three weighted arms mounted above the three-blade rotor.

The anticipated performance of the CL-595 and the demonstrated advantages of the CL-475 attracted the attention of both the US Army and Navy and these Services joined in ordering from Lockheed prototypes of a high-performance research helicopter, with the Navy issuing Contract NOw 62-0665 in February 1962. Bearing the military designation XH-51A and assigned BuNos 151262 and 151263, the two Model 186s differed from the CL-595 design in being fitted as two-seaters to provide space for test instrumentation. Both XH-51As were powered by the 550 shp Pratt & Whitney (Canada) PT6B-9 shaft-turbine and carried 80 US gal (303 litres) of fuel. First flight was made by BuNo 151262 on 2 November, 1962, and, after replacement of the original three-blade rotor with a four-blade unit, the type proved reliable and easy to fly during eighteen months of joint Army–Navy evaluation. In particular, the XH-51As were very stable, without the use of either autopilot or artificial stabilization device, and pilots without rotorcraft experience could convert more rapidly than to standard helicopters.

With its top speed of 174 mph (280 km/h) the XH-51A was already quite fast, yet its rotor system had the potential for operation at substantially higher speed.

427

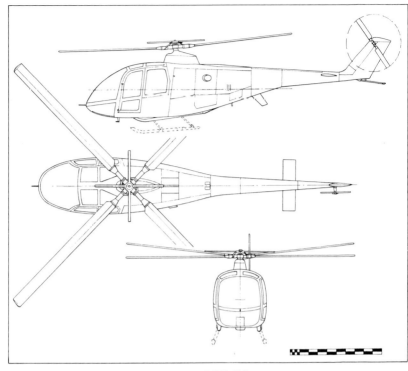

Lockheed XH-51A

Accordingly, the Army funded the modification of the second machine as a compound helicopter with mid-mounted 17 ft (5·18 m)-span wing and a 2,900 lb (1,315 kg) thrust Pratt & Whitney J60-P-2 turbojet on the port side of the fuselage. These modifications resulted in an increase in gross weight from 4,100 to 4,500 lb (1,860 to 2,041 kg). First flown in September 1964 without its turbojet, the XH-51A Compound reached a speed of 272 mph (438 km/h) in May 1965 after its J60 had been installed. Its performance envelope was then progressively expanded until 29 June, 1967, when it set an unofficial speed record for its class of 302·6 mph (486·9 km/h). Both this compound helicopter and the original XH-51A are now preserved in the collection of the US Army Aviation Museum at Fort Rucker, Alabama.

Another Model 186 was built in 1964 and, designated XH-51N, was delivered to NASA at the end of that year. As NASA 531, this five-seater was operated by the Langley Research Center at Hampton, Virginia, for testing advanced helicopter systems. Finally, Lockheed built two Model 286s as five-seat commercial demonstrators. FAA certification was obtained in June 1966 and the Model 286s flew over 150,000 miles (more than 240,000 km) and carried more than 5,000 guests on demonstrations in the United States and Europe. Unfortunately, and in spite of having demonstrated exceptional manoeuvrability and performance (for example, its top speed of 206 mph/331 km/h comfortably exceeded the 136 mph/ 220 km/h maximum speed of the contemporary Aérospatiale Alouette III,

The XH-51A compound helicopter with Pratt & Whitney J60-P-2 turbojet on the port side and stub wing. (*Lockheed*)

which was in the same size and power class), the Model 286 failed to attract civil customers. In particular, without the benefit of military orders over which to spread part of the development cost, the price could not be made competitive. Moreover, a tentative Netherlands order for twelve derivatives of the Model 286, which were to have been fitted for anti-submarine operations, proved insufficient to warrant production of the type.

Related Temporary Design Designations: CL-532, CL-595, CL-703, CL-711, CL-713/CL-715, CL-720/CL-721, CL-744/CL-745, CL-825, CL-864, CL-872/CL-873, CL-877/CL-878, CL-940, CL-956, CL-999, CL-1022, CL-1024, CL-1048, CL-1075, CL-1105, CL-1107/CL-1108, CL-1118, CL-1275 and CL-1710

Length 42 ft 1 in (12·83 m); height 8 ft 1½ in (2·48 m); rotor diameter 35 ft (10·67 m). Empty weight 2,640 lb (1,197 kg); loaded weight 4,100 lb (1,860 kg); power loading 7·5 lb/shp (3·4 kg/shp).
Maximum speed 174 mph (280 km/h) at sea level; cruising speed 160 mph (257 km/h); initial rate of climb 2,000 ft/min (610 m/min); hover ceiling out of ground effect 13,000 ft (3,960 m); hover ceiling in ground effect 16,000 ft (4,875 m); range 350 miles (565 km).
Data for the XH-51A.

Lockheed C-141 StarLifter

By the end of 1960—more than eight years after the start of the abbreviated service life of the de Havilland Comet 1 and more than two years after the debut in airline service of the Comet 4 and Boeing 707-120—the world's air carriers had taken delivery of 399 jetliners produced in the United States, the United Kingdom and France. Yet, at the same time the USAF's jet transport fleet was made up of only three Boeing VC-137As (707-120s operated as Presidential and VIP transports by the Special Air Missions unit at Andrews AFB, Maryland). The backbone of the Military Air Transport Service's inventory were still piston-

A C-141A StarLifter of the 60th Military Airlift Wing touching down at Travis AFB, California. (*Peter J. Mancus/Cloud 9 Photography*)

engined Boeing C-97s, Douglas C-118s and C-124s, and Lockheed C-121s, with less than fifty propeller-turbine powered Douglas C-133A/Bs providing the only modern component of MATS large fleet. Clearly, there existed an urgent need for modernization. Following the change of administration in January 1961, plans to proceed with the upgrading of the MATS fleet were accelerated, and Boeing C-135A/Bs and Lockheed C-130Es were ordered as interim equipment while the development of a modern jet-powered long-range freighter was undertaken. Indeed, its timing proved most fortunate as within four months of its entry into service the jet freighter was heavily committed to providing airlift for the rapidly increasing US involvement in Southeast Asia.

Seeking to obtain a jet transport, the USAF had issued in May 1960 a Specific Operational Requirement (SOR 182) for an aircraft capable of carrying a maximum load of over 60,000 lb (27,215 kg) over 3,500 naut miles (6,480 km), and in December 1960 it circulated a Request for Proposals for the Logistics Transport System 476L. Proposals were submitted by Boeing, Convair, Douglas, and Lockheed, in January 1961 and on 13 March Lockheed was declared the winner. Authorization to Proceed was granted on 5 April, 1961, and a Letter of Intent for five RDT&E (Research, Development, Test and Evaluation) prototypes was issued.

Whereas contemporary jetliners were all of low-wing configuration, the design team at Lockheed-Georgia decided to retain for its Model 300 StarLifter jet transport the high-wing layout of its C-130 Hercules in order to place the floor of the aircraft at truck-bed height and thus avoid the need for complicated loading and unloading devices. Also inherited from the Hercules were the basic fuselage cross-section (10 ft 4 in/3·15 m wide and 9 ft 1¼ in/2·77 m high) and the twin-wheel nose undercarriage. Cargo compartment length was set at 70 ft (21·34 m), with usable volume being 6,530·5 cu ft (184·9 cu m). For cargo loading and unloading a multi-segment, hydraulically-operated clamshell door was provided in the aft fuselage and incorporated a vehicle ramp. The main four-wheel undercarriage bogies were made to retract forward into pods on the sides of the centre-fuselage section, with the port pod also housing an AiResearch APU (auxiliary power unit) while the starboard one provided space for the outlet and piping for the single-point refuelling of the aircraft. The four 21,000 lb (9,525 kg) thrust Pratt & Whitney TF33-P-7 turbofans were underslung on the wing in individual nacelles and were fed from twelve wing tanks with a total capacity of 23,592 US gal (89,306 litres). Normal crew consisted of pilot, co-pilot, flight engineer, navigator and loadmaster, with accommodation being provided for either 138 troops in aft-facing seats, 124 paratroops on side-facing bucket seats, 80 litters and 23 attendants, or 62,717 lb (28,448 kg) of military cargo. Other notable design features included T tail surfaces, 1·2 degrees of wing anhedral, and lift spoilers on the upper wing surface extending from the ailerons to the fuselage.

The definitive contract for the C-141 was signed in May 1962 and the first of two C-141A-1-LMs (serial 61-2775) was flown at Marietta on 17 December, 1963 (the 60th anniversary of the first powered flights by the Wright brothers). Deliveries to the USAF began in October 1964 and the type became operational with the Military Airlift Command on 23 April, 1965. By then Lockheed had received contracts for 132 StarLifters while later awards raised total production to 285 aircraft comprising one civil aircraft (of which more later) and 284 C-141As (61-2775/61-2779, 63-8075/63-8090, 64-609/64-653, 65-216/65-281, 65-9397/65-9414, 66-126/66-209, 66-7944/66-7959, 67-001/67-031 and 67-164/67-166). The last C-141A was delivered in February 1968 and most went to equip fourteen Air Transport Squadrons while one became an NC-141A (61-2777) after being modified for special tests. A few C-141As were completed with strengthened airframes to enable them to carry the Minuteman ICBM; the 86,207 lb (39,103 kg) weight of this missile in its special container exceeded by more than a third the payload of standard C-141As and the modified StarLifters were restricted to a manoeuvring load factor of 2·25 g instead of the 2.5 g load standard for MAC aircraft.

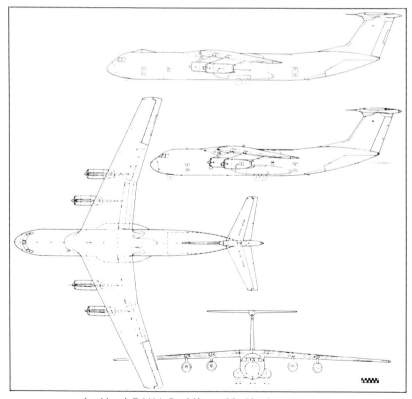

Lockheed C-141A StarLifter, with side view of C-141B

A C-141B, with stretched fuselage and air refuelling receptacle in the hump aft of the cockpit, landing at Marietta. (*Lockheed*)

The C-141A had barely been established in squadron service when, beginning in August 1965, it was called to play a major role in the airlift of personnel, equipment, and supplies to, from and within Southeast Asia. Initially most westbound flights departed from Travis AFB, California; however, as the volume of operations increased, new APOEs (Aerial Ports of Embarkation) were set up not only on the West Coast (Norton and McChord AFBs) but also in the Southwest (Tinker and Kelly AFBs) and the Eastern United States (Charleston, Dover and McGuire AFBs). On their return from Southeast Asia, the StarLifters were frequently used for aeromedical evacuations (flying some 6,000 such missions between July 1965 and December 1972) and for the grimmer task of bringing home the bodies of US personnel killed in action. In the final stage of the war, C-141As were selected to return the 588 POW released from North Vietnam between 12 February and 29 March, 1973. Their final role in this war was the evacuation of Vietnamese refugees in 1975. In more peaceful roles, in 1969 the StarLifter transported the isolation capsule carrying the first moon-landing astronaut team from Hawaii to Texas, and on countless occasions the type brought relief to victims of natural disasters worldwide.

The month-long US airlift during the 1973 Yom Kippur War, when C-141As flew 421 missions and delivered more than 10,000 tons of equipment and supplies to Israel in spite of the fact that most European staging points were denied to MAC transports, clearly demonstrated the need for providing these aircraft with air refuelling capability and for increasing the airlift volume which the Command

Lockheed C-141B StarLifter, with flaps lowered. This view shows to advantage the wing droop when the aircraft is on the ground. (*Phil Francillon*)

432

could provide in time of emergency. Budgetary limitations, which were particularly stiff in the post-Vietnam era, precluded the acquisition of new aircraft. However, Lockheed and the USAF were able to devise a scheme to fulfil at minimum cost these two requirements. By inserting a 13 ft 4 in (4·06 m) fuselage plug forward of the wing and a 10 ft (3·05 m) plug aft of the wing, usable volume was increased by nearly 75 per cent to 11,399 cu ft (322·8 cu m), while the addition of an air refuelling boom receptacle atop the fuselage gave the StarLifter greatly increased operational flexibility. Contract for the design of this improvement package and the modification of a C-141A (serial 66-186) as a YC-141B prototype was awarded in 1976. This aircraft began flight trials on 24 March, 1977, and subsequently the manufacturer was funded for modifying all existing C-141As to the C-141B configuration. The first production C-141B was accepted by MAC on 4 December, 1979, and entered service with the 57th Military Air Transport

The C-141A (N714NA, c/n 300-6110) operated by the Ames Research Center at Moffett Field, California. The opening for the 36-inch telescope can be seen forward of the wing. (*NASA*)

Squadron at Altus AFB, Oklahoma, in January 1980. During that year nearly thirty per cent of the StarLifter fleet was brought up to C-141B standard and the modified aircraft served alongside C-141As in one training and thirteen operational MAC squadrons. Four of the first five C-141As were also operated on special duties by the Aeronautical Systems Division of the Air Force Systems Command at Wright-Patterson AFB.

One of the goals in the design of the Model 300 had been to have it comply not only with military requirements but also with those of the Federal Aviation Agency for commercial aircraft. Accordingly, the StarLifter had been put through the FAA certification programme and had received a Type Certificate in January 1965. Slick Airways ordered the type; but the absorption of this carrier by Airlift International spelled the end for the commercial StarLifter programme, as other airlines, which operated from major airports where the availability of ground equipment negated the advantage of truck-bed loading offered by the Model 300, preferred the freighter versions of the Boeing 707 and Douglas DC-8 with their fifty per cent greater payload and better operating economics.

One C-141A (the L-300-50A, c/n 300-6110) was flown with the civil registration N4141A but later was delivered to the Ames Research Center of the National Aeronautics and Space Administration. With NASA this aircraft continues to be

433

operated, with the registration N714NA, as an airborne infra-red laboratory and has been fitted with a 36-inch (91·4 cm) telescope aimed through a hatch on top of the fuselage, just ahead of the wing.

Related Temporary Design Designations: CL-1522, GL-258, GL-286, GL-289/ GL-292, GL-299, GL-311, GL-315/GL-316, GL-321/GL-322, GL-324, GL-333/ GL-335, GL-344/GL-345, GL-384, GL-388, GL-390, LG-141-101/LG141-145, LG151-001, LG161-001, LG200-001/LG200-016, LG200-019, LG200-101/ LG200-102 and LG300-101/LG300-104

C-141A

Span 160 ft (48·77 m); length 145 ft (44·2 m); height 39 ft 4 in (11·99 m); wing area 3,228·1 sq ft (299·901 sq m).

Empty weight 136,900 lb (62,097 kg); maximum take-off weight 323,100 lb (146,556 kg); wing loading 100·1 lb/sq ft (488·7 kg/sq m); power loading 3·8 lb/lb st.

Maximum speed 565 mph at 24,400 ft (909 km/h at 7,440 m); cruising speed 478 mph (769 km/h); initial rate of climb 7,925 ft/min (2,416 m/min); service ceiling 51,700 ft (15,760 m); range with maximum payload of 62,717 lb (28,448 kg) 4,155 miles (6,685 km); ferry range without payload 6,575 miles (10,580 km).

C-141B

Dimensions as C-141A except for length 168 ft 3½ in (51·29 m); Empty weight 153,350 lb (69,558 kg).

Initial rate of climb 2,990 ft/min (911 m/min); range with maximum payload of 89,152 lb (40,439 kg) 3,200 miles (5,150 km); and maximum unrefuelled range without payload 6,385 miles (10,275 km).

Lockheed QT-2, Q-Star and YO-3A

Better known for its missile (Polaris, Poseidon, Trident, etc) and space (Agena booster, Apollo escape rocket, Space Shuttle insulating tiles, etc) activities, Lockheed Missiles & Space Company (LMSC) ventured but once into the aeronautical field. It did so as the result of a unique requirement created by the Southeast Asia War, and the outgrowth of this venture was as far removed from its usual line of business as it could possibly be.

Guerrilla operations by Viet Cong units, which quickly faded back into the jungle after striking, brought the need to devise means of more reliable tracking of enemy movements. For this purpose a variety of sensors already existed, or were quickly developed, but their short detection range inhibited their effective use from conventional platforms. Accordingly, in its search for solutions, the Department of Defense (DoD) turned to industry. Various approaches were used and among those known to have seen actual use in Southeast Asia were the Pave Eagle (combining sensor-equipped Beech QU-22B drones and Lockheed EC-121R relay aircraft) and Prize Crew programmes, the latter based on the LMSC-developed aircraft.

To bring sensors within effective range without the vehicle being detected by the enemy, engineers in the Advanced Programs Directorate of LMSC conceived in early 1966 the idea of mounting sensors on an aerodynamically-efficient aircraft powered by a muffler-equipped engine driving a slow-turning propeller. To

The Wankel-powered Q-Star with three-blade propeller. (*Lockheed*)

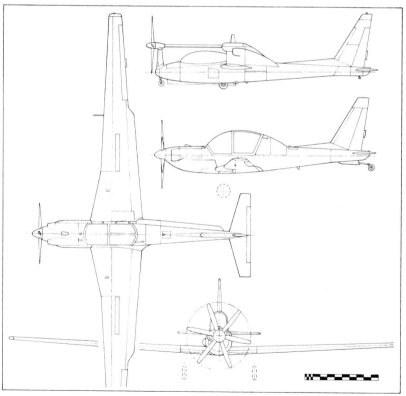

Lockheed YO-3A, with side view (*top*) of QT-2

demonstrate the feasibility of this concept, LMSC proposed to the DoD Advanced Research Projects Agency that a Schweizer SGS 2-32 two/three-seat glider be modified as the QT-1 (Quiet Thruster, single-seat) prototype powered by a 57 hp engine mounted in the fuselage aft of the pilot and driving a tractor propeller by means of a pylon-mounted extension shaft. The Army was interested, but wanted the aircraft to be QT-2 two-seaters, and arranged for the transfer to Lockheed of two Schweizer X-26A sailplanes—SGS 2-32s ordered by the Navy for use in the training programme at the Naval Test Pilot School, N A S Patuxent River, Maryland.

To produce the QT-2 demonstrators, modifications of the Schweizer sailplane were kept to a minimum and essentially centred on the powerplant installation. It

Experimental installation of a six-blade propeller on a YO-3A. (*Lockheed*)

consisted of placing aft of the cockpit a 100 hp Continental O-200-A four-cylinder air-cooled engine which was fitted with outsize mufflers and drove a four-blade wooden propeller by means of a long extension shaft running over the two-seat cockpit. Built by personnel of Lockheed Aircraft Service Company under the direction of Stanley Hall and his LMSC project team, and bearing the civil registration N2471W, the first QT-2 was tested in great secrecy from a remote airstrip in the Mojave Desert, beginning in July 1967. Results were excellent, as the QT-2 proved outstandingly quiet, and the two aircraft were hurriedly fitted with their sensor packages to be airlifted to Vietnam for operational evaluation by the US Army. Arriving in the war theatre in December 1967, the two QT-2PCs (the initials PC, Prize Crew, referring to the code name of the project)

The second YO-3A (69-18001). The pilot sat in the aft cockpit. (*Lockheed*)

demonstrated their effectiveness during the January 1968 Tet offensive. After a few months they were brought back to the United States, where one of them was cannibalized to provide spares for the other which was used at the Naval Test Pilot School as the X-26B, in Navy markings. Later this aircraft returned to the Army and was further evaluated before being placed on display at the US Army Aviation Museum at Fort Rucker.

While the QT-2PCs were tested in Vietnam, Lockheed modified more extensively a third SGS 2-32 which was fitted with a conventional fixed under-carriage instead of the bicycle type used on the previously modified sailplanes. Designated Q-Star and registered N5713S, this demonstrator initially retained the Continental O-200-A engine installation of the QT-2s but was used to test at least nine different types of propellers, including three-blade constant-speed and four- and six-blade fixed-pitch units. Later, in a programme funded by Lockheed, the Curtiss-Wright Corporation, and the US Navy, it was re-engined with a Wright RC2-60 liquid-cooled Wankel-type rotary combustion engine. The use of this powerplant, which was derated from 200 to 185 hp and cooled by an automobile radiator mounted in the nose, was the first aeronautical application of a Wankel-type engine and was first flown with its novel engine in September 1969.

YO-3A 69-18002 in US Army service. The sensors beneath the nose and rear fuselage as well as the viewing scope for the forward crew member can be seen. (*US Army*)

437

YO-3A (NASA 718/N718NA, ex-69-18010) used by the Ames Research Center as an airborne platform for measuring helicopter noise levels. It is seen at Moffett Field on 10 June, 1981. (*René J. Francillon*)

The Q-Star was put in store within less than two years and eventually donated to a private museum.

The successful operational evaluation of the QT-2PCs in Vietnam prompted the US Army Aviation Systems Command to award a $2 million contract to Lockheed in July 1968 for fourteen YO-3A production aircraft (serials 69-18000/ 69-18013). Still retaining the basic Schweizer sailplane all-metal structure, the YO-3A had a conventional undercarriage—with its main legs retracting inwardly into the wing—and a single-piece, upward-hinged canopy and windshield. The main difference between the production aircraft and the earlier demonstrators was in the powerplant, with the YO-3As being powered by a nose-mounted 210 hp Continental IO-360D six-cylinder air-cooled engine. Initially this engine drove a six-blade fixed-pitch propeller but this was later replaced by a three-blade variable-pitch unit. Wing area was also later increased by the addition of a trailing-edge extension over the inner half of the span.

After completing its manufacturer's trials, the first YO-3A was retained for further testing by the Army while the other thirteen aircraft were shipped to Vietnam in early 1970 for use by the 1st Army Security Agency Company at Long Binh. On 30 April, 1972, the unit was deactivated and its YO-3As were returned to the United States. Subsequently two of these aircraft were acquired by the State of Louisiana Department of Wildlife and Fisheries and, registered N14425/N14426, used to track down poachers. In 1980 four other YO-3As were on the US civil register: one was privately-owned in Connecticut, two were operated by the Federal Bureau of Investigation from Oxnard, California, and one, registered N718NA, was used by NASA as a microphone-carrying vehicle to measure rotor-blade noise as part of the helicopter research programme undertaken by the Ames Research Center.

QT-2/X-26B
Span 57 ft 1 in (17·4 m); length 30 ft 10 in (9·4 m); height 9 ft 3 in (2·82 m); wing area 180 sq ft (16·723 sq m).

Empty weight 1,576 lb (715 kg); loaded weight 2,182 lb (990 kg); wing loading 12·1 lb/sq ft (59·2 kg/sq m); power loading 21·8 lb/hp (9·9 kg/hp).

Maximum speed 115 mph (185 km/h); cruising speed 75 mph (121 km/h); ceiling 18,500 ft (5,640 m); range 350 miles (565 km).

YO-3A
Span 57 ft (17·37 m); length 29 ft 4 in (8·94 m); height 9 ft 1 in (2·77 m); wing area 205 sq ft (19·045 sq m).

Empty weight 3,129 lb (1,419 kg); loaded weight 3,519 lb (1,596 kg); maximum weight 3,800 lb (1,724 kg); wing loading 17·2 lb/sq ft (83·8 kg/sq m).

Maximum speed 138 mph (222 km/h) at sea level; cruising speed 110 mph (177 km/h); initial rate of climb 615 ft/min (187 m/min); service ceiling 14,000 ft (4,265 m); endurance at sea level 4·4 hr.

Lockheed AH-56A Cheyenne

The US Army's extensive use of troop-carrying helicopters in Vietnam soon revealed the pressing need for supplementing the escort helicopters—with Bell UH-1Bs and UH-1Cs being armed for that purpose with side guns and rocket launchers—with specialized gunships. Accordingly, in late 1964 the Army initiated the AAFSS (Advanced Aerial Fire Support System) design competition for fast, armoured and heavily-armed helicopters, and shortly after began procuring Bell AH-1G Hueycobras as interim gunships. In the event, the temporary became permanent as at the onset of the 1980s the Hueycobras had still to be joined in service by a specially designed helicopter gunship. Meanwhile, the AAFSS programme turned into a nightmare for both the US Army and the Lockheed Aircraft Corporation.

By the standards of the time, the requirements for the AAFSS were extremely demanding with the helicopter being anticipated to have a top speed of 220 kt (407 km/h), to hover out of ground effect at 6,000 ft (1,830 m) when ambient temperature was 95°F (35°C), and to have a ferry range of 2,100 naut miles (3,890 km)—sufficient for flights between California and Hawaii. Nevertheless, twelve companies submitted AAFSS proposals, with the Army selecting two finalists.

YAH-56A Cheyenne during armament trials at Yuma, Arizona. (*Lockheed*)

This view of the Cheyenne shows the layout of the fixed wing and the tail configuration.
(*Lockheed*)

Thus, in September 1965 six-month study contracts were awarded to Sikorsky, for its S-66, and to Lockheed, for its CL-840.

Declared the winner in November of that year, Lockheed received on 23 March, 1966, a contract for engineering development of the AH-56 attack helicopter. Ten AH-56A-LOs (serials 66-8826/66-8835) were ordered soon after. The first of these helicopters was named Cheyenne — in the US Army tradition of selecting names of Indian tribes for its aircraft, instead of a star name as most other Lockheed types — when it was rolled out at Van Nuys on 3 May, 1967.

The sleek-looking Cheyenne was characterized by its long slim fuselage, with side fairings in which the single-wheel main undercarriage units retracted aft. Small wings, with a span of 26 ft 8½ in (8·14 m) and an area of 195 sq ft (18·116 sq m), were attached to these fairings to off-load the rotor during high-speed flight. Its tail surfaces consisted of fixed tailplane and a ventral fin incorporating a castoring non-retractable wheel at its base. The General Electric T64-GE-16 shaft-turbine, which had its maximum rating progressively increased from 3,435 to 3,925 shp, drove a four-blade rigid rotor, a four-blade anti-torque rotor mounted on the port tailplane, and a three-blade, reverse-pitch, pusher propeller. The crew of two — pilot and gunner/co-pilot — sat in tandem in an enclosed cockpit, with the gunner sitting in front on a stabilized platform which could swivel through 360 deg. Armament consisted of either a 7·62 mm Minigun, a 30 mm Aeronutronic XM140 cannon, or a 40 mm Aeronutronic XM129 grenade launcher, in a nose turret, and six underwing attachment points for Hughes TOW anti-tank missiles and/or 2·75 mm rocket pods. The sophisticated weapon sighting system included night vision equipment and a helmet gun sight.

Following completion of dynamic testing on the ground with c/n 186-1001, flight trials were begun at Van Nuys on 21 September, 1967, with the second prototype, c/n 186-1002. Three and a half months later the US Army ordered an initial production batch of 375 AH-56As. Unfortunately, the hopes of Lockheed and the Army were soon dashed when the full performance envelope of the Cheyenne began to be explored. Initial lack of stability with the AH-56A close to the ground was quickly corrected, but instability at speeds in excess of 200 mph (322 km/h) proved more stubborn. In spite of trying various palliatives, no satisfactory cure had been found when on 12 March, 1969, the third Cheyenne (66-8828) crashed near Carpinteria, California, when its rotor hit the aft fuselage. The other

Cheyennes were immediately grounded and on 10 April, 1969, the Army sent a 'cure' letter to the manufacturer. Notwithstanding a confident answer by Lockheed on 28 April, the programme's production phase was cancelled on 19 May, 1969, six months before the scheduled delivery date of the first production AH-56A.

Flight trials of the evaluation aircraft were resumed in July 1969 to test a number of modifications, but on 17 September the tenth AH-56A (66-8835) was severely damaged in wind-tunnel tests at the NASA Ames Research Center when, once again, the rotor hit the fuselage. None-the-less, by then progress was being made and the end of the teething troubles was in sight. Moreover, trials with all types of weapons proved that the Cheyenne was both a stable firing platform and a highly manoeuvrable helicopter. Funds for advanced production engineering were again included in the defence budget for Fiscal Years 1972 and 1973 but by then the controversy surrounding the programme, together with the budgetary pinch created by the Southeast Asia War and the lack of project

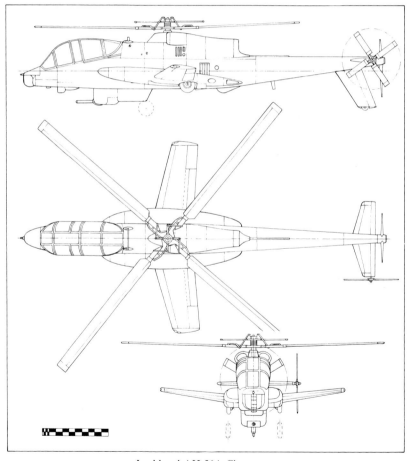

Lockheed AH-56A Cheyenne

441

management experience of the Army Aviation Systems Command combined to doom the Cheyenne.

Finally, the development contract was terminated in August 1972 and the AH-56As were grounded permanently. Today only the fifth Cheyenne (66–8830) survives in the US Army Aviation Museum at Ft Rucker. With the demise of the Cheyenne, Lockheed was forced to abandon the development of advanced civil derivatives—including the 30-seat CL-1026 and 95-seat CL-1090, with gross weights of 23,000 lb (10,433 kg) and 80,000 lb (36,287 kg) respectively—and to bow out, temporarily at least, of the helicopter field. However, in the early 1980s the firm was again active in helicopter technology research and was taking part in the DARPA/Navy funded 'X'-wing (four-blade stopped rotor) programme, with test systems being run at the Rye Canyon facilities.

Related Temporary Design Designations: CL-1025/CL-1027, CL-1029, CL-1031/CL-1033, CL-1050/CL-1052, CL-1055, CL-1059, CL-1077/CL-1078, CL-1081, CL-1084, CL-1091, CL-1093/CL-1094, CL-1096, CL-1111/CL-1113, CL-1117, CL-1122/CL-1123, CL-1214 and CL-1275

Fuselage length 54 ft 7 in (16·64 m); overall length 60 ft 1 in (18·31 m); height 13 ft 8½ in (4·18 m); rotor diameter 50 ft 5 in (15·37 m).

Empty weight 12,215 lb (5,541 kg); loaded weight 18,300 lb (8,301 kg); maximum weight 25,880 lb (11,739 kg) for STOL operation only; power loading 4·7 lb/shp (2·1 kg/shp).

Maximum speed 253 mph (407 km/h) at sea level; cruising speed 247 mph (397 km/h); initial rate of climb 3,420 ft/min (1,042 m/min); service ceiling 25,000 ft (7,620 m); hover ceiling out of ground effect 9,300 ft (2,835 m); maximum range 1,225 miles (1,970 km).

Lockheed C-5 Galaxy

The USAF Specific Operational Requirement to which the C-141A StarLifter was designed had failed to provide for a fuselage cross-section of sufficient size to enable the carriage of large pieces of Army equipment, such as heavy tanks and troop-carrying helicopters. Thus, while the C-141A proved a reliable aircraft and markedly augmented Military Air Transport Service's airlift capability, it did not provide the level of flexibility required to implement fully President Kennedy's policy of offsetting reductions in overseas-based US troops with greater flexibility of home-based forces. To a certain extent this deficiency could be overcome by pre-positioning heavy and bulky items of equipment at selected overseas depots—with personnel and lighter equipment to be flown in by C-130s and C-141s in time of emergency—but the Army still wished for the Air Force to be capable of airlifting a larger percentage of its combat weapons. Consequently, to obtain the necessary aircraft the USAF and the industry began working during 1963 on parametric design studies for the CX-4.

Progressively these studies enabled the Air Force to define more accurately its requirements for the CX-HLS (Cargo Experimental-Heavy Logistics System) and by mid-1964 evaluation of industry preliminary proposals led to the award of contracts for three-month design studies to three airframe manufacturers (Boeing, Douglas and Lockheed) and two engine companies (General Electric and Pratt & Whitney). By then the Department of Defense had developed its 'total-package procurement' (TPP) concept which required the manufacturers to

The Galaxy, first flown on 30 June, 1968, was the world's first aircraft to be powered by high-bypass-ratio turbofans. (*Cloud 9 Photography*)

compete for a whole programme—research, development, testing, evaluation and production—under a single contract, clearly setting price, schedule and performance commitments. Accordingly, in December 1964 the three airframe companies were given additional contracts to prepare TPP proposals for the design, construction and testing of five aircraft, for a 'Run A' of 53 production aircraft, and for a conditional 'Run B' for a further 57 aircraft. Requirements included (1) take-off at maximum weight from an 8,000 ft (2,440 m) runway, (2) landing on a 4,000 ft (1,220 m) semi-prepared strip, (3) carrying 125,000 lb (56,700 kg) on stage length of 8,000 miles (12,875 km), (4) maximum payload of 250,000 lb (113,400 kg), and (5) design life of 30,000 flying hours. At the same time the engine companies were funded to prepare TPP proposals for the powerplant.

The five proposals were submitted to USAF Systems Command in April 1965 and in August of that year General Electric was announced winner of the engine competition with its GE1/6 to go in production as the TF39-GE-1, the world's first high-bypass-ratio turbofan in the 40,000 lb (18,140 kg) plus thrust class. Less than two months later Lockheed won the airframe competition, as its $1·9 billion bid

C-5A Galaxy (69-010) of the 60th MAW at Travis AFB, California. Details of the four-wheel nose unit, and twenty-four-wheel main undercarriage are noteworthy. (*Peter J. Mancus/Cloud 9 Photography*)

443

was lower than that of Douglas ($2 billion) and that of Boeing ($2·3 billion). Rapid price escalation, optimistic cost estimates, the lack of flexibility inherent in the TPP-type contract, Air Force-initiated design changes, and a reduction in 'Run B' from 57 to 23 aircraft combined eventually to raise the total cost to over $5·2 billion. Moreover, Air Force unwillingness to accept design changes recommended by Lockheed resulted in an aircraft, the C-5A, which did not meet some of the CX-HLS specifications. In particular, unmodified C-5As were limited to a maximum life of 8,000 flying hours while unrefuelled range with a payload of 100,000 lb (45,359 kg) was only 6,720 miles (10,815 km).

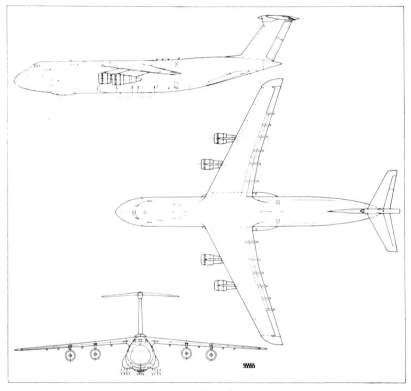

Lockheed C-5A Galaxy

The winner of the C-5 competition, the Model 500 Galaxy, appeared externally as a much enlarged C-141 as it retained the basic StarLifter's configuration, with high-mounted wing, T-tail surfaces, four underslung engine nacelles, and main undercarriage retracting into pods on the sides of the centre fuselage. However, with maximum take-off weight more than twice that of its stablemate and the required ability to operate from semi-prepared airfields, the C-5A had to have an unusually complex undercarriage consisting of a four-wheel nose unit and four six-wheel main bogies. Straight-through loading and unloading of vehicles—up to the size of the M-60 heavy tank and the Boeing Vertol CH-47 Chinook medium transport helicopter— was achieved by using ramps in the aft fuselage and in the nose. The aft ramp was provided with clamshell doors, while Lockheed devised an upward-lifting visor nose which could be raised above the cockpit to enable the aircraft to taxi with the door open. The main cargo compartment was designed with a length of 121 ft 1½ in (36·92 m), a width of 19 ft (5·79 m), a height ranging from 9 ft 6 in (2·96 m) beneath the wing to 13 ft 6 in (4·11 m) in the aft section, and a total usable volume of 34,796 cu ft (985·3 cu m) — more than five times the capacity of the C-141A's compartment. Normally intended to carry vehicles and outsize loads up to a total weight of 265,000 lb (120,200 kg), the aircraft had a fifteen-man relief crew compartment on the upper deck, aft of the cockpit, to supplement its active crew of five. For troop-carrying purposes, a rear

The nose visor and loading ramp of C-5A 69-007 of 60th MAW, Travis AFB, California, photographed on 2 July, 1981. (*Phil Francillon*)

upper-deck compartment with 75 aft-facing seats could be installed — but this reduced the height of the main cargo deck to 9 ft 6 in (2·96 m) — while 290 more troops could be carried if necessary on the main deck.

Powered by four 41,000 lb (18,597 kg) thrust General Electric YTF39-GE-1 turbofans, whereas production aircraft had 41,100 lb (18,643 kg) thrust TF39-GE-1s, the first C-5A Galaxy (66-8303) was flown at Marietta on 30 June, 1968, USAF acceptance began in December 1969 and continued until May 1973 when the 81st aircraft was completed. Serials assigned to the five RDT&E aircraft were 66-8303/66-8307, those for 'Run A' aircraft were 67-167/67-174, 68-211/68-228 and 69-001/69-027, and those for 'Run B' C-5As were 70-445/70-467.

Soon after the C-5A had begun its flight trial programme, wing cracks appeared in the fatigue-test airframe and the aircraft's well-publicized main deficiency came to light. Lockheed devised a number of corrective programmes but until recently the Air Force was reluctant to accept the company's recommendations as it lacked funds and had to contend with the already sizeable cost overrun. In spite of the retrofitting of active ailerons to the fleet of C-5As during 1975–77, these aircraft have a life barely over 25 per cent of the design goal of 30,000 flying hours. Furthermore, under normal operating procedures their payload is limited to 50,000 lb (22,680 kg), which is less than one-fifth of the maximum payload; this limit is withdrawn during emergency operations. However, in early 1978 the USAF finally approved construction and testing — both in flight and on a test rig — of two new wing sets, with the first flight on a modified C-5A being made on 15 August, 1980. All Galaxies are to be fitted by July 1987 with a new wing box manufactured by Avco Structures from stronger and thicker aluminium alloy skin. They will then be able to reach their full design life but, in the meantime, the unmodified C-5As are to continue operation under existing restrictions.

Notwithstanding its structural problem, the C-5A was in great demand during the later phases of the Southeast Asia War as it could airlift about 98 per cent of the Army's equipment. The type, which had entered MAC service in early 1970, flew its first mission to Vietnam in August of that year and, as more became available, the C-5As played an increasingly significant part in the overall airlift in support of the war. Within ten months of the end of this conflict the Galaxies used to good advantage their inflight-refuelling capability — for which a boom receptacle had been provided aft of the cockpit during construction — to airlift tanks, aircraft parts, guns and ammunition to Israel during the critical days of the Yom Kippur War of 1973. They were also flown back to Vietnam at the time of the final evacuation of refugees in April 1975; tragically, one of these aircraft (68-218), which carried orphans and attendants, crashed near Saïgon on the 4th of that month. Overall, however, the C-5A has had a good safety record, and in early 1981, 77 of the 81 aircraft built remained in service with two squadrons in each of the 60th Military Airlift Wing at Travis AFB, California, and the 436th MAW at Dover AFB, Delaware, and with a training squadron at Altus AFB, Oklahoma.

In September 1981 Lockheed proposed to the USAF that forty-four C-5Ns (for New) should be built in lieu of the McDonnell Douglas C-17A, the 1981 winner of the CX design competition.

Like the C-141A, the C-5A had been designed to meet both military and civil requirements, and Lockheed marketed the Galaxy as a commercial freighter and as a 1,000-seat jetliner. However, the aircraft's capacity in either role was excessive for existing traffic levels and the airlines were not interested.

Related Temporary Design Designations: CL-531, CL-1129, GL-358, GL-365, GL-500, LG5-101/LG5-130, LG5-176/LG5-217, LG500-101/LG500-119 and LGM-008

Span 222 ft 8½ in (67·88 m); length 247 ft 9½ in (75·53 m); height 65 ft 1¼ in (19·84 m); wing area 6,200 sq ft (576 sq m).
Empty weight 321,000 lb (145,603 kg); maximum take-off weight 769,000 lb (348,812 kg); wing loading 124 lb/sq ft (605·6 kg/sq m); power loading 4·7 lb/lb st.
Maximum speed 564 mph at 25,000 ft (907 km/h at 7,620 m); cruising speed 506 mph (814 km/h); initial rate of climb 5,840 ft/min (1,780 m/min); service ceiling 47,700 ft (14,540 m); range with maximum payload of 265,000 lb (120,200 kg) 1,875 miles (3,015 km); maximum unrefuelled range without payload 8,400 miles (13,520 km).

Lockheed L-1011 TriStar

The advent of the generation of wide-bodied transport aircraft provided Lockheed with an opportunity to re-enter the commercial aircraft market, and Rolls-Royce with access to the US market. However, this became a period of extraordinary turmoil for both the airframe manufacturer and the engine company, with only the former coming out alive, albeit weakened. Fortunately, ten years after the maiden flight of the RB.211-powered TriStar, Rolls-Royce (1971) Ltd and Lockheed were finally able to look with pride on what was still the most advanced jetliner in service. Success in airline service, however, could not overcome the effects of a world-wide industry recession and, on 7 December, 1981, Lockheed announced its intention to terminate L-1011 production in 1984.

In the early 1960s, while the Lockheed-Georgia design team was concentrating on the CX-4/CX-HLS/C-5 evolutionary programme, Lockheed-California had been preparing preliminary design studies for a large twinjet ASW aircraft for the US Navy. Whereas the former was successful in winning the C-5 competition, the latter's jet-powered project became a non-starter when the Navy decided to rely on the P-3 Orion. Nevertheless, the combined experience gained by the Georgia team, with the use of high-bypass turbofans, and by the California team with large twinjet designs, had well prepared Lockheed to answer an American Airlines'

N701DA (c/n 193C-1041), the first L-1011-1 for Delta Air Lines, at Palmdale before delivery. (*Delta Air Lines*)

requirement for a 250-seat wide-bodied jetliner for use on US domestic routes. Specific sectors identified by this carrier were Chicago–Los Angeles (1,750 naut miles/3,240 km) and New York (LaGuardia)–Chicago (640 naut miles/1,185 km). Significantly, the use of LaGuardia Airport, with its runways extending over Flushing Bay and limiting aircraft weight to 270,000 lb (122,470 kg), and with the configuration of its passenger terminal fingers restricting aircraft length to a maximum of 185 ft (56·38 m), provided the key design parameters. Moreover, American Airlines specified the use of two high-bypass turbofans in the 40,000 lb/18,150 kg thrust class such as the General Electric CTF39, the Pratt & Whitney JT9D, or Rolls-Royce RB.178-51.

To meet this requirement, in the spring of 1966 Lockheed-California assembled a team led by project engineer William M. Hannan. This team was soon ready to show American Airlines and other prospective customers preliminary design studies for an aircraft able to carry 250 passengers in a wide, twin-aisle cabin. Two turbofans in nacelles underslung beneath the wing would provide the power. Several of the airlines—notably TWA, with its many routes over the Rocky Mountains, and Eastern, with its overwater routes to Puerto Rico—then expressed their concern over carrying so many passengers in an aircraft having only two engines. Therefore, like their competitors at Douglas working on the DC-10 design, the Lockheed engineers switched to a three-engined design, with the third engine installed in the aft fuselage and fed through an S-duct with the intake at the base of the fin. Weights, capacity and installed thrust grew progressively, as they did with the DC-10 design, but Lockheed was confident of winning American Airlines' launching order for the wide-bodied trijet; it was thus a shock for the company when on 19 February, 1968, the airline selected the DC-10.

The gloom in Burbank was of short duration as on 29 March, 1968, Lockheed was able to announce a spectacular launch for the L-1011 TriStar with 144 orders and options from Eastern (25 firm and 25 option), TWA (33 and 11), and Air Holdings (50). The Air Holdings order was a clever off-set deal organized by Lockheed and British interests to defuse public and congressional protest in the United States over the selection of the Rolls-Royce RB.211 engine in preference to the General Electric CF6 and Pratt & Whitney JT9D. The aircraft ordered by Air Holdings were for re-sale to carriers in the Commonwealth and, thus, TriStars eventually acquired by Air Canada, British Airways and Cathay Pacific Airways were deducted from the Air Holdings order. On the strength of these massive orders, to which were soon added orders from Delta, Northeast, PSA and two aircraft leasing companies, the L-1011 was put into production, with final assembly to take place in new facilities built in Palmdale.

Although TriStars ordered up to that time were all medium-range aircraft optimized for use in the United States, Lockheed was aware that a sizeable market existed overseas for longer-ranged jetliners combining wide-bodied comfort with a capacity falling between that of the stretched Douglas DC-8 and that of the Boeing 747. Space for additional fuel tanks and more engine thrust as required by a longer-ranged version were available but the increased take-off weight could not be absorbed by the L-1011's existing undercarriage. Accordingly, Lockheed proposed the L-1011-8 in which six-wheel main undercarriage bogies were to replace the four-wheel units of the original TriStar, and the wing was to be redesigned to house the larger undercarriage and improve performance at higher weights. The price of the L-1011-8, however, exceeded that of the more straightforward long-range versions of the DC-10 (the Series 30 and 40) and Lockheed could not find a launching customer for this version.

Air Canada L-1011-1 TriStar (CF-TNF, c/n 193E-1047) over Mirabel Airport, Montreal. (*Air Canada*)

449

The main, and very colourful, cabin of a Gulf Air TriStar. (*Gulf Air*)

In spite of this setback, construction of the first TriStar (c/n 193A-1001, N1011) progressed on schedule and this company-owned aircraft was rolled out at Palmdale on 15 September, 1970. Following ground testing, it was first flown on 16 November, 1970, by H. B. Dees, pilot, R. C. Cokeley, co-pilot, G. E. Fisher, flight engineer, and R. C. Bray, research and development engineer. Performance and handling characteristics gave complete satisfaction, while the Rolls-Royce RB.211-22 turbofans — then derated to provide a maximum thrust of 36,500 lb (16,556 kg) — endowed the TriStar with remarkably low noise levels and exceptionally good fuel consumption. Unfortunately, the technical success of the RB.211 was not matched by the business acumen of its manufacturer; Rolls-Royce, which had underpriced the RB.211, was forced to go into receivership on 4 February, 1971. Consideration was then given to re-engining the TriStar with either CF6s* or JT9Ds but the cost of redesigning the S-duct and starting a new certification programme was found to be excessive, while programme delays — and resulting late-delivery penalties — were unacceptable. Moreover, by then Lockheed itself was on the brink of bankruptcy and only a concerted effort between the British and US Governments, the lenders, the customers and Lockheed — as detailed in the first chapter of this book — saved the L-1011, the RB.211 and their manufacturers.

Type certification was received in the United States on 14 April, 1972, and in the United Kingdom on 30 June, 1972. Since then the TriStar has appeared in the following versions and, with production still underway, a total of one hundred and ninety-five L-1011s had been delivered by the end of 1980.

*During the summer of 1981 the 50,000 lb (22,670 kg) thrust CF6-80A was again offered to Lockheed for advanced models of the TriStar.

450

L-1011-1: The basic medium-range version of the TriStar, as originally designed to satisfy the needs of US domestic trunk carriers, is powered by three 42,000 lb (19,051 kg) thrust RB.211-22B or -22C turbofans. Meeting the same requirements as the DC-10, the L-1011 is quite similar externally to its McDonnell Douglas rival. However, it incorporates several distinguishing features such as the S-duct for its centre engine and its 'flying' tailplane designed to provide more sensitive and positive control at critical attitudes. Typical accommodation in mixed-class is for 256 passengers (52F/204Y), with a flight crew of three and six cabin attendants; however, the L-1011-1 has been certificated to carry up to 400 passengers in high-density configuration. Galleys are normally positioned beneath the main deck, with food-serving carts being brought up by means of lifts; alternatively, the galleys can be installed on the main deck if a customer wishes to make full use of the 3,268 cu ft (92·5 cu m) underfloor compartments to carry cargo. Optional arrangements include a self-contained airstair, which stows into the rear baggage compartment on the starboard side of the fuselage, and a lounge beneath the forward cabin. This latter feature, which so far has only been incorporated in the TriStars ordered but not taken up by PSA, requires the addition of local strengthening elements beneath the nose of the aircraft. Deliveries began on 5 April, 1972, and since then L-1011-1s have been produced for Air Canada, All Nippon Airways, British Airways, Court Line, Delta, Eastern, LTU, PSA and TWA. A number of these aircraft have been modified after delivery to L-1011-100 or L-1011-200 standard.

The first TriStar, which first flew on 16 November, 1970, with RB.211s rated at only 36,500 lb (16,556 kg), has been successively fitted with more powerful engines to serve as a testbed for improved models of the L-1011. As the Advanced TriStar, it has been used, and continues to be used, by Lockheed for testing such features as automatic landing equipment, automatic brakes, flight management systems, etc. More significantly—beginning in 1977 under a NASA-funded Aircraft Energy Efficiency programme—it has flight tested wings of increased span (164 ft 4 in/50·09 m versus 155 ft 4 in/47·35 m) incorporating active aileron control to enable operations at higher gross weights and significantly improve fuel economy. Additional improvements in this area have been obtained through redesign of the engine nacelles and the installation of a new fairing at the base of the fin, just forward of the air intake for the centre engine. The installation of this fairing has also resulted in a marked reduction in perceived noise in the aft cabin.

After first placing a tentative order for DC-10s through Mitsui & Company, All Nippon Airways switched to the L-1011-1, thus sparking a major controversy. JA8501 (c/n 193P-1053) is illustrated. (*Lockheed*)

451

L-1011-100: Retaining the external dimensions of the L-1011-1, this version is basically certificated to operate at higher gross weights, thus enabling heavy payloads to be carried further without exceeding take-off weight limitations. Standard gross take-off weight for the L-1011-100 is 450,000 lb (204,117 kg), versus 430,000 lb (195,045 kg) for the L-1011-1. With the addition of tanks in the centre-section, fuel capacity can be increased to 23,815 US gal (90,150 litres) — as opposed to 22,985 gal for the L-1011-1s and the L-1011-100s without the additional tanks — and gross weight is increased to 466,000 lb (211,374 kg). Engines are either 42,000 lb (19,051 kg) thrust RB.211-22Bs or 43,500 lb (19,731 kg) thrust RB.211-22Fs. Lockheed has built L-1011-100s for Cathay Pacific, Gulf Air, and Saudi Arabian Airlines (Saudia), and others have been obtained by Air Canada, Delta, Eastern, LTU, and TWA, by modifying existing L-1011-1s.

L-1011-200: Specially developed for carriers operating from airports with either high ambient temperature or high elevation, this version differs from the L-1011-100 in being powered by three 48,000 lb (21,772 kg) thrust RB.211-524 engines. The same gross-weight and fuel-capacity options as offered for the L-1011-100s are available, and L-1011-200s have been built for British Airways, Gulf Air, and Saudia, and will be delivered later to Trans Caribbean and Alia — The Royal Jordanian Airline. Furthermore, Saudia has had two ex-TWA L-1011-1s and three of its own L-1011-100s converted to this standard.

L-1011-500: After an intense competitive battle against a proposed RB.211-powered version of the DC-10-30, the L-1011-500 won its launch customer in August 1976 when British Airways ordered an initial batch of six aircraft. This long-range version of the TriStar powered by 50,000 lb (22,680 kg) thrust RB.211-524Bs reduces seating capacity in exchange for increased range. Its fuselage is shortened by 13 ft 6 in (4·11 m), and its galleys are normally located on the main deck to allow accommodation in mixed-class for 246 passengers (24F/222Y), or for 300 passengers in the high-density configuration. Gross weight is increased to 496,000 lb (224,982 kg) while maximum fuel capacity is raised to 31,642 US gal (119,779 litres). Flight trials of the L-1011-500 began on 16 October, 1978, and this version was certificated in April 1979. Whereas the initial production L-1011-500s — as ordered by British Airways and other carriers — retain the original TriStar wing, later production aircraft — as first ordered by Pan American in April 1978 — are fitted with the longer-span wing incorporating active ailerons as tested on the Advanced TriStar testbed. This feature, which reduces fuel con-

Pan American's TriStar 500 N64911 with active ailerons and noise attenuating Frisbee fairing forward of the No.2 intake. (*Pan American World Airways*)

L-1011 N10112 (c/n 193L-1064), built for PSA. With the unique external reinforcement of the forward fuselage to enable carriage of passengers in the lower deck lounge, this TriStar was refitted by Lockheed Aircraft Service before delivery to AeroPeru. (*Lockheed*)

sumption significantly, can be retrofitted to earlier aircraft. In addition to being ordered by existing TriStar customers—including AeroPeru, Air Canada, Alia —The Royal Jordanian Airline, British Airways, Delta, LTU, and TWA— L-1011-500s have been purchased by Air-India, BWIA, Pan American, and TAP/Air Portugal.

Unbuilt versions: Over the years Lockheed has actively marketed several other versions of the TriStar. The L-1011-250 was to have been a medium-to-long range version combining the fuselage of the L-1011-200 with the engines, fuel capacity and gross weight of the L-1011-500. The L-1011-300—which still appeared, even in early 1981, to have had the best chance to receive the go-ahead— was a proposed stretched TriStar with fuselage lengthened by 14 to 30 ft (4·26 to 9·14 m), gross weight of 600,000 lb (272,155 kg) and more powerful RB.211s. The L-1011-400A and -400MP were to have been medium-range aircraft with the reduced capacity of the -500, improved equipment, active aileron control, and reduced operating weights. Two twin-engined derivatives, the L-1011-600 and -600A, were also proposed but stood little chance of success against the Boeing 767 and Airbus A310. Finally, the TriStar has formed the basis for the Lockheed proposal to develop and operate experimentally a liquid-hydrogen fuelled cargo transport; this exotic project no longer appears likely to be funded.

On 26 April, 1972, three weeks after taking delivery of its first L-1011-1 (c/n 193A-1007, N306EA) on 5 April, 1972, Eastern Air Lines introduced the TriStar on scheduled service on its New York–Miami route. On 25 June the type also made its debut with TWA. Since then, Eastern and TWA, as planned when they had jointly ordered TriStars, have regularly exchanged aircraft since their peak traffic periods do not coincide.* The only other L-1011 domestic operator in the United States, Delta Air Lines, initially hedged its bets by leasing five DC-10s when Lockheed and Rolls-Royce ran into trouble. This airline, however, soon regained full confidence in the TriStar and has now become its largest user, with service within the United States, to the Caribbean and to Europe with L-1011-1s, -100s and -500s.

*There was also an exchange agreement between Eastern Air Lines and Air Canada.

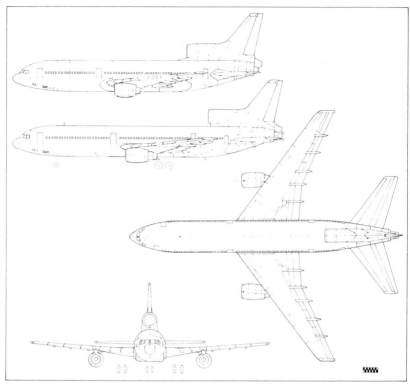

Lockheed L-1011-1 TriStar, with side view (*top*) of L-1011-500

Being powered by British built engines, the TriStar held a distinct advantage over the DC-10 when it came to being acquired by carriers within the Commonwealth as its powerplants were exempt from customs duties. Thus, L-1011s have been bought by Air Canada, British Airways and Cathay Pacific, while Gulf Air's aircraft were originally British-registered. Another early overseas customer, All Nippon Airways, had initially intended to acquire DC-10s but was induced into switching to the L-1011-1s, the manocuvring behind this sale contributing much to Lockheed's notoriety with regard to foreign sales practice. On the other hand, the acquisition of TriStars by Saudia was a straightforward commercial deal influenced by the fact that TWA—an already established L-1011 customer—had a technical/management agreement with the Saudi Arabian carrier.

In service the TriStar has proved to be an extremely reliable aircraft and its limited sales cannot be traced to technical defects or to lack of product support. However, the timing of the financial difficulties experienced by both Lockheed and Rolls-Royce, together with the former's initial inability to launch a long-range version of its trijet, have played havoc with the L-1011's potential market. Consequently, during the critical period when airlines were initially in the market for wide-bodied aircraft smaller than the Boeing 747, McDonnell Douglas was able to walk away from its old rival. Thus, even after the DC-10 had experienced difficulties, Lockheed was never able to catch up. Later, both types of wide-

454

bodied trijets began running into competition from the new generation of fuel-efficient aircraft exemplified by the Airbus A300/A310 and the Boeing 767.

Lockheed's last chance to regain some degree of initiative in this market came in 1976 when it undertook the development of the L-1011-500, which entered service with British Airways on 7 May, 1974, on the London–Abu Dhabi service. Combining good long-range operating characteristics with moderate capacity— respectively 10 per cent below that of the DC-10-30 and 35 per cent below that of the Boeing 747—the Dash 500 presented itself as a nearly ideal replacement for the Boeing 707s and Douglas DC-8s still operated over the so-called 'long and thin' routes. Sanguine hopes for the future of the L-1011-500, which were sparked by Pan American's selection of the type in 1978, have not yet fully materialized. Thus, notwithstanding its technical prowess, the TriStar remained in 1981 a heavy drain on Lockheed's finances.

Related Temporary Design Designations: CL-1011, CL-1208, CL-1211, CL-1219, CL-1266/CL-1268, CL-1296, CL-1302, CL-1315, CL-1319/CL-1322, CL-1327, CL-1332/CL-1333, CL-1335, CL-1560, CL-1600 and LGM-008

L-1011-1
Span 155 ft 4 in (47·35 m); length 178 ft 8 in (54·46 m); height 55 ft 4 in (16·87 m); wing area 3,456 sq ft (321·074 sq m).

Operating weight empty 234,275 lb (106,265 kg); maximum take-off weight 430,000 lb (195,045 kg); wing loading 124·4 lb/sq ft (607·5 kg/sq m); power loading 3·4 lb/lb st.

Maximum speed 545 mph at 30,000 ft (877 km/h at 9,145 m); cruising speed 495 mph (796 km/h); initial rate of climb 2,800 ft/min (853 m/min); service ceiling 42,000 ft (12,800 m); range with maximum payload of 90,725 lb (41,152 kg) 2,880 miles (4,635 km); range with maximum fuel and payload of 40,000 lb (18,144 kg) 4,465 miles (7,185 km).

L-1011-500
(with active ailerons)
Span 164 ft 4 in (50·09 m); length 164 ft 2½ in (50·05 m); height 55 ft 9½ in (17·01 m); wing area 3,541 sq ft (328·971 sq m).

Operating weight empty 242,967 lb (110,208 kg); maximum take-off weight 496,000 lb (224,982 kg); wing loading 140·1 lb/sq ft (683·9 kg/sq m); power loading 3·3 lb/lb st.

Maximum speed 545 mph at 30,000 ft (877 km/h at 9,145 m); cruising speed 484 mph (779 km/h); initial rate of climb 3,050 ft/min (930 m/min); service ceiling 43,500 ft (13,260 m); range with maximum payload of 74,960 lb (34,001 kg) 4,310 miles (6,935 km).

Lockheed S-3 Viking

Even though the US Navy was already contemplating the retirement of its specialized CVS (anti-submarine aircraft carriers), the Service still had a requirement for carrier-borne anti-submarine aircraft to be assigned as part of the normal complement of its carrier air wings (CVWs). This requirement was strengthened by the desirability of phasing-out the piston-powered Grumman S-2 Tracker, and its C-1 Trader carrier-on-board delivery version, in order to dispense with storing highly-volatile avgas on board aircraft carriers. Furthermore, the increased threat posed by Soviet nuclear-powered submarines stressed the need to provide the Fleet with more capable ASW weapons, including high-performance aircraft

A pair of S-3A Vikings of Antisubmarine Squadron 41 (VS-41) above their home base, NAS North Island, California, in 1975. (*R. L. Lawson/US Navy*)

fitted with advanced electronic and acoustic detection systems. Accordingly, after first circulating in mid-1964 its VSX (Experimental carrier-based ASW aircraft) concept to the industry, the Navy released its Specific Operational Requirement for the VSX during the winter of 1966. A formal Request for Proposals was answered in April 1968 by industry teams. Finally, four months later a joint Convair Division of General Dynamic/Grumman team and one led by Lockheed were requested to refine their proposals.

Even before the issuance of the RFP Lockheed had realized that, while it had the best ASW expertise in the industry, it was short of experience with the design of carrier-based aircraft (its only carrier type to have reached production was the T2V-1/T-1A, a jet trainer lacking wing-folding mechanism and some other specialized naval items). By joining forces with LTV Aerospace Corporation, a leader in the design of carrier-based aircraft, and with the Univac Federal Systems Division of Sperry Rand, a specialist in ASW systems, Lockheed was able to lead a formidable team fully capable of matching the strength of its General Dynamics/Grumman/IBM competitor.

The team studied various configurations—all to be powered by two General Electric TF34 high-bypass-ratio turbofans—with these mounted either in pods beneath or above the wings, on the lower sides of the fuselage, on the aft fuselage sides, or in conventional wing nacelles. It also considered single and triple vertical tail surfaces—the latter to try to avoid folding the fin and rudder when storing the aircraft beneath deck—and even briefly studied the merit of using variable-sweep wings to combine high transit speed with long loiter time at low altitude. Lockheed finally settled on a fairly conservative configuration characterized by shoulder-mounted, folding, wings with moderate sweep (15 deg at quarter

456

chord), pod-mounted turbofans beneath the wings, and tall folding vertical tail surfaces. Crew was to consist of pilot and co-pilot, side by side on the flight deck, tactical co-ordinator (TACCO) and sensor operator (SENSO) in the fuselage, just aft of the pilots. After review by the Naval Air Systems Command of the proposals submitted in December 1968 by the two teams, Lockheed was declared the winner on 4 August, 1969. An initial batch of six flight-test and two static-test machines—later changed to have all eight aircraft flyable—was ordered as YS-3As (BuNos 157992/157999).

Working with its team members—LTV (Vought Corporation after January 1976), which had a 24 per cent share of the total programme, and Univac, with its 10 per cent share—and with numerous sub-contractors, which accounted for a further 37 per cent of the programme, Lockheed proceeded with the detailed design and construction of the eight pre-production aircraft. Powered by two 9,275 lb (4,207 kg) thrust General Electric TF34-GE-2 turbofans, the first YS-3A (BuNo 157992) was completed in November 1971. After completing its taxi-ing and systems trials at the Lockheed Air Terminal, the aircraft was transported to Palmdale where, on 21 January, 1972, it was taken up for its 90-minute maiden flight by John Christiansen and Lyle Schaefer.

During the course of the ensuing 26-month trial programme, the eight YS-3As shared the development work with, as customary in such instances, individual aircraft being assigned for specific tests. Thus, for example, the fourth aircraft (BuNo 157995) was used for carrier system-compatibility tests at Patuxent River, Maryland. Board of Inspection and Survey (BIS) trials began in October 1973 and carrier suitability tests were first undertaken aboard the uss *Forrestal* in December of that year. Performance and handling characteristics lived up to expectations and the only airframe modification found necessary consisted of the addition

S-3A Vikings of VS-29 *Vikings* on the starboard forward elevator of the uss *Kitty Hawk* during a training exercise off Southern California on 19 January, 1981. (*Schnell/US Navy*)

457

of small metal strips on the wing leading-edge, between the fuselage and engine pylons, to improve stall characteristics.

Barely three months into its trial programme the S-3A Viking was put into production, when in April 1972 the Navy ordered thirteen aircraft (BuNos 158861/158873). Subsequent contracts brought the total Viking production to 187 aircraft, including the pre-production YS-3As. The last S-3A (BuNo 160607) was delivered in August 1978, but tooling was set aside for possible resumption of production. The first batch of S-3As retained the TF34-GE-2 turbofans as fitted to the pre-production aircraft but, beginning in early 1975, later aircraft were delivered with TF34-GE-400As with the same take-off thrust: 9,275 lb (4,207 kg).

The S-3As are equipped with a Univac AN/AYK-10 digital computer and their principal non-acoustic sensors include Texas Instrument AN/APS-116 radar in the nose and a Texas Instrument OR-89 FLIR (forward-looking infra-red scanner) in a retractable ventral cupola. It also carries a Texas Instrument AN/ASQ-81 magnetic anomaly detection (MAD) sensor in a retractable tailboom and an IBM AN/ALR-47 electronic countermeasures system. Primary acoustic sensors consist of sixty sonobuoys carried in the aft fuselage, with chutes slanted rearward. Offensive load is carried in a ventral bomb bay (up to 2,000 lb/907 kg of bombs, torpedoes, destructors, or depth bombs) or on wing racks (including bombs, rockets or ZAGM-84A Harpoon anti-shipping missiles). Internal fuel capacity of 1,900 US gal (7,192 litres) can be supplemented by two 300-gal (1,136-litre) drop tanks; a retractable inflight-refuelling probe is mounted within the fuselage on the top centreline.

Lockheed S-3A Viking

A YS-3A leading the one-off US-3A and KS-3A. (*Lockheed*)

Service use began in February 1974 when VS-41, the designated S-3A training squadron at NAS North Island, San Diego, received its first Vikings. The first operational unit, VS-21 also at NAS North Island, acquired S-3As in July 1974; one year later it took Vikings aboard the USS *John F. Kennedy* for the type's first carrier deployment. Since then, S-3As have been delivered to VS-29, VS-33, VS-37 and VS-38, also at North Island, and to VS-22, VS-24, VS-28, VS-30, VS-31 and VS-32, at NAS Cecil Field, Jacksonville. The last unit to receive Vikings was VS-37 which began acquiring the type in December 1976. Since then the S-3A has performed reliably and effectively with these twelve squadrons. In particular, it has proved a commendably safe aircraft in spite of being responsible for difficult missions: maintaining control of the sea and, in wartime, denying its use to the enemy by countering the submarine threat. In addition, as demonstrated by VS-24 during a record-length (260-day) 1979-80 cruise aboard the USS *Nimitz* in the Mediterranean and the Indian Ocean, the Viking can also provide logistic support for its carriers.

The latter role—carrier-on-board (COD) delivery—had been identified earlier by Lockheed and the Navy as one for which the Viking could provide an effective replacement for the piston-powered Grumman C-1 Trader. Modifications to the seventh YS-3A (BuNo 157998) to serve as a prototype for the proposed COD version were begun in July 1975 and covered by a supplemental contract awarded on 15 December, 1975. Its ASW equipment was removed to provide room for a crew of three (pilot, co-pilot, and crew-chief/loadmaster) and up to six passengers and/or cargo. Maximum cargo load of 5,750 lb (2,608 kg) could be carried in the modified bomb bay and in two 90-cu ft (2·5 cu m) pods attached to the external wing pylons. Redesignated US-3A and first flown on 2 July, 1976, the modified Viking had a maximum gross weight reduced from 52,539 lb (23,831 kg) for the S-3A to 47,602 lb (21,592 kg). After completion of its trials—including a deployment with VS-33 aboard the USS *Kitty Hawk* in autumn 1977—it was temporarily used as a trainer by VS-41 before being operated once again as a COD aircraft. In this role the US-3A has been joined by three partially modified YS-3As. However, even though the Grumman C-1s are the last avgas-burning aircraft aboard US carriers, Lockheed has been unable up to 1981 to secure a production contract for the COD-version of the Viking—with a fuselage stretched 5 ft 10 in (1·78 m) to accommodate up to 11 passengers. Nevertheless, retaining the necessary tooling, the manufacturer still hopes to have the COD aircraft ordered into production along with a proposed air tanker version (a KS-3A demonstrator, BuNo 157996, was modified from a YS-3A and fitted with probe-and-drogue refuelling equipment in the bomb bay). In 1981 this aircraft was still operated by VS-41, the Viking Replacement Air Group at NAS North Island.

Under a $14·5-mn contract Lockheed will upgrade two Vikings to the S-3B configuration with improved acoustic processing, expanded electronic support measure coverage, increased radar processing capabilities, a new sonobuoy receiver system, and provision for carrying Harpoon air-to-surface missiles. These two aircraft are to be tested beginning in 1985 and, if the modifications prove successful, the Navy plans to have a further 158 aircraft brought up to the S-3B standard between 1987 and 1991.

Related Temporary Design Designations: CL-995, CL-1002, CL-1220, CL-1224, CL-1231, CL-1234/CL-1243, CL-1251/CL-1252, CL-1276/CL-1286, CL-1551/CL-1559, CL-1616, CL-1650/CL-1661, CL-1663, CL-1666/CL-1669, CL-1671, CL-1673/CL-1674, CL-1676, CL-1709, CL-1760/CL-1763, CL-1770/CL-1783, CL-1950/CL-1952, CL-1956, CL-1970, CL-1990/CL-1991 and CL-1995/CL-1999

Span 68 ft 8 in (20·93 m) or 29 ft 6 in (8·99 m) with wings folded; length 53 ft 4 in (16·26 m); height 22 ft 9 in (6·93 m) or 15 ft 3 in (4·65 m) with tail folded; wing area 598 sq ft (55·55 sq m).

Empty weight 26,650 lb (12,088 kg); loaded weight 43,491 lb (19,727 kg); maximum weight 52,539 lb (23,831 kg); wing loading 72·7 lb/sq ft (355·1 kg/sq m); power loading 1·4 lb/lb st.

Maximum speed 518 mph at 25,000 ft (833 km/h at 7,620 m); cruising speed 403 mph (648 km/h); initial rate of climb 4,200 ft/min (1,280 m/min); service ceiling 35,000 ft (10,668 m); normal range 2,000 miles (3,220 km); maximum range 3,454 miles (5,555 km); endurance 4½ hr at radius of 530 miles (850 km).

Data for production S-3A Viking.

APPENDIX A

Lockheed Aircraft Model Designations and Projects

Early aircraft developed by the Loughead brothers were given designations which did not follow a set pattern. Thus, their first aircraft was designated Model G to imply that it was their seventh design, whereas the F-1 and S-1 designations indicated respectively that they identified their first flying-boat and first sportsplane designs. Since then, however, designations given by Lockheed to their aircraft have appeared to be even more confusing to the uninitiated.

The purposes of this appendix are (1) to explain the complex, but logical, aircraft designation systems in use since the late 1930s; (2) to provide a summary of these various systems; and (3) to illustrate seventeen of the most interesting projects not covered in the main section of this book.

As detailed further on, Lockheed began in the late 1930s to assign a Temporary Design Designation (L- or V- followed by a number) during the preliminary phase of each project. Already at that time, this initial identification was replaced by an Airplane Model Designation—consisting of a Basic Model Number (or Modified Basic Model Number), a Power Plant Identification Number, and an Interior Arrangement Identification Number—when the project was formalized and/or committed to production. These methods of designation are best illustrated by giving the example of the Lockheed Neptune.

Initial design studies for this maritime patrol aircraft were undertaken by the Vega Aircraft Corporation under the Temporary Design Designation V-135. Subsequent studies were identified at Vega as the V-146 (the proposal for the XP2V-1), V-148 (a proposed cargo version) and V-200 (a follow-on to the V-148). All additional studies emanated from Lockheed itself and received the following L- and CL- Temporary Design Designations:

Number	Purpose of study
L-165	Civil cargo transport
L-174	Photographic-reconnaissance version with new fuselage
L-175	Compound engine installation (led to P2V-4 version)
L-178	Proposed carrier-borne version
L-184	Powerplant installation interchangeable with that of the Constellation
L-194	Minimum change version
L-198	High-altitude version with propeller-turbines
L-218	Longer fuselage version
L-220	Became Model 726 (P2V-7)
CL-258	Proposed P2V-8, lighter and with better performance
CL-260	Long-range rescue version of P2V-7
CL-301	P2V-7 derivative
CL-305	P2V-8 study
CL-353	Four-engined derivative with low wing
CL-423	P2V-7 derivative for Japan
CL-431	P2V derivative for MAP-delivery to South American customers
CL-438	Standoff fighter with long-range Eagle air-to-air missiles

CL-476	P2V-7 modernization
CL-495	Version proposed to Royal Netherlands Navy in competition with Breguet Atlantic
CL-557	Re-arranged Julie/Jezebel configuration
CL-798	P2V-7KAI proposal for development by Kawasaki
CL-806	Further development of CL-798
CL-886	ASW version with airborne radiation measuring equipment
CL-1018	Project TRIM (AP-2H)
CL-1019	Improved crew emergency escape provision
CL-1020	Project TRICEPTS: electronic countermeasure modification of SP-2H
CL-1034	Project PRACTICE 9: high-altitude monitoring modification
CL-1041	Revised AP-2H (Project TRIM)
CL-1043	Advanced TRIM version
CL-1046	Modernized P-2 with quiet propeller-turbines, turbofans or ducted fan engines
CL-1062	More easily produced TRIM version
CL-1065	Gunship conversion of SP-2E
CL-1066	Proposed replacement of J34 turbojets with General Electric J85s
CL-1068	Improved TRIM armament proposal
CL-1151	Project KLIP: proposed P-2 modification for coastal search
CL-1190	Proposed SP-2H conversion as sensor testbed

The original V-135 and V-146 studies led to the production by Lockheed of 1,051 aircraft in the Model 26 group. The prototype, designated XP2V-1 by the US Navy Bureau of Aeronautics, was given by Lockheed the Airplane Model Designation 026-49-01 in which (1) the Basic Model Number 026 indicated that it was the first version of the Model 26, (2) the Power Plant Identification Number 49 identified the use of Wright R-3350-8 engines, and (3) the Interior Arrangement Identification Number 01 specified the original accommodation for a crew of eight. As new versions were developed, they were given revised Airplane Model Designations, with Modified Basic Model Numbers ranging from 026 to 826, as follows:

026-49-01: XP2V-1 prototype and P2V-1 production model with R-3350-8s and crew of eight.

026-52-01: XP2V-2 with R-3350-24Ws.

026-52-02: P2V-2 production model with R-3350-24Ws, crew of seven, and six cannon in the nose.

126-52-02: Same as above but tail turret with 20 mm cannon.

126-52-07: P2V-2 modified after delivery as P2V-2N, special all-weather photographic configuration.

126-52-08: P2V-2 modified after delivery for more efficient four-crew arrangement.

226-52-03: P2V-2S prototype with APS-20 radar.

326-59-02: P2V-3 production model; same as 026-52-02 (P2V-2) but with R-3350 26Ws.

326-59-04: P2V-3W; AEW version with R-3350-26Ws and crew of nine.

326-59-05: P2V-3C; modification of 326-59-02 for carrier operations; crew of seven.

326-59-09: P2V-3 modified after delivery as P2V-3Z combat transport.

426-59-03: P2V-4 delivered with R-3350-26Ws but with provisions for subsequent installation of R-3350-30Ws.

426-42-03: P2V-4 with R-3350-30Ws and crew of seven.

426-42-06: P2V-5 with R-3350-30Ws, crew of eight and nose turret.

426-42-11: P2V-5; same as above but crew increased to nine, and separate ECM and radio-operator stations.

426-42-13: P2V-5; same as 426-42-11 but tail turret replaced by MAD equipment.

426-42-15: P2V-5; same as 426-42-11 but observer station in lieu of nose turret.

426-42-16: P2V-5; same as 426-42-11 but fixed cannon in nose and separate aircraft-captain station.

426-45-15: P2V-5; same as 426-42-15 but R-3350-32Ws.

526-59-04: P2V-3W; designation later changed to 326-59-04.
626-42-12: P2V-6; same as 426-42-11 but with longer bomb bay and revised wingtip pods.
726-45-14: P2V-7; redesigned flight deck; R-3350Ws and crew of nine, or eight when dorsal turret not installed.
726-45-17: P2V-7; as above but redesigned crew (9) stations; no gun turret.
726-45-18: P2V-7B; same as 726-45-14 but crew of eight and six cannon in the nose.
826-45-14: P2V-7; same as 726-45-14 but no underwing jet pods.

The Lockheed designations described herein have appeared, and continue to appear, on official intra- and inter-departmental records, correspondence and reports, as well as in other official Lockheed documents addressed to various branches of the United States and Foreign governments dealing with aircraft. They are also used in all negotiations with commercial customers, both domestic and foreign. In negotiations with military or civil customers, the Lockheed designations are used interchangeably with those assigned by the customers.

Temporary Design Designations

From inception of preliminary study, each aircraft—be it a completely new design or redesign of a previous model—is assigned a Temporary Design Designation number (TDN). This system, which was first used in the late 1930s by the Lockheed Aircraft Corporation and the Vega Aircraft Corporation, initially consisted of a three-digit number prefixed by the letter L (or formerly V in the case of Vega models) and selected chronologically since 1938 in consecutive numerical order beginning with L-100—a proposed Lockheed Hudson development with American armament—and V-100—a proposed development of the Vega Starliner feeder-liner to be powered by a Pratt & Whitney Wasp Jr engine.

The last V- Temporary Design Designation assigned by Vega was V-313—a proposed three-seat liaison version of the Model 34 Big Dipper—whereas L- numbers continue to be assigned by Lockheed-California and had reached CL-2105 by mid-1981. Since the 1950s, when the Georgia Division came into being, these L-numbers have been prefixed by C (*e.g.* CL-282, the forebear of the U-2) for projects originating in California.

At Lockheed-Georgia a similar system was used from 1954 until 1965 and ran from GL-101 (an assault transport version of the C-130A) to GL-402 (another C-130 derivative). Moreover, the TDN GL-500 was used for a proposed commercial version of the C-5A. From 1966 until 1970 the GL-numbers were replaced by LG numbers as follows:

LG4-101 to LG4-102:	Derivatives of the Hummingbird
LG5-101 to LG5-217:	Military derivatives of the C-5A
LG100-100 to LG100-137:	Civil derivatives of the Hercules (replaced LG382 designations in 1969; still in use)
LG130-101 to LG130-214:	Military derivatives of the C-130
LG140-101 to LG140-116:	Military derivatives of the C-140 JetStar
LG141-101 to LG141-145,	
LG151-001 and LG161-001:	Military derivatives of the C-141
LG200-001 to LG200-019 and LG200-101 to LG200-102:	Civil derivatives of the StarLifter
LG2XX and subsequent	Sundry civil projects
LG300-101 to LG300-104:	Projected civil stretched version of the StarLifter
LG382-101 to LG382-104:	Civil derivatives of the Hercules (replaced by LG100 designations in 1969)
LG400-101 to LG400-104:	Projected twin-engined versions of the Hercules
LG500-101 to LG500-119:	Proposed commercial derivatives of the Galaxy
LG1329-101 to LG1329-110, LG2329-101 to LG2329-106 and LG3329-101 to LG3329-102:	Civil derivatives of the JetStar.

The system currently in use at Lockheed-Georgia was introduced in 1970 and consists of the following TDNs:

LGC001A and up: Commercial preliminary designs
LGM001A and up: Military preliminary designs
LGS001A and up: Support systems preliminary designs
LGX001A and up: Advanced concepts

These various TDN systems account for over 3,000 designs. However, it should be noted that many were nothing but cursory concept analyses while quite a few more were not aircraft related. The latter included items such as monorails, space systems and sonobuoys.

Airplane Model Designation

When a design study identified by a Temporary Design Designation leads either to the preparation of detailed drawings, to the submission of a formal proposal to military or commercial customers, or to the receipt of a development contract, Lockheed assigns a three-part Airplane Model Designation (Basic or Modified Basic Model Number—Power Plant Identification Number—Interior Arrangement Identification Number). Thus, in the previously quoted example, the V-146 proposal study formed the basis for the Model 026-49-01—military designation XP2V-1—in which 026 was the Modified Basic Model Number in the Model 26 group, 49 identified the use of Wright R-3350-8 radials, and 01 identified the original interior arrangement for a crew of eight.

Lockheed's Basic Model Numbers started with the Model 1—the original Vega with Wright Whirlwind radial—and have since been assigned in consecutive order. Initially, new versions of an established type were identified by new Basic Model Numbers (e.g. 2 and 5 for versions of the Vega). Later, the Basic Model Number was retained for all versions but these were identified by a suffix letter (e.g. Models 10-A, 10-B, etc). Finally, begun during the course of production of the Model 12 Electra Junior, the use of Modified Basic Model Number was adopted to identify versions of an established type. The Modified Basic Model Number then already consisted of the Basic Model Number prefixed by a number selected chronologically beginning with the number 0 (e.g., for the Model 49 series: 049, 149, . . . 1649). Lesser changes or post-delivery modifications were identified by adding a suffix letter after the Modified Basic Model Number—but before the hyphenated Power Plant Identification Number (e.g., 1049A, 1049B, . . . 1049G and 1049H).

In the following listing of Basic Model Numbers those followed by an asterisk identify aircraft produced by AiRover/Vega. Records of numerous projects, notably in the 40 to 60 range, are no longer available.

1   Vega with Wright Whirlwind J5 engine
2   Vega with Wright Whirlwind J6 engine
3   Air Express
4   Explorer
5   Vega with Pratt & Whitney Wasp engine
5* Engine nacelle design study for the Armstrong Whitworth Ensign
6   Possibly the Speed Vega (Y1C-17)
6* Cowling design study for the Handley Page Hampden
7   Explorer with wing dihedral
8   Sirius and Altair
9   Orion
10 Electra
11 Proposed twin-engined fighter (XPB-3/XFM-2); not built and Model Number used on some documents for a proposed Lockheed-built, Unitwin-powered design with conventional undercarriage
11* Altair 8G with Unitwin engine
12 Electra Junior
13 Not assigned

14	Super Electra and Hudson
15	Proposed twin-engined transport; developed postwar into the Model 75
15*	PV-2 Harpoon
16	Proposed twin-engined, twelve-seat transport derived from the Model 10
17*	B-17, XB-38 and XB-40 Flying Fortress
18	Lodestar
19	Proposed twin-engined, fourteen-seat transport derived from the Model 18
20	Initially assigned in 1938 to a proposed twin-engined transport; re-assigned to the XP-58 Chain Lightning
21*	Initial designation for the B-34 Ventura
22	P-38/F-4/F-5 Lightning
22*	Unitwin-powered Starliner
23	XP-49; later redesignated Model 522-66-07 in the Model 22 group
24	Proposed lighter and smaller development of P-38 for US Navy
25	Not used
26*	P2V Neptune
27	Proposed twin-engined, 24/35-seat transport with canard surfaces
28	Not used
29	Proposed twin-engined attack bomber
30	Proposed twin-engined attack bomber with canard surfaces
31	Proposed export version of the Model 29
32	Proposed twin-engined reconnaissance bomber version of the Model 18
33*	Little Dipper
34*	Big Dipper
35*	Single-engined primary trainer derived from the North American NA-35
36	Not used
37*	Ventura
38	Not used
39	Not used
40*	Pilotless aerial target; five built
41*	Proposed pilotless aerial target
42*	Proposed pilotless aerial target
43	No records
44	Proposed Excalibur four-engined transport
45	Proposed radio-controlled vehicle
46 to 48	No records
49	Constellation and Super Constellation
50*	Proposed single-engined liaison aircraft
51	Proposed XB-30 four-engined bomber derived from the Model 49 Constellation
52	Proposed single-seat fighter
53 to 59	No records
60*	Proposed twin-engined crew trainer
61*	Proposed twin-engined crew trainer
62*	Proposed twin-engined crew trainer
63 to 70	No records
71 to 73	Open for assignment by GELAC
74	No records
75	Saturn
76 to 79	Open for assignment by GELAC
80	F-80/T-33/F-94/T2V series
81	XFV-1
82	C-130 Hercules
83	F-104 Starfighter
84	W2V-1; cancelled during construction of prototype
85	P-3 Orion
86	XH-51

87   AH-56 Cheyenne
88   Propeller-turbine powered Electra
89   Constitution
90   XF-90
90* Several bomber studies
91   Supersonic transport (SST)
92   Proposed civil helicopter
93   L-1011 TriStar
94   S-3 Viking
95 to 98 No records
99   Interceptor fighter for the USAF; cancelled in January 1951.

The Power Plant Identification Number—the second element in the complete Airplane Model Designation—was assigned by Lockheed to identify each type of engine contemplated for installation. It consisted of a two-digit number selected chronologically in consecutive numerical order beginning with 01. Many Power Plant Identification Numbers were assigned more than once when the type of engine originally so identified was no longer used.

The Interior Arrangement Identification Number—the third and final element in a full Airplane Model Designation—consisted also of a two-digit number assigned in consecutive numerical order beginning with 01 for each Basic Model Number. Thus, for example, the number 01 identified the original eight-seat arrangement of the Model 26 (XP2V-1), the single-seat cockpit installation of the Model 22 (XP-38), and the original arrangement of the Model 82 (YC-130) interior. Therefore, a complete listing of Interior Arrangement Identification Numbers assigned to actual or proposed versions of all types would be excessively long to be quoted here.

Selected Projects

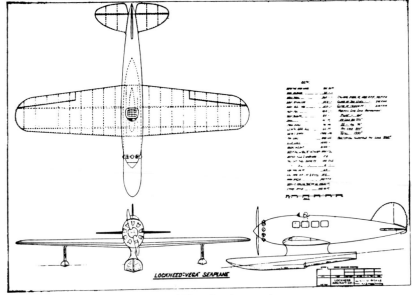

Lockheed Vega Seaplane project

466

Lockheed Vega Seaplane

Shortly after completing the design of the original Vega, Jack Northrop prepared plans for a low-wing version with central main float and wing-mounted stabilizing floats. The basic Vega fuselage and tail were matched to a new wing faired into the lower section of the fuselage. A mock-up was built and attracted the attention of Captain George Hubert Wilkins but, in the end, the noted explorer acquired two conventional Vegas. This design, however, provided the basis from which later Lockheed low-wing monoplanes, from the Explorer to the Orion, were developed. Powered by a 220 hp Wright Whirlwind J5, the projected seaplane had the following characteristics: span 41 ft (12·5 m), length 32 ft (9·75 m), wing area 235 sq ft (21·832 sq m), empty weight 1,750 lb (794 kg), loaded weight 3,100 lb (1,406 kg), maximum speed 130 mph (209 km/h), cruising speed 110 mph (177 km/h), initial rate of climb 775 ft/min (236 m/min), and service ceiling 14,500 ft (4,420 m).

Lockheed Model 27

The highly unusual Model 27, with its canard surfaces, was one of several twin-engined transports studied by Lockheed during the late 1930s. To be powered by 2,000 hp radial engines, the Model 27 was proposed with accommodation for either 24 (three-abreast seating) or 35 day passengers (four-abreast), or 16 passengers in sleeping berths. It attracted some airline interest but, as its novel configuration also caused some concern, it remained on the drawing board. Data from an August 1938 report: span 105 ft (32 m), length 76 ft 8 in (23·37 m), wing area 1,200 sq ft (111·48 sq m), empty weight 22,885 lb (10,380 kg), loaded weight 35,000 lb (15,876 kg), maximum speed 285 mph at 16,500 ft (459 km/h at 5,030 m), cruising speed 240 mph (386 km/h), initial rate of climb 1,520 ft/min (463 m/min), service ceiling 26,050 ft (7,940 m), range 1,500 miles (2,415 km) with 24 passengers and 1,217 lb (552 kg) of cargo.

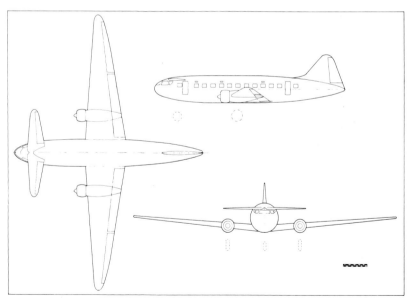

Lockheed Model 27 project

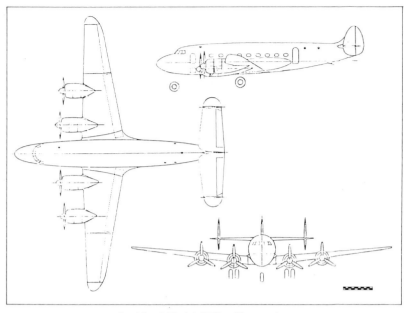

Lockheed Model 44 Excalibur project

Lockheed Model 44 Excalibur

The first four-engined Lockheed design, the Model 44 transport, came close to being ordered by Pan American Airways during 1939. However, development of the Model 49 for TWA rendered the Excalibur still-born. During the design period, the Model 44 grew steadily in size, weight, performance and capacity, and its tail configuration was changed from twin fins and rudders to triple surfaces. The following data are extracted from a June 1940 report and applies to the Model 44-14-01 with four 1,200 hp Pratt & Whitney Twin Wasp S4C4-Gs and daytime accommodation for 32 passengers: span 95 ft (28·96 m), length 74 ft 11½ in (22·85 m), wing area 1,000 sq ft (92·903 sq m), empty weight 26,424 lb (11,986 kg), and loaded weight 40,000 lb (18,144 kg).

Lockheed L-133

Preliminary concepts for a fighter powered by two of the company-designed L-1000 turbojets were prepared at Lockheed during 1941–42. Initial configuration called for a generally conventional design, but with the pilot being accommodated on a reclining seat in a glazed nose. This was changed, first for a canard design with air intakes on the upper fuselage sides, aft of the canard surfaces and cockpit, and then to a generally similar design, but with intakes moved to a nose position and surface cooling on most of the centre fuselage, the fin and the wing. This latter design, the Model 133-02-01, is illustrated. Its characteristics are as published in a February 1942 report: span 46 ft 8 in (14·22 m), length 48 ft 4 in (14·73 m), wing area 325 sq ft (30·194 sq m), and maximum speed 600 mph (965 km/h). Proposed armament: four nose-mounted 20 mm cannon with 90 rpg. Optimistic performance calculations failed to impress the USAF but Lockheed's pioneering jet propulsion work led the Army Air Forces to order the XP-80.

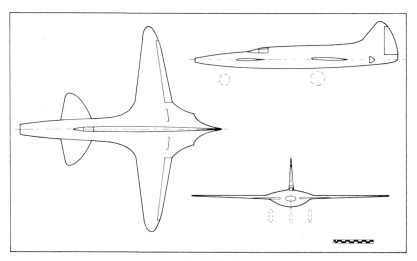

Lockheed L-133-02-01 project

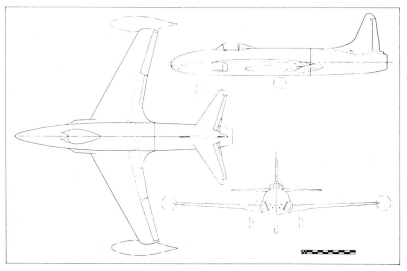

Lockheed L-181-1 (P-80E) project

Lockheed L-181 (P-80E)

The development of the Republic P-84 and North American P-86 threatened Lockheed's lead as the USAF's major supplier of jet fighters, and prompted the company to propose an advanced version of the P-80C. Studied under the Temporary Design Designation L-181 and proposed as the P-80E, the new version retained the nose, centre fuselage, vertical tail surfaces and armament of the P-80C. Its aft fuselage was enlarged to house an afterburning Allison J33-A-27 turbojet. The P-80E was to be fitted with thinner wing and tailplane with a sweep of 35 deg. Unfortunately for Lockheed, the USAF was well satisfied with the P-86

469

(F-86 after June 1948) and did not have any need for the P-80E. The following data are from a May 1948 report: span 37 ft (11·28 m), length 38 ft 10¼ in (11·84 m), wing area 248 sq ft (23·04 sq m), maximum weight 15,200 lb (6,895 kg), maximum speed 662 mph (1,065 km/h) at sea level, cruising speed 480 mph (772 km/h), initial rate of climb 3,720 ft/min (1,134 m/min), service ceiling 37,800 ft (11,520 m), and combat range 1,760 miles (2,830 km).

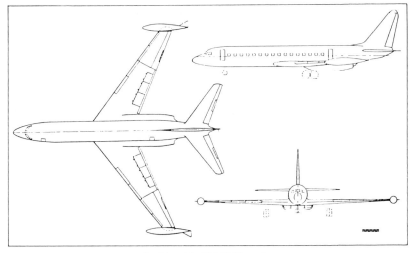

Lockheed L-193-02-01 project

Lockheed L-193

To an even greater extent than Convair, Lockheed underestimated the traffic-stimulation effect of the jetliners. Consequently, its jet transport studies of the early fifties all called for aircraft smaller than the Boeing 707 and Douglas DC-8, and even had in most instances lower seating capacity than the Convair 880. All these studies came to nothing and the company failed to produce a first-generation jetliner. Technically, the Lockheed jetliner studies of that period were quite advanced. Notably, they featured unconventional engine installations such as a staggered configuration with four turbojets mounted on the aft fuselage sides, with the inboard engines mounted aft of the outboard pair but fed by side-by-side intakes. Another configuration had either four or five turbojets mounted side by side beneath the fuselage. The version illustrated here was an early concept, as described in a March 1950 report, which had the following characteristics: span 104 ft (31·7 m) without tip tanks or 111 ft 4 in (33·93 m) with tip tanks, length 112 ft 2 in (34·19 m), wing area 1,615 sq ft (150·039 sq m), empty weight 74,500 lb (33,793 kg), and loaded weight 148,000 lb (67,132 kg). It was to be powered by four 12,200-lb (5,534-kg) thrust turbojets mounted beneath the fuselage, and was to carry only 64 passengers and a crew of five.

Lockheed L-204

Seeking to exploit fully the potential of its F-94 Starfire—the design of which had been undertaken in 1948 to provide the USAF with an interim all-weather jet interceptor, and which in 1949 had already undergone a major redesign to emerge in its F-94C version—Lockheed proposed in July 1950 a noteworthy development. Under the Temporary Design Designations L-204-1 to L-204-3 the manufacturer studied ways to increase performance, notably top speed and range, by revising the cockpit for single-crew operation and adding a

143·5 US gal (543 litre) saddle tank behind the revised cockpit. The L-204-2 was to have a new wing with thickness-to-chord ratio reduced from 10 to 6 per cent, while the L-204-3 was to have a low-aspect-ratio, highly-tapered wing of 6 per cent thickness. The L-204-1, however, was the most promising variant. Its design represented a bold departure from the contemporary state-of-the-art as performance improvements were to be derived from the use of a variable-geometry wing. Its sweep could be changed in flight from 0 deg to 55 deg by means of two pivot points and hydraulically-operated screw drives. Two schemes were proposed for its all-moving horizontal tail surfaces. In one instance they were to be mounted atop the aft fuselage, below the conventional swept fin and rudder, whereas the alternative called for rigidly attaching the horizontal tail surfaces to vertical surfaces which could be pivoted fore and aft to change the stabilizer incidence. Even though the L-204-1 was anticipated to become the first combat aircraft capable of exceeding the speed of sound at all altitudes from sea level to 43,500 ft (13,260 m), it remained at the preliminary design stages because the USAF preferred the all-new Convair F-102. Data for the L-204-1 were as follows: span 37·6 ft (11·46 m) unswept, or 25·3 ft (7·71 m) fully swept; wing area ranging from 233 sq ft (21·646 sq m) unswept to 271 sq ft (25·177 sq m) fully swept. Zero-fuel weight 14,573 lb (6,610 kg); loaded weight 18,896 lb (8,571 kg); maximum weight 22,186 lb (10,063 kg). Maximum speed 765 mph (1,231 km/h) at sea level and 702 mph at 31,700 ft (1,130 km/h at 9,660 m); initial rate of climb 6,200 ft/min (1,890 m/min); service ceiling 50,000 ft (15,240 m); combat range 1,530 miles (2,460 km).

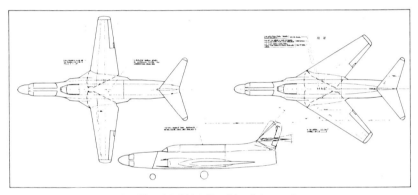

Lockheed L-204-1 (*Lockheed drawing*)

Lockheed L-205 (Model 99)

In answer to a Request for Proposal issued by the Air Force in September 1950, Lockheed developed the L-205 all-weather interceptor. Powered by a 15,000-lb (6,804-kg) thrust afterburning General Electric XJ53-GE-X10 turbojet, this aircraft won the design competition and two prototypes were ordered. Following the contract award, the Temporary Design Designation L-205 gave place to the Basic Model Number 99 and detailed design of the prototypes was undertaken. Armament was to consist of six MX-904 air-to-air guided missiles carried in a fuselage bay beneath and aft of the dorsal intake, and twenty 2·75-in FFAR rockets on the sides of the armament bay. However, concern over anticipated weight increases and resultant downgrading of performance led to the cancellation of the contract in January 1951. Span 30 ft 4 in (9·25 m) without tip tanks, length 63 ft 9¼ in (19·44 m), wing area 300 sq ft (27·871 sq m), empty weight 20,055 lb (9,097 kg), loaded weight 25,400 lb (11,521 kg), maximum weight 32,125 lb (14,572 kg), maximum speed 1,252 mph at 35,000 ft (2,015 km/h at 10,670 m), climb to 40,000 ft (12,190 m) in 1·6 min, combat ceiling 63,000 ft (19,200 m), and ferry range 1,760 miles (2,830 km).

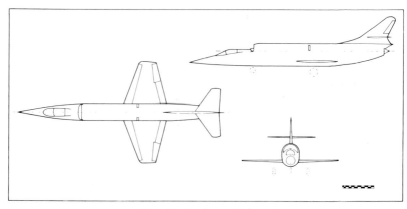

Lockheed L-205 (Model 99) project

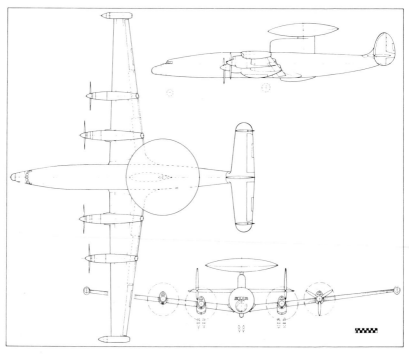

Lockheed W2V-1 project

472

Lockheed W2V-1

Designated CL-257 during the preliminary design phase, the W2V-1 (Lockheed Model 84) was an airborne early-warning version of the Model 1649 Starliner. It was proposed with either the three vertical fins and rudders of the Model 1649 or with enlarged twin vertical surfaces, and was to have been powered by four Allison T56-A-7 propeller-turbines and two wingtip-mounted Westinghouse J34 turbojets. Radar installation was to have combined the dorsal radome of the WV-2 with the rotodome of the WV-2E. Two W2V-1s were ordered by the US Navy during the spring of 1957 but the contract was cancelled in July of that year when the US military budget was drastically reduced. The development of a proposed CL-344 version, which was offered to the USAF as an RC-121 successor, did not even reach that stage. Data for the W2V-1: span 151 ft (46·02 m), length 116 ft 8 in (35·56 m), height 30 ft 3 in (9·22 m), wing area 1,850 sq ft (171·87 sq m), loaded weight 175,000 lb (79,379 kg).

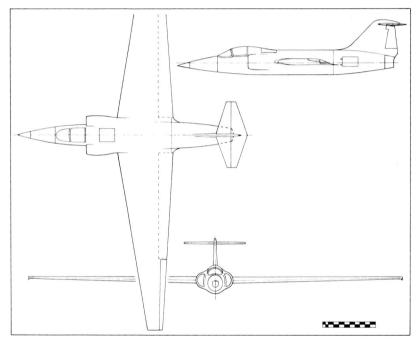

Lockheed CL-282 project

Lockheed CL-282

Designed in February 1954 as a private venture, the CL-282 was conceived as a high-altitude reconnaissance version of the XF-104 to meet the needs of the USAF and CIA. It was intended to be powered by a 9,300-lb (4,218-kg) thrust General Electric J73-GE-X52 turbojet fed from four wing tanks and one fuselage tank with a total capacity of 925 US gal (3,501 litres). For ground handling and take-off it was to rest on a jettisonable dolly—as used with the wartime Messerschmitt Me 163—and was to land on skis. The pilot was to be enclosed in an unpressurized cockpit, with 600 lb (272 kg) of mission payload being carried in a 15 cu ft (0·42 cu m) bay aft of the cockpit. The CL-282 provided the basis of the development of the U-2. Span 70 ft 8 in (21·54 m), length 44 ft (13·41 m), wing area 500 sq ft (46·45 sq m).

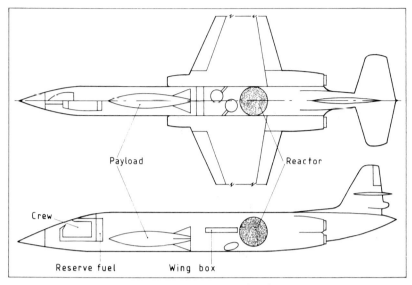

Payload

Reactor

Crew

Reserve fuel

Wing box

Lockheed nuclear-powered project

Lockheed Nuclear-Powered Bomber

As early as 1949 Lockheed explored the principles of nuclear-powered flight. This work led to Lockheed-California initiating preliminary studies for nuclear-powered bombers, some of them being identified by the Temporary Design Designations CL-225, 263, 284, 286, 293, 313 and 319. This research was then transferred to Lockheed-Georgia where work to meet the requirements of the USAF's Weapon System 125 was done under a variety of Temporary Design Designations beginning with GL-145. The use of nuclear propulsion proved unfeasible with the technology of the 1950s and Lockheed ended its efforts. The concept illustrated here called for the installation of the reactor in the centre fuselage, with the crew grouped in the nose and the bombload carried in the fuselage aft of the cockpit and ahead of the reactor.

Lockheed CL-352

To provide air defence for anti-submarine aircraft carriers (CVS class), in 1956 Lockheed proposed to develop an all-weather interceptor fighter from its T2V-1 advanced trainer. Lighter than contemporary naval fighters, the CL-352 benefited also from the SeaStar boundary layer control to operate easily from smaller decks. It was proposed to install a modified AN/APQ-50 radar fire control system in a recontoured nose. Armament was to have consisted of either two Sparrow III guided missiles and two Sidewinder infra-red missiles, or of two Sidewinders and two 19-rocket pods, on underwing pylons. The CL-352 was not adopted by the Navy as this Service preferred to use Sidewinder-armed McDonnell Douglas A-4 Skyhawks to equip its CVS carriers. Two versions of the CL-352 had been proposed, one retaining the Allison J33-A-24 turbojet of the SeaStar, and one with a lighter and more powerful Westinghouse J54-WE-2 turbojet. The following data applies to the J33-powered version. Span 42 ft 11 in (13·08 m); length 39 ft 11 in (12·17 m); wing area 232·8 sq ft (21·628 sq m). Loaded weight 20,500 lb (9,299 kg). Maximum speed 552 mph at 5,000 ft (888 km/h at 1,525 m); initial rate of climb 5,000 ft/min (1,525 m/min); combat range 580 miles

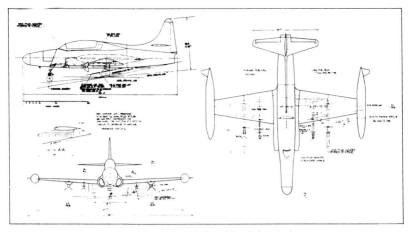

Lockheed CL-352 (*Lockheed drawing*)

(935 km); maximum range 1,075 miles (1,730 km). With the J54 turbojet, loaded weight was reduced to 19,620 lb (8,899 kg), top speed was boosted to 570 mph (917 km/h), and range was increased by 75 per cent.

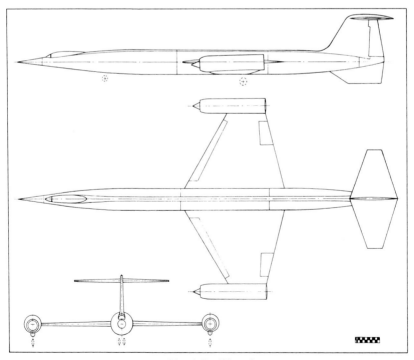

Lockheed CL-400 project

Lockheed CL-400

To meet the requirements for a U-2 successor, in early 1956 Kelly Johnson submitted to the USAF a proposal for a hydrogen-fuelled, high-altitude supersonic reconnaissance aircraft. An initial contract for two CL-400 prototypes was awarded in April 1956 and was followed soon after by an order for six more aircraft. Powered by two 9,500-lb (4,309-kg) thrust Pratt & Whitney 304-2 hydrogen-fuelled engines mounted at the tips of its thin trapezoidal wings, the CL-400 was a two-seat aircraft with span of 83 ft 9 in (25·53 m), length of 164 ft 10 in (50·24 m) and take-off weight of 69,955 lb (31,731 kg). Cruising at Mach 2·5 at between 95,000 and 100,000 ft (28,950 and 30,480 m), it was to reach targets within 1,100 naut miles (2,035 km) in fifty minutes. Engine development proceeded smoothly and manufacture was begun. However, Kelly Johnson and the Air Force were not satisfied with its short range. As 36,000 US gal (136,275 litres) of liquid hydrogen were already to be carried in three fuselage tanks, there appeared no feasible way to stretch range by increasing fuel capacity. Accordingly, the project was terminated in October 1957 and the almost completed prototypes were scrapped.

Lockheed CL-520

Proposed as a land-based Fleet air defence weapon system, the CL-520 was a derivative of the P-3 Orion. Its electronic equipment was to have included nose-mounted AN/APS-96 radar, a search and IFF aerial in a 24 ft (7·32 m) rotodome, ECM in a ventral radome, and a retractable Doppler antenna in the aft fuselage. Flying stand-off patrols over or near Allied vessels, the CL-520 was to engage enemy aircraft with long-range Bendix Eagle missiles; three of these missiles were to be carried in the Orion bomb bay and seven more could be carried beneath the wing centre section. Anticipated performance included a top speed of 420 mph (676 km/h), and a patrol endurance of 4·4 hours at 575 miles (925 km) from base when carrying ten missiles, or 3·5 hours at 1,035 miles (1,665 km) from base when carrying six missiles.

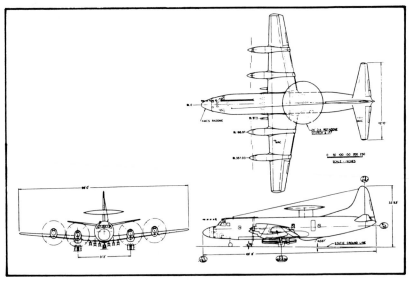

Lockheed CL-520 (*Lockheed drawing*)

Full-scale mock-up of the CL-760 counter-insurgency (COIN) project. (*Lockheed*)

Lockheed CL-760

In answer to a Tri-Service (USA/USAF/USN) requirement for a Light Armed Reconnaissance Aircraft (LARA), in March 1964 Lockheed-California submitted a proposal for its CL-760 counter-insurgency aircraft. Eight other manufacturers entered competitive COIN designs, and the US Navy, which acted as Project Systems Manager for the Department of Defense, selected the North American NA-300 (military designation OV-10 Bronco) in August 1964. The losing Lockheed entry was to have been powered by two 600 shp Garrett T76 propeller-turbines. Fuselage blisters were to house the retractable main undercarriage units and four 7·62 mm machine-guns; offensive stores were to be carried on multiple racks beneath the fuselage and wing. The crew of two was to be seated in tandem forward of the wing and, for troop transport/assault missions, eight fully-armed infantrymen could be carried in the fuselage. Span 30 ft (9·14 m), length 40 ft 3½ in (12·28 m), empty weight 5,106 lb (2,316 kg), loaded weight 9,270 lb (4,205 kg), and maximum speed 325 mph (523 km/h).

Lockheed L-2000

In June 1963 President John F. Kennedy announced his support for a US supersonic transport project and two months later, on 15 August, the FAA requested design proposals for a 125-160 passenger SST and its engines. Phase I proposals were submitted by Boeing, Lockheed (CL-823 design) and North American, with engine designs submitted by General Electric and Pratt & Whitney. Only North American was eliminated before Phases 2A and 2B, during which Boeing and Lockheed refined their designs. By August 1965 the programme had moved into its Phase 2C which extended through December 1966. At that time Lockheed submitted details for its L-2000-7A, with accommodation for up to 273 passengers in all-tourist configuration, and stretched L-2000-7B, with 308 seats. Although it was rumoured that most airlines favoured the Lockheed design, on 31 December, 1966, the FAA announced its selection of the Boeing entry. The following data for the L-2000-7A, with either four afterburning General Electric GE4/J5M or Pratt & Whitney JTF17A-21L engines, were published by Lockheed in a September 1966 report: span 116 ft (35·36 m), length 273 ft 2 in (83·26 m), wing area 8,486 sq ft (788·378 sq m), operating weight empty 238,000 lb (107,955 kg), maximum take-off weight 590,000 lb (267,620 kg), cruise Mach 2·7 at 70,000 ft (21,375 m), and range of 4,000 miles (6,435 km) with payload of 58,450 lb (26,512 kg) equivalent to 258 passengers (typical mixed-class configuration: 28 First +230 Economy) and 6,850 lb (3,107 kg) of cargo.

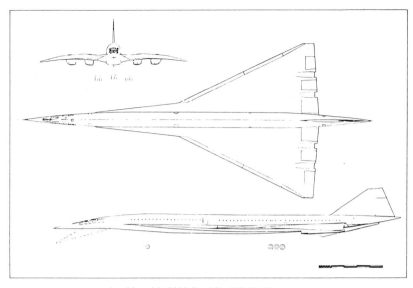

Lockheed L-2000-7A (CL-823-42-1) project

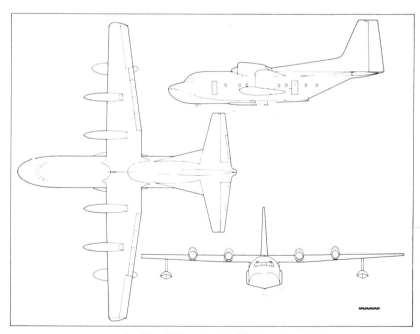

Lockheed Hercules Amphibian project

478

Lockheed Hercules Amphibian

To improve still further the versatility of its C-130, Lockheed-Georgia undertook, between 1964 and 1973, several studies of an amphibian version. The basic principles of the conversion were proved during the course of a 1968 US Navy contract for which a one-sixth dynamically-scaled, radio-controlled model was used as a development tool. Retaining the basic C-130 airframe and undercarriage, the HOW (Hercules-On-Water) was to be fitted with a retractable hydro-ski beneath the fuselage, a false hull beneath the existing pressurized fuselage, and two auxiliary floats each housing 400 US gal (1,514 litres) of fuel. Furthermore, the nacelles for its Allison T56 engines were to be inverted to take the propellers and intakes away from the water spray. The design was improved during the following four years and the version illustrated here had enlarged tail surfaces, double-slotted flaps and spoilers. Various configurations were offered to military users and airlines—the type being proposed as a city centre-to-city centre transport operating from waterways available in most major cities in the United States—but no production contracts were received. Data for this version are extracted from an October 1972 brochure: span 132 ft 7 in (40·41 m), length 100 ft 10¾ in (30·75 m), wing area 1,745·5 sq ft (162·163 sq m), loaded weight 155,000 lb (70,307 kg), maximum payload 36,250 lb (16,443 kg), cruising speed 345 mph (555 km/h), and ferry range 4,300 miles (6,920 km).

APPENDIX B

Production Details and Constructor's Numbers

Only original serials or registrations given.
Abbreviations used include: AF-Air Force, AL-Airline/s, AS-Air Service/s, AT-Air Transport and AW-Airway/s.　　　　　　　　　　Accurate to 31 December, 1980.

LOUGHEAD MODEL G (Number built: 1)

---	Model G	Co. owned	---	1

LOUGHEAD F-1 (Number built: 1)

---	F-1	Co. owned	---	1

CURTISS HS-2L (Number built: 2 by Loughead, plus 754 by other manufacturers)

---	HS-2L	USN	A4228/A4229	2

LOUGHEAD S-1 (Number built: 1)

---	S-1	Co. owned	---	1

LOCKHEED VEGA (Number built: 115 by Lockheed, plus 9 by Detroit Aircraft Corp. and 4 by others)

1	Vega 1	Co. owned	2788	1
3	Vega 1	Co. owned	X3625	1
4	Vega 1	G.H. Wilkins	X3903	1
6	Vega 1	E.P. Halliburton	NC4097	1
7	Vega 5	H.J. Tucker	X4769	1
8	Vega 1	Air Associates	X5885	1
9	Vega 1	Maddux AL	NC6526	1
10	Vega 1	Air Associates	NC6911	1
11	Vega 1	Maddux AL	NC7044	1
12	Vega 1	Texas Pipe Line	7162	1
12B	Vega 1	Chadbourne Aircraft	NC7425	1
14	Vega 1	Universal AL	NC7426	1
15	Vega 1	Santa Maria AL	NC7427	1
16	Vega 1	Continental Air	NC7428	1
17	Vega 1	Sir Hubert Wilkins	X7439	1
18	Vega 5	E.P. Halliburton	X7429	1
19	Vega	Lt. Col. W. Thaw	X7430	1
20	Vega 5	Standard Oil	X7440	1

21	Vega 5	Schlee-Brock	X7441	1
22	Vega 5	Co. owned	NC7952	1
23	Vega 5	Universal AL	NC7953	1
24	Vega 5	F.C. Hall	NC7954	1
25	Vega 5	Schlee-Brock	NC194E	1
26	Vega 5	Nevada AL	NC195E	1
27	Vega 5	Co. owned	196E	1
28	Vega 1	Cromwell-Hunt AS	NC7805	1
29	Vega 1	Schlee-Brock	NC7894	1
30	Vega 1	Commercial AW	7895	1
31	Vega 1	Schlee-Brock	NC7896	1
32	Vega 1	Schlee-Brock	NC7973	1
33	Vega 1	California AT	NC32E	1
34	Vega 1	Bryde & Dahl	NR33E	1
35	Vega 1	Co. owned	NC34E	1
36	Vega 1	Co. owned	NC31E	1
37	Vega 1	Co. owned	NC35E	1
38	Vega 1	Co. owned	NC197E	1
39	Vega 1	Co. owned	198E	1
40	Vega 1	Montana Dev.	NC199E	1
41	Vega 1	Alaska-Wash. AW	NC200E	1
42/47	Vega	Parts only	---	0
48	Vega 5	Alaska-Wash. AW	NC432E	1
49/50	Vega 5	Nevada AL	NC433E/NC434E	2
51	Vega 5	E.P. Halliburton	NC435E	1
52	Vega 5	Schlee-Brock	NC513E	1
53	Vega 5	E.P. Halliburton	NC624E	1
54	Vega 5	Alaska-Wash. AW	NC657E	1
55	Vega 5	E.P. Halliburton	NC658E	1
56	Vega 2	Co. owned	606	1
57/58	Vega 2	Schlee-Brock	NC574E, NC623E	2
59	Vega 5	C.A.T.	NC2874	1
60	Vega 2	Schlee-Brock	NC2875	1
61/62	Vega 5B	C.A.T.	NC2845/NC2846	2
63	Vega 5	Marland Production	NC625E	1
64	Vega 2	Schlee-Brock	NC857E	1
66	Vega 5B	Co. owned	NC858E	1
67	Vega 5	Major J.P. Wood	C859E	1
68	Vega 5B	Co. owned	NC868E	1
69	Vega 5	Schlee-Brock	NC869E	1
70	Vega 5	Middle States AL	NC870E	1
71	Vega 5	Schlee-Brock	NC871E	1
72	Vega 5A	Independent Oil	NC898E	1
73	Vega 5	Schlee-Brock	NC891E	1
74	Vega 5B	Schlee-Brock	NC892E	1
76	Vega 5C	Rapid AL	NC306H	(1)
78	Vega 5	U.S. Air Transport	NC9424	1
79	Vega 5A	B.F. Goodrich	NC308H	1
80	Vega 5A	W. Gibbs McAdoo	NC309H	1
81	Vega 5	Co. owned	NC366H	1
82	Vega 5	U.S. Air Transport	NC397H	1
83	Vega 2	Co. owned	NC505K	1
84	Vega 5	C.A.T.	NC392H	1
85	Vega 5	Co. owned	R393H	1
86	Vega	Parts only	---	0
87	Vega 5	Dr. W.M. Cross	NC394H	1
88	Vega 5A	A. Belmont & Co.	NC395H	1
89	Vega 5A	Co. owned	NC396H	1
90	Vega 5B	C.A.T.	NC504K	1
94	Vega 5	Alaska-Wash. AW	NC974H	1
95	Vega	Parts only	---	0
96	Vega 5A	W.H. Dunning	NC975H	1
97	Vega 5	C.A.T.	NC46M	1
98	Vega 5	Beardsley & Piper	NC31M	1
99	Vega 5	Julian Oil Co.	NC47M	1
100	Vega 5B	C.A.T.	NC48M	1
101	Vega 5B	Asa Candler Jr.	NC49M	1
102	Vega Special	Evening News	NC32M	1
103	Vega 5B	C.A.T.	NC534M	1
104	Vega	Parts only	---	0
105	Vega 5B	Asa Candler Jr.	NC536M	1
106	Vega 5B	Wedell-Williams AS	NC537M	1
107	Vega 5A	Co. owned	NC538M	1

108	Vega 5A	Shell Petroleum	NC539M	1
109	Vega 5B	Wedell-Williams AS	NC540M	1
110/111	Vega	Parts only	---	0
112	Vega 5B	J.H. Mears	NR500V	1
113/115	Vega	Parts only	---	0
117/118	Vega 5B	Standard Oil	NC105N/NC106N	2
119/120	Vega 5B	Alaska-Wash. AW	NC102W/NC103W	2
121	Vega 5B	Wedell-Williams AS	NC104W	1
122	Vega 5B	F.C. Hall	NC105W	1
123	Vega 5B	Julian Oil Co.	NC106W	1
124	Vega 5B	W.T. Ponder	NC107W	1
125	Vega 5B	Beardsley & Piper	NC152W	1
126/127	Vega 5B	Bowen AL	NC160W/NC161W	2
128	Vega 5B	W.H. Dunning	NC162W	1
129	Vega 5B	Bowen AL	NC176W	1
132	Vega 5A	McAleer Manuf.	NC904Y	1
133	Vega 5B	Kessler Oil & Gas	NC905Y	1
134	Vega 5B	Shell Oil	NC926Y	1
135	DL-1	Co. owned	NC497H	1
136/137	DL-1B	Co. owned	NC483M, NC288W	2
138	Vega 5C	Margaret Durant	NC934Y	1
154	DL-1B	Co. owned	NC8497	1
155	DL-1 Special	Lt. Cdr. G. Kidston	G-ABGK	1
156/157	DL-1	Bowen AL	NC8495/NC8496	2
158	Y1C-12	USAAC	31-405	1
159	Y1C-17	USAAC	31-408	1
160	Vega 5C	Parks Air College	NC972Y	1
170	Vega 5C	Prest-O-Lite	NC959Y	1
171	Vega 5C Special	J.H. Mears	NR965Y	1
194	Vega 5C Special	Continental Oil	NC12282	1
203	Vega 5C	Shell Aviation	NC13705	1
210	Vega 5C	W.P. Fuller Sr.	NC14236	1

Vegas assembled by others were as follows:

139	Vega 5B	Wedell-Williams AS	NC997N	1
161	DL-1B Special	John Morrell	NC12288	1
191	Vega 5C	Braniff	NC980Y	1
619	Vega 5 Special	W.S. Brock	NR496M	1

LOCKHEED AIR EXPRESS (Number built: 7)

5	Air Express	WAE	4897	1
65	Air Express	NYRBA	NC514E	1
75	Air Express	Co. owned	NR3057	1
76	Air Express	TAT	NC306H	1
77	Air Express	NYRBA	NC307H	1
91	Air Express	Parts only	---	0
92	Air Express	R.L. Brooks	NC522K	1
93	Air Express	Parts only	---	0
130	Air Express Special	Atlantic Exhib.	NR974Y	1
131	Air Express	Parts only	---	0
EX-2	Air Express	Co. owned	7955	(1)

LOCKHEED EXPLORER (Number built: 4)

2	Explorer 4	A.H. Bromley	NR856H	1
116	Explorer 4	A.H. Bromley	NR856H	1
147	Explorer 7	A.H. Bromley	NR100W	1
148	Explorer 7	Pure Oil Co.	NR101W	1

LOCKHEED SIRIUS (Number built: 14 by Lockheed, plus 1 by Detroit Aircraft Corp.)

140	Sirius 8	C.A. Lindbergh	---	1
141	Sirius 8	Shell Oil	NC349V	1
142	Sirius 8	Co. owned	NR12W	1
143	Sirius 8A	Joan Fay Shankle	NC13W	1
144	Sirius 8	Co. owned	NC14W	1
145	Sirius 8A	Co. owned	NC15W	1
146	Sirius 8A	S.L. Lambert	NC16W	1
149	Sirius 8	Col. R. Fierro	X-BADA	1
150	Sirius 8C	H.W. Blumenthal	NR116W	1
151	Sirius 8A	Air Services	NC117W	1
152	Sirius 8A	Capt. G.R. Hutchinson	NR118W	1
153	Sirius 8A	Co. owned	X119W	1
165	DL-2	Co. owned	X8494	1
166	Sirius 8A	Emil Salay	NR115W	1
167	Sirius 8A	Wedell-Williams AS	NC167W	1

```
LOCKHEED ALTAIR (Number built:  3 by Lockheed, plus 2 by Detroit Aircraft Corp.
                        and 1 by AiRover)
143             Altair 8D         C. Chamberlin       NC13W           (1)
145             Altair            J. Goodwin Hall     NR15W           (1)
152             Altair 8D         Co. owned           X118W           (1)
153             Altair            Co. owned           X119W           (1)
165             Altair DL-2A      Co. owned           NR8494          (1)
176             Altair Special    Macfadden Publ.     NR998Y          1
179             XRO-1             USN                 9054            1
180             DL-2A             Co. owned           X12222          1
188             Altair 8E         Mainichi Shimbun    X12230          1
213             Altair 8F         Mainichi Shimbun    X14209          1
1 (AiRover)     Altair 8G         Co. owned           NX18149         1

LOCKHEED ORION (Number built:  35)
168             Orion 9           Co. owned           X960Y           1
169             Orion 9           Bowen AL            NC964Y          1
172/173         Orion 9           NY & Western AL     NC975Y, NC984Y  2
174             Orion 9           A.G. Candler Jr.    NC988Y          1
175             Orion 9           Continental AW      NC991Y          1
177             Orion 9           Continental AW      NR12220         1
178             Orion 9           NY, Phil. & Wash. AW NC12221        1
180             Orion 9C Special  Shell Aviation      NC12222         (1)
181/186         Orion 9           Varney AS           NC12223/NC12228 6
187             Orion 9A Special  Hal Roach Studios   X12229          1
189/190         Orion 9B          Swissair            X12231/X12232   2
192             Orion 9 Special   Co. owned           NC12277         1
193             Orion 9E          TWA                 NC12278         1
195             Orion 9E          TWA                 NC12283         1
196             Orion 9F          G.A. MacDonald      NC12284         1
197/199         Orion 9D          American            NC12285/NC12287 3
200/202         Orion 9D          American            NC229Y/NC231Y   3
204             Orion 9D-1        J. Mabee            NC232Y          1
205/207         Orion 9D          Northwest           NC13747/NC13749 3
208             Orion 9D-2        Evening News        X799W           1
209             Orion 9D          M. Detroyat         F-AKHC          1
211             Orion 9D Special  Laura Ingalls       NR14222         1
212             Orion 9F-1        Phillips Petroleum  NC14246         1

DETROIT-LOCKHEED XP-900 (Number built:  1)
- - -           XP-900            USAAC               32-320          1

LOCKHEED 10 ELECTRA (Number built:  149)
1001            10-A              Co. owned           X233Y           1
1002/1003       10-A              Northwest           NC14243/NC14244 2
1004            10-C              Co. owned           X14257          1
1005/1006       10-C              PAA                 NC14258/NC14259 2
1007/1008       10-C              Aerovias Centrales  XA-BEO/XA-BEP   2
1009            10-C              Co. owned           NC13762         1
1010/1011       10-A              Northwest           NC14263, NC14260 2
1012            10-A              W.I. Inman          NC3138          1
1013/1015       10-A              Northwest           NC14261/NC14262
                                                      & NC14900        3
1016            10-A              Continental Oil     NC14901         1
1017            10-A              Okura & Co.         ---             1
1018            10-A              Braniff             NC14905         1
1019            10-C              PAA                 NC14906         1
1020/1021       10-A              Northwest           NC14907, NC14915 2
1022            10-C              Aerovias Centrales  XA-BEQ          1
1023/1025       10-A              Northwest           NC14934/NC14936 3
1026/1031       10-A              Braniff             NC14937/NC14942 6
1032            10-A              M.C. Fleischmann    NC14945         1
1033            10-A              C.H. Beal           NC14946         1
1034            10-A              Mesta Mach. Co.     NC14947         1
1035            10-A              R.W. Norton         NC14948         1
1036            10-B              Co. owned           NX14958         1
1037/1040       10-B              North American      NC14959/NC14962 4
1041            10-E              Co. owned           NX14971         1
1042/1043       10-E              PAA                 NC14972/NC14973 2
1044            10-A              Westchester Airplane NC14981        1
1045/1048       10-A              LOT                 SP-AYA/SP-AYD   4
1049/1051       10-B              Delta               NC14990/NC14992 3
1052            XR20-1            USN                 0267            1
```

482

1053	XR30-1	USCG	383	1
1054	10-E	Varney AT	NC14994	1
1055	10-E	Amelia Earhart	NR16020	1
1056/1059	10-B	C & S	NC16021/NC16024	4
1060	10-A	Guinea AW	VH-UXH	1
1061	10-A	Mid-Continent	NC16050	1
1062	10-A	A. Kudner Inc.	NC16051	1
1063/1064	10-A	Canadian AW	CF-AZY, CF-BAF	2
1065	10-E	H.S. Vanderbilt	NC16059	1
1066	10-B	Dr. J.R. Brinkley	NC16054	1
1067	10-B	C & S	NC16022	1
1068	10-A	Bata Shoe Co.	NC16078	1
1069/1070	10-A	National	NC16055/NC16056	2
1071	Y1C-36	USAAC	37-65	1
1072	10-A	Idaho Mar. Mines	NC16084	1
1073/1074	Y1C-36	USAAC	37-66/37-67	2
1075	10-A	R. Wolf Kahn	NC1700	1
1076	10-A	R.R.M. Carpenter	NC20Y	1
1077	10-B	Delta	NC16053	1
1078/1079	10-A	Min. de Comm.	YV-ACE, YV-ACI	2
1080/1083	10-A	British AW	G-AEPN/G-AEPP	
			& G-AEPR	4
1084	10-A	Westchester Airplane	NC16058	1
1085/1088	10-A	LOT	SP-BGE/SP-BGH	4
1089/1090	10-A	LARES	YR-LEA/YR-LEB	2
1091	10-A	Bata Shoe Co.	NC17380	1
1092	10-A	Union AW of NZ	ZK-AFC	1
1093/1094	10-A	LARES	YR-LEC/YR-LED	2
1095	10-A	Union AW of NZ	ZK-AFD	1
1096	10-A	Hanford AL	NC17375	1
1097/1098	10-A	Aeroput	YU-SAV, YU-SAZ	2
1099/1100	10-A	LOT	SP-BGJ/SP-BGK	2
1101	10-A	Fain Drilling Co.	NC17391	1
1102	10-A	British AW	G-AESY	1
1103	10-A	Union AW of NZ	ZK-AFE	1
1104	Y1C-37	NGB	37-376	1
1105	10-A	Guinea AW	VH-UXI	1
1106/1107	10-B	Ansett	VH-UZN/VH-UZO	2
1108	10-A	Guinea AW	VH-AAU	1
1109	10-B	Ansett	VH-UZP	1
1110/1111	10-A	LAV	YV-ACO, YV-ACU	2
1112/1113	10-A	TCA	CF-TCA/CF-TCB	2
1114	10-A	Bata Shoe Co.	OK-CTA	1
1115	10-E	Aviacion Naval	M.M.1	1
1116	10-A	TCA	CF-TCC	1
1117	10-E	Braniff	NC18139	1
1118	10-E	Republic Steel	NC19982	1
1119/1121	10-A	LARES	YR-LEE/YR-LEG	3
1122	10-A	British AW	G-AFEB	1
1123/1124	10-A	Aeroput	YU-SBA/YU-SBB	2
1125	10-E	Aviacion Militar	163	1
1126	10-E	LAV	YV-ADA	1
1127/1128	10-A	Union AW of NZ	ZK-AGJ/ZK-AGK	2
1129	10-E	Idaho Mar. Mines	NC18987	1
1130/1131	10-A	MacRobertson Miller	VH-ABV/VH-ABW	2
1132	10-A	LAV	YV-ADE	1
1133/1134	10-E	SACO	C-10/C-11	2
1135/1137	10-A	Aeroput	YU-SBC/YU-SBE	3
1138	10-A	Standard Oil	NC21735	1
1139	10-A	Aeroput	YU-SDA	1
1140	10-E	Delta	NC21791	1
1141/1142	10-A	LAN	CC-224/CC-225	2
1143/1144	10-A	LAV	YV-ADU, YV-AFA	2
1145/1148	10-A	LAN	CC-226/CC-229	4
3501	XC-35	USAAC	36-353	1

LOCKHEED 12 ELECTRA JUNIOR (Number built: 130)

1201	12-A	Co. owned	NX16052	1
1202	12-A	Tela RR Co.	NC16076	1
1203	12-A	Herschbach Drilling	NC16077	1
1204	12-A	CAA	NC17	1
1205	12-A	Continental Oil	NC16079	1
1206	12-A	Lord Beaverbrook	G-AEMZ	1

1207	12-A	Loffland Bros.	NC58Y	1
1208	12-A	H.E. Talbott & Co.	NC2072	1
1209	12-A	Santa Maria AL	NC17309	1
1210	12-A	Humble Oil	NC17310	1
1211	12-A	Walgreen Drug Co.	NC17311	1
1212	12-A	Brian Allen Av.	G-AEOI	1
1213	12-A	Powell Crossley Jr.	NC16057	1
1214	12-A	E.P. Halliburton	NC16085	1
1215	12-A	Byrd-Frost AT	NC17341	1
1216	12-A	Lang Transp. Co.	NC17342	1
1217	12-A	J.C. Shafter Drilling	NC17373	1
1218	12-A	Superior Oil	NC1/374	1
1219	12-A	Dept. of Transport	CF-CCT	1
1220	12-A	P.G. Thompson	NC17376	1
1221	12-A	J. W. Thorpe	NC18127	1
1222/1223	12-A	Varney AT	NC18125/NC18126	2
1224	12-A	Standard Oil	NC17379	1
1225	12-A	Republic Oil	NR869E	1
1226	12-A	F.C. Hall	NC18130	1
1227	JO-1	USN	1053	1
1228	12-B	Aviacion Militar	---	1
1229	12-A	Varney AT	N18137	1
1230/1233	JO-2	USN	1048/1051	4
1234/1235	12-A	D. Ae.	D.Ae. 01/02	2
1236	12-A	Associated AL	VH-ABH	1
1237	12-A	H.H. Maharajah of Jodhpur	VT-AJN	1
1238	12-A	Aero. Research & Sales	G-AFCO	1
1239	12-A	Dept. de Ferrocarril	XB-ABW	1
1240	12-A	McClanahan Oil	NC18946	1
1241	12-A	W.D. May	NC18947	1
1242	12-A	A. Spreckels	NC18948	1
1243	12-A	Western	NC18955	1
1244	12-A	Johnson & Johnson	NC18956	1
1245	12-A	J.W. Thorpe	NC18957	1
1246	12-A	E.H. Moore	NC18958	1
1247	12-A	Co. owned	NC18965	1
1248	12-A	Min. de Guerra y Marina	---	1
1249	12-B	Aviacion Militar	---	1
1250	12-A	Phillips Petroleum	NC18970	1
1251	12-A	Republic Steel	NC18976	1
1252	12-A	Continental Oil	NC18996	1
1253	XJO-3	USN	1267	1
1254/1255	C-40	USAAC	38-537/38-538	2
1256/1265	C-40A	USAAC	38-539/38-548	10
1266	C-40B	USAAC	38-582	1
1267	12-A	British AW	G-AFKR	1
1268	12-A	NACA	NACA 97	1
1269	12-A	Reiss-Premier	NC17397	1
1270	12-A	British AW	G-AFPF	1
1271	12-A	Phillips Petroleum	NC17399	1
1272	12-A	TVA	NX18964	1
1273	12-A	H.M. Naylor	NC21770	1
1274	12-A	Aero. Research & Sales	G-AFXP	1
1275	12-A	Pittsburgh Steel	NC18977	1
1276	12-A	Sky Kraft Corp.	NC18147	1
1277	12-A	Nevada Devel.	NC18900	1
1278/1279	12-A	D.Ae.	D.Ae. 03/04	2
1280	12-A	Swiftlite Corp.	NC4000	1
1281	12-A	Socony-Vacuum Oil	NC2630	1
1282	12-A	Vaucluse Av. Corp.	NC19967	1
1283	JO-2	USN	2541	1
1284	12-A	Belle Baruch	NC2002	1
1285	12-A	Cunliffe-Owen	G-AGBJ*	1
1286	12-A	Humble Oil	NC25624	1
1287	12-A	Sky Kraft Corp.	NC33615	1
1288/1291	12-A	D.Ae.	D.Ae. 05/08	4
1292	12-A	NACA	NACA 99	1
1293	12-25	Square D Co.	NC34965	1
1294	12-25	Continental Oil	NC33650	1
1295/1314	12-26	N.E.I. Gov't.	L227/L246	20
212-01/-12	212	N.E.I. Air Force	L201/L212	12

| 212-13 | 212 | Co. owned | NX18955 | (1) |
| 212-14/-17 | 212 | N.E.I. Air Force | L213/L216 | 4 |

* wrongly registered, changed to G-AGDT

LOCKHEED 14 SUPER ELECTRA (Number built: 112 by Lockheed, plus 64 by Tachikawa and 55 by Kawasaki)

1401	14-H	Co. owned	X17382	1
1402/1408	14-H	Northwest	NC17383/NC17389	7
1409	14-H	Northwest	NC17382	1
1410	14-F62	KLM	PJ-AIP	1
1411	14-F62	KNILM	PK-AFM	1
1412	14-F62	KLM	PJ-AIT	1
1413	14-F62	KLM	PH-APE	1
1414/1415	14-F62	KNILM	PK-AFN/PK-AFO	2
1416	14-G105	All American Av.	NC18138	1
1417	14-G105	H.S. Vanderbilt	NC2333	1
1418	14-H	Guinea AW	VH-ABI	1
1419	14-G102	Hughes Aircraft	NX18973	1
1420/1425	14-H	LOT	SP-BNE/SP-BNH & SP-BNJ/SP-BNK	6
1426/1428	14-G3B	Tachikawa	---	3
1429/1430	14-H2	TCA	CF-TCD/CF-TCE	2
1431/1432	14-H2	Northwest	NC17392/NC17393	2
1433/1438	14-G3B	Tachikawa	---	6
1439	14-H2	Co. owned	NC17394	1
1439A	14-H2	Northwest	NC18994	1
1440/1441	14-F62	KLM	PJ-AIK, PJ-AIM	2
1442/1443	14-F62	KNILM	PK-AFP/PK-AFQ	2
1444	14-F62	KLM	PH-ASL	1
1445/1446	14-G3B	Tachikawa	---	2
1447/1449	14-G3B	Nihon Koku	---	3
1450/1451	14-H2	TCA	CF-TCF/CF-TCG	2
1452	14-G3B	Tachikawa	---	1
1453/1454	14-G3B	Nihon Koku	---	2
1455/1462	14-G3B	Tachikawa	---	8
1463/1466	14-G3B	LARES	YR-LIB, YR-LID, & YR-LIR/YR-LIS	4
1467/1470	14-F62	British AW	G-AFGN/G-AFGP & G-AFGR	4
1471/1476	14-H2	TCA	CF-TCH/CF-TCM	6
1477/1481	14-G3B	Nihon Koku	---	5
1482	XR40-1	USN	1441	1
1483	14-H2	Santa Maria AL	NC18993	1
1484/1485	14-F62	British AW	G-AFKD/G-AFKE	2
1486	14-H2	M.C. Fleischmann	NC17395	1
1487/1489	14-H2	Air Afrique	F-ARIU/F-ARIV & F-ARIY	3
1490/1491	14-F62	British AW	G-AFMO, G-AFMR	2
1492/1495	14-H	LOT	SP-BPK/SP-BPN	4
1496	14-G105	Superior Oil	NC17398	1
1497/1498	14-F62	Aer Lingus	EI-ABV/EI-ABW	2
1499/1504	14-H2	TCA	CF-TCN/CF-TCS	6
1505/1506	14-H2	Air Afrique	F-ARRE/F-ARRF	2
1507/1508	14-H2	DETA	CR-AAV, CR-AAX	2
1509/1510	14-H2	LAV	YV-ADI, YV-ADO	2
1511	14-H2	DETA	CR-AAZ	1

LOCKHEED HUDSON (Number built: 2,941)

B14L-1601/1739	Hudson Mk.I	RAF	N7205/N7343	139
B14L-1740/1746	Hudson Mk.I	RCAF	759/765	7
B14L-1747	Hudson Mk.I	RAF	N7351	1
B14L-1748	Hudson Mk.I	RCAF	766	1
B14L-1749	Hudson Mk.I	RAF	N7353	1
B14S-1750	Hudson Mk.IV	RAAF	A16-1	1
B14L-1751/1753	Hudson Mk.I	RCAF	767/769	3
B14L-1754/1756	Hudson Mk.I	RAF	N7357/N7359	3
B14L-1757	Hudson Mk.I	RCAF	770	1
B14L-1758/1766	Hudson Mk.I	RAF	N7361/N7369	9
B14L-1767/1768	Hudson Mk.I	RCAF	771/772	2
B14L-1769	Hudson Mk.I	RAF	N7372	1
B14L-1770	Hudson Mk.I	RCAF	776	1
B14L-1771	Hudson Mk.I	RAF	N7374	1

B14L-1772	Hudson Mk.I	RCAF	773	1
B14L-1773/1776	Hudson Mk.I	RAF	N7376/N7379	4
B14L-1777	Hudson Mk.I	RCAF	774	1
B14S-1778/1779	Hudson Mk.IV	RAAF	A16-2/A16-3	2
B14L-1780	Hudson Mk.I	RCAF	775	1
B14L-1781	Hudson Mk.I	RCAF	777	1
B14L-1782	Hudson Mk.I	RCAF	779	1
B14L-1783	Hudson Mk.I	RCAF	778	1
B14L-1784	Hudson Mk.I	RCAF	781	1
B14l-1785	Hudson Mk.I	RCAF	782	1
B14L-1786	Hudson Mk.I	RCAF	780	1
B14L-1787/1790	Hudson Mk.I	RCAF	783/786	4
B14L-1791/1803	Hudson Mk.I	RAF	N7392/N7404	13
B14L-1804	Hudson Mk.I	RAF	R4059	1
B14L-1805/1851	Hudson Mk.I	RAF	P5116/P5162	47
B14L-1852/1853	Hudson Mk.I	So. Africa	P5163/P5164	2
B14L-1854	Hudson Mk.I	RAF	P5165	1
B14S-1855/1900	Hudson Mk.IV	RAAF	A16-4/A16-49	46
B14S-1903/1929	Hudson Mk.IV	RAAF	A16-50/A16-76	27
B14S-1930	Hudson	Sperry Gyroscope	NX21771	1
B14S-1931/1953	Hudson Mk.IV	RAAF	A16-77/A16-99	23
B14S-1955	Hudson Mk.IV	RAAF	A16-100	1
214-2301/2400	Hudson Mk.I	RAF	T9266/T9365	100
414-2401/2419	Hudson Mk.II	RAF	T9366/T9384	19
414-2420	Hudson Mk.II	RCAF	T9385	1
414-2421/2482	Hudson Mk.III	RAF	T9386/T9447	62
414-2483/2500	Hudson Mk.IV	RAF	AE609/AE626	18
414-2501/2518	Hudson Mk.III	RAF	T9448/T9465	18
414-2519/2543	Hudson Mk.III	RAF	V8975/V8999	25
414-2544/2589	Hudson Mk.III	RAF	V9020/V9065	46
414-2590/2601	Hudson Mk.IV	RAF	AE627/AE638	12
414-2602/2991	Hudson Mk.V	RAF	AM520/AM909	390
414-2992/2999	Hudson Mk.V	RAF	AE639/AE646	8
414-3700/3710	Hudson Mk.V	RAF	AE647/AE657	11
414-3711/3713	Hudson Mk.III	RAF	V9066/V9068	3
414-3714	Hudson Mk.III	RCAF	V9069	1
414-3715/3754	Hudson Mk.III	RAF	V9090/V9129	40
414-3755/3775	Hudson Mk.III	RAF	V9150/V9170	21
414-3776	Hudson Mk.III	RCAF	V9171	1
414-3777/3804	Hudson Mk.III	RAF	V9172/V9199	28
414-3805/3807	Hudson Mk.III	RAF	V9220/V9222	3
414-3808	Hudson Mk.III	RCAF	V9223	1
414-3809/3819	Hudson Mk.III	RAF	V9224/V9234	11
414-3820/3837	Hudson Mk.III	RNZAF	NZ2001/NZ2018	18
414-3838/3839	Hudson Mk.III	RAF	V9253/V9254	2
414-3840/3844	Hudson Mk.III	RAF	AE485/AE489	5
414-3845	Hudson Mk.III	RNZAF	NZ2025	1
414-3846/3848	Hudson Mk.III	RAF	AE491/AE493	3
414-3849/3859	Hudson Mk.III	RNZAF	NZ2026/NZ2036	11
414-3860/3963	Hudson Mk.III	RAF	AE505/AE608	104
414-3964/3987	Hudson Mk.III	RNZAF	---	24
414-5988/6029	A-29-LO	USAAF	41-23223/41-23264	42
414-6030/6081	A-28-LO	USAAF	41-23171/41-23222	52
414-6082/6445	A-29-LO	USAAF	41-23265/41-23628	364
414-6446	A-29A-LO	USAAF	41-23629	1
414-6447/6456	A-29-LO	USAAF	41-23630/41-23639	10
414-6457/6656	A-29-LO	USAAF	41-36968/41-37167	200
414-6657/6756	A-29A-LO	USAAF	41-37168/41-37267	100
414-6757/6856	A-28A-LO	USAAF	42-6582/42-6681	100
414-6857/7206	A-28A-LO	USAAF	42-46937/42-47286	350
414-7207/7289	AT-18A-LO	USAAF	42-55485/42-55567	83
414-7290/7506	AT-18-LO	USAAF	42-55568/42-55784	217
414-7507/7589	A-29A-LO	USAAF	42-47287/42-47369	83

LOCKHEED P-38 LIGHTNING (Number built: 9,924 by Lockheed, plus 113 by Consolidated-Vultee)

022-2201	XP-38-LO	USAAC	37-457	1
122-2202/2214	YP-38-LO	USAAC	39-689/39-701	13
222-2215/2232	P-38-LO	USAAC	40-744/40-761	18
222-2234/2244	P-38-LO	USAAC	40-763/40-773	11
222-2245/2280	P-38D-LO	USAAC	40-774/40-809	36
222-5201/5315	P-38E-LO	USAAC	41-1983/41-2097	115
222-5316/5317	F-4-1-LO	USAAC	41-2098/41-2099	2

222-5318/5338	P-38E-LO	USAAC
222-5339/5374	F-4-1-LO	USAAC
222-5375	F-5A-2-LO	USAAC
222-5376/5389	F-4-1-LO	USAAC
222-5390	P-38E-LO	USAAC
222-5391/5436	F-4-1-LO	USAAC
222-5437	P-38E-LO	USAAC
222-5438	F-4-1-LO	USAAC
222-5439/5510	P-38E-LO	USAAC
222-5511/5539	P-38F-LO	USAAC
222-5540	P-38F-1-LO	USAAC
222-5541/5576	P-38F-LO	USAAC
222-5577/5579	P-38F-1-LO	USAAC
222-5580/5599	F-4A-1-LO	USAAC
222-5600/5604	P-38F-LO	USAAC
222-5605	P-38F-1-LO	USAAC
222-5606/5610	P-38F-LO	USAAC
222-5611/5612	P-38F-1-LO	USAAC
222-5613/5623	P-38F-LO	USAAC
222-5624	P-38F-1-LO	USAAC
222-5625/5640	P-38F-LO	USAAC
222-5641/5642	P-38F-1-LO	USAAC
222-5643/5651	P-38F-LO	USAAC
222-5652	P-38F-1-LO	USAAC
222-5653/5657	P-38F-LO	USAAC
222-5658	P-38F-1-LO	USAAC
222-5659/5661	P-38F-LO	USAAC
222-5622	P-38F-1-LO	USAAC
222-5663/5665	P-38F-LO	USAAC
222-5666/5668	P-38F-1-LO	USAAC
222-5669/5670	P-38F-LO	USAAC
222-5671	P-38F-1-LO	USAAC
222-5672/5674	P-38F-LO	USAAC
222-5675/5677	P-38F-1-LO	USAAC
222-5678	P-38F-LO	USAAC
222-5679/5807	P-38F-1-LO	USAAC
222-7001/7100	P-38F-5-LO	USAAF
222-7101/7120	F-5A-1-LO	USAAF
222-7121/7200	P-38G-1-LO	USAAF
222-7201/7220	F-5A-3-LO	USAAF
222-7221/7232	P-38G-3-LO	USAAF
222-7233/7300	P-38G-5-LO	USAAF
222-7304/7400	P-38G-10-LO	USAAF
222-7401/7420	F-5A-10-LO	USAAF
222-7421/7500	P-38G-10-LO	USAAF
222-7501/7560	F-5A-10-LO	USAAF
222-7561/7700	P-38G-10-LO	USAAF
222-7701/7760	F-5A-10-LO	USAAF
222-7761/7991	P-38G-10-LO	USAAF
322-3001/3003	Lightning I	RAF
322-3004/3143	P-322	USAAF
322-3144/3172	P-38F-13-LO	USAAF
322-3173/3293	P-38F-15-LO	USAAF
322-3294/3467	P-38G-13-LO	USAAF
322-3468/3667	P-38G-15-LO	USAAF
422-1001/1003	P-38J-1-LO	USAAF
422-1004	P-38K-1-LO	USAAF
422-1005	P-38H-1-LO	USAAF
422-1006/1012	P-38J-1-LO	USAAF
422-1013/1237	P-38H-1-LO	USAAF
422-1238/1612	P-38H-5-LO	USAAF
422-1613/1822	P-38J-5-LO	USAAF
422-1823/1912	F-5B-1-LO	USAAF
422-1913/2702	P-38J-10-LO	USAAF
422-2703/2812	F-5B-1-LO	USAAF
422-2813/3262	P-38J-15-LO	USAAF
422-3263/4062	P-38J-15-LO	USAAF
422-4063/4212	P-38J-15-LO	USAAF
422-4213/4562	P-38J-20-LO	USAAF
422-4563/4772	P-38J-25-LO	USAAF
422-4773/6062	P-38L-1-LO	USAAF
422-6063/8262	P-38L-5-LO	USAAF
422-8263/8582	P-38L-5-LO	USAAF

41-2100/41-2120	21
41-2121/41-2156	36
41-2157	1
41-2158/41-2171	14
41-2172	1
41-2173/41-2218	46
41-2219	1
41-2220	1
41-2221/41-2292	72
41-2293/41-2321	29
41-2322	1
41-2323/41-2358	36
41-2359/41-2361	3
41-2362/41-2381	20
41-2382/41-2386	5
41-2387	1
41-2388/41-2392	5
41-7484/41-7485	2
41-7486/41-7496	11
41-7497	1
41-7498/41-7513	16
41-7514/41-7515	2
41-7516/41-7524	9
41-7525	1
41-7526/41-7530	5
41-7531	1
41-7532/41-7534	3
41-7535	1
41-7536/41-7538	3
41-7539/41-7541	3
41-7542/41-7543	2
41-7544	1
41-7545/41-7547	3
41-7548/41-7550	3
41-7551	1
41-7552/41-7680	129
42-12567/42-12666	100
42-12667/42-12686	20
42-12687/42-12766	80
42-12767/42-12786	20
42-12787/42-12798	12
42-12799/42-12866	68
42-12870/42-12966	97
42-12967/42-12986	20
42-12987/42-13066	80
42-13067/42-13126	60
42-13127/42-13266	140
42-13267/42-13326	60
42-13327/42-13557	231
AE978/AE980	3
	140
43-2035/43-2063	29
43-2064/43-2184	121
43-2185/43-2358	174
43-2359/43-2558	200
42-12867/42-12869	3
42-13558	1
42-13559	1
42-13560/42-13566	7
42-66502/42-66726	225
42-66727/42-67101	375
42-67102/42-67311	210
42-67312/42-67401	90
42-67402/42-68191	790
42-68192/42-68301	110
42-103979/42-104428	450
43-28248/43-29047	800
44-23059/44-23208	150
44-23209/44-23558	350
44-23559/44-23768	210
44-23769/44-25058	1,290
44-25059/44-27258	2,200
44-53008/44-53327	320

422-8583/9962	P-38L-5-LO	Cancelled	44-53328/44-54707	0
622-2233	XP-38A-LO	USAAF	40-762	1
- - -	P-38L-5-VN	USAAF	43-50226/43-50338	113
- - -	P-38L-5-VN	Cancelled	43-50339/43-52225	0

VEGA STARLINER (Number built: 1)

- - -	Starliner	Co. owned	NX21725	1

LOCKHEED 18 LODESTAR (Number built: 625 by Lockheed, plus 121 Ki-56, by Kawasaki)

10-1954	18	Co. owned	NX17385	(1)
18-1956	18-07	Santa Maria AL	NC18993	(1)
18-1957	18-07	M.C. Fleischmann	NC17395	(1)
18-2001	18-07	Don Marshall	NC25604	1
18-2002/2004	18-07	Mid Continent AL	NC25601/NC25603	3
18-2005/2007	18-07	Air Afrique	F-ARTE/F-ARTG	3
18-2008	XR50-1	USCG	V188	1
18-2009/2011	18-07	Air France	F-ARTJ/F-ARTL	3
18-2012	18-14	R.J. Behan	NC13030	1
18-2013/2014	18-07	Air Afrique	F-ARTM/F-ARTN	2
18-2015/2017	18-08	South African AW	ZS-ASJ/ZS-ASL	3
18-2018	18-07	BOAC	G-AGBO	1
18-2019	18-08	South African AW	ZS-ASM	1
18-2020/2023	18-10	United	NC25630/NC25633	4
18-2024	18-07	BOAC	G-AGBP	1
18-2025	18-08	Inland AL	NC25634	1
18-2026	18-08	South African AW	ZS-ASN	1
18-2027/2028	18-08	Continental AL	NC25635/NC25636	2
18-2029/2030	18-08	South African AW	ZS-ASO/ZS-ASP	2
18-2031	18-08	Continental Oil	NC25640	1
18-2032/2038	18-08	South African AW	ZS-ASR/ZS-ASX	7
18-2039/2040	18-50	National	NC25687/NC25688	2
18-2041	R50-2	USN	7703	1
18-2042	18-50	H.S. Vanderbilt	NC6175	1
18-2043	18-14	Phillips Petroleum	NC28366	1
18-2044/2048	18-08	South African AW	ZS-ASY, ZS-ASZ & ZS-ATA/ZS-ATC	5
18-2049	R50-1	USN	4249	1
18-2050/2058	18-08	South African AW	ZS-ATD/ZS-ATL	9
18-2059/2064	18-10	TCA	CF-TCT/CF-TCY	6
18-2065	R50-1	USN	4250	1
18-2066	18-08	South African AW	ZS-ATM	1
18-2067	18-50	National	NC28336	1
18-2068	18-14	Superior Oil	NC34900	1
18-2069	18-07	Union of So. Africa	F-6	1
18-2070/2071	18-07	BOAC	G-AGBR/G-AGBS	2
18-2072	18-10	Walker Inman	NC3138	1
18-2073/2075	18-10	Continental AL	NC25637/NC25639	3
18-2076	18-07	BOAC	G-AGBT	1
18-2077	18-14	Vaucluse Aviation	NC1611	1
18-2078/2083	18-10	Pan American	NC33663/NC33668	6
18-2084/2086	18-40	Norwegian AF	- - -	3
18-2087/2088	18-10	Dixie AL	NX34901/NX34902	2
18-2089	18-40	Arthur Kudner	NC33669	1
18-2090/2091	18-07	BUAC	G-AGBU/G-AGBV	2
18-2092/2093	18-07	Catalina Air Transport	NC33616/NC33617	2
18-2094/2095	18-07	BOAC	G-AGBW/G-AGBX	2
18-2096/2097	R50-3	USN	01006/01007	2
18-2098/2099	18-10	Yukon Southern AW	CF-BTY/CF-BTZ	2
18-2100	18-10	Panair do Brasil	NC34905	1
18-2101/2110	18-40	NEI	LT9-6/LT9-15	10
18-2111	18-10	Mid Continent AL	NC34964	1
18-2112/2114	18-10	Panair do Brasil	NC34906/NC34908	3
18-2115	C-57-LO	USAAF	41-19730	1
18-2116/2117	18-10	Panair do Brasil	NC34909/NC34910	2
18-2118/2119	C-57-LO	USAAF	41-19731/41-19732	2
18-2120/2129	18-40	NEI	LT9-16/LT9-25	10
18-2130/2136	C-57-LO	USAAF	41-23164/41-23170	7
18-2137	18-07	South African AW	ZS-AVT	1
18-2138/2139	C-60-LO	USAAF	41-29633/41-29634	2
18-2140/2146	C-59-LO	USAAF	41-29623/41-29629	7
18-2147	C-60-LO	USAAF	41-29635	1
18-2148	C-66-LO	DSC (Brasil)	42-13657	1
18-2149/2150	18-40	Navegacao Aerea Bras.	PP-NAE/PP-NAF	2

18-2151/2153	C-59-LO	USAAF	41-29630/41-29632	3
18-2154/2165	C-60-LO	USAAF	41-29636/41-29647	12
18-2166/2171	C-60-LO	USAAF	42-108787/42-108792	6
18-2172/2176	R50-4	USN	05046/05050	5
18-2177/2185	18-50	NEI	LT9-26/LT9-34	9
18-2186/2200	C-60-LO	USAAF	42-32166/42-32180	15
18-2201/2205	C-60A-LO	USAAF	42-32181/42-32185	5
18-2206/2210	C-60A-1-LO	USAAF	42-55845/42-55849	5
18-2211/2217	C-57B-LO	USAAF	43-3271/43-3277	7
18-2218	18-10	LAV	YV-AFO	1
18-2219/2220	18-10	TCA	CF-TDA/CF-TDB	2
18-2221/2222	C-56E-LO	USAAF	43-3278/43-3279	2
18-2223/2231	C-60A-1-LO	USAAF	42-55850/42-55858	9
18-2232/2239	C-60A-LO	USAAF	42-32186/42-32193	8
18-2240/2244	R50-4	USN	12447/12451	5
18-2245/2248	18-10	TCA	CF-TDC/CF-TDF	4
18-2249	C-60A-1-LO	USAAF	42-55859	1
18-2250	XC-60B-LO	USAAF	42-55860	1
18-2251/2278	C-60A-1-LO	USAAF	42-55861/42-55888	28
18-2279/2280	R50-4	USN	12452/12453	2
18-2281/2283	R50-5	USN	12454/12456	3
18-2284/2293	C-60A-LO	USAAF	43-32194/43-32203	10
18-2294/2295	C-60A-1-LO	USAAF	42-55889/42-55890	2
18-2296/2307	C-60A-5-LO	USAAF	42-55891/42-55902	12
18-2308/2317	R50-5	USN	12457/12466	10
18-2318/2337	C-60A-5-LO	USAAF	42-55903/42-55922	20
18-2338/2351	C-60A-LO	USAAF	42-32204/42-32217	14
18-2352/2358	R50-5	USN	12467/12473	7
18-2359	18-10	Pratt & Whitney	N30030	1
18-2360/2402	C-60A-5-LO	USAAF	42-55923/42-55965	43
18-2403	C-57-LO	USAAF	43-34921	1
18-2404/2411	R50-5	USN	12474/12481	8
18-2412/2426	C-60A-LO	USAAF	43-32218/43-32232	15
18-2427/2453	C-60A-5-LO	USAAF	42-55966/42-55992	27
18-2454/2463	R50-5	USN	12482/12491	10
18-2464/2465	C-57-LO	USAAF	43-34922/43-34923	2
18-2466/2511	C-60A-5-LO	USAAF	42-55993/42-56038	46
18-2512/2531	R50-6	USN	39612/39631	20
18-2532/2577	C-60A-5-LO	USAAF	42-56039/42-56084	46
18-2578/2592	R50-6	USN	39632/39646	15
18-2593/2625	C-60A-5-LO	USAAF	43-16433/43-16465	33

VEGA 35 (Number built: 4)

- - -	35	Co. owned	NX21760 & NX28351/NX28353	4

LOCKHEED-VEGA VENTURA AND HARPOON (Number built: 3,028)

37-4001/4188	Ventura Mk.I	RAF	AE658/AE845	188
137-4189/4300	Ventura Mk.II	RAF	AE846/AE957	112
137-4301/4675	Ventura Mk.II	RAF	AJ163/AJ537	375
137-4676/4875	B-34-VE	USAAF	41-38020/41-38219	200
237-4876/5075	PV-1	USN	29723/29922	200
237-5076/5475	PV-1	USN	33067/33466	400
237-5476/5887	PV-1	USN	34586/34997	412
237-5888/6175	PV-1	USN	48652/48939	288
237-6176/6475	PV-1	USN	49360/49659	300
437-6476/6493	B-37-LO	USAAF	41-37470/41-37487	18
15-1001/1030	PV-2C	USN	37035/37064	30
15-1031/1500	PV-2	USN	37065/37534	470
15-1501/1516	PV-2D	USN	37535/37550	16
15-1517/1589	PV-2D	Cancelled	37551/37623	0
15-1590/1600	PV-2D	USN	37624/37634	11
15-1601/1608	PV-2D	USN	84057/84064	8
15-1609/2133	PV-2D	Cancelled	84065/84589	0
15-2134/2408	PV-2D	Cancelled	102001/102275	0

LOCKHEED-VEGA FLYING FORTRESS (Number built: 2,750 by Lockheed)

17-6001/6005	B-17F-1-VE	USAAF	42-5705/42-5709	5
17-6006/6020	B-17F-5-VE	USAAF	42-5710/42-5724	15
17-6021/6040	B-17F-10-VE	USAAF	42-5725/42-5744	20
17-6041/6060	B-17F-15-VE	USAAF	42-5745/42-5764	20

17-6061/6100	B-17F-20-VE	USAAF	42-5765/42-5804	40
17-6101/6150	B-17F-25-VE	USAAF	42-5805/42-5854	50
17-6151/6200	B-17F-30-VE	USAAF	42-5855/42-5904	50
17-6201/6250	B-17F-35-VE	USAAF	42-5905/42-5954	50
17-6251/6325	B-17F-40-VE	USAAF	42-5955/42-6029	75
17-6326/6400	B-17F-45-VE	USAAF	42-6030/42-6104	75
17-6401/6500	B-17F-50-VE	USAAF	42-6105/42-6204	100
17-6501/6600	B-17G-1-VE	USAAF	42-39758/42-39857	100
17-6601/6700	B-17G-5-VE	USAAF	42-39858/42-39957	100
17-6701/6800	B-17G-10-VE	USAAF	42-39958/42-40057	100
17-6801/6900	B-1/G-15-VE	USAAF	42-97436/42-97535	100
17-6901/7000	B-17G-20-VE	USAAF	42-97536/42-97635	100
17-7001/7100	B-17G-25-VE	USAAF	42-97636/42-97735	100
17-7101/7200	B-17G-30-VE	USAAF	42-97736/42-97835	100
17-7201/7300	B-17G-35-VE	USAAF	42-97836/42-97935	100
17-7301/7400	B-17G-40-VE	USAAF	42-97936/42-98035	100
17-7401/7500	B-17G-45-VE	USAAF	44-8001/44-8100	100
17-7501/7600	B-17G-50-VE	USAAF	44-8101/44-8200	100
17-7601/7700	B-17G-55-VE	USAAF	44-8201/44-8300	100
17-7701/7800	B-17G-60-VE	USAAF	44-8301/44-8400	100
17-7801/7900	B-17G-65-VE	USAAF	44-8401/44-8500	100
17-7901/8000	B-17G-70-VE	USAAF	44-8501/44-8600	100
17-8001/8100	B-17G-75-VE	USAAF	44-8601/44-8700	100
17-8101/8200	B-17G-80-VE	USAAF	44-8701/44-8800	100
17-8201/8300	B-17G-85-VE	USAAF	44-8801/44-8900	100
17-8301/8400	B-17G-90-VE	USAAF	44-8901/44-9000	100
17-8401/8500	B-17G-95-VE	USAAF	44-85492/44-85591	100
17-8501/8600	B-17G-100-VE	USAAF	44-85592/44-85691	100
17-8601/8700	B-17G-105-VE	USAAF	44-85692/44-85791	100
17-8701/8750	B-17G-110-VE	USAAF	44-85792/44-85841	50
117-	XB-38-BO	USAAF	41-2401	(1)
217-	XB-40-BO	USAAF	41-24341	(1)

LOCKHEED XP-49 (Number built: 1)

522-	XP-49-LO	USAAF	40-3055	1

LOCKHEED CONSTELLATION (Number built: 233)

049-1961	049	Co. owned	NX25600	1
049-1962/1969	C-69-1-LO	USAAF	43-10310/43-10317	8
049-1970	C-69-1-LO	USAAF	42-94549	1
049-1971	C-69C-1-LO	USAAF	42-94550	1
049-1972/1975	C-69-5-LO	USAAF	42-94551/42-94554	4
049-1976/1978	049	BOAC	G-AHEK/G-AHEM	3
049-1979	049	TWA	N86536	1
049-1980	049	BOAC	G-AHEN	1
049-2021/2030	049	TWA	N86500/N86509	10
049-2031/2033	049	PAA	N88831/N88833	3
049-2034/2035	049	TWA	N86510/N86511	2
049-2036/2038	049	PAA	N88836/N88838	3
042-2039/2044	049	TWA	N86512/N86517	6
049-2045/2050	049	PAA	N88845/N88850	6
049-2051/2054	049	AOA	N90921/N90924	4
049-2055/2062	049	PAA	N88855/N88862	8
049-2063/2065	049	AOA	N90925/N90927	3
049-2066/2067	049	PAA	N88854, N88868	2
049-2068/2071	049	KLM	PH-TAU/PH-TAX	4
049-2072/2075	049	Air France	F-BAZA/F-BAZD	4
049-2076/2080	049	TWA	N90814/N90818	5
049-2081/2082	049	LAV	Y V-C-AME & -AMI	2
049-2083/2084	049	KLM	PH-TEN/PH-TEO	2
049-2085/2088	049	TWA	N90823/N90826	4
749-2503	749	Co. owned	NC86520	1
749-2504/2506	749	Air-India	VT-CQS, VT-CQR & VT-CQP	3
749-2512	749	Air France	F-BAZQ	1
749-2513/2515	749	Air France	F-BAZI/F-BAZK	3
649-2518/2524	649	Eastern	N101A/N107A	7
749-2525/2528	749	PAA	N86527/N86530	4
649-2529/2535	649	Eastern	N108A/N114A	7
749-2538	749	Air France	B-BAZL	1
749-2540/2541	749	KLM	PH-TEP & PH-TER	2
749-2544	749	KLM	PH-TDB	1
749-2545/2547	749	Air France	F-BAZM/F-BAZO	3

749-2548/2549	749	Aer Linte	EI-ACR/EI-ACS	2
749-2550	749	Air France	F-BAZP	1
749-2551/2553	749	KLM	PH-TDC, -TES & -TET	3
749-2554/2555	749	Aer Linte	EI-ADA, EI-ADD	2
749-2556/2559	749	KLM	PH-TDD/PH-TDG	4
749-2560/2561	749	LAV	YV-C-AMA, -AMU	2
749-2562	749	Qantas	VH-EAA	1
749-2564	749	KLM	PH-TDH	1
749-2565	749	Qantas	VH-EAB	1
749-2566	749	Aer Linte	EI-ADE	1
749-2572/2573	749	Qantas	VH-EAC/VH-EAD	2
749-2577/2588	749	TWA	N91201/N91212	12
749-2589/2590	749	KLM	PH-TDI, PH-TDK	2
749-2600	VC-121B	USAF	48-608	1
749-2601/2609	C-121A	USAF	48-609/48-617	9
749-2610/2611	749	Eastern	N115A/N116A	2
749-2612/2613	PO-1W	USN	124437/124438	2
749-2614/2618	749	Eastern	N117A/N121A	5
749-2619/2620	749A	Air-India	VT-DAR/VT-DAS	2
749-2621/2622	749A	KLM	PH-TDN/PH-TDO	2
749-2623	749A	SAA	ZS-DBR	1
749-2624/2629	749A	Air France	F-BAZE/F-BAZH &	
			F-BAZS/F-BAZT	6
749-2630/2632	749A	SAA	ZS-DBS/ZS-DBU	3
749-2633/2637	749A	TWA	N6001C/N6005C	5
749-2638	749A	KLM	PH-TDP	1
749-2639	749A	TWA	N6006C	1
749-2640/2641	749A	KLM	PH-TFD/PH-TFE	2
749-2642	749A	C&S	N86521	1
749-2643/2651	749A	TWA	N6007C/N6015C	9
749-2652	749A	KLM	PH-TFF	1
749-2653	749A	C&S	N86522	1
749-2654/2658	749A	TWA	N6016C/N6020C	5
749-2659/2660	749A	C&S	N86523/N86524	2
749-2661	749A	KLM	PH-TFG	1
749-2662	749A	C&S	N86525	1
749-2663/2664	749A	Avianca	HK-162/HK-163	2
749-2665/2666	749A	Air-India	VT-DEO/VT-DEP	2
749-2667/2672	749A	TWA	N6021C/N6026C	6
749-2673	749A	C&S	N86535	1
749-2674/2677	749A	Air France	F-BAZZ & F-BBDT/	
			F-BBDV	4

LOCKHEED P-80 (F-80) SHOOTING STAR (Number built: 1,732)

140-1001	XP-80-LO	USAAF	44-83020	1
141-1001/1002	XP-80A-LO	USAAF	44-83021/44-83022	2
080-1002	XP-80A-LO	USAAF	44-83023	1
080-1003	XF-14-LO	USAAF	44-83024	1
080-1004/1014	YP-80A-LO	USAAF	44-83025/44-83035	11
080-1015/1222	P-80A-1-LO	USAAF	44-84992/44-85199	208
080-1223	XP-80B-LO	USAAF	44-85200	1
080-1224/1359	P-80A-1-LO	USAAF	44-85201/44-85336	136
080-1360/1405	P-80A-5-LO	USAAF	44-85337/44-85382	46
080-1406	FP-80A-5-LO	USAAF	44-85383	1
080-1407	P-80A-5-LO	USAAF	44-85384	1
080-1408	FP-80A-5-LO	USAAF	44-85385	1
080-1409/1421	P-80A-5-LO	USAAF	44-85386/44-85398	13
080-1422	FP-80A-5-LO	USAAF	44-85399	1
080-1423/1447	P-80A-5-LO	USAAF	44-85400/44-85424	25
080-1448	FP-80A-5-LO	USAAF	44-85425	1
080-1449/1455	P-80A-5-LO	USAAF	44-85426/44-85432	7
080-1456	FP-80A-5-LO	USAAF	44-85433	1
080-1457/1461	P-80A-5-LO	USAAF	44-85434/44-85438	5
080-1462	FP-80A-5-LO	USAAF	44-85439	1
080-1463/1465	P-80A-5-LO	USAAF	44-85440/44-85442	3
080-1466	FP-80A-5-LO	USAAF	44-85443	1
080-1467	P-80A-5-LO	USAAF	44-85444	1
080-1468	FP-80A-5-LO	USAAF	44-85445	1
080-1469	P-80A-5-LO	USAAF	44-85446	1
080-1470	FP-80A-5-LO	USAAF	44-85447	1
080-1471	P-80A-5-LO	USAAF	44-85448	1
080-1472	FP-80A-5-LO	USAAF	44-85449	1
080-1473	P-80A-5-LO	USAAF	44-85450	1

080-1474	FP-80A-5-LO	USAAF	44-85451	1
080-1475	P-80A-5-LO	USAAF	44-85452	1
080-1476	FP-80A-5-LO	USAAF	44-85453	1
080-1477	P-80A-5-LO	USAAF	44-85454	1
080-1478	FP-80A-5-LO	USAAF	44-85455	1
080-1479	P-80A-5-LO	USAAF	44-84456	1
080-1480	FP-80A-5-LO	USAAF	44-85457	1
080-1481	P-80A-5-LO	USAAF	44-84458	1
080-1482	FP-80A-5-LO	USAAF	44-85459	1
080-1483	P-80A-5-LO	USAAF	44-84460	1
080-1484	FP-80A-5-LO	USAAF	44-85461	1
080-1485	P-80A-5-LO	USAAF	44-85462	1
080-1486	FP-80A-5-LO	USAAF	44-85463	1
080-1487	P-80A-5-LO	USAAF	44-85464	1
080-1488	FP-80A-5-LO	USAAF	44-85465	1
080-1489	P-80A-5-LO	USAAF	44-85466	1
080-1490	FP-80A-5-LO	USAAF	44-85467	1
080-1491	P-80A-5-LO	USAAF	44-85468	1
080-1492	FP-801-5-LO	USAAF	44-85469	1
080-1493	P-80A-5-LO	USAAF	44-85470	1
080-1494	FP-80A-5-LO	USAAF	44-85471	1
080-1495	P-80A-5-LO	USAAF	44-85472	1
080-1496	FP-80A-5-LO	USAAF	44-85473	1
080-1497	P-80A-5-LO	USAAF	44-85474	1
080-1498	FP-80A-5-LO	USAAF	44-85475	1
080-1499	P-80A-5-LO	USAAF	44-85476	1
080-1500	FP-80A-5-LO	USAAF	44-85477	1
080-1501	P-80A-5-LO	USAAF	44-85478	1
080-1502	FP-80A-5-LO	USAAF	44-85479	1
080-1503	P-80A-5-LO	USAAF	44-85480	1
080-1504	FP-80A-5-LO	USAAF	44-85481	1
080-1505	P-80A-5-LO	USAAF	44-85482	1
080-1506	FP-80A-5-LO	USAAF	44-85483	1
080-1507	P-80A-5-LO	USAAF	44-85484	1
080-1508	FP-80A-5-LO	USAAF	44-85485	1
080-1509	P-80A-5-LO	USAAF	44-85486	1
080-1510	FP-80A-5-LO	USAAF	44-85487	1
080-1511	P-80A-5-LO	USAAF	44-85488	1
080-1512	FP-80A-5-LO	USAAF	44-85489	1
080-1513	P-80A-5-LO	USAAF	44-85490	1
080-1514	FP-80A-5-LO	USAAF	44-85491	1
080-1515	P-80A-5-LO	USAAF	45-8301	1
080-1516	FP-80A-5-LO	USAAF	45-8302	1
080-1517	P-80A-5-LO	USAAF	45-8303	1
080-1518	FP-80A-5-LO	USAAF	45-8304	1
080-1519	P-80A-5-LO	USAAF	45-8305	1
080-1520	FP-80A-5-LO	USAAF	45-8306	1
080-1521	P-80A-5-LO	USAAF	45-8307	1
080-1522	FP-80A-5-LO	USAAF	45-8308	1
080-1523	P-80A-5-LO	USAAF	45-8309	1
080-1524	FP-80A-5-LO	USAAF	45-8310	1
080-1525	P-80A-5-LO	USAAF	45-8311	1
080-1526	FP-80A-5-LO	USAAF	45-8312	1
080-1527	P-80A-5-LO	USAAF	45-8313	1
080-1528	FP-80A-5-LO	USAAF	45-8314	1
080-1529/1577	P-80A-5-LO	USAAF	45-8315/45-8363	49
080-1578/1691	FP-80A-5-LO	USAAF	45-8364/45-8477	114
080-1692/1694	P-80B-1-LO	USAAF	45-8478/45-8480	3
080-1695	P-80B-5-LO	USAAF	45-8481	1
080-1696/1779	P-80B-1-LO	USAAF	45-8482/45-8565	84
080-1780/1809	P-80B-5-LO	USAAF	45-8566/45-8595	30
080-1810/1931	P-80B-1-LO	USAAF	45-8596/45-8717	122
080-1932/1978	P-80C-1-LO	USAAF	47-171/47-217	47
080-1979/1986	TO-1	USN	33821/33828	8
080-1987/2061	P-80C-5-LO	USAAF	47-526/47-600	75
080-2062/2080	TO-1	USN	33829/33847	19
080-2081	P-80C-1-LO	USAAF	47-1395	1
080-2082/2104	TO-1	USN	33848/33870	23
080-2105/2119	F-80C-1-LO	USAF	48-382/48-396	15
080-2120/2169	F-80C-1-LO	USAF	48-863/48-912	50
080-2170/2626	F-80C-10-LO	USAF	49-422/49-878	457
080-2627/2726	F-80C-10-LO	USAF	49-1800/49-1899	100
080-2727/2730	F-80C-10-LO	USAF	49-3597/49-3600	4

492

LOCKHEED XP-58 CHAIN LIGHTNING (Number built: 1)

020-1526	XP-58-LO	USAAF	41-2670	1

LOCKHEED 33 LITTLE DIPPER (Number built: 1)

33-1001	Model 33	Co. owned	NX18935	1

LOCKHEED P2V (P-2) NEPTUNE (Number built: 1,051 by Lockheed--including 48 assembled by Kawasaki--and 82 P-2Js by Kawasaki)

26-1001/1002	XP2V-1	USN	48237/48238	2
26-1003/1006	P2V-1	USN	89082/89085	4
26-1007	XP2V-2	USN	89086	1
26-1008/1017	P2V-1	USN	89087/89096	10
26-1018/1019	P2V-2	USN	39318/39319	2
226-1020	P2V-2S	USN	39320	1
26-1021/1026	P2V-2	USN	39321/39326	6
126-1027/1068	P2V-2	USN	39327/39368	42
126-1069/1095	P2V-2	USN	122438/122464	27
126-1096/1097	P2V-2N	USN	122465/122466	2
126-1098	P2V-2	USN	122467	1
326-1099/1127	P2V-3	USN	122923/122951	29
326-1128/1151	P2V-3	USN	122964/122987	24
326-1152/1175	P2V-3W	USN	124268/124291	24
326-1176/1181	P2V-3W	USN	124354/124359	6
426-2001/2052	P2V-4	USN	124211/124262	52
426-5001/5020	P2V-5	USN	124865/124884	20
426-5021/5022	P2V-5	RAAF	A89-302 & A89-301	2
426-5023/5027	P2V-5	USN	124885/124889	5
426-5028/5029	Neptune M.R.1	RAF	51-15914/51-15915	2
426-5030/5049	P2V-5	USN	124890/124909	20
426-5050	Neptune M.R.1	RAF	51-15916	1
426-5051/5055	P2V-5	USN	127720/127724	5
426-5056	Neptune M.R.1	RAF	51-15917	1
426-5057/5062	P2V-5	USN	127725/127730	6
426-5063	Neptune M.R.1	RAF	51-15918	1
426-5064/5069	P2V-5	USN	127731/127736	6
426-5070	Neptune M.R.1	RAF	51-15919	1
426-5071/5085	P2V-5	USN	127737/127751	15
426-5086/5088	P2V-5	RAAF	A89-305, -308 & -307	3
426-5089/5091	P2V-5	USN	127752/127754	3
426-5092/5094	P2V-5	RAAF	A89-304, -303 & -306	3
426-5095/5099	Neptune M.R.1	RAF	51-15920/51-15924	5
426-5100/5104	P2V-5	USN	127755/127759	5
426-5105/5109	Neptune M.R.1	RAF	51-15925/51-15929	5
426-5110/5112	P2V-5	RAAF	A89-309/A89-311	3
426-5113/5116	P2V-5	USN	127760/127763	4
426-5117/5121	Neptune M.R.1	RAF	51-15930/51-15934	5
426-5122	P2V-5	RAAF	A89-312	1
426-5123/5130	P2V-5	USN	127764/127771	8
426-5131/5135	Neptune M.R.1	RAF	51-15935/51-15939	5
426-5136/5144	P2V-5	USN	127772/127780	9
426-5145/5170	Neptune M.R.1	RAF	51-15940/51-15965	26
426-5171/5172	P2V-5	USN	127781/127782	2
426-5173/5268	P2V-5	USN	128327/128422	96
426-5269/5272	P2V-5	USN	131400/131403	4
426-5273/5284	P2V-5	MLD	19-21/19-32	12
426-5285/5424	P2V-5	USN	131404/131543	140
626-6001	P2V-6	Aeronavale	126514	1
626-6002/6008	P2V-6	USN	126515/126521	7
626-6009	P2V-6	Aeronavale	126522	1
626-6010/6023	P2V-6	USN	126523/126536	14
626-6024	P2V-6	Aeronavale	126537	1
626-6025	P2V-6	USN	126538	1
626-6026/6027	P2V-6	Aeronavale	126539/126540	2
626-6028/6034	P2V-6	USN	126541/126547	7
626-6035/6060	P2V-6	Aeronavale	134638/134663	26
626-6061/6067	P2V-6	USN	131544/131550	7
626-6068/6083	P2V-6M	USN	131551/131566	16
726-7001/7021	P2V-7	USN	135544/135564	21
726-7022/7026	P2V-7	USN	135566/135570	5
726-7027	P2V-7	USN	135572	1
726-7028	P2V-7	USN	135574	1
726-7029	P2V-7	USN	135576	1
726-7030	P2V-7	USN	135578	1

726-7031	P2V-7	USN	135580	1
726-7032	P2V-7	USN	135582	1
726-7033	P2V-7	USN	135584	1
726-7034	P2V-7	USN	135586	1
726-7035	P2V-7	USN	135588	1
726-7036	P2V-7	USN	135590	1
726-7037	P2V-7	USN	135592	1
726-7038	P2V-7	USN	135594	1
726-7039	P2V-7	USN	135596	1
726-7040	P2V-7	USN	135598	1
726-7041	P2V-7	USN	135600	1
726-7042	P2V-7	USN	135602	1
726-7043	P2V-7	USN	135604	1
726-7044	P2V-7	USN	135606	1
726-7045	P2V-7	USN	135608	1
726-7046	P2V-7	USN	135610	1
726-7047	P2V-7U	USAF	54-4037	1
726-7048	P2V-7	USN	135614	1
726-7049	P2V-7	USN	135616	1
726-7050/7053	P2V-7	USN	135618/135621	4
726-7054/7063	P2V-7	USN	140151/140160	10
726-7064/7069	P2V-7	USN	140962/140967	6
726-7070	P2V-7	JMSDF	4601	1
726-7071	P2V-7	USN	140969	1
726-7072	P2V-7	JMSDF	4602	1
726-7073/7074	P2V-7	USN	140971/140972	2
726-7075	P2V-7	JMSDF	4603	1
726-7076/7077	P2V-7	USN	140974/140975	2
726-7078	P2V-7	JMSDF	4604	1
726-7079/7080	P2V-7	USN	140977/140978	2
726-7081	P2V-7	JMSDF	4605	1
726-7082	P2V-7	USN	140980	1
726-7083	P2V-7	JMSDF	4606	1
726-7084/7092	P2V-7	USN	140982/140990	9
726-7093	P2V-7LP	USN	140434	1
726-7094	P2V-7S	USN	140435	1
726-7095/7096	P2V-7LP	USN	140436/140437	2
726-7097	P2V-7U	USAF	54-4038	1
726-7098	P2V-7LP	USN	140439	1
726-7099	P2V-7U	USAF	54-4039	1
726-7100	P2V-7	USN	140441	1
726-7101	P2V-7U	USAF	54-4040	1
726-7102	P2V-7	USN	140443	1
726-7103/7104	P2V-7	USN	141231/141232	2
726-7105	P2V-7U	USAF	54-4041	1
726-7106/7115	P2V-7	USN	141234/141243	10
726-7116/7117	P2V-7	JMSDF	4607/4608	2
726-7118/7123	P2V-7	USN	141246/141251	6
726-7124/7127	P2V-7	USN	142542/142545	4
726-7128/7132	P2V-7	USN	143172/143176	5
726-7133	P2V-7	JMSDF	4609	1
726-7134	P2V-7	USN	143178	1
726-7135	P2V-7	JMSDF	4610	1
726-7136/7143	P2V-7	Aeronavale	144685/144692	8
726-7144/7145	P2V-7	Aeronavale	146431/146432	2
726-7146/7151	P2V-7	JMSDF	4611/4616	6
726-7152/7157	P2V-7	Aeronavale	146433/146438	6
726-7158/7161	P2V-7	USN	144681/144684	4
726-7162/7173	P2V-7	USN	145900/145911	12
726-7174	P2V-7	Aeronavale	147562	1
726-7175/7176	P2V-7	USN	145912/145913	2
726-7177	P2V-7	Aeronavale	147563	1
726-7178	P2V-7	USN	145914	1
726-7179	P2V-7	Aeronavale	147564	1
726-7180	P2V-7	USN	145915	1
726-7181	P2V-7	Aeronavale	147565	1
726-7182	P2V-7	USN	145916	1
726-7183	P2V-7	Aeronavale	147566	1
726-7184	P2V-7	USN	145917	1
726-7185	P2V-7	Aeronavale	147567	1
726-7186	P2V-7	USN	145918	1
726-7187	P2V-7	Aeronavale	147568	1
726-7188	P2V-7	USN	145919	1

726-7189	P2V-7	Aeronavale	147569	1
726-7190	P2V-7	USN	145920	1
726-7191	P2V-7	Aeronavale	147570	1
726-7192	P2V-7	USN	145921	1
726-7193	P2V-7	Aeronavale	147571	1
726-7194/7195	P2V-7	USN	145922/145923	2
726-7196/7221	P2V-7	USN	147946/147971	26
726-7222/7237	P2V-7	USN	148337/148352	16
726-7238	P2V-7B	MLD	200	1
726-7239	P2V-7	USN	148353	1
726-7240	P2V-7	Aeronavale	148330	1
726-7241	P2V-7B	MDL	201	1
726-7242/7243	P2V-7	USN	148354/148355	2
726-7244	P2V-7	Aeronavale	148331	1
726-7245	P2V-7B	MLD	202	1
726-7246/7247	P2V-7	USN	148356/148357	2
726-7248	P2V-7B	MLD	203	1
726-7249	P2V-7	Aeronavale	148332	1
726-7250	P2V-7	USN	148358	1
726-7251/7252	P2V-7B	MLD	204/205	2
726-7253	P2V-7	Aeronavale	148333	1
726-7254	P2V-7B	MLD	206	1
726-7255/7256	P2V-7	USN	148359/148360	2
726-7257	P2V-7B	MLD	207	1
726-7258	P2V-7	USN	148361	1
726-7259	P2V-7B	MLD	208	1
726-7260	P2V-7	USN	148362	1
726-7261	P2V-7B	MLD	209	1
726-7262	P2V-7	Aeronavale	148334	1
726-7263	P2V-7B	MLD	210	1
726-7264	P2V-7	Aeronavale	148335	1
726-7265	P2V-7B	MLD	211	1
726-7266	P2V-7	Aeronavale	148336	1
726-7267/7269	P2V-7B	MLD	212/214	3
726-7270/7281	P2V-7	RAAF	A89-270/A89-281	12
726-7282/7286	P2V-7	USN	150279/150283	5
826-8001/8025	P2V-7	RCAF	24101/24125	25
- - -	P2V-7	JMSDF	4617/4658	42
- - -	P2V-7	JMSDF	4659/4664	6
- - -	P-2J	JMSDF	4702/4783	82

LOCKHEED 34 BIG DIPPER (Number built: 1)

34-1001	34	Co. owned		1

LOCKHEED 75 SATURN (Number built: 2)

075-1001	Saturn	Co. owned	NX90801	1
075-1002	Saturn	Co. owned		1

LOCKHEED R60-1 CONSTITUTION (Number built: 2)

089-1001/1002	XR60-1	USN	85163/85164	2

LOCKHEED T-33 (Number built: 5,691 by Lockheed; plus 210 by Kawasaki and 656 by Canadair)

580-5001/5020	TF-80C-1-LO	USAF	48-356/48-375	20
580-5021/5028	TF-80C-1-LO	USAF	48-913/48-920	8
580-5029/5083	TF-80C-1-LO	USAF	49-879/49-933	55
580-5084	TO-2	USN	124570	1
580-5085/5156	TF-80C-1-LO	USAF	49-935/49-1006	72
580-5157	T-33A-1-LO	USAF	49-2757	1
580-5158/5172	TO-2	USN	124571/124585	15
580-5173/5284	T-33A-1-LO	USAF	50-320/50-431	112
580-5286/5297	T-33A-1-LO	USAF	50-433/50-444	12
580-5298/5307	TO-2	USN	124930/124939	10
580-5308/5312	T-33A-1-LO	USAF	50-1272/50-1276	5
580-5313/5318	TV-2	USN	126583/126588	6
580-5319/5324	T-33A-1-LO	USAF	51-4025/51-4030	6
580-5325/5330	TV-2	USN	126589/126594	6
580-5331/5345	T-33A-1-LO	USAF	51-4037/51-4051	15
580-5346/5351	TV-2	USN	126595/126600	6
580-5352/5371	T-33A-1-LO	USAF	51-4058/51-4077	20
580-5372/5377	TV-2	USN	126601/126606	6
580-5378/5397	T-33A-1-LO	USAF	51-4084/51-4103	20
580-5398/5403	TV-2	USN	126607/126612	6
580-5404/5430	T-33A-1-LO	USAF	51-4110/51-4136	27

580-5431/5436	TV-2	USN	126613/126618	6	
580-5437/5467	T-33A-1-LO	USAF	51-4143/51-4173	31	
580-5468/5473	TV-2	USN	126619/126624	6	
580-5474/5527	T-33A-1-LO	USAF	51-4180/51-4233	54	
580-5528	T-33A-1-LO	USAF	50-432	1	
580-5529/5531	T-33A-1-LO	USAF	51-4234/51-4236	3	
580-5532/5533	TV-2	USN	126625/126626	2	
580-5534/5538	TV-2	USN	128661/128665	5	
580-5539/5582	T-33A-1-LO	USAF	51-4244/51-4287	44	
580-5583/5589	TV-2	USN	128666/128672	7	
580-5590/5592	T-33A-1-LO	USAF	51-4295/51-4297	3	
580-5593/5649	T-33A-1-LO	USAF	51-4298/51-4354	57	
580-5650/5659	TV-2	USN	128673/128682	10	
580-5660/5719	T-33A-1-LO	USAF	51-4365/51-4424	60	
580-5720/5729	TV-2	USN	128683/128692	10	
580-5730/5809	T-33A-1-LO	USAF	51-4435/51-4514	80	
580-5810/5819	TV-2	USN	128693/128702	10	
580-5820/5828	T-33A-1-LO	USAF	51-4525/51-4533	9	
580-5829/5909	T-33A-1-LO	USAF	51-6497/51-6577	81	
580-5910/5919	TV-2	USN	128703/128712	10	
580-5920/5996	T-33A-1-LO	USAF	51-6588/51-6664	77	
580-5997/6006	TV-2	USN	128713/128722	10	
580-6007/6289	T-33A-1-LO	USAF	51-6675/51-6957	283	
580-6290/6301	T-33A-1-LO	USAF	51-8506/51-8517	12	
580-6302/6325	TV-2	USN	131725/131748	24	
580-6326/6419	T-33A-1-LO	USAF	51-8542/51-8635	94	
580-6420/6435	TV-2	USN	131749/131764	16	
580-6436/6512	T-33A-1-LO	USAF	51-8652/51-8728	77	
580-6513/6533	TV-2	USN	131765/131785	21	
580-6534/6619	T-33A-1-LO	USAF	51-8750/51-8835	86	
580-6620/6654	TV-2	USN	131786/131820	35	
580-6655/6723	T-33A-1-LO	USAF	51-8871/51-8939	69	
580-6724/6737	TV-2	USN	131821/131834	14	
580-6738/6823	T-33A-1-LO	USAF	51-8954/51-9039	86	
580-6824/6859	TV-2	USN	131835/131870	36	
580-6860/6933	T-33A-1-LO	USAF	51-9076/51-9149	74	
580-6934/6951	TV-2	USN	131871/131888	18	
580-6952/7094	T-33A-1-LO	USAF	51-9168/51-9310	143	
580-7095/7114	T-33A-1-LO	USAF	51-16976/51-16995	20	
580-7115/7136	T-33A-1-LO	USAF	51-17388/51-17409	22	
580-7137/7148	T-33A-1-LO	USAF	51-17444/51-17455	12	
580-7149/7182	T-33A-1-LO	USAF	51-17410/51-17443	34	
580-7183/7246	T-33A-1-LO	USAF	52-9129/52-9192	64	
580-7247/7258	T-33A-1-LO	USAF	51-17456/51-17467	12	
580-7259/7361	T-33A-1-LO	USAF	52-9193/52-9295	103	
580-7362/7380	T-33A-1-LO	USAF	51-17468/51-17486	19	
580-7381/7466	T-33A-1-LO	USAF	52-9296/52-9381	86	
580-7467/7491	T-33A-1-LO	USAF	51-17487/51-17511	25	
580-7492/7571	T-33A-1-LO	USAF	52-9382/52-9461	80	
580-7572/7596	T-33A-1-LO	USAF	51-17512/51-17536	25	
580-7597/7681	T-33A-1-LO	USAF	52-9462/52-9546	85	
580-7682/7701	T-33A-1-LO	USAF	51-17537/51-17556	20	
580-7702/7706	T-33A-1-LO	USAF	52-9876/52-9880	5	
580-7707/7776	T-33A-1-LO	USAF	52-9547/52-9616	70	
580-7777/7801	T-33A-1-LO	USAF	52-9881/52-9905	25	
580-7802/7876	T-33A-1-LO	USAF	52-9617/52-9691	75	
580-7877/7896	T-33A-1-LO	USAF	52-9906/52-9925	20	
580-7897/7916	TV-2	USN	136793/136812	20	
580-7917/7976	T-33A-1-LO	USAF	52-9692/52-9751	60	
580-7977/7991	T-33A-1-LO	USAF	52-9926/52-9940	15	
580-7992/8011	TV-2	USN	136813/136832	20	
580-8012/8086	T-33A-1-LO	USAF	52-9752/52-9826	75	
580-8087/8096	T-33A-1-LO	USAF	52-9941/52-9950	10	
580-8097/8132	TV-2	USN	136833/136868	36	
580-8133/8181	T-33A-1-LO	USAF	52-9827/52-9875	49	
580-8182/8206	T-33A-1-LO	USAF	52-9951/52-9975	25	
580-8207/8224	TV-2	USN	136869/136886	18	
580-8225/8428	T-33A-1-LO	USAF	53-4886/53-5089	204	
580-8429	RT-33A-1-LO	USAF	53-5090	1	
580-8430/8512	T-33A-1-LO	USAF	53-5091/53-5173	83	
580-8513	RT-33A-1-LO	USAF	53-5174	1	
580-8514/8547	T-33A-1-LO	USAF	53-5175/53-5208	34	
580-8548	RT-33A-1-LO	USAF	53-5209	1	

496

580-8549/8575	T-33A-1-L0	USAF	53-5210/53-5236	27
580-8576/8578	RT-33A-1-L0	USAF	53-5237/53-5239	3
580-8579	T-33A-1-L0	USAF	53-5240	1
580-8580/8582	TV-2	USN	137934/137936	3
580-8583/8595	T-33A-1-L0	USAF	53-5244/53-5256	13
580-8596	RT-33A-1-L0	USAF	53-5257	1
580-8597/8611	T-33A-1-L0	USAF	53-5258/53-5272	15
580-8612	RT-33A-1-L0	USAF	53-5273	1
580-8613/8629	T-33A-1-L0	USAF	53-5274/53-5290	17
580-8630	RT-33A-1-L0	USAF	53-5291	1
580-8631/8646	T-33A-1-L0	USAF	53-5292/53-5307	16
580-8647	RT-33A-1-L0	USAF	53-5308	1
580-8648	T-33A-1-L0	USAF	53-5309	1
580-8649/8656	TV-2	USN	137937/137944	8
580-8657/8660	T-33A-1-L0	USAF	53-5318/53-5321	4
580-8661	RT-33A-1-L0	USAF	53-5322	1
580-8662/8673	T-33A-1-L0	USAF	53-5323/53-5334	12
580-8674	RT-33A-1-L0	USAF	53-5335	1
580-8675/8685	T-33A-1-L0	USAF	53-5336/53-5346	11
580-8686	RT-33A-1-L0	USAF	53-5347	1
580-8687/8689	T-33A-1-L0	USAF	53-5348/53-5350	3
580-8690/8697	TV-2	USN	137945/137952	8
580-8698	RT-33A-1-L0	USAF	53-5359	1
580-8699/8702	TV-2	USN	137953/137956	4
580-8703/8709	T-33A-1-L0	USAF	53-5364/53-5370	7
580-8710	RT-33A-1-L0	USAF	53-5371	1
580-8711/8713	T-33A-1-L0	USAF	53-5372/53-5374	3
580-8714/8722	TV-2	USN	137957/137965	9
580-8723	RT-33A-1-L0	USAF	53-5384	1
580-8724/8726	TV-2	USN	137966/137968	3
580-8727/8734	T-33A-1-L0	USAF	53-5388/53-5395	8
580-8735	RT-33A-1-L0	USAF	53-5396	1
580-8736/8747	T-33A-1-L0	USAF	53-5397/53-5408	12
580-8748	RT-33A-1-L0	USAF	53-5409	1
580-8749/8758	T-33A-1-L0	USAF	53-5410/53-5419	10
580-8759	RT-33A-1-L0	USAF	53-5420	1
580-8760/8768	T-33A-1-L0	USAF	53-5421/53-5429	9
580-8769	RT-33A-1-L0	USAF	53-5430	1
580-8770/8775	T-33A-1-L0	USAF	53-5431/53-5436	6
580-8776/8779	TV-2	USN	137969/137972	4
580-8780	RT-33A-1-L0	USAF	53-5441	1
580-8781/8787	TV-2	USN	137973/137979	7
580-8788	RT-33A-1-L0	USAF	53-5449	1
580-8789/8795	TV-2	USN	137980/137986	7
580-8796	RT-33A-1-L0	USAF	53-5457	1
580-8797/8799	TV-2	USN	137987/137989	3
580-8800/8804	T-33A-1-L0	USAF	53-5461/53-5465	5
580-8805	RT-33A-1-L0	USAF	53-5466	1
580-8806/8812	T-33A-1-L0	USAF	53-5467/53-5473	7
580-8813	RT-33A-1-L0	USAF	53-5474	1
580-8814/8820	T-33A-1-L0	USAF	53-5475/53-5481	7
580-8821	RT-33A-1-L0	USAF	53-5482	1
580-8822/8829	T-33A-1-L0	USAF	53-5483/53-5490	8
580-8830	RT-33A-1-L0	USAF	53-5491	1
580-8831/8837	T-33A-1-L0	USAF	53-5492/53-5498	7
580-8838	RT-33A-1-L0	USAF	53-5499	1
580-8839/8843	T-33A-1-L0	USAF	53-5500/53-5504	5
580-8844/8846	TV-2	USN	137990/137992	3
580-8847	RT-33A-1-L0	USAF	53-5508	1
580-8848/8855	TV-2	USN	137993/138000	8
580-8856	RT-33A-1-L0	USAF	53-5517	1
580-8857/8863	TV-2	USN	138001/138007	7
580-8864	RT-33A-1-L0	USAF	53-5525	1
580-8865/8871	TV-2	USN	138008/138014	7
580-8872	RT-33A-1-L0	USAF	53-5533	1
580-8873	TV-2	USN	138015	1
580-8874/8877	T-33A-1-L0	USAF	53-5535/53-5538	4
580-8878	RT-33A-1-L0	USAF	53-5539	1
580-8879/8884	T-33A-1-L0	USAF	53-5540/53-5545	6
580-8885	RT-33A-1-L0	USAF	53-5546	1
580-8886/8891	T-33A-1-L0	USAF	53-5547/53-5552	6
580-8892	RT-33A-1-L0	USAF	53-5553	1
580-8893/8898	T-33A-1-L0	USAᶜ	53-5554/53-5559	6

580-8899	RT-33A-1-LO	USAF	
580-8900/8905	T-33A-1-LO	USAF	
580-8906	RT-33A-1-LO	USAF	
580-8907/8908	T-33A-1-LO	USAF	
580-8909/8912	TV-2	USN	
580-8913	RT-33A-1-LO	USAF	
580-8914/8919	TV-2	USN	
580-8920	RT-33A-1-LO	USAF	
580-8921/8925	TV-2	USN	
580-8926	RT-33A-1-LO	USAF	
580-8927/8932	TV-2	USN	
580-8933	RT-33A-1-LO	USAF	
580-8934/8938	TV-2	USN	
580-8939	RT-33A-1-LO	USAF	
580-8940/8942	TV-2	USN	
580-8943/8945	T-33A-1-LO	USAF	
580-8946	RT-33A-1-LO	USAF	
580-8947/8951	T-33A-1-LO	USAF	
580-8952	RT-33A-1-LO	USAF	
580-8953/8957	T-33A-1-LO	USAF	
580-8958	RT-33A-1-LO	USAF	
580-8959/8964	T-33A-1-LO	USAF	
580-8965	RT-33A-1-LO	USAF	
580-8966/8969	T-33A-1-LO	USAF	
580-8970	RT-33A-1-LO	USAF	
580-8971/8976	T-33A-1-LO	USAF	
580-8977	RT-33A-1-LO	USAF	
580-8978/8980	T-33A-1-LO	USAF	
580-8981/8982	TV-2	USN	
580-8983	RT-33A-1-LO	USAF	
580-8984/8988	TV-2	USN	
580-8989	RT-33A-1-LO	USAF	
580-8990/8994	TV-2	USN	
580-8995	RT-33A-1-LO	USAF	
580-8996/9000	TV-2	USN	
580-9001	RT-33A-1-LO	USAF	
580-9002/9006	TV-2	USN	
580-9007	RT-33A-1-LO	USAF	
580-9008/9013	TV-2	USN	
580-9014	RT-33A-1-LO	USAF	
580-9015/9019	TV-2	USN	
580-9020	RT-33A-1-LO	USAF	
580-9021/9025	TV-2	USN	
580-9026	RT-33A-1-LO	USAF	
580-9027/9031	TV-2	USN	
580-9032	RT-33A-1-LO	USAF	
580-9033/9037	TV-2	USN	
580-9038	RT-33A-1-LO	USAF	
580-9039/9043	TV-2	USN	
580-9044	RT-33A-1-LO	USAF	
580-9045/9048	TV-2	USN	
580-9049	RT-33A-1-LO	USAF	
580-9050/9054	TV-2	USN	
580-9055	RT-33A-1-LO	USAF	
580-9056/9058	TV-2	USN	
580-9059	T-33A-1-LO	USAF	
580-9060	RT-33A-1-LO	USAF	
580-9061/9065	T-33A-1-LO	USAF	
580-9066	RT-33A-1-LO	USAF	
580-9067/9071	T-33A-1-LO	USAF	
580-9072	RT-33A-1-LO	USAF	
580-9073/9077	T-33A-1-LO	USAF	
580-9078	RT-33A-1-LO	USAF	
580-9079/9083	T-33A-1-LO	USAF	
580-9084	RT-33A-1-LO	USAF	
580-9085/9089	T-33A-1-LO	USAF	
580-9090	RT-33A-1-LO	USAF	
580-9091/9094	T-33A-1-LO	USAF	
580-9095	RT-33A-1-LO	USAF	
580-9096/9101	T-33A-1-LO	USAF	
580-9102	RT-33A-1-LO	USAF	
580-9103/9106	T-33A-1-LO	USAF	
580-9107	RT-33A-1-LO	USAF	

53-5560	1
53-5561/53-5566	6
53-5567	1
53-5568/53-5569	2
138016/138019	4
53-5574	1
138020/138025	6
53-5581	1
138026/138030	5
53-5587	1
138031/138036	6
53-5594	1
138037/138041	5
53-5600	1
138042/138044	3
53-5604/53-5606	3
53-5607	1
53-5608/53-5612	5
53-5613	1
53-5614/53-5618	5
53-5619	1
53-5620/53-5625	6
53-5626	1
53-5627/53-5630	4
53-5631	1
53-5632/53-5637	6
53-5638	1
53-5639/53-5641	3
138045/138046	2
53-5644	1
138047/138051	5
53-5650	1
138052/138056	5
53-5656	1
138057/138061	5
53-5662	1
138062/138066	5
53-5668	1
138067/138072	6
53-5675	1
138073/138077	5
53-5681	1
138078/138082	5
53-5687	1
138083/138087	5
53-5693	1
138088/138092	5
53-5699	1
138093/138097	5
53-5705	1
141490/141493	4
53-5710	1
141494/141498	5
53-5716	1
141499/141501	3
53-5720	1
53-5721	1
53-5722/53-5726	5
53-5727	1
53-5728/53-5732	5
53-5733	1
53-5734/53-5738	5
53-5739	1
53-5740/53-5744	5
53-5745	1
53-5746/53-5750	5
53-5751	1
53-5752/53-5755	4
53-5756	1
53-5757/53-5762	6
53-5763	1
53-5764/53-5767	4
53-5768	1

580-9108/9111	T-33A-1-LO	USAF	53-5769/53-5772	4
580-9112	RT-33A-1-LO	USAF	53-5773	1
580-9113/9117	T-33A-1-LO	USAF	53-5774/53-5778	5
580-9118	RT-33A-1-LO	USAF	53-5779	1
580-9119/9123	T-33A-1-LO	USAF	53-5780/53-5784	5
580-9124	RT-33A-1-LO	USAF	53-5785	1
580-9125/9128	T-33A-1-LO	USAF	53-5786/53-5789	4
580-9129	RT-33A-1-LO	USAF	53-5790	1
580-9130/9133	T-33A-1-LO	USAF	53-5791/53-5794	4
580-9134	RT-33A-1-LO	USAF	53-5795	1
580-9135/9138	T-33A-1-LO	USAF	53-5796/53-5799	4
580-9139	RT-33A-1-LO	USAF	54-1522	1
580-9140/9143	T-33A-1-LO	USAF	54-1523/54-1526	4
580-9144	RT-33A-1-LO	USAF	54-1527	1
580-9145/9148	T-33A-1-LO	USAF	54-1528/54-1531	4
580-9149	RT-33A-1-LO	USAF	54-1532	1
580-9150/9153	T-33A-1-LO	USAF	54-1533/54-1536	4
580-9154	RT-33A-1-LO	USAF	54-1537	1
580-9155/9156	T-33A-1-LO	USAF	54-1538/54-1539	2
580-9157/9158	T-33A-1-LO	USAF	53-5800/53-5801	2
580-9159	RT-33A-1-LO	USAF	54-1540	1
580-9160/9163	T-33A-1-LO	USAF	53-5802/53-5805	4
580-9164	RT-33A-1-LO	USAF	54-1541	1
580-9165/9168	T-33A-1-LO	USAF	53-5806/53-5809	4
580-9169	RT-33A-1-LO	USAF	54-1542	1
580-9170/9173	T-33A-1-LO	USAF	53-5810/53-5813	4
580-9174	RT-33A-1-LO	USAF	54-1543	1
580-9175/9178	T-33A-1-LO	USAF	54-1544/54-1547	4
580-9179	RT-33A-1-LO	USAF	54-1548	1
580-9180/9183	T-33A-1-LO	USAF	54-1549/54-1552	4
580-9184	RT-33A-1-LO	USAF	54-1553	1
580-9185/9192	T-33A-1-LO	USAF	54-1554/54-1561	8
580-9193/9214	TV-2	USN	138977/138998	22
580-9215/9250	T-33A-1-LO	USAF	53-5814/53-5849	36
580-9251/9272	T-33A-1-LO	USAF	54-1562/54-1583	22
580-9273/9290	TV-2	USN	138999/139016	18
580-9291/9319	T-33A-1-LO	USAF	53-5850/53-5878	29
580-9320/9354	T-33A-1-LO	USAF	54-1584/54-1618	35
580-9355/9394	T-33A-1-LO	USAF	53-5879/53-5918	40
580-9395/9449	T-33A-5-LO	USAF	53-5919/53-5973	55
580-9450/9455	T-33A-1-LO	USAF	54-2950/54-2955	6
580-9456/9475	T-33A-5-LO	USAF	53-5974/53-5993	20
580-9476/9480	T-33A-1-LO	USAF	55-2979/55-2983	5
580-9481/9513	TV-2	USN	141502/141534	33
580-9514/9525	T-33A-5-LO	USAF	55-3017/55-3028	12
580-9526/9569	T-33A-5-LO	USAF	53-5994/53-6037	44
580-9560/9590	T-33A-1-LO	USAF	55-3029/55-3049	21
580-9591/9614	TV-2	USN	141535/141558	24
580-9615/9640	T-33A-1-LO	USAF	55-3074/55-3099	26
580-9641/9669	T-33A-5-LO	USAF	53-6038/53-6066	29
580-9670/9685	T-33A-1-LO	USAF	53-3100/55-3115	16
580-9686/9687	T-33A-1-LO	USAF	54-4035/54-4036	2
580-9688/9773	T-33A-5-LO	USAF	53-6067/53-6152	86
580-9774/9775	T-33A-1-LO	USAF	55-3116/55-3117	2
580-9776/9868	T-33A-5-LO	USAF	55-4332/55-4424	93
580-9869/9900	T-33A-1-LO	USAF	55-4425/55-4456	32
580-9901/9904	T-33A-1-LO	USAF	55-4807/55-4810	4
580-9905/9922	T-33A-1-LO	USAF	55-4945/55-4962	18
580-9923/9996	T-33A-1-LO	USAF	56-1573/56-1646	74
580-9997	TV-2	USN	143014	1
580-9998/9999	T-33A-1-LO	USAF	56-1648/56-1649	2
580-1000	T-33A-1-LO	USAF	56-1650	1
580-1001	TV-2	USN	143015	1
580-1002/1004	T-33A-1-LO	USAF	56-1652/56-1654	3
580-1005	TV-2	USN	143016	1
580-1006/1008	T-33A-1-LO	USAF	56-1656/56-1658	3
580-1009	TV-2	USN	143017	1
580-1010/1012	T-33A-1-LO	USAF	56-1660/56-1662	3
580-1013	TV-2	USN	143018	1
580-1014/1016	T-33A-1-LO	USAF	56-1664/56-1666	3
580-1017	TV-2	USN	143019	1
580-1018/1020	T-33A-1-LO	USAF	56-1668/56-1670	3
580-1021	TV-2	USN	143020	1

499

580-1022/1024	T-33A-1-LO	USAF	56-1672/56-1674	3
580-1025	TV-2	USN	143021	1
580-1026/1028	T-33A-1-LO	USAF	56-1676/56-1678	3
580-1029	TV-2	USN	143022	1
580-1030/1032	T-33A-1-LO	USAF	56-1680/56-1682	3
580-1033	TV-2	USN	143023	1
580-1034/1036	T-33A-1-LO	USAF	56-1684/56-1686	3
580-1037	TV-2	USN	143024	1
580-1038/1040	T-33A-1-LO	USAF	56-1688/56-1690	3
580-1041	TV 2	USN	143025	1
580-1042/1044	T-33A-1-LO	USAF	56 1692/56-1694	3
580-1045	TV-2	USN	143026	1
580-1046/1048	T-33A-1-LO	USAF	56-1696/56-1698	3
580-1049	TV-2	USN	143027	1
580-1050/1052	T-33A-1-LO	USAF	56-1700/56-1702	3
580-1053	TV-2	USN	143028	1
580-1054/1056	T-33A-1-LO	USAF	56-1704/56-1706	3
580-1057	TV-2	USN	143029	1
580-1058/1060	T-33A-1-LO	USAF	56-1708/56-1710	3
580-1061	TV-2	USN	143030	1
580-1062/1064	T-33A-1-LO	USAF	56-1712/56-1714	3
580-1065	TV-2	USN	143031	1
580-1066/1068	T-33A-1-LO	USAF	56-1716/56-1718	3
580-1069	TV-2	USN	143032	1
580-1070/1072	T-33A-1-LO	USAF	56-1720/56-1722	3
580-1073	TV-2	USN	143033	1
580-1074/1076	T-33A-1-LO	USAF	56-1724/56-1726	3
580-1077	TV-2	USN	143034	1
580-1078/1080	T-33A-1-LO	USAF	56-1728/56-1730	3
580-1081	TV-2	USN	143035	1
580-1082/1084	T-33A-1-LO	USAF	56-1732/56-1734	3
580-1085	TV-2	USN	143036	1
580-1086/1088	T-33A-1-LO	USAF	56-1736/56-1738	3
580-1089	TV-2	USN	143037	1
580-1090/1093	T-33A-1-LO	USAF	56-1740/56-1743	4
580-1094	TV-2	USN	143038	1
580-1095/1097	T-33A-1-LO	USAF	56-1745/56-1747	3
580-1098	TV-2	USN	143039	1
580-1099/1101	T-33A-1-LO	USAF	56-1749/56-1751	3
580-1102	TV-2	USN	143040	1
580-1103/1105	T-33A-1-LO	USAF	56-1753/56-1755	3
580-1106	TV-2	USN	143041	1
580-1107/1109	T-33A-1-LO	USAF	56-1757/56-1759	3
580-1110	TV-2	USN	143042	1
580-1111/1113	T-33A-1-LO	USAF	56-1761/56-1763	3
580-1114	TV-2	USN	143043	1
580-1115/1117	T-33A-1-LO	USAF	56-1765/56-1767	3
580-1118	TV-2	USN	143044	1
580-1119/1121	T-33A-1-LO	USAF	56-1769/56-1771	3
580-1122	TV-2	USN	143045	1
580-1123/1125	T-33A-1-LO	USAF	56-1773/56-1775	3
580-1126	TV-2	USN	143046	1
580-1127/1129	T-33A-1-LO	USAF	56-1777/56-1779	3
580-1130	TV-2	USN	143047	1
580-1131/1133	T-33A-1-LO	USAF	56-1781/56-1783	3
580-1134	TV-2	USN	143048	1
580-1135/1137	T-33A-1-LO	USAF	56-1785/56-1787	3
580-1138	TV-2	USN	143049	1
580-1139/1142	T-33A-1-LO	USAF	56-1789/56-1792	4
580-1143/1178	T-33A-5-LO	USAF	56-3659/56-3694	36
580-1259/1498	T-33A-5-LO	USAF	57-530/57-769	240
580-1499/1759	T-33A-5-LO	USAF	58-450/58-710	261
580-1760/1772	T-33A-5-LO	USAF	58-2094/58-2106	13
- - -	T-33A-1-LO	Cancelled	55-5155/55-5234	0
- - -	T-33A-5-LO	Cancelled	57-6308/57-6337	0
- - -	T-33AN	RCAF	21001/21656	656
- - -	T-33A	Koku Jieitai	61-5201/61-5230	30
- - -	T-33A	Koku Jieitai	71-5231/71-5326	96
- - -	T-33A	Koku Jieitai	81-5327/81-5397	71
- - -	T-33A	Koku Jieitai	91-5398/91-5410	13

```
LOCKHEED F-94 STARFIRE (Number built:  854)
780-5001/5002    YF-94-LO       USAF        48-356/48-357        (2)
780-7001/7017    F-94A-1-LO     USAF        49-2479/49-2495       17
780-7018         F-94A-5-LO     USAF        49-2496                1
780-7019         YF-94B-LO      USAF        49-2497                1
780-7020/7110    F-94A-5-LO     USAF        49-2498/49-2588       91
780-7111/7182    F-94B-1-LO     USAF        50-805/50-876         72
780-7183         YF-97A-LO      USAF        50-877                 1
780-7184/7260    F-94B-1-LO     USAF        50-878/50-954         77
880-8000         YF-97A-LO      USAF        50-955                 1
880-8001/8108    F-94C-1-LO     USAF        50-956/50-1063       108
780-7261/7466    F-94B-5-LO     USAF        51-5307/51-5512      206
880-8109/8294    F-94C-1-LO     USAF        51-5513/51-5698      186
880-8295/8387    F-94C-1-LO     USAF        51-13511/51-13603     93
- - -            F-94D-LO       Cancelled   51-13604/51-13716      0

LOCKHEED XF-90 (Number built:  2)
090-1001/1002    XF-90-LO       USAF        46-687/46-688          2

LOCKHEED SUPER CONSTELLATION (Number built:  579)
1049-1961S       1049           Co. owned   NX67900              (1)
1049-4001/4014   1049           Eastern     N6201C/N6214C         14
1049-4015/4024   1049           TWA         N6901C/N6910C         10
1049B-4101/4111  R70-1          USN         128434/128444         11
1049B-4112/4121  RC-121C        USAF        51-3836/51-3845       10
1049B-4122/4130  R7V-1          USN         131621/131629          9
1249A-4131/4132  R7V-2          USN         131630/131631          2
1049B-4133/4150  R7V-1          USN         131632/131649         18
1049B-4151       VC-121E        USAF        53-7885                1
1049B-4152/4160  R7V-1          USN         131651/131659          9
1249A-4161/4162  R7V-2          USN         131660/131661          2
1049D-4163/4166  1049D          S & W       N6501C/N6504C          4
1049B-4167/4169  R7V-1          USN         140311/140313          3
1049F-4170/4202  C-121C         USAF        54-151/54-183         33
1049A-4301/4302  WV-2           USN         126512/126513          2
1049A-4303/4306  WV-2           USN         128323/128326          4
1049A-4307/4312  WV-2           USN         131387/131392          6
- - -            WV-2           Cancelled   131393/131399          0
1049A-4313/4328  WV-2           USN         135746/135761         16
1049A-4329/4343  RC-121D        USAF        52-3411/52-3425       15
1049A-4344/4347  WV-2           USN         137887/137890          4
1049A-4348/4371  RC-121D        USAF        53-533/53-556         24
1049A-4372/4377  RC-121D        USAF        53-3398/53-3403        6
1049A-4378/4385  WV-3           USN         137891/137898          8
1049A-4386/4390  RC-121D        USAF        54-2304/54-2308        5
1049A-4391/4412  RC-121D        USAF        55-118/55-139         22
1049A-4413/4457  WV-2           USN         141289/141333         45
1049A-4458/4499  WV-2           USN         143184/143225         42
1049C-4501/4509  1049C          KLM         PH-TFP & PH-TFR/ PH-TFY  9
1049C-4510/4519  1049C          Air France  F-BGNA/F-BGNJ         10
1049C-4520/4522  1049C          PIA         AP-AFQ/AP-AFS          3
1049C-4523/4538  1049C          Eastern     N6215C/N6230C         16
1049C-4539       1049C          Qantas      VH-EAG                 1
1049C-4540/4544  1049C          TCA         CF-TGA/CF-TGE          5
1049C-4545/4546  1049C          Qantas      VH-EAH/VH-EAI          2
1049C-4547/4548  1049C          Air-India   VT-DGL/VT-DGM          2
1049E-4549       1049E          Qantas      VH-EAJ                 1
1049E-4550/4552  1049E          Iberia      EC-AIN/EC-AIP          3
1049E-4553       1049E          KLM         PH-TFZ                 1
1049E-4554/4556  1049E          Avianca     HK-175/HK-177          3
1049E-4557       1049E          Cubana      CU-P-573               1
1049E-4558/4560  1049E          KLM         PH-TGK/PH-TGM          3
1049E-4561/4562  1049E          LAV         YV-C-AMS & -AMR        2
1049E-4563/4565  1049E          TCA         CF-TGF/CF-TGH          3
1049E-4566/4571  Not Built      ---         - - -                 0
1049G-4572       1049G          Northwest   N5172V                 1
1049E-4573/4574  1049E          Qantas      VH-EAK/VH-EAL          2
1049G-4575/4577  1049G          Northwest   N5173V/N5175V          3
1049E-4578/4581  1049E          Qantas      VH-EAE, -EAF, -EAA& -EAB  4
1049G-4582/4601  1049G          TWA         N7101C/N7120C         20
1049G-4602/4605  1049G          Lufthansa   D-ALAK,EM,IN,OP        4
```

501

1049E-4606/4607	1049E	Qantas	VH-EAC/VH-EAD	2
1049E-4608/4609	Not Built	---	- - -	0
1049G-4610/4612	1049G	Varig	PP-VDA/PP-VDC	3
1049E-4613/4615	1049E	Air-India	VT-DHL/VT-DHN	3
1049G-4616/4618	1049G	TAP	CS-TLA/CS-TLC	3
1049G-4619	1049G	Hughes Tool		1
1049G-4620/4627	1049G	Air France	F-BHBA/F-BHBH	8
1049G-4628	1049G	Avianca	HK-184	1
1049G-4629/4631	1049G	KLM	PH-LKE/PH-LKG	3
1049G 4632/4633	1049G	Cubana	CU-C-602	2
1049G-4634	1049G	Air France	F-BHBI	1
1049G-4635	1049G	KLM	PH-LKH	1
1049G-4636	1049G	LAV	YV-C-AME	1
1049G-4637	1049G	Lufthansa	D-ALAP	1
1049G-4638	Not Built	- - -	- - -	0
1049G-4639	1049G	Air France	F-BHBJ	1
1049G-4640	1049G	Lufthansa	D-ALEC	1
1049G-4641	1049G	TCA	CF-TEU	1
1049G-4642	1049G	Lufthansa	D-ALOF	1
1049G-4643	1049G	TCA	CF-TEV	1
1049G-4644/4645	1049G	KLM	PH-LKI, PH-LKK	2
1049G-4646	1049G	Air-India	VT-DIL	1
1049G-4647	1049G	Lufthansa	D-ALID	1
1049G-4648/4652	1049G	TWA	N7122C/N7126C	5
1049G-4653	1049G	Eastern	N6231G	1
1049G-4654	1049G	TWA	N7126C	1
1049G-4655	1049G	Eastern	N6232G	1
1049G-4656	1049G	TWA	N7127C	1
1049G-4657	1049G	Eastern	N6233G	1
1049G-4658	1049G	TWA	N7128C	1
1049G-4659/4665	1049G	Eastern	N6234G/N6240G	7
1049G-4666/4667	1049G	Air-India	VT-DIM/VT-DIN	2
1049G-4668/4671	1049G	Air France	F-BHMI/F-BHML	4
1049G-4672	1049G	Thai Airways	HS-TCA	1
1049G-4673	1049G	Iberia	EC-AMP	1
1049G-4674	1049G	LAV	YV-C-AMI	1
1049G-4675	1049G	Cubana	CU-C-631	1
1049G-4676	1049G	Iberia	EC-AMQ	1
1049G-4677/4678	1049G	Thai Airways	HS-TCB/HS-TCC	2
1049G-4679/4680	1049G	Qantas	VH-EAO/VH-EAP	2
1049G-4681	1049G	Varig	PP-VDD	1
1049G-4682/4683	1049G	TCA	CF-TEW/CF-TEX	2
1049G-4684/4685	1049G	Varig	PP-VDE/PP-VDF	2
1049G-4686/4687	1049G	Air-India	VT-DJW/VT-DJX	2
1049H-4801	1049H	Qantas	VH-EAM	1
1049H-4802	1049H	S & W	N1006C	1
1049H-4803	1049H	Qantas	VH-EAN	1
1049H-4804	1049H	Flying Tigers	N6911C	1
1049H-4805/4808	1049H	S & W	N1007C/N1010C	4
1049H-4809/4812	1049H	Flying Tigers	N6912C/N6915C	4
1049H-4813	1049H	Cal Eastern	N6931C	1
1049H-4814/4816	1049H	Flying Tigers	N6916C/N6918C	3
1049H-4017	1049H	Air Finance Corp.	N6921C	1
1049H-4818	1049H	Resort	N101R	1
1049H-4819	1049H	Flying Tigers	N6919C	1
1049H-4820	1049H	Dollar Airlines	N1880	1
1049H-4821	1049H	Air Finance Corp.	N1927H	1
1049H-4822	1049H	Flying Tigers	N6920C	1
1049H-4823	1049H	Cal Eastern	N6932C	1
1049H-4824	1049H	Resort	N102R	1
1049H-4825	1049H	Air Finance Corp.	N6922C	1
1049H-4826	1049H	Cal Eastern	N6933C	1
1049H-4827	1049H	Flying Tigers	N6923C	1
1049H-4828/4829	1049H	National	N7131C/N7132C	2
1049H-4830	1049H	Slick Airways	N6937C	1
1049H-4831/4832	1049H	National	N7133C/N7134C	2
1049H-4833/4834	1049H	Aerovias Real	PP-YSA/PP-YSB	2
1049H-4835/4836	1049H	PIA	AP-AJY/AP-AJZ	2
1049H-4837/4838	1049H	Aerovias Real	PP-YSC/PP-YSD	2
1049H-4839	1049H	TWA	N5401V	1
1049H-4840/4841	1049H	KLM	PH-LKL/PH-LKM	2
1049H-4842	1049H	TWA	N5402V	1
1049H-4843	1049H	KLM	PH-LKN	1

```
1049H-4844/4845    1049H            TWA                N5403V/N5404V                    2
1049H-4846/4847    1049H            Cal Eastern        N488C/N469C                      2
1049H-4848/4849    1049H            Slick Airways      N6935C/N6936C                    2
1049H-4850/4851    1049H            TCA                CF-TEY/CF-TEZ                    2
1049H-4852/4853    1049H            Flying Tigers      N6924C/N6925C                    2
1049A-5500/5504    WV-2             USN                143226/143230                    5
1049A-5505/5522    WV-2             USN                145924/145941                   18
- - -              WV-2             Cancelled          145942/145956                    0
```

BOEING B-47 STRATOJET (Number built by Lockheed: 394)
```
                   B-47B-30-LM*     USAF               51-2197                          1
                   B-47B-40-LM*     USAF               51-2204, -2210,
                                                       -2217, -2224, -2231,
                                                       -2237 & -2243                    7
                   B-47E-5-LM       USAF               51-15804/51-15810                7
                   B-47E-10-LM      USAF               51-15811/51-15812                2
                   B-47E-10-LM      USAF               52-202/52-207                    6
                   B-47E-15-LM      USAF               52-208/52-220                   13
                   B-47E-20-LM      USAF               52-221/52-235                   15
                   B-47E-25-LM      USAF               52-236/52-260                   25
                   B-47E-30-LM      USAF               52-261/52-292                   32
                   B-47E-35-LM      USAF               52-293/52-330                   38
                   B-47E-40-LM      USAF               52-331/52-362                   32
                   B-47E-45-LM      USAF               52-363/52-393                   31
                   B-47E-50-LM      USAF               52-3343/52-3373                 31
                   B-47E-55-LM      USAF               53-1819/53-1849                 31
                   B-47E-60-LM      USAF               53-1850/53-1880                 31
                   B-47E-65-LM      USAF               53-1881/53-1911                 31
                   B-47E-70-LM      USAF               53-1912/53-1942                 31
                   B-47E-75-LM      USAF               53-1943/53-1972                 30
```

* Assembled in Marietta from components built by Boeing in Wichita.

LOCKHEED T2V-1 (T-1A) SEASTAR (Number built: 150)
```
1080-1000          L-245            Co. owned          N125D                          (1)
1080-1001/1008     T2V-1            USN                142261/142268                    8
1080-1009/1011     T2V-1            USN                142397/142399                    3
1080-1012/1020     T2V-1            USN                142533/142541                    9
1080-1021/1120     T2V-1            USN                144117/144216                  100
1080-1121/1150     T2V-1            USN                144735/144764                   30
- - -              T2V-1            Cancelled          144765/144824                    0
- - -              T2V-1            Cancelled          146058/146237                    0
```

LOCKHEED F-104 STARFIGHTER (Number built: 741 by Lockheed plus 48 co-produced by
                           Lockheed & European consortium, 340 by Canadair, 444 by Fiat,
                           350 by Fokker, 50 by MBB, 210 by Messerschmitt, 207 by
                           Mitsubishi, and 188 by SABCA)
```
083-1001/1002      XF-104-LO        USAF               53-7786/53-7787                  2
183-1001/1017      YF-104-LO        USAF               55-2955/55-2971                 17
183-1018/1024      F-104A-1-LO      USAF               56-730/56-736                    7
183-1025/1035      F-104A-5-LO      USAF               56-737/56-747                   11
183-1036/1051      F-104A-10-LO     USAF               56-748/56-763                   16
183-1052/1076      F-104A-15-LO     USAF               56-764/56-788                   25
183-1077/1113      F-104A-20-LO     USAF               56-789/56-825                   37
183-1114/1165      F-104A-25-LO     USAF               56-826/56-877                   52
183-1166/1170      F-104A-30-LO     USAF               56-878/56-882                    5
283-5000/5005      F-104B-1-LO      USAF               56-3719/56-3724                  6
283-5006/5014      F-104B-5-LO      USAF               57-1294/57-1302                  9
283-5015/5023      F-104B-10-LO     USAF               57-1303/57-1311                  9
283-5024/5025      F-104B-15-LO     USAF               57-1312/57-1313                  2
383-1171/1226      F-104C-5-LO      USAF               56-883/56-938                   56
383-1227/1247      F-104C-10-LO     USAF               57-910/57-930                   21
483-5026/5032      F-104D-5-LO      USAF               57-1314/57-1320                  7
483-5033/5040      F-104D-10-LO     USAF               57-1321/57-1328                  8
483-5041/5046      F-104D-15-LO     USAF               57-1329/57-1334                  6
483-5047/5076      F-104F-LO        Luftwaffe          59-4994/59-5023                 30
583A-5301/5338     CF-104D          RCAF               12631/12668                     38
583B-5401/5420     F-104DJ          Koku Jieitai       16-5001/16-5020                 20
583C-5501/5506     TF-104G-LO       USAF (MAP)         61-3025/61-3030                  6
583C-5507/5524     TF-104G-LO       USAF (MAP)         62-12262/62-12279               18
583C-5525/5528     TF-104G-LO       USAF (MAP)         63-12681/63-12684                4
583C-5529          TF-104G-LO       USAF (MAP)         65-9415                          1
583D-5701          TF-104G-LO       Luftwaffe (MSP)    61-3031                          1
```

583D-5702	TF-104G-LO	Co. owned	N104L	1
583D-5703/5755	TF-104G-LO	Luftwaffe (MSP)	61-3032/61-3084	53
583D-5756/5766	TF-104G-LO	Luftwaffe (MSP)	63-8452/63-8462	11
583D-5767	TF-104G-LO	AMI (MAP)	63-12685	1
583D-5768	TF-104G-LO	Luftwaffe (MAP)	63-8463	1
583D-5769	TF-104G-LO	AMI (MAP)	63-12686	1
583D-5770/5771	TF-104G-LO	Luftwaffe (MAP)	63-8464/63-8465	2
583D-5772	TF-104G-LO	AMI (MAP)	63-12687	1
583D-5773	TF-104G-LO	Luftwaffe (MAP)	63-8466	1
583D-5774	TF-104G-LO	AMI (MAP)	63-12688	1
583D-5775	TF-104G-LO	Luftwaffe (MSP)	63-8467	1
583D-5776	TF-104G-LO	AMI (MAP)	63-12689	1
583D-5777	TF-104G-LO	Luftwaffe (MSP)	63-8468	1
583D-5778	TF-104G-LO	AMI (MAP)	63-12690	1
583D-5779	TF-104G-LO	Luftwaffe (MSP)	63-8469	1
583D-5780/5785	TF-104G-LO	AMI (MAP)	63-12691/63-12696	6
583D-5786/5788	TF-104G-LO	FAeB (MSP)	64-15104/64-15106	3
583E-5801/5813	TF-104G-LO	KLu	D-5801/D-5813	13
583E-5814/5817	TF-104G-LO	KLu (co-prod)	D-5814/D-5817	4
583F-5901/5932	TF-104G-LO	Luftwaffe	KF201/KF232	32
583F-5933/5942	TF-104G-LO	Luftwaffe	66-13622/66-13631	10
583F-5943/5965	TF-104G-LO	Luftwaffe (co-prod)	KE201/KE223	23
583G-5101/5109	TF-104G-LO	FAeB (co-prod)	FC-04/FC-12	9
583H-5201/5212	TF-104G-LO	AMI (co-prod)		12
683-2001/2009	F-104G-LO	Luftwaffe	KF101/KF109	9
683-2010	F-104G-LO	Luftwaffe	63-13259	1
683-2011/2016	F-104G-LO	Luftwaffe	63-13230/63-13235	6
683-2017	F-104G-LO	Luftwaffe	KF117	1
683-2018	F-104G-LO	Luftwaffe	63-13236	1
683-2019	F-104G-LO	Luftwaffe	KF199	1
683-2020/2028	F-104G-LO	Luftwaffe	63-13237/63-13245	9
683-2029	F-104G-LO	Luftwaffe	KF129	1
683-2030/2042	F-104G-LO	Luftwaffe	63-13246/63-13258	13
683-2043/2050	F-104G-LO	Luftwaffe	KF143/KF150	8
683-2051	F-104G-LO			0
683-2052/2075	F-104G-LO	Luftwaffe	KF151/KF174	24
683-2076	F-104G-LO	Luftwaffe	63-13260	1
683-2077/2085	F-104G-LO	Luftwaffe	KF176/KF184	9
683-2086	F-104G-LO	Luftwaffe	63-13262	1
683-2087/2090	F-104G-LO	Luftwaffe	KF186/KF189	4
683-2091/2093	F-104G-LO	Luftwaffe	63-13263/63-13265	3
683-2094	F-104G-LO	Luftwaffe	KF193	1
683-2095/2097	F-104G-LO	Luftwaffe	63-13266/63-13268	3
683-	F-104G-LO	Pattern a/c for Italy	MM6501	1
683-	F-104G-LO	Pattern a/c for Belgium	63-13274	1
683B-3001/3003	F-104J	Koku Jieitai	26-8501/26-8503	3
683C-4001/4023	F-104G-LO	Greece/Turkey (MAP)	61-2601/61-2623	23
683C-4024	RF-104G-LO	Greece (MAP)	61-2624	1
683C-4025/4033	RF-104G-LO	Norway (MAP)	61-2625/61-2633	9
683C-4034/4044	RF-104G-LO	(MAP)	62-12232/62-12242	11
683C-4045	F-104N-LO	NASA	811	1
683C-4046/4052	RF-104G-LO	(MAP)	62-12243/62-12249	7
683C-4053	F-104N-LO	NASA	812	1
683C-4054/4057	RF-104G-LO	(MAP)	62-12250/62-12253	4
683C-4058	F-104N-LO	NASA	813	1
683C-4059/4066	RF-104G-LO	(MAP)	62-12254/62-12261	8
683C-4067/4084	F-104G-LO	(MAP)	62-12214/62-12231	18

LICENCE-BUILT STARFIGHTERS

Canadair

1001/1200	CF-104	RCAF	12701/12900	200
6001/6048	F-104G	(MAP)	62-12302/62-12349	48
6049/6086	F-104G	(MAP)	62-12697/62-12734	38
6087/6096	F-104G	(MAP)	63-13638/63-13647	10
6097/6140	F-104G	(MAP)	64-17752/64-17795	44

Fiat

6502/6599	F-104G	AMI	MM6502/MM6599	98
6600	F-104G	Luftwaffe	KC101	1
6601	F-104G	AMI	MM6601	1
6602	F-104G	Luftwaffe	KC102	1
6603	F-104G	AMI	MM6603	1
6604/6607	F-104G	Luftwaffe	KC103/KC106	4
6608/6611	F-104G	AMI	MM6608/MM6611	4

6612/6620	F-104G	Luftwaffe	KC107/KC115	9
6621/6630	RF-104G	Luftwaffe	KC116/KC125	10
6631/6638	F-104G	AMI	MM6631/MM6638	8
6639/6642	RF-104G	Luftwaffe	KC126/KC129	4
6643/6651	F-104G	AMI	MM6643/MM6651	9
6652/6657	F-104G	KLu	D-6652/3-6657	6
6658/6660	F-104G	AMI	MM6658/MM6660	3
6658	F-104S	AMI	MM6658	(1)
6660	F-104S	AMI	MM6660	(1)
6661/6665	RF-104G	Luftwaffe	KC130/KC134	5
6666/6671	F-104G	Klu	D-6666/D-6671	6
6672/6679	RF-104G	Luftwaffe	KC135/KC142	8
6680/6685	F-104G	Klu	D-6680/D-6685	6
6686/6693	RF-104G	Luftwaffe	KC143/KC150	8
6694/6700	F-104G	KLu	D-6694/D-6700	7
6701/6850	F-104S	AMI	MM6701/MM6850	150
6851/6868	F-104S	Turkish AF	- - -	18
6869/6883	F-104S	AMI	MM6869/MM6883	15
6884/6889	F-104S	Turkish AF	- - -	6
6890	F-104S	AMI	MM6890	1
6891/6896	F-104S	Turkish AF	- - -	6
	F-104S	AMI		39
	F-104S	Turkish AF	- - -	10

Fokker

8001	F-104G	Luftwaffe	KG101	1
8002/8003	F-104G	Luftwaffe	63-13269/63-13270	2
8004/8006	F-104G	Luftwaffe	KG104/KG106	3
8007/8009	F-104G	Luftwaffe	63-13271/63-13273	3
8010/8012	F-104G	Luftwaffe	KG110/KG112	3
8013	F-104G	KLu	D-8013	1
8014/8020	F-104G	Luftwaffe	KG114/KG120	7
8021	F-104G	Luftwaffe	64-12746	1
8022	F-104G	KLu	D-8022	1
8023/8044	F-104G	Luftwaffe	KG123/KG144	22
8045	F-104G	KLu	D-8045	1
8046	F-104G	Luftwaffe	KG146	1
8047/8053	F-104G	KLu	D-8047/D-8053	7
8054/8055	F-104G	Luftwaffe	KG154/KG155	2
8056	F-104G	Luftwaffe	63-13229	1
8057/8063	F-104G	KLu	D-8057/D-8063	7
8064	F-104G	Luftwaffe	64-12749	1
8065/8066	F-104G	KLu	D-8065/D-8066	2
8067/8069	F-104G	Luftwaffe	64-12750/64-12752	3
8070	F-104G	Luftwaffe	KG170	1
8071	F-104G	Luftwaffe	64-12753	1
8072/8076	F-104G	Luftwaffe	KG172/KG176	5
8077	F-104G	Luftwaffe	64-12754	1
8078/8081	F-104G	Luftwaffe	KG178/KG181	4
8082/8084	F-104G	KLu	D-8082/D-8084	3
8085/8087	RF-104G	Luftwaffe	KG185/KG187	3
8088	F-104G	Luftwaffe	KG188	1
8089/8091	F-104G	KLu	D-8089/D-8091	3
8092	F-104G	Luftwaffe	KG192	1
8093	F-104G	KLu	D-8093	1
8094/8095	RF-104G	Luftwaffe	KG194/KG195	2
8096/8097	F-104G	Luftwaffe	KG196/KG197	2
8098/8099	F-104G	KLu	D-8098/D-8099	2
8100	F-104G	Luftwaffe	KG200	1
8101	RF-104G	KLu	D-8101	1
8102	RF-104G	Luftwaffe	KG202	1
8103	RF-104G	KLu	D-8103	1
8104/8105	F-104G	KLu	D-8104/D-8105	2
8106	RF-104G	Luftwaffe	KG206	1
8107	RF-104G	KLu	D-8107	1
8108	RF-104G	Luftwaffe	KG208	1
8109/8110	F-104G	KLu	D-8109/D-8110	2
8111	RF-104G	Luftwaffe	KG211	1
8112	RF-104G	KLu	D-8112	1
8113	RF-104G	Luftwaffe	KG213	1
8114/8115	F-104G	KLu	D-8114/D-8115	2
8116	RF-104G	Luftwaffe	KG216	1
8117	RF-104G	KLu	D-8117	1
8118	RF-104G	Luftwaffe	KG218	1

8119	RF-104G	KLu	D-8119	1
8120/8121	F-104G	KLu	D-8120/D-8121	2
8122	RF-104G	Luftwaffe	KG222	1
8123	RF-104G	KLu	D-8123	1
8124	RF-104G	Luftwaffe	KG224	1
8125	RF-104G	KLu	D-8125	1
8126	RF-104G	Luftwaffe	KG226	1
8127	RF-104G	KLu	D-8127	1
8128	RF-104G	Luftwaffe	KG228	1
8129	RF-104G	KLu	D-8129	1
8130	RF-104G	Luftwaffe	KG230	1
8131	RF-104G	KLu	D-8131	1
8132	RF-104G	Luftwaffe	KG232	1
8133	RF-104G	KLu	D-8133	1
8134	RF-104G	Luftwaffe	KG234	1
8135	RF-104G	KLu	D-8135	1
8136/8137	RF-104G	Luftwaffe	KG236/KG237	2
8138	RF-104G	KLu	D-8138	1
8139/8140	RF-104G	Luftwaffe	KG239/KG240	2
8141	RF-104G	KLu	D-8141	1
8142	RF-104G	Luftwaffe	KG242	1
8143	RF-104G	KLu	D-8143	1
8144	RF-104G	Luftwaffe	KG244	1
8145	RF-104G	KLu	D-8145	1
8146	RF-104G	Luftwaffe	KG246	1
8147	RF-104G	KLu	D-8147	1
8148/8161	RF-104G	Luftwaffe	KG248/KG261	14
8162	F-104G	Luftwaffe	KG262	1
8163/8165	RF-104G	Luftwaffe	KG263/KG265	3
8166	F-104G	Luftwaffe	KG266	1
8167	RF-104G	Luftwaffe	KG267	1
8168/8170	F-104G	Luftwaffe	KG268/KG270	3
8171	RF-104G	Luftwaffe	KG271	1
8172	F-104G	Luftwaffe	KG272	1
8173/8174	RF-104G	Luftwaffe	KG273/KG274	2
8175	F-104G	Luftwaffe	KG275	1
8176	RF-104G	Luftwaffe	KG276	1
8177	F-104G	Luftwaffe	67-14893	1
8178	F-104G	Luftwaffe	KG278	1
8179/8181	RF-104G	Luftwaffe	KG279/KG281	3
8182	F-104G	Luftwaffe	KG282	1
8183	F-104G	Luftwaffe	63-13690	1
8184/8187	F-104G	Luftwaffe	KG284/KG287	4
8188	F-104G	Luftwaffe	63-13691	1
8189/8190	F-104G	Luftwaffe	KG289/KG290	2
8191/8192	RF-104G	Luftwaffe	67-14890/67-14891	2
8193/8195	F-104G	Luftwaffe	KG293/KG295	3
8196	F-104G	Luftwaffe	63-13261	1
8197/8203	F-104G	Luftwaffe	KG297/KG303	7
8204	RF-104G	Luftwaffe	67-14890	1
8205/8206	RF-104G	Luftwaffe	KG305/KG306	2
8207	F-104G	Luftwaffe	KG307	1
8208/8211	RF-104G	Luftwaffe	KG308/KG311	4
8212	F-104G	Luftwaffe	KG312	1
8213/8215	RF-104G	Luftwaffe	KG313/KG315	3
8216	F-104G	Luftwaffe	KG316	1
8217/8219	RF-104G	Luftwaffe	KG317/KG319	3
8220	F-104G	Luftwaffe	KG320	1
8221/8223	RF-104G	Luftwaffe	KG321/KG323	3
8224	F-104G	Luftwaffe	KG324	1
8225/8227	RF-104G	Luftwaffe	KG325/KG327	3
8228	F-104G	Luftwaffe	KG328	1
8229/8230	RF-104G	Luftwaffe	KG329/KG330	2
8231	F-104G	Luftwaffe	KG331	1
8232/8233	RF-104G	Luftwaffe	KG332/KG333	2
8234	F-104G	Luftwaffe	KG334	1
8235/8236	RF-104G	Luftwaffe	KG335/KG336	2
8237	F-104G	Luftwaffe	KG337	1
8238/8242	RF-104G	Luftwaffe	KG338/KG342	5
8243/8245	F-104G	KLu	D-8243/D-8245	3
8246/8249	RF-104G	Luftwaffe	KG346/KG349	4
8250	F-104G	Luftwaffe	KG350	1
8251/8255	RF-104G	Luftwaffe	KG351/KG355	5

8256/8260	F-104G	KLu	D-8256/D-8260	5
8261/8262	RF-104G	Luftwaffe	KG361/KG362	2
8263	F-104G	Luftwaffe	KG363	1
8264/8265	RF-104G	Luftwaffe	KG364/KG365	2
8266/8268	F-104G	KLu	D-8266/D-8268	3
8269/8271	RF-104G	Luftwaffe	KG369/KG371	3
8272/8273	F-104G	KLu	D-8272/D-8273	2
8274	RF-104G	Luftwaffe	KG374	1
8275	F-104G	Luftwaffe	KG375	1
8276	RF-104G	Luftwaffe	KG376	1
8277/8278	F-104G	Luftwaffe	KG377/KG378	2
8279/8283	F-104G	KLu	D-8279/D-8283	5
8284/8285	F-104G	Luftwaffe	KG384/KG385	2
8286	F-104G	KLu	D-8286	1
8287	F-104G	Luftwaffe	KG387	1
8288	F-104G	KLu	D-8288	1
8289/8292	F-104G	Luftwaffe	KG389/KG392	4
8293/8294	F-104G	KLu	D-8293/D-8294	2
8295/8296	F-104G	Luftwaffe	KG395/KG396	2
8297	F-104G	KLu	D-8297	1
8298/8299	F-104G	Luftwaffe	KG398/KG399	2
8300	F-104G	KLu	D-8300	1
8301/8303	F-104G	Luftwaffe	KG401/KG403	3
8304	F-104G	KLu	D-8304	1
8305/8307	F-104G	Luftwaffe	KG405/KG407	3
8308	F-104G	KLu	D-8308	1
8309/8310	F-104G	Luftwaffe	KG409/KG410	2
8311/8312	F-104G	KLu	D-8311/D-8312	2
8313/8317	F-104G	Luftwaffe	KG413/KG417	5
8318/8319	F-104G	KLu	D-8318/D-8319	2
8320/8323	F-104G	Luftwaffe	KG420/KG423	4
8324/8326	F-104G	KLu	D-8324/D-8326	3
8327/8330	F-104G	Luftwaffe	KG427/KG430	4
8331/8332	F-104G	KLu	D-8331/D-8332	2
8333/8335	F-104G	Luftwaffe	KG433/KG435	3
8336/8338	F-104G	KLu	D-8336/D-8338	3
8339/8340	F-104G	Luftwaffe	KG439/KG440	2
8341/8343	F-104G	KLu	D-8341/D-8343	3
8344/8350	F-104G	Luftwaffe	KG444/KG450	7
MBB				
7301/7314	F-104G	Luftwaffe	2641/2654	14
7401/7436	F-104G	Luftwaffe	2655/2690	36
Messerschmitt				
7001	F-104G	Luftwaffe	64-12745	1
7002/7006	F-104G	Luftwaffe	KE302/KE306	5
7007	F-104G	Luftwaffe	67-14888	1
7008/7014	F-104G	Luftwaffe	KE308/KE314	7
7015	F-104G	Luftwaffe	67-14889	1
7016/7022	F-104G	Luftwaffe	KE316/KE322	7
7023	F-104G	Luftwaffe	67-14886	1
7024/7038	F-104G	Luftwaffe	KE324/KE338	15
7039	F-104G	Luftwaffe	64-12748	1
7040/7097	F-104G	Luftwaffe	KE340/KE397	58
7098	F-104G	Luftwaffe	64-12747	1
7099/7119	F-104G	Luftwaffe	KE399/KE419	21
7120	F-104G	Luftwaffe	66-13524	1
7121/7131	F-104G	Luftwaffe	KE421/KE431	11
7132/7133	F-104G	Luftwaffe	66-13525 & 67-14885	2
7134/7176	F-104G	Luftwaffe	KE434/KE476	43
7177	F-104G	Luftwaffe	63-13526	1
7178/7210	F-104G	Luftwaffe	KE478/KE510	33
Mitsubishi				
683B-3001/3003	F-104J	Koku Jieitai	26-8501/26-8503	(3)
683B-3004/3007	F-104J	Koku Jieitai	26-8504/26-8507	4
683B-3008/3063	F-104J	Koku Jieitai	36-8508/36-8563	56
683B-3064/3158	F-104J	Koku Jieitai	46-8564/46-8658	95
683B-3159/3180	F-104J	Koku Jieitai	56-8659/56-8680	22
683B-3181/3210	F-104J	Koku Jieitai	76-8681/76-8710	30
SABCA				
9002/9005	F-104G	Luftwaffe	63-13275/63-13278	4
9006/9015	F-104G	Luftwaffe	KH106/KH115	10
9016/9024	F-104G	FAeB	FX-1/FX-9	9
9025/9026	F-104G	Luftwaffe	KH116/KH117	2

9027/9029	F-104G	FAeB	FX-10/FX-12	3
9030/9031	F-104G	Luftwaffe	KH118/KH119	2
9032/9034	F-104G	FAeB	FX-13/FX-15	3
9035/9037	F-104G	Luftwaffe	KH120/KH122	3
9038/9040	F-104G	FAeB	FX-16/FX-18	3
9041/9043	F-104G	Luftwaffe	KH123/KH125	3
9044/9046	F-104G	FAeB	FX-19/FX-21	3
9047/9049	F-104G	Luftwaffe	KH126/KH128	3
9050/9052	F-104G	FAeB	FX-22/FX-24	3
9053/9055	F-104G	Luftwaffe	KH129/KH131	3
9056/9058	F-104G	FAeB	FX-25/FX-27	3
9059/9061	F-104G	Luftwaffe	KH132/KH134	3
9062/9064	F-104G	FAeB	FX-28/FX-30	3
9065/9067	F-104G	Luftwaffe	KH135/KH137	3
9068/9073	F-104G	FAeB	FX-31/FX-36	6
9074/9076	F-104G	Luftwaffe	KH138/KH140	3
9077/9079	F-104G	FAeB	FX-37/FX-39	3
9080/9081	F-104G	Luftwaffe	KH141/KH142	2
9082	F-104G	FAeb	FX-27	1
9083/9109	F-104G	FAeB	FX-40/FX-66	27
9110/9112	F-104G	Luftwaffe	KH143/KH145	3
9113/9115	F-104G	FAeB	FX-67/FX-69	3
9116/9118	F-104G	Luftwaffe	KH146/KH148	3
9119/9121	F-104G	FAeB	FX-70/FX-72	3
9122/9124	F-104G	Luftwaffe	KH149/KH151	3
9125/9127	F-104G	FAeB	FX-73/FX-75	3
9128/9130	F-104G	Luftwaffe	KH152/KH154	3
9131/9133	F-104G	FAeB	FX-76/FX-78	3
9134/9136	F-104G	Luftwaffe	KH155/KH157	3
9137/9142	F-104G	FAeB	FX-79/FX-84	6
9143/9145	F-104G	Luftwaffe	KH158/KH160	3
9146/9148	F-104G	FAeB	FX-85/FX-87	3
9149/9151	F-104G	Luftwaffe	KH161/KH163	3
9152/9154	F-104G	FAeB	FX-88/FX-90	3
9155/9157	F-104G	Luftwaffe	KH164/KH166	3
9158/9160	F-104G	FAeB	FX-91/FX-93	3
9161/9163	F-104G	Luftwaffe	KH167/KH169	3
9164/9166	F-104G	FAeB	FX-94/FX-96	3
9167/9169	F-104G	Luftwaffe	KH170/KH172	3
9170/9172	F-104G	FAeB	FX-97/FX-99	3
9173/9175	F-104G	Luftwaffe	KH173/KH175	3
9176	F-104G	FAeB	FX-100	1
9177/9189	F-104G	Luftwaffe	KH176/KH188	13

LOCKHEED XFV-1 (Number built: 2, of which only one was completed)

081-1001/1002	XFV-1	USN	138657/138658	2

LOCKHEED C-130 HERCULES (Number built: 1,604 up to end of 1980; still in production)

082-1001/1002	YC-130-LO	USAF	53-3396/53-3397	2
182-3001/3007	C-130A-LM	USAF	53-3129/53-3135	7
182-3008/3027	C-130A-LM	USAF	54-1621/54-1640	20
182-3028/3072	C-130A-LM	USAF	55-001/55-045	45
182-3073/3075	C-130A-20-LM	USAF	55-046/55-048	3
182-3076/3096	C-130A-6-LM	USAF	56-468/56-488	21
182-3097/3117	C-130A-7-LM	USAF	56-489/56-509	21
182-3118/3138	C-130A-8-LM	USAF	56-510/56-530	21
182-3139/3159	C-130A-9-LM	USAF	56-531/56-551	21
182-3160/3190	C-130A-45-LM	USAF	57-453/57-483	31
182-3191/3202	C-130D- -LM	USAF	57-484/57-495	12
182-3203/3204	C-130A-45-LM	USAF	57-496/57-497	2
182-3205/3216	C-130A-50-LM	RAAF	A97-205/A97-216	12
182-3217/3231	RC-130A-LM	USAF	57-510/57-524	15
282-3501/3505	C-130B-1-LM	USAF	57-525/57-529	5
282-3506/3528	C-130B- -LM	USAF	58-711/58-733	23
282-3529	SC-130B- -LM	USCG	1339	1
282-3530/3532	C-130B- -LM	USAF	58-734/58-736	3
282-3533	SC-130B- -LM	USCG	1340	1
282-3534/3541	C-130B- -LM	USAF	58-737/58-744	8
282-3542	SC-130B- -LM	USCG	1341	1
282-3543/3545	C-130B- -LM	USAF	58-745/58-747	3
282-3546	C-130B- -LM	TNIAU	T-1301	1
282-3547	C-130B- -LM	USAF	58-749	1
282-3548	SC-130B- -LM	USCG	1342	1

282-3549/3553	C-130B- -LM	USAF	58-750/58-754	5
282-3554/3555	GV-1	USMC	147572/147573	2
282-3556/3559	C-130B- -LM	USAF	58-755/58-758	4
282-3560/3561	C-130B- -LM	USAF	59-1524/59-1525	2
282-3562	UV-1L	USN	14ɔ318	1
282-3563	C-130B- -LM	USAF	59-1526	1
282-3564/3565	UV-1L	USN	148319/148320	2
282-3566	GV-1	USMC	148246	1
282-3567	UV-1L	USN	148321	1
282-3568	C-130B- -LM	USAF	59-1527	1
282-3569	C-130B- -LM	USAF	59-1529	1
282-3570	C-130B- -LM	USAF	59-1534	1
282-3571	C-130B- -LM	USAF	59-1528	1
282-3572	C-130B- -LM	RCAF	10301	1
282-3573/3574	GV-1	USMC	148247/148248	2
282-3575	C-130B- -LM	RCAF	10302	1
282-3576	C-130B- -LM	USAF	59-1530	1
282-3577	GV-1	USMC	148249	1
282-3578	C-130B- -LM	TNIAU	T-1302	1
282-3579	C-130B- -LM	USAF	59-1531	1
282-3580	C-130B- -LM	TNIAU	T-1303	1
282-3581	C-130B- -LM	USAF	59-1532	1
282-3582/3583	C-130B- -LM	TNIAU	T-1304/T-1305	2
282-3584	C-130B- -LM	USAF	59-5957	1
282-3585	C-130B- -LM	USAF	59-1535	1
282-3586	C-130B- -LM	USAF	59-1533	1
282-3587	C-130B- -LM	RCAF	10303	1
282-3588/3589	C-130B- -LM	USAF	59-1536/59-1537	2
282-3590	C-130B- -LM	RCAF	10304	1
282-3591	C-130B- -LM	USAF	60-293	1
282-3592	GV-1	USMC	148890	1
282-3593	C-130B- -LM	USAF	60-294	1
282-3594/3595	SC-130B- -LM	USCG	1344/1345	2
282-3596/3597	C-130B- -LM	USAF	60-295/60-296	2
282-3598/3599	C-130B- -LM	TNIAU	T-1306/T-1307	2
282-3600	C-130B- -LM	USAF	60-297	1
282-3601	C-130B- -LM	TNIAU	T-1308	1
282-3602/3604	C-130B- -LM	USAF	60-298/60-300	3
282-3605/3608	GV-1	USMC	148891/148894	4
382-3609	C-130E- -LM	USAF	61-2358	1
282-3610	C-130B- -LM	Jordanian AF	141	1
282-3611	C-130B- -LM	USAF	60-302	1
282-3612	C-130B- -LM	Jordanian AF	140	1
282-3613	C-130B- -LM	USAF	60-303	1
282-3614	C-130B- -LM	USAF	60-305	1
282-3615/3616	C-130B- -LM	TNIAU	T-1309/T-1310	2
282-3617/3618	C-130B- -LM	USAF	60-306/60-307	2
282-3619	GV-1	USMC	148895	1
282-3620/3622	C-130B- -LM	USAF	60-308/60-310	3
282-3623	GV-1	USMC	148896	1
282-3624/3626	C-130B- -LM	USAF	61-948/61-950	3
282-3627	GV-1	USMC	148897	1
282-3628/3630	C-130B- -LM	USAF	61-951/61-953	3
282-3631/3632	GV-1	USMC	148898/148899	2
282-3633/3635	C-130B- -LM	USAF	61-954/61-956	3
282-3636	GV-1U	USN	149787	1
282-3637	C-130B- -LM	USAF	61-957	1
282-3638	SC-130B- -LM	USCG	1346	1
282-3639	C-130B- -LM	USAF	61-958	1
282-3640	GV-1	USMC	149788	1
282-3641	SC-130B- -LM	USCG	1347	1
282-3642/3643	C-130B- -LM	USAF	61-959/61-960	2
282-3644	GV-1	USMC	149789	1
282-3645	GV-1U	USN	149790	1
282-3646/3649	C-130B- -LM	USAF	61-961/61-964	4
282-3650	SC-130B - LM	USCG	1348	1
382-3651	C-130E- -LM	USAF	61-2359	1
282-3652/3656	C-130B- -LM	USAF	61-965/61-969	5
282-3657/3658	GV-1	USMC	149791/149792	2
382-3659	C-130E- -LM	USAF	61-2360	1
282-3660/3661	GV-1U	USN	149793/149794	2
382-3662/3663	C-130E- -LM	USAF	61-2361/61-2362	2
282-3664/3665	GV-1	USMC	149795/149796	2

509

282-3666	GV-1U	USN	149797	1
282-3667/3669	C-130B- -LM	USAF	61-970/61-972	3
282-3670/3679	C-130B- -LM	USAF	61-2634/61-2643	10
282-3680	GV-1	USMC	149798	1
382-3681	C-130E- -LM	USAF	61-2363	1
282-3682/3683	C-130B- -LM	USAF	61-2644/61-2645	2
282-3684/3685	GV-1	USMC	149799/149800	2
282-3686	GV-1U	USN	149801	1
382-3687/3688	C-130E- -LM	USAF	61-2364/61-2365	2
282-3689	C-130B- -LM	Pakistan AF	61-2646	1
282-3690	C-130B- -LM	USAF	61-2647	1
282-3691	C-130B- -LM	Pakistan AF	61-2648	1
282-3692	C-130B- -LM	USAF	61-2649	1
282-3693/3695	GV-1	USMC	149802/149804	3
282-3696	GV-1U	USN	149805	1
282-3697	C-130B- -LM	USAF	62-3487	1
282-3698/3701	C-130B- -LM	IIAF	5-101/5-104	4
282-3702	WC-130B- -LM	USAF	62-3492	1
282-3703/3705	GV-1	USMC	149806/149808	3
382-3706	C-130E- -LM	USAF	61-2366	1
282-3707/3708	WC-130B- -LM	USAF	62-3493/62-3494	2
282-3709/3711	GV-1	USMC	149809/149811	3
382-3712/3717	C-130E- -LM	USAF	61-2367/61-2372	6
282-3718/3719	GV-1	USMC	149812/149813	2
382-3720	C-130E- -LM	USAF	61-2373	1
282-3721/3722	WC-130B- -LM	USAF	62-3495/62-3496	2
282-3723	GV-1	USMC	149814	1
282-3724	C-130B- -LM	SAAF	401	1
282-3725/3726	GV-1	USMC	149815/194816	2
282-3727/3728	GV-1	USMC	150684/150685	2
382-3729/3732	C-130E- -LM	USAF	62-1784/62-1787	4
282-3733/3734	GV-1	USMC	150686/150687	2
382-3735/3739	C-130E- -LM	USAF	62-1788/62-1792	5
282-3740/3742	GV-1	USMC	150688/150690	3
382-3743/3744	C-130E- -LM	USAF	62-1793/62-1794	2
282-3745	SC-130B- -LM	USCG	1349	1
382-3746/3748	C-130E- -LM	USAF	62-1795/62-1797	3
282-3749/3750	C-130B- -LM	SAAF	402/403	2
282-3751	C-130B- -LM	Pakistan AF	62-4140	1
382-3752/3762	C-130E- -LM	USAF	62-1798/62-1808	11
282-3763	SC-130B- -LM	USCG	1350	1
282-3764/3765	C-130B- -LM	SAAF	404/405	2
282-3766	C-130B- -LM	Pakistan AF	62-4141	1
282-3767	C-130B- -LM	SAAF	406	1
282-3768	C-130B- -LM	Pakistan AF	62-4142	1
282-3769	C-130B- -LM	SAAF	407	1
382-3770/3772	C-130E- -LM	USAF	62-1809/62-1811	3
282-3773	SC-130B- -LM	USCG	1351	1
382-3774/3780	C-130E- -LM	USAF	62-1812/62-1818	7
282-3781		Pakistan AF	62-4143	1
382-3782/3812	C-130E- -LM	USAF	62-1819/62-1849	31
382-3813	C-130E- -LM	USAF	63-7764	1
382-3014/3830	C-130F- -LM	USAF	62-1850/62-1866	17
382-3831/3848	C-130E- -LM	USAF	63-7765/63-7782	18
382-3849	C-130G- -LM	USN	151888	1
382-3850/3857	C-130E- -LM	USAF	63-7783/63-7790	8
382-3858	C-130G- -LM	USN	151889	1
382-3859/3860	C-130E- -LM	USAF	63-7791/63-7792	2
382-3861/3870	C-130E- -LM	USAF	63-7795/63-7804	10
382-3871	C-130G- -LM	USN	151890	1
382-3872/3873	C-130E- -LM	USAF	63-7793/63-7794	2
382-3874/3877	C-130E- -LM	USAF	63-7805/63-7808	4
382-3878	C-130G- -LM	USN	151891	1
382-3879/3883	C-130E- -LM	USAF	63-7809/63-7813	5
382-3884/3887	C-130E- -LM	USAF	63-7818/63-7821	4
382-3888/3889	C-130E- -LM	USAF	63-7814/63-7815	2
382-3890/3893	C-130E- -LM	USAF	63-7822/63-7825	4
382-3894/3895	C-130E- -LM	USAF	63-7816/63-7817	2
382-3896/3902	C-130E- -LM	USAF	63-7828/63-7834	7
382-3903/3904	C-130E- -LM	USAF	63-7826/63-7827	2
382-3905/3907	C-130E- -LM	USAF	63-7835/63-7837	3
382-3908/3912	C-130E- -LM	USAF	63-7838/63-7842	5
382-3913/3926	C-130E- -LM	USAF	63-7843/63-7856	14

510

382-3927/3931	C-130E- -LM	USAF	63-7857/63-7861	5
382-3932	C-130E- -LM	USAF	63-7862	1
382-3933/3938	C-130E- -LM	USAF	63-7863/63-7868	6
382-3939/3945	C-130E- -LM	USAF	63-7869/63-7875	7
382-3946	L-100	Co. owned	N1130E	1
382-3947/3952	C-130E- -LM	USAF	63-7876/63-7881	6
382-3953/3954	C-130E- -LM	USAF	63-7882/63-7883	2
382-3955/3958	C-130E- -LM	USAF	63-7884/63-7887	4
382-3959/3965	C-130E- -LM	USAF	63-7888/63-7894	7
382-3966/3970	C-130E- -LM	USAF	63-7895/63-7899	5
382-3971/3973	C-130E- -LM	USAF	63-9810/63-9812	3
382-3974/3976	C-130E- -LM	USAF	63-9813/63-9815	3
382-3977/3978	C-130E- -LM	USAF	63-9816/63-9818	2
382-3979/3984	C-130E- -LM	USAF	64-495/64-500	6
382-3985/3987	C-130E- -LM	USAF	64-501/64-503	3
382-3988/4010	C-130E- -LM	USAF	64-504/64-526	23
382-4011/4012	C-130E- -LM	Turkish AF	ETI-186/ETI-187	2
382-4013/4014	C-130E- -LM	USAF	64-527/64-528	2
382-4015/4016	C-130E- -LM	Turkish AF	ETI-188/ETI-189	2
382-4017/4019	C-130E- -LM	USAF	64-529/64-531	3
382-4020	C-130E- -LM	RCAF	10305	1
382-4021/4025	C-130E- -LM	USAF	64-532/64-536	5
382-4026	C-130E- -LM	RCAF	10306	1
382-4027/4035	C-130E- -LM	USAF	64-537/64-545	9
382-4036/4038	HC-130H- -LM	USAF	64-14852/64-14854	3
382-4039	C-130E- -LM	Swedish AF	84001	1
382-4040	C-130E- -LM	USAF	64-547	1
382-4041/4042	C-130E- -LM	RCAF	10307/10308	2
382-4043/4046	C-130E- -LM	USAF	64-548/64-551	4
382-4047/4049	C-130E- -LM	USAF	64-552/64-554	3
382-4050/4051	C-130E- -LM	RCAF	10309/10310	2
382-4052/4054	C-130H- -LM	RNZAF	NZ7001/NZ7003	3
382-4055	HC-130H- -LM	USAF	64-14855	1
382-4056/4059	C-130E- -LM	USAF	64-555/64-558	4
382-4060/4061	C-130E- -LM	RCAF	10311/10312	2
382-4062/4063	C-130E- -LM	USAF	64-559/64-560	2
382-4064	C-130E- -LM	USAF	64-17680	1
382-4065	C-130E- -LM	USAF	64-561	1
382-4066/4067	C-130E- -LM	RCAF	10313/10314	2
382-4068	C-130E- -LM	USAF	64-562	1
382-4069	C-130E- -LM	USAF	64-17681	1
382-4070	C-130E- -LM	RCAF	10315	1
382-4071	C-130E- -LM	USAF	64-563	1
382-4072/4073	HC-130H- -LM	USAF	64-14856/64-14857	2
382-4074	C-130E- -LM	USAF	64-564	1
382-4075	C-130E- -LM	RCAF	10316	1
382-4076	C-130E- -LM	R Saudi AF	451	1
382-4077	C-130E- -LM	USAF	64-565	1
382-4078	C-130E- -LM	R Saudi AF	452	1
382-4079	C-130E- -LM	USAF	64-569	1
382-4080	C-130E- -LM	USAF	64-566	1
382-4081/4082	HC-130H- -LM	USAF	64-14858/64-14859	2
382-4083	C-130E- -LM	USAF	64-567	1
382-4084	HC-130H- -LM	USAF	64-14860	1
382-4085	C-130E- -LM	USAF	64-570	1
382-4086	C-130E- -LM	USAF	64-568	1
382-4087	C-130E- -LM	USAF	64-571	1
382-4088/4089	HC-130H- -LM	USAF	64-14861/64-14862	2
382-4090	C-130E- -LM	USAF	64-572	1
382-4091/4093	C-130E- -LM	Brazilian AF	2450/2452	3
382-4094	HC-130H- -LM	USAF	64-14863	1
382-4095/4096	C-130E- -LM	RCAF	10319/10320	2
382-4097/4099	HC-103H- -LM	USAF	64-14864/64-14866	3
382-4100	C-130E- -LM	Turkish AF	ETI-949	1
382-4101	L-100	Continental AS	N9260R	1
382-4102/4104	HC-130H- -LM	USAF	65-962/65-964	3
382-4105	C-130E- -LM	USAF	64-18240	1
382-4106/4108	HC-130H- -LM	USAF	65-965/65-967	3
382-4109	L-100	Continental AS	N9261R	1
382-4110/4112	HC-130H- -LM	USAF	65-968/65-970	3
382-4113/4114	C-130E- -LM	Brazilian AF	2453/2454	2
382-4115	C-130E- -LM	IIAF	5-105	1
382-4116	HC-130H- -LM	USAF	65-971	1

382-4117/4119	C-130E- -LM	IIAF	5-106/5-108	3
382-4120/4121	HC-130H- -LM	USAF	65-972/65-973	2
382-4122	C-130E- -LM	RCAF	10317	1
382-4123	HC-130H- -LM	USAF	65-974	1
382-4124	C-130E- -LM	RCAF	10318	1
382-4125/4127	HC-130H- -LM	USAF	65-975/65-977	3
382-4128	C-130E- -LM	R Saudi AF	453	1
382-4129	L-100	Zambian AC	9J-RBW	1
382-4130/4133	HC-130H- -LM	USAF	65-978/65-981	4
382-4134	L-100	Co. owned	N9263R	1
382-4135	HC-130H- -LM	USAF	65-982	1
382-4136	C-130E- -LM	R Saudi AF	454	1
382-4137	L-100	Zambian AC	9J-RBX	1
382-4138/4142	HC-130H- -LM	USAF	65-983/65-987	5
382-4143	HC-130P-125-LM	USAF	65-988	1
382-4144/4145	L-100	PIA	AP-AUT/AP-AUU	2
382-4146	L-100	Int. Aerodyne	N9267R	1
382-4147	L-100	Delta	N9268R	1
382-4148/4149	C-130E- -LM	IIAF	5-109/5-110	2
382-4150/4151	HC-130H- -LM	USAF	65-989/65-990	2
382-4152	HC-130P-125-LM	USAF	65-991	1
382-4153/4154	C-130E- -LM	IIAF	5-111/5-112	2
382-4155/4157	HC-130P-125-LM	USAF	65-992/65-994	3
382-4158	EC-130E- -LM	USCG	1414	1
382-4159/4160	C-130E- -LM	RAAF	A97-159/A97-160	2
382-4161/4166	HC-130P-130-LM	USAF	66-211/66-216	6
382-4167/4168	C-130E- -LM	RAAF	A97-167/A97-168	2
382-4169	C-130K- -LM	RAF	XV176	1
382-4170	L-100	Delta	N9258R	1
382-4171/4172	C-130E- -LM	RAAF	A97-171/A97-172	2
382-4173/4175	HC-130P-130-LM	USAF	66-217/66-219	3
382-4176	L-100	Delta	N9259R	1
382-4177/4178	C-130E- -LM	RAAF	A97-177/A97-178	2
382-4179	HC-130P-130-LM	USAF	66-220	1
382-4180/4181	C-130E- -LM	RAAF	A97-180/A97-181	2
382-4182	C-130K- -LM	RAF	XV177	1
382-4183/4187	HC-130P-130-LM	USAF	66-221/66-225	5
382-4188	C-130K- -LM	RAF	XV178	1
382-4189/4190	C-130E- -LM	RAAF	A97-189/A97-190	2
382-4191/4194	C-130E- -LM	RCAF	10321/10324	4
382-4195/4196	C-130K- -LM	RAF	XV179/XV180	2
382-4197	L-100	Co. owned	N9269R	1
382-4198/4201	C-130K- -LM	RAF	XV181/XV184	4
382-4202	C-130E- -LM	Brazilian AF	2455	1
382-4203/4207	C-130K- -LM	RAF	XV185/XV189	5
382-4208	L-100	Alaska AL	N9227R	1
382-4209	L-100	Gov. of Zambia	9J-REZ	1
382-4210/4214	C-130K- -LM	RAF	XV190/XV194	5
382-4215	C-130E- -LM	R Saudi AF	455	1
382-4216/4220	C-130K- -LM	RAF	XV195/XV199	5
382-4221/4222	L-100	Airlift	N9248R, N9254R	2
382-4223/4224	C-130K- -LM	RAF	XV200/XV201	2
382-4225	L-100	Airlift	N759AL	1
382-4226/4228	C-130K- -LM	RAF	XV202/XV204	3
382-4229	L-100	Airlift	N760AL	1
382-4230/4233	C-130K- -LM	RAF	XV205/XV208	4
382-4234	L-100	Co. owned	N7999S	1
382-4235/4238	C-130K- -LM	RAF	XV209/XV212	4
382-4239	EC-130Q- -LM	USN	156170	1
382-4240/4247	C-130K- -LM	RAF	XV213/XV220	8
382-4248	L-100	Int. Aerodyne	N9262R	1
382-4249	EC-130Q- -LM	USN	156171	1
382-4250	L-100	NAL	N9266R	1
382-4251/4253	C-130K- -LM	RAF	XV221/XV223	3
382-4254	C-130K- -LM	RAF	XV290	1
382-4255	HC-130H- -LM	USCG	1452	1
382-4256/4259	C-130K- -LM	RAF	XV291/XV294	4
382-4260	HC-130H- -LM	USCG	1453	1
382-4261/4264	C-130K- -LM	RAF	XV295/XV298	4
382-4265	HC-130H- -LM	USCG	1454	1
382-4266/4268	C-130K- -LM	RAF	XV299/XV301	3
382-4269	EC-130Q- -LM	USN	156172	1
382-4270/4275	C-130K- -LM	RAF	XV302/XV307	6

382-4276	C-130E-	-LM	IIAF	5-113	1
382-4277/4281	EC-130Q-	-LM	USN	156173/156177	5
382-4282/4284	C-130E-	-LM	IIAF	5-114/5-116	3
382-4285/4286	C-130E-	-LM	RCAF	10325/10326	2
382-4287	C-130E-	-LM	Brazilian AF	2456	1
382-4288/4289	C-130E-	-LM	RCAF	10327/10328	2
382-4290/4293	C-130E-	-LM	Brazilian AF	2457/2460	4
382-4294/4298	C-130E-	-LM	IIAF	5-117/5-121	5
382-4299	L-100-20		Co. owned	N9232R	1
382-4300	L-100-20		First Nat. Chicago	N9265R	1
382-4301	L-100-20		Air America	N7951S	1
382-4302/4303	L-100-20		Flying W AW	N7952S, N9237R	2
382-4304	C-130E-	-LM	R Saudi AF	1606	1
382-4305	LC-130R-	-LM	USN	155917	1
382-4306/4307	C-130E-	-LM	R Saudi AF	1607/1608	2
382-4308/4310	C-130E-	-LM	Argentine AF	TC-61/TC-63	3
382-4311	C-130E-	-LM	R Saudi AF	1609	1
382-4312/4313	C-130H-	-LM	RNZAF	NZ7004/NZ7005	2
382-4314/4331	C-130E-	-LM	USAF	68-10934/68-10951	18
382-4332	C-130E-	-LM	Swedish AF	84002	1
382-4333	L-100-20		Co. owned	N7957S	1
382-4334/4339	C-130H-	-LM	Norwegian AF	BW-A/BW-F	6
382-4340/4349	C-130E-	-LM	USAF	69-6566/69-6575	10
382-4350	L-100-20		Co. owned	N7954S	1
382-4351/4354	C-130E-	-LM	USAF	69-6576/69-6579	4
382-4355	L-100-20		Co. owned	N7960S	1
382-4356/4357	C-130E-	-LM	USAF	69-6580/69-6581	2
382-4358	L-100-20		Co. owned	N7985S	1
382-4359/4360	C-130E-	-LM	USAF	69-6582/69-6583	2
382-4361/4362	L-100-20		Co. owned	N7982S, N7984S	2
382-4363	HC-130N-	-LM	USAF	69-5819	1
382-4364	L-100-20		Co. owned	N7986S	1
382-4365	C-130E-	-LM	IIAF	5-122	1
382-4366	C-130H-	-LM	Libyan AF	111	1
382-4367/4368	HC-130N-	-LM	USAF	69-5820/69-5821	2
382-4369	C-130H-	-LM	Libyan AF	112	1
382-4370/4372	HC-130N-	-LM	USAF	69-5822/69-5824	3
382-4373	C-130H-	-LM	Libyan AF	113	1
382-4374/4382	HC-130H-	-LM	USAF	69-5825/69-5833	9
382-4383/4384	L-100-30		Saturn	N10ST/N11ST	2
382-4385	L-100-20		Safair	ZS-GSK	1
382-4386/4387	C-130E-	-LM	IIAF	5-123/5-124	2
382-4388	L-100-30		Co. owned	N7988S	1
382-4389/4390	C-130E-	-LM	IIAF	5-125/5-126	2
382-4391	L-100-30		Saturn	N15ST	1
382-4392/4394	C-130E-	-LM	IIAF	5-127/5-129	3
382-4395	C-130H-	-LM	Libyan AF	114	1
382-4396/4397	C-130E-	-LM	R Saudi AF	1610/1611	2
382-4398/4399	C-130E-	-LM	IIAF	5-130/5-131	2
382-4400/4401	C-130E-	-LM	Libyan AF	115/116	2
382-4402	C-130E-	-LM	IIAF	5-132	1
382-4403	C-130H-	-LM	Libyan AF	117	1
382-4404	C-130E-	-LM	USAF	70-1259	1
382-4405	C-130H-	-LM	Libyan AF	118	1
382-4406/4409	C-130H-	-LM	Venez. AF	3556, 4951, 7772 & 9508	4
382-4410	C-130E-	-LM	USAF	70-1260	1
382-4411	C-130H-	-LM	Zaire	9T-TCA	1
382-4412	L-100-20		Kuwait	318	1
382-4413/4415	C-130E-	-LM	USAF	70-1261/70-1263	3
382-4416	C-130H-	-LM	Zaire	9T-TCB	1
382-4417/4421	C-130E-	-LM	USAF	70-1264/70-1268	5
382-4422	C-130H-	-LM	Zaire	9T-TCD	1
382-4423/4426	C-130E-	-LM	USAF	70-1269/70-1272	4
382-4427	C-130E-	-LM	Turkish AF	ETI-947	1
382-4428/4429	C-130E-	-LM	USAF	70-1273/70-1274	2
382-4430/4431	C-130H-	-LM	Israeli AF	4X-JUA/4X-JUB	2
382-4432/4433	C-130H-	-LM	IIAF	5-133/5-134	2
382-4434/4435	C-130E-	-LM	USAF	70-1275/70-1276	2
382-4436/4437	C-130H-	-LM	Argentine AF	TC-64/TC-65	2
382-4438/4440	C-130H-	-LM	IIAF	5-135/5-137	3
382-4441	C-130H-	-LM	Italian AF	MM61988	1
382-4442	C-130H-	-LM	IIAF	5-138	1
382-4443	C-130H-	-LM	Italian AF	**MM61989**	1

382-4444/4445	C-130H-	-LM	IIAF	5-139/5-140	2
382-4446/4447	C-130H-	-LM	Italian AF	MM61990/MM61991	2
382-4448	C-130H-	-LM	IIAF	5-141	1
382-4449	C-130H-	-LM	Italian AF	MM61992	1
382-4450	L-100-20		Peruvian AF	FAP396	1
382-4451/4452	C-130H-	-LM	Italian AF	MM61993/MM61994	2
382-4453	C-130H-	-LM	Chilean AF	995	1
382-4454	C-130H-	-LM	IIAF	5-142	1
382-4455	C-130H-	-LM	Belgian AF	CH-01	1
382-4456/4459	C-130H-	-IM	IIAF	5-143/5-146	4
382-4460/4461	C-130H-	-LM	Belgian AF	CH-02/CH-03	2
382-4462/4463	C-130H-	-LM	IIAF	5-147/5-148	2
382-4464	C-130H-	-LM	Argentine AF	TC-66	1
382-4465/4466	C-130H-	-LM	IIAF	5-149/5-150	2
382-4467	C-130H-	-LM	Belgian AF	CH-04	1
382-4468/4469	C-130H-	-LM	IIAF	5-151/5-152	2
382-4470	C-130H-	-LM	Belgian AF	CH-05	1
382-4471	C-130H-	-LM	IIAF	5-153	1
382-4472	L-100-30		Safair	ZS-RSB	1
382-4473	C-130H-	-LM	Belgian AF	CH-06	1
382-4474	C-130H-	-LM	IIAF	5-154	1
382-4475	L-100-30		Safair	ZS-RSC	1
382-4476	C-130H-	-LM	Belgian AF	CH-07	1
382-4477	L-100-30		Safair	ZS-RSD	1
382-4478/4479	C-130H-	-LM	Belgian AF	CH-08/CH-09	2
382-4480	C-130H-	-LM	IIAF	5-155	1
382-4481/4483	C-130H-	-LM	Belgian AF	CH-10/CH-12	3
382-4484/4490	C-130H-	-LM	IIAF	5-156/5-162	7
382-4491/4495	C-130H-	-LM	Italian AF	MM61995/MM61999	5
382-4496	C-130H-	-LM	Chilean AF	996	1
382-4497/4498	C-130H-	-LM	Italian AF	MM62000/MM62001	2
382-4499/4500	C-130E-	-LM	USAF	72-1288/72-1289	2
382-4501	HC-130H-	-LM	USCG	1500	1
382-4502	C-130H-	-LM	USAF	72-1290	1
382-4503	KC-130H-	-LM	R Saudi AF	456	1
382-4504/4506	C-130E-	-LM	USAF	72-1291/72-1293	3
382-4507	HC-130H-	-LM	USCG	1501	1
382-4508	LC-130R-	-LM	USN	159129	1
382-4509/4510	C-130H-	-LM	USAF	72-1294/72-1295	2
382-4511	KC-130H-	-LM	R Saudi AF	457	1
382-4512	L-100-20		Co. owned	N7967S	1
382-4513	HC-130H-	-LM	USCG	1502	1
382-4514	C-130E-	-LM	Turkish AF	ETI-468	1
382-4515	C-130H-	-LM	Libyan AF	119	1
382-4516	LC-130R-	-LM	USN	159130	1
382-4517	C-130E-	-LM	USAF	72-1296	1
382-4518	C-130H-	-LM	Libyan AF	120	1
382-4519	C-130E-	-LM	USAF	72-1297	1
382-4520	C-130H-	-LM	Spanish AF	T10-1	1
382-4521	C-130E-	-LM	USAF	72-1298	1
382-4522	LC-130R-	-LM	USN	159131	1
382-4523	C-130H-	-LM	Libyan AF	121	1
382-4524	C-130E-	-LM	Turkish AF	ETI-991	1
382-4525	C-130H-	-LM	Libyan AF	122	1
382-4526	C-130H-	-LM	Spanish AF	T10-2	1
382-4527	C-130E-	-LM	USAF	72-1299	1
382-4528/4529	HC-130H-	-LM	USCG	1503/1504	2
382-4530	C-130H-	-LM	Israeli AF	4X-FBC	1
382-4531	C-130H-	-LM	Spanish AF	T10-3	1
382-4532	KC-130H-	-LM	R Saudi AF	458	1
382-4533	C-130H-	-LM	Israeli AF	4X-FBD	1
382-4534	C-130H-	-LM	Spanish AF	T10-4	1
382-4535	C-130H-	-LM	Gov. of Morocco	CN-AOA	1
382-4536	C-130H-	-LM	Libyan AF	123	1
382-4537	C-130H-	-LM	Gov. of Morocco	CN-AOB	1
382-4538	C-130H-	-LM	Libyan AF	124	1
382-4539	KC-130H-	-LM	R Saudi AF	459	1
382-4540/4541	C-130H-	-LM	Libyan AF	125/126	2
382-4542/4550	C-130H-	-LM	USAF	73-1580/73-1588	9
382-4551	C-130H-	-LM	Gov. of Morocco	CN-AOC	1
382-4552	C-130H-	-LM	R Saudi AF	1612	1
382-4553	C-130H-	-LM	Can. Forces	130329	1
382-4554	C-130H-	-LM	USAF	73-1590	1

382-4555	C-130H-	-LM	Can. Forces	130330	1
382-4556	C-130H-	-LM	Venezuelan AF	4224	1
382-4557	C-130H-	-LM	USAF	73-1592	1
382-4558	L-100-30		Safair	ZS-RSE	1
382-4559	C-130H-	-LM	Can. Forces	130331	1
382-4560	C-130H-	-LM	R Saudi AF	1614	1
382-4561	L-100-30		Saturn	N20ST	1
382-4562	L-100-30		Safair	ZS-RSF	1
382-4563/4564	C-130H-	-LM	USAF	73-1594/73-1595	2
382-4565	L-100-30		Safair	ZS-RSF	1
382-4566/4567	C-130H-	-LM	R Saudi AF	460/461	2
382-4568	C-130H-	-LM	Can. Forces	130332	1
382-4569	C-130H-	-LM	Zaire	9T-TCE	1
382-4570	C-130H-	-LM	Brazilian AF	2463	1
382-4571	C-130H-	-LM	USAF	73-1597	1
382-4572	C-130H-	-LM	Danish AF	678	1
382-4573	C-130H-	-LM	USAF	73-1598	1
382-4574	C-130H-	-LM	Can. Forces	130333	1
382-4575	C-130H-	-LM	Gov. of Morocco	CN-AOD	1
382-4576	C-130H-	-LM	Argentine AF	TC-67	1
382-4577	C-130H-	-LM	Venezuelan AF	5320	1
382-4578	C-130H-	-LM	Argentine AF	TC-68	1
382-4579	C-130H-	-LM	USAF	74-1658	1
382-4580	C-130H-	-LM	Abu Dhabi AF	1211	1
382-4581	C-130H-	-LM	Gov. of Morocco	CN-AOE	1
382-4582	L-100-30		Gabon	TR-KKA	1
382-4583	C-130H-	-LM	Gov. of Morocco	CN-AOF	1
382-4584	C-130H-	-LM	Abu Dhabi AF	1212	1
382-4585	C-130H-	-LM	USAF	74-1659	1
382-4586	L-100-30		Saturn	N21ST	1
382-4587	C-130H-	-LM	Danish AF	679	1
382-4588/4589	C-130H-	-LM	Zaire	9T-TCF/9T-TCG	2
382-4590	L-100-30		Safair	ZS-RSH	1
382-4591	C-130H-	-LM	IIAF	5-157	1
382-4592	C-130H-	-LM	USAF	74-1660	1
382-4593	L-100-20		Phil. Aero. Dev.	RP-C101	1
382-4594	C-130H-	-LM	IIAF	5-158	1
382-4595	EC-130Q-	-LM	USN	159469	1
382-4596/4598	C-130H-	-LM	USAF	74-1661/74-1663	3
382-4599	C-130H-	-LM	Danish AF	680	1
382-4600	L-100-30		Safair	ZS-RSI	1
382-4601	EC-130Q-	-LM	USN	159348	1
382-4602	C-130H-	-LM	Brazilian AF	2464	1
382-4603/4604	C-130H-	-LM	USAF	74-1664/74-1665	2
382-4605	C-130H-	-LM	R Saudi AF	102	1
382-4606	L-100-30		Safair	ZS-RSJ	1
382-4607/4609	C-130H-	-LM	R Saudi AF	463/465	3
382-4610	L-100-30		Alaska Int.	N108AK	1
382-4611	C-130H-	-LM	USAF	74-1666	1
382-4612	C-130H-	-LM	R Saudi AF	1601	1
382-4613	C-130H-	-LM	USAF	74-1667	1
382-4614	C-130H-	-LM	R Saudi AF	1602	1
382-4615	KC-130R-	-LM	USMC	160013	1
382-4616/4617	C-130H-	-LM	USAF	74-1668/74-1669	2
382-4618	C-130H-	-LM	R Saudi AF	1603	1
382-4619	C-130H-	-LM	Nigerian AF	910	1
382-4620/4621	C-130H-	-LM	USAF	74-1670/74-1671	2
382-4622	C-130H-	-LM	Hellenic AF	741	1
382-4623	C-130H-	-LM	USAF	74-1672	1
382-4624	C-130H-	-LM	Nigerian AF	911	1
382-4625	KC-130H-	-LM	Brazilian AF	2461	1
382-4626	KC-130R-	-LM	USMC	160014	1
382-4627	C-130H-	-LM	USAF	74-1673	1
382-4628	C-130H-	-LM	Swedish AF	84003	1
382-4629	KC-130R-	-LM	USMC	160015	1
382-4630	C-130H-	-LM	Brazilian AF	2465	1
382-4631	C-130H-	-LM	USAF	74-1674	1
382-4632	C-130H-	-LM	Hellenic AF	742	1
382-4633/4634	C-130H-	-LM	R Saudi AF	1604/1605	2
382-4635	KC-130R-	-LM	USMC	160016	1
382-4636	KC-130H-	-LM	Brazilian AF	2462	1
382-4637	C-130H-	-LM	R Saudi AF	462	1
382-4638/4639	C-130H-	-LM	Nigerian AF	912/913	2

382-4640/4641	C-130H-	-LM	USAF	74-1675/74-1676	2
382-4642	KC-130H-	-LM	Spanish AF	TK10-5	1
382-4643	C-130H-	-LM	USAF	74-1677	1
382-4644	C-130H-	-LM	USAF	74-2061	1
382-4645/4646	C-130H-	-LM	USAF	74-1678/74-1679	2
382-4647	C-130H-	-LM	USAF	74-2062	1
382-4648	KC-130H-	-LM	Spanish AF	TK10-6	1
382-4649/4650	C-130H-	-LM	Nigerian AF	914/915	2
382-4651	C-130H-	-LM	USAF	74-1680	1
382-4652	KC-130H-	-LM	Spanish AF	TK10-7	1
382-4653	C-130H-	-LM	Israeli AF	4X-FBQ	1
382-4654	C-130H-	-LM	USAF	74-1681	1
382-4655	C-130H-	-LM	USAF	74-2063	1
382-4656	C-130H-	-LM	R Malaysian AF	FM2401	1
382-4657/4658	C-130H-	-LM	USAF	74-1682/74-1683	2
382-4659	C-130H-	-LM	USAF	74-2064	1
382-4660	KC-130H-	-LM	Israeli AF	4X-FBY	1
382-4661	C-130H-	-LM	R Malaysian AF	FM2402	1
382-4662	C-130H-	-LM	Israeli AF	4X-FBS	1
382-4663	C-130H-	-LM	USAF	74-1684	1
382-4664	KC-130H-	-LM	Israeli AF	4X-FBZ	1
382-4665	C-130H-	-LM	Hellenic AF	743	1
382-4666	C-130H-	-LM	USAF	74-1685	1
382-4667	C-130H-	-LM	USAF	74-2065	1
382-4668	C-130H-	-LM	Israeli AF	4X-FBT	1
382-4669/4670	C-130H-	-LM	USAF	74-1686/74-1687	2
382-4671	C-130H-	-LM	USAF	74-2066	1
382-4672	C-130H-	-LM	Hellenic AF	744	1
382-4673	L-100-30		Safair	ZS-JIV	1
382-4674	C-130H-	-LM	R Malaysian AF	FM2403	1
382-4675	C-130H-	-LM	USAF	74-1688	1
382-4676	L-100-30		Safair	ZS-JVL	1
382-4677	KC-130R-	-LM	USMC	160017	1
382-4678	C-130H-	-LM	USAF	74-2067	1
382-4679	L-100-30		Safair	ZS-JIW	1
382-4680	C-130H-	-LM	Israeli AF	4X-FBU	1
382-4681/4682	C-130H-	-LM	USAF	74-1689/74-1690	2
382-4683	KC-130R-	-LM	USMC	160018	1
382-4684	L-100-30		Safair	ZS-JIX	1
382-4685	C-130H-	-LM	R Malaysian AF	FM2404	1
382-4686	C-130H-	-LM	Israeli AF	4X-FBW	1
382-4687/4688	C-130H-	-LM	USAF	74-1691/74-1692	2
382-4689	KC-130R-	-LM	USMC	160019	1
382-4690	C-130H-	-LM	R Malaysian AF	FM2405	1
382-4691	L-100-30		Safair	ZS-JIY	1
382-4692	C-130H-	-LM	Israeli AF	4X-FBX	1
382-4693	C-130H-	-LM	USAF	74-1693	1
382-4694	C-130H-	-LM	USAF	74-2068	1
382-4695	L-100-30		Safair	ZS-JIZ	1
382-4696	KC-130R-	-LM	USMC	160020	1
382-4697	C-130H-	-LM	R Malaysian AF	FM2406	1
382-4698	L-100-30		Safair	ZS-JJA	1
382-4699/4700	C-130H-	-LM	USAF	74-2069/74-2070	2
382-4701	L-100-30		Safair	ZS-JVM	1
382-4702	KC-130R-	-LM	USMC	160021	1
382-4703	C-130H-	-LM	USAF	74-2071	1
382-4704	C-130H-	-LM	Phil. Gov.	4704	1
382-4705	C-130H-	-LM	USAF	74-2072	1
382-4706	L-100-20		Peruvian AF	FAP382	1
382-4707	C-130H-	-LM	Egyptian AF	SU-BAA	1
382-4708	L-100-20		Peruvian AF	FAP383	1
382-4709	C-130H-	-LM	Egyptian AF	SU-BAB	1
382-4710	L-100-20		Gabon	TR-KKB	1
382-4711	C-130H-	-LM	USAF	74-2130	1
382-4712	KC-130R-	-LM	USMC	160240	1
382-4713	C-130H-	-LM	Gov. of Morocco	CN-AOG	1
382-4714	C-130H-	-LM	Egyptian AF	SU-BAC	1
382-4715	L-100-20		Peruvian AF	FAP384	1
382-4716	C-130H-	-LM	Hellenic AF	745	1
382-4717	C-130H-	-LM	Gov. of Morocco	CN-AOH	1
382-4718	C-130H-	-LM	USAF	74-2131	1
382-4719	C-130H-	-LM	Egyptian AF	SU-BAD	1
382-4720	C-130H-	-LM	Hellenic AF	746	1

516

382-4721	C-130H-	-LM	Egyptian AF	SU-BAE	1
382-4722	C-130H-	-LM	USAF	74-2132	1
382-4723/4724	C-130H-	-LM	Hellenic AF	747/748	2
382-4725	LC-130R-	-LM	Nat. Science Found.	160740	1
382-4726	C-130H-	-LM	Phil. Gov.	4726	1
382-4727	C-130H-	-LM	Hellenic AF	749	1
382-4728	C-130H-	-LM	Egyptian AF	SU-BAF	1
382-4729	C-130H-	-LM	Hellenic AF	750	1
382-4730	C-130H-	-LM	USAF	74-2133	1
382-4731	LC-130R-	-LM	Nat. Science Found.	160741	1
382-4732	C-130H-	-LM	Hellenic AF	751	1
382-4733	C-130H-	-LM	Gov. of Morocco	CN-AOI	1
382-4734	C-130H-	-LM	Hellenic AF	752	1
382-4735	C-130H-	-LM	USAF	74-2134	1
382-4736	C-130H-	-LM	Zaire	9T-TCG	1
382-4737	VC-130H-	-LM	R Saudi AF	112	1
382-4738/4739	C-130H-	-LM	Gov. of Morocco	CN-AOJ/CN-AOK	2
382-4740/4741	C-130H-	-LM	R Saudi AF	466/467	2
382-4742	C-130H-	-LM	Gov. of Morocco	CN-AOL	1
382-4743	C-130H-	-LM	Ecuadorian AF	743	1
382-4744	C-130H-	-LM	Bolivian AF	TAM-90	1
382-4745	C-130H-	-LM	R Saudi AF	1615	1
382-4746	KC-130H-	-LM	R Saudi AF	1616	1
382-4747	C-130H-	-LM	Cameroon AF	TJ-XAC	1
382-4748	C-130H-	-LM	Ecuadorian AF	748	1
382-4749	C-130H-	-LM	Portuguese AF	6801	1
382-4750	KC-130H-	-LM	R Saudi AF	1617	1
382-4751	C-130H-	-LM	R Saudi AF	468	1
382-4752	C-130H-	-LM	Cameroon AF	TJ-XAD	1
382-4753	C-130H-	-LM	Portuguese AF	6802	1
382-4754	C-130H-	-LM	R Saudi AF	469	1
382-4755/4756	C-130H-	-LM	R Saudi AF	1618/1619´	2
382-4757	HC-130H-	-LM	USCG	1603	1
382-4758	C-130H-	-LM	R Saudi AF	470	1
382-4759	C-130H-	-LM	Bolivian AF	TAM-91	1
382-4760	HC-130H-	-LM	USCG	1602	1
382-4761	C-130H-	-LM	Phil. Gov.	4761	1
382-4762	HC-130H-	-LM	USCG	1601	1
382-4763	L-100-30		Alaska Int.	N108AK	1
382-4764	HC-130H-	-LM	USCG	1600	1
382-4765	L-100-20		Gabon	TR-KKC	1
382-4766/4767	C-130H-	-LM	Sudanese AF	1101/1102	2
382-4768	KC-130R-	-LM	USMC	160625	1
382-4769	C-130H-	-LM	Sudanese AF	1103	1
382-4770	KC-130R-	-LM	USMC	160626	1
382-4771	C-130H-	-LM	Sudanese AF	1104	1
382-4772	C-130H-	-LM	Portuguese AF	6803	1
382-4773	KC-130R-	-LM	USMC	160627	1
382-4774/4775	C-130H-	-LM	Sudanese AF	1105/1106	2
382-4776	KC-130R-	-LM	USMC	160628	1
382-4777/4778	C-130H-	-LM	Portuguese AF	6804/6805	2
382-4779	C-130H-	-LM	Jordanian AF	144	1
382-4780	C-130H-	-LM	RAAF	A97-001	1
382-4781	EC-130Q-	-LM	USN	160608	1
382-4782/4791	C-130H-	-LM	RAAF	A97-002/A97-011	10
382-7492	C-130H-	-LM	Egyptian AF	SU-BAH	1
382-4793	C-130H-	-LM	RAAF	A97-012	1
382-4794/4795	C-130H-	-LM	Egyptian AF	SU-BAI/SU-BAJ	2
382-4796	L-100-30		SCIBE	9Q-CBJ	1
382-4797	C-130H-	-LM	Egyptian AF	SU-BAK	1
382-4798	L-100-30		Alaska Int.	N510AK	1
382-4799	L-100-30		Pac. Western AL	C-GHPW	1
382-4800	L-100-30		TNIAU	A-1314	1
382-4801	C-130H-	-LM	Venezuelan AF	3134	1
382-4802/4811	C-130H-	-LM	Egyptian AF	SU-BAL/SU-BAN, SU-BAP/SU-BAV	10
382-4812	C-130H-	-LM	Ecuadorian AF	812	1
382-4813	C-130H-	-LM	Jordanian AF	345	1
382-4814	KC-130H-	-LM	Argentine AF	TC-69	1
382-4815	C-130H-	-LM	ANG	78-806	1
382-4816	KC-130H-	-LM	Argentine AF	TC-70	1
382-4817/4823	C-130H-	-LM	ANG	78-807/78-813	7
382-4824	L-100-30		Indonesian Gov.	PK-PLU	1

517

382-4825	C-130H- -LM	Yemen Arab Rep.	1150	1
382-4826	L-100-30	Indonesian Gov.	PK-PLV	1
382-4827	C-130H- -LM	Yemen Arab Rep.	1160	1
382-4828	L-100-30	Indonesian Gov.	PK-PLW	1
382-4829	C-130H- -LM	Niger Gov.	5U-MBD	1
382-4830	L-100-20	Angola AL	D2-EAS	1
382-4831	C-130H- -LM	Niger Gov.	5U-MBH	1
382-4832	L-100-20	Angola AL	D2-THA	1
382-4833	L-100-30	Bolivian Gov.	CP-1564	1
382-4834	L-100-30			1
382-4835/4836	C-130H- -LM	Spanish AF	T10-8/T10-9	2
382-4837	C-130H- -LM	R Saudi AF		1
382-4838	C-130H- -LM	TNIAU	A-1315	1
382-4839	L-100-30			1
382-4840	C-130H- -LM	TNIAU	A-1316	1
382-4841	C-130H- -LM	Spanish AF	T10-10	1
382-4842	C-130H- -LM	Singapore AF	730	1
382-4843	C-130H- -LM	R Saudi AF		1
382-4844	C-130H- -LM	Singapore AF	731	1
382-4845	C-130H- -LM	R Saudi AF		1
382-4846	C-130H- -LM	Singapore AF	732	1
382-4847	C-130H- -LM	R Malaysian AF	FM2451	1
382-4848	C-130H- -LM	Singapore AF	733	1
382-4849	C-130H- -LM	R Malaysian AF	FM2452	1
382-4850	L-100-20			1
382-4851	L-100-30			1
382-4852	C-130H- -LM	ANG	79-473	1
382-4853	L-100-20			1
382-4854/4860	C-130H- -LM	ANG	79-474/79-480	7
382-4861/4863	C-130H- -LM	R Thai AF	60101/60103	3
382-4864/4865	C-130H(S)- -LM	TNIAU	A-1317/A-1318	2
382-4866	C-130H- -LM	R Malaysian AF	FM2453	1
382-4867	EC-130Q- -LM	USN	161223	1
382-4868/4870	C-130H(S)- -LM	TNIAU	A-1319/A-1321	3
382-4871	KC-130H- -LM	Spanish AF	TK10-11	1
382-4872/4873	KC-130H- -LM	R Saudi AF		2
382-4874	KC-130H- -LM	Spanish AF	TK10-12	1

LOCKHEED U-2 AND TR-1 (Number built: at least 114 according to released information)

	U-2A	USAF	56-6675/56-6722	48
	U-2D	USAF	56-6951/56-6955	5
	U-2R	USAF	68-10329/68-10353	25
	ER-2	NASA	80-1063	1
	TR-1A/TR-1B	USAF	- - -	35

LOCKHEED 1649 STARLINER (Number built: 44)

1649-1001	1649A	Co. owned	N1649	1
1649-1002/1010	1649A	TWA	N7301C/N7309C	9
1649-1011	1649A	Air France	F-BHBK	1
1649-1012/1019	1649A	TWA	N7310C/N/317C	8
1649-1020	1649A	Air France	F-BHBL	1
1649-1021/1025	1649A	TWA	N7318C/N7322C	5
1649-1026	1649A	TWA	N8081H	1
1649-1027/1028	1649A	Air France	F-BHBM/F-BHBN	2
1649-1029/1030	1649A	TWA	N7323C/N7324C	2
1649-1031/1033	1649A	Air France	F-BHBO/F-BHBQ	3
1649-1034	1649A	Lufthansa	D-ALUB	1
1649-1035	1649A	TWA	N7325C	1
1649-1036	1649A	Air France	F-BHBR	1
1649-1037/1039	1649A	TWA	N8082H/N8084H	3
1649-1040/1042	1649A	Lufthansa	D-ALAN. -ALER & -ALOL	3
1649-1043	1649A	Cancelled	- - - -	0
1649-1044/1045	1649A	Air France	F-BHBS/F-BHBT	2

LOCKHEED JETSTAR (Number built: 204) (* = modified as JetStar 731)

329-1001	JetStar	Co. owned	N329J	1
329-1002	JetStar	Co. owned	N329K	1
1329-5001*	JetStar 6	FAA	N1	1
1329-5002	JetStar 6			1
1329-5003	JetStar 6	NASA	NASA 14	1
1329-5004	JetStar 6	United Aircraft Corp.	N13304	1
1329-5005	JetStar 6	McDonnell Aircraft	N12121	1
1329-5006*	JetStar 6			1

1329-5007*	JetStar 6	Gulf Oil Corp.	N110G	1
1329-5008	JetStar 6	Intratex Gas Co.	N500Z	1
1329-5009	JetStar 6	Continental Oil Co.	N540G	1
1329-5010	C-140A-LM	USAF	59-5958	1
1329-5011*	JetStar 6	Indonesian AF	T17845	1
1329-5012	JetStar 6		D-BABE	1
1329-5013	JetStar 6	Ford Motor Co.	N322K	1
1329-5014	JetStar 6	Corning Glass	N58CG	1
1329-5015	JetStar 6	NASA	NASA 4	1
1329-5016	JetStar 6	Morton International	N2222R	1
1329-5017	VC-140B-LM	USAF	61-2488	1
1329-5018	JetStar 6			1
1329-5019	JetStar 6	General Mills Inc.	N105GM	1
1329-5020	JetStar 6			1
1329-5021	JetStar 6	Canadian MOT	C-FETN	1
1329-5022	VC-140B-LM	USAF	61-2489	1
1329-5023	JetStar 6	Soc. Naz. Metanodotti	I-SNAL	1
1329-5024	VC-140B-LM	USAF	61-2490	1
1329-5025	JetStar 6	Luftwaffe	CA101	1
1329-5026	C-140A-LM	USAF	59-5959	1
1329-5027	VC-140B-LM	USAF	61-2491	1
1329-5028	C-140A-LM	USAF	59-5960	1
1329-5029*	JetStar 6	National Steel Corp.	N340NS	1
1329-5030	C-140A-LM	USAF	59-5961	1
1329-5031	VC-140B-LM	USAF	61-2492	1
1329-5032	C-140A-LM	USAF	59-5962	1
1329-5033	JetStar 6	Texaco Inc.	N1620	1
1329-5034	VC-140B-LM	USAF	61-2493	1
1329-5035	JetStar 6	Luftwaffe	CA102	1
1329-5036*	JetStar 6	Texaco Inc.	N1622	1
1329-5037*	JetStar 6	Mobil Oil Corp.	N2600	1
1329-5038	JetStar 6	National Steel Corp.	N341NS	1
1329-5039	JetStar 6	Johnson & Johnson	N600J	1
1329-5040	JetStar 6			1
1329-5041/5045	C-140B-LM	USAF	62-4197/62-4201	5
1329-5046	JetStar 6	Indonesian AF	T9446	1
1329-5047	JetStar 6	Martin Marietta Corp.	N409M	1
1329-5048	JetStar 6		N4N	1
1329-5049	JetStar 6	Tracy Investment Co.	N1230R	1
1329-5050*	JetStar 6	Co. owned	N207L	1
1329-5051	JetStar 6	Kimberly-Clark Corp.	N400KC	1
1329-5052	JetStar 6	Nat'l. Distillers	N300P	1
1329-5053*	JetStar 6	National Equities Inc.	N12R	1
1329-5054	JetStar 6	Union Oil Co.	N7600J	1
1329-5055*	JetStar 6	Atlantic Richfield	N296AR	1
1329-5056	JetStar 6	Gulf Oil Corp.	N105G	1
1329-5057	JetStar 6	Security 1st Nat'l Bank	N1007	1
1329-5058*	JetStar 6	Exxon Corp.	N100A	1
1329-5059	JetStar 6	Indonesian AF	T1645	1
1329-5060	JetStar 6	Firestone Tire & Rubber	N31F	1
1329-5061*	JetStar 6	Tenneco Inc.	N506T	1
1329-5062*	JetStar 6	Coca Cola Co.	N679R	1
1329-5063	JetStar 6	Avco Corp.	N420L	1
1329-5064*	JetStar 6	Georgia Pacific Corp.	N184GP	1
1329-5065	JetStar 6	Ethyl Corp.	N1966G	1
1329-5066*	JetStar 6	AFLC Inc.	N288Y	1
1329-5067	JetStar 6	Co. owned	N207L	1
1329-5068*	JetStar 6	Exxon Corp.	N9231R	1
1329-5069*	JetStar 6	Standard Oil Realty	N910M	1
1329-5070*	JetStar 6	Reynolds Metal Co.	N922	1
1329-5071	JetStar 6	Luftwaffe	CA103	1
1329-5072*	JetStar 6	Superior Oil Co.	N500Z	1
1329-5073	JetStar 6			1
1329-5074*	JetStar 6	Federated Stores Inc.	N67B	1
1329-5075*	JetStar 6	Continental Oil Co.	N540G	1
1329-5076*	JetStar 6	Copley Press Inc.	N100C	1
1329-5077	JetStar 6	First Nat'l Bank of Chicago	N1924V	1
1329-5078*	JetStar 6	Co. owned	N7105	1
1329-5079*	JetStar 6	Santa Fe Int'l.	N9238R	1
1329-5080	JetStar 6	Xerox Corp.	N914X	1
1329-5081	JetStar 6	Exxon Corp.	N200A	1
1329-5082*	JetStar 6	Texasgulf Inc.	N320S	1

519

1329-5083*	JetStar 6	Co. owned	N141LM	1
1329-5084*	JetStar 6	3M Co.	N83M	1
1329-5085	JetStar 6	Bendix Corp.	N586	1
1329-5086	JetStar 6	Johnson & Johnson	N27R	1
1329-5087*	JetStar 6	Union Carbide Corp.	N41N	1
1329-5088	JetStar 6	Canadian MOT	C-FDTF	1
1329-5089	JetStar 6	Ford Motor Co.	N324K	1
1329-5090	JetStar 6	Gulf Oil Corp.	N106G	1
1329-5091	JetStar 6	Gulf Oil Corp.	N107G	1
1329-5092	JetStar 6	Hercules Inc.	N372H	1
1329-5093	JetStar 6	Cargill Inc.	N500C	1
1329-5094	JetStar 6	Republic Steel Corp.	N3030	1
1329-5095*	JetStar 6	Mesa Petroleum Co.	N78MP	1
1329-5096*	JetStar 6	Continental Oil Co.	N530G	1
1329-5097	JetStar 8	Triangle Publ. Inc.	N300L	1
1329-5098*	JetStar 8	GT&E Service	N1967G	1
1329-5099*	JetStar 8	Security 1st Nat'l Bank	N533EJ	1
1329-5100*	JetStar 8	Co. owned	N207L	1
1329-5101*	JetStar 8	B. F. Goodrich Co.	N7008	1
1329-5102	JetStar 8	Ford Motor Co.	N326K	1
1329-5103	JetStar 8	3M Co.	N23M	1
1329-5104*	JetStar 8	Westinghouse	N902K	1
1329-5105	JetStar 8	Trunkline Gas Co.	N277T	1
1329-5106*	JetStar 8	Air Combustion Inc.	N238U	1
1329-5107	JetStar 8	Kaiser Industries Corp.	N118K	1
1329-5108	JetStar 8	Pennzoil Co.	N1207Z	1
1329-5109*	JetStar 8	Great Northern Railway	N968GN	1
1329-5110*	JetStar 8	Mobil Oil Corp.	N2600	1
1329-5111	JetStar 8	Amerada Hess Corp.	N5111H	1
1329-5112*	JetStar 8	Standard Oil Realty	N910G	1
1329-5113*	JetStar 8	Celtran Inc.	N505C	1
1329-5114*	JetStar 8	McKnight WL	N930MT	1
1329-5115*	JetStar 8	Lorillard Corp.	N933LC	1
1329-5116	JetStar 8		N222QA	1
1329-5117*	JetStar 8	Exxon Corp.	N7962S	1
1329-5118	JetStar 8	Kaneb Services Inc.	N333KN	1
1329-5119*	JetStar 8	Houston Oil & Minerals	N11HM	1
1329-5120*	JetStar 8			1
1329-5121	JetStar 8	Luftwaffe	1102	1
1329-5122	JetStar 8	Pennzoil Co.	N1107Z	1
1329-5123*	JetStar 8	State Mutual Life	N1844S	1
1329-5124	JetStar 8	Hunt Oil Co.	N46F	1
1329-5125*	JetStar 8	Union Camp Corp.	N47UC	1
1329-5126	JetStar 8	Honeywell Inc.	N955H	1
1329-5127	JetStar 8	Bankers Life	N42G	1
1329-5128*	JetStar 8	Sun Oil Co.	N26S	1
1329-5129/5130	JetStar 8	R. Saudi AF	101/102	2
1329-5131	JetStar 8	RCA Corp.	N3ORP	1
1329-5132	JetStar 8	Texaco Inc.	N1620	1
1329-5133	JetStar 8	Ford Motor Co.	N329K	1
1329-5134*	JetStar 8	Atlantic Richfield	N295AR	1
1329-5135	JetStar 8	E. F. MacDonald Co.	N636	1
1329-5136	JetStar 8	Libyan Air Force	001	1
1329-5137	JetStar 8	Shah of Persia	EP-VRP	1
1329-5138	JetStar 8	J. C. Penney Co.	N1301P	1
1329-5139	JetStar 8	Reynolds Metals Co.	N991	1
1329-5140	JetStar 8	Cerveceria Moctezuma	XB-V1W	1
1329-5141	JetStar 8			1
1329-5142	JetStar 8	Amerada Hess Corp.	N5113H	1
1329-5143*	JetStar 8		N100UA	1
1329-5144	JetStar 8			1
1329-5145	JetStar 8	Koppers Co.	N46K	1
1329-5146	JetStar 8	General Mills Inc.	N80GM	1
1329-5147	JetStar 8	United Systems	N744UT	1
1329-5148	JetStar 8	Chase Manhattan Bank	N964M	1
1329-5149*	JetStar 8		N157JF	1
1329-5150*	JetStar 8		N516WC	1
1329-5151	JetStar 8		N46KJ	1
1329-5152	JetStar 8	John Deere & Co.	N500JD	1
1329-5153	JetStar 8	Louisiana Land Expl.	N711JS	1
1329-5154	JetStar 8			1
1329-5155*	JetStar 8	Aeropersonal SA	XA-FES	1
1329-5156	JetStar 8	Kuwaiti Gov't.	9K-ACO	1

1329-5157	JetStar 8		N9WP	1
1329-5158	JetStar 8		N516DM	1
1329-5159	JetStar 8	Marathon Oil Co.	N520M	1
1329-5160	JetStar 8	Royal Bank of Canada	C-FRBC	1
1329-5161*	JetStar 8	Esmark Inc.	N22ES	1
1329-5162	JetStar 8	Clorox Co.	N10CX	1
2329-5201	JetStar II	Co. owned	N5527L	1
2329-5202	JetStar II	Allied Stores	N717	1
2329-5203	JetStar II	Shah of Persia	EP-VLP	1
2329-5204	JetStar II	Esmark Inc.	N19ES	1
2329-5205	JetStar II	Cargill Inc.	N5000C	1
2329-5206	JetStar II	General Mills Inc.	N107GM	1
2329-5207	JetStar II	Burlington Northern Inc.	N176BN	1
2329-5208	JetStar II	Campbell Soup Co.	N322CS	1
2329-5209	JetStar II	Oilfield Aviation Corp.	N500S	1
2329-5210	JetStar II	Kimberly-Clark Corp.	N400KC	1
2329-5211	JetStar II	Tenneco Inc.	N500T	1
2329-5212	JetStar II	Republic Steel Co.	N3030	1
2329-5213	JetStar II	Tenneco Inc.	N510T	1
2329-5214	JetStar II	Marathon Oil Co.	N530M	1
2329-5215	JetStar II	Bowaters Inc.	N4BR	1
2329-5216	JetStar II	Burlington Ind.	N95BA	1
2329-5217	JetStar II	Gulf Oil Corp.	N106G	1
2329-5218	JetStar II	Readers Digest	N716RD	1
2329-5219	JetStar II	Bowaters Inc.	N4BR	1
2329-5220	JetStar II	Knight-Ridder Newspapers	N32KR	1
2329-5221	JetStar II	Libyan Gov't.	5A-DAR	1
2329-5222	JetStar II	Tenneco Inc.	N509T	1
2329-5223	JetStar II	Gulf Oil Corp.	N105G	1
2329-5224	JetStar II	Ideal Basic Ind.	N1924G	1
2329-5225	JetStar II	United Telecom	N746UT	1
2329-5226	JetStar II	Morrison-Knudsen Co.	N2MK	1
2329-5227	JetStar II	US Tobacco Co.	N211PA	1
2329-5228	JetStar II	Hercules Inc.	N372H	1
2329-5229	JetStar II	Northwest Pipeline	N7NP	1
2329-5230	JetStar II	H. J. Heinz Co.	N257H	1
2329-5231	JetStar II	Kansas City Life	N196KC	1
2329-5232	JetStar II	Chesebrough-Ponds Inc.	N90CP	1
2329-5233	JetStar II	Iraqi Gov't.	YI-AKA	1
2329-5234	JetStar II	H. J. Heinz Co.	N357H	1
2329-5235	JetStar II	Iraqi Gov't.	YI-AKB	1
2329-5236	JetStar II	Marathon Oil Co.	N531M	1
2329-5237/5240	JetStar II	Iraqi Gov't.	TI-AKC/YI-AKF	4

LOCKHEED 188 ELECTRA (Number built: 170)

188-1001/1004	188A	Co. owned	N1881/N1884	4
188-1005	188A	Eastern	N5501	1
188-1006	188A	Gen. Motors	N5501V	1
188-1007/1012	188A	Eastern	N5502/N5507	6
188-1013/1014	188A	Eastern	N5509/N5510	2
188-1015	188A	American	N6101A	1
188-1016/1018	188A	Eastern	N5511/N5513	3
188-1019	188A	American	N6102A	1
188-1020/1023	188A	Eastern	N5514/N5517	4
188-1024/1025	188A	American	N6103A/N6104A	2
188-1026	188A	Eastern	N5518	1
188-1027/1028	188A	American	N6105A/N6106A	2
188-1029/1030	188A	Eastern	N5519/N5520	2
188-1031	188A	American	N6107A	1
188-1032/1034	188A	Eastern	N5521/N5523	3
188-1035	188A	National	N5001K	1
188-1036	188A	Eastern	N5524	1
188-1037	188A	American	N6108A	1
188-1038	188A	Eastern	N5525	1
188-1039	188A	Ansett-ANA	VH-RMA	1
188-1040	188A	Braniff	N9701C	1
188-1041	188A	American	N6109A	1
188-1042/1043	188A	Eastern	N5526/N5527	2
188-1044	188A	Co. leased	N1883	1
188-1045	188A	Eastern	N5528	1
188-1046	188A	Western	N7135C	1
188-1047	188A	Ansett-ANA	VH-RMB	1
188-1048	188A	Eastern	N5529	1

521

188-1049/1051	188A	American	N6110A/N6112A	3
188-1052	188A	Braniff	N9702C	1
188-1053	188A	Eastern	N5530	1
188-1054	188A	American	N6113A	1
188-1055	188A	Eastern	N5531	1
188-1056	188A	American	N6114A	1
188-1057	188C	Northwest	N121US	1
188-1058	188A	American	N6115A	1
188-1059	188A	National	N5002K	1
188-1060	188A	Eastern	N5532	1
188-1061	188A	TAA	VH-TLA	1
188-1062	188A	Eastern	N5533	1
188-1063	188A	American	N6116A	1
188-1064	188A	National	N5003K	1
188-1065	188A	American	N6117A	1
188-1066	188A	Eastern	N5534	1
188-1067	188A	Braniff	N9703C	1
188-1068	188A	Eastern	N5535	1
188-1069	188A	TAA	VH-TLB	1
188-1070	188A	Western	N7136C	1
188-1071	188A	Eastern	N5536	1
188-1072/1073	188A	American	N6118A/N6119A	2
188-1074	188A	Western	N7137C	1
188-1075	188C	Eastern	N5537	1
188-1076	188A	National	N5004K	1
188-1077	188C	Northwest	N122US	1
188-1078	188C	Eastern	N5538	1
188-1079	188A	National	N5005K	1
188-1080	188C	Eastern	N5539	1
188-1081	188A	American	N6120A	1
188-1082	188C	Northwest	N123US	1
188-1083	188A	American	N6121A	1
188-1084	188A	National	N5006K	1
188-1085	188C	Northwest	N124US	1
188-1086	188A	Braniff	N9704C	1
188-1087	188A	Western	N7138C	1
188-1088	188C	Eastern	N5540	1
188-1089	188A	National	N5007K	1
188-1090	188A	Braniff	N9705C	1
188-1091	188C	PSA	N171PS	1
188-1092	188A	National	N5008K	1
188-1093	188A	American	N6122A	1
188-1094	188A	Western	N7139C	1
188-1095	188A	Braniff	N9706C	1
188-1096/1097	188A	National	N5009K/N5010K	2
188-1098	188C	Eastern	N5541	1
188-1099	188A	Braniff	N9707C	1
188-1100	188A	American	N6123A	1
188-1101	188C	Northwest	N125US	1
188-1102	188A	American	N6124A	1
188-1103	188C	Co. leased	N9725C	1
188-1104	188A	National	N5011K	1
188-1105	188C	Northwest	N126US	1
188-1106	188A	Braniff	N9708C	1
188-1107	188A	National	N5012K	1
188-1108	188C	Northwest	N127US	1
188-1109/1110	188C	PSA	N172PS/N173PS	2
188-1111/1113	188C	Northwest	N128US/N130US	3
188-1114	188A	Braniff	N9709C	1
188-1115/1117	188A	American	N6125A/N6127A	3
188-1118	188A	Western	N7140C	1
188-1119/1126	188A	American	N6128A/N6135A	8
188-1127/1129	188A	Western	N7141C/N7143C	3
188-1130	188C	Capital	N181H	1
188-1131/1132	188C	Northwest	N131US/N132US	2
188-1133/1136	188C	Capital	N182H/N185H	4
188-1137/1139	188C	Northwest	N133US/N135US	3
188-1140	188A	Western	N9144C	1
188-1141/1142	188C	Northwest	N136US/N137US	2
188-1143	188A	Western	N9145C	1
188-1144	188C	Northwest	N138US	1
188-1145	188A	Western	N9746C	1
188-1146	188A	National	N5013K	1

188-1147	188A	TAA	VH-TLC	1
188-1148	188A	National	N5014K	1
188-1149/1168	188A	Cancelled	- - -	0
188-2001	188C	Co. leased	N6934C	1
188-2002	188C	Qantas	VH-ECA	1
188-2003	188C	KLM	PH-LLB	1
188-2004	188C	Qantas	VH-ECB	1
188-2005	188C	Co. leased	N9724C	1
188-2006	188C	KLM	PH-LLC	1
188-2007/2008	188C	Qantas	VH-ECC/VH-ECD	2
188-2009	188C	KLM	PH-LLD	1
188-2010/2011	188C	TEAL	ZK-TEB/ZK-TEC	2
188-2012/2016	188C	KLM	PH-LLE/PH-LLI	5
188-2017/2019	188C	KLM	PH-LLK/PH-LLM	3
188-2020/2022	188C	Garuda	PK-GLA/PK-GLC	3

LOCKHEED LASA-60 (Number built: 2 by Lockheed; plus 18 by Lockheed-Azcarate SA)

	LASA-60	Co. owned	N601L & N602L	2

LOCKHEED P-3 ORION (Number built: 522 up to end of 1980; still in production)

185-1003	YP3V-1	USN	148276	(1)
185-5001/5003	P-3A-1-LO	USN	148883/148885	3
185-5004/5007	P-3A-5-LO	USN	148886/148889	4
185-5008/5013	P-3A-10-LO	USN	149667/149672	6
185-5014/5019	P-3A-15-LO	USN	149673/149678	6
185-5020/5031	P-3A-20-LO	USN	150494/150505	12
185-5032/5046	P-3A-25-LO	USN	150506/150520	15
185-5047/5055	P-3A-30-LO	USN	150521/150529	9
185-5056/5061	P-3A-30-LO	USN	150604/150609	6
185-5062/5073	P-3A-35-LO	USN	151349/151360	12
185-5074/5089	P-3A-40-LO	USN	151361/151376	16
185-5090/5109	P-3A-45-LO	USN	151377/151396	20
185-5110/5125	P-3A-50-LO	USN	152140/152155	16
185-5126/5141	P-3A-55-LO	USN	152156/152171	16
185-5142/5157	P-3A-60-LO	USN	152172/152187	16
185-5158/5173	P-3B-65-LO	USN	152718/152733	16
185-5174/5189	P-3B-70-LO	USN	152734/152749	16
185-5190	P-3B-70-LO	RNZAF	NZ4201	1
185-5191	P-3B-70-LO	USN	152750	1
185-5192	P-3B-70-LO	RNZAF	NZ4202	1
185-5193/5199	P-3B-75-LO	USN	152751/152757	7
185-5200	P-3B-75-LO	RNZAF	NZ4203	1
185-5201	P-3B-75-LO	USN	152758	1
185-5202	P-3B-75-LO	RNZAF	NZ4204	1
185-5203/5207	P-3B-75-LO	USN	152759/152763	5
185-5208	P-3B-75-LO	RNZAF	NZ4205	1
185-5209/5210	P-3B-75-LO	USN	152764/152765	2
185-5211/5225	P-3B-80-LO	USN	153414/153428	15
185-5226/5238	P-3B-85-LO	USN	153429/153441	13
185-5239	P-3B-90-LO	USN	153442	1
185-5240/5254	P-3B-90-LO	USN	153444/153458	15
185-5255/5261	P-3B-95-LO	USN	154574/154580	7
185-5262/5272	P-3B-100-LO	USN	154581/154591	11
185-5273/5285	P-3B-105-LO	USN	154592/154604	13
185-5286	P-3B-105-LO	USN (RAAF)	154605 (A9-605)	1
185C-5301/5305	P-3B- -LO	Norwegian AF	KK-L/KK-P	5
185B-5401/5405	P-3B- -LO	RAAF	A9-291/A9-295	5
185B-5406	P-3B- -LO	RAAF (destroyed)	A9-296	1
185B-5407/5410	P-3B- -LO	RAAF	A9-297/A9-300	4
285A-5500	YP-3C-LO	USN	153443	1
285A-5501/5515	P-3C-110-LO	USN	156507/156521	15
285A-5516/5524	P-3C-115-LO	USN	156522/156530	9
285A-5525/5535	P-3C-120-LO	USN	157310/157320	11
285A-5536/5547	P-3C-125-LO	USN	157321/157332	12
285A-5548/5550	P-3C-130-LO	USN	158204/158206	3
285A-5551	RP-3D- -LO	USN	158227	1
285A-5552/5559	P-3C-130-LO	USN	158207/158214	8
285A-5560/5571	P-3C-135-LO	USN	158215/158226	12
285A-5572/5583	P-3C-140-LO	USN	158563/158574	12
285A-5584/5601	P-3C-145-LO	USN	158912/158929	18
285A-5602/5607	P-3C-150-LO	USN	158930/158935	6
285A-5608/5617	P-3C-155-LO	USN	159318/159327	10
285A-5618/5619	P-3C-160-LO	USN	159328/159329	2
285A-5620/5621	P-3C-165-LO	USN	159503/159504	2

285A-5622	WP-3D- -LO	NOAA	159773 (N42RF)	1
285A-5623/5632	P-3C-165-LO	USN	159505/159514	10
285A-5633	WP-3D- -LO	NOAA	159875 (N43RF)	1
285A-5634/5645	P-3C-170-LO	USN	159883/159894	12
285A-5646/5652	P-3C-175-LO	USN	160283/160289	7
285A-5653/5657	P-3C-180-LO	USN	160290/160294	5
285D-	P-3C- -LO	RAAF	A9-751/A9-760	10
285B-	CP-140	Can. Forces	140101/140118	18
785A-7001/7003	P-3C- -LO	JMSDF	4801/4803	3
785A-7004/7007	P-3C- -LO	JMSDF	4804/4807	4
785A-7008/7045	P-3C- -LO	JMSDF	4808/4845	38
285E-	P-3C- -LO	MLD		13
685A-6001/6006	P-3F- -LO	IIAF	5-256/5-261	6

LOCKHEED CL-475 (Number built: 1)

	CL-475	Co. owned	N6940C	1

LOCKHEED YF-12 and SR-71 (Number built: at least 57 according to released information)

	A-11	USAF	60-6924/60-6933	10
	YF-12A-LO	USAF	60-6934/60-6936	3
	YF-12C-LO	USAF	60-6937	1
	A-11	USAF	60-6938/60-6948	11
	SR-71A-LO	USAF	64-17950	1
	SR-71B-LO	USAF	64-17951	1
	SR-71A-LO	USAF	64-17952/64-17955	4
	SR-71B-LO	USAF	64-17956	1
	SR-71A-LO	USAF	64-17957/64-17980	24
	SR-71C-LO	USAF	64-17981	1
	SR-71A-LO	Cancelled?	64-17982/64-17984	0

LOCKHEED HUMMINGBIRD (Number built: 2)

	VZ-10-LO	USA	62-4503/62-4504	2

LOCKHEED 186 and 286 (Number built: 5)

186-1001/1002	XH-51A-LO	USA/USN	151262/151263	2
186-1003	XH-51N-LO	NASA	NASA 531	1
286-1004/1005	286	Co. owned	N286L & ?	2

LOCKHEED C-141 STARLIFTER (Number built: 285)

300-6001/6002	C-141A-1-LM	USAF	61-2775/61-2776	2
300-6003/6005	C-141A-5-LM	USAF	61-2777/61-2779	3
300-6006/6021	C-141A-10-LM	USAF	63-8075/63-8090	16
300-6022/6046	C-141A-15-LM	USAF	64-609/64-633	25
300-6047/6066	C-141A-20-LM	USAF	64-634/64-653	20
300-6067/6109	C-141A- -LM	USAF	65-216/65-258	43
300-6110	L-300-50A	Demonstrator	N4141A	1
300-6111/6133	C-141A- -LM	USAF	65-259/65-281	23
300-6134/6151	C-141A- -LM	USAF	65-9397/65-9414	18
300-6152/6235	C-141A- -LM	USAF	66-126/66-209	84
300-6236/6251	C-141A- -LM	USAF	66-7944/66-7959	16
300-6252/6282	C-141A- -LM	USAF	67-001/67-031	31
300-6283/6285	C-141A- -LM	USAF	67-164/67-166	3

LOCKHEED Q-STAR and YO-3A (Number built: 17)

- - -	QT-2	Co. owned	N2471W & N2472W	2
- - -	Q-Star	Co. owned	N5713S	1
001/014	YO-3A-LM	USA	69-18000/69-18013	14

LOCKHEED AH-56 CHEYENNE (Number built: 10)

187-1001/1010	AH-56A-LO	USA	66-8826/66-8835	10

LOCKHEED C-5 GALAXY (Number built: 81)

500-0001/0005	C-5A- -LM	USAF	66-8303/66-8307	5
500-0006/0013	C-5A- -LM	USAF	67-167/67-174	8
500-0014/0031	C-5A- -LM	USAF	68-211/68-228	18
500-0032/0058	C-5A- -LM	USAF	69-001/69-027	27
500-0059/0081	C-5A- -LM	USAF	70-445/70-467	23

LOCKHEED L-1011 TRISTAR (Number built: 195 up to end of 1980; still in production)

193A-1001	L-1011-1	Co. owned	N1011	1
193A-1002	L-1011-1	Eastern	N301EA (N1031L)	1
193A-1003	L-1011-1	Eastern	N302EA (N301EA)	1
193A-1004	L-1011-1	Eastern	N303EA	1
193A-1005	L-1011-1	Eastern	N304EA (N6752)	1

193A-1006/1012	L-1011-1	Eastern	N305EA/N311EA	7
193B-1013	L-1011-1	TWA	N31001	1
193B-1014/1018	L-1011-1	TWA	N11002/N11006	5
193M-1019	L-1011-1	Haas-Turner	N312EA	1
193A-1020	L-1011-1	Eastern	N313EA	1
193E-1021	L-1011-1	Air Canada	C-FTNB	1
193A-1022	L-1011-1	Eastern	N314EA	1
193M-1023	L-1011-1	Haas-Turner	N315EA	1
193K-1024	L-1011-1	Court Line	G-BAAA	1
193E-1025	L-1011-1	Air Canada	C-FTND	1
193B-1026	L-1011-1	TWA	N31007	1
193E-1027	L-1011-1	Air Canada	C-FTNE	1
193B-1028/1031	L-1011-1	TWA	N31008/N31011	4
193K-1032	L-1011-1	Court Line	G-BAAB	1
193R-1033	L-1011-1	LTU	D-AERA	1
193B-1034	L-1011-1	TWA	N41012	1
193B-1035/1036	L-1011-1	TWA	N31013/N31014	2
193A-1037/1040	L-1011-1	Eastern	N316EA/N319EA	4
193C-1041	L-1011-1	Delta	N701DA	1
193A-1042/1045	L-1011-1	Eastern	N320EA/N323EA	4
193C-1046	L-1011-1	Delta	N702DA	1
193E-1047/1049	L-1011-1	Air Canada	C-FTNF/C-FTNH	3
193A-1050/1051	L-1011-1	Eastern	N324EA/N325EA	2
193C-1052	L-1011-1	Delta	N703DA	1
193P-1053	L-1011-1	All Nippon	JA8501	1
193A-1054/1056	L-1011-1	Eastern	N326EA/N328EA	3
193C-1057	L-1011-1	Delta	N704DA	1
193E-1058	L-1011-1	Air Canada	C-FTNI	1
193B-1059	L-1011-1	TWA	N31015	1
193B-1060	L-1011-1	TWA	N41016	1
193P-1061/1062	L-1011-1	All Nippon	JA8502/JA8503	2
193B-1063	L-1011-1	TWA	N51017	1
193L-1064	L-1011-1	PSA	N10112	1
193B-1065/1066	L-1011-1	TWA	N31018/N31019	2
193E-1067	L-1011-1	Air Canada	C-FTNJ	1
193P-1068	L-1011-1	All Nippon	JA8505	1
193E-1069	L-1011-1	Air Canada	C-FTNK	1
193P-1070	L-1011-1	All Nippon	JA8506	1
193C-1071	L-1011-1	Delta	N705DA	1
193B-1072	L-1011-1	TWA	N41020	1
193E-1073	L-1011-1	Air Canada	C-FTNL	1
193C-1074	L-1011-1	Delta	N706DA	1
193B-1075/1076	L-1011-1	TWA	N31021/N31022	2
193C-1077/1078	L-1011-1	Delta	N707DA/N708DA	2
193L-1079	L-1011-1	PSA	N10114	1
193B-1080	L-1011-1	TWA	N31023	1
193C-1081	L-1011-1	Delta	N709DA	1
193P-1082	L-1011-1	All Nippon	JA8507	1
193N-1083	L-1011-1	British AW	G-BBAE	1
193C-1084	L-1011-1	Delta	N710DA	1
193A-1085	L-1011-1	Eastern	N329EA	1
193C-1086	L-1011-1	Delta	N711DA	1
193A-1087	L-1011-1	Eastern	N330EA	1
193C-1088/1090	L-1011-1	Delta	N712DA/N714DA	3
193B-1091	L-1011-1	TWA	N31024	1
193C-1092	L-1011-1	Delta	N715DA	1
193N-1093/1094	L-1011-1	British AW	G-BBAF/G-BBAG	2
193C-1095/1097	L-1011-1	Delta	N716DA/N718DA	3
193B-1098	L-1011-1	TWA	N81025	1
193P-1099/1100	L-1011-1	All Nippon	JA8508/JA8509	2
193N-1101/1102	L-1011-1	British AW	G-BBAH/G-BBAI	2
193P-1103	L-1011-1	All Nippon	JA8510	1
193B-1104	L-1011-1	TWA	N81026	1
193P-1105	L-1011-1	All Nippon	JA8511	1
193N-1106	L-1011-1	British AW	G-BBAJ	1
193B-1107/1108	L-1011-1	TWA	N81027/N81028	2
193B-1109	L-1011-1	TWA	N31029	1
193S-1110	L-1011-100	Saudia	HZ-AHA	1
193B-1111	L-1011-1	TWA	N31030	1
193P-1112/1113	L-1011-1	All Nippon	JA8512/JA8513	2
193L-1114	L-1011-1	PSA	N10115	1
193B-1115	L-1011-1	TWA	N31031	1
193S-1116	L-1011-100	Saudia	HZ-AHB	1

193P-1117	L-1011-1	All Nippon	JA8514	1
193T-1118	L-1011-100	Cathay	VR-HHK	1
193P-1119	I-1011-1	All Nippon	JA8515	1
193L-1120	L-1011-1	LTU	D-AERE	1
193A-1121	L-1011-1	Eastern	N331EA	1
193T-1122	L-1011-100	Cathay	VR-HHL	1
193A-1123	L-1011-1	Eastern	N332EA	1
193B-1124	L-1011-1	TWA	N31032	1
193L-1125	L-1011-1	LTU	D-AERU	1
193A-1126	L-1011-1	Eastern	N333EA	1
193P-1127/1129	L-1011-1	All Nippon	JA8516/JA8518	3
193B-1130	L-1011-1	TWA	N31033	1
193U-1131	L-1011-100	Gulf Air	G-BDCW	1
193N-1132	L-1011-1	British AW	G-BEAK	1
193U-1133	L-1011-100	Gulf Air	G-BDCX	1
193P-1134	L-1011-1	All Nippon	JA8519	1
193C-1135/1136	L-1011-1	Delta	N719DA/N720DA	2
193S-1137	L-1011-100	Saudia	HZ-AHC	1
193U-1138	L-1011-100	Gulf Air	G-BDCY	1
193C-1139	L-1011-1	Delta	N721DA	1
193U-1140	L-1011-100	Gulf Air	G-BDCZ	1
193A-1141/1143	L-1011-1	Eastern	N334EA/N336EA	3
193S-1144	L-1011-100	Saudia	HZ-AHD	1
193N-1145/1146	L-1011-1	British AW	G-BEAL/G-BEAM	2
193C-1147	L-1011-1	Delta	N722DA	1
193S-1148/1149	L-1011-100	Saudia	HZ-AHG/HZ-AHH	2
193C-1150/1151	L-1011-1	Delta	N723DA/N724DA	2
193A-1152/1153	L-1011-1	Eastern	N337EA/N338EA	2
193P-1154/1156	L-1011-1	All Nippon	JA8520/JA8522	3
193V-1157	L-1011-500	British AW	G-BFCA	1
193A-1158	L-1011-1	Eastern	N339EA	1
193V-1159	L-1011-500	British AW	G-BFCB	1
193S-1160/1161	L-1011-100	Saudia	HZ-AHI/HZ-AHJ	2
193C-1162/1163	L-1011-1	Delta	N725DA/N726DA	2
193V-1164/1165	L-1011-500	British AW	G-BFCC/G-BFCD	2
193W-1166	L-1011-500	Delta	N751DA	1
193C-1167	L-1011-1	Delta	N727DA	1
193V-1168	L-1011-500	British AW	G-BFCE	1
193S-1169/1171	L-1011-100	Saudia	HZ-AHK/HZ-AHM	3
193W-1172	L-1011-500	Delta	N752DA	1
193C-1173	L-1011-1	Delta	N728DA	1
193V-1174	L-1011-500	British AW	G-BFCF	1
193S-1175	L-1011-200	Saudia	HZ-AHN	1
193Y-1176/1177	L-1011-500	Pan Am	N501PA & N503PA	2
193N-1778	L-1011-200	British AW	G-BGBB	1
193G-1179	L-1011-500	BWIA	9Y-TGJ	1
193C-1180	L-1011-1	Delta	N729DA	1
193Y-1181	L-1011-500	Pan Am	N504PA	1
193N-1182	L-1011-200	British AW	G-BGBC	1
193J-1183	L-1011-500	LTU	D-AERT	1
193Y-1184/1186	L-1011-500	Pan Am	N505PA & N507PA/N508PA	3
193S-1187	L-1011-200	Saudia	HZ-AHO	1
193Y-1188	L-1011-500	Pan Am	N509PA	1
193W-1189	L-1011-500	Delta	N753DA	1
193S-1190	L-1011-200	Saudia	HZ-AHP	1
193G-1191	L-1011-500	BWIA	9Y-TGN	1
193S-1192	L-1011-200	Saudia	HZ-AHQ	1
193N-1193	L-1011-200	British AW	G-BHBL	1
193Y-1194/1195	L-1011-500	Pan Am	N510PA/N511PA	2
193J-1196	L-1011-500	LTU	D-AERL	1
193Y-1197	L-1011-500	Pan Am	N512PA	1
193N-1198	L-1011-200	British AW	G-BHBM	1
193C-1199/1200	L-1011-1	Delta	N730DA/N731DA	2

LOCKHEED S-3 VIKING (Number built: 187)

394A-1001/1008	YS-3A	USN	157992/157999	8
- - -	S-3A	Cancelled	158859/158860	0
394A-1009/1021	S-3A	USN	158861/158873	13
394A-1022/1056	S-3A	USN	159386/159420	35
394A-1057/1101	S-3A	USN	159728/159772	45
394A-1102/1146	S-3A	USN	160120/160164	45
394A-1147/1187	S-3A	USN	160567/160607	41